MANAGING ECONOMIC VOLATILITY AND CRISES

A Practitioner's Guide

Over the past ten years, economic volatility has come into its own after being treated for decades as a secondary phenomenon in the business cycle literature. This evolution has been driven by the recognition that nonlinearities, long buried by the economist's penchant for linearity, magnify the negative effects of volatility on long-run growth and inequality, especially in poor countries. Good times do not offset the negative impact of bad times, which leads to permanent negative effects that are reinforced by incomplete markets, sovereign risk, divisive politics, inefficient taxation, procyclical fiscal policy, and weak financial market institutions. The same phenomena that make volatility difficult to cope with also drive economic crises. This book organizes empirical and policy results for economists and development policy practitioners into four parts: basic features, including the impact of volatility on growth and poverty; commodity price volatility; the financial sector's dual role as an absorber and amplifier of shocks; and the management and prevention of macroeconomic crises. The latter section includes a cross-country study, case studies on Argentina and Russia, and lessons from the debt default episodes of the 1980s and 1990s.

Joshua Aizenman is Professor of Economics at the University of California, Santa Cruz. Prior to his appointment at UCSC, he was Champion Professor of International Economics at Dartmouth College. Professor Aizenman's other affiliations have included teaching and research positions at the University of Pennsylvania, the University of Chicago Graduate School of Business, and the Hebrew University in Jerusalem. He has held consultancies with the International Monetary Fund, the World Bank, the Inter-American Development Bank, and the Federal Reserve Bank of San Francisco. His research covers a range of issues in open economy including commercial and financial policies, crises in emerging markets, foreign direct investment, capital controls, and exchange rate regimes. Professor Aizenman also serves as a Research Associate for the National Bureau of Economic Research.

Brian Pinto has been at the World Bank, Washington, DC, for more than 20 years. He is currently Economic Adviser in the Economic Policy and Debt Department, Poverty Reduction and Economic Management Anchor. Past assignments in the World Bank Group include stints in borrowing operations, the International Finance Corporation, and the Europe and Central Asia Region. Dr. Pinto lived and worked in Poland at the start of its momentous reforms (1990–92) and subsequently in Russia during a period which covered its 1998 crisis and subsequent recovery (1998–2001). His areas of expertise include policy-oriented analyses of macroeconomic crises and recovery, public debt dynamics, and transition economics. His publications have appeared in numerous professional journals.

MANAGING ECONOMIC VOLATILITY AND CRISES

A Practitioner's Guide

Edited by

JOSHUA AIZENMAN
University of California, Santa Cruz

BRIAN PINTO
The World Bank

CAMBRIDGE
UNIVERSITY PRESS

CAMBRIDGE UNIVERSITY PRESS
Cambridge, New York, Melbourne, Madrid, Cape Town, Singapore,
São Paulo, Delhi, Dubai, Tokyo, Mexico City

Cambridge University Press
The Edinburgh Building, Cambridge CB2 8RU, UK

Published in the United States of America by Cambridge University Press, New York

www.cambridge.org
Information on this title: www.cambridge.org/9780521168595

First published 2005
First paperback edition 2010

A catalogue record for this publication is available from the British Library.

Library of Congress Cataloging in Publication Data

Managing economic volatility and crises : a practitioner's guide /
edited by Joshua Aizenman, Brian Pinto.
p. cm.
Includes bibliographical references and index.
ISBN 0-521-85524-1 (hardcover)
1. Business cycles. 2. Financial crises. 3. Economic development.
I. Aizenman, Joshua. II. Pinto, Brian. III. Title.
HB3711.M352 2005
338.54′2 – dc22   2005012972

ISBN 978-0-521-85524-2 Hardback
ISBN 978-0-521-16859-5 Paperback

To Michal and our daughters, Avi and Anbar
To my mother, Praxedes, and the memory of my father, Hugh Pinto

Contents

Contributors

Joshua Aizenman Professor of Economics, University of California, Santa Cruz

Punam Chuhan Lead Economist, Global Monitoring Secretariat, The World Bank

Stijn Claessens Senior Adviser, Financial Sector Operations & Policy, The World Bank, and Professor of International Finance Policy, University of Amsterdam

Jan Dehn Fund Manager, Ashmore Group Limited, London, UK

Julia Devlin Partnership Coordinator, Middle East and North Africa Region, The World Bank

Jeffrey Frankel James W. Harpel Professor of Capital Formation and Growth, Kennedy School of Government, Harvard University

Christopher Gilbert Professor, GRADE and Department of Economics, University of Trento, Italy, and Consultant, Agriculture and Rural Development Department, The World Bank

Evsey Gurvich Head of the Economic Expert Group, Ministry of Finance of The Russian Federation, Moscow

Viktoria Hnatkovska Ph.D. Candidate in Economics, Georgetown University

Thomas Laursen Lead Economist, Poverty Reduction and Economic Management Department, Europe and Central Asia Region, The World Bank

Michael Lewin Senior Economist, Oil, Gas and Mining Policy Division, The World Bank

Norman Loayza Lead Economist, Development Research Group, The World Bank

Sandeep Mahajan Senior Economist, Poverty Reduction and Economic Management Department, South Asia Region, The World Bank

John J. Merrick, Jr. Richard S. Reynolds Associate Professor of Business, College of William and Mary

Guillermo Perry Chief Economist, Latin America & Caribbean Region, The World Bank

Brian Pinto Economic Adviser, Economic Policy & Debt Department, Poverty Reduction and Economic Management Anchor, The World Bank

Luis Servén Research Manager, Development Research Group, The World Bank

Federico Sturzenegger Business School, Universidad Torcuato Di Tella, Argentina, and Visiting Professor of Public Affairs, Kennedy School of Government, Harvard University

Sergei Ulatov Economist, Poverty Reduction and Economic Management Department, Europe and Central Asia Region, The World Bank

Panos Varangis Vice President, Greek Agricultural Bank, Athens, Greece, on leave from Agriculture and Rural Development Department, The World Bank

Shang-Jin Wei Chief, Trade and Investment Division, Research Department, International Monetary Fund

Holger Wolf Associate Professor in the School of Foreign Service, Georgetown University

Acknowledgments

We thank Zia Qureshi, whose idea this book was, and Yaw Ansu, Indermit Gill, Danny Leipziger, Gobind Nankani, and Vikram Nehru for continuing to support the endeavor. We are indebted to the Debt and Volatility Thematic Group and the Economic Policy and Debt Department, Poverty Reduction and Economic Management Anchor, of the World Bank for generous financial support.

Sarah Lipscomb prevented us from lapsing into utter disorganization by expertly handling the contracts and seminar logistics related to this book. Marketa Jonasova's tireless efforts on graphs, tables, references, and formatting were instrumental in producing the chapters on time – she also contributed a box on options for the chapter on managing oil booms. Duane Chilton, Maria Gomes, and Debbie Sturgess cheerfully chipped in whenever needed. Gaobo Pang and Xiaohan Hu helped finalize the manuscript. Jesica Seacor, who was at the time with the Bank's Office of the Publisher, negotiated the contract with Cambridge University Press (CUP). We thank them.

Nancy Morrison proved an outstanding editor. Her meticulous work ensured minimal delay once the manuscript was submitted to CUP. We are grateful to Scott Parris of CUP for inviting us to submit the manuscript and turning it around so quickly. We also thank him and Simina Calin of CUP for patiently and promptly fielding our questions. Ken Karpinski and colleagues at TechBooks did a superb job of producing the book.

A volume such as this involves a complex production function and could quickly degenerate into a coordination nightmare. We sincerely thank the chapter authors, most of all for their contributions, for meeting deadlines, and for putting up with our constant queries and suggestions. The volume benefited from peer reviews of the various chapters by Robert J. Anderson, Jr., Francois Bourguignon, Nina Budina, Craig Burnside, Ricardo Caballero, Mauricio Carrizosa, Paul Cashin, Asli Demirgüç-Kunt, Barry Eichengreen, Bob Flood, Homi Kharas, Donald Larson, Ross Levine, Ashoka Mody, Rolando Ossowksi, Eswar Prasad, Martin Ravallion, Sergio Schmukler, Sergei Vasiliev, and John Williamson. Luc Laeven and Claudio Raddatz also commented on one of the chapters.

The chapters served as a basis for seminars at the Bank and outside. We sincerely thank Morris Goldstein and Michael Mussa for participating in these seminars and sharing their formidable experience. Frank Diebold and Bill Ethier of the

University of Pennsylvania invited us to present an overview of the results at a joint econometrics-international workshop. Our thanks to them.

We owe a special debt of gratitude to Bob Flood, who crossed 19th Street (the trip from the International Monetary Fund to the World Bank) several times in support of this volume. He peer-reviewed both the concept paper and overall volume and was an inspiration throughout the challenging task of putting this volume together.

The views contained in this book are those of the authors and should not be attributed to any particular institution, including those the authors may be associated with, such as the World Bank, the International Monetary Fund, and the NBER.

Joshua Aizenman
Brian Pinto

Foreword

The last half century has seen an unprecedented number of financial crises and periods of great price and output volatility. Slightly removed in time from the events, researchers are now carefully documenting the events and learning from them. This volume is a landmark in that research process. Joshua Aizenman and Brian Pinto have put together a group of cutting-edge researchers and had them stand back and assess what has been learned. Since it is my specialty, I will concentrate my remarks on the crisis part of this volume.

Country particulars and fine technical points aside, two simple lessons seem robust. One lesson is that financial crisis and volatility come in waves. First they hit one country, then the next in close succession. The second lesson is that the next wave of crises is sure to be different from the last. Studying past financial turmoil has an important element in common with studying past wars. Military historians record and analyze battles to discover how they could have been fought better. Potential enemies do the same. The next war, therefore, will surely be different from the last one and it will be different in ways intended to surprise the participants. The great lesson we draw from studying military history is to expect surprises. This lesson turns out to extend to financial crises. Money is made and money is lost in the crises. Those who lost money set up protections, like deposit insurance, so as not to lose in the same way twice. As institutions evolve, those who would make money on crises and other volatility need to look elsewhere for weak points. From this simple dynamic, it follows that the next set of crises will be different from the last.

The precise adversaries are harder to identify in crises than in wars. On one side in a speculative attack on a fixed exchange rate, for example, typically stands a government backing an ill-conceived price-fixing promise. On the other side stand anonymous speculators betting against the government's ability to fulfill the promise. A weak government promise turns speculators against other taxpayers. Walt Kelly on his famous Earth Day poster depicting Pogo overlooking woods filled with trash said: "We have met the enemy and he is us." So it is with financial crises. Poor institutional design creates financial adversaries from those who might have been cooperating to build a stronger economy. Resources are redistributed during the crises, but society as a whole seems frequently to come out of the crises with fewer resources and slower growth than it had on entry. On the plus side, crises do tend to stimulate fiscal and institutional reform.

While crises have existed throughout financial history, for many years we really did not study them much – perhaps because they were looked on as irrational anomalies beyond the bounds of our maximizing-agent-based modeling. This changed when Stephen Salant and Dale Henderson (SH, 1978) presented a rational-agent model of a speculative attack on a government's gold-price fixing scheme. Following on the heels of this seminal work, Paul Krugman (1979) ingeniously applied the SH methods to study an attack on a government currency-price fixing scheme. Once Krugman's paper was published, the floodgates opened; economists used the SH methods in widespread new theory work and fit the models in empirical applications. The SH methods worked well on the 1970s' speculative attacks. These attacks were one-way bets against price fixing schemes that were destined to fail eventually because of other, more powerful, forces inconsistent with the fixed price. These methods were applied with success to speculative attacks in Mexico (1976, 1982), Brazil (1983), and Israel (1974), among others.

Following the theme of successive crisis waves being different, the attacks on fixed parities leading to monetary union in the EMU (The European Monetary System [EMS] came under speculative attack between 1992 and 1993) had little in common with those in Mexico and Brazil except for the profits made by speculators at the expense of other taxpayers. The countries that came under attack (all EMS countries but Germany and the Netherlands) had sound fiscal and monetary policies completely consistent with the adopted parities. It seemed that the speculative attacks were the result of a mind game between speculators, like George Soros, and the countries' monetary authorities concerning the appropriate parity at which to enter the union. This type of speculative gaming was modeled by Maurice Obstfeld (1996) and became known as the second generation of speculative attacks. (Flood and Marion (1999) provide a survey of the first two crisis generations.)

The middle and late 1990s brought crises in East Asia and Latin America. As usual, the new crises looked different from those in the past. The crises still involved governments and speculators, to be sure, but now the solvency of private firms was thrown into the mix. Often, as it turned out, the crisis countries' private firms had borrowed heavily from abroad with their debts denominated in foreign currency. This set up a nightmarish balance-sheet constraint on governments' reactions to adverse shocks. On the one hand, if governments met the shocks with interest rate reductions or monetary expansions, the value of the countries' currencies would decline, exacerbating the private sector's debt burden. Fiscal expansion, on the other hand, would increase domestic-currency interest rates, thereby increasing the domestic-currency debt service burden on already-strapped firms. It was a new crisis type, sometimes called the third-generation crisis. In these crises, the private sector was tied into currency and government solvency crises as never before. After the crises, the attacked countries realized that large crisis war chests in the form of liquid international reserves might have forestalled their problems. As witness to evolving structure following crises, one need only study the gigantic post-crisis reserve buildup in many East Asian countries.

The above is a much-abbreviated version of the modern-crisis history part of the task Joshua Aizenman and Brian Pinto and the authors they invited to participate have taken on in this volume. Their job is accomplished in three steps. First they set out for the reader the problems from which lessons will be drawn. Second they give the reader the intellectual tools with which to study the data. The third and final step is the most rewarding. It is to use the relevant analytical tools to study the crisis case histories in Argentina and Russia. These case histories are the real payoff in this volume. They correspond to the military historian's recounting and dissecting battles.

This volume is like a military history but applied to crises and other volatility; it lays out what happened and why. The authors do not, however, attempt to predict where crises and other volatility will next appear. Instead they remind us to be ready for surprises.

Robert P. Flood, Jr.
Editor, *IMF Staff Papers*
International Monetary Fund
Washington, D.C.

REFERENCES

Flood, Robert, and Nancy Marion. 1999. "Perspectives on the Recent Currency Crisis Literature." *International Journal of Finance and Economics* 4:1–26.

Krugman, Paul. 1979. "A Model of Balance-of-Payments Crises." *Journal of Money, Credit and Banking* 11:311–25.

Obstfeld, Maurice. 1996. "Models of Currency Crises with Self-Fulfilling Features." *European Economic Review* 40:1037–47.

Salant, Stephen, and Dale Henderson. 1978. "Market Anticipations of Government Policies and the Price of Gold." *Journal of Political Economy* 86(August):627–48.

MANAGING ECONOMIC VOLATILITY AND CRISES

A Practitioner's Guide

OVERVIEW

Managing Economic Volatility and Crises:
A Practitioner's Guide

Joshua Aizenman and Brian Pinto

ABSTRACT: This overview introduces and summarizes the findings of a practical volume on managing volatility and crises. The interest in these topics stems from the growing recognition that non-linearities tend to magnify the impact of economic volatility, leading to large output and economic growth costs, especially in poor countries. Good times tend not to offset the negative impact of bad times, which leads to permanent negative effects. Such asymmetry is reinforced by incomplete markets, sovereign risk, divisive politics, inefficient taxation, procyclical fiscal policy, and weak financial market institutions – factors that are more problematic in developing countries. The same phenomena that make it difficult to cope with volatility also drive crises. Hence, this volume also focuses on the prevention and management of crises. It is a user-friendly compilation of empirical and policy results aimed at development-policy practitioners and is divided into four modules: (i) the basics of volatility and its impact on growth and poverty; (ii) managing commodity price volatility, including agricultural commodities and oil; (iii) the financial sector, and its roles both as an absorber and amplifier of volatility and shocks; and (iv) the management and prevention of macroeconomic crises, including a cross-country study, case studies on Argentina and Russia, and lessons from the debt default episodes of the 1980s and 1990s. A Technical Appendix is also available.

WHAT IS VOLATILITY?

To a world still recovering from the bursting of the Internet bubble in 2001, the image most immediately conjured up by the word "volatile" might be that of an unstable stock market; or, in view of the balance-of-payments crises of the late 1990s, of unpredictable capital flows driven by fickle market sentiment to emerging market countries. But "volatile" could equally be applied to the weather. In India, for example, even though the share of agriculture in national output has dropped from one-half in the 1960s to one-quarter today, a good monsoon can still make a significant difference to GDP growth. "Volatile" can also be used to describe a political climate, such as that prevailing in Iraq or Haiti; or the procyclical response of fiscal policy to fluctuations in the price of oil for an oil exporter such as Nigeria; or even the behavior of a crowd in downtown Buenos Aires, Argentina, protesting the *corralito* or freeze on bank deposits in December 2001.

Depending upon how one looks at it, volatility in mainstream economics has either been around for a long time or else is of more recent vintage. The first view would assert that volatility dates to the time that the study of business cycles began – although it might be more correct to say that the concern there was more with decomposing economic growth into a cyclical and trend component than with

1

volatility per se. The second view is that volatility began to develop into an independent field of inquiry in macroeconomics only over the last decade. Up to then, it was regarded as an oscillation around an independent growth trend, a second-order issue of interest mainly to industrial economies concerned about smoothing the fluctuations of the business cycle. It is now beginning to occupy a central position in development economics.

What has catapulted volatility into this prominence? First, following the seminal paper of Garey Ramey and Valerie Ramey in 1995,[1] cross-country studies have consistently found that volatility exerts a significant negative impact on long-run (trend) growth, which is exacerbated in poorer countries. Second, the inclusion of volatility in the growth literature can be regarded as a continuation of the trend that began in the mid-1980s with endogenous growth theory. This theory linked technological progress to the capital stock in an attempt to explain why returns to capital may not diminish in rich, capital-abundant countries, and thereby perpetuate income gaps between rich and poor countries. More recently, attention has turned to the so-called deep determinants of growth: geography, trade openness, and institutions, and their impact on total factor productivity. "Institutions" refers to the quality of governance, the integrity of the legal system, and property rights. Financial market institutions, including creditor and shareholder rights and vigilant supervision, are accorded particular prominence. Empirical investigation increasingly shows that weak policies and institutions in developing countries may magnify the negative effects of volatility on growth and lead to permanent setbacks relative to richer countries. Therefore, understanding the nature of volatility and anticipating and managing its consequences should be of considerable interest to policymakers in developing countries.

Defining and Calculating Volatility

In common parlance, making a distinction among volatility, uncertainty, risk, variability, fluctuation, or oscillation would be considered splitting hairs; but, going back to Frank Knight's classic 1921 work, *Risk, Uncertainty, and Profit*, there is a subtle difference in economics. *Uncertainty* describes a situation where several possible outcomes are associated with an event, but the assignment of probabilities to the outcomes is not possible.[2] *Risk*, in contrast, permits the assignment of probabilities to the different outcomes. *Volatility* is allied to risk in that it provides a measure of the possible variation or movement in a particular economic variable or some function of that variable, such as a growth rate. It is usually measured based on observed realizations of a random variable over some historical period. This is referred to as *realized volatility*, to distinguish it from the *implicit* volatility calculated, say, from the Black–Scholes formula for the price of a European call option on a stock.[3]

---

[1] At about the same time, the Inter-American Development Bank (IDB 1995) conducted a pioneering study of volatility in Latin America under the leadership of Ricardo Hausmann and Michael Gavin.
[2] The Bayesian approach would deal with this situation by assigning a uniform prior to the possible outcomes.
[3] A European call option confers the right (without any obligation) to buy a stock on a given date at a predetermined price, called the strike price. Among other variables, its premium or price depends on the volatility of the stock price.

Realized volatility, or more simply, volatility, is most commonly measured by a standard deviation based on the history of an economic variable. In this volume, there will always be either an explicit or implicit reference to an underlying probability distribution for the variables of concern. Hence it will abstract from Knightian uncertainty. However, if components or trends in the underlying variable are predictable, then calculating volatility based on measured ex post total variability may overestimate risk. For example, one could regard total variability as the sum of predictable variability and pure risk.[4] This presents two options for computing volatility: it can be measured by the standard deviation (std.dev.) of total variability or on the std.dev. of pure risk, which can be obtained as the residual from a forecasting equation for total variability.[5]

An additional question arises. Is the volatility (variance or std.dev.) of the pure risk component constant, or does it vary over time? The idea that volatility tends to cluster – that is, that there may be serial correlation in it – and modeling this in a tractable way using autoregressive conditional heteroskedasticity, were among the contributions leading to the Nobel Prize in economics for Robert F. Engle in 2003.[6] In general, the empirical work in this book will focus on volatility measured by the standard deviation of total variability, although there are exceptions. For example, Chapter 2 on growth uses two different measures of volatility, and Chapter 4 on commodity price volatility isolates shocks based on the unpredictable component of price movements. The discussion now turns to shocks and crisis.

Volatility, Shocks, and Crisis

Since part of the variability in an economic variable may be anticipated, the residual, which captures pure risk or uncertainty, is by definition unanticipated, and constitutes a "shock." Speaking practically, however, economists usually concentrate only on large or extreme shocks, which are defined as those residuals, positive and negative, exceeding a certain cut-off point in magnitude.[7] The size and persistence of shocks can pose major challenges to economic management. A large negative shock is typically more serious than a small one because credit constraints may prevent it from being financed, or it may exhaust a finite buffer stock, which then has knock-on effects. For example, a country may use up its foreign exchange reserves defending a fixed exchange rate following a large negative terms-of-trade (ToT) shock and then be forced to float the currency, leading to additional, possibly disruptive, costs associated with balance sheet currency mismatches for banks and firms. Likewise, a more persistent adverse shock is going to be more costly. A coffee-exporting country, for example, may be able to cope with a onetime ToT shock of 10 percent. If the ToT does not subsequently recover, however, and a large negative shock persists say,

---

[4] As noted, this volume abstracts from Knightian uncertainty and instead takes a Bayesian approach, occasionally using pure risk and uncertainty interchangeably. See Epstein and Wang (1994) and the references there for recent developments in modeling Knightian uncertainty.
[5] Servén (1998) uses this approach when examining the effects of macroeconomic uncertainty on private investment.
[6] An interesting account of Engle's contributions is contained in Diebold (2004).
[7] This is the approach taken in Chapter 4.

for three years, the capacity of the country to cope may be exhausted and lead to economic disruption.

The preceding examples raise a fundamental question: Are there any links between volatility and crises? This volume argues that there are good reasons to consider volatility and crises together. First, the literature tends to compute volatility over long periods of time, such as the standard deviation of real per capita GDP growth from 1960 to 2000. Such computation tends to lump what may be regarded as "normal" and "crisis" volatility together. The distinction between the two is largely one of size; normal output oscillations versus what might be regarded as large swings in output, with declines being defined as "crises". Disentangling the two shows that crisis volatility matters more for the negative impact on growth explored in depth in Chapter 2. This result is reinforced by a casual examination of economic history. As William Easterly, Roumeen Islam, and Joseph Stiglitz (2002, p. 191) note:

> Crises have been a constant of market capitalism – from the bursting of the British South Sea bubble and the French Mississippi bubble in 1720 (which at least one economic historian claims delayed the industrial revolution by 50 years), to the depressions of the 1870s and 1930s in the industrial economies, to the debt crises of the middle-income Latin American countries and low-income African countries in the 1980s, the collapse of output in the formerly socialist economies in the 1990s, and the East Asian financial crisis in 1997–98.

Second, volatility and crises are driven by the same fundamental phenomena. Consider a situation where weak fiscal institutions and inconsistent macroeconomic policies magnify output volatility. It may well be that such circumstances tend to attract short-term, speculative capital inflows, creating a vulnerability to a "sudden stop"[8] and hence a crisis down the road. Thus volatility could evolve into a crisis. As another example, the asymmetry argument – presented in the next section to explain why volatility tends to have permanent negative effects in developing economies – wields much greater force when shocks are larger and the ability to cope with them smaller. If permanent negative effects cumulate, then a country might set itself up for a future crisis. Conversely, a crisis may serve as a catalyst for change, for example, in countries where weak fiscal institutions and politics either increase inequality or lead to procyclical fiscal policies and the excessive buildup of government debt. In this case, a byproduct of a crisis might be stronger fiscal institutions and greater transparency (see Chapter 9, on Russia).

HOW VOLATILITY AFFECTS GROWTH

The consistent empirical finding that volatility exerts a negative impact on growth has prompted research on the precise channels through which this effect operates. Channels identified in Chapter 1 include factor accumulation, trade, the financial system, and even politics. For example, macroeconomic uncertainty can affect growth through investment. For developing country oil exporters, the effects of a price boom are typically transmitted through fiscal policy, which could enhance real exchange rate appreciation and volatility and thus reduce investment in the

[8] Calvo and Reinhart (2001).

non-oil traded goods sector, notably, agriculture and manufacturing. The resultant reduced diversification of production would increase the vulnerability to future ToT shocks, magnifying the long-run costs of ToT volatility. ToT shocks get transmitted through trade links and are proportional to the degree of openness, which is usually measured as the ratio of exports plus imports to GDP. A rise in U.S. interest rates might result in reduced capital flows to an emerging market Latin American country. This effect would be transmitted through the financial system, and the shock could be amplified by vulnerable bank and corporate balance sheets; recession could set in if large-scale bankruptcies occurred. The precise nature of how various channels work and reinforce one another is a topic of ongoing research. Two concepts help to explain the impact of volatility on growth: *concavity* and *asymmetry*. These are considered in turn below.

Why Volatility Is of First-Order Importance: Concavity

Nonlinearity, of which concavity is a specific instance, explains why volatility should be of first-order importance. Suppose the reduced form of the association between real GDP growth (g) and a productivity shock (ε) is summarized by $g = g(\varepsilon)$, where the expected value of the shock is zero. Imposing a linear structure as is often done in economics for simplicity would lead to an equation of the form $g = a + b \cdot \varepsilon$, where a and b are the coefficients that the econometrician would estimate. Assume that a and b are both positive. Then taking expectations yields:

$$E(g) = a + b \cdot E(\varepsilon) = a + b \cdot 0 = a.$$

That is, the expected value of growth is a, or expressed equivalently, growth fluctuates around a trend value of a and is above (below) it when ε is greater (less) than zero. In this case, the variance of ε is relevant only to the extent that it influences the size of the variation above or below a; it does not affect trend growth itself. In other words, the expected growth rate is *independent* of volatility measured by the variance of ε; it is of second-order importance.

A better approximation would allow for nonlinear effects: $g = a + b. \varepsilon + c \cdot \varepsilon^2$. Further, when the association between the shocks and growth is concave, that is, when $c < 0$, this results in a negative impact of volatility on growth. In this case,

$$E(g) = a + b \cdot E(\varepsilon) + c \cdot E(\varepsilon^2) = a + b \cdot 0 + c \cdot V(\varepsilon) = a + c \cdot V(\varepsilon) < a,$$

where $V(\varepsilon)$ is the variance of ε. In this case, trend growth is less than a because of nonlinearity and concavity ($c < 0$); volatility is now a matter of first-order importance. The discussion below will review several possible channels leading to such concavity.

Figure 1 illustrates this for the simplest case, where the shock has only two possible values, plus or minus δ, with equal probabilities, and the realized growth would be either $g(\delta)$ or $g(-\delta)$. The empirical evidence suggests a concave association ($c < 0$), implying that the volatility of the shock reduces the expected growth below a by the bold segment, λ.[9] Had we estimated the growth with a linear specification, we would fail to detect this effect and conclude that it is not worth making an effort to

---

[9] It is easy to show that $\lambda = -c\delta^2 > 0$, where $\delta^2 = V(\varepsilon)$.

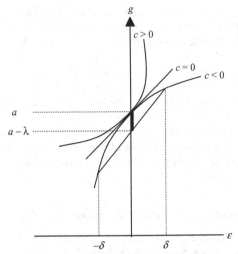

Figure 1. Shocks, Growth, and Welfare.

reduce volatility or manage its consequences.[10] But the realization that eliminating volatility would raise growth by λ (which would call for a nonlinear specification) would create an incentive to take volatility more seriously.

While the discussion above focused on the *empirical* challenges associated with identifying volatility, similar considerations impact the *theoretical* discussions. A useful analytical methodology is linearizing complex models around the equilibrium. This is frequently done in neoclassical frameworks, which rely on Leonard Savage's (1954) expected utility paradigm. That is, only the first moment of the distribution matters; the second, which would bring volatility into the picture, is minuscule and therefore irrelevant. Imposing this structure allows tractable reduced-form solutions of more complex problems; but it a priori rules out large first order effects of volatility on welfare, saving, and optimal buffer stocks. For example, David Newbery and Joseph Stiglitz (1981) showed that for a consumer maximizing the conventional expected utility, the gains from optimal buffer stocks are small, and may not be worth the cost. This result does not hold if agents are loss-averse: namely, if they attach a greater weight to the utility loss from a drop in consumption than to the utility gain from a comparable increase in consumption. In this case, the welfare gain from optimal buffer stocks is sizable, making the improvement of insurance and capital markets a high priority.[11]

Why should volatility have a particularly negative impact on developing countries compared to industrial countries? One way of thinking about this is in terms of the determinants of c in the nonlinear growth-shock specification. Two key determinants of c are likely to be the ability to conduct countercyclical fiscal policy and the state of financial sector development. In industrial countries, both would tend

[10] The heavy reliance on log linear modeling and estimation may also explain why the earlier literature "conveniently" overlooked the possible adverse growth effects of volatility.

[11] See Aizenman (1998) and Bowman, Minehart, and Rabin (1999). See also Obstfeld (1994) for analysis of the potential growth gains from diversification of shocks.

to lower *c* and thereby raise the expected value of growth for a given shock process. Both reflect institutional development, which is a key factor explaining why volatility matters and why its effects may be exacerbated in developing countries. If a country is able to expand deficits during a downturn by, say, maintaining government expenditure while tax revenues contract, this would help dampen the impact of a downturn; but this ability depends fundamentally upon access to credit markets and sovereign risk for given inflation targets. Similarly, well-developed financial systems may help to decouple consumption from output volatility, allowing consumption to be smoothed over time and thereby helping to preserve aggregate demand during a negative output shock.

Why Shocks Have Permanent Effects: Asymmetry

The concave association between shocks and growth may stem from interactions among various structural factors that result in an asymmetric response to good times versus bad times. Good times do not offset the negative effects of bad times, so that shocks tend to have a permanent negative effect. Examples of asymmetry, frequently reinforced by concavity, include:

EXAMPLE 1: WEAK INSTITUTIONS AND THE INVESTMENT CHANNEL. The quality of institutions may not matter in good times; but in bad times countries suffering from institutional deficiencies are likely to suffer more from adverse shocks of the same magnitude than countries that have strong institutions, as argued by Dani Rodrik (1999). Weak institutions, manifested in poorly enforced contracts and property rights, low protection of creditors and inadequate supervision of the financial system, may inhibit the formation of financial markets (de Soto 2000). In financing investment, firms can turn to *external* sources, such as bank loans, equity, or corporate bonds, or rely on *internal* funds, such as retained earnings; but capital markets tend to be thin or nonexistent when institutions are weak, constraining investment to be funded internally, or by banks. Robert Townsend (1979) and Ben Bernanke and Mark Gertler (1989), have shown that more costly verification and enforcement of contracts – symptomatic of weak institutions – and higher economic volatility can increase the cost of external funds, and thereby reduce investment.[12] And when recessions occur, internal funds drop, which leads to a greater contraction of investment than would occur with well-functioning capital markets, thus inducing concavity in the association between shocks and investment.

Garey Ramey and Valerie Ramey (1995) found investment unimportant as a channel for the impact of volatility on growth. Joshua Aizenman and Nancy Marion (1999) applied Ramey and Ramey's methodology to the case where investment is disaggregated into private and public components. They found that, unlike pubic investment, volatility has large adverse effects on private investment, which turns out to be an important channel for the negative effects of volatility on growth.[13]

---

[12] See Aizenman and Powell (2003) for more on the impact of volatility on investment with costly state verification and limited enforceability of contracts.

[13] This result is consistent with the finding that the marginal impact of public investment on growth in developing countries is much lower than that of private (see Khan and Kumar 1997; Bouton and

EXAMPLE 2. INCOMPLETE CAPITAL MARKETS AND SOVEREIGN RISK. Limited integration with the global capital market may induce asymmetries over the business cycle. A simple example is when the aggregate savings schedule is elastic at small levels of debt but becomes vertical at a particular credit ceiling, reflecting sovereign risk: the country can borrow freely at the prevailing interest rate, but only up to a point. In this case, the higher the volatility of investment demand, the lower is expected investment: the increase in investment in good times is constrained relative to the drop in bad times.[14]

To illustrate this channel, suppose the supply of credit facing a country is given by an inverted L-shaped graph, shown in Figure 2, Panel A, where S_0 is the credit ceiling. Let I^d be the demand for investment. Actual investment is given by $I = Min\{I^d(r_0), S_0\}$, where $I^d(r_0) \equiv I_0$ is investment demand at $r = r_0$. Suppose the demand for investment fluctuates between a high state, $I_h^d = I_0 + \varepsilon$, and a low state, $I_l^d = I_0 - \varepsilon$, while the credit ceiling remains S_0. Realized investment is plotted in Figure 2, Panel B. The credit ceiling hampers investment expansion in the high demand state without moderating the drop in investment in the low demand state. Thus volatile investment demand reduces average investment in the presence of credit rationing. In the example, if the probability of each state of nature is 0.5, volatility reduces expected investment from I_0 to $I' = I_0 - 0.5\varepsilon$, which is smaller the higher ε is (see Figure 2, Panel B).[15]

The eventual growth effects of volatility transmitted by investment may be dealt with more comprehensively in endogenous growth models. While the ultimate effects of volatility on growth in such models are ambiguous, one can identify circumstances under which the association would be negative. For example, if riskier technologies are associated with higher productivity but the markets for risk sharing are imperfect, higher economic volatility would induce the adoption of safer but (on average) less productive technologies in endogenous growth models.[16] Alternatively, with a binding credit ceiling, policy-induced uncertainty that has an impact on the tax on capital would tend to reduce growth (Aizenman and Marion 1993). In these models, stabilization of shocks may lead to a higher growth rate.

EXAMPLE 3. VOLATILITY, INCOME INEQUALITY, AND GROWTH. Uncertainty tends to increase income inequality.[17] Income inequality in turn may affect growth through several channels. For example, investment in human capital is frequently

---

Sumlinski 2000; and Everhart and Sumlinski 2001). A possible explanation for this finding is that in countries characterized by weak institutions, public investment is inflated by rent-seeking and corruption.

[14] This result holds even with a stochastic supply of savings, as long as the correlation between the supply of and the demand for savings is less than one.

[15] This result is not modified even if one allows for stochastic credit ceilings and investment where the realized investment is given by $Min\{I_r, S_r\}$. Provided the correlation of shocks affecting the supply of credit and demand for investment is less than 1, volatility will reduce expected investment, with a larger drop the lower the correlation.

[16] Obstfeld (1994) presents an endogenous model growth illustrating this. For further discussion, see Jones, Manuelli, and Stacchetti (1999) and Barlevy (2003).

[17] Higher uncertainty raises income inequality in the presence of specific factors of production (like specific capital), and in the absence of complete asset markets that allow pooling and risk diversification. See also Chapter 3.

Panel A. *Saving, Investment Demand, and the Interest Rate*

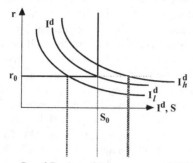

Panel B. *Actual Investment and the Investment Demand*

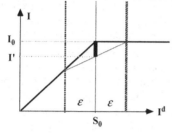

Figure 2. Investment in the Face of a Credit Ceiling.

self-financed, due to the inability to use future earnings as traded collateral against which to borrow. Hence the ability to finance investment in human capital is tied to the wealth of the household. A household with low net worth will find that the credit ceiling is binding, investing less than that warranted without such a ceiling. This leads to a concave dependency of investment in human capital on the credit ceiling facing a household. In the absence of complete insurance markets, greater volatility tends to increase the dispersion of income among households, leading to a drop in average investment because more households face credit ceilings, thereby reducing the accumulation of human capital and, ultimately, growth.[18]

These results are summarized in the following interaction:

Volatile shocks → greater inequality → more credit constraints for poorer people (an effect magnified by bad institutions) → adverse effects on human capital → lower growth.

Inadequate investment in human capital would inhibit the diversification of production, which in turn would tend to increase the impact of shocks. This would reinforce the adverse effects of volatility on growth and could create a vicious cycle.

---

[18] For more details, see Galor and Zeira (1993). See also Flug, Spilimbergo, and Wachtenheim (1998) for empirical confirmation of the adverse impact of volatility on investment in human capital.

EXAMPLE 4. DIVISIVE POLITICS, INEFFICIENT TAXATION, AND PROCYCLICAL FISCAL POLICY. To cite another complex interaction, weak institutions and non-cooperative behavior among competing pressure groups frequently imply inefficient tax systems. Policymakers may have short horizons, either because they may lose the next election or because there is no internalization of the welfare of unborn generations (as is frequently the case in overlapping-generations models). In countries where distributional conflicts are important, the political process may produce policies that tax investment and growth-promoting activities so as to redistribute income in favor of groups linked to the political incumbents. A common feature of developing countries is the scarcity of fiscal instruments, which leads to the inflation tax and customs tariffs as "easy" ways of raising revenue. Alex Cukierman, Sebastian Edwards, and Guido Tabellini (1992) pointed out that the backwardness of the tax structure itself may be the outcome of distributional conflicts between competing political groups. Their menu of taxes includes income taxes, associated with distortions and collection costs, and seigniorage, associated only with distortions. They consider the case where the government is formed by two competing parties that prefer two different types of public goods. As a result of implementation lags, the current tax system was determined one political period ago. If the current government has a low probability of survival, it has the incentive to jeopardize the ability of the future government to spend on the public goods that it does not value. A way to accomplish this is to adopt a narrow tax base, not to include income tax, in order to restrict the revenue of the future administration. Applying this logic, one concludes that countries with more unstable and polarized political systems rely more heavily on seigniorage and import tariffs as a source of revenue than do more stable and homogenous societies. The resultant distortions (high inflation, underinvestment because of costly imports of capital goods, and currency substitution that further diminishes the tax base) may ultimately lead to lower private investment and lower growth. Conversely, greater stability and lower polarization would induce countries to replace the inflation tax and customs tariffs with income and value added taxes, thereby widening the tax base.[19] Procyclical fiscal policy can be interpreted as a byproduct of underdeveloped fiscal systems and sovereign risk, implying that the decline in the output growth rate during recessions would tend to exceed the increase during expansions, inducing another concave association between shocks and growth. These results are summarized in the following interaction:

Weak institutions + noncooperative behavior → inefficient tax system and sovereign risk → procyclical fiscal policy → concave association between shocks, investment, and growth.

[19] While trade taxes and seigniorage are associated with zero (or low) collection costs, these taxes frequently end up with higher distortions and narrower tax bases than income and valued added taxes. The narrowness results from growing smuggling and currency substitution. The development pattern of the United States is similar to the OECD countries, where in the 20th century, public finances switched away from trade taxes to income and sales taxes.

Empirical Challenges

The nonlinearities described above and the interactions among the various channels leading to a concave link between shocks and growth pose challenges to empirical investigation:

- The attempt to identify stable associations between uncertainty and growth using regressions is not easy. This is both because of the difficulty of adequately measuring relevant fundamental variables (including the quality of institutions and capital market imperfections) and the presence of nonlinearities.
- One expects a robust positive association between most volatility measures. Hence the estimations of the impact of each source of volatility tends to be imprecise.
- The association between volatility and growth may go both ways. Volatility may reduce growth, and lower growth may increase volatility, as would be the case if lower growth intensifies fights about the division of the national pie. In these circumstances, volatility and growth may be endogenously and simultaneously determined. The causal impact of volatility on growth can be accurately ascertained only if one is able to identify the exogenous component of volatility (that is, the volatility component that is independent of the growth rate). Isolating this exogenous component may be accomplished by relying on instrumental variables (IV). Ideal IV should explain volatility, while at the same time have an impact on long-run growth only through volatility and the other control variables. Hence identifying the causal impact of volatility requires using variables that are correlated with volatility, but uncorrelated with the residual from the growth regression that measures the association between volatility and the conventional controls and growth. Short of having ideal IV (i.e., *instrumental variables* that meet the above stringent criteria), one should interpret econometric results cautiously.

Impact on Welfare

The ultimate cost of volatility is determined by the interaction between volatility and the structure of the market, and by the eventual impact on consumption. Considerations like the completeness of financial markets, the depth of insurance markets, and consumer preferences would determine the welfare cost of uncertainty. Hence there is no one-to-one transformation from the empirical results to the welfare cost of volatility. For example, with complete insurance markets, and with full integration into international capital markets, a risk-averse consumer living in a commodity-exporting country would be fully insured against terms of trade shocks. Hence, volatility and ToT trends would not influence the consumer's consumption patterns. In practice, sovereign risk and shallow financial markets preempt this rosy scenario. In these circumstances, the ultimate welfare cost of ToT uncertainty hinges on the consumers' valuation of this exposure.

As Robert Shiller (1993, 2003) has argued, the lack of deep insurance markets has adverse welfare consequences even in the OECD countries. One expects these effects to be substantially greater in developing countries, where the insurance markets are underdeveloped, and frequently missing. The position of developing countries is further compromised by the inability to borrow externally in their own currency (the "original sin" point articulated by Barry Eichengreen and Ricardo Hausmann 2003), and by their limited access to the capital market due to sovereign risk.

Some of the deficiencies imposed by the lack of insurance markets may be overcome by self-insurance. This self-insurance may take various forms, such as hoarding international reserves at the country level (Aizenman and Marion 2004) or hoarding gold at the household level. Yet these solutions are costly, and may be inhibited in countries characterized by weak institutions. As by Ricardo Caballero and Stavros Panageas (2003) illustrated, insuring macroeconomic shocks at the global level is not feasible, and would require developing large new financial markets. Needless to say, we are far from understanding the obstacles preventing quicker formation of such markets.

A complete assessment of the welfare cost of volatility would require a structural model, and possibly further advances in modeling economic behavior. To elaborate, recall that Garey Ramey and Valerie Ramey (1995) suggest that the welfare costs are of first-order magnitude, in contrast to Robert Lucas (1987), who argues that welfare costs are second-order. As concisely illustrated by Robert Lucas's 2003 presidential address to the American Economic Association, eliminating the cost of business cycle volatility in a typical neoclassical model leads to welfare gains that are akin to the Arrow–Pratt risk premium. In terms of Figure 1, suppose that the utility of the risk-averse agent consuming $(1 + \varepsilon)$ is $U = U(1 + \varepsilon)$, where ε is a random variable. In these circumstances, the utility is represented by the concave curve, $U \cong a + b \cdot \varepsilon + c \cdot \varepsilon^2$, with $c < 0$.[20] Suppose that the business cycle leads consumption to fluctuate between high and low levels, say one plus or minus δ, with equal probability, which gives $EU = U(1) + c\delta^2 = U(1) - \lambda$. The gain from stabilizing these fluctuations is the bold segment λ corresponding approximately to the Arrow–Pratt risk premium.[21] These gains are trivial using conventional measures of risk aversion. The calibration puts these gains at 0.0005 of average consumption (see Equation 4 in Lucas 2003).[22]

Applying a similar rationale to Lucas (1987), one may conclude that the gains from optimal buffer stocks may not be worth the cost (Newbery and Stiglitz, 1981, chapter 29). The potential redundancy of stabilization policies is consistent with studies that show that competitive firms with full access to the capital market would welcome volatility, as it would increase expected profits and investment.[23] This

---

[20] The proper interpretation of the parameters is $a = U(1); b = U'; c = 0.5U''$, corresponding to a second order Taylor approximation of U around 1.

[21] The risk premium is $0.5\gamma\sigma^2$, where γ is the Arrow–Pratt relative risk aversion measure ($\gamma = -U''/U'$), and σ is the standard deviation of the shocks: in our example, $\sigma = \delta$.

[22] Hence the calibration predicts that the consumer would be willing to pay only a trivial sum (0.05 percent of his or her average consumption) for the benefit of insuring against business cycle risk.

[23] To illustrate, note that the producer surplus has a triangular shape, whose area is a quadratic function of the price facing the producers. (That is, the surplus is proportional to the square of the price of the product, corresponding to the case where in Figure 1, the curve corresponding to $c > 0$ plots the association between the price and profits.) In these circumstances, the profit function is convex with respect to the price of the product, and higher price volatility would increase expected profits, supporting higher investment. See Hartman (1972) and Abel (1983).

Box 1. On the Link Between Uncertainty and Expected Investment

This box illustrates the conflicting forces shaping the association between uncertainty and investment.

Investment under irreversibilities (McDonald and Siegel 1986, Pindyck and Solimano 1993, Dixit and Pindyck 1994).

- *Irreversible investment* arises where investment involves irreversible costs, and the firm cannot disinvest, and some investment expenditure cannot be recovered even if the producer can resell his plant. *Uncertainty* implies that in certain states of nature the firm finds itself with too much capital ex post. Ex ante, the firm internalizes this and requires the expected marginal profit of capital to exceed the marginal cost of investment.
- *Investment and the option value of waiting*: To induce investment, the expected marginal profit of capital should exceed the cost of investment by the value of the option to postpone investment. A key result of the literature is that the option value of waiting increases with uncertainty. The greater the uncertainty, therefore, the higher the productivity of capital required to justify investment.
- *Uncertainty and expected investment*: The implications of this for the average level of investment, however, are ambiguous. Higher volatility may delay investment, but when the investment actually takes place, its magnitude is adjusted to reflect the delay and the irreversibility. Hence the net effect of volatility on *average* investment is determined by elasticity considerations. Volatility would reduce average investment only if the increase in realized investment when the productivity of capital is above the threshold leading to investment does not compensate on average for the lower frequency of investment.
- *Conclusion*: The association between uncertainty and expected investment is ambiguous in the presence of irreversibilities.

Uncertainty, investment, and market power (Caballero 1991).
The ultimate effect of a mean-preserving increase in demand volatility on the profits of a risk-neutral producer is determined by the curvature of the profit function. With constant employment and relative prices, the profit function of a producer using labor and capital with a constant-returns-to-scale (CRS) technology is linear with respect to capital. Employment expansion in good times works to further increase the revenue, inducing convexity of the revenue function, whereas the drop in the relative price due to the higher production level works toward reducing the increase in revenue, which induces concavity of the revenue function. The employment expansion effect is more powerful the greater the flexibility of production, as captured by the share of the variable input. The downward price adjustment effect is larger the smaller the demand elasticity. Ultimately, the balance of these two effects determines the curvature, and thereby the investment effects of volatility.

- *Conclusion*: Perfect competition and constant returns to scale induce a positive association between volatility and investment, whereas decreasing returns to scale or imperfect competition or both induce a negative association.

particular interpretation about the trivial cost of business cycle fluctuations has led to two different reactions. Lucas (1987) inferred that stabilization policies are redundant. An alternative view argues for the need to amend our models of behavior under risk, in order to reflect a more complex environment where the costs of economic fluctuations are greater than those captured by the Arrow–Pratt risk premium.

The complexity of modeling the welfare effects of volatility is illustrated by the elusive effects of uncertainty on investment in neoclassical models. Ricardo Caballero (1991) noted that "the relationship between changes in price uncertainty and capital investment under risk neutrality is not robust . . . It is very likely that it will be necessary to turn back to risk aversion, incomplete markets, and lack of diversification to obtain a sturdier negative relationship between investment and uncertainty." Box 1 provides further technical detail. Caballero's insightful remarks outline a useful agenda for advancing the research about the welfare effects of volatility, which are closely linked to output, and hence consumption, dynamics as influenced by investment behavior. The empirical research reported in this book validates the importance of accomplishing this task.

OVERVIEW OF THE VOLUME

Box 2 sets the stage by providing a list of key empirical studies in the volatility literature. A chapter-by-chapter description of this volume follows.

Box 2. Key Empirical Studies on Volatility

The selection of studies presented here illustrates distinct stages in the understanding of the nature and impact of volatility.

Ricardo Caballero (1991) highlighted the fragility of the theoretical relationship between uncertainty and capital investment, pointing out the need to turn back to risk aversion, incomplete markets, and lack of diversification to obtain a sturdier negative relationship between investment and uncertainty. Caballero (2003) surveys the desirable features of insurance and hedging instruments against capital flow volatility and discusses steps to facilitate the creation of these markets.

Joshua Aizenman and Nancy Marion (1993) showed that policy uncertainty is negatively associated with private investment and growth in developing countries.

Garey Ramey and Valerie Ramey (1995) were the first to show the negative association between growth and volatility in a comprehensive study that included the OECD and developing countries, thereby arguing that the welfare costs of business cycle volatility were of first-order magnitude.

A detailed 1995 study of Latin America and the Caribbean by the **Inter-American Development Bank (IDB 1995)** led by Ricardo Hausmann and Michael Gavin explored the underlying causes and sources of volatility, its costs, and corrective policy regimes.

Dani Rodrik (1999) identified weak institutions and latent social conflict as the main reason for the negative impact of volatility on growth. He examined

(Box continues on the following page)

Box 2 (*continued*)

the drop in growth for various sets of countries between 1960–75 and 1975–89 and found that shocks are secondary as an explanation for the drop in growth, as are various measures capturing the stance of economic policy. What matters ultimately is the capacity to respond to shocks in terms of fiscal adjustment and relative price changes. This is critically influenced by the strength of domestic institutions of conflict management: Strong institutions dampen volatility, while weak ones enhance its negative consequences.

William Easterly, Roumeen Islam, and Joseph Stiglitz (2000) honed in on the financial system as the prime factor in growth volatility. They found that up to a point, greater financial depth is associated with lower growth volatility; but as financial depth and leverage grow, the financial sector could become a source of macrovulnerability.

Daron Acemoglu, Simon Johnson, James Robinson, and Yunyong Thaichoren (2003) took the primacy of institutions a step further by arguing that crises are caused by bad macroeconomic policies, which increase volatility and lower growth; but bad macroeconomic policies in turn are the product of weak institutions. In order to avoid problems with endogeneity and omitted variables, they develop a technique to isolate the "historically determined component of institutions" based on the colonization strategy pursed by European settlers, and show that this is the critical factor in explaining volatility, crises, and growth.

As befits the topic, the empirical results are also volatile and not always consistent across studies; but the trend indicates that paying attention to volatility and crises has become critical for growth and development.

WHAT IS VOLATILITY AND WHY DOES IT MATTER? (CHAPTERS 1–3)

Chapter 1. Volatility: Definitions and Consequences

Chapter 1 by Holger Wolf is organized around the question, "What is volatility, and why should we care?" The chapter starts with a set of graphs showing that, across countries, a higher volatility of real per capita GDP growth (measured by the standard deviation of the growth rate) is associated with lower average growth rates and greater income inequality.[24] The chapter then discusses alternative definitions of volatility and addresses measurement issues. It also provides a simple framework for analyzing volatility and uses it to discuss various origins of volatility, its welfare consequences, and options for managing it. The material in this overview overlaps in part with Chapter 1.

Chapter 2. Volatility and Growth

Developing countries (where development is measured by per capita income, financial depth, trade openness, institutional development, or the ability to conduct countercyclical fiscal policy) are undeniably more volatile than more developed

---

[24] This chapter draws upon two country datasets: results on volatility and growth use the same dataset as Chapter 2, while results for volatility and inequality use the same dataset as Chapter 3. The appendices to Chapters 2 and 3 describe the datasets and sources.

ones (where volatility is measured either by the standard deviation of the output gap or that of per capita GDP growth).[25] But what is the relationship between volatility and long-run growth? Attempting to answer this question in Chapter 2, Viktoria Hnatkovska and Norman Loayza use a framework inspired by the new growth literature, augmented with measures of volatility. The sample includes 79 countries and the period covered is 1960–2000. They explore four questions. The first is whether the volatility-growth link depends on country and policy characteristics, such as the level of development or trade openness. The second is whether this link goes beyond an association to capture a statistically and economically significant causal effect from volatility to growth. The third examines the stability of this relationship over time. The fourth is whether the volatility-growth connection captures the impact of crises, rather than the overall effect of cyclical fluctuations.

An analysis of cross-country data yields a negative association between macroeconomic volatility and long-run economic growth. This is exacerbated in countries that are poor, institutionally underdeveloped, undergoing intermediate stages of financial development, or unable to conduct countercyclical fiscal policies.

Furthermore, using instrumental variables regressions to isolate the exogenous, causal impact of volatility on growth reveals an even stronger, more harmful effect of volatility on growth. This is true for a worldwide sample of countries, and particularly for low- and middle-income economies. This negative effect has been present since the 1960s, but has intensified over the last two decades, coinciding with the drop in growth rates observed during the 1980s and 1990s compared to the 1960s and 1970s.

When volatility is decomposed into a crisis component that captures the effect of deep recessions and a component that captures normal cyclical fluctuations, the regressions show it is crisis volatility that truly harms long-run growth. These results place a premium on financial, fiscal, and institutional development and the avoidance of crisis as key factors in alleviating the negative impact of volatility on growth.

The study yields a telling quantitative measure of the exogenous impact of volatility on growth. An increase in volatility by one standard deviation of sample volatility (that is, one worldwide, cross-country standard deviation of volatility) causes a sizable 1.3 percentage point drop in the growth rate. This drop deteriorates further to 2.2 percentage points of the per capita GDP growth rate for the same increase in volatility during the 1990s or under a crisis situation.

Chapter 3. Volatility, Income Distribution, and Poverty

Volatility can affect poverty either through growth or inequality. In fact, changes in poverty rates can be broken up into a growth and an inequality component. Most cross-country studies have focused on growth and poverty, finding that faster growth reduces poverty, but has no systematic effect on inequality. A 1995 study by the Inter-American Development Bank (IDB 1995) found that higher volatility was associated with both lower growth and higher inequality, with the latter tending to

---

[25] The empirical results in Chapter 2 suggest a nonlinear relationship between financial depth and the volatility-growth link. Trade openness does not significantly alter it. See Chapter 2.

be highly persistent. The impact of volatility on inequality was transmitted mainly through educational attainment.

In Chapter 3, Thomas Laursen and Sandeep Mahajan examine the links between volatility and inequality, including the role of transmission channels. Inequality is measured by the the income share of the poorest quintile. Based on cross-country data, a regression of the natural logarithm of the share of income of the poorest quintile, LQ1, on its lagged value and GDP volatility shows that across countries, volatility and the income share of the poor are negatively correlated. But this finding is not entirely robust across country groups. Introduction of dummy variables for regions shows that the negative relationship between volatility and the income share of the poor holds for the Eastern and Central Europe, Middle East and North Africa, and Sub-Saharan Africa regions. For the group of industrialized countries and the Latin America and Caribbean region, the relationship is negative but statistically insignificant, while volatility and the income share of the poor are positively correlated for the East Asia and Pacific region. When dummy variables are included by country income level groupings per the World Bank's definition of low-, middle-, and high-income countries (LICs, MICs, and HICs), the negative impact of volatility on LQ1 is the largest and most statistically significant for LICs. Moreover, this link became significant and intensified over the 1980s and 1990s. A test of the hypothesis that dependence on primary exports exacerbates the link shows that this is not the case, although primary exporters exhibit higher inequality albeit with higher convergence. By and large, the qualitative results using ordinary least squares are retained when instrumental variable regressions are used to control for endogeneity. However, the magnitude of the coefficients is much higher, suggesting a highly negative causal relationship between volatility and the income shares of the poor.

When transmission mechanisms are investigated, it is found that inflation, public expenditure on social security, and financial sector depth (proxied by the ratio of broad money, M2, to GDP, M2/GDP) each enters the regression with a significant coefficient. Inflation reduces the income share of the poor, while financial sector depth and public expenditure on social security tend to increase it. But including these variables lowers the size and significance of the coefficient on GDP volatility. This suggests that at least some of the impact of GDP volatility on income of the poor may be flowing through these transmission channels. Public expenditure on education and health, the unemployment rate, and real exchange rate volatility do not appear to play a significant transmission role.

In principle, shocks can be cushioned by the financial system – through insurance or borrowing opportunities, and by labor market institutions – by offering unemployment insurance and various employment programs. However, both are often poorly developed in low-income, highly volatile countries. In any case, they tend to be of limited value to people on the subsistence minimum. Thus, government intervention is warranted by imperfect domestic insurance markets that lead individuals to inefficient self-insurance decisions. Such intervention needs to take the form of permanent policies and programs to automatically protect the poor from short-term fiscal adjustments and income shocks. Accordingly, the pro-poor policy responses to volatility or negative income shocks would contain inflation, deepen financial markets, develop flexible labor markets, and ensure countercyclical social sector spending. Adequate and flexible social safety nets should be in place before a crisis hits. A last point is that while targeted programs have been successful in reaching the poor, these programs tend to contract in response to local political economy factors that seek to protect nonpoor spending from budget cuts.

COMMODITY PRICES AND VOLATILITY (CHAPTERS 4 AND 5)

Chapter 4. Agricultural Commodity Price Volatility

Traded agricultural commodities continue to be an important component of exports, government revenue, and income for poor farmers in many developing countries, especially in Sub-Saharan Africa.[26] In Chapter 4, Jan Dehn, Christopher Gilbert, and Panos Varangis discuss how a growing body of empirical and policy-oriented work has contributed to a change in thinking away from attempting to stabilize prices in international markets toward living with and managing commodity price and yield risks. The authors illustrate this change in approach with new and sometimes experimental programs, with special emphasis on those sponsored by the World Bank.

The authors measure commodity price variability for countries by using Deaton–Miller (D–M) indices, which are geometric averages of commodity export prices using weights in some base year. Calculations lead the authors to conclude that commodity price variability increased over the final decades of the last century.[27] Deflating the nominal indices by dollar import unit values to obtain a measure of real volatility only reinforces the finding that commodity prices have become much more volatile after 1972. Over the entire 1958–97 sample, real variability was highest in Laos and lowest in South Africa. Of the 110 countries considered, 31 experienced real volatilities in excess of 20 percent per year; 54, between 10 and 20 percent; and the remaining 25, less than 10 percent. The 31 high-volatility countries include most of the major oil exporters, but also some very poor non-oil exporting countries (Bhutan, Haiti, Laos, and Uganda). These countries exhibit high export concentration. The 25 low-volatility countries are composed of countries that are net oil importers but are well-diversified. This group includes some countries that are normally considered as suffering from commodity price variability (Cameroon, Fiji, and Ghana) as well as some very large countries (Brazil and India).

The authors identify shocks as the difference between the actual and predicted percentage change in nominal D–M indices and then focus on those shocks

---

[26] According to the International Task Force on Commodity Risk Management in Developing Countries (ITF 1999), 83 countries had primary commodities accounting for more than 50 percent of total export revenues in 1997 (39 African, of which 35 Sub-Saharan African; 15 Middle East and Asian; 17 Latin American and Caribbean; and 12 European and Central Asian). Excluding fuels, the number drops to 59 (32 African, of which 31 Sub-Saharan African; eight Middle East and Asian; 10 Latin American and Caribbean; and nine European and Central Asian).

[27] The authors calculate volatility as the standard deviation of the first difference in logs of the annual nominal dollar D–M indices) averaged across countries for various regions for three periods: 1958–72, 1973–84, and 1985–97.

exceeding a cut-off point that would for a standard normal distribution correspond to the ±2.5 percent of the tails. Positive shocks predominate; there are nearly twice as many over 1958–97 (179 positive shocks compared to 99 negative ones). Extreme shocks affect sufficiently many countries to dispel the notion that shocks affect only a narrow group of countries, such as oil producers.

Are the odds stacked against commodity exporters? The authors review the Prebisch–Singer hypothesis put forward in the 1950s, which argued for various reasons – including organized union power for workers in manufactures and low income elasticity for commodities – that commodity producers were doomed to face a declining terms of trade. Whether intentionally or not, this hypothesis was used to argue for import-substituting industrialization behind protective barriers in many developing countries. Empirically, the IMF index of primary commodity prices deflated by the U.S. producer price index shows a trend decline at 1.20 percent per year over 1960–2000, although this estimate is sensitive to the choice of sample dates. Moreover, the trend decline in the price of agricultural exports – a component of primary commodities – relative to manufactured exports may just be an artifact of not properly accounting for price rises stemming from quality improvements. Such improvements are likely to be more pronounced for manufactures (such as automobiles) than agricultural commodities (such as coffee). The authors side with this view.

What is the impact of price volatility? In surveys, rural households, which face several sources of risk, including weather, crop disease, and illness, tend to rank price risks as the most important. In attempting to manage (ex ante, for example, through activity diversification) and cope with risk (ex post, for example, by running down savings, or informal risk sharing), rural households face severe constraints. They may not have access to credit during downturns, which is when they most need it. Even during good times, they may lack collateral. They could self-insure, for example, by running down precautionary savings or turning to other households; but the first option may be constrained by limited resources to begin with, while the second option may work only when the shock is idiosyncratic and not systematic (such as a macroeconomic crisis affecting everyone). Diversification of activities away from the farm is a common response of farmers; but this too is often constrained by lack of education, skills, or access to working capital.

In looking at member countries of the International Coffee Organization, the authors find the share of coffee in total export revenues for these countries declined substantially over the 1990s. This reflects lower coffee prices, but, in many countries, increased agricultural diversification and growth in the nonagricultural sector. However, several poor countries remain highly dependent on coffee exports: notably Ethiopia, Rwanda, and Uganda in Africa; and El Salvador, Guatemala, Honduras, and Nicaragua in Latin America. Further analysis shows that while Latin American countries have generally managed to reduce the dependence of government revenues on coffee through diversification and market liberalization over 1990–2000, the same is not true for Africa. Four countries in particular have increased their reliance on coffee: Ethiopia, Madagascar, Rwanda, and Uganda.

Concern about the negative effects of commodity price volatility on welfare and growth prompted both developing and developed country governments, as well as multilateral agencies, to attempt to stabilize prices through most of the 20th century, but with limited success, if not outright failure. As a result, starting in the mid-1980s, the policy focus has been undergoing a dramatic shift toward living with volatile market prices and risks (rather than attempting to control them) and exploring risk management tools (such as use of the futures markets, and possible issue of commodity bonds). Markets have been liberalized. However, as the authors note, this is not enough to address the two central issues, which form the heart of the current policy discussion: how to get governments to manage expenditures and revenues prudently in a volatile environment; and how to shield vulnerable rural households. Diversifying tax bases and developing institutions to support countercyclical fiscal policy (that is, saving during booms to have a cushion during busts) are identified as fruitful areas for policy assistance from development agencies in relation to the first issue. Regarding the second, the most accessible risk-coping mechanisms for rural households are diversifying activities and informal risk-sharing across households. The former often forces households into low-risk, low-return activities, while the latter may break down when most needed: during a systematic crisis. Access to formal markets for risk insurance is impeded by a number of factors, including economies of scale, transactions costs, and the maturity and liquidity of contracts. There is therefore a role for public safety nets. The authors also summarize experience from an ongoing World Bank initiative in collaboration with numerous other donor and multilateral agencies, which comprise the International Task Force on Commodity Risk Management, to facilitate the access of small developing country farmers to risk-management instruments available on international markets.

A noteworthy aspect of the new thinking about countries still dependent upon commodities (almost exclusively in Sub-Saharan Africa) is that the issue is not so much a "commodity problem" as a more general challenge of economic and rural development aimed at enabling these countries diversify away from traditional exports.

Chapter 5. Managing Oil Booms and Busts in Developing Countries

While natural resources should be a boon that provides the means for underpinning long-run economic development and greater human welfare, this has not always happened in practice. Nigeria's real per capita GDP in 2000 was not much higher than in 1965, even though it was a big beneficiary of the two oil price shocks of 1973–74 and 1979–80. Venezuela, another big oil exporter, found itself mired in debt and economic stagnation in the mid-1980s after the two oil shocks. In contrast, Chile and Norway are widely regarded as having managed their natural resource wealth to the benefit of their citizens. Botswana is also considered a success story, while Malaysia has managed to grow impressively and diversify away from oil. In Chapter 5, Julia Devlin and Michael Lewin note that explanations for the poor performance of oil exporters fall into two categories. The first emphasizes governance, including corruption and rent-seeking. The second focuses on the economic effects:

that is, on Dutch Disease[28] and the potential for minimizing it through policies and institutional mechanisms. The chapter surveys this latter set of issues in order to provide policy guidance.

The Dutch Disease effects of oil revenues are transmitted via two key variables: the real exchange rate and fiscal policy. A real appreciation is to be expected as part of the equilibrium response to an oil price boom. The demand for nontraded goods goes up. Since these by definition cannot be imported, their relative price must rise to draw the resources in for greater production. This leads to a shrinkage of the non-oil traded goods sector. In most developing countries, the government, as guardian of the natural resource wealth, becomes the conduit through which the higher oil revenues flow into the economy through higher public spending, which is often concentrated on the nontraded goods sector. This would not be a problem if the increased oil revenues lasted forever; but typically they do not. Oil prices are notoriously volatile. Now consider a government that responds to a boom by treating it as permanent, even borrowing to finance additional expenditure over and above that permitted by the higher oil revenue. When oil prices subsequently collapse, two problems arise: The government might find it no longer has access to the international capital markets; and the agricultural and manufacturing sectors, which atrophied during the oil boom, do not instantaneously and miraculously reappear because of so-called hysteresis or persistence effects stemming from adjustment costs, including lost skills and lost markets. This creates a vicious circle, intensifying the dependence of the economy on oil and increasing its vulnerability to future oil price shocks and hurting overall economic growth: the "resource curse."[29]

Not surprisingly in view of the above, the authors note that fiscal policy – in particular, a combination of expenditure restraint and revenue management – is the key to managing booms. They proceed to survey country experiences with oil revenue ("stabilization") funds and fiscal policy rules, mechanisms for self-insurance and asset diversification, and policies to catalyze diversification in the real sector.

The authors stress that delinking fiscal expenditures from current revenue is the key to insulating the economy from oil revenue volatility. Oil funds can help achieve this, but are not a panacea. The oil fund can be subverted, by using it to save during a boom but then borrowing against this saving. Thus what needs to be monitored is the consolidated debt/asset position of the government. A well-designed and well-governed oil fund can increase transparency and accountability. It can stabilize oil revenue flows to the budget within the context of an overall fiscal framework focused on the consolidated net asset position of the government with control over the non-oil deficit (spending minus non-oil revenues), to ensure there is genuine saving during booms. This will permit expenditure to be maintained during busts

---

[28] The term originated in Holland in the 1970s. It was used to describe the appreciation of the real exchange rate and the "deindustrialization" that resulted from the discovery of North Sea gas, which made manufactured imports much cheaper. More generally, it refers to the tendency of the manufacturing and agricultural (non-oil traded goods) sectors to atrophy in response to a real exchange rate appreciation fueled by a booming natural resource sector.

[29] Of course, corruption and favoritism (rent-seeking) in the allocation of oil revenues would make the problem much worse, which has been the case for many oil exporters.

and help minimize real exchange rate volatility. The authors proceed to summarize the mixed empirical evidence on the usefulness of oil funds. They emphasize that if a country decides to establish a fund, its design and operation should be based on transparent integration into the budgetary process to avoid off-budgetary spending. Parliamentary/legislative oversight should be included to avoid sole discretionary powers by the executive over the fund's resources.

Implementing an oil fund and/or fiscal rules can stabilize revenue transfers to the budget and help keep the deficit under control but require some assumption about how oil prices will behave. Medium-term budgeting requires that the oil price path be forecast, which is not easy to do. The decision to add to an oil fund or deplete it must rely on some notion of a long-term reference price: when oil prices exceed this, the surplus revenue should be added to the fund; when prices fall below it, the deficit in revenue should be compensated by withdrawals from the fund. This raises complex issues about the stochastic process governing oil prices: to what extent price changes are permanent or temporary and whether prices are mean-reverting or not. One way of dealing with this is by using the information from futures and swap markets.

The authors also discuss how both exchange-traded and over-the-counter (OTC) risk-management instruments can be used to reduce and manage oil price risk; but note that in practice, risk-management programs are rarely implemented, for a variety of reasons, including lack of familiarity with instruments and unwillingness of public officials to face a situation where, say, they authorized a futures contract to lock in the oil price and prices subsequently rose. Simulation exercises suggest that remaining unhedged might lead to higher expected revenue, but also higher volatility (the standard mean-variance tradeoff one would expect if the market is pricing risk efficiently). This could be costly for the economy if it translates into higher budget deficits. Hence while using risk-management instruments to lower the volatility of the received oil price might lower expected revenues, this may be well worth it if it helps execute more prudent and stable fiscal policy.

A key policy issue pertains to the need to maintain a diversified economy with a strong non-oil traded goods sector. The authors stress that it would be a mistake to subsidize specific manufacturing activities directly because of the possible rent-seeking this would generate, not to mention the familiar difficulty of selecting "winners." While deciding how to proceed depends upon individual country circumstances, a guiding principle is that government expenditure to enhance productivity in the non-oil traded goods sector is likely to be the most effective when focused on public goods such as infrastructure, health, and education.

FINANCE AND VOLATILITY (CHAPTERS 6 AND 7)

Chapter 6. Finance and Volatility

In theory, the financial system should help to mobilize and allocate resources efficiently, while also providing mechanisms to share and manage risks. In practice, the financial system can also increase volatility, for example, by intensifying a credit cycle in real estate by providing funds on too-easy terms, imperfectly monitoring how firms use borrowed funds, or amplifying macroeconomic cycles through the so-called credit channel. In other words, access to funding can be procyclical. Likewise, financial sector policy can be a source of volatility, as when a country decides to liberalize the financial sector to reap the benefits of better resource mobilization and allocation but does not have adequate supervision in place. Systemic financial crises can be particularly damaging because of their impact on the real sector and public finances in the event of government bailouts.

Chapter 6 by Stijn Claessens examines the links between finance and volatility. In general, greater financial development (measured by credit to the private sector as a ratio of GDP) is associated with lower growth volatility. Interestingly, so long as supporting institutions are strong, financial structure – that is, whether the financial system is primarily bank-based or capital market-based – does not make a difference. Both structures can provide effective risk management, provided legal underpinnings (importantly, equity and creditor rights) and other elements (such as accounting standards) are strong. The results on international financial integration are more controversial. Many studies find positive benefits from liberalization and increased integration with world financial markets at the micro level (or firm level) for investment and growth. Some have found little benefit, however, with volatility potentially rising, especially when financial and institutional development are weak.

How can countries move from financially repressed systems to more liberalized, market-oriented ones without increasing risks? Theory and empirics in these areas are still young. While evidence suggests that individual firms stand to benefit from equity market liberalization, asset price volatility also increases. The possibility of contagion – that is, spillovers from other markets – also goes up, especially when there is a common international lender or investor base. This in part arises as there are forces at play that restrict gains for the country from international integration, such as the absence of the equivalent of an international bankruptcy court. Capital inflows can also aggravate domestic credit booms, as domestic asset prices rise and lead to currency mismatches when the domestic financial system is not functioning well. In the case of East Asia, a desire to sterilize capital inflows kept interest differentials high. This, in conjunction with an implicit exchange rate guarantee, led to currency mismatches for banks and corporations. Such a configuration can create a vulnerability to a sudden stop of capital inflows, with severe knock-on effects because of the balance sheet mismatches. If in addition public debt dynamics are unsustainable (as in Argentina in the late 1990s) and banks hold a large fraction of their assets in government paper, a sovereign default could trigger a huge financial and real crisis. In Argentina, "bad macropolicy" trumped the "good financial sector regulation" the country was reputed to have.

In discussing crisis prevention and management, the chapter notes that crises are difficult to predict, and outlines reasons for why Early Warning Systems may not be much better than naïve forecasts. A recent initiative has involved the development of analytical tools to assess macrofinancial risks, based on stress-testing the financial system under different assumptions on exchange rates, interest rates, and growth, in part under the World Bank/IMF Financial Sector Assessment Program. While such exercises can help identify risks, trigger preventive responses and enhance transparency, they are hampered by poor data quality and the difficulty of analytically specifying the necessary relationships. Hence financial crises are going to remain a fact of life.

Responding to a financial crisis can be divided into three phases: containment, an initial period, during which attempts may be made to stabilize the situation and limit the size and costs of the crisis; restructuring of financial institutions and corporations; and structural reforms. In all three phases, politics pose major problems, as does the difficulty in separating unviable from viable entities.

The key issue during the containment phase is the tradeoff between restoring confidence and containing fiscal costs. A study of the fiscal cost of 40 crises in industrial and developing economies from 1980 to 1997 found that higher fiscal costs incurred to contain the crisis do not facilitate subsequent economic growth. Countries that used policies such as liquidity support, blanket guarantees, and particularly costly forbearance – i.e., the relaxing of prudential standards – did not recover faster. Rather, liquidity support appears to prolong the recovery period and increase output losses. This suggests that during the containment phase, it is important to limit liquidity support and not to extend guarantees.

During the restructuring phase, the two major issues are how to allocate costs among shareholders, creditors, workers, the government, and taxpayers; and how to get the financial and real sectors up and running as soon as possible. This must be done in conjunction with macroeconomic reform, because of the many interdependencies. Evidence suggests that it is not necessary for governments to assume all losses; these can be shared with shareholders and large depositors in the case of banks, for instance.

One major objective is that banks should emerge well-capitalized from the process and properly regulated and supervised, or they may engage only in cosmetic corporate restructuring rather than writing off debts. The restructuring of firms needs to take place alongside that of financial institutions. The question is how to decide which firms are worth restructuring. In an individual case, the decision will be made by the concerned private agents – but what about in a systemic crisis? One step the government can take is to improve the enabling environment. The crisis will typically provide an opportunity to improve bankruptcy legislation, make the judicial system more efficient, liberalize entry for foreign investors, harden budgets for enterprises, and improve corporate governance – structural reforms, which are important for efficient financial and real sectors in any case. But the problem of how to restructure firms and who will lead the process in a way that minimizes fiscal costs and quickly reestablishes going concerns remains a complicated one. Several proposals are discussed in this regard.

A related topic is the creation of a supportive macroeconomic environment. The fiscal-monetary policy mix must be conducive to restructuring, but may be constrained by the indebtedness and balance sheet mismatches of banks and firms, as well as the level of public debt. Raising interest rates to defend the currency could hurt indebted firms, as well as public debt dynamics. Letting the exchange rate go could be problematic if liabilities are denominated in foreign currency and hedges are unavailable. Similarly, liquidity support, especially to insolvent institutions, could both increase fiscal costs and contribute to a free fall of the currency if the liquidity made available is used to buy the central bank's foreign exchange reserves. On the other hand, a credit crunch may deprive firms of working capital and slow down restructuring. There are no easy answers; but the empirical evidence shows clearly that lowering the risks of a financial crisis in the first place – by emphasizing

macroeconomic fundamentals, creditor and property rights, and proper and adequate
regulation and supervision – is well worth it.

Chapter 7. Evaluating Price Signals from the Bond Markets

Sovereign bond issues by emerging market countries in Latin America and elsewhere
are largely a phenomenon of the 1990s and after. An important feature of these bonds
is that they are continuously traded in the secondary markets. In Chapter 7, John
Merrick discusses how bond prices can be used to gauge market sentiment and in
particular, how yield spreads can be interpreted as signals of default probability.
Emerging market bond spreads can be thought of as determined by four sets of
factors: macroeconomic fundamentals; debt instrument and country characteristics;
interest rates in "benchmark" countries, particularly the United States; and market
sentiment. A noteworthy finding in empirical studies quoted in the chapter is that
while in "normal" times economic fundamentals explain spreads across countries
well, volatile market sentiment and herd behavior explain short-run variations in
such spreads at times of crisis better than shifts in fundamentals.[30] Whatever the
determinants of spreads, pricing theory suggests that the way emerging market bonds
are priced is informative about how the market views the chances of default.

Consider a simple example based on the chapter: a one-period emerging market
country bond with a coupon of 10 percent and principal or face value of $100 due
after one year. Assume that this bond is priced at $96.38. Its yield, denoted Y, is
simply the discount rate, which equates the present value of the promised future
cash flows of the bond – in this case, $110 after one year – with its price: that is,
$96.38 = 110/(1 + Y)$. This gives $Y = 14.13$ percent.

Now assume the one-year U.S. Treasury zero coupon bond yield is $y = 5$ percent.[31] This is in effect the yield on a default- or risk-free bond. The spread on
the emerging market bond can be obtained as: $1 + s = (1 + Y)/(1 + y)$, which
yields a spread $s = 8.7$ percent, or 870 basis points.[32] A positive spread arises
precisely because there is no guarantee that the promised $110 will actually be
paid; let p denote the probability of repayment. In a risk-neutral framework, this
discounting problem can be equivalently written as $96.38 = p(110)/(1 + y)$, where
the risk-free rate is now used to discount the *expected* cash flow (as opposed to the
promised one). By comparing this equation with the one above, one can see that
$p/(1 + y) = 1/(1 + Y)$, and combining this with the expression for the spread, s,
yields $p = 1/(1 + s)$. This gives a payment probability of 92 percent and a default
probability of 8 percent. But as Merrick cautions, this interpretation holds if and
only if the assumed recovery value in the event of default is zero. In this case, and
assuming a per period default rate of 8 percent, the chances that default would occur
on a 10-year bond would be almost 57 percent![33]

---

[30] But of course there could be shifting perceptions about fundamentals!

[31] A zero-coupon bond is one that pays a lump sum at maturity without any intermediate payments.

[32] The reason for doing this geometrically rather than arithmetically is that it makes it easier to interpret
while discounting. Note that 1 percentage point = 100 basis points.

[33] The probability of default is the sum of default in period 1 plus no default in 1, and default in 2 plus
no default in 1 and 2, but default in 3, up to 10, which eventually gives a probability of $1 - p^{10}$.

Merrick then shows that the simple interpretation above linking s and p no longer holds once a positive default recovery value is assumed. This can be seen immediately by assuming a recovery value of $R > 0$. In this case,

$$96.38 = p\frac{110}{1+y} + (1-p)\frac{R}{1+y},$$

and setting $R = 0$ gives the previous case. There is now no longer a simple one-to-one mapping between s and p even *though* the quoted Y and s remain the same, at 14.13 percent and 870 basis points, respectively. Assuming $R = 50$, this new equation can be solved to give $p = 85$ percent, that is, the default probability almost doubles from 8 percent to 15 percent. Alternatively, if p were kept fixed at 92 percent, the fair price of the bond would be $100.19 (= 0.92[110/1.05] + 0.08[50/1.05])$, reflecting improved perceived treatment in the default state. In this case, the new yield linking the price and promised cash flow would fall from 14.13 percent to 9.8 percent. This 9.8 percent would be the yield quoted by the market; but it is actually a blend of the risk-free rate of 5 percent and the appropriate risky sovereign rate of 14.13 percent. This can be seen by writing the price of the bond $V = (p)110/(1 + y) + (1 - p)R/(1 + y)$, which as already seen, gives $V = 100.19$, when $p = 0.92$, $y = 0.05$ and $R = 50$. The right-hand side of this equation can be rearranged to give: $V = p(110 - R)/(1 + y) + R/(1 + y)$. Given $R = 50$ and defining $p/(1 + y) = 1/(1 + Y)$, this reduces to $V = (110 - 50)/(1 + Y) + 50/(1 + y)$.

Thus the "risky" component of the cash flow, which picks up true sovereign risk, is effectively discounted at 14.13 percent, while the "riskless" recovery value is discounted at the risk-free rate. Once again, the true sovereign yield of 14.13 percent can be linked to the default probability of 8 percent. But here is where the problem arises, as Merrick notes. All one would actually observe would be the blended yield of 9.8 percent, the bond's price of 100.19, and the promised cash flows. The probability of default cannot be inferred without knowing what default recovery value the market is assuming, which is not directly observable.

Merrick extends the above formulation to the n-period bond case and presents a methodology to extract measures of the market's implied recovery value and payment (default) probabilities based on promised cash flows and market bond prices. He applies this to Republic of Argentina's Eurobonds during the market collapse prior to the December 2001 default and contrasts the results with those obtained through a similar exercise covering August to December 1998. The 2001 results are also compared with those that would be obtained assuming a zero-percent recovery value, based on the observed sovereign spreads. The latter depict a much lower default probability than that yielded by the simultaneous extraction of implied recovery values and default probabilities using Merrick's methodology.

MANAGING CRISES (CHAPTERS 8–11)

Chapter 8. Managing Macroeconomic Crises: Policy Lessons

In the last decade, macroeconomic crises have successively hit Mexico, Thailand, Korea, Indonesia, Malaysia, Russia, Brazil, Turkey, and Argentina. Which policies for crisis prevention or crisis management seem to work, and which do not? Using the probability of a currency crisis and the total output lost during crises as the criteria of economic performance, Jeffrey Frankel and Shang-Jin Wei attempt to answer this question in Chapter 8 by linking key lists of macroeconomic variables to models of crisis probability.

These lists of variables are inspired by the "three generations" of crisis models. The *first generation* model attributes balance-of-payments crises to budget deficits financed by domestic credit in a fixed exchange rate regime with perfect capital mobility. This leads to current account deficits and a steady loss of reserves at a rate equal to the pace of credit creation; but a speculative attack resulting in a discrete exhaustion of remaining reserves occurs *before* these would have been used up based on credit expansion alone. A float will then be forced.[34] Such macroeconomic over-expansion and overvaluation were the standard diagnoses of balance-of-payments crises in developing countries before 1995, and were the basis of most adjustment programs administered by the International Monetary Fund. The international debt crisis of the 1980s is an important example.

The *second generation* model argues that there are "crisis" and "no-crisis" multiple equilibria consistent with unchanged fundamentals. This approach was inspired the European Exchange Rate Mechanism (ERM) crises of 1992–93. The speculative attack on France in 1993 was puzzling, because the government had over the preceding years succeeded in attaining a level of macroeconomic discipline comparable to that of Germany, its partner in the ERM. Moreover, after the bands were widened, the crisis passed without a substantial further depreciation of the franc, even though there had been no tightening of macroeconomic policy in the meantime. How then could the fundamentals have been responsible for the earlier speculative pressure? The second generation argument is most simply illustrated by a "prisoner's dilemma". Consider two speculators. Each realizes that if the other sells, the resulting depreciation will reduce the value of his holdings of domestic currency. Neither wants to stand pat if the other might sell. One equilibrium is for both to sell, even though the economy may be worse off after the devaluation.

The *third generation* model was developed as an explanation of the East Asian crisis of 1997–98, where expansionary macroeconomic policy did not seem to be a factor, but a different kind of weakness in fundamentals appeared: structural distortions in the financial system combined with implicit exchange rate guarantees. The phrase "crony capitalism" became popular in 1997 to describe flaws in the structure of Asian financial systems. Well-connected banks and businessmen are able to borrow from abroad to finance risky projects such as real estate development or construction of new factories in the already-glutted steel industry. They are aware of the risk, but confident they will be bailed out by the government if things go badly. The timing of the attack again stems from the calculations of speculators who worry that if they wait too long, there will not be enough foreign exchange reserves

---

[34] The basic insight of the Krugman (1979) and Flood–Garber (1984) models was to show that the speculative attack would happen when remaining reserves are exactly equal to the reduction in the demand for real domestic money balances that occurs when the fixed peg is abandoned. The reduction in money demand would be determined by the rise in the inflation rate (equal to the rate of currency depreciation when the float is forced) needed to generate the seignorage (inflation tax) necessary to finance the fiscal deficit.

to go around. But there is a key difference from the first generation model, where reserves fall in the run-up to crisis. In this case, liabilities artificially encouraged by moral hazard rise to a point at which investors suddenly cash in their investments, fearful that if they wait any longer, they might not be able to get their money out. The speculative attack, as usual, then forces the central bank to abandon the exchange rate.

The data set is based on macrovariables over the period 1990–2002, driven by four sets of considerations:

- Definition of crisis, which is based on a foreign exchange market pressure index defined as the percentage fall in reserves plus the percentage fall in the foreign exchange value of the currency.
- Measures of performance, including number of crises, output lost, and average rate and standard deviation of growth during the period.
- Crisis prevention policies, which prompts consideration of the "deep determinants" of performance, such as institutions/governance, the choice of exchange rate regime, the capital account regime, trade openness, and the composition and use of capital inflows.
- Crisis management policies, such as monetary contraction measured by the change in the real interest rate relative to the change in the real exchange rate, and the relative importance of fiscal contraction measured by the change in the budget surplus relative to the change in the trade balance.

The question is whether there exists some combination of these policies that enables a country to increase its trade balance in response to a sudden stop in capital flows that avoids an output contraction. Perhaps a contraction becomes unavoidable if the period of sudden stop – which might consist of several months rather than a single instant, as models suggest – has already been spent running down reserves to low levels and switching the composition of liabilities toward short-term dollar loans. The formulation here is based on the textbook framework of adjusting to an external imbalance through some combination of expenditure reduction and real devaluation, which remains among the most useful models for developing countries.

A casual inspection of the data for countries that had the most visible crises during the period 1994–2002 and selected noncrisis "control cases" suggests that it may not be possible to neatly separate the crises into first, second, or third generation; elements of all three models played a role. Nor is it easy to take any single variable regarded as crucial and show that it is *the* one driving crisis. For example, crises occurred with hard pegs (Argentina), floating (Brazil after January 1999), and intermediate exchange rate regimes (Mexico, Thailand, Korea, Russia, Turkey). Likewise, while Indonesia scores much higher on corruption than Argentina, both experienced severe crises.

The authors next use probit analysis to search for robust correlates of crisis based on a sample of 62 developing countries. Only two variables qualify as "very likely" contributors: the ratio of short-term external debt to foreign exchange reserves, and expansionary monetary policy (inflation). Two additional variables satisfy the generous definition for a "likely" determinant of crisis: the ratio of FDI and equity inflows to gross foreign liabilities, estimated to decrease the chance of a crisis; and intermediate exchange rate regime, less likely to be associated with crisis than the floating exchange rate regime.

To allow for nonlinear threshold effects, regression tree analysis is employed to potentially nest all threshold and interactive effects. When the ratio of short-term debt to reserves exceeds 157 percent and inflation exceeds 17 percent, there is a 50 percent probability of a crisis. This is the only combination, from the universe of all the variables considered, that would generate a crisis probability of 50 percent or higher. Even in scenarios in which the short-term debt to reserve ratio is below the threshold of 157 percent, a combination of high inflation (exceeding 25 percent per year) and a high ratio of external debt to GDP (exceeding 80 percent) would also place a country in jeopardy. Therefore, the regression tree analysis identifies three variables – the ratio of external debt to GDP, in addition to the ratio of short-term debt to reserves and inflation – as the most important variables that can help classify country-years into high versus low probabilities of crisis.

Equally telling is what was not chosen by the regression tree analysis: financial openness and institutional quality. If there is a hump-shaped relationship between financial openness and currency crisis, or if there is a particular combination of weak institutions, exchange rate regime and high financial openness that would enhance a country's vulnerability, the analysis suggests that these relationships are either not robust or quantitatively unimportant (assuming that these variables are well-measured). Similarly, no decade dummies are selected by the regression tree, implying a lack of strong evidence that one decade is more crisis-prone than any other.

A major issue is that the above variables are endogenous and do not clearly map into an optimal choice of policies. Debt and inflation are endogenous to fiscal and monetary policy. High levels of external debt may not lead to crises on their own, if debt is long-term or used (in part) to bolster reserves. But the composition of inflows is also endogenous. No policymaker deliberately wishes to borrow short term and in dollars. It may be the result of a deeper cause, such as crony capitalism or original sin. Or an adverse shift in composition may result from the response to a sudden stop, for example, a refusal to devalue or raise domestic interest rates after the speculative attack is launched. Such procrastination could result in a country's entering a crisis with a higher proportion of short-term and dollar-denominated debt, which could then lead to a steep recession – no matter what policies are followed.

Some insight into these factors is sought by looking at the effect of the crisis prevention variables on output lost during a crisis. Macrovariables, such as debt/GDP and inflation, do not appear to be significant; nor is capital account openness. But noncorruptness is significant with the expected sign. Overall, countries tend to have fewer or less severe crises if they are free from corruption, and tilt the composition of their capital inflows away from dollar-denomination. When the corners hypothesis (hard peg or float) was tested, it was rejected: that is, corner regimes are not less crisis-prone and intermediate regimes may work better.[35] Nor does exchange rate

---

[35] The corners hypothesis, also known as the bipolar view or two-corner solution, argues that for countries open to international capital flows, "intermediate regimes between hard pegs and free floating are unsustainable" (Fischer 2001). The two corners are free floats and hard pegs, while intermediate regimes include all adjustable pegs and everything else in between, although Stanley Fischer's warning about unsustainability seems to apply only to soft pegs.

flexibility systematically reduce crises. Using average growth over 1990–2002 as the performance variable, a high ratio of short-term debt to equity and FDI shows a statistically significant negative effect. When interaction effects are explored (once again, with crisis output lost as the dependent variable), it is difficult to find support for any of the supposedly "deadly" combinations: namely, open capital markets and high fiscal deficits; open capital markets and short-term debt; or open capital markets and currency mismatch. But the variable that interacts open capital markets and initial income shows a positive sign and is significant at the 95 percent level. This might be rationalized by the possibility that open capital markets can lead to heavy borrowing and thereby to crises in middle-income countries, but are less dangerous in poor countries.

When crisis management (as opposed to prevention) is examined, the first interesting finding is that the average length of the sudden stop (the interval between the month that reserves peak and adjustment to crisis starts) varies between 6 and 13 months.[36] The point is: this is sufficiently long for the policy response to the sudden stop to have a significant impact on key variables such as the composition of capital flows, and thereby on the range of policy options available when the crisis actually hits. To take an important example, whatever the composition of the capital inflows a year or two earlier, if on the day when the crisis occurs the debt is substantially dollar-denominated and short-term, then the country is in trouble regardless what mix of policies it chooses as the means of adjustment. Either a short-term increase in interest rates or a devaluation, or any combination of the two, will sharply worsen the balance sheets of debtor firms and banks, and thereby contribute to bankruptcies and contraction in output and employment. While econometric evidence on this is inconclusive, the authors cite country examples from Mexico and Brazil to make their point.

Perhaps the most interesting question of crisis management is the mix between adjustment by real devaluation versus expenditure reduction. For fiscal policy, the authors found that countries for which the fall in government consumption constituted a large share of the adjustment in the trade balance suffered a smaller output loss, other things equal. The effect, however, was not significant at the 95 percent level. For monetary policy, the authors found that countries that relied heavily on high real interest rates (either absolutely or relative to the preceding year) suffered larger output losses than those that relied on big real depreciations of the currency, a highly significant result statistically.

Chapters 9 and 10. The Russian and Argentine Crises

Russia and Argentina both suffered severe macroeconomic crises in recent years: Russia in 1998, and Argentina in late 2001 and still unresolved.[37] In both cases, public debt dynamics became unsustainable and eventually led to sudden stops in

---

[36] Adjustment is defined as starting in the month of devaluation or a substantial fiscal contraction, or the signing of an IMF agreement.

[37] The Convertibility Plan, under which Argentina had a hard peg at parity with the U.S. dollar, was effectively abandoned in December 2001 when, following runs on banks, withdrawals were restricted under the infamous *corralito*.

capital inflows. In both cases, there was a reprofiling of public debt through market-based swaps, which eventually failed to avert crisis, and might even have accelerated it. Furthermore with the wisdom of hindsight, significant real exchange rate over-valuation had also been a problem in both cases. And both involved defaults. But the aftermath has turned out to be different. Russia rebounded quickly, growing the very next year, and was able to achieve a substantial debt restructuring. Argentina is now showing signs of recovery, but has only recently resolved its debt crisis, some four-and-a-half years after its default. The first main difference is the speed with which the fixed exchange rate was let go, and the related balance sheet currency mismatch. Argentina took much longer to do so and had a severe mismatch, which plunged its banks and corporates into deep trouble when convertibility was finally abandoned.[38] The second main difference pertains to special circumstances that made it much easier for Russia to restructure its debt, which are discussed in Chapter 9.

RUSSIA. The Russian meltdown occurred in August 1998 only six months after single-digit inflation was attained and less than a month after a big rescue plan put together by the international financial institutions (IFIs) took effect in July 1998. A unique feature of the plan was an upfront liquidity injection from the IFIs and a debt swap out of short-term ruble treasury bills (GKOs) into long-term dollar eurobonds in an attempt to boost market confidence and avoid a devaluation. Preserving the fixed exchange rate band was seen as vital for credibility and retaining stabilization gains. The rescue plan was abandoned following a government announcement of emergency measures on August 17, 1998. These included an immediate devaluation with a forced restructuring of ruble-denominated public debt maturing up to the end of 1999. The suspension of the rescue surprised those who believed Russia was "too big to fail" and that an IFI-led bailout would proceed regardless. Another surprise was that the Russian economy recovered much faster than anyone expected, with the crisis becoming a positive turning point in Russia's transition.

In Chapter 9, Brian Pinto, Evsey Gurvich, and Sergei Ulatov use a four-part framework: an analysis of fundamentals, especially fiscal and growth; market signals; potential crisis triggers; and moral hazard issues, to argue that what happened in Russia was not that surprising after all. Indeed, had a decision to let the exchange rate go been made in May instead of August 1998, Russia would have used up $16 billion less of foreign exchange resources (reserves plus new debt) in its futile defense of the ruble: some 8 percent of postcrisis 1999 GDP. This illustrates two of the key ideas from Chapter 8. First, sudden stops are not that sudden. Russia's lasted for about 10 months. Second, the avoidance of procrastination through early decisive action can be beneficial to the economy and to the balance sheets of the government and private sector. Quite apart from the politics, the key to early decisive action is a shared economic assessment of the nature of the crisis, and even this appears hard to achieve.[39]

---

[38] Indeed, the presence of a severe mismatch was one of the reasons the Argentines were reluctant to abandon their hard peg.

[39] Indeed, it might be impossible to separate it from the politics.

The authors ascribe the surprising constancy of the public debt to GDP ratio over 1995–97 to the strong real appreciation that accompanied the exchange rate-based stabilization program launched in mid-1995. This led to capital gains on the dollar-denominated debt of the government, which masked the effect of large deficits and poor growth. By the beginning of 1998, with inflation approaching single-digit levels and the real exchange rate flattening out, public debt dynamics began reflecting their true determinants: namely, high primary fiscal deficits and real interest rates, and weak economic growth. By mid-May 1998, the marginal real interest rate was 27 percent under the macroeconomic program assumptions, compared to zero-growth expectations, and public debt was on an explosive path.

Why did growth not accompany stabilization? First, the real sector was facing a punishing combination of high real interest rates and significant real appreciation that accompanied the stabilization. Second, a unique structural issue arose in the form of the so-called nonpayments problem. Manufacturing enterprises were allowed to run large arrears on their energy and tax dues, which were then settled through various noncash, barter-based means at off-market prices that incorporated significant discounts. Not politically permitted to disconnect nonpaying customers, the energy monopolies became delinquent on their own tax payments, adding to a consistent revenue shortfall for the government and leading to larger debt issues – thereby creating a direct, if hidden, link between nonpayments and public debt dynamics. Why did the government tolerate and even participate in the nonpayments system and its use of noncash settlements? One reason was the high real interest rates. A second, ironically, may have been the fear that the punishing macroeconomic environment would lead to mass bankruptcy and social chaos.

Was the real appreciation an equilibrium phenomenon? The authors note that the real appreciation preceding the 1998 crisis was not accompanied by rising productivity in the traded goods sector and occurred alongside, indeed masked, increasingly unsustainable debt dynamics. Besides, the real exchange rate remained appreciated because of the high real interest rates that accompanied stabilization, followed by the interest rate defense of the ruble after speculative attacks that started in late October 1997. Thus in spite of current account balance, the real appreciation was not an equilibrium phenomenon. Indeed, the biggest threat to the real exchange rate by May 1998 was the possibility that the deficit might have to be monetized and debt inflated away: real interest rates were far higher than expected growth; debt was being frantically rolled over to hold on to inflation gains; and markets were signaling that Russia might have reached its credit ceiling – the classic Sargent–Wallace (1981) conditions.

The authors develop a simple technique for extracting market signals on default and devaluation risk and track their evolution during the months before the meltdown, showing how default risk rose continually during this period. By May 1998, it was clear that Russia was in danger of a fundamentals-based speculative attack. But Russia procrastinated for another 10 weeks. Eventually, the crisis was triggered by a combination of deteriorating liquidity, the vulnerability of banks, and the GKO-Eurobond swap.[40]

---

[40] For an analysis of the destabilizing impact of the swap, see Chapter 9 and Kharas, Pinto, and Ulatov (2001).

Did moral hazard play a role in prolonging the defense of the ruble at great cost after May 1998? The authors suggest that only the prospect of an IFI bailout permitted Russia to increase its dollar-denominated debt by $16 billion between June 1 and the meltdown. The implications are potentially serious for a country. External, hard currency borrowing headroom could be used up in defense of an unsustainable peg rather than to support reforms or defray the social costs of a crisis. And the debt burden becomes more severe when the exchange rate eventually collapses.

While the expectation was that Russia was headed for a political and economic disaster after the August 17, 1998 devaluation and default, it rebounded much faster than anyone expected and grew by more than 5 percent in real terms the very next year. The two immediate factors according to the authors were the large real depreciation, which switched demand toward domestic goods, and the hardening of the government's budget constraint by the default (which shut it out of the capital markets), leading eventually to the dismantling of the costly nonpayments system. Macropolicy objectives moved away from attaining low inflation per se to maintaining a competitive real exchange rate and placing public debt on a stable long-run trajectory. While rising oil prices after 1999 helped, the proceeds were used to rebuild reserves and pay down public debt. Improvements in the quality of fiscal institutions also played a big role, including the implementation of the new treasury system, a new budget code, and elimination of all noncash settlements by 2001.

The authors conclude with a list of lessons. Three are mentioned here. First, it is difficult to design a package to deal with confidence (liquidity) and fundamentals at the same time, especially in the context of a fixed exchange rate. If public debt is on an unsustainable course and the market is signaling high levels of default risk, attempts to bolster liquidity with loans from the IFIs could actually trigger a crisis. More junior debt holders (such as GKO – ruble treasury bills – holders, in the case of Russia) could seize the opportunity to exit, and the temporary increase in liquidity as the result of the IFI loan provides the exit opportunity.

Second, inflation reduction should be viewed with suspicion if it is achieved in an environment of weak growth prospects, an appreciating real exchange rate, and stubbornly large fiscal deficits. This combination can only mean that public debt is either on an obvious or latent explosive trajectory that will eventually cause a collapse in stabilization.

Third, Russia's problem with nonpayments also has lessons for other economies: that macroeconomic stabilization is eventually unsustainable without hard budgets for enterprises.

ARGENTINA. Seldom has an economy gone so rapidly from being the "darling of emerging market finance to the world's leading deadbeat" – to use Michael Mussa's (2002) expression – as Argentina did during the 1990s. Its economy grew rapidly following the adoption in April 1991 of parity with the U.S. dollar under a currency board system, as part of the Convertibility Plan to reverse decades of macroeconomic instability and declining per capita income. It handily survived the "tequila crisis" following the Mexican devaluation of 1994, and continued to perform well until the Russian crisis in 1998 and Brazil's subsequent devaluation. Argentina then plunged into recession and meltdown over 1999–2001.

Luis Serven and Guillermo Perry analyze the reasons why in Chapter 10. It starts by delineating competing hypotheses, illustrating how difficult it is to identify the basic cause(s) of a crisis even ex post. In distinguishing between bad luck and bad policies, it compares the major external shocks suffered by Argentina in the second half of the 1990s with other Latin American countries. Three sources of vulnerability are then examined: the straitjacket imposed by the hard peg, the destabilizing fiscal policy stance, and the fragilities hidden in the financial system.

The first surprise that emerges is that the external shocks suffered by Argentina, including the terms of trade, the impact of global economic slowdown during 2001, and the sudden stop in capital flows triggered by the Russian crisis, were either comparable to or milder than in other Latin American comparators. However, Argentina also suffered from two significant country-specific shocks stemming from the appreciation of the U.S. dollar against the euro and the devaluation of the Brazilian *real* in 1999. These prompted a large real appreciation, which the hard-peg straitjacket could do little to alleviate, adding to the real appreciation that had already occurred earlier during the 1990s as a result of the exchange rate-based stabilization.[41] The authors note the inadvisability of choosing a hard peg to the U.S. dollar based on Optimal Currency Area arguments: trade with the United States was only one-fifth of Argentina's total trade, and the hard peg left Argentina without the flexibility to adjust to shocks that might require a different monetary policy response from the United States.

The question is whether or not the real appreciation of the peso, which occurred alongside growing dollarization in the financial system encouraged by the hard peg, was an equilibrium phenomenon. The authors conclude that the real exchange rate started diverging from its equilibrium level in 1998 and was 45 percent more appreciated than the equilibrium level by 2001. Correcting this was complicated by the hard peg and could explain the slowdown in Argentine growth after 1999.

On the fiscal side, both the federal and provincial governments ran persistent deficits throughout the 1990s. The growing fiscal deficit was the driving force behind the large current account deficits of the 1990s, which led to the steady erosion of Argentina's foreign asset position and to an overvalued real exchange rate. Not surprisingly, public debt rose, from 25 percent of GDP in 1992 to more than 60 percent in 2001. Moreover, a major expansion in fiscal policy during the boom years compelled a contraction during the downturn which began in 1999, further hurting growth. Lower growth meant lower taxes, and in conjunction with rising interest rates, worsened public debt dynamics. Moreover, correcting for the overvaluation in the real exchange rate would have raised the debt/GDP ratio from the measured 60 percent to 90 percent in 2001, with a huge 7 percent of GDP primary *surplus* required to keep the debt/GDP ratio constant, compared to an actual primary *deficit* of 1.4 percent of GDP for that year.

One of the more painful lessons from Argentina pertains to the financial sector. The authorities undertook ambitious prudential and regulatory reforms to build a resilient financial sector, mostly based on dollar-denominated deposits and loans.

---

[41] Using the exchange rate as an anchor to bring inflation down from very high levels commonly leads to a large real appreciation, as inflation tends to come down more slowly than the rate of depreciation, which goes instantaneously to zero with the fixing of the exchange rate.

Absent a lender of last resort (which was ruled out by the currency board), large prudential liquidity buffers were built into the system, sufficient to withstand sizeable liquidity and solvency shocks – including a flight of more than one-third of the system's deposits, as well as a sudden and complete default in up to 10 percent of the loan portfolio – without endangering Convertibility.

But the exchange rate guarantee under Convertibility had encouraged large mismatches in balance sheets. By the late 1990s, 70 percent or more of firms' outstanding debt was dollar-denominated, and the degree of dollarization was particularly high for firms in the nontraded sector. Nearly 80 percent of outstanding mortgage credit was dollar-denominated as well. Time and saving deposits showed also a high (and increasing) degree of dollarization. These large mismatches in the balance sheets of banks' debtors – dollar debts of households and nontraded-sector firms – meant that a nominal devaluation would have rendered many debtors insolvent, and thus wrecked the banking system. But so would a real devaluation, regardless of whether Convertibility was maintained, by hampering the repayment capacity of those with earnings from the nontraded sector. Thus, while the authorities may have been in an awkward position to signal the vulnerability to a nominal devaluation (because of the fears of creating a self-fulfilling prophecy), the failure to recognize the risks posed to the nontraded sector by a real devaluation was a major weakness. To add to the banks' growing exposure to a real devaluation, as the government ran into growing difficulties to finance its deficit through market borrowing, it began increasingly to place its debt with banks after 1998, exposing them to sovereign default risk as well.

One lesson from Argentina may simply be that a hard peg is not consistent with unsustainable public debt dynamics, along the lines of first-generation crisis models. Another pertains to the need to build up a fiscal reserve during boom times that will permit a countercyclical expansion during an adverse shock, such as the global slowdown of 2001, and thereby help to support economic growth. Yet another is about the financial system. While financial sector policy may have been exemplary, it was derailed by the dollarization encouraged by the hard peg and eventually the placing of public debt with financial institutions; bad macropolicy trumps good financial sector policy. Finally, the combination of a hard peg, procyclical fiscal policy, and balance sheet mismatches makes it virtually impossible to address serious real exchange rate overvaluation without a crisis. An exit policy needs to be crafted during "good times," appropriately supported by fiscal policy and financial sector prudential regulation that recognizes the risk to the nontraded goods sector in the event a real depreciation is needed.

Chapter 11. Default Episodes of the 1980s and 1990s

Chapter 11 by Punam Chuhan and Federico Sturzenegger distills lessons from the debt default episodes of the 1980s and 1990s. Not surprisingly, the evolution of debt crises has paralleled – and likely motivated – the development of the three generations of crisis models reviewed in Chapter 8. In this context, the authors note that the 1980s crisis, which came about as a result of recycling petro-dollars by the money center banks to emerging market countries, took over a decade to resolve and was treated as an issue of liquidity, rather than one of solvency for most of this time. The crisis began when Mexico declared a debt moratorium in

1982 following a substantial interest rate hike in the United States. It spread to eventually encompass 47 rescheduling agreements for 27 countries, covering $130 billion in debt over 1982–84. The initial concern was how to contain the systemic risk posed to the international financial system, which appeared vulnerable to collapse. The exposure of U.S. money center banks to countries restructuring debt was 215 percent of banks' capital and 260 percent of equity at end-1982; that of UK and Canadian banks was 275 percent and 195 percent of their respective equity. Only in the third phase (1985–89) of restructuring, when the Baker Plan – named for U.S. Treasury Secretary James A. Baker, III – took hold, was the need for fostering growth recognized. The Baker Plan advocated structural adjustment and market-oriented policies, increased lending by commercial banks, and greater participation of the IMF and World Bank.

While systemic risk to the international financial system was contained, growth did not resume in the defaulting countries and the combination of relatively short-term rescheduling and new money – which fell short of targets – only exacerbated the debt burden. Two related theoretical concepts developed during this time: the debt overhang and the debt Laffer curve. The *debt overhang* was the notion that when external debt is very high and servicing it depends upon future growth and taxes, this may actually discourage investment today, because the debt in effect raises the marginal tax rate on investment. If this leads to a situation where the marginal ability to repay debt actually falls with the level of debt – that is, a *debt Laffer curve* develops – then beyond a point, reducing debt could actually increase repayments and thus benefit both the countries and their creditors. Such reasoning might have played a role when the United States unveiled the Brady Plan (named for then-U.S. Treasury Secretary Nicholas F. Brady) in March 1989, officially recognizing for the first time the need for debt reduction. The Brady Plan presented a menu approach, with a range of instruments to give both cash flow and debt relief; these are discussed in the chapter. The Plan also gave banks a chance to write down debt against taxes, while reducing the risk of the new instruments issued against bank loans through various forms of collateral of principal and interest. The development of a secondary market in Brady bonds (of which the principal was collateralized) also increased liquidity and permitted those banks that wished to do so to exit.

The Brady Plan, which was implemented for 18 countries restructuring $200 billion of bank loans into $154 billion of bonds, was considered a success. However, in the ten years after it was launched, the world has witnessed a series of new debt crises starting with Mexico in 1994 and continuing with East Asia, Russia, Turkey, and Argentina, among others. From a debt restructuring perspective, the story is different now, as it involves a large number of diverse, anonymous bondholders rather than a few large banks; and these crises have been approached on a case-by-case basis, in contrast to the large, multicountry, officially sponsored debt workouts of the 1980s. However, several countries have undertaken bond exchanges quite smoothly. This may be regarded as good news in a situation of about $500 billion in emerging market bonds, of which about 80 percent is public and publicly guaranteed.

One needs to be circumspect, however, because bond exchanges fall into two groups: voluntary, market-based swaps and involuntary exchanges. As a general rule, the ones that have worked smoothly fall into the first group. This should not be surprising because, as the term "market-based swaps" suggests, existing bondholders can effectively bid on the terms of the new exchange, which may involve a lengthening of maturities or a change in currency denomination or both; but no debt reduction in a present value sense, assuming that the market is pricing maturity and currency risks consistently. But involuntary debt restructuring, which typically involves a debt write-down, is quite another matter, as demonstrated by the ongoing debt restructuring negotiations for Argentina stemming from its December 2001 default. In contrast, Russia's involuntary restructuring of ruble-denominated debt instruments and debt owed to the London Club following the 1998 crisis went relatively smoothly even though substantial write-downs were involved; but as Chapter 9 notes, special considerations applied.

Even for market-based exchanges, complexities may arise. In situations where fiscal constraints are severe and the country is at its market-imposed credit limit, a market-based swap may not just be neutral, but could actually bring crisis forward. This could happen for a variety of reasons, including when the new instruments have perceived seniority over existing claims, or imply greater dollarization of liabilities, thereby increasing expected depreciation and raising interest differentials (opposite to the intended effect), or interact negatively with existing exposures of investors, or simply worsen public debt dynamics because interest rates go up visibly. In the case of Argentina, for example, not only did the market-based $29.5 billion megaexchange of June 2001 worsen the debt dynamics, but as the crisis deepened, the new bonds were eventually defaulted upon, together with all other debt instruments.[42]

The recognition that crises are costly has spurred considerable debate on whether suitable mechanisms can be developed to achieve a quick resolution that would benefit both creditors and countries. Two proposals discussed by the chapter are the Sovereign Debt Restructuring Mechanism (SDRM) and collective action clauses (CACs).[43] The SDRM is part of the IMF's effort to improve the international financial architecture. It would seek to address the problem of creditor coordination in debt workouts through a statutory approach analogous to that used for corporate bankruptcies, while facilitating collective action. An insolvent country would activate the SDRM on request; all external debt owed to private creditors would be aggregated. A supermajority of creditors would be able to negotiate a debt restructuring that would be binding for all creditors. Proceeds from litigation would be shared, and disputes would be adjudicated by independent bankruptcy tribunals. While the SDRM has not yet taken root, CACs, which address the creditor holdout problem, have begun appearing in recent sovereign bond issues. In February 2003, Mexico became the first major emerging market borrower to issue a bond with CACs under New York

---

[42] For a formal analysis of why market-based debt exchanges may not work when fiscal fundamentals are weak – motivated by the Russian 1998 debt swap and the Argentine 2001 debt swap – see Aizenman, Kletzer, and Pinto (2005). The Russian debt swap is described in Chapter 9 and also analyzed in Kharas, Pinto, and Ulatov (2001) as a factor triggering the 1998 Russian crisis.

[43] The collective action problem refers to a situation where a small minority of creditors stays out of an agreement reached with the majority: that is, they hold out in the hope of securing a better deal for themselves. In the oft-cited case of *Elliott Associates v. Peru*, Elliott sued for full payment after Peru had reached an agreement with 180 creditors, obtaining a restraining order on restructured payments in the process. Rather than default on its restructured debt, Peru settled out-of-court, paying Elliott $56 million in 2000 for unrestructured debt that had been purchased in the secondary market for $11 million in 1996.

law. The CAC would allow a majority of 75 percent of bondholders to make wide-ranging changes to the terms of the bond contract in the event of a restructuring. While CACs address the creditor coordination problem for individual bond issues, they do not solve the problem of such coordination across bond issues (the so-called aggregation problem) or the problem of creditor coordination for an existing stock of debt (the so-called transition problem). Thus it remains to be seen whether CACs will be sufficient to resolve debt crises or whether additional mechanisms will be needed.

While future sovereign debt crises might differ in the method of resolution from the bank loans crisis of the 1980s, many of the basic questions remain the same. Debate is likely to persist on the nature of the crises, that is, whether the crux of the matter is confidence and liquidity problems, or fundamentals, and whether or not public debt is on an unsustainable course. While CACs might help avoid creditor holdouts, this still requires that an agreement with a majority of creditors be reached in the first place.

CONCLUDING REMARKS

The economist's penchant for linearizing models around equilibria and relying on linear regressions may have obscured the negative impact volatility exerts on growth, uncovered by empirical studies over the past decade. Volatility also has a negative impact on poverty, through growth as well as inequality. These effects are the most damaging in poor countries, where the capacity to manage volatility and shocks is limited by shallow financial sectors and impediments to implementing counter-cyclical fiscal policy. The impediments include credit constraints as well as political economy factors. These impediments could also interfere with attempts to self-insure, for example, by saving during booms as a cushion for busts.

The problem becomes even more serious when countries tend to depend upon just a few agricultural commodities for both exports and taxes, as exemplified by certain Sub-Saharan African countries. Agricultural commodity price volatility presents challenges in terms of smoothing government spending and shielding vulnerable rural households from negative terms of trade shocks and macroeconomic crises. Diversifying tax bases is of considerable importance – even more so as governments slash customs duties, reduce inflation, and give up the implicit taxation from financial repression in pursuit of more efficient financial sectors. Technical assistance in this regard would be fruitful. Likewise, designing and funding social safety nets is also important. The key point is to have adequate social safety nets in place *before* a crisis hits in order to avoid permanent damage. With regard to agricultural commodity exporters in particular, the latest thinking is that it may not be so much a "commodity problem" as a more general challenge of economic and rural development eventually leading to greater diversification.

The by-now familiar problem of how to manage booms and busts comes back with a vengeance in the case of oil exporters, which as a group have suffered from the natural resource curse, exemplified by Nigeria and Venezuela. Oil funds could help, but are not a panacea. For instance, countries could be accumulating money in an oil fund when prices are high, but borrowing against this as collateral – which defeats the purpose. Eventually, it is the fiscal and government debt situation in totality, and the transparency with which public spending decisions are made, that matter. The key challenges are to run a countercyclical fiscal policy that will smooth the path of the real exchange rate, while using some of the oil proceeds to provide those services in particular that will help the manufacturing and agricultural sectors as a whole, including power, transport, trade-related infrastructure, and access to information.

In principle, a liberalized, market-oriented financial sector should help with resource allocation and be a shock absorber; but it can also act to amplify shocks and trigger crises. The question for developing countries therefore is how to liberalize their financial sectors while managing the attendant risks. Various ideas have been spawned by the high-profile crises of the late 1990s on how to deal with asset bubbles and procyclicality in financing; but rectifying microeconomic distortions and creating a robust financial and regulatory system may ultimately be the "best" solution. However, even good financial sector regulation can be trumped by bad macroeconomic policy, as the Argentine crisis showed. There are no easy answers; but taking steps to lower the risks of a financial crisis – by emphasizing macro-economic fundamentals, creditor and property rights, and adequate regulation and supervision – could lay the foundation for substantial long-run benefits.

The preceding discussion illustrates the harmful effects of volatility for poor countries, which also happen to be at a lower stage of development measured by income levels, quality of institutions, financial development, trade openness, or the ability to conduct countercyclical fiscal policy. One might therefore legitimately ask how focusing on volatility alters any of the standard development prescriptions. The answer is that fortunately it does not, but instead reinforces the need for financial, fiscal, and institutional development. The key insight yielded by this wide-ranging look at volatility is that a country does not necessarily have to wait for a crisis to begin reforming institutions: developing countries are more volatile, and this volatility reduces long-run growth and increases inequality irrespective of whether a crisis occurs.

The perspective this volume offers is that of dealing with missing insurance markets. While all countries may benefit from adding such markets, the cost of missing markets is incomparably higher for developing countries. Volatility of the type impacting the OECD countries may induce occasional recessions and unemployment, and temporarily reduce growth rates – whereas volatility of the type afflicting developing countries may lead to famines, riots, stagnation, and long-run economic decline. To develop this thought further, recall that how volatility affects a country depends on the channels through which it is transmitted and how it interacts with policies and institutions. The empirical evidence clearly shows that developing countries are at a disadvantage here. Combining this evidence with the asymmetry result – namely, that positive shocks do not cancel out the deleterious effects of negative shocks, so that there could be permanent setbacks to growth – yields yet another reason for why income levels in poor countries may not converge to those in rich countries. Not only do the latter have an advantage stemming from the endogeneity of technological progress, but they also reap a persistent advantage from having better coping mechanisms for dealing with volatility. And repeated bouts of volatility will perpetuate the gap in income levels between developed and developing countries.

More volatile countries are also likely to be more predisposed to crisis, which can be thought of as large shocks to growth. While crises may spur improvements in fiscal, financial, and judicial institutions, they are also costly and disruptive; as Chapter 2 shows, "crisis" volatility does most of the damage to growth. In conjunction with the pioneering study of Dani Rodrik (1999) on latent social conflict, shocks, and growth, this finding suggests that addressing the management of "normal" volatility needs to be given a higher profile. Developing "social capital" and conflict resolution mechanisms clearly become important.

Turning to exchange rate crises, the empirical analysis highlights two variables in particular as enhancing vulnerability: a high ratio of short-term external debt to reserves (well above 1) and moderately high two-digit inflation rates. Two other variables also receive some prominence: external debt to GDP[44] and the choice of exchange rate regime (intermediate regimes are less crisis-prone). Countries tend to have fewer or less severe crises if they are free of corruption and tilt the composition of their capital inflows away from dollar denomination. In particular, foreign direct investment and equity are preferable to dollar-denominated external debt.

A review of the debt default episodes of the 1980s and 1990s suggests that in certain cases, bond restructurings have proceeded smoothly in spite of the coordination problem posed by a multitude of small, anonymous investors. However, the experience needs to be interpreted carefully. For example, both the Russian GKO-Eurobond exchange of July 1998 and the Argentine megabond swap of June 2001 were hailed as successes; but Russia suffered a meltdown the very next month, defaulting on most of its GKOs, and Argentina's default in December 2001 included the restructured bonds of June 2001. Such cases show that "market friendly debt restructurings" – that is, those where the terms of the exchange are determined by bids placed by the existing investors – may be relatively easy to execute; but do not help countries with fundamental public finance problems or preclude more messy restructurings in the future, also illustrated by the ongoing Argentine experience. The only recent innovation is that of including collective action clauses (CACs) in bond issues, but it remains to be seen how effective these will be.

In conclusion, volatility and crises have particularly damaging effects on growth and on poor people, especially in low-income countries. Their ability to cope is limited by shallow financial sectors and the inability to conduct countercyclical fiscal policy, because of credit constraints and political economy considerations. Understanding the best ways to deal with missing insurance markets, including the development of suitable financial instruments to help low- and middle-income countries, remains a formidable agenda. Short of a generic solution, promising avenues include promoting fiscal, financial, and judicial institutions; and helping build social capital to minimize conflict. These improvements may facilitate the formation of deeper

---

[44] Specifically, Chapter 8 identified the threshold of vulnerability as a combination of a ratio of short-term external debt to reserves exceeding 157 percent and inflation exceeding 17 percent per annum. External debt in excess of 80 percent of GDP could also pose vulnerability in combination with inflation exceeding 25 percent. While these thresholds are sample-specific, they reflect general vulnerabilities. Of course, these are not policy choices but endogenous outcomes determined by a combination of country circumstances, track record, and investor preferences.

markets and allow existing markets to provide more self-insurance opportunities. Another priority is to gain more insight into the preemption and easier resolution of debt crises in the brave new world of bond issues.

REFERENCES

Abel, A. 1983. "Optimal Investment under Uncertainty." *American Economic Review* 73(2):22–33.

Acemoglu, Daron, Simon Johnson, James A. Robinson, and Yunyong Thaicharoen. 2003. "Institutional Causes, Macroeconomic Symptoms: Volatility, Crises, and Growth." *Journal of Monetary Economics* 50(1):49–123.

Aizenman, Joshua. 1998. "Buffer Stocks and Precautionary Savings with Loss Aversion." *Journal of International Money and Finance* 17(12):931–47.

Aizenman, Joshua, and Nancy Marion. 1993. "Policy Uncertainty, Persistence and Growth." *Review of International Economics* 1(9):145–63.

———. 1999. "Volatility and Investment: Interpreting Evidence from Developing Countries." *Economica* 66:157–79.

———. 2004. "International Reserve Holdings with Sovereign Risk and Costly Tax Collection." *Economic Journal* 114(497):569–91.

Aizenman, Joshua, and Andrew Powell. 2003. "Volatility and Financial Intermediation." *Journal of International Money and Finance* 22(5):657–79.

Aizenman, Joshua, Kenneth M. Kletzer, and Brian Pinto. 2005. "Sargent–Wallace Meets Krugman–Flood–Garber Or: Why Sovereign Debt Swaps Don't Avert Macroeconomic Crises." *Economic Journal* 115:343–67.

Barlevy, G. 2003. "The Cost of Business Cycles Under Endogenous Growth." NBER Working Paper 9970. National Bureau of Economic Research, Cambridge, MA.

Bernanke, B., and M. Gertler. 1989. "Agency Costs, Net Worth, and Business Fluctuations." *American Economic Review* 79(1):14–31.

Bouton, Lawrence, and Mariusz Sumlinski. 2000. "Trends in Private Investment in Developing Countries: Statistics for 1970–98." IFC Discussion Paper No. 41. International Finance Corporation, Washington DC.

Bowman D., D. Minehart, and M. Rabin. 1999. "Loss Aversion in a Consumption-Savings Model." *Journal of Economic Behavior and Organization* 38(2):155–78.

Bulow, Jeremy, and Kenneth Rogoff. 1988. "Sovereign Debt Restructurings: Panacea or Pangloss?" NBER Working Paper 2637. National Bureau of Economic Research, Cambridge, MA.

Caballero, Ricardo J. 1991. "On the Sign of the Investment-Uncertainty Relationship." *American Economic Review* 81(1):279–88.

———. 2003. "On the International Financial Architecture: Insuring Emerging Markets." NBER Working Paper 9570. National Bureau of Economic Research, Cambridge, MA.

Caballero, Ricardo J., and S. Panageas. 2003. "Hedging Sudden Stops and Precautionary Recessions: A Quantitative Framework." NBER Working Paper 9778. National Bureau of Economic Research, Cambridge, MA.

Calvo, Guillermo A., and Carmen Reinhart. 2001. "When Capital Inflows Come to a Sudden Stop: Consequences and Policy Options." In Peter Kenen and Alexander Swoboda, eds., *Key Issues in Reform of the International Monetary System.* Washington, DC: International Monetary Fund.

Calvo, Guillermo, Alejandro Izquierdo, and Ernesto Talvi. 2003. "Sudden Stops, the Real Exchange Rate and Fiscal Sustainability: Argentina's Lessons." NBER Working Paper 9828. National Bureau of Economic Research, Cambridge, MA.

Cukierman, A., S. Edwards, and G. Tabellini. 1992. "Seigniorage and Political Instability." *American Economic Review* 82(3):537–55.

de Soto, Hernando. 2000. *The Mystery of Capital: Why Capitalism Triumphs in the West and Fails Everywhere Else.* New York: Basic Books and London: Bantam Press/Random House.

Diebold, Francis X. 2004. "The Nobel Memorial Prize for Robert F. Engle." *Scandinavian Journal of Economics* 106(2)(June):165–85.

Dixit, A., and R. Pindyck. 1994. *Investment under Uncertainty.* Princeton, NJ: Princeton University Press.

Easterly, William, Roumeen Islam, and Joseph E. Stiglitz. 2000. "Shaken and Stirred: Explaining Growth Volatility." In Boris Pleskovic and Joseph E. Stiglitz, eds., *Annual World Bank Conference on Development Economics 2000.* Washington, DC: World Bank.

Eichengreen Barry, Richard Hausmann, and Ugo Panizza. 2003. "The Pain of Original Sin." In Barry Eichangreen and Ricards Hausmann, eds., *Debt Denomination and Financial Instability in Emerging-Market Economics.* Chicago: University of Chicago Press.

Epstein, Larry, and Tan Wang. 1994. "Intertemporal Asset Pricing under Knightian Uncertainty." *Econometrica* 62(2):283–322.

Everhart, Stephen S., and Mariusz A. Sumlinski. 2001. "Trends in Private Investment in Developing Countries Statistics for 1970–2000 and the Impact on Private Investment of Corruption and the Quality of Public Investment." IFC Discussion Paper No. 44. International Finance Corporation, Washington DC.

Fischer, Stanley. 2001. "Exchange Rate Regimes: Is the Bipolar View Correct?" *Finance and Development* 38(2):18–21.

Flood, Robert P., and Peter M. Garber. 1984. "Collapsing Exchange-Rate Regimes: Some Linear Examples." *Journal of International Economics* 17(1–2):1–13.

Flug, K., A. Spilimbergo, and E. Wachtenheim. 1998. "Investment in Education: Do Economic Volatility and Credit Constraints Matter?" *Journal of Development Economics* 55(2):465–81.

Galor O., and J. Zeira. 1993. "Income Distribution and Macroeconomics." *Review of Economic Studies* 60:35–52.

Hartman, R. 1972. "The Effects of Price and Cost Uncertainty on Investment." *Journal of Economic Theory* 5:258–66.

IDB (Inter-American Development Bank). 1995. "Overcoming Volatility." *Economic and Social Progress in Latin America.* 1995 Report. Washington, DC: Inter-American Development Bank.

ITF (International Task Force on Commodity Risk Management in Developing Countries). 1999. "Dealing with Commodity Price Volatility in Developing Countries: A Proposal for a Market-Based Approach." Washington, DC: World Bank.

Jones L., R. Manuelli, and E. Stacchetti. 1999. "Technology (and Policy) Shocks in Models of Endogenous Growth." NBER Working Paper 7063. National Bureau of Economic Research, Cambridge, MA.

Khan M., and M. Kumar. 1997. "Public and Private Investment and the Growth Process in Developing Countries." *Oxford Bulletin of Economics and Statistics* (UK) 59(2): 69–88.

Kharas, Homi J., Brian Pinto, and Sergei Ulatov. 2001. "An Analysis of Russia's 1998 Meltdown: Fundamentals and Market Signals." *Brookings Papers on Economic Activity*, 1:1–68.

Knight, Frank H. 1921. *Risk, Uncertainty, and Profit.* Boston: Houghton Mifflin.

Krugman, Paul. 1979. "A Model of Balance-of-Payments Crises." *Journal of Money, Credit, and Banking* 11(3):311–25.

Lucas, R. 1987. *Models of Business Cycles. 1985 Yrjö Jahnsson Lectures.* Oxford: Basil Blackwell.

———. 2003. "Macroeconomic Priorities." *American Economic Review* 93(1):1–14.

McDonald, R., and D. Siegel. 1986. "The Value of Waiting to Invest." *Quarterly Journal of Economics* 101(4):707–27.

Mussa, Michael. 2002. "Argentina and the Fund: From Triumph to Tragedy." Institute for International Economics, Washington, DC.

Newbery, David, and Joseph Stiglitz. 1981. *The Theory of Commodity Price Stabilization, A Study of the Economics of Risk.* Oxford: Clarendon Press.

Obstfeld, Maurice. 1994. "Risk-taking, Global Diversification and Growth." *American Economic Review* 85 (December):1310–29.

Pindyck R., and A. Solimano. 1993. "Economic Instability and Aggregate Investment." *NBER Macroeconomics Annual.* Cambridge, MA: National Bureau of Economic Research.

Ramey, Garey, and Valerie A. Ramey. 1995. "Cross-country Evidence on the Link between Volatility and Growth." *American Economic Review* 85(5):1138–51.

Rodrik, Dani. 1999. "Where Did All the Growth Go? External Shocks, Social Conflict, and Growth Collapses." *Journal of Economic Growth* 4 (4):385–412.

Sargent, Thomas J., and Neil Wallace. 1981. "Some Unpleasant Monetaristic Arithmetic." *Federal Reserve Bank of Minneapolis Quarterly Review* 5(3):1–17.

Savage, Leonard. J. 1954. *The Foundations of Statistics.* New York: John Wiley and Sons.

Serven, Luis. 1998. "Macroeconomic Uncertainty and Private Investment in LDCs: An Empirical Investigation." World Bank, Washington, DC. World Bank Policy Research Working Paper No. 2035.

Shiller, Robert J. 1993. "The Theory of Index-Based Futures and Options Markets." *Estudios Económicos* (El Colegio de México) 8(2):163–78.

———. 2003. *The New Financial Order: Risk in the 21st Century.* Princeton, NJ: Princeton University Press.

Townsend, R. 1979. "Optimal Contracts and Competitive Markets with Costly State Verification." *Journal of Economic Theory* 21(2):265–93.

1. Volatility: Definitions and Consequences[1]

Holger Wolf

SETTING THE STAGE

Some decades ago, output volatility was perceived mainly as a fleeting business cycle phenomenon of secondary concern for longer-term development objectives. Theoretical advances have since melded short-term and long-term fluctuations into a single framework, while a growing body of research suggests that higher volatility is causally associated with lower growth. Volatility has hence assumed a more central role in the development debate. This chapter introduces some of the themes taken up in more depth in later chapters.

As a background to the discussion, Figures 1.1 through 1.7 illustrate some core linkages for a broad sample of countries.[2] Figure 1.1 plots the volatility of GDP per capita growth (measured as the standard deviation of the growth rate) against the mean growth rate of GDP per capita, revealing the broad negative association that has motivated the increased attention to volatility.[3] Figures 1.2 and 1.3 illustrate the link between output volatility and income inequality: higher growth volatility goes hand in hand with a higher Gini coefficient and a lower income share of the lowest quintile of the population.

Figure 1.4 differentiates the link between growth volatility and growth by income group. While, as Figure 1.1 revealed, the correlation is negative for the full sample, splitting the sample by income groups reveals three distinct relationships. For the group of low-income countries, growth volatility and average growth are negatively associated. For the middle-income group, volatility and average growth are almost uncorrelated, while for the high-income group, there is a positive association.

Figure 1.5 illustrates the change of growth volatility over time, plotting the volatility measure for 1961–80 against the volatility measure for 1981–2000. While

---

[1] The chapter benefited from very helpful comments by Paulo Mauro, Eswar Prasad, Joshua Aizenman, and Brian Pinto. Viktoria Hnatkovska provided very capable research assistance.

[2] Figures 1.1 and 1.4 to 1.6 use the same dataset as Chapter 2, while Figures 1.2 and 1.3 use the same dataset as Chapter 3. The appendices to these chapters describe the datasets.

[3] The classic reference is Ramey and Ramey (1995). See also IDB (1995); Duryea (1998); Aizenman and Marion (1999); Flug, Spilimbergo, and Wachtenheim (1999); Kaminsky and Reinhart (2002); Kose, Prasad, and Terrones (2003). The effect tends to be both statistically and economically significant.

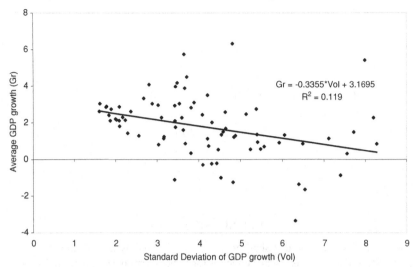

Figure 1.1. GDP Growth versus Volatility, 1960–2000. *Source*: Author's calculations.

no overall pattern emerges, splitting the sample by income group reveals that – with a few exceptions – volatility has declined for high-income countries from the first to the second period. The experience of middle-income and low-income countries is more varied, though a higher fraction of middle-income countries experienced rising volatility.

Figures 1.6 and 1.7 turn to the longer-term evolution of volatility, plotting GDP growth volatility (measured as the nine-year standard deviation) for Brazil, France, and Japan[4] from 1870 to 1994, and for South Africa, the United Kingdom, and the United States for 1955 through 1994. The figures illustrate the prevalence of volatility throughout history and the importance of particular events – notably the two world wars. The postwar evolution shows a trend increase in the volatility of the two middle-income countries and a (muted) decline for the mature economies, consistent with the broader pattern of Figure 1.5.[5] The time path suggests a volatility "life-cycle," driven both by changes in the nature and magnitude of the shocks impinging on the economy and by the availability and usage of coping mechanisms.

In conjunction, Figures 1.1–1.7 establish that crosssectional differences in volatility are related to cross-sectional differences in growth and income distribution. They also suggest that these links are not necessarily constant across country subgroups or time. It is hence instructive to complement cross-country research with studies of individual economies or a group of related economies. Two recent World Bank studies are particularly insightful in this regard. Phillipe Auffret (2003) explores the role of natural disasters for a group of Caribbean countries, while

[4] The spike for Japan reflects a recorded GDP decline of 69 percent in 1945.
[5] See also Buch (2002); Obstfeld and Taylor (2003).

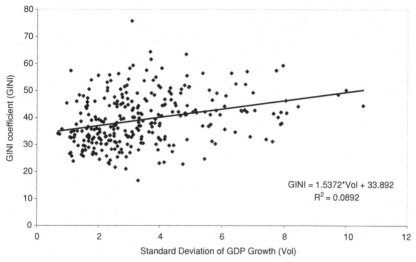

Figure 1.2. Gini and Volatility, 1957–99. *Source*: Author's calculations.

Douglas Addison and his colleagues (2003) provide an in-depth exploration of the causes and consequences of volatility for Nigeria.

If these linkages are causal and if volatility affects consumption, then dealing with volatility becomes part of the broader development challenge. Chapters 2 and 3 take up the growth and poverty linkages in detail. This introductory chapter aims to set the stage by discussing conceptual and measurement issues, reviewing the literature on the sources and effects of volatility, and outlining some of the options available to individuals and governments to reduce and manage excess volatility.

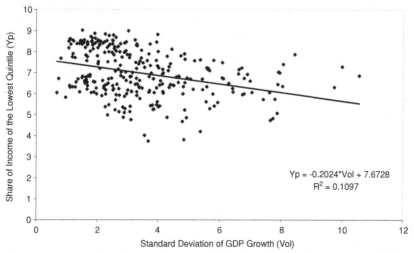

Figure 1.3. Income of the Poorest Quintile and Volatility, 1957–99. *Source*: Author's calculations.

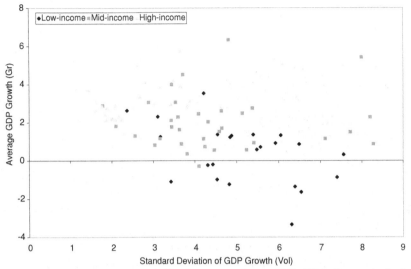

Figure 1.4. GDP Growth and Volatility by Income Group, 1960–2000. *Source*: Author's calculations.

CONCEPTUAL ISSUES

What is meant by the term "volatile"? A look at dictionary definitions yields a range of connotations: "tending to vary often or widely," "unstable," "changing suddenly," "characterized by or prone to sudden change," "unpredictable," and "fickle." Beyond the varying definitions of the term itself, further ambiguities arise from the terms often used in conjunction with volatility, sometimes employed as synonyms, sometimes viewed as implications, such as "crisis," "risk," "fragility," and "vulnerability."

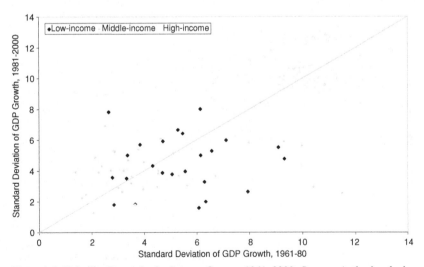

Figure 1.5. Volatility Dynamics by Income Groups, 1961–2000. *Source*: Author's calculations.

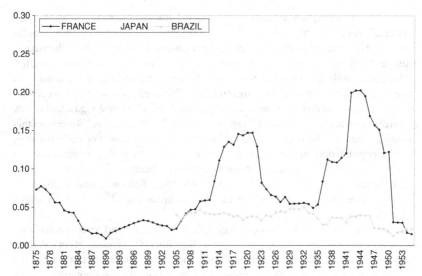

Figure 1.6. Standard Deviation of GDP Growth Rate, 1870–55. *Source*: Author's calculations.

Two key connotations of volatility are *variability* and *uncertainty*. Variability refers to all movement, while uncertainty refers to unknown movement. Conceptually, volatility at a given time can be decomposed into a predictable component and an unpredictable component. The appropriate relative weight of these two features depends on the issue examined. As households and policymakers are typically better able to cope with predictable variation, the primary concern is unpredictable movement.

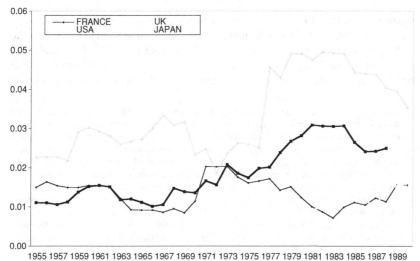

Figure 1.7. Standard Deviation of GDP Growth Rate, 1955–94. *Source*: Author's calculations.

A second distinction is sometimes made between "normal" volatility and "extreme" volatility (or "crisis"). From a conceptual point of view, this separation is problematic. Are extreme events simply observations drawn from the tails of a single distribution, or do they come from a different source? As a practical matter, looking separately at extreme events is sensible since coping mechanisms may fail once shocks exceed some critical threshold size. The likelihood of shocks exceeding these thresholds, and their economic effects, are thus of interest regardless of the researcher's conceptualization of "normal volatility" versus "crisis." To pursue this distinction empirically requires a definition of what constitutes "normal" volatility. Among popular options for defining "extreme" volatility is the imposition of an absolute threshold (for example, commodity price changes of more than 10 percent), the imposition of a distributional threshold (the 5 percent largest declines), or the use of a deviation criterion (observations that are at least 2 standard deviations above the mean).

A third distinction arises between "equilibrium volatility" and "excess volatility." Reducing consumption volatility increases welfare only if the consumption volatility reflects some type of market imperfection. The policy challenge is thus not the reduction of volatility to zero, but rather the elimination of excess volatility.

MEASUREMENT: CONCEPTUAL AND EMPIRICAL ISSUES

How should a practitioner assess "the volatility" of a particular variable? There is no single best measure. In most cases, a multi-pronged approach – built around the standard deviation as a core measure, but augmented by robustness checks – is likely to yield the best results. This section discusses some of the pertinent considerations, only some of which will likely be operational choices for any particular research question.

Operational Choices

CHOICE 1: SAMPLE LENGTH. The appropriate sample length reflects a cost–benefit tradeoff: a longer sample length increases measurement accuracy, but only if the underlying volatility has been stable over the sample period.[6,7] The problem is particularly acute for aggregate variables, as their volatility can change over time both because of a changing volatility of exogenous and endogenous shocks (such as

---

[6] To illustrate, it is widely accepted that the 1970s were a period of relatively higher "volatility" and the early 1990s were a period of relatively low "volatility." To the extent one views these episodes as realizations of a stable underlying process (with a particular pronounced sequence of large realized shocks in the 1970s and a particularly pronounced series of small realized shocks in the early 1990s), the best single measure of volatility over the entire period is obtained by averaging over both periods. Such averaging would be less appropriate if the underlying volatility process itself had changed over the period; for example, reflecting greater financial and real integration.

[7] Time-changing volatility has attracted particular attention in some financial applications. Commencing with Robert Engle's (1982) seminal paper on ARCH models, the finance literature has developed a rich array of parametric and nonparametric techniques allowing, among other features, for asymmetric volatility responses to positive and negative shocks and threshold effects. A complete survey of this literature is beyond the scope of this chapter. For a recent discussion, see Andersen, Bollerslev, and Diebold (2002).

terms of trade shocks) and because of changes in the transmission channels (such as the mechanisms determining the impact of terms of trade shocks on output). Alas, there are few objective gauges, as the sample length typically available for macro applications constrains the use of statistical tests for differences in volatility.

CHOICE 2: MEASUREMENT FREQUENCY. The frequency at which volatility should be calculated depends on the question examined. To assess the impact of the arrival of news on asset price volatility, the appropriate time frame is seconds; for the effect of monetary policy on consumption volatility, a monthly time frame is appropriate; while for an assessment of macroeconomic policy instability on long-term growth, multiyear averages would be reasonable. The choice is not innocuous, as the statistical measure of volatility may differ dramatically depending on the time frame observed.[8]

CHOICE 3: SYMMETRY OR WEIGHTING? The most popular measure of volatility, the standard deviation, treats negative and positive deviations from the mean symmetrically. From a theoretical viewpoint, however, there are good reasons to suspect asymmetric effects for many variables. In particular, a large negative and a large positive shock may have different effects, as evidenced in the asymmetric concern about "crises" and "booms."[9] If such asymmetries are expected, it may be prudent to attach a lower weight to positive shocks in the computation of the volatility measure.

CHOICE 4: REALIZED VERSUS EXPECTED VOLATILITY. Volatility is commonly measured by computing the standard deviation over some time period. It is important to keep in mind that such an ex post measure does not capture the expected volatility at the beginning of the sample period. If the latter measure is more pertinent to the question examined (such as assessing the effect of expected volatility on investment), construction of a predicted volatility series may be possible for some higher frequency series.

CHOICE 5: ALLOWING FOR THRESHOLDS. The potential presence of thresholds at which relationships between input shocks and output changes, or at which coping mechanisms (such as buffer stocks) are overwhelmed, creates another challenge. In such an environment, a complete assessment of volatility must include the likelihood that shocks will exceed the threshold levels at which the economy's coping mechanisms are overwhelmed.

---

[8] As an admittedly trivial example, consider the measurement of "the" volatility of output growth. Intraday, output is extremely volatile: production at 3 AM is dramatically lower than at 3 PM; smaller dips occur around lunchtime and each weekend. The very high volatility of hourly GDP generated by these nightly and weekly "recessions" is however of little concern and indeed is not statistically measured.

[9] For instance, given financial and regulatory structures, a particularly large negative shock may lead to the demise of a firm/bank, whereas a commensurate positive shock would not have a similar discrete effect. In like vein, an external shock which reduces central bank foreign currency reserves to zero under a pegged regime is likely to have more pronounced effects than a commensurate shock which doubles reserves.

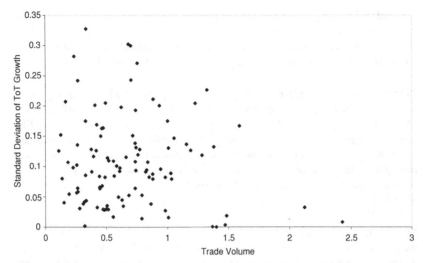

Figure 1.8. Trade Openness and ToT Volatility, 1960–2000. *Source*: Author's calculations.

CHOICE 6: ALLOWING FOR PERSISTENCE AND BUNCHING. If the coping ability of the economy is limited (for example, reflecting a given buffer stock), then the persistence of shocks – that is, the likelihood that a negative shock today is followed by another negative shock tomorrow, building up into a large cumulative shock – is of separate interest.

CHOICE 7: THE LEVEL OF AGGREGATION. The income of an individual household is influenced by both idiosyncratic and shared developments. Aggregation eliminates some of the idiosyncratic, regional, and sectoral shocks. In consequence, household income volatility will generally be greater – and possibly much greater – than aggregate GDP volatility. If households lack access to effective risk diversification and management tools, the typical measure of national income volatility – aggregate GDP volatility – may provide a rather benign picture of the volatility faced by the typical household in developing countries.[10]

Where does that leave the practitioner? None of the existing measures of volatility captures all relevant aspects of volatility. Prudence suggests a multimeasure approach build around the standard deviation as core measure, but adding robustness checks appropriate to the issue examined.

Impact Measures: Assessing the Macroimpact of Micro Volatility

Suppose that the problems raised above have been resolved and that, for a particular shock – say, the terms of trade or world interest rates – an appropriate volatility measure has been constructed. To assess whether this particular microshock "matters" on the aggregate level, the volatility of the shock must be related to a measure of its importance. For the terms of trade, an obvious metric is given by the openness of the

---

[10] The differentiation could be extended further: for example, by distinguishing between shocks to labor and to capital income, or to shocks to particular regions within a country.

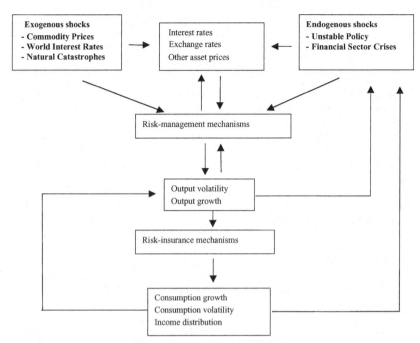

Figure 1.9. Conceptual Framework.

economy. The greater the openness of the economy, the greater is the likely impact of a *given* volatility of terms of trade shocks on the economy. For global interest rate shocks, an appealing metric would be net external floating rate indebtedness.

As an illustration, Figure 1.8 presents evidence on the first of these links, plotting the volatility of the terms of trade against openness (measured as the ratio of the sum of exports and imports to GDP). In this case, no clear pattern arises. In consequence, the ranking of countries by terms of trade (ToT) volatility might not map closely into the mapping of the importance of ToT volatility in determining aggregate output volatility.

CONCEPTUAL FRAMEWORK

Against the background of the above discussion, we turn now to a more systematic treatment of some of the main sources of volatility and their transmission to output and consumption.[11] To provide a structure, Figure 1.9 summarizes some of the links discussed below.

Input Shocks

A first conceptual distinction may be made between two sources of shocks. *Exogenous volatility* derives from sources that – at least in the short term – are outside the control of both households and policymakers. For small open economies, these

---

[11] See Buch (2002) for a comprehensive survey.

Table 1.1. *Input volatilities, 1960–2002*

Input shocks	Low-income economies	Middle-income economies	High-income economies
Terms of Trade (% change)			
Standard deviation	0.162	0.096	0.040
– Standard deviation of deviation from bandwidth filter (level)	0.131	0.084	0.035
– Maximum absolute annual change	−0.146	−0.092	−0.030
– Autocorrelation	−0.118	−0.004	0.079
Inflation rate (%)			
Standard deviation	0.183	0.155	0.051
Standard deviation of deviation from bandwidth filter (level)	0.190	0.159	0.044
Maximum absolute annual change	0.738	0.668	0.209
Autocorrelation	0.441	0.645	0.762
Government expenditure (share of GDP) (% change)			
Standard deviation	0.138	0.089	0.034
Standard deviation of deviation from bandwidth filter (level)	0.112	0.081	0.029
Maximum absolute annual change	0.021	0.130	0.129
Autocorrelation	−0.020	0.085	0.302

Source: Author's calculations.

include commodity price shocks influencing the terms of trade, changes in world interest rates, climate changes, and natural disasters. *Endogenous volatility* sources include unstable macropolicies, political instability, and, to some extent, financial crisis brought about or amplified by domestic market imperfections.

As is often the case, the conceptual distinction does not always map easily into empirics. Many shocks are hybrids. Thus capital flow reversals often have both an external exogenous component, such as changes in world interest rates, and a domestic endogenous component, such as perceived fragility due to maturity or currency mismatch. In like vein, productivity shocks, an important source of volatility, typically reflect both exogenous and endogenous factors.

The empirical evidence suggests that input shocks play a significant role.[12] Table 1.1 provides background information on three input shocks. The volatility of the terms of trade is (in the short run) largely exogenous, while the volatilities of inflation and fiscal spending are to a significant extent a reflection of policy choices. The table reports three alternative volatility measures: the regular standard deviation; the standard deviation of the residuals from a bandwidth filter (allowing for a time varying trend); and the maximum absolute annual change, as an extreme value

[12] To cite two examples, Michael Gavin and Ricardo Hausmann (1996) conclude that long-run growth volatility in a sample of developing countries has been importantly influenced by input volatilities, notably in the terms of trade and the real exchange rate, while Philippe Auffret (2003) highlights the importance of environmental shocks for the Caribbean.

measure. For all three measures, the same pattern emerges: input volatility declines with income. The decline is small between lower- and middle-income countries, and pronounced between middle- and high-income countries. The table also reports the autocorrelation, revealing greater persistence for upper-income economies.

Transmission Channels from Input Shocks to Output Volatility and Output Growth

Input shocks are transmitted to output volatility through a variety of channels. These are briefly reviewed here. Chapter 2 provides an in-depth analysis.

FACTOR ACCUMULATION. The link between input volatility and investment depends on a variety of features, including the reversibility of investment decisions and the alternatives available to firms. Beyond effects on volume, volatility may also affect the type of investment by tilting incentives toward the accumulation of less specialized capital goods with lower expected returns, which can be reallocated more easily in response to shocks. Human capital accumulation may be affected in a similar way (Duryea 1998; Flug, Spilimbergo, and Wachtenheim 1999). Such efficiency effects are consistent with the empirical finding that growth in more volatile economies tends to be lower even after controlling for input quantity.[13]

DOMESTIC FINANCE. Finance plays multiple roles. The financial system can be a source of shocks. In the presence of market imperfections, it can amplify shocks originating both at home and abroad. Yet financial markets also provide the tools to cope with volatility. The empirical literature suggests that for high-income countries, financial development and output volatility are negatively associated. For low- and middle-income economies, the net link is less evident, and may depend on the degree of international financial integration.[14]

TRADE. The role of trade and openness is similarly complex. Greater openness allows better insulation against domestic demand shocks. Yet if accompanied by greater specialization, it may also lead to greater exposure to sectoral shocks, and enhance exposure to external demand and supply shocks. Openness also enhances the role of the real exchange rate, which in turn can act both as a stabilizing element and as a source of additional input volatility. Empirically, a higher volatility of the terms of trade appears to be linked to a higher volatility of output (Agénor,

---

[13] The discussion focuses on the effect of input volatility. In terms of outcome volatility, the reverse causal linkage may arise. For example, one of the major expected benefits of integration comes from specialization in sectors of comparative advantage. Yet such specialization by definition increases exposure to sectoral shocks, and may thus lead to greater output volatility. This volatility is best thought of as the side effect of the benefits of greater specialization. To the degree it can be hedged, it may not be reflected in greater consumption volatility and may be of secondary welfare concern compared with its primary growth effect.

[14] Beck, Levine, and Loayza (2001) explore these links in detail. See also Denizer, Iyigun, and Owen (2002); Buch and Pierdzioch (2003); Kose, Prasad, and Terrones (2003); and Kose, Prasad, Rogoff, and Wei (2003).

McDermott, and Prasad 2000). The link between generic measures of openness and output volatility in contrast is less settled.

CAPITAL MOBILITY. Following the recent spate of emerging market crises, renewed attention has focused on the role of international financial linkages and macroeconomic volatility. Theory suffers from an embarrassment of riches. Greater financial integration allows economies, notably emerging markets, to tap external funding sources to achieve more diversified production structures and thus to reduce their exposure to sector-specific shocks. Yet integration also creates new transmission channels for external shocks and may magnify the effect of domestic distortions.[15] The literatures on collateral problems, on currency mismatch/original sin, and on the resource curse trace many of these potential vulnerabilities. The net effect is ambiguous, and likely to be conditional on both country characteristics and on the nature of shocks.

The evidence is similarly mixed. In a regression framework, the search for a robust cross-country link between financial integration and volatility has proved elusive. Studies by Assaf Razin and Andrew Rose (1994) and by Claudia Buch and Christian Pierdzioch (2003) found no robust link while other authors have found financial integration to be an important determinant of volatility for subgroups. More weakly the evidence suggests a possible reversal of the link between middle- and high-income economies, with middle-income countries experiencing a positive link between financial integration and volatility, and high-income countries, a negative link.[16]

POLITICS. The political system, including the ability to respond in a speedy way to shocks, may affect the sensitivity of aggregate outcomes to input shocks (Rodrik 1999). Evidence on this linkage is as yet sparse but growing. Daron Acemoglu, Simon Johnson, James A. Robinson, and Yunyong Thaicharoen (2002) find that good institutions are associated with reduced output growth volatility. Over time, institutions may themselves become endogenous to volatility, as unsatisfactory performance may enhance the pressure for reform.[17]

Avoidance and Mitigation Strategies

The preceding paragraphs focused on channels by which input shocks are transmitted to output. As emphasized before, not all of the resulting output volatility is undesirable. To the extent that excess volatility is present, or that the ability

---

[15] See Sutherland (1996); Faia (2001); and Buch and Pierzioch (2003).

[16] Thus, Bekaert, Harvey, and Lundblad (2002) find that stock market liberalization is associated with reduced volatility of both consumption and output. Looking at measures of more general capital account openness, they find a positive link between financial integration and both output and consumption growth volatility for emerging markets, but a negative link for mature economies. Kose, Prasad, and Terrones (2003), using both capital account restrictions and capital flows, likewise find a positive link between financial integration and consumption growth volatility for nonindustrialized countries, but a negative link for industrialized countries.

[17] Arguments along this line have been made for post-1991 India and post-1998 Russia.

Table 1.2. *Output and consumption volatility, 1960–2002*

Volatility	Low-income economies	Middle-income economies	High-income economies
GDP per capita growth			
– Standard deviation, full sample	0.0608858	0.0590874	0.0375206
– Standard deviation, 1980–latest	0.0580189	0.052712	0.0313299
– Standard deviation of deviation from bandwidth filter	0.0574366	0.0570887	0.035183
– Maximum absolute annual change	−0.0911258	−0.0021264	0.0611574
– Autocorrelation	0.1137416	0.2855715	0.2916662
Consumption per capita growth			
– Standard deviation	0.0880907	0.0733261	0.0312265
– Standard deviation, 1980–latest	0.087995	0.0703962	0.0275752
– Standard deviation of deviation from bandwidth filter	0.0722855	0.0652268	0.0296149
– Maximum absolute annual change	−0.0574868	0.041073	0.0898115
– Autocorrelation	−0.1011594	0.0721121	0.3092209

Source: Author's calculations.

of households to shield consumption from output volatility is constrained, policy actions taken to reduce output volatility are, however, potentially welfare enhancing. On the most direct level, countercyclical policy can be used to offset demand shocks. Yet accumulating evidence suggests that fiscal policy in emerging markets often exhibits procyclical tendencies and may thus at times act as an additional source of volatility.[18]

Output Volatility

Table 1.2 provides background information on the volatility of GDP per capita.[19] The volatility of output again decreases with income, most notably between the middle-income and the upper-income economies, while persistence, measured by the autocorrelation, increases in the income level.[20]

[18] One contributing factor may be procyclical access to domestic and external debt markets, coupled with overspending incentives reflecting political economy incentives. Alesina, Perotti, and Tavares (1998) provide a partial survey of this growing field. See Martin and Rogers (1997) and Talvi and Vegh (2000). Kose, Prasad, and Terrones (2003) find that total consumption (private plus government) is less volatile than private consumption. Agénor, McDermott, and Prasad (2000) find government consumption to be countercyclical for a fairly small set of noncrisis middle-income countries. The pattern however does not seem to be uniform, with evidence of procyclicality for other country groups. Again, a context dependence may arise, as procyclicality has been attributed to a procyclical borrowing capacity, notably of primary producers. Taking a slightly different approach, Buch and Pierdzioch (2003) find a positive link between higher volatility of government consumption spending and output volatility.

[19] See also Kose, Prasad, and Terrones (2003).

[20] There is also strong evidence that output volatility decreases in the size of economy. See Head (1995) and Crucini (1997). On the challenges facing small countries, see also Harden (1985) and Srinivasan (1986).

Consumption Volatility: Size and Importance

From a welfare perspective, the growth and volatility of consumption is central. Indeed, in a perfect market environment, households could hold diversified portfolios that shield their consumption entirely from local shocks. Before turning to the link between output growth volatility and consumption growth volatility, it is instructive to consider the importance of the welfare effects of consumption volatility. How large a reduction in the permanent growth rate of consumption would a household be willing to accept in return for eliminating consumption volatility? The answer for mature economies appears to be: not much (Lucas 1987). For developing countries, aggregate consumption volatility is higher, however, as are the gains from smoothing (Stéphane Pallage and Michael Robe 2003). Furthermore, as discussed above, volatility as perceived at the level of households is likely to exceed aggregate volatility, as aggregation partly eliminates regional, sectoral, and idiosyncratic factors.

OPTIONS. The link between local income volatility and local consumption volatility is determined by the ability of firms, households, and governments to avoid or hedge risks. At the individual level, responses include the accumulation of precautionary savings, diversification of income sources across household members (including choices about participation of multiple household members in the monetized economy), the utilization of domestic and international financial markets, and insurance mechanisms (Hunter and Smith 2002).[21] Various forms of economywide insurance, such as reserve holdings, buffer stock arrangements, stockpiles of critical products, and an appropriately constructed welfare net, can complement individual access to insurance. National measures in turn can be complemented by multinational mechanisms aimed at alleviating the effect of volatility on consumption and on poverty (Fischer 2002).

EVIDENCE. In the extreme case of perfect markets with no home preferences, idiosyncratic shocks to local production would have negligible effects on local consumption, as households would hold well-diversified portfolios giving them a claim on world output, rather than local output. By extension, local consumption growth would depend more closely on world output growth than on local output growth, and consumption growth rates would exhibit a higher cross-country correlation than income growth rates.

These predictions have not been confirmed by empirical evidence (see also bottom of Table 1.2).[22] First, consumption growth volatility does not appear to be much smaller than output volatility, and indeed in some low- and middle-income countries,

---

[21] As discussed above, however, financial markets may again display a Janus face, with volatility-management opportunities being matched by volatility emanating from the financial sector, creating policy challenges on both the national and the multilateral level. Financial markets may thus act both as a source of volatility and a means of dealing with volatility.

[22] See, for example, Gavin and Hausmann (1996); IDB (1995); Kose, Prasad, and Terrones (2003); Kose, Prasad, Rogoff, and Wei (2003); Buch (2002); Hnatkovska and Loyaza (Chapter 2, this volume).

appears to be higher (Table 1.2, bottom; see also Kose, Prasad, and Terrones 2003). Second, across countries, output growth correlations are comparable to consumption growth correlations. Third, there remains a closer dependency between local output and local consumption than between global output and local consumption. Fourth, portfolio holdings exhibit marked home bias. Rendering these stylized facts consistent with theoretical predictions without large deviations from the complete markets framework has proven challenging (Heathcote and Perri 2002), though data problems may account for at least some of the puzzle (Kose, Prasad, and Terrones 2003).[23]

Volatility and the Poverty of Individuals and Nations

Income distribution consequences of volatility may arise from three distinct channels. First, individuals may be differently affected by input shocks. Second, the transmission channels may affect some income groups more than others. Third, access to risk-management tools may depend on income and wealth. Within countries, individuals living close to or below the poverty level are least likely to hold internationally diversified investment portfolios, or to have the ability to insure themselves against other risks, or the ability to self-insure by means of precautionary savings.[24]

OPTIONS TO MANAGE VOLATILITY

The preceding sections illustrated a variety of linkages between input shocks, growth, and consumption volatility and income distribution. Individuals, firms, and governments can resort to a number of steps to reduce volatility or mitigate its impact. Some of these have been alluded to above; this section draws the options together. Three fundamental responses to volatility can be distinguished:

- *Risk-reduction measures* attempt to directly affect the probability of an event occurring. Examples at the personal level include the acquisition of multiple skills to reduce the likelihood of prolonged unemployment and the adoption of a healthier lifestyle to avoid disease. Firms can reduce fragility by following prudent balance sheet policies regarding maturity and currency mismatch and diversifying their customer base. On the industry or regional/national level, examples include emergency food stocks to counteract famine and the construction of dams to avoid flooding.

---

[23] Theory emphasizes utility smoothing; empirical work measures the volatility of consumption expenditures. Data problems arise to the extent that expenditures are not a good proxy for utility. Among the caveats in this respect is the lumpiness of durables expenditures relative to their utility flow, the treatment of leisure and other nonmarket consumption elements, and the treatment of government consumption.

[24] For example, some evidence points to a negative effect of volatility on educational attainment (Duryea 1998; Flug, Spilimbergo, and Wachtenheim 1999). To the degree that human capital provides an avenue for risk diversification, current volatility may thus influence future vulnerability to volatility.

- *Market insurance* transfers resources across states of nature, in most cases from good to bad states, reducing the exposure of individuals to stochastic events with a well described population distribution (such as fire, earthquakes, and illness) by spreading cost over a large pool of insured individuals.[25] *Public insurance* has a similar function, and is particular prevalent in the areas of health, retirement, and unemployment. Within countries, the scope for insurance is limited by the importance of national shocks. Recent proposals on international risk sharing and GDP indexed bonds extend the principle to the international realm.
- *Self-insurance* reallocates resources over time for an individual, household, or family. A classic example of self-insurance is precautionary savings, building up net savings in good times to be able to sustain consumption in bad times. Other examples include the maintenance of a backup vegetable garden and the international diversification of portfolios to insulate nonwage income from national shocks. At the household level, having several members active in different parts of the monetary economy provides some protection against misfortune befalling any one individual member.

In practice, a range of options is often available. For example, a healthy individual concerned about income losses or additional costs due to illness might buy health insurance or long-term care insurance (market insurance, pooling across individuals); might increase precautionary savings (self-insurance); or alter his/her diet and lifestyle (risk reduction). Preparing for any specific risk may thus involve a mix of steps (World Bank 2000). In addition, these individual steps may be complemented by public mechanisms. Thus, in an economy subject to volatile terms of trade, individuals may insure themselves by appropriate diversification of their portfolios, while governments or producer organizations may develop stabilization funds or tax/subsidy scheme correlated to the price in question, possibly with external assistance.

The measures can reduce both output and consumption volatility. As discussed above, steps to reduce output volatility are warranted only if such volatility is excessive, or if tools to deal with consumption volatility are not available. It is also worth noting that a given policy step can have quite asymmetric effects on consumption and output volatility. For example, steps taken to enhance financial and trade integration may increase output volatility (by encouraging greater specialization, and thus exposure to sectoral shocks) but reduce consumption volatility (by enhancing acccess to and use of risk-management tools).

---

[25] For some risks, such as earthquakes and flooding, the exogeneity of the original event is near complete. Even in these cases, however, individual responses to obtaining insurance might influence the probability distribution of damages, for example, through increased building in areas susceptible to earthquakes and flooding. In other cases, insurance providers have to incorporate both endogenous responses to the provision of insurance (such as insured drivers driving more aggressively) and, for voluntary insurance schemes, the likelihood that individuals with a higher expected probability of facing the adverse event are more likely to seek insurance. Both moral hazard and adverse selection problems can partly be addressed through the structure of the insurance contract.

CONCLUDING REMARKS

While the web spun by volatility sources, transmission channels, and coping mechanisms is complex, differences in consumption volatility across countries reflect three main factors. First is the relative incidence of input shocks. Second is the ability of the economy to accommodate shocks (or its tendency to aggravate them). Third is the ability of households and economies to insulate consumption from temporary shocks. The following chapters take up these themes in greater depth.

REFERENCES

Acemoglu, Daron, Simon Johnson, James A. Robinson, and Yunyong Thaicharoen. 2002. "Institutional Causes, Macroeconomic Symptoms: Volatility, Crises, and Growth." CEPR Working Paper 3575. Centre for Economic Policy Research, London.

Addison, Douglas (Team Leader). 2003. "Nigeria: Policy Options for Growth and Stability." PREM 3 Report No. 26215-NGA. World Bank, Washington, DC.

Agénor, Pierre Richard. 2002. "Does Globalization Hurt the Poor?" Policy Research Working Paper 2922. World Bank, Washington, DC.

Agénor, Pierre Richard, C. McDermott, and Eswar Prasad. 2000. "Macroeconomic Fluctuations in Developing Countries." *World Bank Economic Review* 14:251–85.

Aghion, Phillipe, and Gilles St. Paul. 1998. "On The Virtues of Bad Times." *Macroeconomic Dynamics* 2(3):322–44.

Aghion, Phillipe, Abhijit Banerjee, and Thomas Picketty. 1999. "Dualism and Macroeconomic Volatility." *Quarterly Journal of Economics* (November):1359–97.

Aizenman, Joshua. 1998. "Buffer Stocks and Precautionary Savings with Loss Aversion." *Journal of International Money and Finance* 17(6):931–47.

———. 2002. "Volatility, Employment and the Patterns of FDI in Emerging Markets." NBER Working Paper 9397. National Bureau of Economic Research, Cambridge, MA.

Aizenman, Joshua, and Nancy Marion. 1999. "Volatility and Investment: Interpreting Evidence from Developing Countries." *Economica* 66:157–79.

———. 2002. "International Reserve Holdings with Sovereign Risk and Costly Tax Collection." NBER Working Paper 9151. National Bureau of Economic Research, Cambridge, MA.

Alesina, Alberto, Roberto Perotti, and Jose Tavares. 1998. "The Political Economy of Fiscal Adjustments." *Brookings Papers on Economic Activity* 1:197–248.

Andersen, Torben, Tim Bollerslev, and Francis Diebold. 2002. "Parametric and Nonparametric Volatility Measurement." NBER Technical Working Paper 279. National Bureau of Economic Research, Cambridge, MA.

Auffret, Philippe. 2003. "High Consumption Volatility: The Impact of Natural Disasters." Policy Research Working Paper 2962. World Bank, Washington, DC.

Baldacci, Emanuele, Luiz de Mello, and Gabriela Inchauste. 2002. "Financial Crises, Poverty, and Income Distribution." *Finance and Development* 39(2):24–27.

Beck, Thorsten, Ross Levine and Norman Loayza. 2000. "Financial Intermediation and Growth: Causality and Causes." *Journal of Monetary Economics* 46:31–77.

Beck, Thorsten, Mattias Lundberg, and Giovanni Majnoni. 2001. "Financial Development and Economic Volatility: Does Finance Dampen or Magnify Shocks?" Policy Research Working Paper 2707. World Bank, Washington, DC.

Bekaert, Geert, Campbell Harvey, and Christian Lundblad. 2004. "Growth Volatility and Financial Liberalization." NBER Working Paper 10560.

Bourguignon, Francois, J., Luiz Pereira da Silva, and Nicholas H. Stern. 2002. "Evaluating the Poverty Impact of Economic Policies: Some Analytical Challenges." Paper presented at the IMF Conference on Macroeconomic Policies and Poverty Reduction, March. International Monetary Fund, Washington, DC.

Buch, Claudia. 2002. "Business Cycle Volatility and Globalization: A Survey." Kiel Working Paper No. 1107. Kiel Institute for World Economics, Kiel.

Buch, Claudia, and Christian Pierdzioch. 2003. "The Integration of Imperfect Financial Markets: Implications for Business Cycle Volatility." Working Paper No. 1161. Kiel Institute for World Economics, Kiel.

Caballero, Ricardo, and M. Hammour. 1994. "The Cleansing Effect of Recessions." *American Economic Review* 84(5):1350–68.

Caballero, Ricardo, and A. Krishnamurthy. 2001. "International and Domestic Collateral Constraint in a Model of Emerging Market Crisis." *Journal of Monetary Economics* 48: 513–48.

Caballero, Ricardo, and R. Pindyck. 1996. "Uncertainty, Investment, and Industry Evolution." *International Economic Review* 37(3):641–62.

Crucini, Mario. 1997. "Country Size and Economic Fluctuations." *Review of International Economics* 5(2):204–20.

Dalsgaard, T., J. Elmeskov, and C. Y. Park. 2002. "Ongoing Changes in the Business Cycle." OECD Working Paper No. 315. Organization for Economic Cooperation and Development, Paris.

Davis, Jeffrey, Rolando Ossowski, James Daniel, and Steven Barnett. 2001. "Stabilization and Savings Funds for Nonrenewable Resources: Experience and Fiscal Policy Implications." IMF Occasional Paper 205. International Monetary Fund, Washington, DC.

Dehn, Jan. 2000. "The Effects on Growth of Commodity Price Uncertainty and Shocks." Policy Research Working Paper 2455. World Bank, Washington, DC.

Denizer, Cevdet, M. Iyigun, and A. Owen. 2002. "Finance and Macroeconomic Volatility." *Contributions to Macroeconomics* 2(1):1–30.

Dollar, David, and Aart Kraay. 2001. "Growth Is Good for the Poor." Policy Research Working Paper 2587. World Bank, Washington, DC.

Duryea, Suzanne. 1998. "Children's Advancement through School in Brazil: The Role of Transitory Shocks to Household Income." IDB Working Paper 376. Inter-American Development Bank, Washington, DC.

Eble, Stephanie, and Petra Koeva. 2001. "The Distributional Effects of Macroeconomic Crises: Microeconomic Evidence from Russia." Paper presented at the IMF workshop on Macroeconomic Policies and Poverty Reduction, Washington, DC. April.

Engle, Robert. 1982. "Autoregressive Conditional Heteroskedasticity with Estimates of the Variance of the United Kingdom Inflation." *Econometrica* 50(4):987–1008.

Faia, E. 2001. "Stabilization Policy in a Two Country Model and the Role of Financial Frictions." Working Paper 56. European Central Bank, Frankfurt.

Fischer, Stanley. 2002. "Financial Crises and Reform of the International Financial System." NBER Working Paper 9297. National Bureau of Economic Research, Cambridge, MA.

Flug, Karnit, Antonio Spilimbergo, and Eric Wachtenheim. 1999. "Investment in Education: Do Economic Volatility and Credit Constraints Matter?" *Journal of Development Economics* 55(2):465–81.

Frankenberg, Elizabeth, J. P. Smith, and Duncan Thomas. 2002. "Economic Shocks, Wealth, and Welfare." Paper presented to IMF conference on Macroeconomic Policies and Poverty Reduction, March.

Gavin, Michael, and Ricardo Hausmann. 1996. "Sources of Macroeconomic Volatility in Developing Countries." IDB Working Paper. Inter-American Development Bank, Washington, DC.

Harden, Sheila. 1985. *Small Is Dangerous: Micro States in a Macro World*. London: Frances Pinter.

Hausmann, Ricardo. 2002. "Volatility and Development: What Have We Learned?" Paper prepared for the Thematic Group on Growth and Volatility Workshop, June 17. World Bank, Washington, DC.

Hausmann, Ricardo, and Michael Gavin. 1996. "Securing Stability and Growth in a Shock Prone Region: The Policy Challenge for Latin America." IDB Working Paper 315. Inter-American Development Bank, Washington, D.C.

Head, A. 1995. "Country Size, Aggregate Fluctuations, and International Risk Sharing." *Canadian Journal of Economics* 28(4b):1096–119.

Heathcote, Jonathan, and Fabrizio Perri. 2002. "Financial Globalization and Real Regionalization" NBER Working Paper 9292. National Bureau of Economic Research, Cambridge, MA.

Hnatkovska, Viktoria, and Norman Loayza. 2004. "Volatility and Growth." Chapter 2 of this volume.

Hunter, William, and Stephen Smith. 2002. "Risk Management in the Global Economy." *Journal of Banking and Finance* 26(2–3):205–21.

Imbs, Jean. 2002. "Why the Link between Volatility and Growth Is Both Positive and Negative." CEPR Discussion Paper 3561. Centre for Economic Policy Research, London.

Inter-American Development Bank (IDB). 1995. *Overcoming Volatility. Economic and Social Progress in Latin America*. 1995 Report. Washington, DC.

Kaminsky, Graciela, and Carmen Reinhart. 2002. "Financial Markets in Times of Stress." *Journal of Development Economics* 69(2):451–70.

Karras, G., and F. Song. 1996. "Sources of Business Cycle Volatility." *Journal of Macroeconomics* 18(4):621–37.

Kose, Ayhan, Eswar Prasad, and Marco Terrones. 2003. "Financial Integration and Macroeconomic Volatility." *IMF Staff Papers* 50:119–42.

Kose, Ayhan, Eswar Prasad, Kenneth Rogoff, and Shang-Jin Wei. 2003. "Effects of Financial Globalization on Developing Countries: Some Empirical Evidence." International Monetary Fund, Washington, DC.

Kraay, Aart, and Jaume Ventura. 2002. "Trade Integration and Risk Sharing." *European Economic Review* (Netherlands) 46(6):1023–48.

Lucas, Robert. 1987. *Models of Business Cycles*. New York: Blackwell.

Martin, P., and C. A. Rogers. 1997. "Stabilization Policy, Learning By Doing, and Economic Growth." *Oxford Economic Papers* 49:152–66.

Obstfeld, Maurice, and Alan Taylor. 2004. *Global Capital Markets: Integration, Crisis and Growth*. Cambridge, UK: Cambridge University Press.

Pallage, Stéphane, and Michael Robe. 2003. "On the Welfare Costs of Economic Fluctuations in Developing Countries." *International Economic Review* 44(2):677–98.

Ramey, Garey, and Valerie A. Ramey. 1995. "Cross-Country Evidence on the Link between Volatility and Growth." *American Economic Review* 85(5):1138–51.

Razin, Assaf, and Andrew Rose. 1994. "Business Cycle Volatility and Openness." In Leonardo Leiderman and Assaf Razin, eds., *Capital Mobility*. Cambridge, UK: Cambridge University Press.

Rodrik, Dani. 1999. "Where Did All the Growth Go? External Shocks, Social Conflict and Growth Collapses." *Journal of Economic Growth* 4(4):385–412.

Srinivasan, T. N. 1986. "The Cost and Benefits of Being a Small, Remote, Island, Landlocked or Mini-State Economy." *Research Observer* 1(2):205–18.

Sutherland, Alan. 1996. "Financial Market Integration and Macroeconomic Volatility." *Scandinavian Journal of Economics* (Sweden) 98(4):521–39.

Talvi, Ernesto, and Carlos Vegh. 2000. "Tax Base Variability and Procyclical Fiscal Response." NBER Working Paper 7499. National Bureau of Economic Research, Cambridge, MA.

World Bank. 2000. *Securing Our Future*. Washington, DC.

———. 2001. *World Development Report 2000–2001*. Washington, DC.

———. 2002. *Finance for Growth: Policy Choices in a Volatile World*. Washington, DC.

2. Volatility and Growth[1]

Viktoria Hnatkovska and Norman Loayza

ABSTRACT: This study examines the empirical, cross-country relationship between macroeconomic volatility and long-run economic growth. It addresses four central questions. The first is whether the volatility–growth link depends on country and policy characteristics, such as the level of development or trade openness. The second is whether the link reflects a causal effect from volatility to growth and, if so, whether this effect is statistically and economically significant. The third question concerns the stability of this relationship over time and, in particular, whether the relationship between volatility and growth has become stronger in recent decades. The fourth is whether the volatility–growth connection actually reveals the negative impact of crises, rather than the overall effect of cyclical fluctuations.

The study finds that indeed macroeconomic volatility and long-run economic growth are negatively related. This negative link is exacerbated in countries that are poor, institutionally underdeveloped, undergoing intermediate stages of financial development, or unable to conduct countercyclical fiscal policies. The study finds evidence that this negative relationship actually reflects the harmful effect from volatility to growth. Furthermore, the study finds that the negative effect of volatility on growth has become considerably larger in the last two decades and that it is due mostly to large recessions, rather than to normal cyclical fluctuations.

VOLATILITY AND GROWTH

In the last four decades, the 40 most volatile countries of the 79 sampled in this study have been developing economies (see Tables 2.1 and 2.2).[2] Among the most volatile are not just small economies, like the Dominican Republic and Togo, but also large

---

[1] We thank Megumi Kubota for able research assistance in the preparation of the database used in the study. We are grateful to Joshua Aizenman, Edgardo Favaro, Sandeep Mahajan, Brian Pinto, Holger Wolf, and especially to our discussants, Ricardo Caballero and Luis Servén, for comments and suggestions. Viktoria Hnatkovska is affiliated with Georgetown University, and Norman Loayza, with the World Bank. The findings, interpretations, and conclusions expressed in this chapter are entirely those of the authors. They do not necessarily represent the view of the World Bank, its Executive Directors, or the countries they represent.

[2] Appendix A presents average per capita GDP growth, the standard deviation of the output gap, and the standard deviation of per capita GDP growth in the 1960–2000 period for each country in the sample. As explained below, the latter two variables are the measures of volatility used in the chapter. Table 2.1 presents summary statistics of the growth rate and the two volatility measures by decades in the sample. Table 2.2 presents correlation coefficients between average per capita GDP growth, the standard deviation of output gap, and the standard deviation of per capita GDP growth in the 1960–2000 period by various groups of countries.

Table 2.1. *Growth and volatility by decades.* Sample: 79 countries, 1960–2000

	GDP per capita growth	Volatility, standard deviation of output gap	Volatility, standard deviation of GDP growth
Mean			
1960–70	2.772	2.467	3.782
1971–80	2.285	2.651	4.079
1981–90	0.710	2.354	3.559
1991–2000	1.359	1.879	3.075
Std. dev.			
1960–70	1.884	1.796	2.801
1971–80	2.383	1.435	2.275
1981–90	2.414	1.245	1.854
1991–2000	2.364	1.229	1.920
Min			
1960–70	−1.485	0.569	0.811
1971–80	−2.842	0.885	0.720
1981–90	−4.060	0.663	1.037
1991–2000	−8.861	0.417	0.545
Max			
1960–70	8.907	9.414	14.520
1971–80	10.503	8.277	12.223
1981–90	7.423	6.349	8.435
1991–2000	8.563	5.834	9.465

Source: Authors' calculations.

countries, like China and Argentina. Many are predominantly commodity exporters, like Nigeria and Ecuador, but some are also rapidly industrializing countries, like Chile and Indonesia (see Appendix A). At the other extreme of the spectrum, nine of the 10 least volatile countries in the world belong to the OECD. The connection between volatility and lack of development is undeniable, but is volatility also related to economic growth? Judging by simple cross-country correlations, there appears to be a negative relationship between the average and the standard deviation of per capita GDP growth, both calculated over long periods (see Figure 2.1). However, this connection is not uniform; it seems to depend on structural country characteristics. For example, while the correlation between volatility and growth is negative for poor countries, it is basically zero for middle-income countries, and even positive for the group of rich economies (see Figure 2.2).[3]

From academic and policy perspectives, this chapter addresses four central questions on the relationship between volatility and growth. The first is whether this link depends on country and policy characteristics, such as the level of development or trade openness. The second is whether the link reflects a causal effect from volatility to growth and, if so, whether this effect is statistically and economically significant. The third question concerns the stability of this relationship over time, and in particular whether the relationship between volatility and growth has become

[3] This grouping follows the World Bank income classification.

Table 2.2. *Simple correlations, cross-sectional analysis. Sample: 79 countries, 1960–2000*

	No. Obs.	Average GDP per capita growth and		Standard deviation of output gap and
		Standard deviation of output gap	Standard deviation of GDP per capita growth	Standard deviation of GDP per capita growth
Full sample:	79	−0.3538	−0.3450	0.980
By income:				
High-income (OECD countries + Israel)	22	0.4558	0.6043	0.8947
Middle-income (Upper- and lower-middle income countries)	34	0.0356	0.0540	0.9807
Low-income (low-income countries)	23	−0.3852	−0.4425	0.9673
By financial development:				
High financial development (countries with private domestic credit/GDP > 41%)	26	0.2542	0.2691	0.9783
Medium financial development (countries with private domestic credit/GDP > 21% And <41%)	26	−0.4936	−0.4448	0.98
Low financial development (countries with private domestic credit/GDP < 21%)	27	−0.2543	−0.2473	0.9703
By trade openness:				
High trade openness (countries with trade volume/GDP > 71%)	26	−0.417	−0.3787	0.977
Medium trade openness (countries with trade volume/GDP > 45% And <71%)	26	−0.484	−0.4758	0.9952
Low trade openness (countries with trade volume/GDP < 45%)	27	−0.1495	−0.1563	0.9673
By institutional development:				
High level of institutional development (above 57% of ICRG index range)	26	0.1118	0.2815	0.9447
Medium level of institutional development (between 36% And 57% of ICRG index range)	26	−0.1383	−0.1417	0.9664
Low level of institutional development (between 36% of ICRG index range)	27	−0.1933	−0.2355	0.9829
By degree of fiscal policy procyclicality:				
Highly procyclical fiscal policy (corr[ΔY, ΔGC] > −10%)	26	−0.0756	−0.1402	0.9847
Medium procyclical fiscal policy (corr[ΔY, ΔGC] > −24% And < −10%)	26	−0.5875	−0.5506	0.9774
Countercyclical fiscal policy (corr[ΔY, ΔGC] < −24%)	27	−0.3253	−0.2763	0.9834

Source: Authors' calculations.

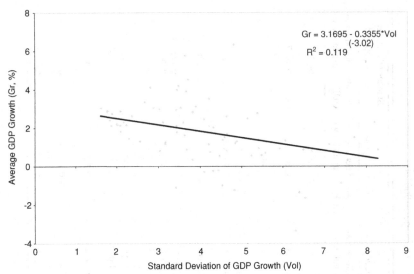

Figure 2.1. Growth and Volatility, 1960–2000. *Source*: Authors' calculations.

stronger in recent decades. The fourth question is whether the volatility–growth connection actually reveals the negative impact of crises, rather than the overall effect of cyclical fluctuations.

With these questions in mind, this study documents the relationship between macroeconomic volatility and long-run economic growth. Its approach is mostly empirical and relies on cross-country comparisons. To help understand and put the

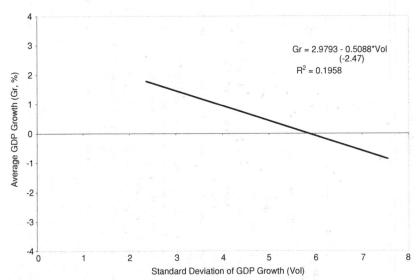

Figure 2.2a. Growth and Volatility, 1960–2000, Low-Income Economies. *Source*: Authors' calculations.

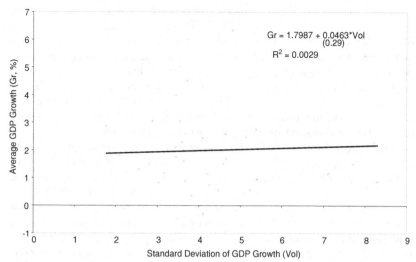

Figure 2.2b. Growth and Volatility, 1960–2000, Middle-Income Economies. *Source*: Authors' calculations.

empirical results into context, the first section of the chapter selectively reviews the analytical literature on the volatility–growth relationship. The second section describes the data and econometric methodologies used in the empirical sections of the study. Of special importance is the discussion on the various measures of volatility and economic crises.

The third section presents new empirical results, following the questions outlined above. Using interaction terms in the regression analysis, the study first attempts to

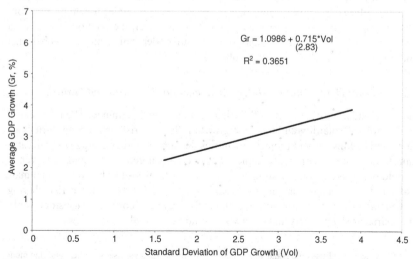

Figure 2.2c. Growth and Volatility, 1960–2000, High-Income Economies. *Source*: Authors' calculations.

determine whether there is a significant link between volatility and growth under various structural country characteristics. These characteristics are the country's overall level of development as indicated by average income, the degree of openness to international trade, the extent of financial depth, the level of institutional development, and the degree of fiscal policy procyclicality.

Second, using instrumental variables inspired from the causes-of-volatility literature, the analysis accounts for the likely endogeneity of volatility with respect to economic growth and its determinants. In this way, the study tries to ascertain the causal effect from macroeconomic volatility to long-run growth.

Third, the volatility–growth link is compared for the four decades since the 1960s, paying special attention to the break that researchers have observed before and after the 1980s. The decade comparison is done two ways: by ignoring the potential endogeneity of macroeconomic volatility and by accounting for it.

Finally, the study analyzes whether the negative connection between volatility and growth may be due to the consequences of economic crises. This is done by contrasting the growth effects of repeated but small cyclical fluctuations ("normal volatility") with large and lasting negative macroeconomic fluctuations ("crises").

The fourth and final section offers selected concluding remarks, together with some practical quantifications of the relationship between macroeconomic volatility and long-run economic growth.

ANALYTICAL BACKGROUND

Traditionally, the literatures on long-run growth and business cycles have remained separate. Recently, however, this approach has been challenged by theories and evidence that establish a strong connection between business cycle behavior and long-run performance.[4] One aspect of this relationship is the link between macroeconomic volatility and economic growth. In theory, this link could result from the joint determination of volatility and growth as endogenous variables or could stem from a causal effect from one variable to the other. Moreover, the relationship between volatility and growth may be positive or negative, depending on the mechanisms driving the relationship (see Imbs 2002).

Joint Determination (Interdependence) of Volatility and Growth

First, consider the case when both variables are jointly determined. Their link could be positive if volatility and long-run growth reflect the risk and mean return characteristics of investment projects: countries that aim at higher average growth rates must accept correspondingly higher risks. For this argument to hold, however, it would be necessary for countries to have sufficiently well-developed financial markets and government institutions, including judicial courts. Without risk-sharing mechanisms and proper monitoring and enforcement of contracts, investors would not pursue risky projects that otherwise would be optimal.

---

[4] For reviews, see Fatás (2002) and Wolf (2004). For theoretical analyses, see Caballero and Hammour (1994) and Aghion and Saint-Paul (1998). For empirical evidence, see Ramey and Ramey (1995), Martin and Rogers (2000), Kroft and Lloyd-Ellis (2002), and Servén (2003).

A different approach to analyze the joint determination of volatility and growth derives from considering asymmetric effects of business-cycle fluctuations. On the one hand, a positive link could develop as follows. If volatility is associated with the occurrence of recessions, and if recessions lead to higher research and development and/or the destruction of least productive firms, then higher long-run growth can occur alongside higher volatility. This is the "creative destruction" view that dates back at least to Joseph Schumpeter (1939).[5] Again, this argument requires deep financial markets, active firm turnover, and the ability to conduct countercyclical educational and innovation expenditures – characteristics that are usually associated with developed economies.

On the other hand, a negative link between volatility and growth could occur if recessions are tied to a worsening of financial and fiscal constraints, which is more likely to occur in developing countries. In this case, recessions can lead to less human capital development – (by decreasing learning-by-doing or producing cuts in expenditures on public health and education, for instance) – lower productivity-enhancing expenditures at the firm level, and thus lower growth rates (see Martin and Rogers 1997; Talvi and Végh 2000). Moreover, aversion to economic recessions could prompt governments to adopt policies that make firms less flexible and willing to innovate, such as labor market restrictions. This in turn could deepen a negative link between volatility and long-run growth.

Causality from Volatility to Growth

The connection between volatility and growth can also result from a causal relationship. This study concentrates on the potential impact of volatility on growth. This effect will be mostly negative when volatility is associated with economic uncertainty, whether this comes from political insecurity (Alesina, Roubini, and Swagel 1996), macroeconomic instability (Judson and Orphanides 1996), or institutional weaknesses (Rodrik 1991; Servén 1997). The theoretical underpinnings for a negative effect of uncertainty on economic growth operate through conditions of risk aversion, aversion to bad outcomes, lumpiness, and irreversibility associated with the investment process. Under these conditions, uncertainty is likely to lead firms to underinvest or to invest in the "wrong" projects (see Bertola and Caballero 1994).[6] Some structural country characteristics are bound to worsen the impact of volatility and uncertainty on economic growth, such as a poor level of financial development, deficient rule of law, and procyclical fiscal policy, which usually accompany large public indebtedness (see Caballero 2000).

This study is interested in the empirical regularities dealing with both the *overall relationship* between volatility and growth and the *causal effect* from volatility to growth. Against the analytical background just summarized, this chapter considers both the role of structural country characteristics in shaping this mutual relationship

---

[5] For a modern treatment of this view, see Shleifer (1986), Hall (1991), Caballero and Hammour (1994), and Aghion and Saint-Paul (1998).

[6] This study does not analyze the channels through which volatility affects economic growth. A possible interesting extension would then be assessing whether volatility's effect runs through factor accumulation (physical or human capital investment) or total factor productivity growth.

and the role of factors that drive volatility in order to estimate the exogenous impact of volatility on growth.

METHODOLOGY AND DATA

This study is interested in describing the empirical, cross-country connection between macroeconomic volatility and long-run economic growth. For this purpose, it examines a variety of empirical models in which a country's economic growth is the dependent variable and its volatility is the main explanatory variable. The statistical units are given by country observations with data representing averages over relatively long periods. The majority of the empirical exercises are conducted using only cross-sectional data: specifically, country-averages over the 1960–2000 period. Since this study is also interested in testing the stability of the volatility–growth relationship over time, in some cases it works with country averages by decades, spanning the same period. The next sections describe the study's empirical strategy and data in detail.

Empirical Methodology

The analysis follows the main strand of the new growth literature in the choice of both the dependent and explanatory variables, to which a volatility measure is added (see Barro 1991). It starts by examining the simple correlation of the growth rate of per capita GDP with each of two measures of macroeconomic volatility (defined below). This is done for the full sample of countries and for various country groupings determined by criteria such as the level of overall development, financial depth, trade openness, institutional development, and fiscal policy procyclicality.

Next, the link between volatility and growth is assessed after controlling for other variables that affect a country's growth process. This allows the analysis to examine whether the simple link between volatility and growth is channeled through regular growth determinants. The corresponding growth regression is given by

$$gr_i = \beta_0 + \beta_1 vol_i + \beta_2 X_i + \varepsilon_i, \tag{1}$$

where gr represents average growth rate of per capita GDP, vol is a volatility measure, X represents a set of control variables, ε is the regression residual, and i is a country index. The set of control variables includes the initial level of GDP per capita (to account for transitional convergence effects), the average ratio of domestic private credit to GDP (as proxy for financial development), and the average secondary school enrollment ratio (to account for human capital investment). These control variables are chosen in consideration of their robust role in the new empirical growth literature (see Levine and Renelt 1992).[7]

The regression analysis is then extended by considering whether the size and statistical significance of the volatility–growth relationship is magnified or diminished by the structural characteristics mentioned above. These effects are taken into

[7] An expanded set of control variables was also considered, including measures of trade openness, government consumption, and institutional development. Although in some cases these variables presented significant coefficients, their inclusion did not alter the volatility-related results discussed in this study.

account through both continuous and categorical interactions (explained below) between volatility and country structural characteristics in the corresponding growth regressions. The corresponding regression equations are given by

$$gr_i = \beta_0 + \beta_1 vol_i + \beta_2 vol_i * Struct_i + \beta_3 X_i + \varepsilon_i, \qquad (2)$$

where *Struct* represents, in turn, the following structural country characteristics: overall economic development, financial depth, international trade openness, the level of institutional development, and the degree of fiscal policy procyclicality.[8]

The country characteristics represented in *Struct* are interacted with volatility in two ways. The first one is standard and consists of *Struct* taking the actual values of the corresponding measures for each country. This is the case of a "continuous" interaction with volatility (or simple multiplicative effect). The second way of accounting for structural characteristics is through country groups (or categories) derived from the cross-country ranking for each characteristic. In each case, three similarly sized groups of countries are used: low, medium, and high. The variable *Struct* acts as a "dummy" variable that indicates whether or not a country belongs to a given group.[9] This is the case of a "categorical" interaction with volatility, and it allows for a nonmonotonic relationship between volatility and growth.

Next, attempting to go beyond the description of mutual relationships, the analysis takes into account the possibility that volatility may be endogenously determined together with long-run growth. An instrumental-variable procedure is used to isolate exogenous changes in volatility and thus gauge their causal impact on per capita GDP growth. The regression model then becomes

$$gr_i = \beta_0 + \beta_1 vol_i + \beta_2 X_i + \varepsilon_i \qquad (3)$$
$$vol_i = \gamma_i I V_i + u_i$$
$$E(vol_i * \varepsilon_i) \neq 0, \quad but \ E(I V_i * \varepsilon_i) = 0,$$

where *IV* represents a set of instrumental variables for volatility, whose desired properties are that they help explain volatility but at the same time affect long-run growth only through volatility (and the other control variables). The set of instrumental variables was chosen for their importance in the macroeconomic stabilization literature. They are the standard deviation of the inflation rate, a measure of real exchange rate misalignment, the standard deviation of terms of trade shocks, and the frequency of systemic banking crises. These variables highlight the point that macroeconomic volatility can be driven by nonpolicy factors (such as the volatility of terms of trade shocks) or a combination of policy and nonpolicy elements (all the rest).

The regression analysis is then applied – with and without interaction terms and instrumental variables – to the database organized as country averages by decades. For the majority of countries, the analysis works with four observations each, corresponding to the 1960s, 1970s, 1980s, and 1990s. The objective is to assess how

---

[8] The study also considered the production structure of the economy: specifically, the share of agricultural value added in GDP. However, this structural characteristic did not seem to affect the volatility–growth relationship in a robust or significant manner.

[9] For example, in the case of the interaction with economic development, countries were divided into three groups based on income level – low, medium, and high – as in Figure 2.2. The effect of volatility on growth was then estimated for each group in the context of regression equation, Equation 3.

the volatility–growth connection has changed over time, and in particular, whether it has increased in the 1980s and 1990s. For this purpose, the pooled cross-section, time series data were used to estimate jointly the coefficients on volatility for each decade and then test whether their differences are statistically significant. The pooled regression model is given by

$$gr_{i,t} = \beta_{0,t} + \beta_{1,t}vol_{i,t} + \beta_2 X_{i,t} + \varepsilon_{i,t}, \tag{4}$$

where the subscript t denotes time periods (decades). Note that the analysis allows the volatility coefficient to be different across decades. As mentioned above, this regression was extended to account for the joint endogeneity of volatility and for the dependence of the volatility–growth relationship on the average level of income.

Finally, the study examines whether the negative association between volatility and growth could reflect the harmful impact of sharp negative fluctuations (crisis volatility) rather than the effect of repeated but small cyclical movements (normal volatility). For this purpose, the regression analysis was modified by replacing the (overall) volatility measure by two of its components: one related to "normal volatility" and the other representing "crisis volatility." The measurement of these volatility components is described in the next section. The growth regression equation then becomes

$$gr_i = \beta_0 + \beta_1 NormalVol_i + \beta_2 CrisisVol_i + \beta_3 X_i + \varepsilon_i, \tag{5}$$

where *NormalVol* and *CrisisVol* represent the normal and crisis components of volatility, respectively. This regression was estimated two ways, both ignoring the potential endogeneity of the volatility components and accounting for such endogeneity. The set of instruments was expanded by generating the "crisis" versions of the instruments and adding them to the regular set.

Sample and Data

Both a single cross-section of countries and a pooled sample of country and time-series observations were used. In the case of a single cross-section, the observations correspond to country averages for the 1960–2000 period. The pooled sample consists of decade averages per country, corresponding to 1961–70, 1971–80, 1981–90, and 1991–2000. The pooled dataset is almost fully balanced in the sense that for nearly 95 percent of the countries, complete data are available for each of the four decades. The resulting sample consists of 79 countries, of which 22 are industrial. Among the developing countries, the regional breakdown is as follows: Latin America and the Caribbean, 21; Sub-Saharan Africa, 18; the Middle East and North Africa, seven; East Asia and the Pacific, six; South Asia, four; and Eastern and Central Europe, one (see Appendix A).

Macroeconomic volatility was measured two ways. Both focus on overall output volatility, as a summary proxy. Both intend to capture the variability of cyclical macroeconomic fluctuations: around a constant mean, in one case, and a time-varying trend, in the other. Following most of the empirical literature on volatility, the first measure is the standard deviation of per capita GDP growth, calculated for each country over the corresponding sample period. The second measure follows the real business cycle literature and consists of the standard deviation of the per capita GDP gap. This involves estimating the trend (or potential level) of each

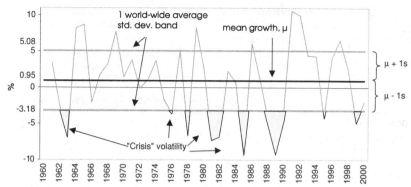

Figure 2.3. Volatility Decomposition, Example: Argentina, GDP per capita growth rate. (*Note*: s is a worldwide average of standard deviations of per capita GDP growth rates.) *Source*: Authors' calculations.

country's per capita GDP series, obtaining the gap between actual and trend GDP, and then calculating the standard deviation of the gap series. Each country's trend per capita GDP was estimated by applying the bandpass filter developed by Baxter and King (1999) to the country's per capita GDP series.

The first volatility measure implicitly assumes that the trend rate of per capita GDP growth is constant for each country (and equal to its mean), whereas the second measure allows trend per capita GDP to follow a richer, time-dependent and country-dependent process. The standard deviation of per capita GDP growth would exaggerate macro volatility if actual per capita GDP growth has an upward or downward trend (which is the case for economies in transition to their long-run steady state). On the other hand, the standard deviation of the per capita output gap may underestimate macroeconomic volatility if the trend series follows the actual one too closely. In practice, however, the two volatility measures are highly correlated in the cross-country dimension and render quite similar results in this study. The coefficient of correlation between the two volatility measures is 0.98 for the full sample and above 0.89 for any of the country groups (see Table 2.2).

The measures of "normal" and "crisis" volatilities are obtained from the same distribution as the overall volatility measure. "Crisis" volatility is defined as the portion of the standard deviation of per capita GDP growth or output gap that corresponds to downward deviations below a certain threshold. This threshold is set equal to the mean of the world distribution of overall volatility measures; thus it is common to all countries. Using a common threshold generates absolute crisis measures, as opposed to relative, country-specific ones. Thus it facilitates cross-country comparisons.

"Normal" volatility is then defined as the portion of the standard deviation of per capita GDP growth or output gap corresponding to deviations that fall within the threshold. For example, consider the case of annual per capita GDP growth in Argentina over the 1961–2000 period (see Figure 2.3). Argentina's volatility, measured as the standard deviation of per capita GDP growth, was 5.41. With the average world volatility during the same period being 4.13, the study calculates 0.62 for "crisis" and 4.33 for "normal" volatility, which amounts to respectively

Table 2.3. *Simple correlations with "components" of standard deviation,
cross-sectional analysis.* Sample: 79 countries, 1960–2000

| | Mean growth | (A). Volatility: Standard deviation of output gap | | |
		Aggregate volatility	"Crisis" volatility	"Normal" volatility
Mean Growth	1	–	–	–
Aggregate Volatility: std. dev. of output gap	−0.3538	1	–	–
"Crisis" Volatility: std. dev. of output gap	−0.2431	0.8556	1	–
"Normal" Volatility: std. dev. of output gap	−0.3553	0.9041	0.6049	1

| | (B). Volatility: Standard deviation of GDP per capita growth | | |
	Aggregate volatility	"Crisis" volatility	"Normal" volatility
Aggregate Volatility: std. dev. of GDP per capita growth	−0.345	1	–	–
"Crisis" Volatility: std. dev. of GDP per capita growth	−0.2294	0.8073	1	–
"Normal" Volatility: std. dev. of GDP per capita growth	−0.3549	0.8815	0.5242	1

Source: Authors' calculations.

12 percent and 80 percent of the country's volatility measure (the remaining 8 percent corresponds to volatility related to extreme positive fluctuations).

Table 2.3 shows the cross-country correlations between the per capita GDP growth rate and the overall, "crisis," and "normal" volatility measures. Overall volatility is highly correlated (at least 80 percent) with any of its components, "crisis" or "normal." The correlation coefficient between "crisis" and "normal" volatilities is around 55 percent, which is high enough to denote a strong link but not so high as to render one of them redundant. Including each of them in the analysis will provide independent informational content.

Finally, note that the correlation between per capita GDP growth and the volatility measures is always negative, in the neighborhood of −35 percent for overall and "normal" volatilities, and around −23 percent for "crisis" volatility. The smaller (in absolute value) correlation between growth and the "crisis" component could indicate that, when competing as explanatory variables for growth, "normal" volatility would prevail. As noted at the end of next section, this is not the case.

Regarding the *dependent variable*, the growth rate of per capita GDP is calculated as the annualized log difference of the period's final and initial real per capita GDP. The *control variables* are the period's initial level of real per capita GDP, the average ratio of domestic private credit to GDP, and the average secondary school enrollment ratio.

The *instrumental variables* are calculated as follows. The volatility of inflation and terms of trade shocks are calculated as the standard deviation of, the growth

Table 2.4. *Correlations between the structural variables.* Sample: 79 countries,
1960–2000

	Average GDP per capita	Trade openness	Financial development	Institutional development	Fiscal policy procyclicality
Average GDP per capita	1	–	–	–	–
Trade openness	−0.2573	1	–	–	–
Financial development	0.7446	−0.2178	1	–	–
Institutional development	0.8374	−0.1793	0.7296	1	–
Fiscal policy procyclicality	−0.1915	−0.1265	−0.1532	−0.2442	1

Source: Authors' calculations.

rates respectively of the consumer price index and the terms of trade over the corresponding period. The measure of real exchange misalignment is calculated as the absolute difference of the real exchange rate and its equilibrium level – where this is obtained by fitting a country's dollar price of a common basket of goods (relative to the price in the United States) on its average income (again relative to that of the United States), population density, and region-specific factors. The frequency of banking crises is given by the ratio of years a country experienced a systemic banking crises to the total number of years in the period.

The *structural variables* used in the interactions with volatility are measured as follows. Overall economic development is proxied by average output per capita. Financial depth is measured as the ratio of private domestic credit to GDP. International trade openness is represented by the ratio of real exports plus imports to real GDP. The level of institutional development is proxied by a subjective index of investor perceptions, the International Country Risk Guide (ICRG) index. The degree of fiscal policy procyclicality is approximated by the correlation coefficient between the growth rate of GDP and the growth rate of government consumption as share to GDP (see Table 2.4).[10] For more details on variable definitions and data sources, see Appendix B.

RESULTS

This section presents the empirical results on the relationship between macroeconomic volatility and economic growth. For this purpose, the outline explained in the methodological section is followed.

Simple Correlations

Table 2.2 presents the bivariate correlation coefficients between the two measures of volatility with each other and with the growth rate of GDP per capita for various

[10] Table 2.4 presents the coefficients of correlation between the measures of the structural variables. Output per capita is strongly positively correlated with financial depth and institutional development and negatively correlated with trade openness and fiscal policy procyclicality. There is enough difference between these measures so as to make the exercises with each of them informative.

samples of countries. For the full sample of countries, the correlation between the growth rate and the two measures of volatility is negative. This is not always the case for different subsamples of countries, however. The correlation between volatility and growth appears to decline as average income decreases. It is positive for high-income countries, close to zero for the medium-income group, and negative for low-income countries.

A somewhat different pattern emerges when countries are grouped according to financial development. The correlation between volatility and growth is positive for countries of high financial development. It becomes large and negative in the medium group, and it remains negative but of smaller magnitude for countries of low financial development. Therefore, when breaking the sample according to financial development, the correlations describe a nonlinear "U" pattern.

In the case of trade openness, the correlations between volatility and growth are negative for all groups, but more so for medium- and highly-open economies. It would appear that the negative association between volatility and growth increases with openness. As discussed later, this result does not survive the inclusion of additional determinants for economic growth.

When breaking the sample by the degree of institutional development, the pattern of correlations resembles that by income levels: that is, it becomes less negative as development occurs. However, in this case, the differences across groups are not as noticeable as when the sample is divided by income.

Finally, when the sample is split by the degree of fiscal policy procyclicality, the correlation results are surprising. It would appear that highly procyclical countries have the smallest negative association between growth and volatility. This result is unexpected because procyclical fiscal policies tend to magnify the effect of macroeconomic shocks. However, as discussed below, this result is overturned when the analysis controls for other growth determinants.

Regression Analysis: Homogeneous Effect of Volatility on Growth

Table 2.5 presents the regression coefficients, associated t-statistics, and other estimation results for simple and multiple regressions of the growth rate of GDP per capita on the volatility measures (one by one) and the control variables.

The simple regression (Columns 1 and 4) indicates a negative and statistically significant association between either measure of volatility and economic growth. The size and statistical significance of the volatility coefficient decline only marginally when the study controls for initial GDP per capita. In fact, after including the full set of controls, the volatility coefficient declines only slightly from its simple-regression value and retains its statistical significance at usual confidence levels. It appears, then, that the direct link between volatility and growth is not captured by standard growth determinants. Note that the control variables are all statistically significant and present coefficients that have the expected signs. The coefficient on initial income suggests that there is conditional convergence; and the results on both human capital investment and financial depth indicate a positive effect on growth.

The following sections consider, in turn, four avenues for a deeper study of the volatility–growth connection. First, the link between volatility and growth may

Table 2.5. *Homogeneous effect of volatility on growth, cross-sectional regression analysis, 1960–2000*

	Dependent variable: Growth rate of GDP per capita					
	Panel A. Volatility: Standard deviation of output gap			Panel B. Volatility: Standard deviation of GDP per capita growth		
	(1)	(2)	(3)	(4)	(5)	(6)
Volatility	−0.5507	−0.4996	−0.4383	−0.3355	−0.2994	−0.2605
	−2.89	−2.63	−3.24	−2.87	−2.57	−3.02
Control variables						
Initial GDP per capita	–	0.0672	−0.9358	–	0.0759	−0.9276
(in logs)	–	0.57	−5.89	–	0.64	−6.01
Education	–	–	1.6119	–	–	1.6188
(secondary enrollment, in logs)	–	–	4.89	–	–	4.92
Financial Depth	–	–	1.1664	–	–	1.1617
(private domestic credit/GDP, in logs)	–	–	4.37	–	–	4.48
R-squared	0.1251	0.1274	0.5823	0.1190	0.1219	0.5772
No. Countries / No. Observations	79/79	79/79	79/79	79/79	79/79	79/79

Note: t-Statistics are presented below the corresponding coefficient.
Intercept is included in all estimations but not reported.
Standard errors are corrected for potential heteroscedasticity using Newey–West procedure.
Source: Authors' calculations.

change depending on the structure of the economy. Second, volatility may be jointly endogenous with economic growth. Third, the volatility–growth link may have changed over time. Fourth, large and negative fluctuations may explain the negative volatility–growth link.

Regression Analysis: Heterogeneous Effect of Volatility on Growth Depending on Various Country Characteristics

In contrast to the previous set of regressions, here the empirical link between volatility and growth is allowed to vary according to some country structural characteristics. These are the overall level of development (proxied by the level of per capita income), the depth of financial markets, the openness of international trade, the level of institutional development, and the degree of fiscal policy procyclicality. As explained in the methodological section, heterogeneous volatility–growth links can be accounted for through "continuous" and "categorical" interactions.

CONTINUOUS INTERACTION EFFECTS. These effects are measured through the coefficient on the multiplicative term between each volatility measure and the proxy for a given structural characteristic. Table 2.6, Panels A and B, reports these results. There is strong evidence that the level of (average) income affects the relationship

Table 2.6. *Heterogeneous effect of volatility on growth, continuous interaction effects, cross-sectional regression analysis, 1960–2000*

	Dependent variable: Growth rate of GDP per capita				
	Panel A. Volatility: Standard deviation of output gap, volatility interacted with:				
	Average income [1]	Trade openness [2]	Fin. development [3]	Instit. development [4]	Fiscal Policy procyclicality [5]
Volatility (standard deviation of output gap)	−2.4417 −3.2	−0.3321 −2.16	−0.8258 −1.43	−0.2341 −1.91	−0.4369 −3.08
Volatility interaction (volatility × corresponding structural variable)	0.2912 2.92	−0.0014 −1.24	0.1188 0.71	0.2116 3.72	−0.2190 −1.35
Control variables					
Initial income (GDP per capita in 1960, in logs)	−1.3904 −5.79	−0.9425 −6.09	−0.8833 −5.07	−1.1638 −6.63	−0.9508 −5.54
Education (secondary enrollment, in logs)	1.2835 3.87	1.6207 4.94	1.5827 4.55	1.8383 −5.88	1.6378 4.89
Financial depth (private domestic credit/GDP, in logs)	1.1630 4.4	1.1493 4.28	0.8289 1.85	0.6935 2.62	1.1829 4.34
R-squared	0.6515	0.5876	0.5851	0.6751	0.5927
No. countries / No. observations	79/79	79/79	79/79	79/79	79/79

	Panel B. Volatility: Standard deviation of GDP per capita growth, volatility interacted with:				
	Average income [1]	Trade openness [2]	Fin. development [3]	Instit. development [4]	Fiscal policy procyclicality [5]
Volatility (standard deviation of GDP per capita growth)	−1.6746 −3.62	−0.2015 −1.96	−0.5158 −1.35	−0.1139 −1.32	−0.2605 −2.95
Volatility Interaction (volatility × corresponding structural variable)	0.2064 3.33	−0.0007 −0.99	0.0789 0.72	0.1386 3.74	−0.1519 −1.55

Panel B. Volatility: Standard deviation of GDP per capita
growth, volatility interacted with:

	Average income [1]	Trade openness [2]	Fin. development [3]	Instit. development [4]	Fiscal policy procyclicality [5]
Control variables					
Initial income	−1.4342	−0.9310	−0.8715	−1.1556	−0.9428
(GDP Per Capita in 1960, in logs)	−6.29	−6.15	−4.96	−6.73	−5.67
Education	1.2356	1.6269	1.5900	1.8437	1.6397
(secondary enrollment, in logs)	3.84	4.96	4.55	5.90	4.92
Financial depth	1.0990	1.1467	0.7873	0.6337	1.1839
(private domestic credit/GDP, in logs)	4.20	4.38	1.66	2.37	4.50
R-squared	0.6658	0.5808	0.5805	0.6813	0.5906
No. countries / No. observations	79/79	79/79	79/79	79/79	79/79

Note: *t*-statistics are presented below the corresponding coefficient.
Intercept is included in all estimations but not reported.
Standard errors are corrected for potential heteroscedasticity using Newey–West procedure.
Source: Authors' calculations.

between volatility and growth, in the sense that it tends to be less negative for higher income countries (see Column 1 in Panels A and B). As is the case for most of this study's findings, the two measures of volatility render the same qualitative results. When the study interacts volatility with institutional development (see Column 4 in panels A and B), the negative link between volatility and growth weakens in a statistically significant fashion as institutional development improves.

In the case of financial depth (see Column 3 in Panels A and B), the coefficient on volatility remains negative but loses significance when the interaction term is included. The coefficient on the interaction term itself is positive but lacks statistical significance. However, as discussed in the following section, once nonlinear effects are allowed for by looking at categorical interactions, financial depth becomes significant, as anticipated by the correlation analysis.

In the case of fiscal procyclicality (see Column 5 in Panels A and B), the interaction term is negative, indicating that more procyclical fiscal policies worsen the negative link between volatility and growth. However, this result is significant – and marginally so – only in the case of the standard deviation of GDP growth as the measure of volatility. As in the case of financial development, this appears to indicate a more complicated pattern for the effect that fiscal policy procyclicality has on the volatility–growth link, as shall be discussed in the next section.

Finally, when volatility is interacted with trade openness (see Column 2 in Panels A and B), although the coefficient on volatility remains negative and statistically significant, the coefficient on the interaction is not significant. Contrary to the cases of financial development or fiscal procyclicality, the lack of significance of the trade interaction simply reflects the fact that openness has no impact on the volatility–growth relationship.

CATEGORICAL INTERACTION EFFECTS. As mentioned above, the lack of significant results on some of the continuous interactions may be due to the fact that they impose a monotonic relationship between the volatility–growth link and a given structural characteristic. (For instance, the effect of volatility on growth must decline, stay constant, or increase with financial development, but it cannot describe a nonmonotonic, "U"-type of pattern.) In this section, the study allows for nonmonotonic effects through categorical interactions.

Categorical interaction effects are measured through the coefficient on the multiplicative term between each volatility measure and the binary variable that indicates whether or not the country belongs to a given group. As explained in the methodological section, for each structural characteristic, the sample is divided into three groups of similar size (groups of low, medium, and high values for the corresponding structural characteristic). The volatility coefficients for each of the three groups are estimated, which allows the study to test whether each of them is statistically significant.[11] In addition, the analysis tests whether the coefficients for the low and medium groups are different from the high group, which, therefore, acts as the benchmark. Table 2.7, Panels A and B, reports the regression estimation results and related tests.

Regarding the level of income (Column 1), there is no significant relationship between volatility and growth for medium- and high-income economies. In contrast, the volatility–growth link is significantly negative for poor countries. In the case of institutional development (Column 4), the result is similar. That is, the relationship between volatility and growth is significantly negative only in the group of poorly developed countries. A likely interpretation for these results is that as countries develop, they have the means – from stabilization policies, institutional safeguards, and insurance markets – to neutralize the long-run effects of volatility (see Fatás 2002). Note that the volatility coefficient for medium-income countries is negative, as it is for low-income countries, but it fails to be significant. The study reexamines the growth effect of volatility at various income levels below, when it controls for the potential endogeneity of volatility.

Regarding financial development (Column 3), there is no significant link between growth and volatility in countries that are either highly or poorly financially developed. However, there is strong evidence of a negative relationship for countries in the middle of the financial development spectrum. This result is consistent with the literature that indicates a larger macroeconomic vulnerability in countries that have just liberalized their financial systems (see Gaytán and Ranciere 2002).

---

[11] To obtain the significance of the volatility coefficients for each group, the interactive terms between volatility and each dummy are included, but volatility by itself is omitted in order to avoid perfect colinearity. Significance of the differences between the groups is tested using a Wald test.

Table 2.7. *Heterogeneous effect of volatility on growth, categorical interaction effects, cross-sectional regression analysis, 1960–2000*

	Dependent variable: Growth rate of GDP per capita				
	Panel A. Volatility: Standard deviation of output gap, categories by:				
	Income [1]	Trade openness [2]	Fin. development [3]	Instit. development [4]	Fiscal policy procyclicality [5]
Categorical interactions					
Volatility, low category	−0.5565	−0.3680	−0.3222	−0.5222	−0.3425
(volatility × [dummy = 1 if low category country])	−2.89	−1.89	−1.55	−2.59	−1.00
Volatility, medium category	−0.1769	−0.4622	−0.6354	−0.1921	−0.5592
(volatility × [dummy = 1 if medium category country])	−1.31	−1.91	−3.43	−0.88	−3.48
Volatility, high category	0.1986	−0.4610	−0.2810	0.3172	−0.3251
(volatility × [dummy = 1 if high category country])	0.86	−2.39	−1.04	0.99	−1.9
Control Variables					
Initial GDP per capita	−1.2652	−0.9287	−0.9049	−1.1064	−0.9010
(in logs)	−7.01	−5.76	−5.22	−7.00	−5.62
Education	0.8137	1.5869	1.5866	1.8167	1.5415
(secondary enrollment, in logs)	3.24	4.64	4.77	5.29	4.5
Financial depth	0.7873	1.1834	1.1802	0.8612	1.1196
(private domestic credit/GDP, in logs)	2.97	4.37	2.39	2.67	4.15
R-squared	0.8674	0.8082	0.8149	0.8493	0.8155
No. countries/No. observations	79/79	79/79	79/79	79/79	79/79
TESTS (*P*-values)					
(a) Ho: Volatility coefficient for high = Volatility coefficient for medium	0.122	0.996	0.257	0.163	0.260
(b) Ho: Volatility coefficient for high = Volatility coefficient for low	0.018	0.717	0.901	0.037	0.962

(continued)

83

Table 2.7 (continued)

	Dependent variable: Growth rate of GDP per capita				
	Panel B. Volatility: Standard deviation of GDP per capita growth, categories by:				
	Income [1]	Trade openness [2]	Fin. development [3]	Instit. development [4]	Fiscal policy procyclicality [5]
Categorical Interactions					
Volatility, low category	-0.3865	-0.2551	-0.1931	-0.3310	-0.1375
(volatility × [dummy = 1 if low category country])	-2.97	-1.65	-1.40	-2.41	-0.66
Volatility, medium category	-0.0974	-0.2786	-0.3569	-0.1243	-0.3684
(volatility × [dummy = 1 if medium category country])	-1.12	-1.84	-3.07	-0.86	-3.61
Volatility, high category	0.2041	-0.2466	-0.1764	0.3764	-0.2248
(volatility × [dummy = 1 if high category economy])	-1.25	-2.13	-0.95	-1.59	-2.04
Control Variables					
Initial GDP Per Capita	-1.2407	-0.9279	-1.9011	-1.0489	-0.8971
(in logs)	-6.8	-5.66	-5.03	-7.41	-5.75
Education	0.8198	1.6081	1.6003	1.8161	1.5581
(secondary enrollment, in logs)	3.36	4.73	4.77	5.29	4.63
Financial depth	0.7641	1.1788	1.1779	0.8695	1.1337
(private domestic credit/GDP, in logs)	3.04	4.46	2.47	2.85	4.36
R-squared	0.8704	0.8058	0.8113	0.8544	0.8149
No. countries / No. observations	79/79	79/79	79/79	79/79	79/79
TESTS (*P*-values)					
(a) Ho: Volatility coefficient for high = Volatility coefficient for medium	0.087	0.854	0.387	0.056	0.275
(b) Ho: Volatility coefficient for high = Volatility coefficient for low	0.009	0.964	0.942	0.015	0.698

Note: t-statistics are presented below the corresponding coefficient.
Intercept is included in all estimations but not reported.
Standard errors are corrected for potential heteroscedasticity using Newey–West procedure.
Source: Authors' calculations.

When trade openness is considered as the structural characteristic of interest (Column 2), the volatility coefficient is significantly negative in all country groups at the 10 percent significance level and the differences across groups are not statistically different from zero. Together with the result on the continuous interaction, this indicates that openness has no bearing on the volatility–growth link. That is, open countries are as likely to deal with their volatile environment and neutralize it as closed economies are.

Finally, when countries are classified by their degree of fiscal policy procyclicality (Column 5), the study finds that only in those countries that conduct relatively more countercyclical policies does volatility have no statistically significant link with growth (see Imbs 2002). This is particularly noticeable when volatility is measured as the standard deviation of GDP growth. Moreover, the negative coefficient on volatility tends to be larger (although not statistically so) for medium fiscal procyclical economies than for high ones. One interpretation for this result is that medium countries are also the most uncertain regarding how governments react to shocks, and it is this uncertainty that worsens the volatility–growth connection.

In sum, the types of countries where volatility and growth appear to be negatively related are those that are relatively poor, institutionally underdeveloped, undergoing intermediate stages of financial development, and that conduct mixed or highly procyclical fiscal policies. The level of trade openness does not appear to worsen or improve the negative relationship between volatility and growth.

Instrumental Variable Regression Analysis: Controlling for the Endogeneity of Volatility

Here our study attempts to estimate the causal effect of volatility on growth. This is done by extracting the exogenous component of volatility through the use of instrumental variables. The analysis also allows for interaction effects (both continuous and categorical) but related only to the level of average income, the most relevant indicator of overall development. Table 2.8, Panels A and B, reports the results when the study does not allow for interaction effects (Column 1) as well as when it considers continuous (Column 2) and categorical (Column 3) interaction effects between volatility and level of income.

The set of instrumental variables used in the analysis consists of real exchange rate misalignment; frequency of banking crises; price volatility, proxied by the standard deviation of inflation rate; and volatility of terms of trade shocks.

Before discussing the estimation results, the first issue to consider is whether there are grounds to believe that the volatility measures may be subject to joint endogeneity. For this, a Hausman-type test was conducted, reported at the bottom of Table 2.8. Under the null hypothesis that volatility is exogenous, the ordinary-least-squares (OLS) estimates are both consistent and efficient, and the instrumental-variable (IV) estimates are consistent but not efficient.[12] In contrast, under the alternative hypothesis, only the IV estimates are consistent. The test results lead

[12] Recall that consistency of the estimator requires asymptotic unbisedness and asymptotically vanishing variance in large samples and refers to its closeness to the true population parameter, while efficiency denotes the property of minimum variance.

Table 2.8. *Instrumental variable estimation, cross-sectional regression analysis,
1960–2000*

	Dependent variable: Growth rate of GDP per capita		
	Panel A. Volatility: Standard deviation of output gap		
	Homogeneous effect [1]	Continuous interaction [2]	Categorical interaction [3]
Volatility	−1.1950	−3.2805	−
(standard deviation of output gap)	−4.09	−3.31	−
Volatility interaction with income	−	0.3201	−
(volatility × log average income)	−	2.57	−
Volatility, low income	−	−	−1.2355
(volatility × [dummy = 1 if low income country])	−	−	−2.03
Volatility, medium income	−	−	−0.6484
(volatility × [dummy = 1 if medium income country])	−	−	−2.9100
Volatility, high income	−	−	−0.0020
(volatility × [dummy = 1 if high income country])	−	−	−0.01
Control Variables			
Initial GDP per capita	−1.2388	−1.6918	−1.3061
(in logs)	−4.7	−5.15	−6.14
Education	1.6871	1.3145	0.9940
(secondary enrollment, in logs)	4.08	3.02	3.31
Financial depth	1.0318	1.0489	0.7856
(private domestic credit/GDP, in logs)	3.33	3.31	3.21
R-squared	0.7345	0.7868	0.8359
No. countries / No. observations	79/79	79/79	79/79
R-squared 1st stage (average)	0.4782	0.4860	0.8176
SPECIFICATION TESTS (*p*-values)			
(a) Durbin–Wu–Hausman test	0.0001	0.0007	0.0086
(b) Hansen J-Test for overidentifying restrictions	0.9446	0.8234	0.6623
	Panel B. Volatility: Standard deviation of GDP per capita growth		
	Homogeneous effect [1]	Continuous interaction [2]	Categorical interaction [3]
Volatility	−0.6917	−2.0698	−
(standard deviation of GDP per capita growth)	−4.25	−4.01	−
Volatility interaction with income	−	0.2098	−
(volatility × log average income)	−	3.16	−

	Panel B. Volatility: Standard deviation of GDP per capita growth		
	Homogeneous effect [1]	Continuous interaction [2]	Categorical interaction [3]
Volatility, low income	–	–	−0.7321
(volatility × [dummy = 1 if low income country])	–	–	−2.53
Volatility, medium income	–	–	−0.3839
(volatility × [dummy = 1 if medium income country])	–	–	−2.9100
Volatility, high income	–	–	0.1790
(volatility × [dummy = 1 if high income country])	–	–	0.62
Control Variables			
Initial GDP per capita	−1.2044	−1.6812	−1.2771
(in logs)	−4.93	−5.64	−6.09
Education	1.7023	1.3011	0.9808
(secondary enrollment, in logs)	4.19	3.18	3.42
Financial depth	1.0248	0.9800	0.7527
(private domestic credit/GDP, in logs)	3.5	3.23	3.18
R-squared	0.7445	0.8009	0.8443
No. countries/No. observations	79/79	79/79	79/79
R-squared 1st stage (average)	0.5157	0.5164	0.8200
SPECIFICATION TESTS (*p*-values)			
(a) Durbin–Wu–Hausman test	0.0001	0.0006	0.0124
(b) Hansen J-Test for overidentifying restrictions	0.8490	0.8082	0.7339

Note: *t*-statistics are presented below the corresponding coefficient.
Intercept is included in all estimations but not reported.
Standard errors are corrected for potential heteroscedasticity using Newey–West procedure.
Source: Authors' calculations.

to a strong rejection of the null hypothesis of exogenous volatility and point to the use of instrumental variables to estimate the causal impact of volatility on growth.

Next, the analysis needs to make sure that the instrumental-variable procedure is appropriate. This depends, first, on whether the instrumental variables can explain a large share of the variation in volatility and, second, whether they are related to economic growth only through the explanatory variables in the regression (so that the instruments' correlation with the regression residual is zero). In order to show the instrumental variables' strong explanatory power on the volatility measures, the R-squared coefficients of the first-stage regression are reported. They are about 50 percent in the first two columns and jump considerably when the study allows for categorical interaction effects. The full first-stage regression (not reported) indicates that all instruments exhibit the expected positive coefficient, and all are statistically significant, except for the frequency of banking crises. Then, to assess whether the instrumental variables are not correlated with the regression residual, the study conducted a Hansen test of overidentifying restrictions and reported its *p*-value. Fortunately, the test clearly indicates that the hypothesis that there is no correlation between the instrumental variables and the error term should not be rejected.

The general result from the IV estimation is that the coefficient on volatility becomes larger in magnitude and stronger in statistical significance than the corresponding OLS estimate. Apparently, there is a positive association between volatility and growth that comes from either simultaneous causation from third variables or a positive feedback from growth to volatility. Once this positive link is removed, the negative effect from volatility to growth is revealed to be larger in magnitude. In fact, comparing Table 2.8 (Column 1) with Table 2.5 (Columns 3 and 6), the IV volatility coefficients are more than twice as large as the OLS coefficients, whether the standard deviation of the output gap or per capita GDP growth is considered as the measure of volatility. The economic significance of the estimated effect of volatility on growth is discussed in the concluding section.

When income interaction effects are considered (Columns 2 and 3), it is also the case that the volatility coefficient under IV is larger than its OLS counterpart. This is particularly noticeable when the study allows for categorical interactions. Now, volatility has a negative impact on growth not only in poor countries but also in medium-income economies (although more so in the former group). Nevertheless, it is still the case that for rich countries, volatility has no significant effect on growth.

Pooled Regression Analysis: The Stability of the Volatility–Growth Relationship over Time

The study now considers whether the link between volatility and growth has changed in recent decades. As explained in the methodological section, for this purpose the analysis conducted pooled regression analysis on country observations corresponding to the four decades since the 1960s to the 1990s. The analysis was carried out first ignoring and then allowing for income interactions. The results are reported in Tables 2.9 and 2.10, respectively. In both cases, the regression coefficients were obtained through OLS and IV estimators.

First consider the results in Table 2.9, which ignore income interactions. For both OLS and IV estimators, the largest volatility coefficients occur in the 1980s. Focusing on the IV estimates, there is a sharp and statistically significant increase in the size of the volatility effect on growth from the 1970s to the 1980s, continuing a trend already present since the 1960s. The 1990s coefficient is only a little smaller than that of the 1980s, and the difference is not statistically significant. The marked change between the first two decades and the latter two does not appear to be related to a major change in the cross-country mean or variance of either volatility measure. What seems to drive the change is the substantial decrease in the mean growth rate, which dropped to less than one third from the 1960s to the 1980s and less than one

Table 2.9. *Homogeneous effect of volatility on growth: OLS and IV estimation, regression analysis of decades, 1960–2000*

	Dependent variable: Growth rate of GDP per capita			
	Panel A. Volatility: Standard deviation of output gap		Panel B. Volatility: Standard deviation of GDP per capita growth	
	OLS [1]	IV [2]	OLS [3]	IV [4]
Volatility, 1960s	−0.0415	−0.6451	−0.0406	−0.4159
(Volatility × [Dummy = 1 if year 1961–70)	−0.48	−1.66	−0.72	−1.79
Volatility, 1970s	−0.4022	−1.0453	−0.2359	−0.6752
(Volatility × [Dummy = 1 if year 1971–80)	−1.77	−3.29	−1.55	−3.29
Volatility, 1980s	−0.7146	−2.4869	−0.5309	−1.2976
(Volatility × [Dummy = 1 if year 1981–90)	−6.50	−2.87	−5.85	−3.73
Volatility, 1990s	−0.3193	−2.0165	−0.2126	−1.1917
(Volatility × [Dummy = 1 if year 1991–2000)	−1.53	−3.68	−1.57	−3.75
Control Variables				
Initial GDP per capita	−0.6800	−0.8634	−0.7148	−0.9003
(in logs)	−4.65	−4.55	−4.99	−5.07
Education	1.1780	1.0970	1.2076	1.1202
(secondary enrollment, in logs)	5.48	3.75	5.59	4.05
Financial depth	1.1872	0.8642	1.1900	0.9455
(private domestic credit/GDP, in logs)	4.87	2.85	4.90	3.45
R-squared	0.6087	0.3273	0.6117	0.4266
No. countries/No. observations	79/310	79/309	310	309
R-squared 1st stage (average)	–	0.7906	–	0.7985
TESTS (*p*-values)				
(a) Ho: Volatility coefficient for 1960s = Volatility coefficient for 1970s	0.1220	0.336	0.210	0.312
(b) Ho: Volatility coefficient for 1960s = Volatility coefficient for 1980s	0.0000	0.030	0.000	0.015
(c) Ho: Volatility coefficient for 1960s = Volatility coefficient for 1990s	0.2161	0.019	0.240	0.024
(d) Ho: Volatility coefficient for 1970s = Volatility coefficient for 1980s	0.2132	0.082	0.094	0.075
(e) Ho: Volatility coefficient for 1980s = Volatility coefficient for 1990s	0.0942	0.595	0.049	0.794
SPECIFICATION TESTS (*p*-values)				
(a) Durbin–Wu–Hausman test	–	0.0000	–	0.0001
(b) Hansen J-Test for overidentifying restrictions	–	0.7525	–	0.6841

Note: *t*-statistics are presented below the corresponding coefficient.
Intercept is included in all estimations but not reported.
Standard errors are corrected for potential heteroscedasticity using Newey–West procedure.
Source: Authors' calculations.

Table 2.10. *Heterogeneous effect of volatility on growth, continuous interaction effects: OLS and IV, regression analysis of decades, 1960–2000*

	Dependent Variable: Growth rate of GDP per capita			
	Panel A. Volatility: Standard deviation of output gap		Panel B. Volatility: Standard deviation of GDP per capita growth	
	OLS [1]	IV [2]	OLS [3]	IV [4]
Volatility, 1960s	−1.5392	−3.7136	−1.0594	−2.3899
(Volatility × [Dummy = 1 if year 1961–70])	−3.01	−3.57	−3.15	−3.38
Volatility, 1970s	−1.5855	−4.0515	−0.9555	−2.4480
(Volatility × [Dummy = 1 if year 971–80])	−2.79	−4.89	−2.55	−4.55
Volatility, 1980s	−2.6642	−6.2465	−1.5623	−3.5250
(Volatility × [Dummy = 1 if year 1981–90])	−4.48	−5.33	−4.49	−4.32
Volatility, 1990s	−3.4670	−6.3728	−1.9633	−3.7489
(Volatility × [Dummy = 1 if year 1991–2000])	−5.03	−4.81	−4.50	−4.54
Continuous interactions between volatility and average income				
Volatility interaction, 1960s	0.2249	0.3533	0.1557	0.2357
(volatility × average income × [Dummy = 1 if year 1961–70])	2.84	2.46	2.97	2.47
Volatility interaction, 1970s	0.1613	0.4133	0.0973	0.2426
(volatility × average income × [Dummy = 1 if year 1971–80])	2.03	3.64	1.82	3.11
Volatility interaction, 1980s	0.2573	0.6045	0.1374	0.3175
(volatility × average income × [Dummy = 1 if year 1981–90])	3.23	4.28	2.89	3.20
Volatility interaction, 1990s	0.4784	0.8006	0.2670	0.4849
(volatility × average income × [Dummy = 1 if year 1991–2000])	5.13	3.86	4.55	3.45
Control Variables				
Initial GDP Per Capita	−1.0623	−1.5513	−1.0743	−1.5600
(in logs)	−6.91	5.87	−7.19	−5.98
Education	1.0641	0.6399	1.1095	0.7517
(secondary enrollment, in logs)	4.73	1.89	4.92	2.24
Financial Depth	1.0509	0.7796	1.0648	0.8119
(private domestic credit/GDP, in logs)	5.00	3.16	5.04	3.37
R-squared	0.6445	0.4333	0.6435	0.4538
No. countries/No. observations	79/310	79/309	79/310	79/309
R-squared 1st stage (average)	–	0.8187	–	0.8230

Dependent Variable: Growth rate of
GDP per capita

	Panel A. Volatility: Standard deviation of output gap		Panel B. Volatility: Standard deviation of GDP per capita growth	
	OLS [1]	IV [2]	OLS [3]	IV [4]
TESTS (*p*-values)				
(a) Ho: Volatility coefficient for 1960s = Volatility coefficient for 1970s	0.937	0.683	0.787	0.914
(b) Ho: Volatility coefficient for 1960s = Volatility coefficient for 1980s	0.068	0.010	0.179	0.088
(c) Ho: Volatility coefficient for 1960s = Volatility coefficient for 1990s	0.007	0.016	0.043	0.046
(d) Ho: Volatility coefficient for 1970s = Volatility coefficient for 1980s	0.090	0.008	0.123	0.058
(e) Ho: Volatility coefficient for 1980s = Volatility coefficient for 1990s	0.256	0.892	0.351	0.712
(a) Ho: Interaction coefficient for 1960s = Volatility coefficient for 1970s	0.486	0.667	0.335	0.939
(b) Ho: Interaction coefficient for 1960s = Volatility coefficient for 1980s	0.722	0.103	0.750	0.423
(c) Ho: Interaction coefficient for 1960s = Volatility coefficient for 1990s	0.015	0.029	0.090	0.061
(d) Ho: Interaction coefficient for 1970s = Volatility coefficient for 1980s	0.280	0.115	0.485	0.381
(e) Ho: Interaction coefficient for 1980s = Volatility coefficient for 1990s	0.024	0.242	0.034	0.133
SPECIFICATION TESTS (*p*-values)				
(a) Durbin–Wu–Hausman Test	–	0.0000	–	0.0000
(b) Hansen J-Test for Overidentifying Restrictions:	–	0.6448	–	0.5304

Note: *t*-statistics are presented below the corresponding coefficient.
Intercept is included in all estimations but not reported.
Standard errors are correlated for potential heteroscedasticity using Newey–West procedure.
Source: Authors' calculations.

half from the 1960s to the 1990s (see Table 2.1 for summary statistics on growth and volatility by decades). The world is not more volatile now than 30 years ago, but volatility is taking a larger toll on growth.[13]

[13] An alternative explanation is that although total volatility has not risen, the "crisis" portion of volatility has increased in the last two decades. As noted below, it is this component that explains the negative effect of volatility of growth. The authors thank Luis Servén for this observation.

Table 2.11. *Homogeneous effect of volatility and crisis on growth, cross-sectional regression analysis, 1960–2000*

	Dependent variable: Growth rate of GDP per capita			
	Panel A. Volatility: Standard deviation of output gap		Panel B. Volatility: Standard deviation of GDP per capita growth	
	OLS [1]	IV [2]	OLS [3]	IV [4]
"Normal" volatility	−0.1207	−0.5311	−0.0017	−0.7033
(volatility within the worldwide 1-std. dev. threshold)	−0.38	−0.53	−0.01	−1.36
"Crisis" volatility	−0.7913	−2.0111	−0.5722	−0.8559
(volatility below the worldwide 1-std. dev. threshold)	−2.45	−2.17	−2.38	−1.82
Control Variables				
Initial GDP per capita	−0.9307	−1.2205	−0.9692	−1.1676
(in logs)	−5.80	−4.71	−5.49	−4.16
Education	1.6069	1.6579	1.6895	1.6710
(secondary enrollment, in logs)	4.76	4.10	4.80	3.72
Financial depth	1.2775	1.2988	1.2825	1.1186
(private domestic credit/GDP, in logs)	4.75	3.85	4.79	3.37
R-squared	0.5820	0.7377	0.5876	0.7581
No. countries/No. observations	79/79	79/79	79/79	79/79
R-squared 1st stage (average)	–	0.4761	–	0.5302
SPECIFICATION TESTS (*p*-values)				
(a) Durbin–Wu–Hausman test	–	0.0009	–	0.00057
(b) Hansen J-Test for overidentifying restrictions:	–	0.7344	–	0.9021

Note: *t*-statistics are presented below the corresponding coefficient
Intercept is included in all estimations but not reported
Standard errors are correlated for potential heteroscedasticity using Newey–West procedure
Source: Authors' calculations.

Table 2.10 tells a similar story, implying that the volatility interaction with income cannot explain the changes in recent decades. The coefficients on volatility and on the income interaction term are remarkably similar between the 1960s and the 1970s, and also between the 1980s and the 1990s, but a break occurs in the 1980s. The difference between the first two decades and the latter two is notable and statistically significant. The fact that the coefficients on volatility and on the interaction term change by roughly the same proportion indicates that the overall growth effect of a change in volatility also changes proportionally, provided income stays constant. The gains from an increase in income – in terms of a diminished *indirect* effect of volatility on growth – are larger in the latter decades, but so is the negative *direct* effect of volatility.

Regression Analysis: Volatility and Crises

It can be shown that a high measure of volatility can result from large but infrequent swings in per capita GDP as well as from small but frequent fluctuations. However, their respective real effects could be sharply different (see Caballero 2002). The measures of volatility used up to now in this study combine normal and crisis fluctuations. This section focuses on the components of volatility to answer the last question posed in this study. This is whether the negative relationship between volatility and growth is actually due to the harmful impact of large negative fluctuations ("crisis" volatility) and not really to the effect of repeated but small fluctuations around the trend ("normal" volatility).

Here the analysis takes the basic model (Table 2.5, Columns 3 and 4) and replaces overall volatility by measures of "normal" and "crisis" volatilities. Then it estimates the model by OLS and IV estimators. The results are reported in Table 2.11. Although both forms of volatility present negative coefficients, only "crisis" volatility is statistically significant. This is true whether the output gap or per capita GDP growth is used as the proxy for macroeconomic fluctuations, but the contrast between "crisis" and "normal" volatility effects is sharper in the case of the output gap. As before, the IV estimates render larger coefficients for either type of volatility, but only the "crisis" one is statistically significant. In the case of the output gap, the effect of "crisis" volatility is almost twice as large as that of overall volatility (compare Table 2.8, Panel A, Column 1 with Table 2.11, Column 2).

CONCLUSIONS

Analyzing cross-country data, this study concludes that macroeconomic volatility and long-run economic growth are negatively related. This negative link is exacerbated in countries that are poor, institutionally underdeveloped, undergoing intermediate stages of financial development, or unable to conduct countercyclical fiscal policies. On the other hand, the volatility–growth association does not appear to depend on a country's level of openness to international trade.

Furthermore, the negative global relationship between macroeconomic volatility and long-run growth actually reflects an even stronger, harmful effect from volatility to growth. This is true for a worldwide sample of countries, and particularly so for low-income and middle-income economies. The negative effect of volatility on growth has been present since the 1960s, but it has become considerably larger in the last two decades. This does not reflect a change in volatility trends over time; rather, it is due to the reduction in growth in the 1980s and 1990s and the countries' inability to deal with volatility in that lower-growth context.

Examining the components of volatility, the study finds that its negative impact on growth is not the effect of small repeated cyclical deviations but of large drops below the output trend. Therefore, it is the volatility due to crisis that harms the economy's long-run growth performance, not the volatility due to normal fluctuations.

Table 2.12. *Growth effects of volatility*

Growth effect of 1 standard deviation increase in volatility[a]	
OLS[b]	−0.4681[c]
IV	−1.2762
IV-1990s	−2.1535
"Crisis"	−2.1479

Notes:

[a] The measure of volatility is the standard deviation of the output gap. The worldwide std. dev. of volatility used in the calculations is 1.068.

[b] The corresponding volatility coefficients are the following. OLS:−0.4383, IV:−1.195, IV−1990s:−2.0165, "Crisis":−2.0111.

[c] The growth effects of volatility are obtained as products of the corresponding regression coeffcient and worldwide std. dev. of volatility.

Source: Authors' calculations.

The effects just described are not only statistically significant; their magnitude leads one to believe that they are also economically significant. To illustrate volatility's long-run impact, Table 2.12 reports the growth effect of a change in volatility under various conditions. In order to make the table figures comparable with one another, the same benchmark change in volatility is applied in all exercises. It is set equal to one worldwide, cross-country standard deviation of volatility, measured for each country as the standard deviation of its output gap over 1960–2000. To make this benchmark change in volatility more concrete, consider the following two examples of sequences of countries. In each sequence, countries are presented in ascending order of volatility, and the separation between two consecutive countries is about one standard deviation of volatility. The first sequence, which covers almost the full spectrum of countries in the sample, is France, Egypt, Uruguay, Jordan, and Nigeria. The second example, which covers countries toward the middle of the volatility distribution, is Japan, Botswana, and Argentina.

If the endogeneity of volatility is ignored, the growth decline due to a one-standard-deviation increase in volatility appears to be modest: about 0.5 percentage points of the growth rate. However, once simultaneous and reverse causation in the volatility–growth relationship is accounted for, the same increase in volatility is found to lead to a 1.3 percentage-point drop in the growth rate – which already represents a sizable loss. This decline in growth is magnified even further if one considers the same change in volatility in the 1990s or under a crisis situation. In both cases, the loss would amount to about 2.2 percentage points of the per capita GDP growth rate. For the government and the private sector alike, macroeconomic volatility should be not only a source of short-run concern but also a constant preoccupation for the achievement of long-run goals.

Appendix A: *Sample of countries.* Sample: 79 countries, 1960–2000

Country	Average GDP per captia growth (%)	Volatility standard deviation of output gap	Volatility standard deviation of GDP growth	Commodity exporter	Region	Income group
France	2.606	0.759	1.608	0	ind	High
Norway	3.037	1.058	1.621	0	ind	High
Austria	2.846	0.929	1.767	0	ind	High
Sri Lanka	2.882	1.079	1.780	0	SA	Mid
Netherlands	2.409	1.076	1.840	0	ind	High
United Kingdom	2.121	1.323	1.872	0	ind	High
Belgium	2.746	1.040	1.892	0	ind	High
United States	2.210	1.407	2.002	0	ind	High
Sweden	2.168	1.210	2.022	0	ind	High
Australia	2.128	1.342	2.086	0	ind	High
Italy	2.877	1.162	2.089	0	ind	High
Colombia	1.818	1.270	2.098	0	LAC	Mid
Canada	2.307	1.346	2.168	0	ind	High
Denmark	2.148	1.336	2.234	0	ind	High
Switzerland	1.445	1.422	2.292	0	ind	High
Pakistan	2.620	1.368	2.366	0	SA	Low
Guatemala	1.301	1.277	2.560	1	LAC	Mid
Spain	3.339	1.171	2.676	0	ind	High
Ireland	4.095	1.527	2.809	0	ind	High
Egypt, Arab Rep.	3.047	1.892	2.883	0	MENA	Mid
Finland	2.972	1.919	3.027	0	ind	High
Honduras	0.815	2.017	3.037	1	LAC	Mid
India	2.296	1.938	3.109	0	SA	Low
Philippiness	1.158	2.045	3.163	0	EAP	Mid
Burkina Faso	1.249	2.035	3.171	0	SSA	Low
Madagascar	−1.108	2.200	3.423	1	SSA	Low
Israel	2.944	2.134	3.427	0	ind	High
Mexico	2.106	2.133	3.437	0	LAC	Mid
Malaysia	3.983	2.251	3.446	0	EAP	Mid
Costa Rica	1.765	2.133	3.447	0	LAC	Mid
Japan	4.184	1.465	3.485	0	ind	High
Tunisia	3.047	2.157	3.538	0	MENA	Mid
Turkey	2.285	2.331	3.595	0	ECA	Mid
Paraguay	1.619	2.053	3.632	1	LAC	Mid
Korea, Rep.	5.747	2.321	3.649	0	ind	High
Portugal	3.897	2.254	3.633	0	ind	High
South Africa	0.877	2.270	3.678	0	SSA	Mid
Thailand	4.512	2.337	3.716	0	EAP	Mid
Bolivia	0.347	2.186	3.816	1	LAC	Mid
Iceland	2.825	2.568	3.819	1	ind	High
Greece	3.112	1.935	3.891	0	ind	High
Brazil	2.442	2.339	4.091	0	LAC	Mid
Venezuela, RB	−0.299	2.633	4.099	1	LAC	Mid

(continued)

Appendix A (*continued*)

Country	Average GDP per captia growth (%)	Volatility standard deviation of output gap	Volatility standard deviation of GDP growth	Commodity exporter	Region	Income group
Uruguay	1.137	2.920	4.211	0	LAC	Mid
Indonesia	3.512	2.580	4.212	0	EAP	Low
El Salvador	0.738	2.453	4.241	0	LAC	Mid
Senegal	−0.239	2.765	4.311	0	SSA	Low
Panama	2.022	2.781	4.319	0	LAC	Mid
Ghana	−0.210	2.891	4.433	1	SSA	Low
Jamaica	0.541	2.523	4.469	0	LAC	Mid
Haiti	−0.995	2.639	4.534	0	LAC	Low
Bangladesh	1.359	2.943	4.545	0	SA	Low
Ecuador	1.517	2.633	4.587	0	LAC	Mid
Trinidad and Tobago	2.588	2.281	4.637	1	LAC	Mid
Morocco	1.691	2.759	4.648	0	MENA	Mid
Botswana	6.326	2.615	4.812	1	SSA	Mid
Zambia	−1.246	3.000	4.825	1	SSA	Low
Kenya	1.225	3.046	4.844	0	SSA	Low
Papua New Guinea	1.302	3.078	4.882	1	EAP	Low
Chile	2.479	3.239	5.135	1	LAC	Mid
Peru	0.557	3.546	5.239	1	LAC	Mid
Dominican Republic	2.754	3.259	5.378	0	LAC	Mid
Malawi	1.363	3.452	5.397	1	SSA	Low
Argentiva	0.947	3.675	5.412	1	SSA	Mid
Cote d'Ivoire	0.573	2.998	5.482	1	SSA	Low
Zimbabwe	0.707	3.617	5.570	1	SSA	Low
Gambia, The	0.918	3.227	5.972	0	SSA	Low
Congo, Rep.	1.329	3.677	6.053	1	SSA	Low
Congo, Dem. Rep.	−3.348	3.551	6.309	1	SSA	Low
Sierra Leone	−1.363	3.453	6.393	0	SSA	Low
Togo	0.860	3.912	6.493	1	SSA	Low
Niger	−1.645	4.148	6.541	1	SSA	Low
Jordan	1.151	4.124	7.113	0	MENA	Mid
Nicaragua	−0.874	4.436	7.339	1	LAC	Low
Nigeria	0.316	5.041	7.556	1	SSA	Low
Iran, Islamic Rep.	1.500	4.689	7.718	1	MENA	Mid
China	5.421	5.125	7.994	0	EAP	Mid
Syrian Arab Republic	2.278	4.808	8.204	0	MENA	Mid
Algeria	0.861	5.043	8.285	1	MENA	Mid
Mean	**1.785**	**2.501**	**4.128**			
Standard deviation	**1.662**	**1.068**	**1.710**			

Note: Countries are sorted by volatility (std. dev. of GDP growth) in ascending order.
Source: Authors' calculations.

Appendix B: *Definitions and sources of variables used in correlation and regression analysis*

Basic variables	Definition and construction	Source
Real per capita GDP (in 1985 US$ PPP)	Ratio of total GDP to total population. GDP is in 1985 PPP-adjusted US$. Growth rates are obtained from constant 1995 US$ per capita GDP series.	Authors' construction, using Summers, Heston, and Aten (2002) and The World Bank (2002)
Output gap	Difference between the log of actual GDP and (the log of) potential (trend) GDP. In order to decompose the log of GDP, the Baxter–King filter is used.	Authors' calculations
Gross secondary-school enrollment	Ratio of total secondary enrollment, regardless of age, to the population of the age group that officially corresponds to that level of education.	World Development Network (2002) and The World Bank (2002)
Domestic credit to the private sector (% of GDP)	Ratio to GDP of the stock of claims on the private sector by deposit money banks and other financial institutions.	Beck, Demirguc-Kunt, and Levine (2000)
Trade openness (% of GDP)	Ratio of exports and imports (in 1995 US$) to GDP (in 1995 US$).	World Development Network (2002) and The World Bank (2002)
Structural Variables		
Index of institutional development	First principal component of four indicators: prevalence of law and order, quality of bureaucracy, absence of corruption, and accountability of public officials.	International Country Risk Guide (ICRG)
Government consumption (% GDP)	Ratio of government consumption to GDP.	Summers, Heston, and Aten (2002)
Fiscal policy procyclicality	Correlation between GDP growth rate and growth rate of government consumption as percent of GDP.	Authors' calculations
Instrumental Variables		
Volatility of inflation	Measured by the standard deviation of the rate of change in the consumer price index: annual percentage change in the cost to the average consumer of acquiring a fixed basket of goods and services.	The World Bank (2002)

(continued)

Appendix B *(continued)*

Basic variables	Definition and construction	Source
Real Exchange Rate Misalignment	Absolute deviation of the real exchange rate overvaluation from the equilibrium real exchange rate (set to 1). The extent of real exchange rate disequilibrium is defined as the difference between actual real effective exchange rate and its equilibrium level, given by cross-country purchasing power parity comparisons.	Authors' calculations
Systemic Banking Crises	Number of years in which a country underwent a systemic banking crisis, as a fraction of the number of years in the corresponding period.	Authors' calculations using data from Caprio and Klingebiel (1999) and Kaminsky, Lizondo, and Reinhart (1998)
Volatility of Terms of Trade Shocks	Standard deviation of the log difference of the terms of trade.	The World Bank (2000) "World Development indicators"

REFERENCES

Aghion, P., and G. Saint-Paul. 1998. "Virtues of Bad Times: Interaction between Productivity Growth and Economic Fluctuations." *Macroeconomic Dynamics* 2(3):322–44.

Alesina, A., S. Ozler, N. Roubini, and P. Swagel. 1996. "Political Instability and Economic Growth." *Journal of Economic Growth* 1(2):189–213.

Barro, R. J. 1991. "Economic Growth in a Cross Section of Countries." *Quarterly Journal of Economics* 106(2):407–43.

Baxter, M., and R. G. King. 1999. "Measuring Business Cycles: Approximate Band-Pass Filters for Economic Time Series." *Review of Economics and Statistics* 81(4):575–93.

Beck, T., A. Demirguc-Kunt, and R. Levine. 2000. "A New Database on the Structure and Development of the Financial Sector." *World Bank Economic Review* 14(3):597–605.

Bertola, G., and R. J. Caballero. 1994. "Irreversibility and Aggregate Investment." *Review of Economic Studies* 61(2):223–46.

Caballero, R. J. 2000. "Macroeconomic Volatility in Latin America: A View and Three Case Studies." *Economia* 1(1):31–108.

———. 2001. *Macroeconomic Volatility in Reformed Latin America: Diagnosis and Policy Proposals.* Inter-American Development Bank, Washington, DC.

———. 2002. "Coping with Chile's External Vulnerability: A Financial Problem." In Norman Loayza and Raimundo Soto, eds., *Economic Growth: Sources, Trends, and Cycles.* Santiago: Banco Central de Chile.

Caballero, R. J., and M. L. Hammour. 1994. "The Cleansing Effect of Recessions." *American Economic Review* 84(5):1350–68.

———. 1996. "On the Timing and Efficiency of Creative Destruction." *Quarterly Journal of Economics* 111(3):805–52.

Caprio, G. Jr., and D. Klingebiel. 1996. "Bank Insolvencies: Cross Country Experience." Policy Research Working Paper No. 1620, the World Bank.

Easterly, W., R. Islam, and J. E. Stiglitz. 2000. "Shaken and Stirred: Explaining Growth Volatility." In *The World Bank Annual Conference on Economic Development*. Washington, DC: World Bank.

Fatás, A. 2000a. "Endogenous Growth and Stochastic Trends." *Journal of Monetary Economics* 45(1):107–28.

———. 2000b. "Do Business Cycles Cast Long Shadows? Short-Run Persistence and Economic Growth." *Journal of Economic Growth* 5(2):147–62.

———. 2001. "The Effects of Business Cycles on Growth." INSEAD, Fontainebleau.

———. 2002. "The Effects of Business Cycles on Growth." In *Economic Growth: Sources, Trends and Cycles*, Eds. Norman Loayza and Raimundo Soto. Central Bank of Chile.

Fischer, Stanley. 1993. "The Role of Macroeconomic Factors in Growth." *Journal of Monetary Economics* 32(3):485–511.

Gaytán, A. and R. Ranciere. 2002. "Liquidity, Financial Intermediation, and Growth." Working paper, New York University, New York.

Hall, Robert E. 1991. "Labor Demand, Labor Supply, and Employment Volatility." *NBER Macroeconomics Annual 1991*: 17–46.

———. 1993. "Macro Theory and the Recession of 1990–1991." Papers and Proceedings of the Hundred and Fifth Annual Meeting of the American Economic Association. *American Economic Review* 83(2): 275–79.

Heston, Alan, Robert Summers, and Bettina Aten. 2002. "Penn World Table Version 6.1." Center for International Comparisons at the University of Pennsylvania (CICUP), Philadelphia.

Imbs, J. 2002. "Why the Link between Volatility and Growth Is Both Positive and Negative." CEPR Discussion Paper No. 3561.

International Country Risk Guide (ICRG). Various years. The PRS Group, Inc. East Syracuse, N.Y.

International Monetary Fund (IMF). 2002. *World Economic Outlook*. Washington, DC.

Judson, R., and A. Orphanides. 1996. "Inflation, Volatility and Growth." *Finance and Economics Discussion Series No. 19*. Board of Governors of the Federal Reserve Bank, Washington, DC.

Kaminsky, G., S. Lizondo, and C. Reinhart. 1998. "Leading Indicators of Currency Crises." *International Monetary Fund Staff Papers* 45(1):1–48.

Kroft, K. and H. Lloyd-Ellis. 2002. "Further Cross-Country Evidence on the Link between Growth, Volatility and Business Cycles." Mimeo, Queen's University.

Levine, R., and D. Renelt. 1992. "A Sensitivity Analysis of Cross-Country Growth Regressions." *American Economic Review* 82(4):942–63.

Martin, P., and C. A. Rogers. 1997. "Stabilization Policy, Learning by Doing, and Economic Growth." *Oxford Economic Papers* 49:152–66.

———. 2000. "Long-Term Growth and Short-Term Economic Instability." *European Economic Review* 44(2):359–81.

Mills, T. C. 1999. "Business Cycle Volatility and Economic Growth: A Reassessment." Business Cycle Volatility and Economic Growth Recearch Paper No. 99/2, Loughborough University.

Ramey, G., and V. Ramey. 1995. "Cross-Country Evidence on the Link between Volatility and Growth." *American Economic Review* 85(5):1138–50.

Ranciere, R., and A. Gaytán. 2004. "Banks, Liquidity Crises and Economic Growth." Econometric Society 2004 North American Summer Meetings 399, Econometric Society.

Rodrik, D. 1991. "Policy Uncertainty and Private Investment in Developing Countries." *Journal of Development Economics* 36(2):229–42.

Schumpeter, J. A. 1939. *Business Cycle: A Theoretical, Historical, and Statistical Analysis of the Capitalist Process*. New York: McGraw-Hill.

Servén. 1997. "Irreversibility, Uncertainty, and Private Investment: Analytical Issues and Some Lessons for Africa." *Journal of African Economies* 6(3):229–68.

Servén, L. 2003. "Real-Exchange-Rate Uncertainty and Private Investment in LDCs." *Review of Economics and Statistics* 85(1):212–18.

Shleifer, A. 1986. "Implementation Cycles." *Journal of Political Economy* 94(6):1163–90.

Summers, R., and A. Heston. 1991. "The Penn World Table (Mark 5): An Expanded Set of International Comparisons, 1950–1988." *Quarterly Journal of Economics* 106(2):327–68.

Talvi, E., and C. A. Végh. 2000. "Tax Base Variability and Procyclical Fiscal Policy." NBER Working Paper No. 7499. Cambridge, MA.

Trends in International Mathematics and Science Study (TIMSS). 2000. *The TIMSS 1999 International Database*. Boston, MA: Boston University.

Wolf, Holger. 2005. "Volatility: Definitions and Consequences." Chapter 1, this volume.

World Bank. 1997. *World Development Indicators*. Washington, DC.

———. 2000. *World Development Indicators*. Washington, DC.

———. 2002. *Global Economic Prospects*. Washington, DC.

3. Volatility, Income Distribution, and Poverty

Thomas Laursen and Sandeep Mahajan[1]

ABSTRACT: This study examines the link between macroeconomic volatility and income distribution, including potential transmission channels. Few cross-country studies have directly examined this link: most have explored either the relation between growth and poverty or between growth and income distribution, and, in some cases, between volatility and growth. Analyzing the volatility–inequality link confronts the well-known challenge of linking the macro- and micro-sides of an economy; this study does not attempt to push the envelope in that direction. Rather, the study uses a cross-country regression framework and finds that output volatility has a negative impact on equality (the income share of the bottom quintile), although this finding is not entirely robust across country groups. The study also finds empirical support for some of the presumed main transmission channels, notably inflation, financial sector depth, and government social security expenditures. Accordingly, the main pro-poor policy responses to volatility or negative income shocks would be to contain inflation, develop financial markets, and ensure countercyclical social security spending. Developing labor markets and establishing well-targeted social safety nets are also key ongoing challenges in this regard, to reduce the vulnerability of low-income groups.

INTRODUCTION

Macroeconomic volatility can affect poverty through its impact on *growth* as well as its impact on *income distribution*. Conversely, changes in poverty may be decomposed into a *growth effect* and an *income distribution effect*. (See Box 3.1.) Both effects depend on the initial levels of development and income distribution. Furthermore, there may be a link between growth and changes in the income distribution. If a deterioration in income distribution also reduces a country's growth rate, this could result in a "double whammy" for the poor to the extent that volatility has a negative effect on income distribution.

The previous chapter documented a pronounced negative link between output volatility and growth for low-income countries. This chapter focuses on the relationship between volatility and income distribution or inequality. Combining the two

---

[1] Respectively from the Economic Policy Unit of the Poverty Reduction and Economic Management Network Anchor (PRMEP) and the Poverty Reduction and Economic Management Network Sector Unit of the South Asia Region (SASPR), the World Bank. Viktoria Hnatkovska, Georgetown University, has provided excellent research assistance to the chapter. We would like to thank Francois Bourguignon, Francisco Ferreira, Aart Kraay, Brian Pinto, and Martin Ravallion for helpful suggestions and comments. Remaining errors are of course ours.

Box 3.1. Decomposing Changes in Poverty into Growth and Changing Income Distribution Effects

Any change in income poverty can be decomposed into a growth effect and income distribution effect, as demonstrated in Datt and Ravallion (1992) and Kakwani (1993) (for a clear exposition, see also Bourguignon 2003 and Cline 2002). The growth effect in turn can be decomposed into growth in average income; and the elasticity of poverty with respect to growth in average income. These effects can be assessed either with full knowledge of the income distribution or assuming some specific form for it.

These effects are shown in the figure below. Income levels (in logarithms) are ordered along the bottom axis, from lowest to highest. The vertical axis shows the shares of the population that correspond to each income level. Income distribution in Figure 3.0 is assumed to be log-normal. The growth effect is shown by the rightward shift in the initial income distribution function to the point where average income equals that of the new income distribution. The share of the population below the poverty line (normalized at 1) has obviously decreased due to this shift.

The income distribution effect is shown as the change in the income distribution at the new average income level (the "taller" curve shows a new distribution with less dispersion around the mean income – a reduction in inequality). This further reduces poverty. Of course, there is some path dependence in this decomposition. One could alternatively have evaluated the distribution effect at the initial average income level and the growth effect on the basis of the new income distribution. This might yield quite different results, except for very small changes.

Decomposition of change in poverty into growth and distributional effects

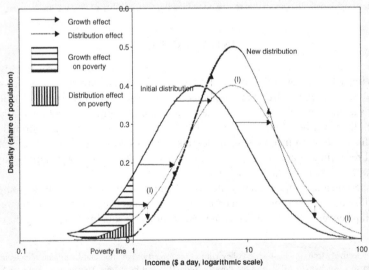

Figure 3.0. *Source*: Bourguignon (2003).

(*Box continues on the following page*)

> **Box 3.1** (*continued*)
>
> Assuming a log-normal or Pareto form for the income distribution, the elasticity of poverty (headcount index) with respect to growth can be shown to be a simple increasing function of the level of development (as measured by average income relative to the poverty line) and a decreasing function of the initial degree of inequality. It can be shown that a growth-poverty elasticity of −2, found in many studies, is consistent with a Pareto-distribution in which the poverty threshold is set at half the average income and the initial distribution has a Gini coefficient of 0.5 (or a log-normal distribution where the respective values are 40 percent and 0.4). The elasticity of poverty with respect to changes in income distribution is more complex.

effects, and taking into account potential linkages between growth and income distribution, would yield the total impact of volatility on poverty. Analyzing the volatility–inequality link confronts the well-known challenge of linking the macro- and micro-sides of an economy; this study does not attempt to push the envelope in that direction. Nevertheless, a better understanding of the impact of volatility on growth, income distribution, and poverty is critical to designing appropriate institutions and policies to protect the poor.

Few studies have examined the link between volatility and inequality. Most cross-country studies have explored either the relation between growth and poverty,[2] or between growth and income distribution.[3] The former have found that typically income of the poor tends to grow one-to-one with average income, and that the average elasticity of poverty with respect to growth is around minus 2; that is, a 1 percent increase in mean income, on average, leads to a 2 percent reduction in the poverty rate. The latter type of study has not found any systematic relationship between growth and inequality. A smaller set of studies has focused on the links between volatility and inequality. One major study of Latin American countries in the 1970s and 1980s found that higher output volatility was associated with both lower output growth and higher inequality, with significant inequality persistence (IDB 1995). Output growth and inflation, on the other hand, had no significant impact on differences in inequality among these countries. The link between volatility and inequality was found to work mainly through educational attainment.

Some studies have focused on financial crises and find that crises are systematically associated with increases in poverty; but this has been mainly due to the general declines in income, with no systematic change in income distribution.[4] In a cross-country study, Emanuele Baldacci, Luiz de Mello, and Maria Inchauste (2002) do find crises be to associated with a worsening of the income distribution – mainly through retrenchment of government social spending. But, results from most country-level studies do not seem to support this. For instance, studies of the crisis in Mexico 1994–95 (Lopez-Acevedo and Salinas 2000) and Brazil 1998–99 (Ferreira

---

[2] For example, Chen and Ravallion (1997, 2000); Dollar and Kraay (2001); World Bank (2001a); Ghura and others (2002).

[3] For example, Deininger and Squire (1998).

[4] Using the elasticity estimate above, Cline (2002) calculates that the recent crises (Mexico, Thailand, Korea, Brazil, Turkey, Indonesia, Russia, and Argentina) increased the poor population by 40–60 million (with most of the increase occurring in Indonesia).

Table 3.1. *Data characteristics*

Regional features of LQ1 data							
	EAP	ECA	MNA	LAC	SA	SSA	IND
# of Obs	45	27	14	62	23	21	82
Min	4.4	4.2	4.7	2.2	6.9	2.4	4.6
Max	10.1	12.0	9.4	8.1	9.3	8.2	10.5
Average	6.9	8.3	6.4	4.6	8.4	5.2	7.5

Regional features of GDP volatility data							
	EAP	ECA	MNA	LAC	SA	SSA	IND
# of Obs	45	27	14	62	23	21	82
Min	0.4	1.6	2.0	1.1	0.8	0.5	0.5
Max	7.7	13.1	10.8	10.6	6.9	11	6.5
Average	3.2	5.9	4.5	4.0	2.6	4.6	2.2

Source: Authors' calculations.

and others 2002) do not find evidence of any systematic increase in inequality. There is some evidence, however, from these and other Latin American countries that the poor suffer relatively more than other income groups during deep economic downturns (while the opposite is true in moderate recessions), possibly reflecting rapid draw-down of assets and loss of income (World Bank 2000b). Similarly, studies of the 1997–98 East Asia crisis countries generally found that inequality if anything declined, although these findings are clouded by the concurrent severe climatic shock (El Niño) affecting several of these countries.[5] Evidence from the 1998 Russia crisis also suggests that inequality declined, with the poor suffering relatively less than the nonpoor – reflecting to a large extent improved targeting of social spending (Lokshin and Ravallion 2000). On the whole, the evidence from crisis countries appears consistent with the cross-country findings of no systematic relationship between growth and inequality.

The rest of this chapter first explores the link between volatility and inequality and discusses possible transmission channels, mainly at the macrolevel. Next, cross-country econometric results are presented, including the role of transmission channels. Finally, policies to address the poverty implications of volatility are discussed.

STYLIZED FACTS

This section looks at the cross-country correlations between volatility and inequality. The volatility measure considered is the standard deviation of the annual growth rate of real GDP. Given this study's primary interest in the linkage between volatility and poverty, the inequality measure considered here is the logarithm of the share of income earned by the bottom quintile (LQ1).[6] The dataset covers 90 countries over the period 1950–99 (see Table 3.1 and Appendix A for further details).

[5] See Pritchett et al. (2002) for Indonesia; Datt and Hoogeven (2000) for the Philippines.
[6] This measure is closely correlated with the Gini coefficient.

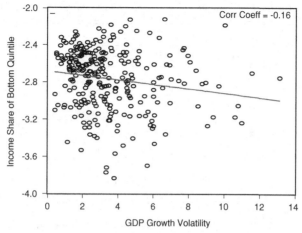

Figure 3.1. Correlation between LQ1 and Volatility (full sample). *Source*: Authors' calculations.

For the cross-country sample, the correlation coefficient between volatility and the income share of the poor is negative and statistically significant (Figure 3.1). However, this obviously does not establish causality, which may run both ways. For example, an increase in volatility could lower incentives for accumulation of human capital, which a number of studies find to be a determinant of the level of inequality. On the other hand, inequality could increase social instability and hence increase GDP volatility (Alesina and Perotti 1996). A more rigorous econometric analysis is applied later in the chapter to test for causality. Between different country groupings, the negative relationship between volatility and the income share of the poor is most visible for the Eastern and Central Europe (ECA), Middle East and North Africa (MNA), and Sub-Saharan Africa (SSA) regions, as well as the groups of low-income and high-income countries (Figure 3.2). The relationship is positive and statistically significant for the East Asia and Pacific (EAP) region, and statistically insignificant for the Latin America and Caribbean (LCR) and South Asia (SAR) regions, as well as the group of middle-income countries.

As seen in Table 3.2 below, volatility affects different income segments differently. The bottom four quintiles seem to suffer consistently as a result of higher volatility, while the top quintile typically benefits from volatility. This could be reflecting the lack of diversification opportunities available to all but the very rich, who are able to arbitrage this phenomenon to their gain.

TRANSMISSION CHANNELS

Conceptually, one can distinguish between five different (but overlapping) direct channels through which macroeconomic volatility or shocks may affect income distribution (Baldacci, De Mello, and Inchauste 2002; Agenor 2002a): relative prices between different goods and services or between factor inputs and outputs; labor demand and employment; returns on physical assets and capital gains or

Table 3.2. *Correlation between volatility and quintile shares in national income*

	Q1	Q2	Q3	Q4	Q5
GDP Volatility	−0.12	−0.19	−0.16	−0.12	0.17

Source: Authors' calculations.

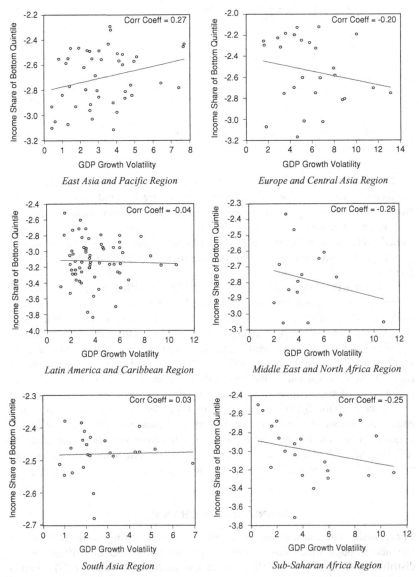

Figure 3.2a. Correlation between LQ1 and Volatility (by Region). *Source*: Authors' calculations.

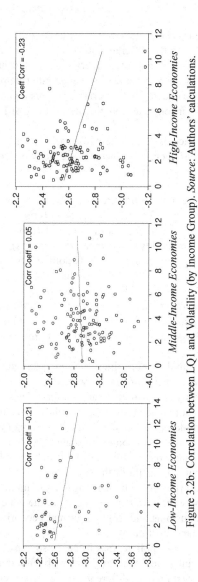

Figure 3.2b. Correlation between LQ1 and Volatility (by Income Group). *Source:* Authors' calculations.

losses; public or private transfers; and community environment effects. These channels in turn can be traced to the different sources of household income, the prices households face when purchasing goods and services, and their ability to access these goods and services. Inflation and the real exchange rate (the price between traded and nontraded goods) are two key macrovariables in this regard, as they affect real wage, capital, or transfer incomes and employment among different income groups and economic sectors.

The relative importance of these different "generic" transmission channels and the extent to which they affect relative incomes are likely to depend on a number of key factors:

- *The source and nature of volatility or shocks.* As discussed in Chapter 1, output volatility may have very different characteristics (crisis versus trend volatility, for example). Further, it is the result of input volatility, which in turn may be exogenous (such as commodity prices or natural disasters), semiexogenous (such as terms of trade), or endogenous (such as political or policy) shocks. These different forms and sources of volatility are likely to affect income distribution through different channels and with different intensity. For example, one would expect negative commodity price shocks and natural disasters to have a larger impact on the rural population through a decline in labor income, while financial crises may have a larger effect on better-off urban residents through declining asset prices.

- *Initial conditions.* Initial or prevailing economic, structural, and institutional conditions and characteristics of a country are likely to be fundamental factors affecting how volatility is transmitted and absorbed. These include the macroeconomic environment (exchange-rate regime, the degree of international integration including trade openness and access to international capital markets, the existing level of macroeconomic imbalances including inflation and fiscal/external deficits, and the existing levels of public and external debt); the level of development and health of the financial system; labor market institutions and conditions (the flexibility of wages and employment contracts, the mobility of labor between different sectors,[7] and the education and skill level of workers); social customs and formal/informal networks; and the quality of political and budgetary institutions.

- *Policy response.* Economic policies may be both a source of episodes of macroeconomic volatility and a response to them, with important bearings on how this volatility is transmitted to different groups in the economy.[8] Structural policies (such as the existence or establishment of targeted social safety nets)

---

[7] Labor mobility in turn may be affected by a range of factors such as the allocation of responsibilities for providing social insurance and housing policies.

[8] One of the main theoretical models for analyzing the impact of macroeconomic adjustment on different income groups/sectors has been the "dependent economy model" (Cashin and others 2001). A real depreciation would raise real incomes of the poor in the long run to the extent that they possess labor in abundance, labor is mobile between traded and nontraded goods sectors, and the traded goods sector is more labor-intensive than the nontraded goods sector (the Stolper–Samuelson theorem). Disaggregated CGE (Computable General Equilibrium) models comprising groups of representative households are usually built along these lines.

are important initial conditions and have relatively longer-term implications. Macroeconomic policies (such as the adjustment of fiscal and monetary policies in the face of a financial crisis) are key in the shorter term. The extent to which overall fiscal policy and income transfer programs are countercyclical is particularly important in this respect. The conduct of monetary policy clearly also matters for what happens to the exchange rate and inflation.

* *Private smoothing mechanisms.* Households may employ a variety of both formal and informal risk management and risk coping strategies that will protect income or consumption during periods of economic turmoil (World Bank 2002). Risk-management strategies include income and asset diversification (such as working multiple jobs); investing in human, physical, and social capital; precautionary savings; and participating in formal or informal insurance arrangements. Risk-coping strategies include drawing down financial assets or borrowing, selling, or mortgaging real assets, changes in labor supply (hours worked or number of family members working, including possibly taking children out of school to work), migration, and support from family members or the local community. The development of labor markets, financial/insurance markets, and household/community organization are clearly important for how well such strategies can work. Private coping strategies are likely to be more successful in case of idiosyncratic shocks, as opposed to economy-wide ones, as risk can more easily be shared within a community or country.

The transmission channels, the factors affecting them, and the impact on income distribution clearly depend on the time dimension employed, and asymmetries become a critical condition for the existence of permanent effects. Negative income shocks or crises may affect income distribution either temporarily (during the downturn) or permanently, potentially exacerbating "transient" or "chronic" poverty, respectively. Most crisis studies mentioned above have focused on temporary effects. Permanent effects of crises and volatility must somehow be related to asymmetric responses to economic downturns and upturns relative to a country's potential growth path.[9] (In the case of crises, these reflect the initial income decline and subsequent recovery, while in the case of volatility, one would think of these as an ongoing process of mean-reverting deviations of output from its trend path.) The faster an economy recovers from a crisis, the less severe is the impact on transient poverty – but presumably so are any permanent effects.

Pierre-Richard Agenor (2001 and 2002a) distinguishes among five classes of explanations supporting the idea that there are asymmetric effects of cycles and crises. First, effects on human capital might be irreversible. Second, expectations and confidence factors might play a larger role during downturns; for example, leading to capital outflows that may not be easily reversed. Third, financial crises typically produce adverse selection and credit crunches that can irreversibly damage the industrial and social fabric. Fourth, household assets may be drawn down, reducing the ability of households to smooth future income swings. Fifth, "labor hoarding" might lead to laying off unskilled workers as firms protect their skilled labor force

---

[9] To detect patterns of such asymmetries, Appendix C tracks the movements of some key economic variables over relatively large economic upturns and downturns.

because of higher turnover costs associated with skilled workers. As a result, some workers may become permanently unemployed.

There are a number of reasons to believe that the lower-income groups may be more vulnerable to volatility or shocks than the better off (see also Agenor 2001). First, their income sources are likely to be less diversified. The lowest income groups are likely to be mainly unskilled laborers in the private formal or informal sector. Accordingly, the main sources of their income are labor earnings and government transfers (net of taxes). Second, their lower levels of education and skills are likely to reduce their mobility across sectors and regions. Third, their lower levels of assets and limited access to financial markets make it more difficult to protect against adverse income and employment shocks. Fourth, the lower income groups depend more on public transfers and social services, notably health and education, exposing them more directly to cuts in government spending (including in real terms through inflation).[10] Several studies have found that both overall fiscal policy and social spending tend to be procyclical in middle- and low-income countries reflecting both procyclical financing opportunities and political economy factors. This may result in lower quantity or quality of social spending in more volatile countries. In addition, low-income families may be forced to take children out of school to cope with temporary income shortfalls. Erosion of human capital affects income earning capacities over the longer run and is thus a potentially important asymmetric and permanent effect.

While the discussion above has implied that causality runs from volatility to income distribution, it is conceivable that causality could also run the other way: that is, that a worsening of the income distribution could lead to increased macroeconomic volatility (for example, through social unrest). Most likely, there will be some interaction between the two. Furthermore, there are other factors at play that must be adequately accounted for in order to isolate the impact of volatility. Some of these may affect income distribution but not volatility, while others may affect both. For example, many of the Asian crisis countries were simultaneously experiencing severe climatic shocks in the form of drought induced by El Niño, which severely impacted the agricultural sector. Political economy factors may also be important determinants of both volatility and income distribution. Furthermore, there may be ongoing nonsystemic shocks affecting sectors, villages, households, or individuals. Evidence suggests that such "idiosyncratic" shocks may be more important at the microlevel than macrorelated shocks. Finally, there may be a problem of measurement error. Countries with poor data may record more volatile output growth, while measurement error in household surveys may accentuate measured inequality.

While insights into how macro volatility affects income distribution (and poverty) at an aggregate level are important, designing specific policies to mitigate the impact on the poor or vulnerable requires an understanding of which groups are affected. Even if there were little overall impact of volatility on the income share of

---

[10] GDP volatility and inflation are highly correlated in our data sample, and several studies have found that higher inflation in turn is associated with higher inequality and poverty (Easterly and Fischer 2001; Romer and Romer 1998). This reflects the greater difficulties of the lower income groups in protecting their incomes and assets against inflation.

the lowest income group, there is likely to be considerable "churning," with some moving up the income ladder and others down. Different villages or households within the same socioeconomic group may be affected very differently, as indeed may individuals within the same household. Representing this heterogeneity properly is a formidable challenge. The techniques for addressing these issues have gone through various phases, while becoming increasingly sophisticated (see Bourguignon, Pereira da Silva, and Stern 2002 for an excellent overview). They have generally been developed in the context of evaluating the distributional and poverty effects of economic policies and all rely on household survey data.[11]

ECONOMETRIC ANALYSIS

Ordinary Least Squares Estimation

The economic literature, in general, finds no robust determinants of income inequality. David Dollar and Aart Kraay (2001), for example, try various combinations of policy and institutional variables that are typically identified in the literature as determinants of growth and poverty and find that none of these significantly (at the 5 percent level) impacts LQ1.[12] At the same time, the stylized facts presented above show a strong, negative correlation between GDP growth volatility (which Dollar–Kraay do not test for) and LQ1, which prompts the following more systematic examination of this relation.

The analytical exercise that follows builds on the framework by Ronald Benabou (1996) and Martin Ravallion (2002a), who show evidence of convergence in inequality across countries: that is, countries with higher initial inequality tend to have lower increases in inequality. Figure 3.3 substantiates this result for the dataset used in this chapter.

To test for the impact of volatility on inequality, we add GDP volatility as a regressor to the unconditional inequality convergence regression used by Benabou and Ravallion:

$$LQ1_{it} = a + b^*LQ1_{i0} + c^*VOL_{it} + e_{it}, \tag{1}$$

where LQ1 is the log of the income share of the bottom quintile, measured at $t = 0$ and $t = T$, and VOL_{it} is GDP volatility between and including $t = 0$ and $t = T$; $T \geq 5$ years. Each measure of volatility therefore covers at least six annual observations on GDP growth.

Column 1 in Appendix Table B-1 shows the results of estimating Equation 1 using ordinary least squares (OLS). The estimated value of b is 0.7, which is significantly less than 1.0 and confirms earlier findings of inequality convergence. In addition,

---

[11] Several microdata sources may be available in a given country: labor-force surveys; income and expenditure surveys; and demographic and health surveys. In general, however, their coverage of the information needed for accurately measuring individual welfare and evaluating microoriented public policies is often partial. Multipurpose surveys that gather information not only on households but also on their economic and social environment are thus highly desirable. There is significant experience acquired in this field since the mid-1980s with the LSMS surveys.

[12] Dollar and Kraay find the impact of inflation and government consumption as a share of GDP on LQ1 to be significant at the 10 percent level when all growth variables were included in the estimation.

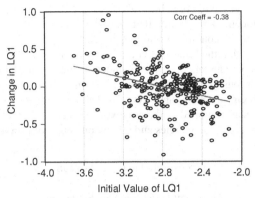

Figure 3.3. Correlation between LQ1 and Its Lagged Value. *Source*: Authors' calculations.

the estimated value of c is -0.03, which is significant at the 1 percent-level and supports the hypothesis that, across countries, volatility and the income share of the poor are negatively correlated. This negative relationship is presented in Figure 3.4, which shows the partial scatter between volatility and inequality.

Next we consider various modifications of the basic specification in Equation 1 to test for differences across regions, income groups, time, and between primary commodity exporters and more diversified exporters.

Regression 2 (Column 2, Appendix Table B-1) adds intercept dummies for each region and also interacts the regional dummies with the lagged inequality and volatility measures. The intercept dummies for the group of industrialized countries (IND) and the regions of EAP, LCR, SAR, and SSA are negative and significant, at least at the 5 percent-level. The intercepts for the ECA and MNA regions are negative but statistically insignificant. The intercept dummies for LCR and SAR are significantly lower and the dummies for the ECA and MNA regions significantly higher than the dummy for the IND countries, reflecting higher inequality in LCR and SAR and lower inequality in ECA and MNA relative to industrialized countries.

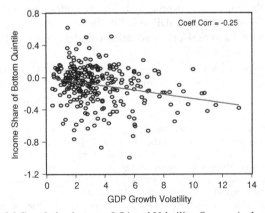

Figure 3.4. Partial Correlation between LQ1 and Volatility. *Source*: Authors' calculations.

The negative relationship between volatility and the income share of the poor holds for the regions of ECA, MNA, and SSA. For the EAP region, the coefficient of the volatility variable is positive and significant, while the coefficients for the IND and LCR countries are negative but not significant. Inequality convergence is seen in all regions but LCR and SAR. The coefficient of lagged LQ1 is significantly higher for the ECA region and statistically not different for the EAP, MNA, and SSA regions relative to the IND countries; reflecting slower inequality convergence in the ECA region relative to the IND countries. Only for the EAP region is the volatility coefficient significantly different than for IND countries. This implies that barring the EAP region, regional characteristics do not seem to shape the adverse impact that volatility has on inequality.

Similarly, Regression 3 (Column 3, Appendix Table B-1) includes intercept and slope dummies for low-, middle-, and high-income economies (LICs, MICs, and HICs) to test whether the level of income has any bearing on inequality convergence and on the volatility–inequality relationship. The intercept dummies for the MICs and HICs are negative and significant at the 1 percent-level, while the dummy for the LICs is negative but statistically insignificant. There is strong evidence of inequality convergence in each income group, with the rate of convergence significantly slower (at the 10 percent-level) in MICs and LICs relative to HICs. Volatility has a negative impact on LQ1 in the LICs (significant at the 1 percent-level) and in HICs (significant at the 10 percent-level), but surprisingly not in MICs. The negative impact of volatility on the income share of the poor is more pronounced in LICs than in HICs.

Regression 4 (Appendix Table B-1) tests whether the nature of these relationships has changed over time. For this, the test adds an intercept dummy for the decades of 1960s, 1970s, 1980s, and 1990s, and also interacts the decade dummies with the lagged inequality and volatility measures. The intercept dummies for all decades are negative, and are significant at the 5 percent-level for the 1970s, 1980s, and 1990s. The magnitudes of the intercept term for each decade are not statistically different. Inequality convergence is seen for the last three decades, while the negative relationship between volatility and the income share of the poor is significant only for the 1980s and 1990s. The coefficients on lagged inequality and volatility are stable over the 1970–90 period.

It may be the case that the negative relationship between inequality and volatility across countries is driven by the nature of countries' exports: overdependence on primary exports may cause both higher inequality and higher volatility. To test if this is the case, Regression 5 (Appendix Table B-1) introduces intercept and slope dummies for the group of countries that are primary commodity exporters and those that are not. The intercept terms for both groups are negative and highly significant, with the dummy for the former group significantly lower than that for the latter group, reflecting higher inequality on average in primary exporters. Results on inequality convergence are also highly significant for both groups, with the convergence rate significantly faster for primary exporters. The slope coefficients on the volatility measure are negative and highly significant for both groups and statistically there is no difference between them. It does not appear therefore that the volatility–inequality relationship is exogenously being driven by the export composition of countries.

Two-stage Least Squares Estimation

The consistency of the OLS estimates in Appendix Table B-1 may suffer from problems related to endogeneity of the volatility measure, omitted regressors, and/or measurement errors. There are several potential sources of biased results. First, volatility may be correlated with some omitted factors (possibly policy variables such as interest rates and inflation) that may also affect the income share of the poor, thus leading to the omitted variables problem. Second, volatility may be determined by the level of inequality, resulting in a simultaneity problem. Indeed, the Durbin–Wu–Hausman statistics derived in Appendix Table B-2 suggest that, at the 5 percent-level, endogeneity of lagged LQ1 and volatility cannot be rejected under some of the specifications used in Appendix Table B-1. This calls for estimation of the model by two-stage least squares estimation (2SLS).

Lagged LQ1 is instrumented for by the lagged change in LQ1 (that is, lagged LQ1 minus twice lagged LQ1). This appears to be a valid instrument: given that estimation of Equation 1 finds a significant value for b, by construction, the lagged change in LQ1 is correlated with lagged LQ1. Further, a priori there is no reason to believe that this instrument would be correlated with the contemporaneous error term. For GDP volatility, the standard deviations of annual terms of trade (ToT), growth, annual CPI inflation (covering the same time period as the corresponding GDP volatility measure), and the ratio of total trade (imports + exports) to GDP are used as the instruments. The first and second instruments are found to be valid instruments and used by Viktoria Hnatkovska and Norman Loayza in the previous chapter on growth and volatility. William Easterly, Roumeen Islam, and Joseph Stiglitz (2000) find the trade/GDP ratio to be the variable most robustly correlated with output volatility.[13] As seen in results for the basic specification (Regression 1' in Appendix Table B-2), the first-stage R-squared is 23 percent and the Hansen J-Test for overidentifying restrictions shows that the hypothesis of no correlation between the instruments and the second-stage error term cannot be rejected even at the 10 percent level.

Regressions 1'–3' and 5' in Appendix Table B-2 correspond to Regressions 1–3 and 5 in Appendix Table B-1 and show the results with and without the use of instrumental variables, with the sample size of the latter restricted to be the same as that of the former.[14] As seen in results for the basic specification in Regression 1', the coefficient on the volatility variable remains significant (at the 5 percent-level) with IV technique for estimation. While significant in appendix table B-1 the coefficients of the volatility slope dummies become insignificant (at the 10 percent-level) for ECA and MNA regions (Regression 2'), and for the group of nonprimary exporters (Regression 5') under the IV specification. However, these modifications

---

[13] There may be some concern that the trade/GDP ratio is correlated with the second stage error term, which would make it an invalid instrument. However, the literature is far from conclusive on this. While Barro (2000), for example, finds a positive correlation between trade openness and inequality, Edwards (1997) and Dollar and Kraay (2001) find no evidence of a relationship between the two measures. Additionally, results in this study do not change significantly if this instrument is dropped.

[14] Due to estimation problems related to lack of sufficient data points for the earlier decades, we do not perform the IV estimation for the differentiation by decade (corresponding to Regression 4 in Table C-1).

appear to be driven mainly by the change in sample size when using instruments, since, qualitatively, the results are virtually the same in the OLS regressions (using the restricted sample) in Appendix Table B-2. At the same time, while the OLS estimate of the coefficient of the volatility slope dummy for the IND group of countries is not significant (in the unrestricted and restricted samples), it becomes highly significant in the IV estimation. Similarly, the volatility slope dummies for the LIC and HIC groups are not significant in the OLS restricted sample regressions, but become significant in the IV regression. Broadly, most qualitative results of the OLS estimations are replicated by their IV counterparts.

In terms of magnitude, the coefficient on the volatility variable increases more than threefold in the IV estimation of the basic specification (Regression 1′) relative to its OLS counterpart. This suggests that the volatility–inequality relationship may be driven, at least in part, by other variables, and/or there may be some causal effect of inequality on volatility. Explicitly accounting for this by using appropriate instruments results in a significant magnification of the negative causal impact of volatility on inequality.

Transmission Channels

Next, some of the main transmission channels discussed above are tested for. The average inflation rate, public expenditure on social security, health and education, the unemployment rate, financial sector depth, and real effective exchange rate volatility are used as proxies for the transmission channels. The strategy is to add these variables one-by-one as regressors to Regression 1. The expectation is that if any of these variables plays the transmission role, then using it in the regression would make the impact of volatility insignificant (or at least substantially less significant).

Due to problems associated with multicollinearity among several of the transmission channels and relatively small common samples when multiple transmission channels are included in a single regression, the impact of each transmission channel is considered separately. For each transmission channel, first the results of the OLS regression of LQ1 on lagged LQ1 and volatility are reported, and then holding the sample constant, the results with the addition of a particular transmission channel as a regressor are reported (Appendix Table B-3). The inflation rate, public expenditure on social security, and financial sector depth (proxied by M2/GDP) each enters the regression with a significant coefficient,[15] but in the process weakens the significance of the coefficient on GDP volatility.

This suggests that at least some of the impact of GDP volatility on income of the poor may be flowing through each of these transmission channels. Public expenditure on education and health, the unemployment rate, and real effective exchange rate (REER) volatility do not appear to be playing a significant transmission role since each enters the regression with an insignificant coefficient and, with the exception of the latter, does not seem to influence the significance of the coefficient on GDP volatility much.

---

[15] Ceteris paribus, inflation reduces the income share of the poor while financial sector depth and public expenditure on social security tend to increase it.

Testing for Asymmetries during Episodes of Large Income Swings

In Appendix C, we track the movement of some key economic variables (potential transmission channels) during large deviations of GDP around its long-term trend to detect any patterns of asymmetric responses of these during large economic upturns and downturns. As discussed earlier, the presence of asymmetries can help explain the negative relationship between volatility and income distribution.

The suggestive findings in Appendix C are broadly consistent with the longer-term results on the likely role of transmission channels. In particular, inequality tends to increase during episodes of both large upturns and downturns, which suggests that large deviations of income in either direction can hurt poverty – in the case of upturns, this would happen if the rise in inequality offsets the impact of the increase in the overall income. During both upturns and downturns, public sector capital expenditures tend to be cut (which can harm long run growth) as do expenditures on wages and salaries (which could harm the lower middle class). In a majority of downturns, governments were unable to protect social spending on health, education, and social security and unemployment rose, which helps explain why the poor tend to suffer relatively more during these periods, and also why temporary downturns can lead to permanent adverse effects on important poverty determinants such as human capital and employment. Inflation typically increases during boom periods and could be a large part of the reason why inequality rises during large upturns.

POLICY IMPLICATIONS

The discussion and analysis above provides reasonably robust evidence that higher macroeconomic volatility leads to higher inequality (lower income share of the bottom quintile). This amplifies the impact on the poor of the negative relationship between volatility and growth found in the previous chapter. In addition, evidence from other studies suggests that poor people in developing countries face significant income risk due not only to macroeconomic or systemic volatility or shocks, but also due to shocks at the regional, village, or household level.[16]

The findings in this chapter on the link between volatility and inequality, combined with earlier studies' findings on crises and poverty, strongly point to the need for carefully considered risk reduction, management, and coping strategies, both by the government and private sector agents.[17] These would include pursuing measures to reduce volatility, establishing institutions to dampen the impact of volatility

---

[16] Many studies have demonstrated the volatility of the income of poor people in developing countries. A great deal of the empirical evidence comes from studies done at the village level (for example, Townsend 1994 for Indonesia; Bliss and Stern 1982 for India; Deaton 1991 for Cote d'Ivoire; and Dercon 2002 for Ethiopia). Although in practice difficult to separate, two types of risk are taken into consideration by these studies: common risks that affect and are covariate within an entire economy, region, or large community; and idiosyncratic risks that affect only a specific household or individual.

[17] Risk management refers to preventive strategies aimed at diversifying income sources, saving, and insuring against risk, while risk coping refers to strategies for dealing with income shortfalls once they occur (see, for example, World Bank 2000b and 2002 and Holzman and Jorgensen 2000 for a good discussion of alternative strategies for dealing with income risk).

on the lowest income groups, and protecting these in the face of prolonged and/or severe negative income shocks (including reducing the risk of permanent effects). As discussed elsewhere in this volume, reducing volatility is an integral part of the development process, and this discussion will not be pursued further here except to note that a prudent conduct of macroeconomic policies plays a dual role in both reducing endogenous input volatility and in managing and coping with volatility. The discussion that follows focuses on risk management and coping strategies, particularly for the lowest income groups.

The fundamental way of dealing with income volatility or potential shocks is through precautionary saving, accumulation of physical and human capital, and insurance. This is true both at the macroeconomic (government) level and at the microeconomic (household) level. Both financial sector and labor market institutions play an important role at the household level. Financial institutions can offer both short- and long-term savings instruments (and potentially borrowing possibilities) and various types of insurance policies, while labor market institutions may offer unemployment insurance or various active employment policies (see Box 3.2 below). However, both financial markets and labor market institutions are often poorly developed in highly volatile countries, and in any case generally are of limited value to people living at the subsistence level.[18] Especially for this group, the accumulation/ownership of some kind of other wealth becomes crucial to deal with temporary income shortfalls. Whether at the macro- or micro-level, policies or actions that reduce the accumulation of human or physical capital (or even worse, deplete it) to cope with short- to medium-term financial problems risk undermining the future long-term income earning potential.

Government intervention is warranted by incomplete or imperfect domestic insurance markets that lead individuals to costly and inefficient self-insurance decisions, or the inability of some to use these markets because of low income. The government's role is to assess who is vulnerable to different types of shocks; strengthen mechanisms used by households to insure against risk of income loss or cope with such losses when they occur (improve the enabling environment); discourage private strategies that may have negative longer-term implications; and provide assistance when private mechanisms are inadequate or undesirable. In general, government programs are needed to deal with systemic or covariate risks and shocks, while it may be possible to rely more on private or market arrangements to deal with idiosyncratic ones.

Fundamentally, pro-poor government policies should aim to put in place permanent institutions that reduce the impact of volatility on the lower-income groups, dampen output swings to the extent possible when they occur, and respond in a way that protects the poor during severe negative income shocks. This includes: promoting flexible labor markets and financial system development; putting in place effective social safety nets; conducting sound macroeconomic policies (low and stable inflation, moderate fiscal and external deficits, and manageable debt burden); and

---

[18] Besley (1995) surveys the theoretical and practical characteristics of credit and insurance markets in developed and developing countries. In the latter, formal credit and insurance markets are typically absent and are replaced by informal mechanisms (such as *tied credit* and *pawning*) requiring less formal collateralization and guarantees but seemingly adjusting well to high-risk environments.

allowing these to adjust in an appropriate manner to large swings in output (including letting the real exchange rate move in line with fundamentals, containing inflation, and permitting automatic fiscal stabilizers, such as an expansion of social safety net spending during downturns) while protecting essential capital and other spending programs. The remainder of this section focuses on the role of fiscal policies in general and social safety nets in particular.

Fiscal Policy

Fiscal policies in developing countries have tended to be procyclical, exacerbating macrovolatility, adding policy risk to the income risk of the poor, and leading to a deficit bias in fiscal policies (Perry 2003). This reflects both the political difficulties in containing spending during good times and problems financing larger deficits during economic downturns when access to international capital markets may be curtailed. Also, financial crises have often occurred against the backdrop of unsustainable fiscal policies, and a key element in dealing with these crises has thus been a significant fiscal adjustment.

Of even more concern is the evidence from Latin America that social spending too has a procyclical element (World Bank 2000b). The share of social spending in total spending tends to rise during booms, and while it is generally maintained during busts, this has not been enough to protect the poor as the level of resources declines and the demand for these increases.

Fiscal rules may be useful to the extent they address both solvency and cyclical concerns and are associated with high exit costs. A good example of this is Chile's structural budget balance rule. While a countercyclical fiscal policy is generally desirable, it may not always be possible to allow automatic stabilizers to operate fully or even partially. In this case it is particularly important that social spending (or more specifically, income transfers) is allowed to work in a countercyclical way – or at the very least, that it is protected from cuts in case of needed fiscal adjustment. This is even more important for programs directly affecting the poor.

At the same time, social spending is a heterogeneous category. It includes spending on such items as pensions, formal unemployment insurance, and higher education – which tend to benefit the nonpoor more than the poor – as well as more pro-poor spending on basic education and health care, social assistance, and active labor market programs. This calls for a more careful assessment of how targeted spending programs have responded to macroeconomic volatility. Evidence from Argentina, Bangladesh, and India suggests that it is program spending on the nonpoor that is protected from budget cuts (Ravallion 2002b). In Argentina, although some programs have been countercyclical, only about 7 percent of social spending is targeted, and within this only 65 percent goes to the poor.

It is important to know the counterfactual incidence of fiscal contractions in order to assess the effectiveness of add-on programs. Evaluations that ignore the political economy of fiscal adjustment can greatly underestimate the impact on poverty of successful add-on programs relative to the counterfactual of no intervention.

All in all, developing countries would do well by instituting permanent policies and programs that can automatically protect the poor from short-term fiscal adjustments and respond endogenously to income shocks facing the low-income groups (both macrocrises and more moderate idiosyncratic risks in normal years). A central social safety fund can potentially play an important role in this regard. The discussion that follows considers issues in the design of social safety nets in more detail.

Social Safety Nets

Social safety nets are particularly important in cushioning the impact of shocks or crises on the poor (for an excellent overview of issues and recent experience, see Chu and Gupta 1998). These include unemployment insurance schemes, income transfers, subsidies, and public works programs. The main role of social safety nets is to provide insurance. The key issue then is whether publicly provided safety nets provide insurance more efficiently and equitably than private mechanisms. The following are main considerations in this regard:

- *Efficiency*. Safety nets should not provide unduly perverse incentives that would increase unemployment or other forms of dependency on public support in the long run. They should be efficient in terms of equalizing the marginal social return relative to other programs.
- *Permanency and countercyclicality*. Programs should be permanent, dealing with issues of transient poverty, localized shocks, and development of poor areas in normal years, but expand during crises to assist those temporarily in need. To ensure that resources are available in case of a crisis, a fund could be set up with regular payments during normal years to accumulate resources for crises. In particular, it is key that adequate and flexible social safety nets are in place before a crisis hits. This requires a thorough assessment of the risks faced by various population groups to different types of shocks (see Tesliuc and Lindert 2002 for an excellent application to Guatemala).
- *Targeting*. In principle, the goal should be to have the best possible targeted means-tested transfers that at the same time create positive incentives to promote the proper accumulation of skills, human capital, and the like. Targeted social spending (income transfers) should be countercyclical (the share of targeted spending in total spending should increase in times of crisis or shock). However, targeting is generally not costless; the most finely targeted programs may not be the best. Political economy arguments suggest that less targeting may mean more money for the poor by providing for a larger budget envelope (Gelbach and Pritchett 1995; de Donder and Hindricks 1998; van de Walle 1998; Ravallion 2003). This is largely an empirical question.
- *Conditionality*. To ensure efficiency, programs should be conditional on certain desirable actions on the part of recipients.
- *Comprehensiveness*. Programs should be able to deal with both macroeconomic crises and idiosyncratic risks in normal years. Generally, an adequate social protection system should consist of self-insurance, unemployment insurance, public works programs (especially for informal sector workers), and targeted programs for the poor. Programs should provide employment for those who are able to work and transfers to those who cannot or should not. There may also be a case for

special micro credit programs, but these need to be carefully designed. Again, a good assessment of who are the vulnerable groups or individuals becomes essential.

- *Unemployment support programs.* These include unemployment insurance, public works or workfare programs, mandatory severance pay, training, and individual savings accounts. The World Bank (2000b) assesses the main income support programs in Latin America according to coverage, cost, incentives, and insurance. They find that the relatively high coverage of programs among those at work is in sharp contrast to the low number of beneficiaries among the unemployed (no more than one out of 10) and that costs often outweigh benefits. The report considers severance pay schemes possibly the worst form of unemployment insurance.

    Workfare programs should be available at all times, but expanded during times of crisis as demand increases. Projects are best proposed by local community groups to ensure relevance and ownership and selected by a central agency. The central government should fund wage and non-wage costs. Also, setting the appropriate wage rate is key. Argentina's Trabajar and India's Employment Guarantee Scheme in the state of Maharashstra are good models.

- *Transfer programs.* These should be aimed at those unable to work in order to mitigate the risk of long-term negative effects of income losses. Such programs include cash or food to specific subgroups of the poor, such as pregnant and lactating women or the elderly, or those who should not work, such as school-age children. Targeted conditional transfer (TCT) programs are means-tested cash transfers conditional on socially desirable behavior, typically health and education for children. Good examples include Bolsa Escola in Brazil, the Food for Education Program in Bangladesh, and Progresa in Mexico (Box 3.2). These programs reduce the volatility of individual incomes and diminish the risk of children leaving school, but may be at the expense of a loss in total family income.

The lessons from targeted programs remain somewhat mixed. While several programs such as Trabajar and Food for Education have been successful in targeting the poor, performance has tended to worsen as programs contracted in response to local political economy factors that sought to protect nonpoor spending from budget cuts. A recent study (Ravallion 2003) revisits the role of targeted transfers in poor countries in light of the new theories on the social costs of uninsured risks and unmitigated inequalities. Market or quasi-market credit and risk-sharing arrangements suffer the problems of asymmetric information. Recent evidence on the heterogeneity in the performance of the same program across different settings, and the lack of heterogeneity in the performance of different programs in the same setting, points to the importance of context and the weak power of generalizations about what works and what does not. There appears to be more scope for generalizations about principles for guiding the design of effective intervention in specific settings. While efficiency concerns about targeting may have been exaggerated, Ravallion notes that in general targeted transfers may not be better than other options such as direct efforts to improve factor markets for the poor, supply-side interventions in schooling and health care, or even untargeted transfers.

Box 3.2. Examples of Successful Social Safety Net Programs

Contingent Transfer Programs

Food for Education (FEE) (Bangladesh). Community-based targeting of food transfers, contingent on families keeping children in school. One of the earliest of many school-enrollment subsidy programs now found in many developing (and developed) countries. Evidence of significant gains in terms of school attendance with only modest forgone income through displaced child labor. Studies show that targeting performance varied greatly between villages and that inequality within villages matters for the relative power of the poor in local decision making.

Progresa (Mexico). Cash transfers targeted to certain demographic groups in poor areas, conditional on regular school attendance and visits to health centers. Studies have found that schooling increased, though the gains appear to be lower than for Food for Education programs (possibly because primary schooling rates were already higher). The program may have been more successful if it had concentrated on those children less likely to attend school in the absence of the program, including by focusing on the transition to secondary school.

Bolsa-Escola (Brazil). Cash transfers targeted to certain demographic groups in poor areas, conditional on regular school attendance and visits to health centers.

In Brazil and Mexico, ex post evaluations of these programs have shown their valuable contribution to poverty reduction. Ex ante evaluation is now being done more extensively and showing that it does contribute to maintaining children in schools, with positive implications for the long-run accumulation of human capital.

Workfare Programs

Trabajar (Argentina). Add-on program set up in the mid-1990s to cope with sharply rising unemployment, especially among the poor. Low-wage work on infrastructure and other projects in poor areas. Donor financed. High degree of targeting, but tends to deteriorate as the program is contracted. Studies have found that foregone income was substantial (around one-half), but indirect gains to the poor were achieved in the areas where public works was done.

Employment Guarantee Scheme (Maharashstra, India). Permanent program launched during the severe drought in 1970–73. Intended to assure income support in rural areas by providing unskilled manual labor at low wages to anyone who wants it. Automatically contracts in good agricultural years and expands in bad years. Financed from local taxes. Program at times jeopardized by excessively large wage increases. Studies have found that forgone income was quite low (around one-quarter).

On the other hand, a case study of Mexico (Baldacci, De Mello, and Inchauste 2002) finds that geographical targeting and greater attention to the most vulnerable (young and elderly) would have worked better in alleviating the effects of the 1994 crisis.

Table A-1. *Data sources*

Variable	Source
Income of the poor and average income	Dollar–Kraay dataset
GDP per capita growth	World Bank data
ToT growth	Global Development Finance and World Development Indicators, and authors' calculations
Trade as a share of GDP	World Bank data, Summers and Heston Penn World Tables
Gross capital formation (% of GDP)	Global Development Finance and World Development Indicators
Population growth	Global Development Finance and World Development Indicators
School enrollment, secondary (% gross)	Global Development Finance and World Development Indicators

APPENDIX A. DATA SAMPLE

The data on LQ1 are from Dollar and Kraay (2001). Drawing on four different data sources (the UN-WIDER World Inequality Database, Deininger and Squire 1996, Chen and Ravallion 2000, and Lundberg and Squire 2000), Dollar and Kraay are able to pull together a sample of 953 observations covering 137 countries over the period 1950–99. As in Dollar–Kraay, our interest is in movement of LQ1 over the medium to long run. Accordingly, following their strategy, we use only those data points that are separated by at least 5 years, starting with the first available observation for each country. This filtering strategy leaves us with a highly unbalanced and irregularly spaced panel of 418 observations on LQ1.[19] The spatial, geographical, and other characteristics of the database are spelled out by Dollar–Kraay.

GDP growth data are from the World Bank's World Development Indicators (WDI) database. GDP volatility corresponding to each observation on Q1 is measured as the standard deviation of annual GDP growth between and including the years in which Q1 and its lagged value are observed. GDP volatility for each observation therefore covers at least six annual observations. This yields 276 measured points each of GDP volatility and LQ1. From this we remove two observations that are extreme outliers – one for volatility and one for LQ1 – leaving a dataset of 274 observations that we use in the rest of this study.

In all, the dataset covers 90 countries, with an average of three observations, a minimum of two observations, and a maximum of seven observations per country. The average value for GDP volatility is 3.5, varying between a minimum of 0.4 and a maximum of 13.1. The average value of LQ1 is −2.8 (Q1 = 6.6 percent), varying between a minimum of −3.8 (Q1 = 2.2 percent) and a maximum of −2.1 (Q1 = 12.2 percent).

---

[19] Dollar and Kraay also make adjustments to the Q1 data for observable differences in survey types and to make income distribution data comparable across countries. The Q1 data used for this study reflect these adjustments.

APPENDIX B. REGRESSION RESULTS

Table B-1. *OLS estimations*

	Regression 1		Regression 2		Regression 3	
	Coeff	*t*-stat	Coeff	*t*-stat	Coeff	*t*-stat
Intercept	−0.75	−5.96				
Lagged LQ1	0.75	14.51				
GDP Volatility	−0.03	−4.96				
Intercept Dummies						
EAP			−1.05	−4.03		
ECA			−0.38	−1.12		
IND			−1.43	−4.44		
MNA			−0.34	−0.42		
LCR			−2.46	−6.35		
SAR			−2.68	−14.46		
SSA			−1.08	−2.29		
Lagged LQ1*EAP			0.66	7.18		
Lagged LQ1*ECA			0.79	6.07		
Lagged LQ1*IND			0.43	3.46		
Lagged LQ1*MNA			0.81	3.02		
Lagged LQ1*LCR			0.21	1.60		
Lagged LQ1*SAR			−0.08	−1.08		
Lagged LQ1*SSA			0.60	3.74		
Volatility*EAP			0.03	3.24		
Volatility*ECA			−0.04	−3.93		
Volatility*IND			−0.02	−1.04		
Volatility*MNA			−0.02	−2.02		
Volatility*LCR			−0.01	−0.39		
Volatility*SAR			0.00	0.06		
Volatility*SSA			−0.04	−2.99		
Intercept Dummies						
LIC					−0.50	−1.51
MIC					−0.95	−4.732
HIC					−1.34	−5.22
Lagged LQ1*LIC					0.76	5.98
Lagged LQ1*MIC					0.68	9.72
Lagged LQ1*HIC					0.46	4.57
Volatility*LIC					−0.05	−5.94
Volatility*MIC					−0.01	−0.64
Volatility*HIC					−0.02	−1.79
# Observations	274		274		274	
Adj. R-Squared	0.49		0.62		0.53	

Standard errors are White-corrected for heteroskedasticity

(*continued*)

Table B-1 (*continued*)

	Regression 4		Regression 5	
	Coeff	t-stat	Coeff	t-stat
Dependent variable: LQ1				
Intercept Dummies				
1960s	−0.08	−0.11		
1970s	−1.09	−4.08		
1980s	−0.92	−4.03		
1990s	−0.51	−2.41		
Lagged LQ1*1960s	1.04	4.14		
Lagged LQ1*1970s	0.59	5.54		
Lagged LQ1*1980s	0.62	6.97		
Lagged LQ1*1990s	0.79	10.21		
Volatility*1960s	0.06	1.06		
Volatility*1970s	−0.02	−1.32		
Volatility*1980s	−0.04	−3.96		
Volatility*1990s	−0.03	−3.89		
Intercept Dummies				
Dummy for Primary Exporters			−1.433	−4.566
Dummy for Nonprimary Exporters			−0.705	−4.587
Lagged LQ1*Dummy for Primary Exporters			0.482	4.6312
Lagged LQ1*Dummy for Nonprimary Exporters			0.717	12.208
Volatility*Dummy for Primary Exporters			−0.028	−2.578
Volatility*Dummy for Nonprimary Exporters			−0.023	−3.548
# Observations	274		274	
Adj. R-Squared	0.50		0.50	

Standard errors are White-corrected for heteroskedasticity

Source: Authors' calculations.

Table B-2. *TSLS estimations*

	Regression 1′ (basic specification)			
	W/out instruments		With instruments	
	Coeff	t-stat	Coeff	z-stat
Dependent variable: LQ1				
Intercept	−0.63	−4.03	−1.07	−2.99
Lagged LQ1	0.75	12.45	0.53	3.53
GDP Volatility	−0.02	−2.35	−0.07	−2.09
Adj. R-Squared		0.56		0.44
# Observations		168		168

First-stage regression				
	Dependent variable:			
	LQ1		Volatility	
	Coeff	*t*-stat	Coeff	*t*-stat
Intercept	−2.55		2.14	7.05
Lagged LQ1 – Twice Lagged LQ1	0.49		0.21	0.43
Std Deviation of TOT growth	−0.01		0.07	3.50
Std Deviation of annual CPI inflation	−1E-05		0.003	4.52
Trade/GDP, %	−0.001		0.002	1.35
1st Stage R-Squared (average)		0.23		
Specification Tests (P-Values)				
Durbin–Wu–Hausman Test (for exogeneity of Lagged LQ1)				0.04
Durbin–Wu–Hausman Test (for Volatility)				0.01
Hansen J-Test for Overidentifying Restrictions				0.9

Standard errors are White-corrected for heteroskedasticity

Dependent variable: LQ1				
	Regression 2′			
	W/out instruments		With instruments	
	Coeff	*t*-stat	Coeff	*z*-stat
Intercept Dummies				
EAP	−0.91	−3.70	−2.03	−3.49
ECA	−0.32	−0.70	−1.06	−1.41
IND	−1.11	−4.04	−1.88	−2.73
MNA	1.69	0.59	−22.59	−0.42
LCR	−2.58	−4.91	−2.37	−2.55
SAR	−2.10	−4.14	−3.91	−2.40
SSA	−1.58	−1.81	−1.10	−0.88
Lagged LQ1*EAP	0.69	7.77	0.31	1.52
Lagged LQ1*ECA	0.92	5.55	0.63	2.31
Lagged LQ1*IND	0.55	5.14	0.23	0.89
Lagged LQ1*MNA	1.43	1.65	−5.70	−0.36
Lagged LQ1*LCR	0.19	1.11	0.19	0.68
Lagged LQ1*SAR	0.15	0.75	−0.55	−0.87
Lagged LQ1*SSA	0.37	1.15	0.52	1.22
Volatility*EAP	0.02	1.98	0.05	1.67
Volatility*ECA	0.00	−0.09	0.01	0.40
Volatility*IND	−0.01	−0.72	−0.05	−5.78
Volatility*MNA	−0.07	−0.88	0.76	0.42
Volatility*LCR	0.01	0.35	−0.04	−0.84

(*continued*)

Table B-2 *(continued)*

Dependent variable: LQ1				
	Regression 2′			
	W/out instruments		With instruments	
	Coeff	*t*-stat	Coeff	*z*-stat
Volatility*SAR	0.00	−0.26	0.03	0.87
Volatility*SSA	−0.09	−2.72	−0.11	−4.11
Adj. R-Squared		0.63		0.44
# Observations		168		168
Specification Test (P-Values)				
Durbin–Wu–Hausman Test (for exogeneity of Lagged LQ1)				0.7
Durbin–Wu–Hausman Test (for Volatility)				0.46
Hansen J-Test for Overidentifying Restrictions				0.60

Standard errors are White-corrected for heteroskedasticity

Dependent variable: LQ1				
	Regression 3′			
	W/out instruments		With instruments	
	Coeff	*t*-stat	Coeff	*z*-stat
Intercept Dummies				
LIC	−0.34	−0.85	−0.28	−0.50
MIC	−0.95	−3.60	−1.63	−2.78
HIC	−1.17	−4.69	−1.34	−2.12
Lagged LQ1*LIC	0.84	5.41	0.81	3.39
Lagged LQ1*MIC	0.68	7.68	0.39	1.96
Lagged LQ1*HIC	0.54	5.53	0.44	1.80
Volatility* LIC	−0.03	−1.15	−0.07	−2.23
Volatility* MIC	0.00	−0.06	−0.04	−0.96
Volatility* HIC	−0.01	−0.61	−0.04	−2.52
Adj R-Squared		0.58		0.50
# Observations		168		169
Specification Tests (P-Values)				
exogeneity of Lagged LQ1) exogeneity of Lagged LQ1)				0.08
Durbin–Wu–Hausman Test (for Volatility)				0.16
Hansan J-Test for Overidentifying Restrictions				0.57

Standard errors are White-corrected for heteroskedasticity

Dependent variable: LQ1				
	Regression 5′			
	W/out instruments		With instruments	
	Coeff	*t*-stat	Coeff	*z*-stat
Intercept Dummies				
Dummy for Primary Exporters	−1.45	−4.98	−0.39	−0.42
Dummy for Nonprimary Exporters	−0.48	−2.52	−1.12	−2.36
Lagged LQ1* Dummy for Primary Exporters	0.44	4.12	0.76	2.60
Lagged LQ1* Dummy for Nonprimary Exporters	0.81	11.27	0.50	2.31
Volatility* Dummy for Primary Exporters	−0.05	−3.26	−0.07	−2.64
Volatility* Dummy for Nonprimary Exporters	−0.02	−1.49	−0.09	−1.05
Adj. R-Squared		0.57		0.38
# Observations		168		168
Specification Tests (P-Values)				
Durbin–Wu–Hausman Test (for exogeneity of Lagged LQ1)				0.03
Durbin–Wu–Hausman Test (for Volatility)				0.01
Hansen J-Test for Overidentifying Restrictions				0.67
Standard errors are White-corrected for heteroskedasticity				

Source: Authors' calculations.

Table B-3. *Testing for transmission channels*

Dependent Variable: LQ1

	Coeff	t-stat	Coeff	t-stat	Coeff	t-stat	Coeff	t-stat	Coeff	t-stat	Coeff	t-stat	Coeff	t-stat	Coeff	t-stat
Intercept	-0.81	-6.35	-0.75	-5.71	-0.62	-4.07	-0.92	-5.11	-0.82	-6.45	-0.85	-6.34	-0.51	-2.46	-0.62	-2.74
Lagged LQ1	0.68	14.83	0.68	14.91	0.76	13.81	0.68	11.36	0.67	14.95	0.67	14.77	0.79	11.25	0.76	10.58
GDP Volatility	-0.03	-4.07	-0.02	-3.01	-0.02	-2.14	-0.01	-1.42	-0.03	-4.00	-0.03	-4.02	-0.03	-3.12	-0.03	-3.01
Average CPI Inflation			-0.02	-1.67												
Public Exp on Social Security, % GDP							0.01	2.95								
Public Exp on Education, % GDP									0.004	0.06						
Public Exp on Health % GDP															0.02	1.21
# Observations	251		251		163		163		254		254		96		96	
Adj R-Squared	0.49		0.49		0.55		0.57		0.48		0.48		0.57		0.57	

	Coeff	t-stat	Coeff	t-stat	Coeff	t-stat	Coeff	t-stat	Coeff	t-stat	Coeff	t-stat
Intercept	-0.70	-4.36	-0.71	-4.37	-0.56	-3.64	-0.56	-3.60	-0.84	-5.55	-1.00	-6.20
Lagged LQ1	0.71	12.03	0.71	11.89	0.77	13.97	0.77	13.38	0.68	12.87	0.66	12.38
GDP Volatility	-0.03	-2.92	-0.02	-2.43	-0.03	-3.88	-0.03	-3.87	-0.02	-3.14	-0.02	-2.82
REER Volatility			-2E-04	-0.47								
Unemployment Rate							0.00	0.05				
M2/GDP, %											0.002	2.62
# Observations	96		96		152		152		202		202	
Adj R-Squared	0.57		0.57		0.57		0.57		0.46		0.48	

Source: Authors' calculations.

128

APPENDIX C. EPISODES OF LARGE INCOME SWINGS

Here we take a closer look at some of the key transmission channel variables by tracking their movement during large swings (upward and downward) of GDP around its long-term trend. Of particular interest are potential asymmetries over the semi-cycles. As discussed in the main text, these are key to the existence of any longer-term negative relations between volatility and income distribution. The methodology used to identify relatively deep semicyclical movements of real GDP around its long-term trend is explained in the box below. The main results are summarized in Tables A-1 and B-1–3.

Key Results: Inverted U Semicycles

- In almost 70 percent of cases, inflation increased over the entire semicycle.
- There appears to be a credit boom during the upswing, which is not reversed during the latter part of the semicycle. In more than 70 percent of the cases, monetary depth rises coming out of the semicycle; a potential source of enhanced financial vulnerability in these situations.

Box 3.3. Note on Identification of Cyclical Movements in GDP

This box describes the identification of relatively deep semicycles, both upward and downward, of GDP around its long-term trend. For this, first the constant price per capita GDP series for each country is detrended using the HP filter. From this detrended series those semicycles are isolated during which the peak is at least 2 standard deviations away from the mean and there is at least one more year for which the difference is at least 1.5 standard deviations.

An example for Russia is illustrated below. Figure 3.5A shows the constant price GDP series and the HP trend, while Figure 3.5B shows the detrended GDP series. Application of the criteria specified above gives us a boom semicycle during 1985–92 and a bust semicycle for the period 1992–99, with their respective peaks in years 1989 and 1994. This exercise was done for all countries for which data are available over the 1960–2000 period. This gives 63 episodes of boom semicycles and 52 episodes of bust semicycles (50 booms and 48 busts each for developing countries).

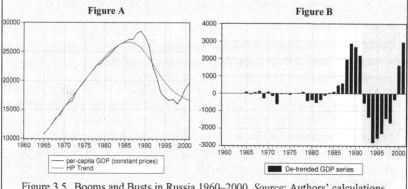

Figure 3.5. Booms and Busts in Russia 1960–2000. *Source*: Authors' calculations.

Thomas Laursen and Sandeep Mahajan

Table C-1A. *Changes in key variables over inverted U-shaped semicycles (Booms)*

	Inverted U semicycle for developing countries								
	Peak relative to start			End relative to peak			End relative to start		
	I	D	U	I	D	U	I	D	U
CPI Inflation	33	18	0	29	22	0	37	14	0
Public Expenditure (% GDP)	25	18	0	27	13	0	25	13	0
Public Sector Current Revenue (% GDP)	26	18	0	19	22	0	26	14	0
Fiscal Balance	16	27	0	13	26	0	12	26	0
Pub Exp on Edu (% GDP)	19	16	0	26	7	0	35	11	0
Pub Exp on Health (% GDP)	7	3	0	13	2	1	10	0	0
Pub Exp on Social Security (% GDP)	18	12	0	25	6	0	20	8	0
Wages & salaries (% of total public exp)	19	18	0	13	22	0	14	18	0
Pub Capital Exp (% GDP)	22	19	0	14	25	0	13	23	0
Unemployment Rate	4	14	1	16	4	0	9	8	2
Gini	5	7	0	9	3	0	10	7	0
Q1 (share of the bottom quintile)	4	6	0	1	8	0	9	10	0
Q2	4	6	0	2	7	0	8	11	0
Q3	7	3	0	3	6	0	5	13	1
Q4	5	5	0	3	6	0	7	12	0
Q5	4	6	0	7	2	0	14	5	0
M2/GDP	33	16	0	32	17	0	34	15	0

Note: "I" indicates number of times an increase took place. Similarly, "D" stands for number of decreases and "U" for number of unchanged values.

- Both fiscal revenues and expenditures (as shares of GDP) tend to increase over the semicycle. However, the increase in the expenditure ratio typically dominates. As a result, the fiscal balance worsens in almost 70 percent of the cases. Revenues and expenditures tend to increase more steeply than GDP during the initial boom (first half) of the semicycle, indicating a procyclical fiscal stance in these cases.
- Public capital expenditure (as a share of GDP) is typically lower at the end of the semicycle compared to the beginning, mainly because of sharp cutbacks during the second half of the semicycle, potentially having an adverse impact on long-run growth.

Table C-1B. *Changes in key variables over U-shaped semicycles (Busts)*

	U-shaped semicycle for developing countries								
	Peak relative to start			End relative to Peak			End relative to start		
	I	D	U	I	D	U	I	D	U
CPI Inflation	18	26	0	17	28	0	18	26	0
Public Expenditure (% GDP)	17	16	0	14	20	0	15	16	0
Public Sector Current Revenue (% GDP)	21	12	0	21	12	0	17	13	0
Fiscal Balance	15	17	0	23	11	0	18	13	0
Pub Exp on Edu (% GDP)	15	15	0	14	15	0	17	17	0
Pub Exp on Health (% GDP)	9	7	2	6	13	0	4	12	0
Pub Exp on Social Security (% GDP)	14	10	0	11	11	0	8	13	0
Wages & salaries (% of total public exp)	9	18	0	10	18	0	8	18	0
Pub Capital Exp (% GDP)	10	22	0	14	20	0	11	19	0
Unemployment Rate	16	6	0	9	14	0	14	9	0
Gini	6	7	0	11	4	0	10	8	0
Q1 (share of the bottom quintile)	4	9	0	7	6	0	8	6	2
Q2	5	8	0	7	6	0	7	8	1
Q3	3	10	0	7	6	0	5	10	1
Q4	6	7	0	8	5	0	7	9	0
Q5	11	2	0	6	7	0	10	6	0
M2/GDP	26	15	0	16	27	0	23	18	0

Source: Authors' calculations.

- Public expenditures on education, health, and social security tend to increase over the semicycle, with the number of increases being more pronounced during the latter part of the semicycle, indicating some procyclicality in these expenditures. Meanwhile, the share of wages and salaries in total expenditures declines in the majority of cases, mainly as a result of a sharper adjustment of this expenditure than of total expenditure during the latter half of the semicycle, when GDP falls toward its trend.
- Unemployment typically decreases during the initial boom and increases as growth reverts to trend. Over the entire semicycle, there is no clear pattern in its movement.

- Inequality typically rises during the semicycle, especially in the latter half. The bottom four quintiles tend to lose, while the top quintile typically gains from such fluctuations in GDP. The contrast in relative gains is particularly stark during the latter half of the semicycle.

U-Shaped Semicycles

- Inflation tends to fall over the entire semicycle.
- Monetary depth typically increases during downturns and falls during the recovery period. Over the entire semicycle, an increases in monetary depth is more typical.
- During the initial downturns (first half of the semicycle), in almost half the cases governments cut their expenditures at least in equal proportion to the decline in GDP. Public spending on wages and salaries takes a disproportionate hit, while expenditure on education as a share of GDP declined in half the cases, and expenditures on health and social security declined in about two-fifths of cases, adversely impacting the poor in particular. In almost two-third of the cases, public capital expenditures declined, potentially harming long-term growth and delaying economic recovery. Revenues tend to hold more steady during this period, perhaps because of the dominance of nontax revenues in the budget.
- During the recovery (second half) period of the semicycle, revenues tend to increase as a share of GDP, while increases in expenditures tend to lag GDP increases. As a result, in almost two-thirds of the cases, the budget balance improves during this phase. The recovery in health, wages and salaries, and capital expenditures is typically less than proportionate to the movement in GDP.
- Overall, over the entire semicycle, in almost half the cases governments emerged with smaller expenditures as share of GDP, while stronger revenue generation improved budget balances. Spending on wages and salaries is curtailed the most, while expenditures on education, health, and social security are protected in only 50 percent, 25 percent, and 40 percent of the cases, respectively. This could have long-term adverse impacts on the poor. Public sector investment rates are also typically curtailed during such episodes, with likely adverse implications for long-run growth.
- Unemployment rises during the downturn, and this is not offset during the recovery. As a result, in a majority of cases the unemployment rate increases over the entire semicycle. This may indicate the existence of poverty hysteresis.
- Inequality typically increases over the semicycle; more starkly during the recovery period. Quintiles 2, 4, and 3 tend to lose, while the bottom and especially top quintiles tend to gain.

In sum, there appear to be significant asymmetries at play during booms and busts over the medium term. In particular, capital expenditures and wages and salaries tend to get cut back, and inequality tends to increase (although there is no clear pattern for the income share of the bottom quintile) during episodes of large upswings and downswings. An asymmetric response of inflation during upswings, which typically results in higher inflation over the entire semicycle, may be a cause of the increased inequality typically seen during these episodes. Also, procyclicality during upturns in social expenditures, on which the poor are more reliant, leaves the poor more vulnerable to the next economic downturn, when these expenditures typically take a disproportionate hit. Similarly, the inability of governments to protect social spending on health, education, and social security in a majority of cases and the tendency of unemployment to increase help explain why the poor tend to suffer relatively more during periods of large downswings. These suggestive findings are consistent with our results over the longer term, but warrant further scrutiny.

REFERENCES

Agenor, Pierre-Richard. 2001. "Business Cycles, Economic Crises, and the Poor: Testing for Asymmetric Effects." Policy Research Working Paper 2700. World Bank, Washington, DC.

————. 2002a. "Macroeconomic Adjustment and the Poor – Analytical Issues and Cross-Country Evidence." Policy Research Working Paper 2788. World Bank, Washington, DC.

————. 2002b. "Does Globalization Hurt the Poor?" Policy Research Working Paper 2922. World Bank, Washington, DC.

Alderman, H., and C. Paxson. 1994. "Do the Poor Insure? A Synthesis of the Literature on Risk and Consumption in Developing Countries." In D. Bacha, ed., *Development, Trade, and the Environment* (Volume 4 of *Economics in a Changing World*). London: Macmillan.

Alesina, Alberto, and Roberto Perotti. 1996. "Income Distribution, Political Instability, and Investment." *European Economic Review* 40(6):1203–28.

Baldacci, Emanuele, Luiz De Mello, and Maria Inchauste. 2002. "Financial Crises, Poverty, and Income Distribution." IMF Working Paper 02/4 (January). International Monetary Fund, Washington, DC.

Barro, Robert J. 2000. "Inequality and Growth in a Panel of Countries." *Journal of Economic Growth* 5(1):5–32.

Benabou, R. 1996. "Inequality and Growth." NBER Working Paper 5658. National Bureau of Economic Research, Cambridge, MA.

Besley, T. 1995. "Nonmarket Institutions for Credit and Risk Sharing in Low-Income Countries." *Journal of Economic Perspectives* 9(3):115–27.

Bliss, C., and N. Stern. 1982. *Palanpur: The Economy of an Indian Village.* Oxford: Oxford University Press.

Bourguignon, F. 2003. "The Growth Elasticity of Poverty Reduction: Explaining Heterogeneity Across Countries and Time Periods." In T. S. Eicher and S. Turnovsky, eds., *Inequality and Growth: Theory and Policy Implications.* Cambridge, MA: MIT Press.

Bourguignon, F., W. H. Branson, and J. de Melo. 1992. "Adjustment and Income Distribution – A Micro-Macro Model for Counterfactual Analysis." *Journal of Development Economics* 38:17–39. Discussion Paper Series 1482 (September). Center for Economic Policy Research, London.

Bourguignon, F., L. Pereira da Silva, and N. Stern. 2002. "Evaluating the Poverty Impact of Economic Policies: Some Analytical Challenges." Paper presented to IMF conference on Macroeconomic Policies and Poverty Reduction, March.

Breen, Richard, and Cecilia Garcia-Penalosa. 1999. "Income Inequality and Macroeconomic Volatility: An Empirical Investigation." European University Institute, Oxford.

Cashin, P., P. Mauro, C. Pattillo, and R. Sahay. 2001. "Macroeconomic Policies and Poverty Reduction: Stylized Facts and an Overview of Research." IMF Working Paper 01/135 (September). International Monetary Fund, Washington, DC.

Chen, S., and M. Ravallion. 1997. "What Can New Survey Data Tell Us about Recent Changes in Distribution and Poverty." *World Bank Economic Review* 11(2):357–82.

———. 2000. "How Did the World's Poorest Fare in the 1990s?" Policy Research Working Paper 2409. World Bank, Washington, DC.

Chu, K., and S. Gupta, eds. 1998. *Social Safety Nets: Issues and Recent Experiences*. International Monetary Fund, Washington, DC.

Cline, W. R. 2002. "Financial Crises and Poverty in Emerging Market Economies." Paper prepared for R. Albert Berry Festschrift, Munk Center for International Studies, University of Toronto, April.

Datt, G., and H. Hoogeveen. 2000. "El Niño or El Peso: Crisis, Poverty, and Income Distribution in the Philippines." Policy Research Working Paper 2466. World Bank, Washington, DC.

Datt, G., and M. Ravallion. 1992. "Growth and Redistribution Components of Changes in Poverty Measures: A Decomposition with Applications to Brazil and India in the 1980s." *Journal of Development Economics* 38(2)(April):275–95.

Deaton, A. 1991. "Savings and Liquid Constraints." *Econometrica* 59(5):1221–48.

———. 1997. *The Analysis of Household Surveys: A Microeconomic Approach*. Baltimore, MD: Johns Hopkins University Press.

De Donder, P., and J. Hindricks. 1998. "The Political Economy of Targeting." *Public Choice* 95(1–2):177–200.

Deininger, K., and L. Squire. 1996. "A New Data Set Measuring Income Inequality." *World Bank Economic Review* 10(3):565–91.

———. 1998. "New Ways of Looking at Old Issues: Asset Inequality and Growth." *Journal of Development Economics* 57:259–87.

Dercon, S. 2002. "Income Risk, Coping Strategies, and Safety Nets." *World Bank Research Observer* 17(2):141–66.

Dollar, David, and A. Kraay. 2001. "Growth Is Good for the Poor." *Journal of Economic Growth* 7(3):195–225.

Easterly, William. 2001. *The Elusive Quest for Growth*. Cambridge, MA: MIT Press.

Easterly, William, and Stanley Fischer. 2001. "Inflation and the Poor." *Journal of Money, Credit, and Banking* 33(2)(May):160–78.

Easterly, William, Roumeen Islam, and Joseph Stiglitz. 2000. "Shaken and Stirred: Explaining Growth Volatility." In *The World Bank Annual Conference on Economic Development*. World Bank: Washington, DC.

Eble, S., and P. Koeva. 2001. "The Distributional Effects of Macroeconomic Crises: Microeconomic Evidence from Russia." Paper presented to IMF workshop on Macroeconomic Policies and Poverty Reduction, April.

Edwards, S. 1997. "Trade Policy, Growth, and Income Distribution." *American Economic Review* 87(2):205–10.

Fallon, P., and R. Lucas. 2002. "The Impact of Financial Crises on Labor Markets, Household Incomes, and Poverty: A Review of Evidence." *World Bank Research Observer* 17(1):21–45.

Ferreira, F., G. Prennushi, and M. Ravallion. 1999. "Protecting the Poor from Macroeconomic Shocks: An Agenda for Action in a Crisis and Beyond." Policy Research Working Paper 2160. World Bank, Washington, DC.

Ferreira, F., P. de Guimaraes Leite, P. Picchetti, and L. Pereira da Silva. 2002. "Aggregate Shocks and Income Distribution: Can Macro-Micro Models Help Identify Winners and Losers from a Devaluation." World Bank, Washington, DC.

Frankel, J., and A. Rose. 1996. "Currency Crashes in Emerging Markets: Empirical Indicators." CEPR Discussion Paper No. 1349. Center for Economic Policy Research, London.

Gelbach, J. B., and L. H. Pritchett. 1995. "Does More for the Poor Mean Less for the Poor?" Policy Research Working Paper 1523. World Bank, Washington, DC.

Ghura, D., C. A. Leite, and C. Tsangarides. 2002. "Is Growth Enough? Macroeconomic Policy and Poverty Reduction." IMF Working Paper 02/188 (July). International Monetary Fund, Washington, DC.

Halac, M., and S. L. Schmukler. 2003. "Distributional Effects of Crises: The Role of Financial Transfers." World Bank, Washington, DC.

Holzman, R., and S. Jorgenson. 2000. "Social Risk Management: A New Conceptual Framework for Social Protection and Beyond." Social Protection Discussion Paper 0006. World Bank, Washington, DC.

IDB (Inter-American Development Bank). 1995. "Economic and Social Progress Report – Overcoming Volatility." Washington, DC.

Kakwani, N. 1993. "Growth and Income Redistribution: A Poverty Decomposition Using an Axiomatic Approach." Discussion Paper 93/2 (March). University of New South Wales, Australia.

Lokshin, M., and M. Ravallion. 2000. "Welfare Impacts of the 1998 Financial Crisis in Russia and the Response of the Public Safety Net." *Economics of Transition* 8(2):269–95. European Bank for Reconstruction and Development, London.

Lopez-Acevedo, G., and A. Salinas. 2000. "How Mexico's Financial Crisis Affected Income Distribution." Policy Research Working Paper 2406. World Bank, Washington, DC.

Lundberg, M., and L. Squire. 2000. "The Simultaneous Evolution of Growth and Inequality." World Bank, Washington, DC.

Lustig, Nora. 2000. "Crises and the Poor: Socially Responsible Macroeconomics." IADB Technical Papers Series (February). Inter-American Development Bank, Washington, DC.

Murdoch, J. 1995. "Income Smoothing and Consumption Smoothing." *Journal of Economic Perspectives* 9(3):103–14.

Perry, G. 2003. "Can Fiscal Rules Help Reduce Macroeconomic Volatility in the Latin American and Caribbean Region?" Policy Research Working Paper 3080. World Bank, Washington, DC.

Pritchett, L., Suryahadi, A., S. Sumarto, and Y. Suharso. 2000. "The Evolution of Poverty During the Crisis in Indonesia 1996–99." Policy Research Working Paper 2435. World Bank, Washington, DC.

Ravallion, M. 2001. "Growth, Inequality, and Poverty: Looking Beyond Averages." Policy Research Working Paper 2558. World Bank, Washington, DC.

———. 2002a. "Inequality Convergence." *Economic Letters* 80:351–56.

———. 2002b. "Who Is Protected? On the Incidence of Fiscal Adjustment." Paper prepared for IMF Conference on Macroeconomic Polices and Poverty Reduction, March.

———. 2003. "Targeted Transfers in Poor Countries: Revisiting the Trade-Offs and Policy Options." Policy Research Working Paper 3048. World Bank, Washington, DC.

Ravallion, M., and S. Chen. 1997. "What Can New Survey Data Tell Us About Recent Changes in Distribution and Poverty." *World Bank Economic Review* 11(2):357–82.

Robilliard, A., F. Bourguignon, and S. Robinson. 2001. "Crisis and Income Distribution – A Micro-Macro Model for Indonesia." Paper presented at a World Bank seminar.

Romer, C., and D. Romer. 1998. "Monetary Policy and the Well-being of the Poor." NBER Working Paper 6793:1–62. National Bureau of Economic Research, Cambridge, MA.

Schady, N. R. 2004. "Do Macroeconomic Crises Always Slow Down Human Capital Accumulation?" *World Bank Economic Review* 18(2).

Tesliuc, E., and K. Lindert. 2002. "Vulnerability: A Quantitative and Qualitative Assessment." Guatemala Poverty Assessment Program. Draft paper presented to World Bank Poverty Day Conference, October.

Townsend, R. 1994. "Risk and Insurance in Village India." *Econometrica* 62(3):539–91.

_____. 1995. "Consumption Insurance: An Evaluation of Risk-Bearing Systems in Low-Income Economies." *Journal of Economic Perspectives* 9(3):83–102.

Van de Walle, D. 1998. "Targeting Revisited." *World Bank Research Observer* 13(2): 231–48.

World Bank. 2000a. "East Asia: Recovery and Beyond." East Asia and Pacific Region Study (June). Washington, DC.

_____. 2000b. "Securing Our Future in a Global Economy." Latin American and Caribbean Studies (June). Washington, DC.

_____. 2001a. *World Development Report 2000–2001: Attacking Poverty*. Washington, DC.

_____. 2001b. "Argentina – Household Risk, Self-Insurance, and Coping Strategies in Urban Argentina." Report No. 22426-AR (October). Washington, DC.

_____. 2002. "Caribbean Economic Overview 2002 – Macroeconomic Volatility, Household Vulnerability, and Institutional and Policy Responses." Report No. 24165–LAC. Discussion Draft (June). Washington, DC.

4. Agricultural Commodity Price Volatility[1]

Jan Dehn, Christopher L. Gilbert, and Panos Varangis

ABSTRACT: Traded agricultural commodities are an important source of export earnings for many developing countries, and an important component of income and expenditure for poor farmers. Thus, policies to manage the negative consequences of volatile commodity markets are a key issue for governments and policymakers. This study considers the origins, incidence, and consequences of commodity price volatility.

Over the past two decades, both the political institutions that structure the markets for internationally traded commodities and the policies that have emerged from these institutions have changed in dramatic ways. Policies based on government or multilateral interventions that had been common for decades have come to be viewed as ineffective and unsustainable. Policies and supporting institutions that were put in place to foster development have come to be viewed as impediments to growth. Nevertheless, because traded agricultural commodities remain an important source of export earnings for many developing countries and an important component of income and expenditure for poor farmers, policies to manage the negative consequences of volatile commodity markets remain a key issue for governments and policymakers.

This chapter reviews the work of applied economists and policymakers and the institutions that have come to characterize the commodity and risk markets since the 1980s. It discusses how a growing body of work has contributed to a change in thinking that has moved policy away from price and revenue stabilization goals toward policies that emphasize the management of commodity risks. The study illustrates this change in approach with new and sometimes experimental programs, with special emphasis on World Bank programs.

[1] Jan Dehn is with Ashmore Group Limited, London, UK. Christopher Gilbert is Professor of Econometrics, Department of Economics, University of Trento (Italy) and consultant to the Agriculture and Rural Development Department, the World Bank. Panos Varangis is Vice President of the Greek Agricultural Bank, Athens (Greece) and is currently on leave from his position as Lead Economist, Agriculture and Rural Development Department, the World Bank. This study draws on Anderson, Larson, and Varangis (2002) and Dehn (2000a, 2000b). We are grateful to Jock Anderson and Donald Larson for allowing us to use our joint work, to Erin Bryla for research assistance, and to Paul Cashin, Julie Dana, Jan Willem Gunning, Brian Pinto, Don Larson, and Ulrich Hess for comments. All errors remain our own responsibility.

COMMODITY PRICE VOLATILITY

The Origin of Commodity Price Volatility

Commodity prices are variable because short-term production and consumption elasticities are low. Production responsiveness is low in agriculture because input decisions are made before new crop prices are known. Similarly, there is a lag of several months between mine production decisions and the sale of refined metal. These decisions depend on expected prices, not realized prices. Price outcomes are seldom so disastrous as to result in the crop being abandoned on the trees or in the ground. Short-term demand elasticities are low because the actual commodity price may not be a large component of the overall value of the final product (cocoa in chocolate – milk and sugar can be more important – or coffee beans in soluble coffee powder, to take two examples).

Elasticities determine the amplitude of fluctuations in commodity prices but their origin is in shocks to production and consumption. Shocks to supply predominantly affect agricultural commodities. Shocks to demand originating in the industrial business cycle predominantly affect industrial commodities, such as metals. Low elasticities imply that small shocks to production can have a large impact on price. The impact of shocks on commodity prices is moderated by stockholding. Low prices, caused either by positive supply shocks, negative demand shocks, or both, imply probable positive returns to stock holding. Consumption demand is therefore augmented by stock demand until such point as the expected return from holding stocks is equal to rate of interest on comparably risky investments. The fall in prices is moderated to the extent that excess supply is absorbed in stocks. Because of stockholding, the impact of a negative shock in one year is extended into the following year or years (Samuelson 1957).[2] The consequence is that, even with shocks that are uncorrelated over time, stock holding induces positive autocorrelation in the resulting prices.

Price Variability

How much do prices vary? In examining commodity price movements, one can either look across markets or across producing countries, averaging across countries. The choice will depend on whether one's focus is on individual commodities (such as coffee or cocoa) or on the position of individual commodity-producing nations (such as Cameroon or Côte d'Ivoire). This study takes a country focus. It follows the approach of Angus Deaton and Ronald Miller (1995) in using geometric Laspeyres (that is, base-weighted) indices. These have the nice property that the percentage change in the index is a weighted average of the percentage change in the component prices. Such indices may either be nominal or real. If real, they may either be deflated by a standard dollar deflator (such as the U.S. producer price index) or by a measure of import prices. In the latter case, they may be interpreted as terms of trade indices for the commodity-producing sector. Such indices will differ from normal terms of

---

[2] See also Wright and Williams (1991), Deaton and Laroque (1992, 1995), and Ng (1996).

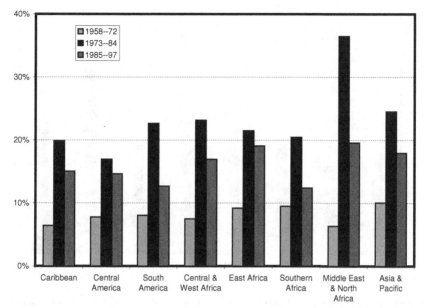

Figure 4.1. Volatility of Nominal Deaton–Miller Indices, 1958–97. *Source*: Authors' calculations, using data from Dehn (2000a, 2000b).

trade indices, obtained as the ratio of export to import prices, in excluding the prices of noncommodity exports. This exclusion will be important for many diversified middle-income commodity-exporting countries.

Jan Dehn (2000a) found that the variability of nominal dollar country-specific Deaton–Miller commodity price indices has increased in the last 30 years. Figure 4.1, which uses Dehn's data, charts the volatility of the annual nominal Deaton–Miller indices for the three periods 1958–72, 1973–84, and 1985–97 averaged across geographical regions. (Volatility is measured as the standard deviation of the changes in the logarithms of the indices.) Because these periods have been chosen such that both the 1973–74 commodity price boom and the two major positive oil shocks are in the second period, it is unsurprising that volatility is greatest in this period in each region distinguished. What is more notable is that although volatility has subsequently declined, it also remains higher in the final 1985–97 period than in the pre-1973 period in every single region.[3] This strongly suggests that nominal commodity price variability increased over the final decades of the century. Dehn (2000a) shows that the same conclusions broadly hold for uncertainty measures, depending on which precise uncertainty measure one adopts.

The annual commodity price volatility figures post-1972, which typically exceed 20 percent, are around twice the level of dollar-yen and dollar-DM exchange rate

---

[3] See also Brunetti and Gilbert (1995), which documented the long-term constancy of metals price volatility from the mid-1970s.

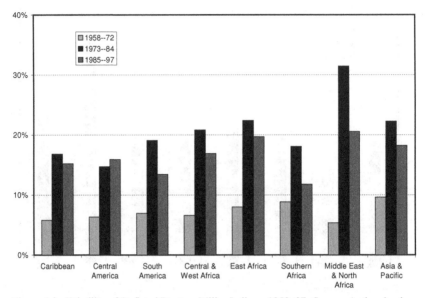

Figure 4.2. Volatility of Deflated Deaton–Miller Indices, 1958–97. *Source*: Authors' calculations, using data from Dehn (2000a, 2000b).

variability over the same period.[4] It is reasonable to conclude that primary commodity prices are among the most volatile prices in the international economy, and that these volatility levels remain high even taking into account the fact that countries average across different export commodities.

Dehn's Deaton–Miller indices are calculated in terms of U.S. dollars. Part of the variability of these indices in the 1970s and 1980s may derive from variability in the value of the dollar. Deflation by dollar import unit values gives a set of real indices. These are charted in Figure 4.2. Deflation tends to reduce the contrast between the 1973–84 and 1985–97 periods, except in the case of the Middle East and North Africa, where the indices are dominated by movements in the oil price. The major contrast is between the calm of the pre-1973 "Bretton Woods period" and the turmoil of the past three decades.

The level of commodity price variability differs across countries, depending on the commodity composition of each country's exports and in particular the extent to which exports are diversified across commodities. Figures 4.1 and 4.2 suggest that these differences tend broadly to average out across regions. The Middle East and North Africa region has suffered the highest variability because of high oil concentration, followed by East Africa, Asia and the Pacific, and Central and West Africa. Variability appears lowest in the Southern African and South American regions. Taking the entire 1959–97 sample, real variability was highest in Laos (27.3 percent)

---

[4] Dollar-yen volatility was 11.4 percent and dollar-DM volatility was 11.7 percent, both at annual rates, over the period 1973–97. The annual volatility of the U.S. Treasury bill rate was 2.6 percent over the same period (authors' calculations using data from IMF, *International Financial Statistics*).

and lowest in South Africa (5.4 percent). Of the 110 countries considered, 31 experienced real volatilities in excess of 20 percent per year, 54 experienced volatilities of between 10 percent and 20 percent, and the remaining 25 had volatilities of less than 10 percent. The first group of high volatility countries includes most of the major oil exporters, but also some very poor non-oil exporting countries (Bhutan, Haiti, Laos, and Uganda). These countries share high export concentration. The final group of low volatility countries is composed of countries that lack oil exports but that are well diversified. This group includes some countries that are normally considered as suffering from commodity price variability (Cameroon, Fiji, and Ghana) as well as some very large countries (Brazil and India). Of course, even if an economy is diversified, farmers in that country may nevertheless suffer from price variability. The fact that a country is well diversified does not imply that individual farmers will be diversified, but it does suggest that the government may have the means to offset the farm level impact of price variability through tax or social security policy.

Uncertainty

Volatility is an unconditional measure of price variability. By contrast, uncertainty is conditional. It conditions the variability measure on factors that can help predict price movements, in particular past volatility levels and shocks to volatility. In any particular period, uncertainty may be either greater or less than realized volatility, but to the extent that volatility has regular, predictable components, uncertainty can be expected to be lower. Much of the seasonal variation in weather is predictable, for example; hence the variability in weather conditions is considerably greater than uncertainty.

Garey Ramey and Valerie Ramey (1995) and Luis Serven (1998) have argued that the variability–uncertainty distinction is important. Crudely, one can think of uncertainty as affecting the plans made by economic agents, whereas variability will be important to the extent that agents are unable or unwilling to smooth expenditures. This suggests that uncertainty is likely to be particularly important in investment decisions where resources are committed in advance of prices being revealed. This includes farmers' decisions on diversifying production and purchasing inputs. By contrast, variability effects will predominate in contexts in which agents are constrained. This focuses attention on deficiencies in credit markets.

Uncertainty measures rely on the model of the volatility processes used to encapsulate agents' perceptions about predictable components of volatility. Dehn (2000a) considered three alternative approaches adopted in the empirical literature:

- Prices and volatility are both unpredictable. In this case, uncertainty is not distinguishable from volatility. A historical volatility measure, based on recent data, provides the best estimate of future volatility.
- Prices are partially predictable, but volatility is unpredictable. In this case, uncertainty relates to the volatility of the price innovations (the unpredictable components of the price series) and not to the prices themselves. (See Ramey and Ramey 1995.) Predictability in price levels may arise either because of mean reversion or because of the presence of local trends. Uncertainty is constant over time but differs from, and will be lower than, price volatility.

142   *Jan Dehn, Christopher L. Gilbert, and Panos Varangis*

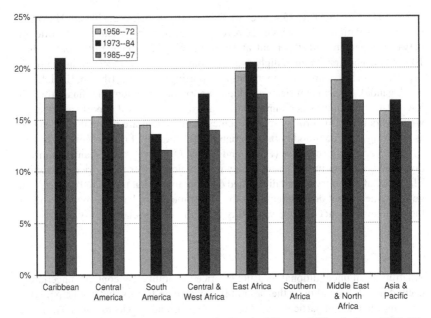

Figure 4.3. GARCH Uncertainty Measures for Nominal Deaton–Miller Indices, 1958–97. *Source*: Authors' calculations, using data from Dehn (2000a, 2000b).

- Volatility tends to be persistent and this allows it to be predicted. This predictability implies that it may be modeled as autoregressive. At high frequencies, GARCH models are often employed. (See Bollerslev 1986 and Serven 1998). Uncertainty now becomes time-varying. At any point of time, it may be greater than or less than current price volatility.

While the first of these three approaches is unconditional, the second and third make uncertainty a conditional measure. The general difficulty with all of these approaches is that any uncertainty measure relies on a particular model used to calculate uncertainty.

Figure 4.3 summarizes Dehn's (2000b) nominal uncertainty estimates by region and time period using the third of these approaches. These estimates were derived by applying a GARCH(1,1) filter to the returns on the nominal Deaton–Miller indices used for the nominal volatility estimates shown in Figure 4.1. In comparison with the numbers graphed in Figure 4.1, there is far less variability in the uncertainty figures either over time or across regions. One reason for the lack of time variability is that, in the standard GARCH model the mean parameter is constant implying that the unconditional variance is constant over time. This will be inappropriate if volatility is tending to increase over time, as in the 1970s and 1980s. It should be possible to improve upon this in future work.

Figure 4.3 may be taken either as supporting the conclusion that uncertainty has been less variable over time than volatility, or that more sophisticated models are required for distinguishing between variability and uncertainty than have been used hitherto. This study favors the latter conclusion.

Exceptional Commodity Price Shocks

Dehn (2000a) finds that three-quarters of the 113 less developed and emerging market economies in his sample exhibit uncertainty profiles, which can be described as periods of relative calm punctuated by extreme shocks. These countries come from all regions of the world and comprise a broad range of commodity producers (not just oil producers). It is possible that these outliers, rather than uncertainty per se, drive any potential negative growth effects associated with commodity price uncertainty.

The literature on commodity price shocks supposes that large and sudden movements in commodity prices have a disproportionately large impact on the economies that are so impacted. If a country has a Deaton–Miller price index P, the period t shock is measured either by the proportional change $\Delta \ln P_t$, corresponding to the simple volatility measures discussed in the price variability section above, or by the unanticipated component $\Delta \ln P_t - E_{t-1} \Delta \ln P_t$, which corresponds to the second uncertainty measure discussed above. The extraordinary shocks hypothesis amounts to an assertion that the impact of shocks is nonlinear. The most extreme version of this hypothesis asserts that only large price shocks have an impact. It is sometimes also claimed that responses to shocks may be asymmetric, differing between favorable and unfavorable shocks. Henceforth this study refers to these large shocks as *exceptional shocks*, and more loosely simply as shocks.

Nonlinear responses might arise because agents (farmers, stabilization authorities, governments) are well-adapted to normal price fluctuations but either do not expect or do not consider it worth making provision against extreme events that arise only with low probability. Asymmetric responses can reflect asymmetry in constraints. For example, borrowing may be constrained while lending is unconstrained.

This raises the question of how one should discriminate between normal and exceptional shocks. One might do this in either of two ways:

- One could regard the largest α percent of shocks (in terms of the absolute value of the price change) as being exceptional, either in each country or over the entire sample.
- One could regard shocks greater than a specified size, say ξ, (in absolute value), as being exceptional.

In any given sample, there will be a value $\xi(\alpha)$ that will make the two definitions equivalent.

Using the same sample as discussed in the price variability section above, this study follows Dehn (2000a) in using the former procedure, applied over the entire sample, in relation to changes in log prices and using a value of $\xi = 1.96$ standard deviations. If the price change distribution were normal, this would correspond to a value of $\alpha = 2.5$ percent, but excess kurtosis (the fact that the price change distribution tends to be fat-tailed) implies a somewhat higher shock frequency. Dehn's criterion allows identification of shock episodes in aggregate country commodity price indices for the same 113 countries over the period 1957 to 1997. It gives a total of 278 shock episodes, averaging 2.5 shocks per country over the full sample period (1959–97), or one major shock every 16 years. However, shocks became more important in the latter part of the sample. Shock incidence increased in the

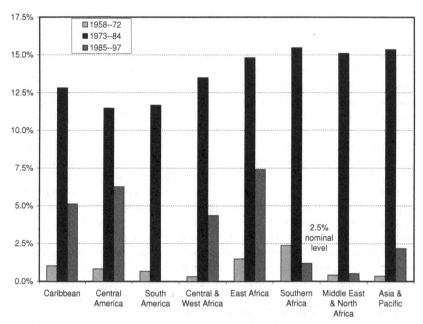

Figure 4.4. Incidence of Extreme (2.5%) Positive Shocks by Region. *Source*: Authors' calculations, using data from Dehn (2000a, 2000b).

1970s and has not returned to pre-1970s levels in the subsequent period. In the most recent part of the sample, countries could expect to receive a major shock every nine years.

The distribution of positive and negative shocks also appears asymmetric, in line with the predictions of theory. Of the 278 shocks identified, 179 are positive shocks while 99 are negative shocks. Nearly one-third of the sampled countries in the sample experienced positive shocks in the 1970s. The incidence of negative shocks also increased in the 1970s, although by less than the incidence of positive shocks. Negative shocks dominate in the 1980s. Forty countries – over one-third of the whole sample – experienced extreme negative shocks in 1986 (more on this below). The 1970s may be characterized as a decade of positive shocks, while the 1980s was dominated by large negative shocks.

This contrast can be seen in Figures 4.4 and 4.5, which show the incidence of extreme positive and negative nominal shocks respectively. Following Dehn (2000a), the cut-off is taken at ±2.5 percent relative to the country-specific standard deviation. This implies that, if shocks were normally distributed, one should expect each region to exhibit 2.5 percent positive and 2.5 percent negative extreme shocks. Instead, the proportion of positive shocks, averaging across the three periods, is well in excess of 2.5 percent (Figure 4.4), while the proportion of extreme negative shocks is well below 2.5 percent in almost all regions (Figure 4.5). Furthermore, extreme positive shocks are concentrated in the 1973–84 period, with some incidence also in the post-1984 period in Central and South America and in sub-Saharan Africa. Similar, but less pronounced results are obtained if one considers extreme real shocks. This

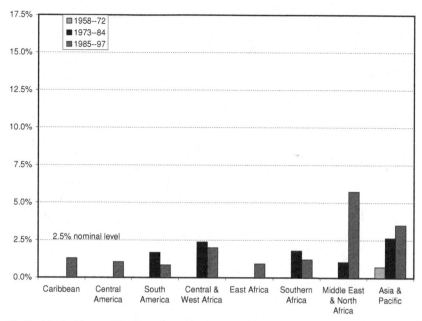

Figure 4.5. Incidence of Extreme (2.5%) Negative Shocks by Region. *Source*: Authors' cal-culations, using data from Dehn (2000a, 2000b).

contrast between the incidence of extreme positive and negative shocks is in line with the Wright and Williams (1991) and Deaton and Laroque (1992) models, in which stockholding generates a right-skewed price distribution.

Extreme shocks affect many countries and commodities sufficiently enough to dispel the notion that shocks are a policy issue that affects only a narrow group of countries, such as oil producers. Consider the relationship between the incidence of oil shocks in the sample and other shocks. The sample's 23 oil producers experienced positive shocks in 1974 and 1979, and a negative shock in 1986. This distribution is similar to the overall distribution of shocks, begging the question whether oil shocks are really driving the overall distribution. In fact, at least half of all the commodity shocks seen in the early 1970s occurred before the first oil shock even showed up in the data. Some 26 countries – and 13 different commodities – were affected by major price outliers in 1973. In 1974 when oil prices spiked, some 33 countries experienced shocks; but this high incidence of country shocks is explained to a considerable extent by price shocks in 15 commodities other than oil. Thus more than twice as many countries experienced shocks in 1973 and 1974 than there are oil producers in the sample (59 versus 23). The same is true for the negative oil shock in the 1980s. Negative price shocks occurred in 10 different commodities in 1986, and 40 countries – almost twice as many as produce oil – experienced negative commodity price shocks in that year. It is also telling that there is no evidence that the second oil shock in 1979 precipitated widespread commodity shocks, as one would expect if oil prices were indeed the cause of the general increase in the incidence of shocks among the non-oil commodities. In fact, shocks in 1979 are

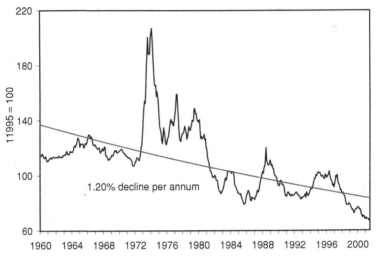

Figure 4.6. Deflated IMF Commodity Price Index, 1960–2000. *Source*: International Monetary Fund, *International Financial Statistics* (cd-rom), and authors' calculations.

confined almost exclusively to oil producers. Only a small number of exporters of other types of commodities experienced positive shocks in that year. More than 40 percent of the 52 agricultural food producers in the sample experienced positive shocks in the 1970s, with many of these shocks occurring in the 1977, the time of the well-documented beverage boom. Well over half of the sample's 18 agricultural nonfood producers witnessed positive shocks in 1973 and nearly 55 percent of this group of countries experienced negative shocks in 1986.

Trend and Cycle

Relative to the price of manufactured goods, primary commodity prices have exhibited a variable but steady downward trend over the past century. Enzo Grilli and Maw Cheng Yang (1988) documented the long-term decline of primary prices. This downward trend is illustrated in Figure 4.6 from 1960. The IMF index of primary commodity prices is used, deflated by the U.S. producer price index (all items). A linear trend fitted to the logarithms of the prices shows a trend decline of 1.20 percent per year, although this estimate is sensitive to the choice of sample dates (see Deaton 1999). No negative trend was evident in the post-1945 data until the 1980s.[5]

Raul Prebisch (1950, 1962) and Hans Singer (1950) independently noticed the tendency for the net barter terms of trade of primary commodity-producing countries to deteriorate over time. On that basis, they asserted the hypothesis that prices for primary commodity exports will fall relative to manufactured imports. Singer argued

---

[5] John Cuddington and Carlos Urzùa (1989) argued that the Grilli and Yang data were better explained by a structural break than a downward trend. However, this view is becoming more difficult to sustain as continued evidence of downward price movements accumulates. See also León and Sato (1997).

that primary commodities typically exhibit lower income elasticities of demand than manufactures and argued that this would imply that relative prices would decline over time. Prebisch claimed that greater union power in developed country manufacturing would raise the price–cost margins in manufacturing with the same result. Neither argument is sound. The long-term impact of low elasticities would be lower commodity production, not lower prices; while the claimed greater union power in manufacturing would, at most, result in a price mark-up of manufactures over primary commodities, but could not generate a continuing trend.

As recognized by Sir Arthur Lewis (1954), any explanation of the long-term trend in commodity prices must start from a discussion of production costs – see also Deaton and Laroque (2003). Lewis saw the prices of tropical agricultural commodities as being determined by subsistence costs – but that is only true so long as labor remains in surplus and so long as productivity levels remain constant. In fact, productivity advances affect tropical agriculture in the same way that they affect manufacturing. The differential price trend appears to be largely the consequence of the different ways that technical advance and productivity change are accounted for in primary and manufactured goods. In manufactured goods, technical change results in quality improvements that are in part matched by price increases, so that a year 2005 automobile is qualitatively superior to its 1975 counterpart. By contrast, a bag of year 2005 coffee beans will, broadly, be indistinguishable from beans from the same origin in 1975, and productivity advances will be reflected solely in lower prices. Analyzing the price trend over the period to the mid-1980s, Robert Lipsey (1994, p. 21) concluded "the case is weak that there has been a long-term deterioration in commodity prices relative to a price index, adjusted for quality change, of manufactured exports from developed countries to developing countries." There is nothing in the recent experience that should lead one to revise this judgment.[6]

The existence of resource rents complicates the position in minerals commodities. These rents drive a wedge between prices and production costs. Harold Hotelling (1931) argued that increased scarcity would drive up resource rents over time in proportion to the interest rate. In fact, low-cost discoveries continue to be made and productivity advances appear to more than offset any scarcity effects (see Slade 1982).

The concern here is with volatility, and not the trend per se. But although trend and cycle are conceptually distinct, in practice it is difficult to distinguish the one from the other. At a formal level, the difficulty in distinguishing trend from cycle follows from acknowledgment that the trend is almost certainly stochastic and not deterministic. This is the counterpart of the observation that, in Figure 4.6, the trend appears visually to be highly variable and therefore not well represented by the fitted constant linear trend. Standard statistical tests are not conclusive.[7]

---

[6] Lipsey's conclusion does not imply that the adverse commodity price trend is a statistical illusion, but rather grounds it in national accounting practices. Arguments such as those advanced by Prebisch (1950, 1962) are simply irrelevant.

[7] An ADF test on the annual logarithmic price series graphed in Figure 4.6 fails to rejects nonstationarity around a deterministic trend ("trend stationarity"). Eliminating the double negative, the test accepts nonstationarity. However, the same test using monthly data over the same sample rejects trend nonstationarity at the 10 percent-level, but not the 5 percent-level.

A more pragmatic approach is to ask what proportion of the variability of commodity prices is permanent and what proportion is temporary (that is, involves reversion to the local trend defined by the cumulated permanent shocks). This view implies a decomposition of commodity price volatility into two components: volatility of the commodity price trend and volatility of commodity price about this variable trend.

Following John Cuddington (1992) and Carmen Reinhart and Peter Wickham (1994), this study applies the procedure used by Stephen Beveridge and Charles. R. Nelson (1981) for decomposing a non-stationary series into a permanent and a transitory component to the IMF series to the data graphed in Figure 4.6. The transitory component accounts for only 18.5 percent of the annual return variance. Equivalently, the standard deviation of the transitory shocks is 43 percent (the square root of 18.5 percent) of that of the returns. A similar result is found by inspection of the moving average representation of the series found using a Wold decomposition: only 19.5 percent of any shock is subsequently reversed. Using monthly data, this rises to 28 percent of a shock cumulated over 12 months. The implication is that between 70 percent and 80 percent of any change to (aggregate) commodity prices should be considered permanent. Failure to distinguish between permanent and transitory shocks can explain the poor performance of commodity price forecasts made by the World Bank (among others) in the 1970s and 1980s.[8] As Paul Cashin and John McDermott (2002, p. 188) state, "trends appear to be widely variable and largely uncertain, and cannot be relied upon as a basis for making forecasts of future commodity prices."

An implication of this observation is that one can only distinguish between trend and cycle with the benefit of hindsight. This has implications for policy aimed at addressing volatility issues. It is generally accepted that producing countries must adjust in the face of secular movements in the prices of the commodities they produce but that they may legitimately act to offset the effects of volatility. However, it will not generally be clear to what extent a price fall, such as those experienced by many producing countries in the mid-1980s, is cyclical and to what extent it is permanent. In that specific instance, overestimation of the tendency to mean reversion was contributory to the failure of a number of domestic and international price stabilization schemes (see Gilbert 1996, 1997). It is tempting to argue that because commodity price volatility is large relative to drift, concerns about long-run declines in price trends are less important than concerns over the implications of increasing price volatility (see Deaton 1999; Cashin and McDermott 2002). The practical difficulty of distinguishing between trend and cyclical movements leads this study to reject that view.

The Beveridge–Nelson procedure can be used to examine the same issues on an individual country basis using Dehn's (2000a,b) Deaton–Miller indices. On an annual basis, these show between 15 percent and 40 percent transitory component in the variance of price returns. There is some degree of regional variation, with the transitory variance lowest in southern Africa, the Middle East and North Africa, and Central America. This is illustrated in Figure 4.7. The figure also shows the extent of reversion, calculated from the Wold decomposition. This statistic shows

---

[8] See Powell (1991), Deaton and Miller (1995), and Deaton (1999).

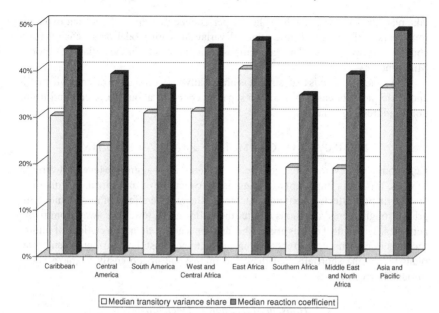

Figure 4.7. Median Reaction and Transitory Variance of Commodity Price Shocks. *Source*: Authors' calculations, using data from Dehn (2000a, 2000b). For definitions, see text. The calculations relate to shocks in the deflated Deaton–Miller indices.

the percentage of any shock that will be reversed. These reversion statistics vary between 34 percent (southern Africa) and 49 percent (Asia and Pacific).[9]

To the extent that there is reversion, how quickly does this take place? Paul Cashin and John McDermott (2002) assert that it takes around three years for half the reversion to take place. However, they report substantial variation across commodities. The half-life of price shocks range from two months for bananas to permanent for robusta coffee, with a median half-life of about four years across the 44 commodities. Their measure depends on the NBER procedure of dating cycles (see Watson 1994; Cashin, Céspendes, and Sahay 2003). The conceptual difficulty with this approach is that, in general, an economic time series will be analyzed in terms of a (possibly infinite) number of cycles each with different periodicities. This study prefers to measure persistence directly from the Wold moving average representation of the returns in each country's Deaton–Miller index. The measure used in this study is the number of years required for full reversion to

---

[9] The Wold decomposition represents the proportionate change in a country's Deaton–Miller index P as an infinite moving average $\Delta \ln P_t = \sum_{j=0}^{\infty} \alpha_j \varepsilon_{t-j}$ where $\alpha_0 = 1$ and the $\{\varepsilon_s\}$ are a set of independent disturbances (see Hamilton 1994, pp. 108–09). We measure reversion as $\rho = -\sum_{j=1}^{\infty} \alpha_j$. The moving average representation of the price change is obtained by inversion of an AR(5) $\Delta \ln P_t = \beta_0 + \sum_{j=1}^{5} \beta_j \Delta \ln P_{t-j} + \varepsilon_t$ estimated over the sample 1963–97. The estimation procedure can give rise to some extreme estimates for countries in which the estimated AR(5) as poor explanatory power. Figure 4.7 therefore reports median estimates and not averages for each region. Countries for which ρ is estimated as negative are omitted from the median statistics.

take place.[10] This gives slightly shorter persistence measures of between two and four years with relatively little regional variation, with modal persistence across countries of two years.[11] The calculations relate to shocks in the deflated Deaton–Miller indices.

The general lesson is that, since it is practically very difficult to disentangle trend and cycle, it is not easily possible to separate concerns about the price trend from policy addressing volatility.

THE IMPACT OF COMMODITY PRICE VARIABILITY

Commodity price variability may affect economies at an aggregate level in a variety of ways. It is again important to distinguish between the ex ante effects of volatility and the ex post effects of extreme outcomes. The ex ante effects of uncertainty will arise through agents' decisions to alter their allocations toward or away from risky activities. The ex post effects arise either as agents adjust their expectations of future incomes in response to current earnings, or as they adjust their current expenditure plans to income shortfalls that they find impossible or too costly to make good through borrowing.

Household Allocation Decisions

Rural households are exposed to many risks that affect their income. Survey results often cite weather-related risks, yield risks, price risks, illness, livestock problems, weak markets/demand to sell their products, and weak demand for their off-farm labor because of economywide shocks. Poorer farmers tend to consider weather-related risks, yield risks, illnesses of household members, and weak demand for their off-farm labor as the main sources of their risks. More commercially oriented farmers with surplus production and cash crop incomes also consider price risks as very important. For example, a 2001 survey of coffee producers in Nicaragua showed price risk as the main source of income risk (ITF 2002a). Similarly, in the Dominican Republic, coffee-producing households consider price risks as most important, followed by illness of household members, lack of credit, and weather and disease-related risks (ITF 2002b; see Table 4.1). The results do not show any significant variation between small (under 5 ha.), medium (5–10 ha.), and large (more than 10 ha.) farmers.

Risks may be considered systematic or idiosyncratic. *Systematic risks* are these that can affect many households at the same time. For example, price shocks and weather shocks (such as droughts and floods) are systematic risks, while illness of household members and livestock problems tend to be more isolated risks and hence *idiosyncratic risks*.

One possible response at the household level is increased precautionary saving. This will lower welfare relative to a world in which there was less uncertainty, or in

---

[10] The statistic is the lowest integer n for which $-\sum_{i=1}^{n} \alpha_i \geq \rho$.

[11] Of the 112 countries analyzed, 50 exhibited reversion in two years, 16 in four years, nine in one year, and eight in three years. One country (Rwanda) showed a five-year reversion. A negative estimated value for ρ, implying no apparent reversion, prevented calculation of this statistic for 28 countries (mostly oil producers).

Table 4.1. *Risks faced by coffee-producing households in the Dominican Republic (% reporting risk as very important)*

Risks	Holding size		
	<5 ha.	5–10 ha.	>10 ha.
Weather-related yield risk	46.5	60.9	49.1
Disease-related yield risk	64.1	67.1	62.5
Price risk	73.2	82.9	81.2
Yield risk in other crops	35.2	46.3	35.7
Loss of employment	30.3	28.1	33.9
Illness	56.3	70.7	60.7
Lack of credit	64.1	78.1	72.3

Source: ITF (2002b).

which credit were more freely available, since households will be required to devote too high a proportion of their income to savings. However, the impact on growth and poverty will be more complicated. Inferences on the direction of change will likely depend on the assumptions made.

Under risk neutrality, the predicted link between uncertainty and investment follows from convexity of the profit function (Hartman 1972). This is a direct implication of the Oi (1961) result that risk-neutral producers benefit from price variability to the extent that they can substitute effort and resources from periods of low prices to periods of high prices. It is more natural to suppose that uncertainty discourages investment. This can be the case either if the profit function becomes nonconvex because of imperfect competition or decreasing returns to scale (Caballero 1991), or because of producer risk aversion (Zeira 1987). Empirically, using a panel of developing countries, Luis Serven (1998) found a negative relationship between private investment and uncertainty (measured from GARCH residuals) relating to inflation, the relative price of capital and labor, the real exchange rate, the terms of trade, and GDP growth.

In countries dependent on the export of tropical agricultural commodities, uncertainty is more likely to have an impact on crop choice than on the level of accumulation per se. Farmers self-insure against both price and weather risks by either diversifying across crops or by diversifying family labor inputs across agricultural and nonagricultural activities. This diversification is effective in reducing risk, but it is costly in that it prevents farmers from exploiting comparative advantage. It also inhibits the development of larger scale farming based on economies of scale and increased mechanization. Uncertainty may therefore retard economic growth by reinforcing the position of traditional agriculture (although other factors are also implicated).

Harold Alderman and Christina Paxson (1994) distinguish between risk management and risk coping. Risk management aims to reduce risk ex ante through diversification and through income skewing, which is achieved by taking low-risk activities even at the cost of low returns. Risk coping actions are those undertaken after the shock has happened, and include self-insurance arrangements and informal risk sharing. Households build up their assets during good years and deplete them during bad years. Risk coping also includes earning extra income in bad times by, for example, increasing labor supply outside the farm or by migration to urban centers or abroad.

First consider risk coping. There are several strategies that households use to cope with risks, including price risks. These include using assets, such as self-insurance through savings, asset accumulation, and accessing credit; income diversification; informal insurance arrangements; and use of formal risk sharing markets.

Angus Deaton (1992) argued that poor households are impatient and that their time preference exceeds the interest rates. Such households cannot achieve the asset accumulation level that would allow them to self-insure against severe crises. Moreover, assets are risky. Rural households have very limited options, so their asset portfolio is highly constrained. Furthermore, in bad crises all households will tend to sell assets at the same time and this will result in lower asset prices. For example, the price of livestock will decline if all farmers need to sell their livestock in response to a collapse in coffee prices. David Bevan, Paul Collier, and Jan Willem Gunning (1987, 1990) found that the price of durable goods increased during the Kenyan coffee price boom of the mid-1970s. Another issue is that assets tend to be "lumpy," making their accumulation and liquidation difficult for poorer farmers. A cow can form a sizeable component of a poor household's asset stock, for example.

Christina Paxson (1993) analyzed the savings patterns of Thai rice farmers in response to revenue variability. The study found that credit can serve as a substitute for insurance, but credit markets are imperfect and they usually imply collateralized lending, making them useful only to those households that already have assets. Furthermore, when a crisis comes, households have less access to credit. When credit is most needed, it is least available. For example, credit has virtually disappeared from the coffee sector in many Central American countries because of the collapse of coffee prices (Varangis, Hess, and Bryla 2003). Households experiencing a shock are less creditworthy.

In the terminology of Alderman and Paxson (1994), diversification is a form of household risk management. Diversification implies entering into other on-farm activities (other crops) or nonfarm activities – the income from which is little correlated with farm incomes. Thomas Reardon, Eric Crawford, and Valerie Kelly (1994) found an average share of 39 percent of income from nonfarm activities in eight West African countries. Surveys among Mexican grain smallholder farmers indicate that no more of 25 percent of their income comes from own-farm activities, while the rest comes from remittances and off-farm labor (labor in nearby farms or nearby towns).

However, correlations among income streams from different sources may be higher in crisis years than normal years as the result of spillover effects, which increase systematic risk components. In a severe economic downturn, caused for example by a collapse of commodity prices or a severe drought, the correlation between nonfarm and farm incomes may increase. Katherine Czukas, Marcel Fafchamps, and Chris Urdy (1998) find that this was the case during West African droughts. Another limitation of diversification is that entry costs associated with other crops and nonagricultural activities may be high. In the case of Ethiopia, for example, Stefan Dercon (2002) notes that lack of working capital, lack of skills, and other requirements create barriers to entry into other activities as means of diversification. Dercon also states that reducing income risk often comes at a cost because it is difficult to diversify the sources of income without reducing the level of mean income. Improved rural banking in conjunction with stable currency values could result in reduced farm-level diversification as farmers move toward intertemporal risk sharing.

Impact on Government Revenues

Many governments of commodity-exporting countries depend heavily on revenues from commodity exports. The linkage between commodity prices and government revenues can either be direct, through export taxation, or indirect, if fluctuations in commodity export revenues are transmitted to the broader economy and thence to government receipts. While uncertainty may lead governments to seek a higher or a lower level of debt ex ante, there is little evidence that this is important. Instead, governments – many of which are constrained in credit markets – are likely to find it difficult to maintain expenditure in the face of revenue shortfalls, and may also find it all too easy to invest windfall gains in political capital, rather than economic capital.

There is a widespread view that liberalization of tropical agricultural markets over the past two decades has diminished the dependency of government revenues on commodity export earnings. A major objective of the liberalization objective has been to ensure that farmers receive a higher share of world prices. Reduction in export taxation, not by itself implied by the liberalization agenda, has been an important means of achieving this end. Governments of commodity-producing countries have tended both to reduce the overall level of commodity export taxation and to move from ad valorem to fixed taxes (which are less susceptible to corruption). It is widely supposed that these changes have reduced direct dependence of government revenues on commodity export revenues, although the extent to which this is the case has not been quantified. But even if this is the case, it does not have any bearing on indirect dependence.

Following Gilbert (2003), this study looks at this issue by considering exports of a set of 21 coffee exporting countries. Coffee is the single most important tropical agricultural commodity both in terms of the value of exports and the number of producing countries. This sample includes all the important coffee-producing member countries of the International Coffee Organization (ICO) for which satisfactory national accounts data are available.[12] Figure 4.8 shows the cross-plot of the volatilities of real coffee export revenues and real government expenditure over the 1966–2000 period. The very considerable variation in revenue variability across countries indicates that the coffee price cannot be the only factor driving export variability (see Gilbert and Tabova 2004). There is a positive relationship, with a correlation coefficient of 0.35. This is marginally significant ($t = 1.67$). However,

---

[12] The two important omissions are Côte d'Ivoire, where national accounts information is inadequate, and Vietnam, which was not a member of the ICO until 2001.

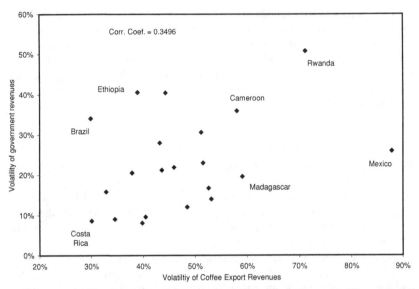

Figure 4.8. Variability of Government Revenues and Coffee Export Revenues. (*Note*: Volatilities are measured using the standard deviations of the deviations of the logarithms of the
relevant variable, deflated by the U.S. producer prices (all items) index, about a linear regression trend.) *Source*: Coffee export revenues, ICO. Export revenues and government revenues,
IMF, *International Financial Statistics*.

the Rwandan experience is particularly influential; with Rwanda omitted, the correlation drops to an insignificant 0.18. This offers weak support for the claim that
variability in commodity export revenues translates into variability of government
revenues. Despite this, the correlation pattern is broadly stable over time and the
correlation itself is higher over the second part of this period than the first (1966–85,
$r = 0.25$; 1986–2000, $r = 0.61$).

It is reasonable to suppose that the impact of variability of commodity export
revenues on government revenues will be broadly proportional to the share of the
commodity exports in overall exports. Figure 4.9, taken from Gilbert (2003), shows
the share of coffee export revenues in total export revenues for these 21 countries for the three final decades of the 20th century. In general terms, these shares
have declined. The unweighted country average over 1970–89 was approximately
30 percent, but was only 19 percent over 1990–99. This decline reflects both the
lower value of coffee exports as coffee prices have fallen, and, in many countries, increased agricultural diversification and growth in the nonagricultural sector. However, a number of the poorest coffee exporters remain highly dependent on coffee exports, notably Ethiopia, Rwanda, and Uganda in Africa, and El
Salvador, Guatemala, Honduras, and Nicaragua in Latin America. These are the
countries in which one would expect to see the greatest impact of commodity revenue
variability.

Gilbert (2003) assumes that the impact of coffee export revenues on government
revenues is proportional to the share of coffee in each country's exports, but he allows

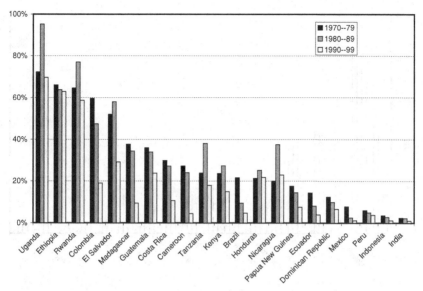

Figure 4.9. Coffee Exports as a Share of Total Exports, 1970–99. *Source*: Gilbert (2003).

the constant of proportionality to vary by continent (Central and South America, Africa, and Asia) and over time. The results are dramatic.

• The impact of coffee export revenue fluctuations is higher in African producing countries than in Latin American countries, even controlling for differences in the importance of coffee in the economy.
• These differences were exacerbated in the 1990s. The data fail to find any dependence of Latin American government revenues on coffee exports in the 1990–2000 period. By contrast, Gilbert's estimates suggest that the dependence may even have increased in African producing countries over that decade.

The hypothesis that the combination of diversification and market liberalization has reduced the dependence of governments on commodity exports over the most recent period appears valid in relation to Latin American coffee exports, but not in relation to African exports.

Gilbert (2003) uses these estimates to compute the marginal impact of changes in coffee prices and revenues on government revenue. The results for the impact of coffee prices are shown in Figure 4.10. The figure shows that, for most coffee producers, coffee price variability now translates much less into government revenues than in earlier decades. The estimated impacts are very small except in African countries where export concentration remains high. While governments in the remainder of the coffee-producing world, governments have managed to reduce their (direct and indirect) reliance on coffee, the estimates show that this reliance has increased in these countries.

Why is it that some African coffee producers have been so much less successful than the Latin American producers in insulating government revenues from variability in the coffee price? The first reason must be their failure to diversify

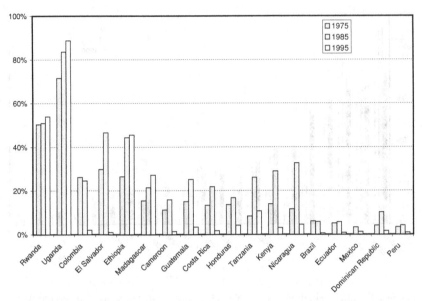

Figure 4.10. The Marginal Impact of Coffee Export Prices on Government Revenue. *Source*:
Gilbert (2003).

sources of export revenue. Where African coffee producers have diversified
(Cameroon, Kenya, Tanzania), government revenues reflect the prosperity of a
number of different industries. This can be the result of diversification into other
crops (vegetables in Kenya) or into nonagricultural activities (tourism in Kenya and
Tanzania, oil in Cameroon).

African governments may also have been less successful in diversifying their
sources of revenue, even conditional on the degree of diversification in the economy,
and may have preferred to remain reliant on taxes on exports of the traditional
commodity industries. This judgment is consistent with the regression results of this
study, which show a higher impact of fluctuations in coffee exports on government
revenues in Africa relative to Latin America, even conditioning on commodity
diversification constant.

Gilbert (2003) concludes that policy in this area should be addressed primarily to
helping the governments of this group of African countries diversify their sources or
revenue, rather than by considering the variability of commodity prices and revenues
as a problem at the macroeconomic level, at least so far as government revenues are
concerned.

Impact on Growth

Despite a substantial and mature literature, it has not been established that there
is either a quantitatively important or statistically significant link between the variability of commodity export prices and economic growth. While the argument that
volatility has reduced investment and has subsequently led to lower rates of growth

in commodity-dependent countries has been appealing, economists have found only weak empirical evidence for a direct link. Using data from Malaysian rubber plantations, an early study by Sir Sidney Caine (1954) challenged the negative link between revenue instability and investment. Alasdair MacBean (1966) also challenged the hypothesis of a negative link using cross-country data, as did Odin Knudsen and Andrew Parnes (1975).[13]

As discussed above, variability measures may conflate ex ante uncertainty (whether conditional or unconditional) with ex post realizations, and this distinction has not always been clearly drawn in the literature. If variability is interpreted as primarily an ex ante uncertainty measure, the lack of any clear result stands. This contrasts with Luis Serven's (1998) claims on the effects of volatility on investment. Extreme shocks, whether based on price changes or residuals from some regression, are unambiguously an ex post realization measure. Angus Deaton (1992) found that that, for Africa overall, periods of expansion for investment and ultimately GDP were greater during periods of increasing export prices than were the contractions during periods of falling prices. Ludger Schuknecht (1996) examined the transmission of windfalls and showed that higher revenues from windfall taxation have been associated with higher fiscal deficits, higher current expenditure, lower shares of health and education expenditures, and lower growth. Paul Collier and Jan Willem Gunning (1996) examined the impact of 19 positive shocks on annual growth rates over the period 1964–91 for a sample of developing countries. They find that initial increases in income are more than reversed in the post-shock period, so that the overall effect over several years is negative. They attribute this to a combination of low-quality public investment projects and policy-induced disincentives for private agents to lock into their saving decisions. Both these studies emphasize that revenue windfalls tend to be dissipated without major growth benefits. As noted above, the incidence of comparably large negative shocks is less acute. Perhaps for this reason, their impact has been less systematically examined.[14]

Jan Dehn (2000b) examined the importance of uncertainty, positive, and negative shocks on growth within the Burnside and Dollar (2000) growth model using a panel of 56 developing countries over the period from 1970 to 1993. Important control variables included policy quality, racial balance, and regional dummies. To abstract from short-term fluctuations, he measured growth over a succession of six 4-year periods. He confirmed the result that commodity price uncertainty is not significantly associated with economic growth. This finding holds for six different measures of commodity price uncertainty and across all sample periods and is robust with respect to the inclusion or exclusion of ex post shocks in the regression specification. He found that extreme negative shocks significantly reduce economic growth rates and that this effect persists. The coefficient on the shock variable implies that an extreme negative shock to a country's Deaton–Miller commodity price index

---

[13] Other contributions include Erb and Schiavo-Campo (1969); Glezakos (1973); Knudsen and Parnes (1975); Yotopoulos and Nugent (1976); Lutz (1994); Dawe (1996); Guillaumont and Chauvet (1998); and Guillaumont, Guillaumont-Jeanneney, and Brun (1999).

[14] Dani Rodrik (1999) compared growth rates in countries before and after the collapse in terms of trade in the mid-1970s. He found that the interaction of social conflicts and shocks with the quality of domestic institutions of conflict management determined the growth-rate response.

(that is, a shock with absolute value in the extreme 5 percent tail) would reduce growth by more than one-half percent over the long term. These results imply that pronounced negative commodity price shocks have significant growth-reducing effects. Further, and in line with the findings of Paul Collier and Jan Willem Gunning (1996), Dehn (2000b) showed that extreme positive shocks have no statistically significant effects on growth.

There must always be a concern in panel-based studies that effects attributed to variables of interest instead reflect the impact of unmeasured factors. To the extent that these unmeasured effects relate to factors that are relatively constant over time but that vary over countries, it is possible to control for this by looking at changes in growth rates over time. This study reexamined Dehn's (2000b) results using the same data, using both a 5 percent and a 10 percent cut-off to define exceptional shocks, but estimating by pooled OLS on the differenced equation. The results are reported in Table 4.2 for two definitions of extreme shocks: 5 percent (first and second columns) and 10 percent (third and fourth columns). In each case, the table reports estimates in which the coefficients on positive and negative shocks are allowed to differ (first and third columns) and estimates in which they are restricted to be equal (second and fourth columns). The Student t statistic tests the restriction. These t statistics are low and the results fail to confirm any asymmetry between the growth impact of positive and negative shocks. These results are robust to the inclusion of time dummies. Inclusion of lagged shocks provides only very weak evidence of rebound effects.[15]

The results reported above implicitly control for other growth effects by differencing, while Dehn's (2000a) results were based on a specific set of controls in a nondifferenced equation. Against that view, one can argue that differencing generates a very substantial loss of information and the tests reported in Table 4.2 are likely to have very low power. Overall, the conclusion must be that further work is required to resolve this issue before the asymmetry hypothesis can be accepted.

Overall, the outcome of the large amount of work that has been devoted to examination of the impact of commodity price variability on growth must be regarded as disappointing. There is no evidence that ex ante variability or uncertainty have any consistent growth impact. Ex post realizations do affect growth and it is clear that negative shocks result in slower growth. Further research is required on the claim that positive terms of trade shocks are dissipated without positive growth impact. If that claim cannot be sustained, one is simply left with the unexciting result that growth

---

[15] The estimated equation is

$$g_{jt} = \alpha + f_j + \beta z_{jt}^+ + \gamma z_{jt}^- + u_{jt},$$

where g_{jt} is the growth rate of country j in (four-year) time period t, z_{jt}^+ is a dummy variable which takes the value one if country j experienced a positive commodity price shock in period t, z_{jt}^- is a dummy variable which takes the value one if country j experienced a negative commodity price shock in period t, f_j is a country-specific fixed growth effect, and u_{jt} is an error term, which we take to be serially independent. The restriction tested in the final row of the equation is $\beta + \gamma = 0$. The equation standard errors reported in the table relate to the levels and not the differences in growth rates.

Table 4.2. *Estimation results*

Dependent variable growth	10% shock cut-off		5% shock cut-off	
	Unrestricted	Restricted	Unrestricted	Restricted
Constant	−0.0025	−0.0025	−0.0027	−0.0027
	(2.55)	(2.51)	(2.70)	(2.67)
Positive shocks	0.0085		0.0068	
	(2.98)	0.0075	(2.12)	0.0062
Negative shocks	−0.0060	(3.47)	−0.0051	(2.47)
	(1.55)		(0.99)	
Restriction test *t*		0.48		0.26
sigma (levels)	0.0363	0.0362	0.0364	0.0364

Note: Pooled panel regression in differences over 635 observations (95 countries with up to seven growth observations).
Source: Authors' calculations, using data from Dehn (2000a, 2000b).

is increased by favorable movements in a country's terms of trade and reduced by unfavorable movements.

A possible reaction to these results is to argue that the link between low growth and volatile commodity markets has more to do with government mismanagement than private investment. Alan Gelb and François Bourguignon (1989) provide evidence for this hypothesis from Venezuela, as has David Bevan, Paul Collier, and Jan Willem Gunning (1990) for Nigeria and Indonesia. Dani Rodrik (1999) argues that the link between short-term economic shocks and growth was determined by the capacity of governments to manage the political conflict engendered by extreme price shocks. If this view is correct, commodity price volatility, including extreme realizations, should be seen as providing opportunities for producing countries, as well as generating problems that they need to overcome.

The Exchange Rate

An important route by which commodity prices can affect economic activity is through the exchange rate. Paul Cashin, Luis Céspendes, and Ratna Sahay (2003, 2004) have documented the relationship between Deaton–Miller commodity price indices and the real exchange rate for 58 commodity-dependent countries, of which 53 are in the developing world. Granger-causality tests clearly show that causation runs from commodity price movements to the real exchange rate. They find that for 22 of these countries, over 80 percent of real exchange rate movement is explained by movements in the prices of their commodity exports. However, the extent to which the real exchange rate responds to commodity prices and the channels through which this happens depend both on the exchange rate regime and institutions and on monetary and exchange rate policies.

One may think of a primary commodity exporting country as producing three goods: primary products for export, other exports (such as manufactures and tourism), and nontraded goods. This study assumes that the country is a price taker

160   *Jan Dehn, Christopher L. Gilbert, and Panos Varangis*

in all traded goods markets. Initially suppose a floating exchange rate. The rise
in dollar export values will immediately generate a nominal appreciation, reducing
the domestic price of imported goods and of nonprimary exports. The dollar cost of
the domestic consumption basket falls. The real exchange rate may be defined as the
dollar price of domestic consumption relative to the dollar price of an international
basket. The decline in the real exchange rate, which follows from the reduced cost
of the domestic basket, amounts to a real appreciation.

One of the most important consequences of the rise in the commodity export
price in a floating rate regime is the effect of the nominal appreciation on noncommodity exports. Profitability in this sector will decline and resources will move into
commodity exports and into the production of nontraded goods. This phenomenon,
in which the booming primary sector crowds out the production of other traded
goods, is known as Dutch Disease.[16]

Turning to the polar opposite case of fixed rates, a rise in the price of the export
commodity will lead to a rise in the price of nontraded goods as marginal products
are equalized across the three sectors (Cashin, Céspendes, and Sahay 2004). This
will be reinforced by income effects, assuming that both the nontraded and import
goods are normal in the sense of having positive income elasticities of demand.
The result is to generalize the benefits from the higher commodity price across the
economy. The real exchange rate will decline, corresponding to a real appreciation.[17]

Although price changes within the producing economy generalize the impact of
the higher commodity price across the economy under both fixed and floating and
regimes, these redistributional effects will typically be both larger and more rapid
in the case of floating rates. Fixed rates will concentrate the benefit of the higher
commodity price on the producers. The major difference in the floating rate case
is that there are losers (producers of nonprimary exports and rural consumers with
low "tastes" for imported goods) as well as beneficiaries (producers of the primary
commodity and urban consumers with high "tastes" for imported goods). Dutch
Disease symptoms will be apparent in both cases. In the case of fixed rates, these
will manifest themselves only through higher labor costs, whereas under floating
rates, producers of nonprimary exports will also experience lower prices in terms
of the domestic currency. Does this imply that a flexible exchange rate exacerbates
the macroeconomic instability caused by commodity price variability? The answer
must depend on the extent of the exchange rate response and on the capacity of the
commodity-producing and exporting sectors to absorb revenue fluctuations relative
to the remainder of the economy. Normally, some degree of risk-sharing is regarded

[16] See Corden (1984) for a survey; Edwards (1984) and Killick (1984) for discussions of coffee in
Colombia and Kenya; and Scherr (1989) for the impact of an oil export boom on agriculture in
Indonesia, Mexico, and Nigeria.
[17] Under fixed rates, a positive commodity price shock will result in a current surplus. If not sterilized
(and this must be the appropriate assumption for a developing economy), the surplus will lead to an
increase in the money supply and hence, over time, inflation. A negative shock will have the reverse
effect. The inflationary processes will produce a rise in the price of nontraded relative to traded goods.
Eventually, the current surplus will be eliminated. Provided that transitional asset accumulation and
decumulation effects are insufficient to generate path dependence, the real exchange rate will be the
same as that which would have resulted under the floating regime. In practice, inflation is more likely
to result from a negative commodity price shock than a positive shock.

Table 4.3. *West African inflation inside and outside the CFA zone*

Period	Average rate of inflation			Inflation standard deviation		
	CFA zone	Non-CFA	Equality test t_9	CFA zone	Non-CFA	Equality test $F_{3,6}$
1970–99	6.6%	22.5%	1.27	15.2%	28.4%	3.50*
1970–79	8.9%	16.0%	0.62	15.7%	22.8%	2.11
1980–89	5.5%	30.1%	2.03**	13.1%	30.3%	5.37**
1990–99	4.5%	21.4%	1.42*	15.1%	25.6%	2.86

Note: The table compares average quarterly CPI inflation rates (at an annual rate) for CFA and non-CFA countries, and the standard deviations of these rates. The variance equality test is the ratio of the non-CFA to CFA variances, scaled in each case by the number of degrees of freedom. The *t* test is the standard equality of means test assuming a common variance. In each case, a single asterisk indicates rejection at the 10 percent-level, and a double asterisk rejection at the 5 percent-level.
CFA zone countries: Burkina Faso, Cameroon, Côte d'Ivoire, Gabon, Niger, Senegal, Togo.
Non-CFA countries: Gambia, Ghana, Nigeria, Sierra Leone. Other West African countries were omitted because of insufficient data.
Source: Authors' calculations, using data from IMF, *International Financial Statistics* (cd-rom).

as welfare-improving, and exchange rate variability may be seen as ameliorating rather than exacerbating instability.

There must be a particular concern that the combination of a floating exchange regime with volatile commodity export prices will result in either higher or more variable inflation, or both. Inflation that is on average higher than under a fixed rate regime could result if those groups that lose from exchange depreciation are able to exert pressure on government or the central bank to protect them from adverse changes. Greater inflation variability is to be expected as shocks to commodity export prices are translated by the floating rate to the prices of nontraded goods.

These hypotheses are difficult to test because inflation has multiple causes. The movable peg system operated by the CFA franc zone allows comparison across a number of otherwise quite similar West African economies. This study compares quarterly inflation rates inside and outside the CFA franc zone in the 11 commodity-dependent West African economies for which sufficient data are available. Results are given in Table 4.3. The table confirms that CFA inflation has been consistently below non-CFA inflation throughout the 1970–99 period, and has also been less variable. However, because of paucity of degrees of freedom, these differences are not statistically significant, with the exception of the 1980s. Despite this lack of overall significance, the results lend support to the view that the CFA arrangements have contained the macroeconomic effects of commodity price variability in the participating countries.[18]

[18] The CFA franc is fixed against the euro, and prior to the advent of the euro was fixed against the French franc. There was a major devaluation in 1994. Using a sample of countries covering the whole of Africa, this study also examined whether the level of inflation and/or its variability was related to commodity concentration, measured as a Herfindahl index. Although there was no apparent relationship for average inflation, there was a weak and statistically insignificant positive association between inflation variability and commodity concentration.

POLICY TOWARD COMMODITY PRICE VARIABILITY

The Welfare Economics of Commodity Price Variability[19]

Commodity price variability imposes welfare costs, but also generates possible welfare-increasing possibilities. This was first established by Friedrich Waugh (1944), who showed that shocks to agricultural supply generate a potential benefit to consumers who can consume more at low prices and less at high prices. Walter Oi (1961) showed the analogous result for producers when the source of price variability shocks is shifts in demand. These effects were synthesized by Benton Massell (1969): producers gain and consumers lose from price stabilization if the source of instability lies on the supply side, while consumers gain and producers lose from price stabilization if the source of instability lies on the demand side. In both cases, gainers could afford to overcompensate the losers, so there are net benefits from price stabilization if this could be costlessly achieved. In that sense, commodity price variability is an economic bad. David Newbery and Joseph Stiglitz (1981), and later Ravi Kanbur (1984), reinforced this conclusion by including risk aversion.

The Massell–Newbery–Stiglitz framework is ultimately unhelpful since there is clearly no costless means of stabilizing prices. Any useful analysis must therefore balance benefits against stabilization costs. Consider buffer stock schemes. Mario Miranda and Peter Helmberger (1988) have shown that public stockholding changes the incentives for the private sector to hold stocks. If such an agency is credibly committed to preventing prices from falling beneath a specified floor, the private sector will focus on the expected rise in price, given that the price distribution is truncated at the floor price. If the excess supply at the stabilization floor price is sufficiently large, the public sector will end up holding this excess supply in its entirety. This was the situation under the sixth International Tin Agreement, which collapsed in 1985 (see Anderson and Gilbert 1988). Floor provisions of this type make buffer stock stabilization extremely expensive.

Comparable problems arise if a buffer stock attempts to defend a fixed ceiling price. To the extent that this commitment is credible, it will reduce the incentive for the private sector to hold stocks by truncating the price distribution at the ceiling price. However, once the commitment ceases to be credible, typically because the agency's stocks are insufficient, the private sector will wish to buy the entirety of the agency's remaining stock. This discontinuity in the private sector's desired inventory as a function of market excess demand gives rise to the phenomenon of "speculative attack" (see Salant 1983). Recognizing this, Brian Wright and Jeffrey Williams (1991) suggested that a stabilization agency should not commit to a ceiling, but should operate a quantity-based rule along the lines set out by Robert Gustafson (1958) and put the whole of their accumulated inventory on the market in every period. Nevertheless, this would still involve public sector stockholding displacing private sector stocks, with the implication that the stabilization objective would be less expensively satisfied by an interest rate subsidy for private storage.

Some economists also argued that the benefits of stabilization were overstated. Milton Friedman (1954) stressed the importance of private savings rather than public

---

[19] The next three sections draw on the discussion in Anderson, Larson, and Varangis (2002).

stabilization schemes in solving the "producer income problem." David Newbery and Joseph Stiglitz (1981) argued that Benton Massell's (1969) findings exaggerated the benefits of stabilization. An important and frequent finding is that the welfare gains that are possible from price stabilization are relatively small.[20] Similarly, John McIntire and Panos Varangis (1999) find that cocoa farmers in the Côte d'Ivoire paid too much for the price stabilization generated by the caisse de stabilisation (stabilization authority). Moreover, the practical implementation of stabilization schemes raises many thorny problems to be overcome by program administrators (Scandizzo, Hazell, and Anderson 1981). These include assessing the supply responsiveness to induced stability, the size of which is difficult to estimate (see Just 1975; Griffiths and Anderson 1978).

Evidence also mounted that many of the interventions, put in place in part to facilitate growth, had instead become an impediment to growth. This was due in part to the fact that stabilization policies limited competition and misdirected resources; it was also due to the inconsistent policy objectives of many developing countries. In many instances, the same governments that sought to protect producers from the negative consequences of volatile commodity markets also taxed their producers directly or indirectly to spur industrialization and favor urban interests. Influential studies by Yair Mundlak, Domingo Cavallo, and Roberto Domenech (1989) and Anne Krueger, Maurice Schiff, and Alberto Valdés (1992) documented the negative consequences of these policies and recommended sweeping reforms, many of which have been implemented.

The Stabilization Agenda

The variability of agricultural prices induced both developed and developing country governments to seek to prevent or offset these movements throughout the 20th century. This process accelerated at the close of World War II as countries attempted to avoid what was seen as a likely relapse into the depressed conditions of the 1930s. In the 1950s and 1960s, newly independent former colonies inherited the control arrangements established by the colonial powers. In Latin America, control arrangements were homegrown.[21] This was an age of fixed exchange rates, and central banks were often motivated to manage shocks in export earnings as part of the business of exchange rate management. At Bretton Woods, John Maynard Keynes (1943) had proposed a world currency based on a price index of the 30 most-traded commodities. By linking currencies to the index, commodity prices and price-related swings in trade earnings would have been stabilized in an automatic fashion. While Keynes's ideas were not incorporated into the charters of the Bretton Woods institutions founded at that time, an alternative approach to link lending with commodity volatility emerged. A succession of proposed internationally backed compensatory financing schemes followed the Bretton Woods conference, including the 1953 Olano proposal for a mutual insurance scheme, the 1961 Development

---

[20] See, for example, Scandizzo, Hazell, and Anderson (1981); Myers and Oehmke (1988); Wright (1988); and Kannapiran (2000).

[21] These developments are discussed in the context of coffee, cocoa, cotton, sugar and grains in Akiyama, Baffes, Larson, and Varangis (2001).

Insurance Fund, the 1962 Organization of American States proposal, the Swedish and Brazilian proposals at the Committee for International Commodity Trade meetings, and the French proposal for market organizations, all in 1963.

Also in 1963, the IMF began to offer compensatory financing to countries experiencing an unexpected temporary decline in export earnings. The ongoing program is based on net export earnings, rather than a single set of commodities, thus taking advantage of any natural portfolio effect that might arise from diversified exports and imports. With modifications, this program remains the primary instrument among the Bretton Woods institutions for handling the effects of volatile commodity trade, although in practice it has not been used very widely. Later, as part of the first Lomé Agreement in 1975, the European Union (EU) offered its own compensatory financing schemes, STABEX and SYSMIN, to African, Caribbean, and Pacific (ACP) countries. These were terminated in February 2000 when the Lomé IV EU-ACP treaty was replaced by the Cotonou Treaty. (The complicated FLEX export compensation provisions in the Cotonou Treaty are currently under review.)

By the 1980s unilateral and multilateral interventions in agricultural commodity markets had therefore become the norm. International commodity organizations employed buffer stocks or managed trade with the intention of bringing order to volatile commodity markets. The United States used support prices and inventories to manage domestic prices. The EU had a similar scheme, but also operated a special set of commodity-specific exchange rates ("green rates") for trade among EU members. Marketing boards and stabilization funds were common in both developed and developing countries, including those for cocoa in Côte d'Ivoire, coffee in Uganda, and wool in Australia.

Interventions could be either through multilateral means or through domestic agencies. International commodity agreements, which acted to stabilize prices through export controls and buffer stock interventions, were successively established for tin, sugar, coffee, cocoa, and natural rubber. Such agreements have been characterized as internationally sanctioned cartels by Alton Law (1975). Consumer country participation allowed consumer governments to moderate the potential monopoly power that a producer cartel might exercise. At the same time, producers gained from the legitimacy bestowed by the inter governmental treaty structure (Gilbert 2004).

In 1968, UNCTAD put forward a proposal that ultimately resulted in a 1975 resolution calling for an Integrated Program for Commodities (IPC), covering 10 core commodities (see UNCTAD 1976). If this endeavor had been successful, it would have made control the norm for the international trade in primary commodities. In conjunction with this development, the IMF established its Buffer Stock Financing Facility in 1969. However, the natural rubber agreement was the only new scheme to emerge from the IPC. In addition, and after long and labored negotiations (see Brown 1980), the Common Fund for Commodities (CFC) was established as an independent member of the United Nations family of organizations to provide liquidity for buffer stocks set up under the integrated program.

In parallel, governments operated domestic stabilization programs. The then-prevailing approaches included buffer stock schemes (for Bangladesh, India, Indonesia, Mexico, the Philippines, and South Korea); buffer funds (for Côte d'Ivoire, Papua New Guinea, and South Korea); marketing boards with monopolies on trade (for most of Africa, Ecuador, India, and Malaysia); and variable tariff schemes (for Chile, Malaysia, and Venezuela) (see Knudsen and Nash 1990).

It would be incorrect to state that the commodity price stabilization agenda was always and everywhere a failure (see Gilbert 1987, 1996). A number of important schemes worked successfully for considerable periods of time, most notably the International Coffee Agreement and (until around 1980) the International Tin Agreement. Marketing board and caisse schemes for the stabilization of the domestic prices of tropical export crop prices also generally functioned well until the 1980s. The difficulties faces by these schemes became exacerbated during the 1980s for a combination of reasons:

- High commodity prices in the mid- and late 1970s, combined with "Limits to Growth" concerns that primary prices would rise inexorably, resulted in a situation in which producers became overoptimistic about the prices they could obtain.
- This overoptimism was underwritten by a perhaps deliberate confusion in the UNCTAD IPC between the objective of price stabilization and that of obtaining higher ("remunerative") prices for producers.
- The inefficiency costs associated with controls became higher over time. In coffee, high prices induced expansion of area in a number of countries (mainly in Africa) with relatively high production costs, while quota restrictions held down production in lower-cost origins such as Brazil. Bureaucracies, such as the Instiuto Brasiliero do Café in Brazil and Cocobod in Ghana, multiplied in size and absorbed much of the benefit of higher prices, and other forms of rent extraction became established (see Bohman, Jarvis, and Barichello 1996).

The consequence was that, as commodity prices fell through the mid-1980s, almost all previously successful intervention schemes succumbed to financial difficulties. The international commodity agreements were unable to adapt to changes in the market, and by 1996 the economic clauses in them had all lapsed or failed, victims of politics and economics (Gilbert 1987, 1996). During the 1980s, the existing international commodity agreements either collapsed, as in the case of the International Tin Agreement in 1985, or lapsed – that is, their intervention clauses were dropped, as in the case of the International Coffee Agreement in 1989 – or became inactive, as with International Cocoa Agreement. The longest lasting scheme was the International Natural Rubber Agreement, suspended in 1999. As a direct consequence, there has never been any call on the IMF or CFC buffer stock facilities to be used for their intended purpose. The IMF eliminated its Buffer Stock Financing Facility in 2000 and the CFC now operates entirely in terms of its "second window," originally considered as supplementary, for project finance in the commodity industries.

The operation of these multilateral stabilization programs is reviewed by Christopher Gilbert (1987, 1996), who concluded that the cocoa and sugar agreements were completely ineffective at either stabilizing or raising prices and the natural rubber agreement generated a modest degree of stabilization. The tin agreements (prior to 1980) and the côffee agreement generated significant stabilization but, in the case of coffee, also raised prices substantially above competitive levels. Coffee was therefore the major and important success story (for a detailed assessment, see Palm and Vogelvang 1991). Even in coffee, taxation and rent extraction implied that farmers were not always major beneficiaries (see Bohman, Jarvis, and Barichello 1996). However, coffee price volatility was lower and coffee-producing countries, taken as a group, were better off under the coffee agreements than after the lapse of its economic clauses.

Domestic stabilization programs were subject to similar problems. Peter Bauer and Frank Paish (1952) noted that the stabilization objectives of most colonial marketing boards were ill-defined and were potentially a guise for taxation. John Quiggin and Jock Anderson (1979, 1981) discussed the limits of price bands and buffer funds. Brian Wright and Jeffrey Williams (1991) noted the widespread failure of domestic stabilization schemes of all sorts and linked the failure to the nature of commodity prices and underlying models of storage. However, the crucial problem, as with the international schemes, was overoptimistic price expectations. Many of these schemes became insolvent in the latter part of the 1980s (see Gilbert 1997; Varangis and Schreiber 2001).

The Move to a Market Approach

As the deteriorating performance of stabilization schemes became more evident, emphasis shifted toward policies that worked within markets, taking market prices as a given, rather than against markets, by attempting to alter prices away from those generated by the market. Ronald McKinnon (1967) explored the use of futures markets as an alternative to buffer stocks. Later, Christopher Gilbert (1985) demonstrated that, in specified circumstances, hedging on forward markets could substitute for some of the welfare gains normally associated with buffer stocks. Gordon Gemmill (1985) argued that futures markets for cocoa, coffee, and sugar would provide an attractive mechanism for hedging export-earnings risks and that forward contracts could be substantially cheaper than buffer-stock operations. Maureen O'Hara (1984) looked at the use of commodity bonds to stabilize consumption. Jacques Rolfo (1980) investigated the use of futures for cocoa producer prices and calculated the optimal hedge ratio in the presence of both production (output) and price volatility. James Overdahl (1987) demonstrated the benefits of oil futures markets for oil-producing states. Robert Myers and Stanley Thompson (1991) provided a model of external debt management that included commodity-linked bonds, and Stijn Claessens (1991) pointed out that commodity bonds can be used to hedge debt-management problems associated with volatile export earnings. Brian Wright and David Newbery (1991) proposed commodity-linked financial instruments to smooth commodity export revenue. Jock Anderson, Donald Larson, and Panos Varangis (2002) looked at the role of partial guarantees and commodity contingency. Stijn Claessens and Ronald Duncan (1993) showed how markets could be used to achieve many of the sectoral stabilization objectives of many existing programs in a sustainable way. Market-based methods were offered as an alternative to unsound price stabilization programs in Costa Rica, Papua New Guinea, and Venezuela.

In the 1980s and 1990s, a pervasive series of reforms aimed at market liberalization was launched, undertaken in part at the urging of multilateral lenders such as the European Union, USAID, and the World Bank. Takamasa Akiyama, John Baffes, Donald Larson, and Panos Varnagis (2001) illustrate the rapid pace of these reforms for Africa. While the reforms swept away many of the ineffective institutions that were mandated to stabilize domestic markets, the reforms did not, nor were the reforms designed to, address two key remaining problems related to commodity risks: the inability of some governments to prudently manage revenue and expenditures that are volatile; and the high cost paid by vulnerable rural households, often in terms of forgone productivity, to limit the consequences of risks. These developments focused attention back onto household strategies for coping with commodity price risk.

A second evolution was to distinguish more clearly than previously between the macroeconomic consequences of commodity price variability, and policies that should address those, and the impact of volatility on individual producer households, and policies aimed at ameliorating their position. This latter distinction arose because it was no longer possible to suppose that governments would always transmit stabilization benefits through to farmers. For example, whether correctly or not, the EU's Stabex compensatory finance was widely perceived in producing countries as providing general budgetary support to government with little impact in the producing areas. In the context of the increased priority for poverty alleviation in the national and multilateral development agenda, policymakers looked for strategies that would impact farmers directly, rather than through governments. The next section looks at macroeconomic policy developments and the section after that examines farm-level initiatives.

Macroeconomic Policy Developments

While many developing countries that were previously dependent on commodity exports have been successful in diversifying their economies and are therefore less sensitive to economy-wide commodity shocks, a number of poor developing countries, mainly in the Africa region, still remain very dependent on a few commodities. These are the countries in which commodity price volatility is likely to throw up the most acute problems.

The major difficulty in addressing macroeconomic policy issues arising out of commodity price volatility is the lack of clear evidence that volatility generally does have adverse long-term consequences, in particular for growth rates. The implication is that some, perhaps even most, primary exporting countries appear to be managing to accommodate price volatility. If that is the case, policy should be addressed toward bringing the remaining countries up to best practice standards rather than attempting to devise new initiatives. There are two specific areas of concern: government revenues and the exchange rate.

The government fiscal position was discussed earlier, where it was noted that most governments of primary producing countries have managed to diversify their tax bases away from the primary sector, even where export concentration remains high. However, a number of governments, mainly in Africa, have failed to make progress in this respect. These governments will continue to find that their ability to fund necessary public expenditure will be restricted in periods in which their export prices are low, unless countercyclical budgetary assistance is forthcoming in a timely manner. One possibility would be for these governments to hedge their revenue positions on the financial markets. There may be merit in exploring this possibility in cases in which there is a liquid futures market in the export commodity and where the government's credit rating will sustain such transactions. However, a more reliable and less dangerous long-term alternative is for government to diversify its tax base away from the traditional primary sector. The authors of this study believe that national and multilateral development agencies should offer greater assistance in this process.

Like other economic agents, governments are well advised to save a large part of windfall revenues when prices are high so that these become available when revenues decline due to prices declines. Reliance on foreign capital markets to borrow when prices and revenues decline may not be an option. Most poorer commodity-dependent countries have little or no access to international lenders, particularly when they need them most: that is, when prices have declined. As noted above, contingent borrowing facilities such as from the IMF and EU have had their problems and they are either under review (IMF) or have been abolished (EU). A standard way to formalize governmental saving is to create a stabilization fund to stabilize government expenditures but not to support or stabilize commodity prices. Such funds tend to be used in relation to oil and metals revenues, where governments capture significant royalty payments (see Devlin and Lewin 2004). Examples are the Norwegian and Oman oil funds and the Chilean copper stabilization fund. The same principle could be applied tax revenues from agricultural export commodities. However, funds can often run into problems because of difficulties in distinguishing between transient and permanent price changes (see section "Trend and Cycle" above) and because of the potential for mismanagement of fund resources.

The second area of governmental concern is the exchange rate. Earlier, this study noted that commodity price variability can translate into variability of the real exchange rate and of inflation, generalizing the initial volatile process across the entire economy. This generalization process may be desirable in part as the burden of adjustment is spread across a larger number of economic agents, each of whom may thus be expected to incur lower proportionate costs. Dutch Disease is problematic because the costs imposed on the nonboom sector can be disproportionately high, perhaps because of higher labor intensity (consider an oil boom) or because of hysteresis effects which imply that, once retired, physical and human capital is lost permanently. For these reasons, governments will look to contain the effects of commodity price volatility from affecting the exchange rate.

Three strategies are available. First, maintenance of a fixed exchange rate insulates the nonboom traded sector until such time as the trade surplus feeds through into inflation. This may take sufficiently long that the commodity price will have fallen. This will either reduce the need for adjustment or, at worst, spread it over time, which will result in lower overall costs under the standard assumption of convexity. However, avoidance of Dutch Disease is only one of many considerations in the decision on the choice of exchange regime, which will also need to take into account issues of feasibility. A more reasonable position is to argue on sequencing grounds that a move away from a fixed rate to follow rather than precede the development of dependable independent central banking.[22]

---

[22] An alternative proposal, which goes to the other extreme, is that commodity-dependent countries should tie their exchange rates to the prices of a basket of export goods. In the case that a country

Second, regional currency zones, such as the West African CFA zone, are an intermediate position between fixed and floating rates. The consequence of pooling within a regional currency bloc is that, provided there is no a dominant member, the bloc commodity concentration will be lower than that of individual member countries and hence Dutch Disease effects will be proportionately lower. This is an effective means of spreading adjustment. It is likely that such a move will increase central bank independence. The cost is that monetary policy will be less well adapted to the individual circumstances of particular member countries. The CFA experience is complicated by the fact that this pooling took place in a system that also pegged the nominal rate. Despite these concerns, the generally favorable CFA experience in relation to inflation suggests that regional currency zones have the potential to offer a degree of insurance against the macroeconomic effects of commodity price variability to other groups of commodity dependent countries, such as those in East Africa.

The third approach is to sterilize windfall earnings through purchase of overseas assets. One possibility is for government to issue foreign currency-denominated bonds. For example, in Colombia during the coffee boom of the 1980s, the central bank issued "coffee bonds" to exporters in exchange for foreign currency earned from exports. However, given liquid capital markets, the holders of such debt can borrow against these bonds to obtain domestic currency, desterilizing the surplus.

If government operates a commodity stabilization fund, it is desirable that the fund be invested overseas. In this way, the current account surplus resulting from high export prices will be offset by capital outflows, thus reducing the required exchange rate appreciation. Conversely, capital inflows will offset the extent of exchange rate depreciation required in periods of low prices in which the fund is drawn down. This potential of a stabilization fund to offset Dutch Disease is a further powerful argument for its adoption. Despite this logic, it may be politically difficult to persuade voters in countries with low capital stocks that the nation's resources are best invested overseas. Governments will often require assistance in educating their citizens in relation to the distinction between resources devoted to stabilization and insurance, which should be insulated from shocks to the domestic economy, and resources to devoted to capital investment, which cannot escape country-specific risk.

Farm-Level Strategies to Reduce Risk Impact

Diversification is the most easily available do-it-yourself insurance policy at the household level. The challenges and preconditions for successful diversification programs to farm and nonfarm activities have been thoroughly investigated (see, for example, Jaffee 1993; Barghouti, Timmer, and Siegel 1990). Poor households are inhibited from entering into riskier higher return activities because the downside risks are simply too great in the event of a crisis. Richer households can borrow

produces a single export commodity, the local currency price of this product would be completely stabilized – but at the expense of forcing the entire adjustment on the remainder of the economy, in particularly on imports. That cannot be sensible, and an intermediate risk-sharing solution must be preferable.

more easily in such periods because they have assets that are available as collateral. If credit is not available, they can smooth their income by selling assets. In contrast, poorer households need to adopt low-risk, low-return strategies. As Stefan Dercon (2002) argues, these results do not follow from differences in risk preferences but reflect the constraints on the risk management and risk-coping strategies that poorer households face. Relaxation of these constraints should make diversification less attractive.

Households also make use of various informal risk-sharing arrangements, usually involving systems of mutual assistance between family networks or within members of a community. Most studies find evidence of partial risk sharing.[23] Poorer households have fewer contacts on which to rely in cases of shocks. Sustainability is also a problem because of the lack of consistent enforcement. Furthermore, systematic shocks, such as price and weather shocks, can cause a breakdown of these arrangements by exposing entire groups of households to the same risk. Informal risk-sharing arrangements are thus important in helping poor households cope with idiosyncratic risks but not with systematic risks.

The literature has argued that public safety nets could be developed to cope with systematic risks and other idiosyncratic risks not covered by informal arrangements (Dercon 2002). At the same time, the literature has highlighted the problem that public transfers might crowd out informal arrangements. This is because public safety nets do not provide full protection to all affected households. Thus, public transfers could change the circumstances and may put pressure on informal arrangements. Some households covered by public safety nets may find incentives to leave informal arrangements, leaving other households less protected in times of crisis. The same could happen if some households within an informal risk-sharing network have access to a new source of risk protection, like a new insurance scheme. Stefan Dercon (2002) argues that one way to reduce this problem is to target groups rather than individuals. This requires information about preexisting informal arrangements. It also requires that communities be encouraged to develop group-based self-insurance schemes, perhaps through the provision of insurance as part of a group-based credit program.

On the specific issue of price risk, public safety nets are little in evidence. Most governments have responded to commodity price crises by using price stabilization mechanisms that have often been short-lived and have failed through lack of resources in the face of prolonged price declines. More recently, some Latin American coffee-producing countries in response to a severe price shock, have provided fixed payments to their coffee farmers per hectare, and in some cases, per kilo. Some of these schemes have targeted smallholder farmers, but most such schemes have been universal (Varangis, Hess, and Bryla 2003).

In addition to informal risk-sharing arrangements, there are markets that allow economic agents to share risks. Formal markets for price risks include forward markets, futures and options markets, and over-the-counter markets. (For weather-related risks, there are insurance markets and weather-risk markets. For illnesses, there is health insurance. For livestock, there are livestock insurance products). The advantage of these formal markets is that they externalize the risk outside the

---

[23] See Coate and Ravallion (1993); Udry (1994); Platteau (1997); and Dercon (2002).

community and even outside the overall economy. However, there are a number of preconditions and issues for producers in developing countries to access these markets.

Formal risk markets have the potential to strengthen and complement existing risk-sharing arrangements within a group of farmers or a community. For example, formal risk management contracts can protect the group against systematic risks, leaving the redistribution of the proceeds or payments to the group in the event of an actual crisis. This principle can be applied to both price hedging (to protect the group against price shocks) and also weather risk markets (to protect against droughts and other negative weather shocks). While not directly related to commodity price risk management, there is evidence pointing to the ability of informal groups to reach many households in periods of crises. Ethan Ligon, Jonathan Thomas, and Tim Worrall (2002) argue that targeting the needy is very difficult. However, given informal risk-sharing arrangements, it is possible that poorly targeted transfers may be redistributed within the risk-sharing group. Stefan Dercon and Pramila Krishnan (2000) present evidence from Ethiopia, where food aid, although poorly targeted, nevertheless reached many poor households. This suggests that price risk management instruments (and also weather insurance) have the potential to be a useful tool to microfinance institutions, mutual farmer insurance groups, and group-based savings groups. However, there may be unintended adverse impacts on households not covered under the risk-hedging program (Dercon 2002).

While market-based tools that insure against price volatility, such as those based on futures and options, already exist and are widely used in high-income countries, the vast majority of agricultural producers in developing countries are unable to access these markets. This is because:

- The minimum size of contracts traded on organized exchanges far exceeds the annual quantity of production of individual small and medium-sized producers.
- Small producers, as well as many market intermediaries in developing countries, lack knowledge of such market-based price insurance instruments and an understanding of how to use them.
- Sellers of such instruments, generally international banks and brokerage houses, are often unwilling to engage with a new and unfamiliar customer base of small-scale producers, characterized by high transaction costs (often increased by regulatory concerns directed at money laundering), diminished access to credit, and performance risk.

For the most part, use of forward, futures, and options contracts in developing countries is confined to large (private or public) organizations and firms, and also some large farmers in countries where these are present. With respect to exportable commodities, such as coffee, cocoa, and sugar, price hedges are undertaken at the point of export. This cover seldom extends back to intermediaries and almost never to smallholder farmers.

It is often argued that the bottom line in any market-based approach to commodity risk management must be the willingness of farmers to pay for the insurance provided. A survey to evaluate the willingness of Nicaraguan coffee farmers to pay for price insurance provided through put options was undertaken by the World Bank in September 2001 (ITF 2002a). The main results are shown in Table 4.4. The table

Table 4.4. *Proportion of Nicaraguan coffee farm households willing to pay to insure $50, September 2001*

Premium level	$5.00	$4.00	$3.00	$2.00	$1.00	No interest
Premium as a percentage of the insured level	10%	8.0%	6.0%	4.0%	2.0%	–
Percent willing to pay	16.7%	11.4%	22.0%	12.9%	12.9%	24.1%
Cumulative percent	16.7%	28.1%	50.1%	63.0%	75.9%	100%

Source: Authors' calculations, based on ITF (2002a).

defines the (subjective) demand curve for price insurance. On September 25, 2001, a 100 lb. put option with March 2002 expiration and strike price of 50 cents/lb. (that is, $50 per option contract) would have cost $3.85, or 7.7 percent of the exercise price. Interpolating from Table 4.4, 31 percent of households would have been willing to pay this premium. As always, one needs to read survey data or this sort with the qualification that stated intentions may not correspond to actual behavior.

Despite this, attempts to retail price insurance directly to farmers have met with little success. As already noted, villages or wider communities tend to self-insure, albeit on an informal basis, and hence individual farmers will tend to purchase suboptimal levels of market insurance, since they will bear the entire cost of such purchases but only partially share in the benefits. Reported valuations may therefore exaggerate willingness to pay. Greater success has been achieved in the intermediation of price risk management to cooperatives and to the local banks which lend both to these cooperatives and also to private sector operators. These activities have the objective of ensuring the continued financial viability of the commodity sector operators and their bankers in the face of adverse commodity price movements. The benefits to the farmers themselves are indirect – financial security and access to credit will ensure an efficient intermediation structure with lower intermediation costs, and hence higher producer prices, than would otherwise have been the case. Farmers benefit from the results of improved risk management at the sectoral level but are not directly assisted in managing their own risk.

The development literature points to the following overall conclusions:

- There is a need for analysis of the price shocks experienced by households and the ways that they currently cope with these shocks. Such work is rarely done in either country-economic or sector-specific economic work and projects.
- Public safety nets can be useful, but crowding out of informal and formal risk management and risk-coping arrangements should be a concern. Thus information about both formal and informal arrangements should be taken into consideration before designing a public safety net. Furthermore, in the case of severe shocks such as price and weather shocks, public safety nets for poorer households could include work programs but also direct income transfers during the period of shock.
- Strengthening group self-insurance, through group-based savings and mutual insurance schemes, for example, is an alternative. However, these schemes could run into problems in the face of large systemic shock, such as in the case of a collapse of commodity prices or a severe drought.

- The market-based approach to commodity risk management may turn out to be more productive for intermediaries (banks, cooperatives, etc.) than for farmers themselves, who will only benefit indirectly from more efficient and hence lower cost intermediation.

The International Task Force on Commodity Risk Management

In 1999, the World Bank – with support from several donor governments, and in collaboration with other international organizations and private sector representatives – initiated a project to make price risk-management instruments available to farmers, particularly smallholder farmers, through cooperatives, producer organizations, banks and other rural financial institutions, and traders. The project provides technical assistance, capacity building, and training to producer organizations and local financial institutions to assist them in purchasing price risk-management instruments from private sector providers. This market-oriented approach provides the growers, producer organizations, and local financiers with the ability to hedge their short-term exposure to price risks, which should improve their business management and access to credit. A number of small transactions had been concluded at the time of writing, benefiting a number of small coffee farmers in three countries. However, scaling up the initiative will require significant operational challenges to be overcome, and it is uncertain that this can be achieved. A larger number of transactions has been completed in cotton assisting cooperatives and the local banks which lend to these cooperatives to protect themselves against adverse intraannual price. Details of the International Task Force (ITF) initiative are given in Box 4.1.

The ITF approach has a number of advantages, but it also has certain inherent limitations. In many countries, there is a lack of reliable and consistent local prices that can be used as a benchmark in commodity risk management transactions (Larson, Varangis, and Yabuki 1998). As agricultural markets have been liberalized, they have moved from fixed to variable prices, and there is little experience with respect to establishing a transparent, liquid, and reliable reporting system. In agricultural markets, grade and quality differentiation can be very important. Developing countries should put special emphasis on the establishment of systems to ensure the availability of reliable, transparent, and usable commodity price series and devise systems that will improve dissemination of price information.

Second, even where there are clear local prices, perhaps because of national auctions, basis risk can pose a serious problem. One may decompose price variability into two orthogonal components. The first component is the variability of an exchange price: for example, the New York Board of Trade (NYBOT) price for arabica coffee. The second component is the variability of the difference between the price obtained by an exporting country – Tanzania, in the case of arabica – and the exchange price. Basis risk is this second risk component. It can arise from changes in transportation costs, from quality differentials, or as the consequence of changes in the domestic policy environment (such as quality controls, export regulations, or the exchange rate regime). Hedging using exchange futures and options affects the only first, exchange, risk component. Its effectiveness depends on the basis risk component being small. In the specific case of Tanzania, the correlation between 12-week changes in the Tanzanian auction price and the NYBOT price varied from a very acceptable 0.90 in the 1999–2000 coffee year to a uselessly

---

Box 4.1. The International Task Force

In 1999, the World Bank initiated a project to make price risk-management instruments available to smallholder farmers, through cooperatives, producer organizations, traders, banks, and other rural financial institutions. This initiative was supported by several donor governments (the European Union, the Netherlands, and Switzerland), and was undertaken in collaboration with other international organizations and private sector representatives under the umbrella of the International Task Force on Commodity Risk Management (ITF). The initiative is described in ITF (1999). The role of the World Bank is seen as that of facilitator, providing technical assistance and capacity building to farmers and intermediary institutions, such as cooperatives, which bear the price risk. Hedging transactions are strictly commercially based and represent direct business between the local intermediary and the provider (seller) of price risk management instruments.

The project entered into the implementation phase in 2002 when several hedging transactions were concluded involving local coffee producer organizations in Nicaragua, Tanzania, and Uganda. These transactions used providers (mainly major international banks) in Europe and the United States. These pilot transactions benefited 250 farmers in Nicaragua, about 450 farmers in Uganda, and a few thousand farmers in Tanzania. The transactions have provided price protection for tonnages ranging from 50 tons to 700 tons. The time period covered by these transactions varied from one to seven months. Transactions typically involved the purchase of average price ("Asian") or exchange traded put options and involved payment of a premium: usually around 3 percent to 6 percent of the international coffee price.

In Tanzania, a large cooperative used the instruments to try to protect the minimum price to farmers between the time it was committed (April/May) and the time that coffee was sold at the auction (August–February). The collapse in coffee prices during the 2001–02 coffee year, which took effect before the cooperative could harvest, had caused severe financial losses because the minimum price guaranteed by the cooperative to its members turned out to be higher than the price the cooperative realized when it sold the coffee. This led to the decision of the cooperative to hedge for the following crop year. In addition, the local bank that was financing the cooperative strongly encouraged the cooperative to seek price protection for its 2002–03 crop.

In Uganda, the pilot transaction involved a cooperative exporter that guaranteed a minimum price to the farmer societies from which it was purchasing coffee. Price hedging was seen as a way to ensure that the cooperative exporter would not lose in the case of a price decline during the crop year. In the Nicaraguan case, the initial transaction involved direct purchase of put options by a group of farmers just before the harvest to cover their price exposure during the sales period later in the crop year. The objective was that farmers should not have to sell immediately following harvest time but could time their sales better throughout the crop year. Although this work has seen initial successes, a combination of problems with coffee basis risk (Tanzania), overoptimistic expectations (generally), slow decision-making processes (a general problem with cooperatives), and

(Box continues on the following page)

Box 4.1 (*continued*)

continuing high demands for technical assistance have limited the take-up of these instruments.

More recently, ITF risk management work has focused on intermediation of price risk instruments to coffee and cotton cooperatives through the banks which finance them which finance them in Tanzania. In the East African cotton and coffee sectors, where ginners and cooperatives offer prices to farmers at the start of the season, carrying the price risk through until time of sale (typically 7–10 months) can threaten the financial viability of these organizations. The ITF has assisted local banks lending to the sector to encourage cooperatives to hedge their exposure, and to hedge the hedge the exposure themselves to the extent that their clients have not done so. The benefit to farmers in both cases comes through the improved ability of commodity sector intermediaries to cope with price volatility, and, as the direct result, to obtain more credit on better terms.

The ITF started to work on weather risk management for farmers in 2003 with three pilot operations for 1,500 farmers in India. In 2004 the ITF expanded these pilots in India to rural finance portfolio insurance based on weather as well. Following the 2003 pilot, other insurance companies sold the weather insurance product to 18,000 farmers. The ITF initiated similar weather risk insurance pilot work at farm, local community, financial intermediary and government levels in Ukraine, Malawi, Zambia, Peru, Nicaragua, Ethiopia, and South Africa. For weather risk insurance, the provision and maintenance of reliable and easily accessible meteorological records is a public good, and the ITF is working with national meteorological services to provide this.

---

low 0.04 in the 2001–02 coffee year.[24] A key issue for producer organizations is to monitor basis risk to identify those market circumstances that are opportune for hedging price risks, and to void those circumstances where hedging would be less appropriate.

Third, a strategy based on protecting farmers against price risk does little or nothing to offset quantity (yield) risk. In many cases, this type of risk may be as important as price risk. If it were possible, insurance of farmers against revenue risk would be preferable, but this would need to be done through insurance rather than financial markets, and in such a way as to avoid moral hazard and adverse selection problems. An approach to deal with quantity risk that to a large extent avoids these problems is based on the concept of weather or area-based yield risk-management

---

[24] World Bank calculations, using data provided by the Tanzanian Coffee Board. Auction prices are averages across all lots. Part of the variability of the auction price may reflect variability in the quality of coffee sold at different weekly auctions. Twelve weeks corresponds to the period of time between a cooperative's purchase of coffee from its farmer members and the receipt of its sales at auction. Basis risk is not a major problem for exporters since they will typically negotiate sales, in the case of Tanzania to Japanese or European grinders, at an agreed premium or discount to the unknown futures price at the date of delivery in the consuming market. It is variations over time in these premia or discounts that give rise to the basis risk experienced by cooperatives and hence farmers. Christopher Gilbert (2002) discusses basis risk in conjunction with the ITF schemes.

instruments. For example, weather events that correlate closely to yield losses can be identified, such as low rainfall in critical plant growth periods. Buyers of weather risk management instruments can receive a payment if for example rainfall falls below a certain threshold level (see Varangis, Hess, and Bryla 2003). The ITF approach has been expanded to include weather (and area-yield) based index risk management instruments based on the results from earlier feasibility studies conducted by the World Bank's research and financial sector departments (see also Skees and others 2001; and Skees and others 2002).

The nature of the existing instruments defines the parameters within which the price risk management strategy can operate. The focus must therefore be on commodities with liquid international markets for risk management. The obvious candidates are cocoa, coffee, cotton, grains, natural rubber, and oilseeds. These are all very important crops for developing countries, but there are many other important commodities for which liquid international markets do not exist.[25] For these other commodities, there is a need to investigate other modes of managing price risks.

The quality of economic policy is also important. Macroeconomic stability, improvements in the functioning of credit and asset markets, and better access of financial markets by poor households could increase the use of assets and credit to provide self-insurance. Where inflation is high and variable, this adds risk in nominal contracts. Controls and regulations, including reporting requirements, on foreign exchange transactions, can increase the costs associated with hedging.

Commodity Policy within a Broader Rural Development Framework

In the long run, the solution to the problem of low and volatile incomes of commodity producers is to be found in accelerated growth and better income-generating opportunities in rural areas. For this reason, policies need to focus on a more holistic approach to rural development. Those countries that remain highly dependent on traditional agricultural commodities are the countries that have failed to diversify into more profitable activities, such as manufacturing, information technology, and tourism, which offer their population an escape from the low incomes and hard toil associated with traditional agriculture. Their comparative advantage is in those products that their more rapidly developing competitors are in the process of discarding. There is not so much a commodity problem as a problem with countries that have failed to develop away from primary commodities.

From this perspective, rural development strategies need to address this failure to develop, rather than the commodity markets themselves. Policy must aim to increase competitiveness and to reduce dependence on a few commodities by broadening the range of commodities produced by the agriculture sector, improving production and marketing systems, and supporting the creation of nonfarm activities. The aim

---

[25] Why are these markets absent? A successful futures market requires a good balance between long and short hedging interest. In the absence of such a balance, speculative positions may need to be larger than can be justified in terms of market liquidity. It will normally be uncertain ex ante whether these conditions exist, and this may make it too risky for an exchange to risk the considerable investment required to create a new market. The absence of a market therefore cannot be taken as indicating market failure. However, policy analysis becomes more complicated since interventions which could not be welfare-improving in the context of complete spanning may raise nevertheless raise welfare conditional on the limited set of markets which do exist – see Newbery and Stiglitz (1981).

should be to produce a modern agricultural and agribusiness sector. But such a sector will also deliver lower employment than traditional agriculture, and so, in the absence of massive emigration, rural development must run in parallel with development of the modern sectors.

Furthermore, the risk-management approach discussed above assists the commodity-producing sector in better managing its risks but it does not give revenue or even price stabilization. In the terminology of Alderman and Paxson (1994), it is a coping strategy. Stabilization schemes adopted the wider objective of reducing revenue variability as well as price risk, although it is debatable whether either objective was achieved. The market-based approach to revenue stabilization, which would complement the risk-management initiative, would be improved rural banking, perhaps through microcredit institutions, such that producers could smooth their consumption streams.

These rural development and rural finance strategies require real investments. These include investments in public infrastructure, market information, quality and standards systems, and research and extension, which would enable the rural sector to grow by adding value to existing commodity sectors and developing alternative activities. This will enable rural sectors to more easily adjust to price (and yield) variations. Rural development provides for the long-run solution. In the short run, there is a need to provide ways for commodity-dependent poor countries to deal with their commodity-related exposures, both at the macro/government and at the micro/household level. The near-term strategy for dealing with volatile commodity markets should consider compensatory financing and other lending instruments to assist countries in dealing with commodity-related macroeconomic shocks, appropriate macroeconomic policies, and microinitiatives to directly assist farmers to insure themselves against short-term price and production shocks.

CONCLUSION

Commodity price variability is caused by shocks to commodity production (typically crop commodities) or to demand (industrially consumed commodities), or both. These shocks become amplified as they are transmitted to prices because of the short-term price inelasticity of production and consumption. That effect is itself attenuated in periods of excess supply as the result of speculative stockholding. The resulting price cycles are flat-bottomed but exhibit occasional sharp peaks. Price volatility in commodities increased sharply in the 1970s from previously low levels, but has been relatively steady since that time. It does not vary substantially across commodity-producing countries or regions.

In analyzing the economic impact, it is important to make two distinctions: that between the ex ante impact of agents' perceptions of price variability, and the ex post impact of large price realizations; and, in relation to ex ante perceptions, the distinction between unconditional volatility measures and conditional uncertainty measures. The latter distinction raises the question of how agents form expectations. Uncertainty measures are necessarily model-specific, whereas unconditional volatility measures are sample estimates of population variances.

Commodity price volatility is superimposed on a downward trend in prices, caused by productivity growth in commodity production and intermediation. Because primary commodities are fairly homogeneous and are generally priced in relation to standardized grades, productivity growth is reflected in lower prices and not high quality. However, the pace of productivity growth is uneven and the trend is therefore stochastic. A large part of the variation in commodity prices is attributable to variations *of* the trend itself rather than variations *around* the trend. This makes it difficult to know whether a particular price movement at any point in time is cyclical or permanent. This study finds that between 60 percent and 70 percent of commodity price movements is permanent. The view that the cyclicality of commodity prices is more important than the trend is, in our view, incorrect. An implication of this observation is that price forecasting is very difficult. It is not altogether surprising that agents have sometimes extrapolated recent prices overoptimistically or overpessimistically.

Turning to the effects of commodity price variability, this study looked at the impact on household decisions, on governments, and, at the level of the macroeconomy, on growth rates. Survey evidence confirms that price risk is one of the most important components of risk faced by rural households in developing countries, but that it is not the only important risk factor. In principle, the substitution possibilities generated by price variability may imply that producers benefit from price movements. In practice, these gains are likely to be small because of the unpredictability of price changes between the production decision and the delivery date. Risk aversion effects will therefore dominate. In the absence of insurance markets, rural households will cope with price variability by saving–dissaving, intragroup risk sharing, and diversification. Poorly developed rural credit markets, together with the frequent absence of collateral and the fact that price risk is systemic when households specialize in the same crops, throws the burden of adjustment on diversification. But this is costly, in the sense that it involves sacrifice of comparative advantage.

Many governments of primary producing countries also remain dependent on commodity export earnings either directly, through the importance of export taxes, or indirectly, as export revenue variability generalizes across the economy. The evidence from the coffee market suggests that many countries dependent on coffee export revenues have managed to substantially reduce the dependence of their tax revenues on coffee, in part through diversification away from coffee, but also by controlling for export concentration. The exceptions are a number of African coffee-producing countries. This raises the question of why tax diversification has been less successful in Africa than in Latin America.

Much effort has been expended in looking at the impact of commodity price variability on growth. The results are generally disappointing and inconclusive. Theory is ambiguous as to whether ex ante variability measures such as uncertainty should increase or decrease growth rates – although most investigators have looked for a negative impact. There is little evidence of any effect, whether positive or negative. The only reasonable conclusion is that if there are such effects, they are either of the second order of importance or are variable across countries or time, or both. Rather larger claims have been made for the impact of large price shocks. One current view is that this impact is asymmetric, so that countries suffer slower growth when hit by a large adverse shock, but fail to benefit, or to benefit commensurately, when they enjoy a large positive shock. Although a number of recent studies have claimed to find this asymmetric impact, this study casts doubt on its validity. Further work is required to determine where the truth lies in this matter.

The long history of interventionist policy in the commodities area stands in contrast to the mixed evidence that commodity price variability has an adverse impact. The history of intervention extends back to Keynes's proposals for managed markets stemming from a fear that otherwise the world would lapse back into the depressed commodity prices of the1930s, and to the marketing practices of British and French colonial administrations. The consequence is that the major tropical commodity products were managed through a set of international commodity agreements and domestic stabilization schemes, and the ambition of the so-called New International Economic Order (UNCTAD 1976) was to extend this system more generally. While it would be incorrect to state that the international agreements and domestic schemes were always and everywhere ineffective at stabilizing prices, it is true that these arrangements did almost universally experience acute problems during the 1980s, which typically ended in their collapse or abandonment. A consequence of the liberalization of many tropical agricultural markets over the subsequent period is that implementation of similar schemes would now no longer be feasible, even if there were a desire to move in that direction.

The consequence of the abandonment of interventionist policy aimed at reducing commodity price volatility is that policy has moved to helping agents live with the volatility that the market generates. This altered direction in policy has been encouraged by the lack of clear evidence that commodity price variability has pervasive and general adverse macroeconomic consequences. Nevertheless, this is quite different from arguing that there are no adverse impacts. Rural households are obliged to undertake costly diversifications in crops and labor time to protect themselves from the possibility of low prices. Governments with overly narrow tax bases may be forced either to curtail socially necessary expenditures or to increase borrowing, often expensively, in the event of export revenue shortfalls. In the event of exceptional shocks, there will indeed be negative consequences for income and growth.

One strand of current policy is that of improved intermediation of risk management instruments to cooperative societies and individual farmers. This not only should have a direct impact of preventing farmers from lapsing into more acute poverty when prices fall to low levels, but it may also allow them to obtain enhanced access to credit and to increase profitable specialization. Initial results are encouraging, but capacity building programs are inevitably slow. A second stand of policy aims is directed at governments, with the aim of making them less dependent on taxes based directly or indirectly on commodity export revenues, and – to the extent that this is not possible – in adjusting the timing of some of their expenditure commitments to more closely match the time pattern of their receipts.

Overall, it would be helpful if there could be less talk of "the commodity problem" and more attention to the problems of those countries that remain primary producers simply because they have not developed alternative and more remunerative activities. The Latin American experience has shown that tropical agricultural export commodities can form an important component of modern agricultural sectors, and that price volatility is no bar to these developments. The poorest economies are those which, almost by definition, have failed to diversify out of traditional exports, in which productivity is advancing more slowly than in their more successful competitors, and which combine high export concentration with slow growth. Many, but by no means all, these economies are in Africa. These countries require assistance – ultimately to escape what appears to be a "dead-end" dependence, and until such time as they can escape, to live with the volatility aspects of this dependence.

Commodity policy should aim to reduce the commodity dependence of these countries in the long term while helping them to live with commodity price volatility in the interim. But that will require viewing commodity policy as an integral part of a holistic rural development strategy.

REFERENCES

Akiyama, Takamasa, John Baffes, Donald Larson, and Panos Varangis. 2001. "Market Reforms: Lessons from Country and Commodity Experiences." In T. Akiyama, J. Baffes, D. Larson, and P. Varangis, eds., *Commodity Market Reforms: Lessons from Two Decades.* Washington, DC: World Bank.

Alderman, Harold, and Christina Paxson. 1994. "Do the Poor Insure? A Synthesis of the Literature on Risk and Consumption in Developing Countries." In Edmar L. Bacha, ed., *Economics in a Changing World*, Volume 4, "Development, Trade, and Environment." London: MacMillan.

Anderson, Ronald W., and Christopher L. Gilbert. 1988. "Commodity Agreements and Commodity Markets: Lessons from Tin." *Economic Journal* 98(389):1–15.

Anderson, Ronald W., Christopher L. Gilbert, and Andrew Powell. 1989. "Securitization and Commodity Contingency in International Lending." *American Journal of Agricultural Economics* 71(Supp.):523–30.

Anderson, Jock R., Donald Larson, and Panos Varangis. 2002. "Managing Risks Rather Than Markets: An Institutional View from the World Bank of Agricultural Risk Management." In Ross Garnault, ed., *Resource Management in Asia Pacific Developing Countries.* Canberra: Asia Pacific Press.

Barghouti, Shawki, Carol Timmer, and Paul Siegel. 1990. "Rural Diversification: Lessons from East Asia." Technical Paper No. 117. World Bank, Washington, DC.

Bauer, Peter, and Paish, Frank W. 1952. "Reduction in the Fluctuations of Incomes of Primary Producers." *Economic Journal* 62(248):750–80.

Bevan, David L., Paul Collier, and Jan Willem Gunning. 1987. "Consequences of a Commodity Boom in a Controlled Economy: Accumulation and Redistribution in Kenya, 1975–1983." *World Bank Economic Review* 1(3):489–514.

———. 1990. *Controlled Open Economies.* Oxford: Oxford University Press.

Beveridge, Stephen, and Charles R. Nelson. 1981. "A New Approach to Decomposition of Economic Time Series into Permanent and Transitory Components with Particular Attention to Measurement of the Business Cycle." *Journal of Monetary Economics* 7(2):151–74.

Bohman, Mary, Lovell Jarvis, and Richard Barichello. 1996. "Rent Seeking and International Commodity Agreements: The Case of Coffee." *Economic Development and Cultural Change* 44(2):379–404.

Bollerslev, Tim. 1986. "Generalized Autoregressive Conditional Heteroscedasticity." *Journal of Econometrics* 31(3):109–16.

Brown, Christopher P. 1980. *The Political and Social Economy of Commodity Control.* Kuala Lumpur: Oxford University Press.

Brunetti, Celso, and Christopher L. Gilbert. 1995. "Metals Price Volatility, 1972–1995." *Resources Policy* 21(4):237–54.

Burnside, Craig, and David Dollar. 2000. "Aid, Policies, and Growth." *American Economic Review* 90(4):847–68.

Caballero, Ricardo J. 1991. "On the Sign of the Investment-Uncertainty Relationship." *American Economic Review* 81(1):279–88.

Caine, Sidney 1954. "Instability of Primary Product Prices: A Protest and a Proposal." *Economic Journal* 64(255):610–14.

Cashin, Paul, and C. John McDermott. 2002. "The Long-Run Behavior of Commodity Prices: Small Trends and Big Variability." *IMF Staff Papers* 49(2):175–99.

Cashin, Paul, Luis Céspendes, and Ratna Sahay. 2003. "Commodity Currencies." *Finance and Development* 40(1):45–48.

_____. 2004. "Commodity Currencies and the Real Exchange Rate." *Journal of Development Economics* 75(1):239–68.

Claessens, Stijn. 1991. "Integrating Commodity and Exchange Rate Risk Management: Implications for External Debt Management." In Theophilos Priovolos and Ronald Duncan, eds., *Commodity Risk Management and Finance*. Oxford: Oxford University Press for the World Bank.

Claessens, Stijn, and Ronald C. Duncan, eds. 1993. *Managing Commodity Price Risk in Developing Countries*. Washington, DC: World Bank.

Coate, Stephen, and Martin Ravallion. 1993. "Reciprocity without Commitment: Characterization of Informal Insurance Arrangements." *Journal of Development Economics* 40(1): 1–23.

Collier, Paul, and Jan Willem Gunning. 1996. "Policy Towards Commodity Shocks in Developing Countries." IMF Working Paper 84. International Monetary Fund, Washington, DC.

Corden, W. Max. 1984. "Booming Sector and Dutch Disease Economics: Survey and Consolidation." *Oxford Economic Papers* 36(3):359–80.

Cuddington, John T. 1992. "Long-Run Trends in 26 Commodity Prices." *Journal of Development Economics* 39(2):207–27.

Cuddington, John T., and Carlos M. Urzùa. 1989. "Trends and Cycles in the Net Barter Terms of Trade: A New Approach." *Economic Journal* 99(396):426–62.

Czukas, Katherine, Marcel Fafchamps, and Chris Udry. 1998. "Drought and Saving in West Africa: Are Livestock a Buffer Stock?" *Journal of Development Economics* 55(2): 278–306.

Dawe, David. 1996. "A New Look at the Effects of Export Instability on Investment and Growth." *World Development* 24(12):1905–14.

Deaton, Angus. 1992. "Saving and Income Smoothing in Côte d'Ivoire." *Journal of African Economies* 1(1):1–24.

_____. 1999. "Commodity Prices and Growth in Africa." *Journal of Economic Perspectives* 13(3):23–40.

Deaton, Angus, and Guy Laroque. 1992. "On the Behaviour of Commodity Prices." *Review of Economic Studies* 59(1):1–23.

_____. 1995. "Estimating a Nonlinear Commodity Price Model with Unobservable State Variables." *Journal of Applied Econometrics* 10(Supp.):S9–40.

_____. 1996. "Competitive Storage and Commodity Price Dynamics." *Journal of Political Economy* 104(5):896–923.

_____. 2003. "A Model of Commodity Prices after Sir Arthur Lewis." *Journal of Development Economics* 71(2):289–310.

Deaton, Angus, and Ronald I. Miller. 1995. "International Commodity Prices, Macroeconomic Performance, and Politics in Sub-Saharan Africa." *Princeton Studies in International Finance* 79.

Dehn, Jan. 2000a. "Commodity Price Uncertainty and Shocks: Implications for Investment and Growth." D. Phil. thesis, Oxford University, unpublished.

_____. 2000b. "The Effects on Growth of Commodity Price Uncertainty and Shocks." Policy Research Working Paper 2455. World Bank, Washington, DC. Forthcoming in *Journal of African Economies*.

Dercon, Stefan. 2002. "Income Risk, Coping Strategies, and Safety Nets." *World Bank Research Observer* 17(2):141–66.

Dercon, Stefan, and Pramila Krishnan. 2000. "In Sickness and in Health: Risk Sharing within Households in Rural Ethiopia." *Journal of Political Economy* 108(4):688–727.

Devlin, Julia, and Michael Lewin. 2004. "Managing Oil Booms and Busts." (Chapter 6, this volume).

Edwards, Sebastian. 1984. "Coffee, Money, and Inflation in Colombia." *World Development* 12(11–12):1107–17.

Erb, Guy F., and Salvatore Schiavo-Campo. 1969. "Export Instability, Level of Development, and Economic Size of Less Developed Countries." *Bulletin of the Oxford University Institute of Economics and Statistics* 31(4):263–83.

Friedman, Milton. 1954. "The Reduction of Fluctuations in the Incomes of Primary Producers: A Critical Comment." *Economic Journal* 64(256):698–703.

Gelb, Alan, and Bourguignon, Francois. 1989. "Venezuela: Absorption without Growth." In Alan Gelb and Associates, eds., *Oil Windfalls – Blessing or Curse?* Oxford: Oxford University Press.

Gemmill, Gordon. 1985. "Forward Contracts or International Buffer Stocks? A Study of Their Relative Efficiencies in Stabilizing Commodity Export Earnings." *Economic Journal* 95(378):400–17.

Gilbert, Christopher L. 1985. "Futures Trading and the Welfare Economics of Commodity Market Stabilization." *Economic Journal* 95(379):637–61.

———. 1987. "International Commodity Agreements: Design and Performance." *World Development* 15(5):591–616.

———. 1996. "International Commodity Agreements: An Obituary Notice." *World Development* 24(1):1–19.

———. 1997. *Cocoa Market Liberalization.* London: Cocoa Association of London.

———. 2002. "Commodity Risk Management: Preliminary Lessons from the International Task Force." In Ross Garnault, ed., *Resource Management in Asia Pacific Developing Countries.* Canberra: Asia Pacific Press.

———. 2003. "The Impact of Commodity Price Variability on Government Revenues." Vrije Universiteit, Amsterdam. Processed.

Gilbert, Christopher L. 2004. "International Commodity Agreements as Internationally Sanctioned Cartels." In P. Z. Gronman, ed., *How Cartels Endure and How They Fail.* Cheltenham: Edward Elgar.

Gilbert, Christopher L., and Alexandra Tabova. 2004. "Commodity Prices and Debt Sustainability." University of Trento (Italy). Processed.

Glezakos, Constantine. 1973. "Export Instability and Economic Growth: A Statistical Verification." *Economic Development and Structural Change* 21(4):670–78.

Griffiths, William E., and Jock R. Anderson. 1978. "Specification of Agricultural Supply Functions – Empirical Evidence on Wheat in Southern N.S.W." *Australian Journal of Agricultural Economics* 22(2–3):115–28.

Grilli, Enzo R., and Maw Cheng Yang. 1988. "Primary Commodity Prices, Manufactured Good Prices and the Terms of Trade of Developing Countries: What the Long Run Shows." *World Bank Economic Review* 2(1):1–47.

Guillaumont, Patrick, and Lisa Chauvet. 1999. "Aid and Performance: A Reassessment." CERDI, Universisité de Clermont-Ferrand I. Processed.

Guillaumont, Patrick, Sylviane Guillaumont-Jeanneney, and Jean-François Brun. 1999. "How Instability Lowers African Growth." *Journal of African Economies* 8(1):87–107.

Gustafson, Robert L. 1958. "Carryover Levels for Grains: A Method for Determining the Amounts Which Are Optimal under Specified Conditions." Technical Bulletin 1178. U.S. Department of Agriculture, Washington, DC.

Hamilton, James D. 1994. *Time Series Analysis.* Princeton: Princeton University Press.

Hartman, Richard. 1972. "The Effects of Price and Cost Uncertainty on Investment." *Journal of Economic Theory* 5(2):258–66.

Hotelling, Harold. 1931. "The Economics of Exhaustible Resources." *Journal of Political Economy* 39(2):137–75.

ITF (International Task Force on Commodity Risk Management in Developing Countries). 1999. *Dealing with Commodity Price Volatility in Developing Countries: A Proposal for a Market-Based Approach.* Washington, DC: World Bank.

———. 2002a. "Nicaragua. Coffee Price Risk Management Phase II Report." Available at http://www.itf-commrisk.org/documents/documents_database/nicaragua.pdf.

———. 2002b. "Dominican Republic: Price Risk Management for Coffee and Cocoa." Commodity Risk Management Group, World Bank, Washington, DC.

Jaffee, Steven. 1993. *Exporting High-Value Food Commodities: Success Stories from Developing Countries.* World Bank Discussion Paper 198. Washington, DC.

Just, Richard E. 1975. "Risk Response Models and Their Use in Agricultural Policy Evaluation." *American Journal of Agricultural Economics* 57:836–43.

Kanbur, S. M. Ravi. 1984. "How to Analyse Commodity Price Stabilisation: A Review Article." *Oxford Economic Papers* 36(3):336–58.

Kannapiran, Chinna A. 2000. "Commodity Price Stabilization: Macroeconomic Impacts and Policy Options." *Agricultural Economics* 23(1):17–30.

Keynes, John Maynard. 1943. "The Objective of International Price Stability." *Economic Journal* 53(210–211):185–87.

Killick, Tony. 1984. "Kenya, 1975–81." In Tony Killick, ed., *The IMF and Stabilization.* London: Heinemann.

Knudsen, Odin, and John Nash. 1990. "Domestic Price Stabilization Schemes in Developing Countries." *Economic Development and Cultural Change* 38(3):539–58.

Knudsen, Odin, and Andrew Parnes. 1975. *Trade Instability and Economic Development.* Lexington, MA: Lexington Books.

Krueger, Anne, Maurice Schiff, and Alberto Valdés. 1992. *The Political Economy of Agricultural Pricing Policy: A Synthesis of the Economics of Developing Countries.* Baltimore: Johns Hopkins University Press.

Larson, Donald, Panos Varangis, and Nanae Yabuki. 1998. "Commodity Risk Management and Development." Policy Research Working Paper 1963. World Bank, Washington, DC.

Law, Alton D. 1975. *International Commodity Agreements.* Lexington, MA: D.C. Heath.

León, Javier, and Raimundo Sato. 1997. "Structural Breaks and Long-Term Trends in Commodity Prices." *Journal of International Development* 9(3):347–66.

Lewis, Arthur. 1954. "Economic Development with Unlimited Supplies of Labour." *Manchester School* 22(2):139–91.

Ligon, Ethan, Jonathon P. Thomas, and Tim Worrall. 2002. "Informal Insurance Arrangements with Limited Commitment: Theory and Evidence from Village Economies." *Review of Economic Studies* 69(1):209–44.

Lipsey, Robert E. 1994. "Quality Change and Other Influences on Measures of Export Prices of Manufactured Goods." Policy Research Working Paper 1348. World Bank, International Economics Department, Washington, DC.

Lutz, Matthias. 1994. "The Effects of Volatility in the Terms of Trade on Output Growth: New Evidence." *World Development* 22(12):1959–75.

MacBean, Alasdair L. 1966. *Export Instability and Economic Development.* London: George Allen and Unwin.

Massell, Benton F. 1969. "Price Stabilization and Welfare." *Quarterly Journal of Economics* 83(2):284–98.

McIntire, Jim, and Panos Varangis. 1999. "Reforming Cote d'Ivoire's Cocoa Marketing and Pricing System." Policy Research Working Paper 2081. World Bank, Washington, DC.

McKinnon, Ronald J. 1967. "Futures Markets, Buffer Stocks, and Income Stability for Primary Producers." *Journal of Political Economy* 75:844–61.

Miranda, Mario J., and Peter G. Helmberger. 1988. "The Effects of Commodity Price Stabilization Programs." *American Economic Review* 78(1):46–58.

Mundlak, Yair, Domingo Cavallo, and Roberto Domenech. 1989. "Agriculture and Economic Growth in Argentina, 1913–1984." Reference Report No. 76, International Food Policy Research Institute, Washington, DC.

Myers, Robert J., and James F. Oehmke. 1988. "Instability and Risk as Rationales for Farm Programs." In Daniel A. Sumner, ed., *Agricultural Stability and Farm Programs: Concepts, Evidence, and Implications*. Boulder: Westview.

Myers, Robert J., and Stanley R. Thompson. 1991. "Optimal External Debt Management with Commodity-Linked Bonds." In Theopilos Priovolos and Ronald C. Duncan, eds., *Commodity Risk Management and Finance*. Washington, DC: Oxford University Press for the World Bank.

Newbery, David M. G., and Joseph E. Stiglitz. 1981. *The Theory of Commodity Price Stabilization*. Oxford: Clarendon Press.

Ng, Serena. 1996. "Looking for Evidence of Speculative Stockholding in Commodity Markets." *Journal of Economic Dynamics and Control* 20(1–3):123–43.

O'Hara, Maureen. 1984. "Commodity Bonds and Consumption Risks." *Journal of Finance* 39(1):193–206.

Oi, Walter Y. 1961. "The Desirability of Price Instability under Perfect Competition." *Econometrica* 29(1):58–64.

Overdahl, James A. 1987. "The Use of Crude Oil Futures by the Governments of Oil Producing States." *Journal of Futures Markets* 7(6):603–17.

Palm, Franz C., and Ben Vogelvang. 1991. "The Effectiveness of the World Coffee Agreement: A Simulation Study Using a Quarterly Model of the World Coffee Market." In Orhan Güvenen, Walter C. Labys, and Jean-Baptiste Lesourd, eds., *International Commodity Market Models*. London: Chapman and Hall.

Paxson, Christina. 1993. "Consumption and Income Seasonality in Thailand." *Journal of Political Economy* 101(1):39–72.

Platteau, Jean-Phillipe. 1997. "Mutual Insurance as an Elusive Concept in Traditional Rural Communities." *Journal of Development Studies* 33(6):764–96.

Powell, Andrew. 1991. "Commodity and Developing Country Terms of Trade: What Does the Long Run Show?" *Economics Journal* 101(409):1485–96.

Prebisch, Raul. 1950, 1962. "The Economic Development of Latin America and Its Principal Problems." *Economic Bulletin for Latin America* 7(1):1–22. Initially released as a separate document by the United Nations.

Quiggin, John, and Jock R. Anderson. 1979. "Stabilisation and Risk Reduction in Australian Agriculture." *Australian Journal of Agricultural Economics* 23(3):191–206.

———. 1981. "Price Bands and Buffer Funds." *Economic Record* 57(156):67–73.

Ramey, Garey, and Valerie A. Ramey. 1995. "Cross-Country Evidence on the Link between Volatility and Growth." *American Economic Review* 85(5):1138–51.

Reardon, Thomas, Eric Crawford, and Valerie Kelly. 1994. "Links Between Nonfarm Income and Farm Investment in African Households: Adding the Capital Market Perspective." *American Journal of Agricultural Economics* 76(5):1172–76.

Reinhart, Carmen M., and Peter Wickham. 1994. "Commodity Prices: Cyclical Weakness or Secular Decline?" *IMF Staff Papers* 41(2):175–213.

Rodrik, Dani. 1999. "Where Did All the Growth Go? External Shocks, Social Conflict, and Growth Collapses." *Journal of Economic Growth* 4(4):358–412.

Rolfo, Jacques. 1980. "Optimal Hedging Under Price and Quantity Uncertainty: The Case of a Cocoa Producer." *Journal of Political Economy* 88(1):100–16.

Salant, Stephen W. 1983. "The Vulnerability of Price Stabilization Schemes to Speculative Attack." *Journal of Political Economy* 91(1):1–38.

Samuelson, Paul A. 1957. "Intertemporal Price Equilibrium: A Prologue to the Theory of Speculation." *Weltwirtschaftliches Archiv* 79:181–219. Reprinted in Joseph E. Stiglitz, ed., 1966. *Collected Scientific Papers of Paul A. Samuelson.* Cambridge, MA: MIT Press.

Scandizzo, Pasquale L., Peter Hazell, and Jock R. Anderson. 1981. "Risky Agricultural Markets: Expectations, Welfare and Intervention." World Bank, Economics and Policy Division, Agriculture and Rural Development Dept., Washington, DC.

Scherr, Sara J. 1989. "Agriculture in an Export Boom Economy: A Comparative Analysis of Policy and Performance in Indonesia, Mexico and Nigeria." *World Development* 17(4):543–60.

Schuknecht, Ludger. 1996. "Fiscal Policies, Natural Resource Rents, and Rent Seeking." Paper presented at the Annual Meeting of the European Public Choice Society, April, Bar Ilan University, Ramat Gan, Israel.

Serven, Luis. 1998. "Macroeconomic Uncertainty and Private Investment in LDCs: An Empirical Investigation." World Bank, Washington, DC. Processed.

Singer, Hans. 1950. "The Distribution of Gains between Investing and Borrowing Countries." *American Economic Review, Papers and Proceedings* 40(2):473–85.

Skees, Jerry, Stephanie Gober, Panos Varangis, Rodney Lester, and Vijay Kalavakonda. 2001. "Developing Rainfall-Based Index Insurance in Morocco." Policy Research Working Paper 2577. World Bank, Washington, DC.

Skees, Jerry, Panos Varangis, Donald Larson, and Paul Siegel. 2002. "Can Financial Markets Be Tapped to Help Poor People Cope with Weather Risks?" Policy Research Working Paper 2812. World Bank, Washington, DC.

Slade, Margaret E. 1982. "Trends in Natural-Resource Commodity Prices: An Analysis in the Time Domain." *Journal of Environmental Economics and Management* 9(2):122–38.

Udry, Chris. 1994. "Risk and Insurance in a Rural Credit Market: An Empirical Investigation in Northern Nigeria." *Review of Economic Studies* 61(3):495–526.

UNCTAD. 1976. *The Integrated Programme for Commodities: Resolution 93(IV).* Geneva: UNCTAD.

Varangis, Panos, and Gotz Schreiber. 2001. "Cocoa Market Reforms in West Africa." In Takamasa Akiyama, John Baffes, Donald Larson, and Panos Varangis, eds., *Commodity Market Reforms: Lessons from Two Decades.* Washington, DC: World Bank.

Varangis Panos, Ulrich Hess, and Erin Bryla. 2003. "Innovative Approaches for Managing Agricultural Risks." In Nigel Scott, ed., *Agribusiness and Commodity Risk: Strategies and Management.* London: Risk Books.

Watson, Mark W. 1994. "Business Cycle Durations and Postwar Stabilization in the U.S. Economy." *American Economic Review* 84(1):24–46.

Waugh, Friedrich V. 1944. "Does the Consumer Benefit from Instability." *Quarterly Journal of Economics* 58(4):602–14.

Wright, Brian D. 1988. "Storage, Stability, and Farm Programs." In Daniel A. Sumner, ed., *Agricultural Stability and Farm Programs: Concepts, Evidence, and Implications.* Boulder: Westview.

Wright, Brian D., and David M. G. Newbery. 1991. "Financial Instruments for Consumption Smoothing by Commodity Dependent Exporters." In Theopilos Priovolos and Ronald C. Duncan, eds., *Commodity Risk Management and Finance.* Oxford: Oxford University Press for the World Bank.

Wright, Brian D., and Jeffrey C. Williams. 1991. *Storage and Commodity Markets.* Cambridge, UK: Cambridge University Press.

Yotopoulos, Pan A., and Jeffrey B. Nugent. 1976. *Economics of Development: An Empirical Investigation.* New York: Harper and Row.

Zeira, Joseph. 1987. "Investment as a Search Process." *Journal of Political Economy* 95(1):204–11.

5. Managing Oil Booms and Busts in Developing Countries

Julia Devlin and Michael Lewin[1]

ABSTRACT: The poor economic performance of oil-rich countries has led to the notion that oil abundance, ideally a blessing, is frequently a "resource curse" which stunts instead of spurring economic growth. Explanations for this phenomenon can be divided into two categories. The first emphasizes governance issues (including rent-seeking and corruption); the second emphasizes the economic effects, often called "the Dutch Disease." This study examines the latter set of issues in oil-exporting developing economies, with an emphasis on the role of fiscal policy. It surveys policies and institutional mechanisms designed to minimize the harmful effects of oil booms and busts through government expenditure management, self-insurance, and asset diversification.

RESOURCE ABUNDANCE: THE PARADOX OF PLENTY?

The weak economic performance and continued poverty of many commodity-dependent economies, particularly oil-exporting ones, continues to pose a challenge to development economists. That resource-poor countries have outperformed resource-rich countries in terms of economic growth has been well documented (see Ranis 1991; Sachs and Warner 1995; Auty 2001).[2]

The explanations for poor growth performance on the part of oil-exporting countries can be roughly divided into two categories. Some focus on governance issues such as corruption, rent-seeking, and bloated public sectors (Karl 1997; Eifert, Gelb, and Tallroth 2003). Others focus on the economic effects: namely, the Dutch Disease and volatility (Gelb and Associates 1988; Corden and Neary 1982; Aizenmann and Marion 1993; Gavin 1997; Hausmann and Rigobon 2003). This study focuses on the latter set of issues. As such, it addresses two main areas: understanding the

---

[1] Julia Devlin is Senior Private Sector Development Specialist in the MENA (Middle East and North Africa) Region and Michael Lewin is Senior Economist in DECDG (Development Economics Development Data Group) of the World Bank. The authors would like to thank Nina Budina and Rolando Ossowski for excellent comments and suggestions, and Brian Pinto and Thilak Ranaweera for many helpful conversations. The authors would also like to thank Marketa Jonasova for her assistance in preparing figures pertaining to options. Alas, we alone are responsible for all remaining deficiencies.

[2] For example, in the period 1960–90, the per capita income of small oil exporting countries grew on average 1.7 percent per year, compared to 2.5 percent and 3.5 percent for small and large resource-poor countries, respectively. For the period 1970–93, the picture is even more stark: 0.8 percent for small oil producers versus 2.1 percent and 3.7 percent for the resource-poor countries (Auty and Mikesell 1998).

macroeconomic effects of oil dependence in the developing country context; and surveying policies and institutional mechanisms to manage oil booms and busts through expenditure restraint, self-insurance, and asset diversification – also in the developing country context. A strong and transparent public governance climate is an essential underpinning for such management.

THE ECONOMIC EFFECTS OF OIL REVENUES

Much of the analytical framework for the Dutch Disease argument was anticipated in the debate in the 1920s over German reparations, which became known as the "transfer problem."[3] Among other things, it was argued that a country receiving reparations payments (a transfer) could be worse-off in the long run as a result. This seemingly paradoxical outcome can occur, it was argued, because in the absence of other capital flows, the receiving country must run a trade deficit to accommodate the transfer (and vice versa for the transferring country.) As an integral part of this process, it will undergo an appreciation of the real exchange rate so that net exports can decline. Exports will fall and imports will rise, the trade deficit being financed by the transfer. Disposable income and consumption in the receiving country will have risen so that the country becomes better off (and vice versa for the payer).

Over the years, however, economists have noted that the fall in exports due to the real appreciation could have deleterious effects beyond the immediate disruption to the sector. In particular, if the transfer is short-lived, then the rise in income and consumption could also be short-lived. However, the decline of the traditional export sector may be difficult to reverse. In contemporary terminology this is sometimes called "deindustrialization." Proponents of this view note that industries and sectors may decline quickly, but are difficult to resuscitate when the transfers cease. Thus, the welfare effects of the transfer depend on whether it is permanent or temporary, and whether spending and hence the real exchange rate are affected by the current level of the transfer or its expected time-path.

The transfer problem offers several insights for the analysis of oil revenues. First, the oil revenue is similar to a transfer in that the oil industry employs negligible domestic resources; thus, the revenues are like a rent to the economy. In most small oil-producing economies, the oil industry is an "enclave" and therefore influences the economy, or is absorbed into the economy, in the same way as a transfer. While not strictly speaking a transfer in the accounting sense, from an analytical point of view its effects are the same. Other things equal, a windfall will be unambiguously welfare-enhancing. Thus, any negative effects from the impact on the real exchange rate would result from the revenue being transitory or volatile.

But real exchange rate movements depend on the conduct of fiscal policy because, as with a transfer, the oil revenue in most countries is paid directly to

---

[3] The well-known issue arose from an exchange between John Maynard Keynes and Bertil Ohlin regarding reparations payments after World War I. The original discussion involved analyzing the effects of reparations on both the transferring country and the recipient. For the purposes of analyzing mineral revenues, it is sufficient to consider only a small receiving economy, the "transfer" being thought of as similar in its effects to mineral revenues.

the government as the guardian of the natural resources. Hence, the government becomes the conduit for the oil revenues into the economy and the effect of the revenues on the real exchange rate depends on the saving/investment behavior it induces.[4] If the revenue is unstable and/or transitory and spills over into fiscal policy, then the real exchange rate will be unstable and the natural resource blessing could become a curse. Over time, these effects will lead to specialization in the economy's productive structure in favor of nontradables. This will make the economy more vulnerable to oil price volatility particularly in the presence of capital market imperfections (Hausmann and Rigobon 2003). Fiscal policy is therefore a key element, for most countries, in causing or preventing the resource curse.[5]

THE IMPACT OF OIL IN A SIMPLE MACROFRAMEWORK

Using a simple analytical framework based on a one-good, small economy model, the macroeconomic impact of oil exports on the economy can be understood in terms of the following scenario:[6] Suppose this is a small developing economy that begins to export oil. As a result of launching oil production – and assuming the simplest case where oil revenue is transferred directly in a lump sum to the private sector and therefore increases disposable income directly – total exports and also imports would be expected to increase because of the income effects. In the absence of any induced capital flows, the real exchange rate will adjust to balance trade following the start of the oil revenue flows.

The Boom

Intuitively, the exogenous increase in export revenue will have the effect of lowering (or appreciating) the real exchange rate, which would bring about trade or current account balance. Since disposable income has increased, with a positive marginal propensity to save, saving would increase, leading to a lower interest rate and, hence, a higher rate of investment and growth.

While it is clear that the benefit of the windfall or transfer is the increase in disposable income and consumption, what is often less well understood is that this goes hand-in-hand with the real appreciation. If prewindfall production was at capacity then the windfall will increase demand for both home and foreign goods,

---

[4] Complete Barro–Ricardo equivalence is said to hold if fiscal deficits and surpluses do not alter aggregate saving and investment in the economy. This study assumes throughout that any Barro–Ricardo effects are at best incomplete.

[5] As noted in the introduction, macroeconomic or real exchange rate effects are not the only possible causes of the resource curse. Governance and institutional issues are likely to play a large role (see Gelb and others 2003).

[6] The details of this argument will depend, among other things, on the degree of capital mobility. In the case of capital market integration, the real interest rate is fixed (in the absence of expected exchange rate changes) and so investment is constant. The additional saving therefore results in a reduction of net foreign liabilities (or an increase in foreign assets). So in addition to the direct benefits of the windfall, there are also benefits over time in the form of reduced interest payments on external debt. Thus, in both the capital autarky and capital integration cases, there is additional growth to disposable income if some of the windfall is saved. For a complete exposition, see Lewin (2003).

raising the relative price of the home good. In the case described above, the increase in exports (the oil revenue) causes a real appreciation and an increase in imports and a decrease in non-oil exports. The increase in domestic consumption is satisfied partly by an increase in imports and partly by increased domestic consumption of the exportable good.[7] To assume an extreme case to illustrate the point, if imports were rationed – by, say, a fixed quota – then the increased demand due to the windfall would have to be satisfied entirely by the home good. This would cause a further rise in domestic prices and all the rise in domestic consumption would be at the expense of non-oil exportable goods. In other words, what would previously have been exported will now be consumed domestically. In both cases, if output is at capacity, the welfare benefits must be accompanied by a real appreciation and a decline in net non-oil exports.

Sterilization of the oil revenue can only delay the real appreciation but not eliminate it, if there is to be any benefit from the oil. Thus, if the full amount of the transfer or windfall were invested offshore, there would be no effect on the balance of payments (the outflow exactly equaling the inflow) and no effect on disposable income. Hence, the real appreciation would be avoided, but there would be no welfare gain until the repatriation of income from the offshore investment began. The effect of this income in each period is exactly the same as in the analysis above: a real appreciation and a decline in net non-oil exports.

The Bust

From the above it would appear that there is no bust, at least not from economic sources (as opposed to governance or institutional ones). However, a fundamental assumption underlying this conclusion is the assumption that the windfall or transfer is constant. In reality, it is likely to be variable for many reasons, but the most important reason is the price of oil, which tends to be highly volatile.[8] Figure 5.1 shows the monthly price of oil from January 1970 through October 2003.

In an oil-dependent economy, the variability of the oil rent will, in the absence of countermeasures, spill over into the real exchange rate. An oil price boom will lead to a real appreciation and a decline in non-oil exports. This is often taken as the main symptom of the Dutch Disease, but is not in and of itself a cause of reduced welfare. The problem arises when the decline in net exports is due to a boom that is short-lived. When the windfall revenue subsequently falls, the real exchange

---

[7] A key assumption of the model is that purchasing power parity does not necessarily hold and that the price of home goods is determined in the domestic market. This introduces the notion of the real exchange rate or competitiveness in meaningful way. This may not be as rich for many purposes as a model with nontraded goods. However, the aggregative model (that is, the one-good model) makes it easier to determine investment and saving variables, which are the main stuff of macroeconomics and key determinants of long-run growth (given technology).

[8] Hausmann and Rigobon (2003, p. 19) note that the standard deviation of oil price changes has been between 30 and 35 percent, so that a one standard deviation fluctuation would result in an income shock of around 6 percent of GDP for a country where oil constitutes 20 percent of GDP. For the period 1983 to 1997, the average monthly price of crude oil was $20/bbl; the median was $18. The price fluctuated between a high of $34.5 (or 171 percent of the average) and $9.6 (or 47 percent of the average) (World Bank 1999).

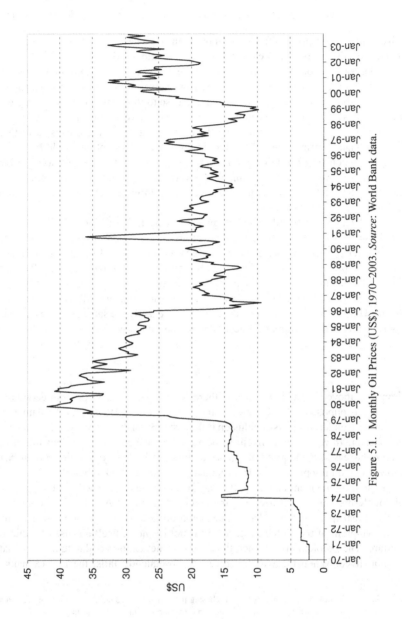

Figure 5.1. Monthly Oil Prices (US$), 1970–2003. *Source:* World Bank data.

rate becomes overvalued. But it may not be possible to recover lost non-oil export markets or resuscitate the relevant sectors, notably, agriculture and manufacturing, in short order *even if* the real overvaluation is corrected by a subsequent depreciation. Additionally, adjustments to the real exchange rate are unlikely to be smooth.

Repeated episodes of booms and busts in oil prices transmitted to the real exchange rate would result in large risk premiums in the non-oil sectors and thus depress investment in those sectors. This may cause a secular decline in productivity, resulting in lower rates of growth or stagnation in the non-oil sectors. Thus, the deleterious outcomes from oil price variability flow from its translation into real exchange rate volatility.[9] The adjustment to a reversal of the windfall may be very costly.

Government as Conduit

In most oil-exporting countries, the government acts as "trustee" of the resources for the country and is the exclusive or almost exclusive recipient of the oil rents. From the analysis above, it is clear that the real economic effects of the mineral revenues are determined by their effect on saving/consumption/investment balances in the economy and the balance of payments. The introduction of government into the analysis opens up other avenues for the absorption of the revenues. The analysis above assumed that the windfall simply reduced the overall level of taxes in all periods, thereby increasing disposable income.[10] Analytically, the difference here between a rise in government spending and a fall in the level of taxes is slight and the change in expenditure does not affect the government budget balance, as it is fully funded by the mineral revenue.

If the government spends more on investment when oil prices rise, then, theoretically, it can increase growth – assuming that the implementation capacity exists and the investments are indeed productive. Governments will also typically increase consumption, such as wages and salaries, and outright subsidies and transfers, as well as expenditures on health and education. This could have lasting effects, in terms of raising public expectations and ratcheting up current and future expenditure commitments limiting the government's ability to adjust fiscal policy when revenues fall. In the smaller exporting countries in particular, government expenditure will constitute a large share of total spending and have a profound influence on aggregate demand.

Hence, much of the economic turbulence in many oil economies is due to overspending during the boom. If the government spends all or most of the windfall revenue, then practically all the increase in aggregate demand due to the windfall is in the form of government expenditure. The government becomes the booming sector. One way or another, if revenue falls, the shock will be transmitted to the rest of the economy. Maintaining expenditure at boom levels will be unsustainable, whereas

---

[9] The exhaustibility of the resource is often given as another harmful factor. However, insofar as this is known, it is possible to take steps in preparation for the decline in resource production. Price variability is more difficult to hedge.

[10] In practice the differences are significant. The government will typically not transfer much of the wealth to the private sector, but will divide the revenue between investment and consumption expenditures.

reducing expenditures in line with lower revenues will affect aggregate demand directly. Thus when government expenditure is determined by current revenue, then if the revenue is volatile, fiscal policy also becomes volatile and so does aggregate demand. These gyrations in fiscal spending spill over into real exchange rate volatility and lead governments to rely more heavily on import tariffs and other trade distorting taxes for revenue generation and management of the resulting loss of competitiveness in the non-oil sectors. This would be in addition to the higher production costs typical of oil-exporting economies.[11] The antidote is clear: governments should set realistic (sustainable) expenditure targets and accumulate assets when prices are above normal (that is, save the windfall) and take opposite measures when prices are below normal. Unfortunately, as pointed out by Max Corden (1995), governments tend to regard boom prices as permanent and low prices as transitory. This leads governments to try and maintain an unsustainable expenditure path financed by borrowing, giving rise to the ironic phenomenon of heavily indebted oil-rich countries. Thus, the key challenge for many oil producing countries is to sever the link between current revenue and expenditure.[12]

Primacy of Fiscal Policy

Since the government is the conduit for the mineral revenues to the rest of the economy, fiscal policy is the key to managing booms. Country experience in this regard suggests that success lies in some combination of expenditure restraint and revenue management – the latter consisting of self-insurance and asset diversification. The aim of these approaches is to eliminate instability in aggregate demand, and consequently the real exchange rate, by smoothing expenditure over time, which implies self-insuring against revenue downfalls. The ability to maintain expenditure during the bust depends on having been prudent during the boom.

Alternatively, oil-producing governments can transfer oil price volatility to private markets by using financial instruments to hedge oil price risk. This approach tends to work better with a combination of short- and long-term instruments that provide opportunities for hedging (such as options and futures), along with asset diversification (through the use of commodity bonds). In reality, however, few countries systematically manage commodity risk with financial instruments – although there are success stories in this regard. Insulating the economy from oil price volatility will, other things equal, allow the non-oil sector to accumulate productive assets through the normal process of saving and investment, thus effectively supplementing the volatile revenue with a more stable source of income over the medium to long term. It is also worth noting that fiscal policy is determined by the *consolidated* government transactions. Saving all the oil revenues (such as in an oil revenue fund; see Box 5.1) does not in itself indicate the net accumulation of assets by the government,

[11] Gelb (2002).

[12] In practice, however, there is considerable, though not insurmountable, difficulty in predicting oil prices from historical data and thus distinguishing between transitory and permanent components. This is discussed in more detail below. It is probably wise to err on the side of caution when it comes to expenditure. While spending too little has real welfare costs, these are probably outweighed by the subsequent costs resulting from the typical boom–bust cycle induced by overspending during booms.

Box 5.1. Oil Funds

The "fiscal link" is the key element in the transmission of oil price volatility to the rest of the economy in most small oil-dependent countries. To insulate the economy from oil revenue volatility requires delinking fiscal expenditures from current revenue. Expenditure should be targeted at a sustainable level akin to the "permanent income" level of consumption theory. This means that the government (the main recipient of oil income in most small economies) should save – that is, accumulate assets – when the oil price is higher than its long-run level, and dissave when the price is low. Thus, the fiscal authority will alternate between net asset and liability accumulation depending on whether the price is above or below its long-run level. So, unless the government spends all of current revenue, the process of managing the revenues will depend on the country's particular institutional arrangements. An "oil revenue fund" (or more generally, a "natural resource fund") is one such institutional mechanism for managing the oil revenues. How these funds operate is elaborated in the text.

- *What an Oil Revenue Fund cannot do.* The oil revenue fund (ORF) is not a panacea. Most importantly, it cannot prevent the fiscal authority from spending the windfalls and financing its expenditure by borrowing. Thus, the fiscal authority can acquire assets on the one hand in the ORF, but liabilities on the other through borrowing. In such a case, the consolidated net asset position of the government would not improve during the boom. Fiscal policy therefore would not be able to insulate the economy from oil price turbulence and the fund would have served no purpose. It is also important to note that although ORFs are often called stabilization funds, they cannot in fact stabilize oil revenue since that depends, inter alia, on oil prices. The most the ORF can do is manage the revenue and ensure stable transfers to the budgetary or fiscal authority.
- *What an Oil Revenue Fund can do.* An appropriately constituted ORF can potentially increase transparency and accountability. It should be designed, at least, to make it possible to keep track of what funds are accumulated, how they are managed, and how much is transferred to the fiscal authority, thus increasing public scrutiny of public finance in general and of oil revenue in particular. Promoters of stabilization funds claim that they help maintain fiscal discipline by giving institutional backing to the idea that a boom should not lead to a spending binge; windfalls should be saved for future use. This could be important given the nature of the typical oil revenue regime, which often leads to opacity and corruption.
- *The verdict.* Critics of ORFs emphasize their deficiencies in terms of controlling overall government expenditure and net asset accumulation. They also argue that ORFs will often be nontransparent and used to mask the true fiscal position. Proponents emphasize the governance failures of oil economies that derive from their being rentiers, arguing that the quality of rent management can influence the quality of its deployment; and, that if properly constituted a fund can improve the quality of rent management. Opinions are divided on whether the empirical evidence supports the view that ORFs achieve their objectives. Additional research would be welcome. In the absence of a conclusive resolution of the debate, economists should not be dogmatic in advising for or against the establishment of ORFs. Particular circumstances should dictate whether and if so what kind of ORF is advisable.

as this can be offset by the accumulation of other liabilities. In monitoring the fiscal stance of a country, it is therefore important to monitor the consolidated debt/asset position of the government.

One way to achieve this is to constrain the non-oil deficit to be consistent over time with the sustainable permanent component of oil revenues.[13] In this case, one can think of the non-oil deficit as being financed by oil revenue and other borrowing; therefore the non-oil deficit measures the total net change in liabilities, including the depletion of oil. This is akin to thinking of oil as an asset. It follows that depletion of the oil is a reduction in national wealth. One can maintain the level of wealth by replacing the depleted oil with other assets, or what Max Corden (1995) has called substituting the assets below the ground with assets above the ground. Thus expenditure from an exhaustible resource can be extended in perpetuity by spending only the income from the assets and maintaining the value of total wealth. (Similarly, one could calculate the present discounted value of the oil revenues, which would, hypothetically, be the value of financial assets the government could get if it were to sell off all the oil. The revenue from these assets would be its permanent income.)

The analogy with the concepts of "permanent income" and "wealth" of consumer theory is clear. This can serve as a guide to policy in the case where intertemporal smoothing is the objective. However, as a rough rule of thumb, it may also serve as a guide to policy in response to price volatility. In this case, one is replacing an uncertain or volatile stream of income (oil revenue) with a more stable one from the assets "above the ground." Thus, for stability and sustainability, expenditure should be targeted at permanent or "expected" income (revenue).[14] Netting out other government borrowing and lending, an accurate measure is obtained of genuine government saving and the amount of the oil rents actually spent and saved.

The following sections survey country experiences with oil revenue ("stabilization") funds and fiscal policy rules, mechanisms for self-insurance and asset diversification, and policies to catalyze diversification in the real sector.

POLICY ISSUES

Stabilization and Savings Funds

An increasing number of oil-exporting developing countries have introduced stabilization and savings funds as a measure of self-insurance to deal with volatile oil revenues. A stabilization fund is designed to stabilize revenue flows and implicitly expenditure. A savings fund is designed to create a store of wealth for future generations by converting a depletable revenue stream into a perpetual income flow.[15]

---

[13] As emphasized by Barnett and Ossowski (2003).

[14] The question of how these quantities may be calculated is beyond the scope of this study.

[15] The nomenclature may be misleading. Strictly speaking, it is not possible to "stabilize" flows *to the fund* as long as oil prices are unstable. The stabilization fund therefore attempts to stabilize the flows *to the budget* by saving during booms and dissaving during busts. The budget revenues will therefore be more stable, allowing the government to maintain a targeted expenditure pattern through

The relatively successful experience of countries such as Kuwait and Norway in the use of stabilization and savings funds to restrict revenue and therefore to limit fiscal spending during oil price booms and to accumulate substantial net savings, has contributed to a proliferation of mineral funds in recent times. During the last decade or so, Azerbaijan, Algeria, Ecuador, Iran, Kazakhstan, Mexico, Nigeria, Venezuela, and others have joined the group of pioneers that introduced funds in the 1960s and 1970s.

Rules for accumulation tend to be price-contingent (accumulation of revenues greater than at a target price), as in the case of the Chile Copper Stabilization Fund (CSF); or revenue-contingent (50 percent of oil revenues), as in the case of the Alaska Permanent Fund; or both (50 percent of all oil revenue above a reference price), as in the case of Venezuela Stabilization Fund Rule. Withdrawal provisions have tended to be more discretionary than rules-based, in terms of transfers to the budget as needed (Alberta, Kuwait, Kiribati, and others), with some control and oversight in most cases by the Ministry of Finance, central bank, and other government officials (Davis and others 2001; Fasano-Filho 2000; Heilbrunn 2002).

Empirically, the effectiveness of funds in mitigating volatility is somewhat ambiguous. An IMF study estimates the impact of commodity revenues on government spending, using time-series analysis and structural break tests to determine whether the establishment of a fund has a significant impact on government spending (Davis and others 2001). Based on time-series data for countries with funds, expenditure appears to be less correlated with changes in revenues than in countries without funds, as would be expected if the funds work as they are supposed to; however, this experience is not uniform. In addition, in countries with funds, the establishment of a fund did not have an identifiable impact on government spending. This suggests that countries with more prudent expenditure policies tended to establish a fund, rather than the fund itself led to increased expenditure restraint.

More recent analysis using pooled crosssection and time-series data builds on this evidence by allowing for a more complete specification of volatility in government expenditure, country-specific effects, and incorporation of the size of fund balances (Crain and Devlin 2002). Using a standard measurement and estimation strategy for fiscal expenditure volatility (Ramey and Ramey 1995), aggregate panel data covering 71 countries for the years 1970 through 2000 suggests four central findings. First, volatility in government spending is costly. A 10 percent reduction in budget volatility generates efficiency gains comparable to a 2.7 percent increase in the level of funding. Second, funds can have the effect of increasing the volatility of government expenditure, particularly in oil-exporting countries, due to their inability to insure overall fiscal restraint. Third, funds appear to have a dampening effect on government spending as a percentage of GDP, but at the cost of higher fiscal deficits during the boom, potentially leading to expenditure volatility. Fourth, implementing a fund appears to raise fixed capital investments as share of GDP by nearly 3 percentage points. There is also a positive relationship between the balances held in the fund and fixed capital investment.

---

thick and thin without resorting to destabilizing or unsustainable borrowing or inflating. Thus, in the language of consumption theory, a single stabilization and savings fund combines both intertemporal and precautionary motives for saving.

In the case of specific countries – Chile, Norway, and Oman[16] – funds appear to deliver a number of favorable outcomes: lower levels of volatility in government expenditure, reduced government expenditure, and higher shares of gross fixed capital investment. This suggests that country-specific circumstances matter a lot and that more specific cases should be studied before any firm conclusions can be drawn.

If the decision is taken to establish a fund, then design and operation of funds should be based on transparent integration into the budgetary process, to avoid off-budgetary spending. Parliamentary/legislative oversight should be included, with the aim of preventing the executive from maintaining sole discretionary powers over the fund's resources. Ideally, there should be no earmarking of fund resources. To ensure proper integration of the funds in the budgetary process, there should be no independent spending authority for funds. Moreover, the fund should be prohibited from holding public debt. Assets in the fund should not be used as collateral to increase uncontrollable fiscal spending. Furthermore, an asset management strategy for the fund needs to be designed that is consistent with the debt management operations of the ministry of finance, the treasury's management of government cash flow, and the financial assets already held as part of the government's balance sheet. This will help ensure that the overall net asset position of the government is maintained in an appropriate way.

Fiscal Rules and Targets

Revenue management is of course only one side of the strategy to insulate the economy from oil price volatility. Good revenue management will come to naught if public spending is out of control. While restricting revenue can put pressure on government to curtail expenditure, it cannot guarantee it. Restraint can be encouraged by well-defined rules to smooth expenditure of oil revenues over time. Fiscal rules, broadly defined, are budgetary institutions or a set of rules and regulations according to which budgets are drafted, approved, and implemented. They have been used in a number of ways to ensure macroeconomic stability (postwar Japan), enhance the credibility of the government's fiscal policy and help in debt consolidation (Canadian provinces), ensure long-term sustainability of fiscal policy (New Zealand), and reduce procyclical bias in fiscal policy (Fiess 2002). For a fiscal rule to be efficient, it should be not too rigid to provide some flexibility to legitimate countercyclical policy when needed. It should be credible: that is, it should be viewed as permanent. And it should be transparent: easy to monitor and difficult to manipulate.

It is important to point out that rules related to fiscal balances or fund accumulation are a means to an end: namely, attaining a medium-term fiscal target. In the case of Chile, for example, the government recently introduced a structural surplus target of 1 percent of GDP.[17] The structural balance takes into account cyclical and

---

[16] It is important to point out that in the case of Chile and Norway, commodity revenues as a percentage of overall government revenues are significantly lower than in most oil-exporting countries implying that the impact of a volatile revenue stream is significantly lower. Copper prices are also less volatile than oil prices, lessening the degree of potential fiscal volatility. These effects were taken into account in Crain and Devlin (2002).

[17] Calculation of the structural surplus is similar to that of OECD methodology, but revenues and expenditures are adjusted for the business cycle and cyclical movements in copper prices.

random effects of changes in the price of copper by reflecting revenue and expenditure achievable on the basis of long-term copper prices. Like a stabilization fund, the fiscal target effectively functions as a measure of self-insurance by adjusting for commodity price fluctuations and transferring resources from booms to busts (Perry 2002; Fiess 2002).

Fiscal policy management in the commodity-exporting developing country context has thus become increasingly characterized as a problem of identifying and applying the appropriate fiscal rule or target in the context of a medium-term fiscal framework (Perry 2002; Bjerkholt 2002; Davis, Ossowski, and Fedelino 2003). However, the reality in many developing countries is such that informal norms and practices tend to have a greater effect on fiscal behavior than formal rules and institutions (Schick 1998). Furthermore, such problems tend to be extreme in oil-exporting developing countries, where the "rentier" nature of oil revenues tends to weaken formal mechanisms of revenue accountability (Eifert, Gelb, and Tallroth 2003).

Hence, an overriding focus on formal fiscal rules and budgetary procedures may miss the point. In weak fiscal environments, a key challenge for strengthening public resource management is to enhance financial incentives in the government overall (Schick 1998). In this regard, the case where funds have proven to be relatively effective may also be related to the fact that management of (in some cases, a sizeable share of) public resources is being effectively outsourced to the market, with favorable repercussions on financial incentives in overall government performance. This may explain why funds tend to do better in helping countries to deal with windfalls and converting nonrenewable wealth into productive assets, in the form of investment (Crain and Devlin 2002; Hannesson 2001).

Financial Incentives

Prudent use of windfalls with a fund requires appropriate governance structures based on transparency and accountability. Time devoted to a well-designed fund may also be an investment in better fiscal policy management overall. Such funds should therefore be designed with built-in mechanisms for accountability, professionalism, and performance benchmarks and transparency (see Box 5.2 on the Tuvalu Trust Fund). With regard to accountability, important elements are oversight by the central bank and/or Ministry of Finance – which also provide an investment strategy for the fund and operational guidelines that define the linkages between the central bank or ministry and the fund manager.

However, it is important to remember that in developing countries, such guidelines need to take into account country-specific circumstances. In many countries, funds have been subject to high levels of discretion by the executive, either directly or indirectly through a board of directors, and in many cases under central bank supervision. It is important to consider who appoints the board of directors. Where the central bank is not independent of the fiscal authority, this leaves fund resources vulnerable to rapid depletion for reasons of political expediency. Furthermore, parliamentary approval regarding use of the fund's resources may be desirable, but it can also be problematic if the legislature is less fiscally conservative than the executive. In this case, a "Ways and Means" committee in the legislature, whose purpose is to

---

Box 5.2. The Tuvalu Trust Fund

Tuvalu is one of the world's smallest countries, consisting of nine coral atolls covering only 25 square km of land spread over a distance of 676 km. It is classified by the United Nations as a least developed country, with a per capita income of $1,329 in 1996. However, following creation of the Tuvalu Trust Fund in 1987 and its subsequent success in capitalizing earnings from the island's "windfall" cash transfer following independence from Britain in 1978, Tuvalu has become one of the most successful examples of long-term development planning on the basis of capitalizing a depletable resource: in this case, the initial onetime cash transfer.* The Tuvalu Trust Fund is also an example of good donor–recipient coordination and partnership, since it has become the primary vehicle for ongoing donor assistance to Tuvalu.

The Tuvalu Trust Fund was set up in 1987, under an international agreement signed by the Government of Tuvalu and development partners – New Zealand, Australia, and the United Kingdom, who initially contributed to the Fund. The initial funding amounted to $27.1 million (Australian currency). Tuvalu's initial contribution was $1.6 million, and each donor contributed $8 million. In terms of shares, Tuvalu's share of initial fund capital was only 6 percent. Today it is nearly 30 percent.

Tuvalu Trust Fund resources are invested internationally in a combination of shares, listed property, fixed interest deposits, and bonds. The primary objective is maintaining the real capital value of the Fund. Seventy percent of assets are in growth areas. Thirty percent are in defensive, conservative allocations. There are two accounts. The A account, or the growth capital account, is managed with the objective of maintaining the real purchasing power of the Fund. Distributions are made from the A account when Fund growth exceeds the rate of inflation. The B account is a buffer fund of unspent distributions.

Over the 13 years of the Fund's existence, the Fund capital (A account) has increased nearly two and a half times, with a market value at $66.6 million in September 2000. In addition to the Fund capital, the Tuvalu government has built up a buffer fund (B account), which totaled $20 million in September 2000. Together the A and B accounts represent a growth in reserves from $27 million to $86 million, which is a compound increase of 9.4 percent per year nominal growth in reserves. In FY 2001, distribution of the fund's earnings to the government was $6.1 million, representing 38 percent of core expenditure.

Several key aspects of the Tuvalu Trust Fund have contributed to its superior performance. First is accountability through a Board of four directors, with Tuvalu in the chair and the other original parties providing members. Second is professional funds management. Third is monitoring of the Fund performance by actuarial consultants (the Fund Monitor). Fourth is auditing of the Fund by international auditors. Finally, an advisory committee monitors Tuvalu's economic performance and provide advice to the Government and the Board.

In the Fund's governance structure, the primary responsibility of Fund management lies with the Board of Directors. The Board consists of four Trust Directors,

(*Box continues on the following page*)

Box 5.2 (*continued*)

representing the governments of Tuvalu (Chair), New Zealand, Australia, and the United Kingdom. The Directors appoint a Fund Monitor to recommend an investment policy and money managers. The objectives of the Fund, and consequently the risk profile of the investments, are laid out in an investment policy, which includes benchmarks and allowable ranges for a balance portfolio. The Fund Monitor then drafts contracts with money managers – namely, 50 percent with County NatWest and 50 percent with JP Morgan Chase – who invest the money on behalf of the Board.

Another body, the Advisory Committee, with representatives from Tuvalu plus New Zealand, Australia and the United Kingdom, prepares an annual report on the performance of the Fund, as well as its impact on the economy. This is also submitted to Parliament. This group meets in Tuvalu twice a year for about 10 days to review the government budget and to provide advice on macro- and micro-issues, similar to an Article IV IMF mission. At the end of each financial year, the Committee calculates the value of the Fund to ensure that Fund capital is maintained in real terms for inflation. If the market value of the Fund is grater than the maintained value, then the difference is automatically transferred to the Tuvalu Government and placed in a buffer fund (the B Account), referred to in the Budget as the Consolidated Investment Fund.

* *Source*: Bell (2001).

have some oversight of the policy and performance of the fund's financial assets, may help to address this issue.

Funds should be professionally managed, ideally with oversight by the Ministry of Finance, board of directors, and/or central bank and should have clear performance benchmarks. In the case of the Norges Fund for Norway, a new department, the Norges Bank Investment Management (NBIM) Group, was established in 1998 to mange the Petroleum Fund. NBIM is organized with Chinese walls to the ordinary central bank functions. The head of the NBIM reports to the governor of the central bank (Norges Bank), but does not take part in the internal discussion of monetary policy. Within the NBIM, roughly 50 percent of the equity portfolio is managed in house, while 15 external managers do the bulk of the active risk taking in portfolio investment decisions. The primary goal of Petroleum Fund management is to outperform the benchmark portfolio defined by the Ministry of Finance (Skancke 2002).

The institutional design of the funds can also make the earnings and use of resource revenues more transparent (Bjerkholt 2002). In the case of the Alaska Permanent Fund, which uses invested oil revenues to distribute annual dividends[18]

[18] Each year, the state of Alaska distributes a share of Permanent Fund earnings from its investments in stocks, bonds, and real estate to every qualified Alaska resident. The size of each year's dividend is calculated using a formula that averages the Fund's earnings over the previous five years. Eligibility requirements for the Permanent Fund Dividends include at least one year's residency in Alaska, no claim of residency in any other state or country, no felony convictions, and at least 72 consecutive hours of physical presence in Alaska in the prior two years.

to all Alaskan citizens, the population can check the monthly earnings and expenditure of the fund to determine the exact amount of dividend checks. Another proposal along these lines is to deposit surplus commodity revenues into pension accounts to encourage more public scrutiny of fund resources (Hannesson 2001). A similar approach is to engage interest groups with a firm stake in better management of oil proceeds, such as environmental groups and traditional exporters (Bates 1997; Karl 1997).

Information on the fund's activities should be publicly available and widely disseminated. Detailed annual reports should describe how the fund is managed and include a list of the companies in which the fund's capital has been invested. Information on total return, benchmark return, and attribution of excess return should be included, along with management costs. Where relevant, information on the selection process for external mangers should also be included. In the case of the Norges Bank, an independent company hired by the Ministry of Finance also makes calculations of the fund's returns and provides an analysis of differences between actual and benchmark returns. These reports, as well as the external audit of the fund, are made publicly available and submitted to Parliament.

The size of the fund matters. For economic and political reasons, larger funds can potentially incur more inefficiencies and distortions. Both theoretical and empirical evidence on the size of funds suggests that the optimal size fund tends to be much smaller than expected, with the determining factor being the statistical properties of oil prices, rather than rules for accumulation and withdrawal (Arrau and Claessens 2001; Crain and Devlin 2002). In the case of the CSF, the copper price is treated as mean-reverting, implying that fluctuations in copper prices are treated as temporary. However, empirical evidence suggests that all copper price changes should be treated as permanent, which may have been a factor in contributing to a slightly larger size CSF than predicted on the basis of theoretical calculations.

Budget Forecasts

An underlying assumption in managing volatile commodity flows is that the fiscal authority is able to accurately forecast revenues and expenditure needs over the medium term. This is not always straightforward, as oil prices have temporary (mean reversion) and permanent (persistence) components. The evidence on the statistical properties of oil prices tends to find relatively more support for mean-reversion (Pindyck 1999; Barnett and Vivanco 2003) than persistence (Cashin, Liang, and McDermott 2002; Engel and Valdés 2000) using unit root tests, although much depends on the time interval under scrutiny.

To deal with this issue, a number of countries use downward-biased estimates in budget preparation to avoid overfunding of planned expenditures. The problem with this approach is that it requires accurate estimates of oil prices, which is difficult in practice. Governments in Indonesia, Kuwait, Mexico Saudi Arabia, and Venezuela, for example, have tended to make huge errors in their revenue forecasts.[19] Robert

---

[19] Pinto (1987 pp. 424) demonstrates the volatility of oil price expectations using as an example the World Bank forecast of the 1985 price of a barrel of oil made at three different points in time: "... the

Weiner (1995) demonstrates that high forecast errors in the budgeting processes of these states were not a result of incompetent forecasting but reflected the difficult task of forecasting volatile mineral prices.

Specifically, there are problems associated with determining a long-term reference price. In Chile, Russia, and other countries, this has frequently resulted in a prolonged process of discussion and dispute over forecasting methods; a process that is also vulnerable to political pressure. In the case of Chile, the copper benchmark price was traditionally determined by a group of experts on an annual basis in a largely nontransparent fashion. A related difficulty is that while oil prices exhibit properties of mean reversion, reversion tends to be slow, and the permanent components to oil prices are significant. This suggests that it is advisable not to base fiscal rules on moving averages of past commodity prices.

One alternative that addresses both these issues is the greater use of futures markets to provide evidence regarding mean reversion tendencies and reference price estimates. With regard to the former, one way to evaluate the relative importance of the temporary and permanent components is to compare the fluctuations in futures and forward prices of various maturities with spot price changes. If price changes are largely temporary (that is, prices tend to revert to some long-run average), long-term futures prices will have substantially less volatility than either short-term futures prices or spot prices. Evidence indicates that long-term futures prices of oil are about half as volatile as short-term futures prices. (Barnett and Vivanco 2003; Smith and Schwartz 2000). With respect to determining longer-term price estimates for budgeting purposes, the price of a five-year swap that locks in prices can be used for medium-term budgeting.

Asset Diversification

With self-insurance, the public sector still ultimately bears the risk of commodity price volatility. In other words, the government is self-insuring against commodity price risk, as opposed to passing this risk on to private markets through the use of risk-management instruments. This is aggravated by increasing specialization in the productive structure over time, as the nontradable sector grows large at the expense of the nonoil tradable sector. For both these reasons, it is critical to implement policies and mechanisms for asset diversification through the use of financial markets and the development of the non-oil tradable sector.

DIVERSIFICATION THROUGH FINANCIAL INSTRUMENTS. The use of market-based financial instruments has long been identified as the first-best solution for dealing with oil price volatility in theory, but in practice, risk-management programs are rarely implemented (Engel and Mellor 1993; Claessens and Duncan 1993; World Bank 1999). Instruments such as swaps, futures, and options make it possible to lock into a known oil price for a given period of time, thus eliminating price uncertainty.

1976 forecast was $21.9; in 1979, following the second oil shock, this number was revised upward to $47.3; and then downward to $29.0 in 1983. . . . These forecasts have a mean of $32.73 and a standard deviation of $10.70 per barrel. . . ."

More importantly financial instruments allow a country to transfer commodity price risk to the market, rather than self-insuring. From a political economy standpoint, a risk management strategy can also make credible the promise not to spend windfall income (Hausmann 1999).

Given that mineral funds can be vulnerable to prolonged periods of price busts, a number of studies also point to the benefits of combining the use of risk management instruments with a mineral fund (Claessens and Varangis 1993). Simulation exercises for Alaska and Venezuela, for example, demonstrate that such a combination may be optimal from the vantage point of using financial instruments to hedge against price booms and busts. When the fund is small, there is a rationale for using financial instruments to avoiding the situation of depleting the fund. In general, the tools for managing mineral price risk, such as futures and swaps, are becoming more sophisticated with the development of derivative and capital markets. For example, futures and options for crude oil and natural gas are traded on the New York Mercantile Exchange (NYMEX), while forward and swap contracts are traded in the Over-the-Counter-Market (OTC).

EXCHANGE-TRADED INSTRUMENTS. Exchange-traded instruments are usually more transparent, more easy to monitor, and more liquid than OTC instruments such as swaps and forwards. Options are similar to taking out an insurance policy to guard against increases or decreases in oil prices.[20]

A *put option* allows the government to create a price floor by buying the right to sell a certain quantity of oil at a specific price for a specific time period. If actual oil prices fall below this floor, the option is "in-the-money" and can be exercised or sold for a profit. To help offset the cost of the premium on a put option, the government can sell *call options*, or the right to buy oil at a specific price over a given time period, establishing an effective ceiling on the price. Various combinations of selling puts and calls are possible so that a government will not have to give up the upside potential: for example, selling a call option and buying a call option at a higher strike price. The "costless collar" is an instrument with which the government can purchase a put option and sell a call option so that the premiums received from selling call options are used to finance the purchase of the put options.

An important factor to take into consideration with the use of futures and options is an adequate assessment of basis risk. Basis risk refers to the difference between the benchmark oil price (such as West Texas Intermediate) that is used to hedge and the mineral price that is actually realized in the exporting country. Although in practice basis risk tends to be much smaller than the overall price risk for oil, the benefits and costs of using risk management instruments are clearly affected by basis risk. In the case of Alaskan oil, oil prices have ranged from $9 to $41, whereas the basis, or the difference with West Texas Intermediate, has ranged from $0.80 to $4.20 (Lindahl 1996a).

---

[20] An option is a contract that conveys to its holder the right, but not the obligation, to buy (in the case of a call) or sell (in the case of a put) a security or a commodity at a specified price (the strike or exercise price) on or before a given date (expiration day). In return for the rights they are granted, options buyers pay options sellers a premium. (A more technical discussion can be found in Blake 1990.)

Mexico is one of the few developing country exporters that used financial instruments to manage oil price risk and during the 1990s. It was able to lock in an effective price of $17/barrel using hedging instruments. A recent simulation (Daniel 2001) of different oil price management strategies for Mexico during this period (1990–2000) demonstrates how this was possible. A simple futures strategy for example, in which the government sells oil through 12-month WTI (West Texas Intermediate) futures rather than on the spot market, results in much less volatile revenue and a slightly lower average price. The effective oil price is then the Mexican spot price plus the gain/loss from holding a 12-month WTI futures contract. In this example, the volatility of the average monthly spot price was roughly 4.5 $/barrel, compared with futures at 1.9 $/barrel (Daniel 2001).

CUSTOMIZED INSTRUMENTS. Compared to exchange trade instruments, OTC instruments, such as swaps and forward contracts, offer greater flexibility because they are customized transactions between the government and the financial intermediary. As such, they can mitigate basis risk, are available in large volumes for single transactions, and frequently cover longer periods. They also eliminate the need for initial deposits and margin calls.

In a swap transaction, the oil-producing government contracts with a private bank to lock in an oil price (say, $20/barrel) for a longer period of time (say, two to three years). The producing government then sells the oil on the open market, and both parties calculate an average sales price every six months. If the average price that the country receives for its oil is less than $20/barrel, the bank pays the producing government the difference. If oil prices increase, the payment flows in the reverse direction.

There are a number of possible variations on this basic approach. A country could also use a swap to establish a price floor at $20/barrel and could sell a cap (say, at $25) to help cover the cost of the floor. In this case, the country would pay the bank any oil revenues received over $25/barrel.

Example: Figure 5.2 illustrates how a "costless collar" works. The country effectively buys a put at a strike price, which becomes the floor, and sells a call at a higher strike price, which becomes the ceiling. The strike prices can be chosen in a way that the premium paid for the put is exactly offset by the premium received for the call. In Figure 5.2, the put establishes a price floor at $20/barrel and the call a ceiling at $25.

Using both exchange-traded and OTC instruments, oil-producing governments can sell their production forward or buy insurance against large price declines. For governments that have not considered the use of financial instruments to manage oil price risk, a good time to start for political economy reasons is when prices are high relative to trend. During a high price period for example, a producing country can lock in revenues at the high price through swaps and protect against low case price scenarios with put options.

PRACTICAL DIFFICULTIES. Although the use of financial instruments will reduce risk and increase efficiency for a country, implementing such a policy may be risky for the government official who makes the decision. Policymakers are likely to be

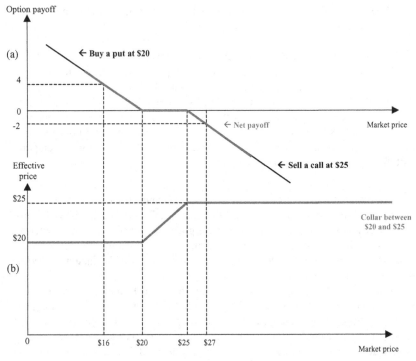

Figure 5.2. A Collar between $20 and $25. Buying a put at $20 and selling a call at $25.

evaluated by how well market-based instruments work relative to the status quo or the case in which risks are not hedged using financial markets.

In addition, government officials are likely to find financial market transactions very risky because they are not very well understood and are difficult to explain. Relevant risks facing these officials include not only the volatility of prices, but also the success of the risk-management decisions: namely, whether the country turns out to be better or worse off as a result of implementing the financial market strategy. In practice, however, there are high penalties for countries not hedging oil price risk, as demonstrated by the sovereign premia for many oil-exporting countries and lack of countercyclical access to capital.

This experience is similar for oil and gas companies. A recent study (Kessler 2002) of the risk management behavior of firms in the oil and gas industry indicates that there are well-defined costs to cash flow volatility for companies that are not captured by standard discounted cash flow models. First, stock markets and rating agencies tend to reward companies that hedge forward cash flow volatility. Second, given that investment decisions depend on cash flow realizations, the implication is that hedging may lead to greater corporate investment or at least protect capital budgets during downswings in commodity prices. Third, producers with upstream exposure (such as refineries) tend to have the greatest incentive to hedge oil prices, given that oil price volatility is significantly higher than refining margin volatility. Fourth, noninvestment grade or highly leveraged institutions are encouraged to hedge by banks to deal with a perceived credit risk. For example, in the oil industry, noninvestment grade acquirers will often hedge target production to secure bank financing (Kessler 2002).

One of the few examples of using market-based instruments to hedge state budgets is the State of Texas Risk Management Program. As such, it offers some important lessons for implementation of a risk management program (Patterson 2001). Texas collects approximately $500 million from production taxes on crude mineral annually. The value of the tax is 4.6 percent of crude mineral production. State budgets are prepared biennially. In the mid-1990s, the state government introduced a risk management program using exchange trade options to hedge approximately 10 percent of its revenue. Three years later the program was expanded to cover 25 percent of revenues, using the strategy of a straddled costless collar. This approach effectively locks in a floor for oil prices, but also provides opportunities for benefiting if prices increase unexpectedly.

Lessons from the Texas case underscore the need to develop a clear philosophy for the program, such as risk management, to deal with fears of speculation. Ideally, a hedging program should be introduced as a way of extending existing responsibilities for treasury operations, rather than creating a new, stand-alone program. Existing staff with high levels of technical expertise and some experience with commodity markets are preferred. Clear operational guidelines for the program should be developed and approved, including authorization to trade, decision making responsibilities, position (stop-loss) limitations, broker constraints, daily monitoring, separation of responsibilities, and internal reporting.

Implementation of a risk-management strategy can begin after four to five alternative risk-management strategies (options, swaps, futures) are evaluated on paper. The strategy can be introduced as a pilot program with a sunset provision if the program loses too much money, and must have clear opportunities for upside potential. The program should be able to make profits, but not be speculative.

Evaluating the effectiveness of risk-management strategies from the vantage point of fiscal stability is an important area for further research. One recent study develops a quantitative measure of risk-management effectiveness, based on the future value of actual revenues (including net option payoffs) and the future value of anticipated taxes (Buttimer, Shaw, and Swidler 1999). (The simulation exercise suggests that a government will realize the highest portion of expected revenue when it does not use market-based instruments.) However, this case also has the highest level of volatility in revenues, and a higher frequency of budget deficits. In the case where financial instruments are employed, option risk management effectively manages extreme downside risk and stops large budget deficits from occurring.

DIVERSIFICATION OF THE REAL SECTOR. If macroeconomic policies to insulate the economy from oil price volatility are implemented, then diversification of the economy away from oil will occur, other things equal, through the normal process of saving and investment. The role of government in promoting such diversification is no different in principle from promoting economic development in general. (See Box 5.3.)

Box 5.3. Guidelines on Diversification.[*]

Promoting a diversified economy by maintaining incentives for a competitive non-oil tradable sector is often the stated goal of policymakers in oil-dependent economies. However, good policy intentions are not enough: the "cure" may act to worsen the ailment. Bearing in mind that each country is different, the following general guidelines sum up three key areas often discussed in this context.

- *Prudent expenditure management is more than half the battle.* The government is often the conduit for oil revenues and therefore the main source of potential instability in relative prices that determines the long-run development of a competitive tradable goods sector. Prudent fiscal policy will limit the volatility and over-appreciation of the real exchange rate. Other things equal, this will preserve resources in the more labor-intensive non-oil, tradable goods sector. Over 1979–81, for example, the Government of Indonesia managed to avoid some of the pitfalls of the oil boom by saving 40 percent of the oil windfall abroad. When increases in private and public consumption and investment threatened to undermine this policy, the government cut public spending and devalued the rupiah.
- *Openness to trade, competition, and creating an enabling environment for productivity growth.* An open trade policy avoids the protectionist antiexport bias and strengthens market forces. Even though oil-abundant countries such as Malaysia and Indonesia intermittently sought to implement heavy, big-push-type industrial development, they ultimately enhanced competitiveness and greater export orientation by developing free trade zones, encouraging foreign investment and reducing protection. Although their policies were not textbook perfect, both countries were able to build up competitive, labor-intensive, export-oriented industries. Productivity growth at the firm level was also supported by eliminating distortions in regulation and licensing, implementing privatization, vigorously promoting education and investment in human capital, and providing critical infrastructure.
- *Subsidies.* Many governments attempt to use subsidies in promoting diversification. Apart from the well-known pitfalls associated with "picking winners," experience shows that such policies can also encourage rent-seeking and inefficiency. Government expenditure to enhance productivity in the non-oil sector is most effective when focused on public goods such as infrastructure, health, and education. Nevertheless, there may be cases where the use of government funds to promote positive spillovers is appropriate. Given the preconditions of sound macroeconomic management and openness to trade and competition, a number of governments have used public funds to lower input costs for non-oil tradable sectors.

In Indonesia, for example, in addition to infrastructure programs, the government lowered costs for agricultural producers by distributing cheap complementary inputs such as fertilizers.

(Box continues on the following page)

Box 5.3 (*continued*)

These guidelines derive from "best practice" policies in the general development context. This is because the "diversification problem" is quintessentially one
of economic development. Policies that are good for economic development in
resource-poor countries will also serve resource-abundant countries well.

---

* For an early comparison of policies in oil-dependent Nigeria and Indonesia see Pinto (1987).
Detailed case studies can be found in Auty (2001) and Auty and Mikesell (1999). See also Gelb
(2002).

CONCLUSION

In the developing country context, oil windfalls clearly have the potential to be a
blessing rather than a curse. Oil revenue can help fund development needs while
containing the tax burden and reducing – or even eliminating – dependence on aid
or external borrowing. However, much depends on the level and pattern of fiscal
spending. Typically, procyclical government spending of oil revenue puts into play
a train of price effects that are difficult to reverse and tend to persist where markets
do not function well. Oil-financed public spending can lead to increased imports
(mainly capital goods) and the excess demand drives up prices of nontradables
(construction, services) relative to tradables (agriculture, manufacturing). In other
words, it leads to an appreciation of the real exchange rate. However, while a once-
and-for-all appreciation in the level of the real exchange rate can be managed, the
continuous volatility of oil prices, transmitted to government spending and then to the
real exchange rate (and accompanying price effects), creates unstable government
programs, risky investment climates, lack of steady growth in productive assets, and
no protection against budget shortfalls.

To deal with these effects, governments should adopt a policy of fiscal restraint
or a fiscal rule or target to avoid transmitting oil price volatility to the rest of
the economy. To the extent that such mechanisms help to "smooth" expenditures,
they can help to insulate (or sterilize) the economy by breaking the link between
volatile and high oil prices and government expenditure levels. The experience
of Botswana, Norway, and others suggests that a stable expenditure plan, based
on permanent (or expected) income, rather than transitory income – either with
or without a stabilization or savings fund – when combined with institutions that
promote financial accountability, can help prevent volatility in fiscal spending and
deteriorating growth performance.

Even under optimal circumstances, however, measures to promote expenditure
smoothing can do little in the way of eliminating oil price risk itself. Financial instruments can help a developing country government manage this risk more efficiently
and credibly. Again, the institutional environment is critical. Governments such as
the State of Texas that have successfully employed risk-management programs have
put in place safeguards to ensure adequate monitoring and control of the program,
together with a public awareness campaign designed to explain the implications
of *not* managing commodity risk. In addition, policymakers must take enabling

measures to diversify the real economy by using oil proceeds to enhance productivity and growth. Such measures need to be combined with exposing these sectors to competition (performance targets) and controlling fiscal spending.

REFERENCES

Aizenman, Joshua, and Nancy Marion. 1993. "Policy Uncertainty, Persistence, and Growth." *Review of International Economics* 1 (June):145–63.

Alier, Max, and Martin Kaufman. 1999. "Nonrenewable Resources: A Case for Persistent Surpluses." International Monetary Fund, Washington, DC.

Arrau, Patricio, and Stijn Claessens. 2001. "Commodity Stabilization Funds." World Bank, Washington, DC.

Auty, Richard. 1997. "Natural Resources, the State and Development Strategy." *Journal of International Development* 9:651–63.

———. 2001. *Resource Abundance and Economic Development.* New York: World Institute for Development Economics Research of the United Nations University and Oxford University Press.

Auty, Richard, and Raymond Mikesell. 1998. *Sustainable Development in Mineral Economies.* New York: Oxford University Press.

Barnett, Steven, and Rolando Ossowski. 2003. "Operational Aspects of Fiscal Policy in Oil Producing Countries." In Jeffrey Davis, Rolando Ossowski, and Annalisa Fedelino, eds., *Fiscal Policy Formulation and Implementation in Oil-Producing Countries.* Washington, DC: International Monetary Fund.

Barnett, Steven, and Alvaro Vivanco. 2003. "Statistical Properties of Oil Price: Implications for Calculating Government Wealth." In Jeffrey Davis, Rolando Ossowski, and Annalisa Fedelino, eds., *Fiscal Policy Formulation and Implementation in Oil-Producing Countries.* Washington, DC: International Monetary Fund.

Bates, R. 1997. *Open-Economy Politics. The Political Economy of the World Coffee Trade.* Princeton, NJ: Princeton University Press.

Bell, Brian. 2001. "Trust Funds for Improved Governance and Economic Performance in Developing Countries." Paper presented at the AARES 45th Annual Conference, January 23–25, Adelaide, South Australia.

Bevan, David, Paul Collier, and Jan Willem Gunning. 1992. *Nigeria, Policy Responses to Shocks, 1970–90.* San Francisco: ICS Press.

Bjerkholt, Olav. 2002. "Fiscal Rule Suggestions for Economies with Nonrenewable Resources." Paper presented at the IMF/World Bank Conference on Rules-Based Fiscal Policy in Emerging Market Economies in Oaxaca, Mexico, February 14–16, 2002.

Blake, David. 1990. *Financial Market Analysis.* Berkshire, UK: McGraw-Hill.

Buttimer, Richard, Ron Shaw, and Steve Swidler. 1999. "Government Risk Management: Motivation, Implementation." *Public Budgeting and Finance* 19 (4):75–90.

Cashin, Paul, and C. John McDermott. 2002. "The Long-Run Behavior of Commodity Prices: Small Trends and Big Variability." *IMF Staff Papers* 49 (2):175–99.

Chalk, Nigel. 1998. "Fiscal Sustainability with Nonrenewable Resources." Working Paper 98/26. International Monetary Fund, Washington, DC.

Claessens, Stijn, and Ronald C. Duncan, eds. 1993. *Managing Commodity Price Risk in Developing Countries.* Baltimore: Johns Hopkins University Press (for the World Bank).

Claessens, Stijn, and Panos Varangis. 1993. "A Mineral Import Risk Management Program in Costa Rica." In Stijn Claessens and Ronald Duncan, eds., *Managing Commodity Price Risk in Developing Countries.* Baltimore: John Hopkins University Press (for the World Bank)

Collier, Paul, and Jan Willem Gunning. 1996. *"Policy towards Commodity Shocks in Developing Countries."* Working Paper 96/84. International Monetary Fund, Washington, DC.

Corden, W. Max. 1984. "Booming Sector and Dutch Disease Economics: Survey and Consolidation." *Oxford Economic Papers* 36 (3):359.

———. 1995. *Economic Policy, Exchange Rates, and the International System.* New York: Oxford University Press.

Corden, Max, and Peter Neary. 1982. "Booming Sector and De-industrialisation in a Small Open Economy," Oxford: *Economics Journal*, 92:825–848.

Crain, Mark, and Julia Devlin. 2002. "Nonrenewable Resource Funds: A Red Herring for Fiscal Stability?" World Bank, Washington DC. Draft working paper.

Dalmazzo, Alberto, and Guido de Blasio. 2001. "Resources and Incentives to Reform: A Model and Some Evidence on Sub-Saharan African Countries." Working Paper 01/88. International Monetary Fund, Washington, DC.

Daniel, James. 2001. "Hedging Government Oil Price Risk." IMF Working Paper 01/185. International Monetary Fund, Washington, DC.

Davis, Jeffrey, Rolando Ossowski, and Annalisa Fedelino. 2003. *Fiscal Policy Formulation and Implementation in Oil-Producing Countries.* Washington, DC: International Monetary Fund.

Davis, Jeffrey, Rolando Ossowski, James Daniel, and Steven Barnett. 2001. "Stabilizationand Savings Funds for Nonrenewable Resources: Experience and Fiscal Policy Implications." IMF Occasional Paper 205. International Monetary Fund, Washington, DC.

Deaton, Angus, and Guy Laroque. 1992. "On the Behavior of Commodity Prices." *Review of Economic Studies* 59(198):1–24.

Devlin, Julia, and Michael Lewin. 2002. "Issues in Oil Revenue Management." Presentation for the World Bank/ESMAP Workshop on Petroleum Revenue Management, October 23–24, Washington, DC.

Eifert, Ben, Alan Gelb, and Nils Borje Tallroth. 2003. "The Political Economy of Fiscal Policy and Economic Management in Mineral Exporting Countries." In Jeffrey Davis, Rolando Ossowski, and Annalisa Fedelino, eds., *Fiscal Policy Formulation and Implementation in Oil-Producing Countries.* Washington, DC: International Monetary Fund.

Engel, Eduardo, and Patricio Meller, eds. 1993. *External Shocks and Stabilization Mechanisms.* Washington, DC: Inter-American Development Bank.

Engel, Eduardo, and Rodrigo Valdés. 2000. "Optimal Fiscal Strategy for Mineral Exporting Countries." Working Paper 00/118. International Monetary Fund, Washington, DC.

Fasano-Filho, Ugo. 2000. "Review of the Experience with Mineral Stabilization and Savings Funds in Selected Countries." Working Paper 00/112. International Monetary Fund, Washington, DC.

Fatas, A., and I. Mihov. 2002. "The Case of Restricting Fiscal Policy Discretion." INSEAD draft report. Fontainbleu, France.

Fiess, N. 2002. "Chile's New Fiscal Rule." World Bank, Washington, DC. Draft report.

Gavin, Michael. 1997. "A Decade of Reform in Latin America: Has It Delivered Lower Volatility?" IADB Working Paper Green Series, No. 349. Inter-American Development Bank, Washington, DC.

Gelb, Alan. 2002."Economic and Export Diversification in Mineral Countries." Presentation to the World Bank Managing Volatility Thematic Group on Best Practice in Diversification Strategies for Mineral Exporting Countries. Washington, DC, January 7, 2002. Available at http://www wbweb.worldbank.org/prem/prmep/economicpolicy/documents/mv/20020107_02.doc.

Gelb, Alan, and associates. 1988. *Mineral Windfalls: Blessing or Curse?* New York: Oxford University Press.

Hannesson, Rögnvaldur. 2001. *Investing for Sustainability: The Management of Mineral Wealth.* Boston: Kluwer Academic Press.

Hausmann Ricardo. 1995. "Overcoming Volatility in Latin America." *International Monetary Fund Seminar Series* (international) August 1995 (34):1–86.

———. 1999. "Managing Terms of Trade Volatility." *PREM Notes* No. 18. World Bank, Poverty Reduction and Economic Policy Group, Washington, DC.

Hausmann, Ricardo, and Roberto Rigobon. 2003. "An Alternative Explanation of the Resource Curse." In Jeffrey Davis, Rolando Ossowski, and Annalisa Fedelino, eds., *Fiscal Policy Formulation and Implementation in Oil-Producing Countries.* Washington, DC: International Monetary Fund.

Hausmann, Ricardo, Andrew Powell, and Roberto Rigobon. 1993. "An Optimal Spending Rule Facing Mineral Income Uncertainty (Venezuela)." In Eduardo Engel and Patricio Meller, eds., *External Shocks and Stabilization Mechanisms.* Washington, DC: Inter-American Development Bank.

Heilbrunn, John R. 2002. "Governance and Mineral Funds." Colorado School of Mines, Golden, Colorado.

Hill, Catherine. 1991. "Managing Commodity Booms in Botswana." *World Development* 19(9):1185–96.

Karl, Terry Lynn. 1997. *The Paradox of Plenty: Mineral Booms and Petro-States.* Berkeley: University of California Press.

Kessler, Alan. 2002. "A View from the Market." Presentation for the IMF Conference on Fiscal Policy Formation and Implementation in Oil Producing Countries, Washington, DC, June 2002.

Lewin, Michael. 2003. "Modeling Oil Windfalls." Draft Working Paper, World Bank, Washington, DC.

Lindahl, Mary. 1996a. "A Risk Management Strategy for Alaska: Learning from the Texas Experience?" *Journal of Energy, Finance, and Development* 1(1):1–8.

Liuksila, Claire, Alejandro García, and Sheila Bassett. 1994. "Fiscal Policy Sustainability in Oil-Producing Countries." Working Paper 94/137. International Monetary Fund, Washington, DC.

Myers, Robert, and Stanley Thompson. 1993. "Managing Mineral Import Price Risk in Costa Rica: Strategies and Benefits." In Stijn Claessens and Ronald Duncan, eds., *Managing Commodity Price Risk in Developing Countries.* Baltimore: John Hopkins University Press (for the World Bank).

Neary, Peter, and Sweder Van Wijnbergen. 1986. *Natural Resources and the Macro Economy.* Cambridge, MA: MIT Press.

Occhiolini, Michael. 1993. "Regulatory Aspects of Commodity-Linked Finance: Implications for Developing Countries." In Stijn Claessens and Ronald Duncan, eds., *Managing Commodity Price Risk in Developing Countries.* Baltimore: John Hopkins University Press (for the World Bank).

Patterson, Linda. 2001. "The State of Texas Risk Management Program: A Long Position and Long Perspective." Presentation for the World Bank Managing Volatility Thematic Group, June 25, Washington, DC.

Perry, Guillermo. 1999. "Measuring Mineral's Role in Latin American Growth." PowerPoint presentation. World Bank, Latin American and Caribbean Region, Office of the Chief Economist, Washington, DC.

———. 2002. "Fiscal Rules." World Bank, Washington, DC.

Pindyck R. 1999. "The Long-Run Evolution of Energy Prices." *Energy Journal* 20(2):1–27.

Pinto, Brian. 1987. "Nigeria During and after the Oil Boom: A Policy Comparison with Indonesia." *World Bank Economic Review* 1(3):419–45.

Ramey, Garey, and Valerie Ramey. 1995. "Cross-Country Evidence on the Link between Volatility and Growth." NBER Working Paper 4959. National Bureau of Economic Research, Cambridge, MA.

Ranis, G. 1991. "Towards a Model of Development." In L. B. Krause and K. Kihwan, eds., *Liberalization in the Process of Economic Development*. Berkeley, CA: University of California Press.

Sachs, J., and A. Warner. 1995. "Economic Convergence and Economic Policy." NBER Working Paper 5039. National Bureau of Economic Research, Cambridge, MA.

Schick, Allen. 1998. "Why Most Developing Countries Should Not Try New Zealand Reforms." *World Bank Research Observer* 13(1):123–31.

Schwartz, Eduardo, and James Smith . 2000. "Short-Term Variations and Long-Term Dynamics in Commodity Prices." *Management Science* 46: 893–911.

Shimko, David. 1995. "Long Term Energy Risk Management in the Alaskan Context." Paper prepared for the Risk Management Workshop, October, University of Alaska-Anchorage, Anchorage, AK.

Skancke, Martin. 2002. "Fiscal Policy and Petroleum Fund Management in Norway." Paper presented at the IMF Conference on Fiscal Policy Formulation and Implementation in Mineral-Producing Countries, June 5–6.

Varangis, Panayotis, and Don Larson. 1996. "Dealing with Commodity Price Uncertainty." Policy Research Working Paper 1667. World Bank, Policy Research Department, Washington, DC.

Verleger, Philip. 1995. "Risk Management Mineral Revenues: The Dilemma for Producers." Paper prepared for the Risk Management Workshop, October, University of Alaska-Anchorage, Anchorage, AK.

Weiner, Robert. 1995. "Petroleum Fiscal Dependence: Revenue Forecasting and Oil Price Volatility." Paper prepared for the Risk Management Workshop, October, University of Alaska-Anchorage, Anchorage, AK.

World Bank. 1999. "Commodity Risk Management in Developing Countries: Proposal for a Market-Based Approach." International Task Force on Commodity Risk Management in Developing Countries, Washington, DC.

6. Finance and Volatility

Stijn Claessens[1]

ABSTRACT: Risk sharing is an important function of any financial system, although there are natural limits to the degree of risk sharing across individuals, corporations, and countries. How effective a financial system is in providing risk diversification can depend on its capitalization and its institutional development, including the quality of its regulation and supervision. A financial system will typically not provide full risk insurance, and may even propagate economic variability or create risks of its own. Before or during a crisis, financial markets and institutions can play a large role in causing or amplifying financial crises because of balance sheet effects and contagion, among others. Following a crisis, the state of the financial sector can impede the efficacy of restructuring policies and the ability to resume growth. This study reviews the literature on these issues and highlights the areas where knowledge is still limited.

CONCEPTS AND DEFINITIONS

Even though the financial sector has long been regarded as a key part of any economy, the importance of its links to economic performance is only coming to be fully appreciated and analyzed in the last decade or so. This statement is even more true of the relationship between finance and volatility. The purpose of this study is to present recent analytical thinking and empirical evidence regarding these topics to practitioners. The chapter opens with the basic concepts explaining why financial contracts, markets, and intermediaries arise (for definitions of terms, see Box 6.1). It then discusses how a perfect or well-functioning financial system deals with risk, reviewing the risk-pooling function of finance. In theory, risk-reduction benefits can be large for households, firms, and countries. Empirical evidence confirms some of these benefits.

In practice, however, risk sharing is often imperfect, within countries but particularly internationally. The financial sector can even propagate economic shocks, rather than mitigate them. This imperfect risk sharing and amplification of shocks

[1] Senior Policy Adviser, World Bank, Professor of International Finance Policy, University of Amsterdam and fellow of CEPR. The study was written while the author was at the University of Amsterdam. Very helpful comments were received from Joshua Aizenman, Asli Demirgüç-Kunt, Jerry Caprio, Ross Levine, Brian Pinto, and Zia Qureshi. Participants in a seminar at the World Bank on March 24, 2004 provided useful feedback. I would especially like to thank Claudio Raddatz for his many useful comments, on which I have drawn in several places. Thanks to Nancy Morrison for excellent editing and Sarah Lipscomb for help with the references.

Box 6.1. Terminology

The term **financial development** usually refers to the *overall size of the financial system* relative to the economy. Measures commonly used include financial "depth" measures, such as the ratio of (private) credit to GDP or stock market capitalization to GDP. Sometimes, the term refers to the efficiency of the financial sector, as measured by the costs of financial intermediation, or the *quality of the provision of financial services*, as measured by the range of financial products available, for example.

Financial systems have evolved differently in various parts of the world, leading broadly to two distinct types of systems. In *bank-based systems*, banks facilitate the bulk of financial intermediation, as in Germany and Japan. In *market-based systems*, stock and bond markets represent the largest share of financial intermediation, as in the United States and the United Kingdom. The term **financial structure** is often used to refer to the relative importance in the country of bank-intermediated versus market-intermediated external financing.

The term **good fundamentals** refers to well functioning and competitive real output and input markets, such as product, labor, energy, and other input and output markets, which jointly determine the value added in the economy. It includes good macro policies.

The term **good institutions** refers to all the institutions needed for a well-functioning market economy. It includes well-defined and enforced property rights, an efficient judicial system, good financial sector regulation and supervision, a high level of transparency and disclosure, availability of high-quality information, active monitoring by third parties, and more generally a good incentive structure, including open and competitive financial and corporate sectors. The term sometimes includes the institutions necessary to support proper macroeconomic management. A common set of good fundamentals and institutions are necessary for financial sector development, in both bank-based and market-based systems.

Still, it is not clear what exactly constitutes good institutions, beyond some key principles. Regulation and supervision in developed countries, for example, differ in many aspects, but it is difficult to argue that these differences affect financial sector development. Furthermore, while there is some commonality among key principles, there is less commonality among outcomes, such as financial structures, and firm balance sheet measures, such as leverage and other risk indicators. Analyzing financial systems on the basis of such indicators must be done carefully and in the context of the particular financial system.

---

is due to both the nature of financial intermediation and possible distortions. Natural impediments include information asymmetries between lenders and borrowers, the fact that banks are highly leveraged and have short-maturity funding, and the decentralized functioning of financial markets. Distortions, such as a large government role or a weak institutional framework, will mean that the financial system cannot always provide risk sharing mechanisms efficiently.

Imperfect risk sharing manifests itself in a variety of ways. If the financial sector provides excessive financing, does not liquidate insolvent firms or otherwise poorly monitors how financial resources are used, firms may take on excessive risk and thus contribute to overall economic risk. The financial sector may, for example, aggravate a credit cycle in real estate lending by providing financing on terms that are too easy. Even when not leading to crises, the financial sector itself can amplify macroeconomic cycles. For example, through the so-called credit channel, banks can adjust their lending to respond more strongly to changes in monetary and other economic conditions than other forms of financial intermediation do. In addition, the role of asset markets has become more important in the last decades. Assets prices can be volatile, and can become misaligned with economic fundamentals, leading to consequences in the real sector through misallocation of resources.

Financial sector policy can also be a source of volatility, particularly in developing countries, where it has often contributed to short-run volatility and even triggered deep crises leading to long periods of slow growth. Financial liberalization can be a risk factor in its own right, leading to both gains and increased risks, especially in the short run. It is not always easy to achieve a proper balance between advancing reforms aimed at improving financial sector functioning and encouraging institutional development, on the one hand, and managing the new risks generated by this very process, on the other hand. Internationally, financial markets can smooth shocks but also to add to volatility.

The exacerbation of shocks by the financial sector can be even more pronounced when a country is faced with a systemic financial crisis: that is, a crisis that affects a large part of the country's financial system and the real sector. This can happen through the many normal channels through which the financial sector operates; but additional channels could come into play, such as the need for fiscal resources to recapitalize banks, which would create a link between the financial sector and fiscal sustainability. These factors justify a separate analysis of the role of the financial sector in creating risks before, during, or immediately after a systemic financial crisis.

FINANCE AND RISKS: THE GENERAL CONCEPTS AND EVIDENCE

A financial system provides the following services to businesses, households, and the government. It mobilizes funds, provides saving instruments, allocates resources, exerts corporate governance, provides payments and other services, and finally facilitates the trading, hedging, pooling, and diversifying of a variety of risks.[2] Financial intermediaries, and the markets they support – such as interbank, money, bond, and equity markets – enhance liquidity: that is, the ability to exchange some assets for others easily. Savers often prefer not to part with their funds for a long time for a variety of reasons. Indeed, early in economic and financial development, this is precisely what savers do. They often shun higher return investments because they require a sizable commitment of resources and they increase the already substantial

---

[2] Much has been written, especially in recent years, on the functioning of the financial sector. This study refers to these analyses (for example, World Bank 2001 and Levine 2005) for more detail and here presents only a general overview of financial sector functioning and development. This particular section draws on Caprio and Claessens (1997).

risks confronting savers. With more liquid markets, more savers will be induced to hold a bundle of assets diversified along the risk and maturity spectrum.

Intermediaries also help by pooling funds, providing liquidity, and dealing with asymmetric information. Direct transacting by individuals would be very costly on these accounts. Banks provide savers with liquidity by offering demandable debt and term savings, which are of shorter maturity than the underlying investments. Equity markets allow claims on investments to be easily traded. Thus, both reduce transaction costs. Savers also know less about how funds will be used and the likelihood of their return than do the recipients of the funds. Financial intermediaries uncover information about underlying investments: banks, in the course of their lending decisions; and equity markets, by revealing the value of firms.

The services financial intermediaries offer can be especially important for new and small- and medium-size enterprises. The entrepreneur who tries out new ideas needs credit and a financial system with a broad set of instruments. The services the financial system offers are not limited to traditional credits or loans but include payment, insurance, and leasing services. Leasing a truck, for example, may be the way for a small enterprise to get started, and improving cash-management may help a recently established firm. The breadth of services a financial system offers is crucial for savings. Through the various savings instruments, the financial system broadens the saving choice, which in turn, leads to a rise in savings and investments.

In addition to pooling resources, financial intermediaries play a role in the allocation of resources and corporate governance. This happens through lending decisions, as well as direct equity investment in some countries. Financial intermediaries offer a variety of debt, equity, and mixed contracts with the goal of maximizing the return to themselves (and repaying their depositors and creditors). As outsiders, they work with a firm's controlling owners to induce the firm's managers to act in the best interests of the owners and outside creditors. Small, outside owners cannot monitor and verify the performance of firm managers efficiently on their own; hence the demand for intermediaries. Banks, which typically offer short-term and long-term financing, can discipline managers by choosing not to renew loans. Liquid equity markets reveal the market's valuation of how a firm is doing and so determine its costs of new capital. Through changes in valuation, equity markets play an important role in corporate governance – with the final threat of management replacement or takeover, should a firm's value slip too low.

Decisions about how to allocate and use resources are important for growth even in economies with large savings because over time, tiny increments in the efficiency with which resources are used can dwarf the effects of more savings and investment. Economizing on the costs of providing these key functions is an important reason for financial intermediation. There is considerable evidence that more developed financial systems allocate resources to more efficient uses and thereby lead to more rapid economic growth. Since intermediaries will look not just for better current uses of resources but also for better future uses, they will encourage innovation – another channel to promote faster growth.

The most quoted function of finance is providing payment services, in particular, providing the unit of account and means of payment, and guaranteeing money as a store of value. This function is often taken for granted; however, it is a key function. Life without finance, such as found in some traditional societies, can be difficult.

Box 6.2. Risk Diversification of Various Financial Systems

Risk-reduction services will vary greatly in form not only by type of financial service, but also by financial system. In comparing financial systems of developed countries, a useful distinction is between intratemporal forms of risk sharing and risk management (within the same period, or cross-sectional) and intertemporal ones (across periods) (Allen and Gale 2000). In a financial system dominated by capital markets, prices and markets are the main mechanisms through which risks are pooled and shocks are absorbed within the same period across various parts of the economy. An example is the United States, where asset markets are the most important mechanism for absorbing, and sometime propagating, risks and shocks – whether from current events or changes in expectations of future events.

In a bank-based system, risk sharing mostly occurs through financial institutions and happens more slowly, as shocks are smoothed through new financing. The spreads on loans and bonds during normal times reflect some markup for the implicit insurance being provided during times of stress. In Germany and Japan and other bank-dominated systems, banks are the more important means of absorbing risks.

These are stylized comparisons. Recently, systems have been converging to more market-based models, as banks are becoming less important in financial intermediation and more financial intermediation is happening through capital markets.

Societies can arrange a number of substitutes: barter to take the place of payments services; children for long-term saving and insurance; multiple income-earners for casualty insurance; rotating savings and credit associations for formal savings institutions. However, such substitutes can entail a number of inefficiencies, as suggested by their more common occurrence mainly in lower income countries.

The Risk-Reduction Function of Finance

How does a well-functioning financial system deal with risk? Risk sharing takes many forms, including explicit insurance contracts; formal hedging contracts; the adjustment of asset prices, lending, or other financing terms; the provision of finance to firms, households, or countries during periods of financial distress, shock, or tightening of financing constraints; and insurance for legal liability claims to help an enterprise operating in a market that is otherwise too risky.

The risk-sharing function is common to any financial system (Box 6.2). As such, a well-developed financial system – irrespective of financial structure – will mean that firms and households incur less risks. Theoretical analyses have shown the gains from increased risk sharing – through reduced overall economic volatility, lower cost of capital, greater availability of financing, and finally higher economic growth – to be large. At the international level, Maurice Obstfeld (1994), for example, estimates that in theory the gains from full risk sharing in terms of overall worldwide economic growth could amount to several percentage points.

THE EMPIRICAL EVIDENCE ON RISK SHARING. The general empirical evidence is that a more developed financial system reduces risks at the level of the individual firm and household. Whether through direct risk sharing – such as through financial

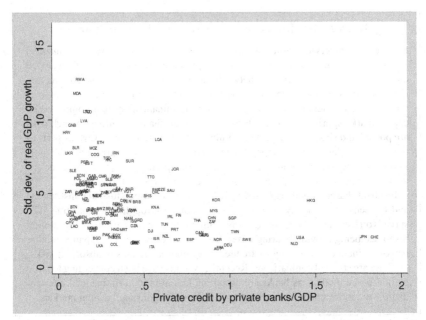

Figure 6.1. The Relationship between Private Credit by Private Banks and Economic Volatility. *Source*: Raddatz (2002).

hedging, derivative contracts, or insurance contracts – or through access to investment and financing opportunities to smooth positive and adverse shocks, households and firms can benefit from a greater access to financial services, a wider variety of financial products, and a more robust financial sector. These effects are economically quite significant and have been reported at the individual firm and households level for many countries in numerous studies. They have also been found for samples of households and firms for a cross section of countries. In turn, the presence of these risk-sharing benefits has been shown to affect performance and economic growth at the firm and sector level (see, for example, Shiller 2003).

At the country level, it has also been found that the more developed the financial system is (as measured by greater levels of credit to GDP), the less volatile output is. Sectors with greater external financing and liquidity needs are less volatile and experience less deep crises when the financial system in the country is deeper, Claudio Raddatz (2002) finds.[3] This is shown in Figure 6.1, which depicts the

[3] The paper follows the Rajan and Zingales (1998) methodology and analyzes the growth at the country's sectoral level. The innovation of Rajan–Zingales approach is that it overcomes some of the identification problems encountered in standard cross-country growth regressions. In case of the original Rajan–Zingales paper, it does this by interacting a country characteristic (financial development of a particular country) with the external financial dependence of a particular industry. This approach is less subject to criticism regarding an omitted variable bias or model specification than traditional approaches that relate financial sector development directly to economic growth, even when considering other country characteristics. It allows Rajan and Zingalis to isolate the impact of financial development on growth. In the regression results explaining sectoral growth, Rajan and Zingales find a positive sign for the interaction between the external financial dependence ratio and the level of financial development. In the paper by Claudio Raddatz (2002), the dependent variable is the volatility of sectoral growth.

negative relationship that Raddatz finds between the ratio of private credit by private banks to GDP (x-axis) – which includes the credit by banks and other financial institutions, but excludes the credit allocated by the central bank – and the volatility (standard deviation) of real GDP growth (y-axis).

Other analyses have found that in systems with greater financial sector development, the financial structure does not affect the lower economic volatility very much. Thorsten Beck, Mattias Lundberg, and Giovanni Majnoni (2001) find no strong evidence that countries' financial structures matter in overall economic or financial volatility. This suggests that both bank and market-oriented systems can provide effective risk-management functions. This confirms the evidence collected in Demirgüç-Kunt and Levine (2001) that differences in financial structure are not as important as are the differences in the legal system (such as well-developed equity and creditor rights) and other foundations (such as proper accounting standards) that allow the financial sector to perform its key necessary functions.

These gains from risk sharing also exist at the international level. More financially integrated countries – that is, countries that have opened themselves up to a greater degree of risk sharing with international financial markets – for example, have higher levels of investment (Henry 2003). Many have found positive overall GDP growth and volatility effects from international risk sharing facilitated through equity market liberalization. Peter Henry (2003) finds positive growth effects from liberalization. And Geert Bekaert, Campbell Harvey, and Christian Lundblad (2002a and b) establish that the volatility of GDP growth does not increase after financial liberalization and consumption volatility actually decreases. More generally, financial liberalization allowing more risk diversification has been found to be risk reducing (for reviews, see Bekaert and Harvey 2003 and Stulz 1999).

The positive effects of international financial integration on volatility and growth, however, are somewhat controversial. Whether results apply to some countries only or are more systematic is unclear. There are difficulties in measuring economic volatility. Some changes to GDP, for example, may not represent external shocks but rather structural changes, and as such should not be considered volatility. In an empirical test, Ross Levine and Sara Zervos (1998) do not find much benefit to growth from financial integration. Andrew Karolyi (2002) finds some recent evidence that increased use of American Depositary Receipts (ADRs) may make stock prices less informative about the true value of firms and may increase price volatility in the local stock market. Many have blamed financial integration for the increase in volatility experienced by emerging markets. Some, like Dani Rodrik (2000) have found little growth benefits of financial integration. The results of international risk sharing are thus not uncontroversial, especially after the East Asian financial crisis. It is likely that under some circumstances, including limited financial development and poor institutional framework, international financial integration may increase volatility.

DEVIATIONS FROM THE PERFECT RISK-SHARING MODEL

A financial system will typically not provide all these risk management services, and, as the previous analysis shows, the degree of financial sector development will determine the risk-reduction gains. A financial sector may even propagate economic

Table 6.1. *Impediments to perfect risk sharing*

Source of deviation	Particular cause
Market source	Information asymmetries, and the resulting credit and net worth channels
	Nature of banks
	Decentralized nature of financial markets and excessive asset price movements
Government and institutional factors	The role of government
	The effect of the financial sector on overall risk taking
	The links between financial liberalization and risk
Imperfections in international financial markets	Various international dimensions and macroeconomic channels

variability or create risks of its own. There are many causes of these "deviations," but they may be classified in two types: because of the nature of financial intermediation; or because of government policies, institutional weaknesses, and the process of liberalization. The dividing line is arbitrary and the two sources of deviations interact as the degree to which markets (can) operate effective will greatly depend on the institutional environment. Nevertheless, this study classifies the consequences of these factors under six headings: three market sources and three government and institutional factors (Table 6.1). The imperfections in international financial markets are analyzed separately.

Information Asymmetries

Information asymmetries refer to differences in information sets between the borrower and the lender on the viability of the project being financed, the type of firm, or the quality and action (effort) of the entrepreneur. With perfect financial markets, the availability of financing would be determined solely by the prospects of the project being financed. With information asymmetries, however, the ability to borrow will depend in part on the borrower's net worth. Different micromodels can lead to this prediction. With information asymmetries, lenders or other suppliers of external financing do not fully know the riskiness of their borrowers. ("External financing" refers to financing from sources outside the firm: that is, other than retained earnings or reinvested profits. It can be obtained from banks, stock markets, other capital markets, or nonbank financial institutions, such as leasing companies.) Price, that is, the interest rate at which to lend, can no longer clear the demand of borrowers with the supply from lenders. At high interest rates, lenders will be less willing to extend financing, as they realize that they will attract only worse borrowers (Stiglitz and Weiss 1981; also see Box 6.3). In these circumstances, lenders will derive comfort from knowing that the borrower's own "money is at stake," thereby making net worth an important part of the lending decision. Principal-agent relationships, that is, managers' (agents) running of firms for the benefit of owners and creditors

---

Box 6.3. The Effect of Information Asymmetries on the Supply of Funds

In any market, market clearing will mean demand meeting supply at the equilibrium price. The effects of a change in quantity supplied will be such that some consumers will adjust their demand. For example, if there is a general decrease in supply and prices increase, the normal expectation in this demand-supply world is that some consumers will no longer demand the product. In the context of financial markets, this would imply that with a rise in interest rates some borrowers will drop out of the market, as their projects or firms are no longer financially attractive at the prevailing interest rate. That is, they are not willing to pay the higher price for capital. But borrowers will not be rationed out of the market by the amount of financing available.

There is an additional effect in financial markets, however, as higher interest rates increase the probability of partial default. Hence repayment is higher only when it happens. The ultimate effect of the higher interest rate on expected repayment depends on the strength of the increase in repayment when it happens and on the decrease in the probability of repayment. Creditors realize these two effects and start to ration credit at some interest rate level. That is, at higher rates they will make less credit available – not more – as otherwise they lower the expected repayments. This effect has been highlighted in the literature dealing with costly state verification and costly enforcement.

In this world, a change in general interest rates will still affect the supply of credit to all types of borrowers, regardless from which financial intermediary they borrow. In the presence of informational asymmetries, however, effects can differ by the type of financial intermediary. Information asymmetries refer to situations where some information is private and revealing it is costly, and sometimes impossible. With information asymmetries, lenders will limit the supply of financing more to some categories of borrowers as they realize that higher spreads to compensate for increased risks will only lead to adverse selection: that is, higher spreads will only attract borrowers with poor credit. This also means the supply curve for credit will be backward bending and quantity-rationed (Stiglitz and Weiss 1981). If interest rate rises, lenders will cut back the supply of loans to borrowers subject to information asymmetries more sharply than to other borrowers. The reason is that lenders will be (even) less willing to extend financing (at any price) as they realize that they will only attract borrowers with poor credit at the higher interest rate. These effects will be more severe for bank lending, since banks are more likely than other lenders to lend to firms that suffer from a greater degree of informational asymmetries.

(principals), can together with informational asymmetries, further make the borrower's net worth an important determinant of the supply of external financing. Another avenue through which net worth can be important is when there are high costs of verifying the true financial conditions of a firm (Townsend 1981). If it is very costly knowing whether a borrower willingly defaults, rather than because of events outside his control, banks will become reluctant to lend, unless the borrower's own net worth is sufficient. These and other micromodels of information asymmetries generate the same reduced form result, namely, that the ability to borrow depends on the borrower's net worth.

This emphasis on borrowers' net worth can make financial markets propagate shocks to the real economy. When the net worth of a firm declines as a result of economic shocks, the supply of external financing may be curtailed, even when the firm has viable new investments. This dependence of external financing on net worth will amplify the effects of shocks, with the severity depending, among others, on the degree of leverage, as for firms that are highly leveraged small shocks can have large effects on borrowers' net worth. More generally, the net worth channel means that firms' balance sheets can determine how economic conditions affect the real sector. There are also analogues to these channels at the international level. Pierre Richard Agenor and Joshua Aizenman (2002), for example, argue that these effects are exemplified in large swings in sovereign spreads of emerging markets, as these economies have greater difficulty in obtaining funds when international financing conditions change even slightly.

The information asymmetries effects will also differ by types of external financing and by types of firms. They will be more severe for bank lending than for capital markets' forms of financing. By pooling savings from uninformed depositors and lending these out while monitoring borrowers carefully, banks become delegated monitors. Given this role, banks will be more likely than others to lend to firms that suffer from a greater degree of informational asymmetries. Furthermore, banks may develop special relationships with their borrowers. They may try to acquire proprietary information by investing resources in firms that are young or otherwise lend to firms that suffer from a greater degree of informational asymmetries. This in turn means that other forms of external financing may not be as readily available as bank loans or may not be close substitutes. This means that favorable shocks can make banks more willing than other lenders to extend new loans. And, conversely in case of adverse shocks, banks will be less willing than other suppliers of external financing to extend financing to borrowers. This makes the form of financial intermediation influence how shocks get translated to the real economy.

This combination of balance sheet and lending channels can affect the transmission of monetary policy. Monetary policy aims to change general conditions of lending. Interest rate changes will not be transmitted directly to borrowers in a straightforward manner when their net worth changes as a consequence of interest changes or may vary by the form of financial intermediation. In this context, Ben Bernanke and Mark Gertler (1987) have drawn attention to the credit channel for the transmission of monetary policy. Changes in interest rates and monetary policy will affect bank lending more than other forms of external financing as banks are more likely lend to borrowers with information asymmetries. When bank lending is a large share of firm external financing, information asymmetries will typically be large and fewer alternative source of external financing may be available. As a consequence, monetary policy will not be straightforward when bank lending is large.

This channel can impact specific classes of borrowers and economic volatility in general. It can mean that small- and medium-size firms may be hit harder by monetary policy changes, as they are more dependent on bank financing, have no close substitutes available, and as lenders find it harder to get information about them. For all type of economies, these channels mean that a disruption of the banking system, induced by an economic shock or changes in regulation, can reduce the access of all types of firms to external financing. And, the state of the banking

---

Box 6.4. Monetary Policy Channel

For most central banks – and assuming a market-determined exchange rate policy is pursued – the main policy instrument is the short-term interest rate. (For those countries with a fixed or pegged exchange rate and an open capital account, monetary policy is largely dictated by the exchange rate policy.) This instrument is set in order to achieve the monetary policy objectives (which, for this analysis, are not assumed to include any exchange rate target).

The monetary policy transmission mechanism consists of all the channels through which the interest rate changes decided by the central bank affect the economy. If the financial markets are well developed and efficient, then monetary policy normally affects household spending through its impact on interest rates and asset prices. Following a change in the interest rate, for example, households may be induced to shift their expenditure patterns through time, advancing or postponing their consumption of goods and services or investments, say in housing. Changes in asset prices can also affect consumption through wealth effects. Moreover, interest rate changes may affect disposable income directly through the proceeds received (or paid) on variable rate contracts. For firms, the transmission mechanism operates through the user cost of capital and the relationship between the market value of capital and its replacement cost, which can affect firms' expenditure in fixed and inventory investment.

Financial development can play an important role for a number of these channels. If the financial markets are incomplete or imperfect, then the effect of using these transmission channels can be amplified by changes in the availability of internal cash flow or of external credit. Using company data, studies have found significant evidence that firms' demand for investment goods depends on the availability of cash flow or liquid assets (for a review, see Bernanke and Gertler 1995).

The structure of the financial system can also matter. If, as in many countries, banks are the main providers of funds for households and enterprises, then monetary policy could affect their (investment) spending by modifying the supply of bank loans. For instance, the availability and value of collateral is a highly relevant factor in lending. If the value of assets falls – for example, as a result of monetary tightening – and thus the value of collateral falls, lenders may be more reluctant to grant new loans for investment. In practice, studies using bank data found some limited evidence of shifts in the supply of loans by banks.

Source: ECB (2002).

---

system and regulation and supervision can affect the degree to which these channels operate. A poorly developed banking system may be more inclined, for example, to lend on a collateral basis and less inclined to lend on a cash flow and project basis, as lenders lacks the skills to analyze uncertain future returns on new projects. Such a financial system may be more affected by balance sheets effects and shocks that reduce borrowers' net worth.

There is much empirical evidence on the links between monetary policy and lending behavior (Gertler and Gilchrist 1994, and Kashyap, Stein, and Wilcox 1993 are classic references for evidence on the U.S.; see Christiano, Eichenbaum, and Evans 1999 for a general review; Box 6.4 provides a recent summary; see also

224 *Stijn Claessens*

Vasquez, 2003 for some recent evidence for emerging economies). The effects of the regulation and the state of the banking system on the severity of the link have also been investigated. The role of prudential regulations has been analyzed extensively in the context of the Basel 1989 Accord, which tightened capital adequacy rules for some classes of internationally active banks. A review of the evidence (BIS 1999) suggests that the effects of these tighter rules have been minimal on aggregate credit provision. There is some evidence, however, that borrowers from weaker banks saw their access to financing more curtailed by tighter regulation and supervision (BIS 1999). There is also some evidence on the occurrence and importance of credit crunches both in the United States (Bernanke and Lown 1991) and in developing countries (Caballero 2000). Credit crunches may have happened in East Asia as bank lending is large in these economies (Ding, Domac, and Ferri 1998). Also, the effects of interest rate increases lowering net worth were important in East Asia as corporate sector leverage was generally high and small shocks had a large effect on borrowers' net worth, resulting in sharp curtailment of credit. In Korea, for example, the average corporate sector leverage (debt to equity ratio) was more than four before the 1997 financial crisis, compared to less than one for most developed countries. As banks dominate financial intermediation in Korea, many borrowers suffered a sharp curtailment in bank financing when they were hit with rising interest rates and their net worth dropped. As such, the state of the banking system can affect the severity of the credit channel.

Nature of Banks as a Source of Volatility

Banks are characterized by specific balance sheet features: they are funded by many, short-term deposits, while they lend for longer-term; and they are highly leveraged. Although the maturity mismatch and leverage is a discipline on banks themselves, thus enhancing their incentives to monitor their own assets, it does create risks as it makes banks subject to runs – that is, fast withdrawals of funds. The possibility of runs is a consequence of a coordination failure among depositors and the information asymmetry on the banks' side (Diamond and Dybvig 1983). Runs force banks to liquidate assets at high costs and recover less than their underlying value (banks cannot differentiate depositors with real liquidity needs from those without; otherwise it could partially suspend convertibility). Sometimes runs are induced by bank weaknesses, and can then be justifiable. But sometimes runs are irrational, as in a self-fulfilling panic, in which case all depositors try to withdraw their deposits, but all can be worse off in case the bank was solvent after all. Either way, these runs create the risks of spillovers in the rest of the financial system and the real economy. Governments have responded to the risk of run by putting in place safety nets, but these can give rise to moral hazard and reduce the incentives of depositors to monitor banks.

The high leverage makes banks vulnerable to shocks. Shocks can cause banks to face a real or perceived capital shortage, whether these shocks are real (such as changes in the terms of trade affecting the creditworthiness of banks' borrowers); financial (such as increases in world interest rates or a decline in external financing); or regulatory (such as the raising of capital adequacy requirements or the tightening of loan classifications). As a result of this capital shortage, banks may become unwilling to lend to even viable firms and instead prefer to invest excess liquidity in safe assets, such as government bonds.

Runs, shocks to the financial sector, and increased uncertainty more generally may affect the provision of credit to the real sector, especially the supply of credit from banks to firms. This curtailment of credit – a so-called credit crunch – can lower financing for investment purposes or even for working capital needs to borrowers that have valuable new investment and trading opportunities. This in turn will hurt firms' performance, potentially making credit crunches self-fulfilling. The state of the financial sector will be a factor affecting how it deals with shocks. Well-capitalized financial systems will be less likely subject to runs, be able to absorb most shocks and will not be a source of volatility. For developed countries where shocks, regulatory changes, and other changes have been relatively small and where there are many alternatives to bank loans, there is little evidence of credit crunches.

In weaker environments, however, the banking system can be a source of risk for the reasons outlined above. There is much empirical evidence on this. The extent of deposit insurance, for example, has been found to affect the probability of a banking crisis (see further the section on the role of the government and institutional factors). Furthermore, when the financial system's viability is already undermined, it is more likely that it will be a source of overall volatility – even to the point of affecting macroeconomic stability or the resumption of such stability, as happened in many crisis countries. Given the unbalanced financial systems in many developing countries, where banks dominate and fewer alternative financing sources are typically available, and the fragile state of some banking systems, the effects of tighter regulatory and supervisory frameworks on credit provision are often more severe. Indeed, there is evidence for this for East Asia following the 1997 financial crisis. The already weak banking sectors in these countries responded to tighter regulations on bank classification standards and loan-loss provisioning, combined with further weakening loan portfolios, by cutting back lending, including to the better borrowers.

Decentralized Nature of Financial Markets

Asset markets have grown in importance in many countries, partly because of financial liberalization. As a consequence, asset prices – such as stock prices, exchange rates, interest rates, and property prices – have become increasingly important in guiding the allocation of resources, both within countries and internationally. The collective actions of anonymous individuals participating in financial markets, however, may not lead to a first best outcome. Markets can over- or under-shoot or experience irrational exuberance or pessimism. When asset prices do not reflect fundamental values, changes in asset prices can amplify changes in the real economy and affect the real economy through a misallocation of resources. Asset price bubbles as far back as the tulip price bubble of the early 17th century and the South Sea bubble of the early 18th century are extreme examples of a manifestation that can lead to serious consequences for the real sector. As has become evident from the last cycle in global stock markets, even in well-developed markets, asset prices can become misaligned with economic fundamentals, with perverse effects on resource allocation of significant economic importance. These abnormal price movements are not limited to bubbles and can manifest themselves over short periods. The sharp drops in asset prices and increases in spreads in many developed countries in the fall of 1998, following the LTCM bankruptcy and the Russia and Brazil financial crisis, for example, are not easily explained, yet had serious consequences.

Why bubbles or sharp price movements occur, or what types of institutions would reduce the chances of them occurring, is not very clear and research has only recently started to address these issues. Certainly, asset price movements are influenced by macroeconomic conditions, but even with the achievement of macroeconomic stability in most developed countries, stability in asset prices has not been assured over the last decade. It has been argued that monetary policy is not a good or even an appropriate tool to deal with asset prices misalignments, as in the debate surrounding the role of the Federal Reserve System in the United States during the recent stock market bubble. Not only is it difficult to identify misalignments of asset prices, but also it is not obvious how monetary policy can stop a severe price misalignment and whether the risks of trying to affect prices outweigh the gains. General macroeconomic policy, including monetary policy, also cannot directly influence the price of a particular asset. These policies will affect all asset prices – bonds, stocks, and real assets – but most often will be too blunt to affect particular asset price movements. Rather, the focus of analysis has been on the role of microfactors in explaining particular asset price behavior.

Microeconomic factors seem to affect the degree of asset price misalignment. (The G-10 Contact Group Report 2002 reviews the literature and recent experiences.) A variety of such factors have been argued to play a role in amplifying credit and asset price cycles in more mature, developed countries, including weaknesses in accounting standards, provisioning standards for classified loans and loan to value ratio requirements, specific tax treatment of loan-loss provisioning and interest expenses (such as the tax deductibility of mortgage financing), and standards for the treatment of impaired loans (Box 6.5).

The G-10 Contact Group (2002) reports specific evidence that the deductibility of interest on housing mortgages from personal income can amplify property prices swings. As income rises, the desire for tax deductions from mortgage financing also rises, accelerating a property boom underway as demand for housing increases. There is also evidence of a procyclical nature of prudential regulation, including rules for loan-loss provisioning being related to the business cycle. Specifically, during economic upswings there will be a tendency to relax bank loan classification and loan-loss provisioning criteria; conversely, there can be a tendency to tighten these during economic downturns (see Borio and Lowe 2002 for a review). This in turn will induce procyclical lending behavior.

While microfactors can affect price and lending behavior, it is not clear that discretionary policies can affect the development of particular asset prices such as property prices or internet stocks at particular times, mainly because such measures are hard to fine-tune. Countercyclical loan classification and loan-loss provisioning rules, for example – tighter provisioning to induce more conservative lending and more caution during good times and more relaxed criteria in bad times – are hard to design. They require the ability to identify the phase in the business cycle

---

Box 6.5. G-10 Report on Micropolicies and Turbulence in Asset Markets

The 2003 report by the Contact Group on Asset Prices,* *Turbulence in Asset Markets: The Role of Micro Policies*, explores how micropolicy measures can increase the risks of excessive and potentially destabilizing asset price movements and their impact on real sector instability. The report draws on case studies and a survey covering industrial countries for which the link between micropolicies and equity and property prices was assumed to be important. Micropolicies covered in the report include taxes and aspects of regulation, such as provisioning that vary by the state of the economy, and market value accounting in the banking industry.

It was found that distortions in property taxation, such as mortgage interest deductibility, and financial transaction taxes, such as turnover taxes, are potentially impinging upon asset market prices. Policy changes, especially in the financial sector, can add to asset price bubbles. Prominent examples of poorly timed policies can be found in the wake of financial market deregulation among developed and developed countries in the 1980s. Although deregulation itself was important, in conjunction with high inflation and strong fiscal incentives for asset purchasing, it led to the build-up of price bubbles. In many cases, measures to cap the inflating bubble came too late, were too abrupt, and were implemented at a time when economic conditions were deteriorating anyway. The asset price drops were often followed by a wave of defaults and bankruptcies, and, in some cases, a major financial crisis. The report argues that these lessons may be important as *dress rehearsals* for policymakers in countries that have yet to complete their deregulation.

The report finds evidence to suggest that unsound incentive structures within the financial sector have contributed to excessive risk taking, both by individual loan managers or traders and by entire financial institutions, as in the case of many savings and loans in the United States in the early 1980s. In addition, many analysts have mentioned the current Basel Capital Accord for commercial banks as a source of procyclicality and financial vulnerability. A distortion, brought about by taxation systems, is the tax deductibility of debt financing. The income effects can be dramatic as countries go from a high-inflation to a low-inflation environment, and may exacerbate the initial asset price drop generated by the rise in real interest rates. The report reviews the effects of limited awareness of the role of these policies and suggests that greater transparency can lead market participants to make more informed assessments and reduce the incidence of such phenomena as disaster myopia and herd behavior.

The report briefly reviews three measures to counter these effects: dynamic provisioning, fair value accounting, and loan-to-value ratios. Dynamic provisioning would involve setting higher provisioning requirements during good times and less during bad times, reducing the procyclicality in lending. Fair value accounting would balance accounting based on market-values with judgments on the underlying value of the firm or project, thus reducing sensitivity to market swings. Finally, regulators could require banks not to extend loans beyond a certain value of the underlying asset and to lower this ratio during good times to reduce the procyclicality in lending.

---

* The Contact Group on Asset Prices was established in April 2001 and comprises the central banks of Australia, Belgium, Canada, Germany, Hong Kong, Ireland, Japan, the Netherlands, Spain, Sweden, Switzerland, and the United Kingdom. The other G-10 participants also contributed to the report. The report was released on January 8, 2003 and served as background for discussion among G-10 Ministers and Governors in September 2003.

correctly and to adjust criteria and regulations relatively quickly. In addition, they can create moral hazard problems. Countercyclical regulations put the supervisor or government in the position to have to make a call on the state of the overall economy or particular sectors. As the government is (seen as actively) involved in private sector decisions, they might create moral hazard. For asset classes that are highly integrated internationally, such as equity, bonds, and loans, there is very little room for policy initiatives on the national level. Transaction taxes are not likely to be a preferred policy tool under any circumstances, particularly at the national level, as they can be easily avoided.

While there may be some scope in adopting measures to counter the sources of procyclicality and financial vulnerability (such as dynamic provisioning, fair value accounting, and loan-to-value ratios), rectifying microeconomic distortions and creating a robust financial and regulatory system may be the only and first-best solution. Tax structures should not unintentionally amplify asset price fluctuations. In this respect, as strong fiscal incentives for asset purchasing often lead to the build-up of price bubbles, the removal or limitation of tax incentives, such as deductions for loans on housing and debt financing more generally, can be effective, although perhaps politically difficult. Loan-loss provisioning should be based on the average riskiness of loans over the whole business cycle and not be relaxed during upswings. A uniformly strict provisioning standard – that is, to eliminate the laxity in good times – might thus be best. In many markets, there will be an increased need for transparency and information disclosure, both from individual firms and from public authorities. In principle, a high level of transparency should lead market participants to make more informed assessments and reduce the incidence of phenomena like disaster myopia, the systematic underestimation of the chances of a large shock, and herd behavior, the tendency of financial markets to follow one another. More generally, authorities should work to increase risk awareness and reduce moral hazard problems within the financial sector.

While research is still evolving, much of (relative) asset prices movements are not easily explained, even in mature markets. In this context, the new, so-called behavioral finance literature has drawn attention to the many deviations from the efficient market and rationality hypotheses, most often investigated for sophisticated markets like the United States. This literature attempts to explain financial phenomena such as prices of shares that deviate persistently from "fundamental" values; differences in values between shares that represent similar cash flow rights on the same company, which nonetheless remain unarbitraged (as in American Depositary Receipts, or ADRs, but also in stocks such as Royal Dutch Shell, which list on two stock exchanges but at different implied prices); the often observed underperformance of mutual fund managers, who still manage to retain the interest of investors; the jump in prices of stocks when they are added to a stock market index, such as the S&P 500 index, although nothing changes in the underlying business of the listed firm; and the role of investor and firm management "sentiment" in driving stock prices, new issue activity, and the like. The literature has developed and tested models in which agents are not fully rational, with the two building working hypotheses being limits to arbitrage and investor psychology. The research is new, and few strong results have yet emerged.

With much unexplained in price movements, expectations for reducing financial and economic volatility must remain modest. Financial asset markets can be unavoidable amplifying factors. Indeed, as the Contact Group on Asset Prices (G-10 2002) points out in its report, *Turbulence in Asset Markets: The Role of Micro Policies*, "A boom and bust in asset prices is perhaps the most common thread running through most financial crises." Importantly for developing countries, many of these weaknesses will arise in the context of (too) rapid financial liberalization, or at least liberalization in some areas ahead of institutional development, and affect the risk of a financial crisis (see more below).

The Role of Government and Institutional Factors

Government policies play a large role in shaping the effectiveness of the financial sector. The prevailing attitude in the 1950s was that finance did not matter. This, coupled with underdeveloped revenue systems, led governments to use financial intermediaries as vehicles for implicitly collecting taxes through financial repression. Reserve and liquidity requirements to be met by cash holdings or investments in government securities were high; deposit interest rates were kept low; credit was allocated in accordance with government plans; and profits were channeled to the fiscal authority.

Over the last two decades or so, many countries have realized the importance of an independent financial sector, have reconsidered the role of the government in the allocation of resources, and have adjusted ownership and policies accordingly. They have also started to put in place the many necessary ingredients for a market-based system of financial intermediation. A well functioning financial system requires good laws, high quality financial information, and a good market structure. Nevertheless, governments have not taken all steps and many distortions can remain. These can be classified under two aspects: the lingering direct role of the government, and the degree to which an institutional framework for a market-based system of financial intermediation is in place. There is much empirical evidence available about the links between the degree and type of government interventions, the quality of the institutional framework, and financial development.

The control of interest rates and credit allocation by the government impedes banks from considering (credit) risk and developing their institutional capacity to assess and manage risks. Empirically, we indeed know that financial controls tend to retard future financial development (Bekaert et al. 2002a). State-owned banks are less likely to have the proper incentives to manage risk than privately owned banks. The degree of state ownership of banks is inversely related to the degree of financial development (La Porta et al. 2002). More generally, a high level of state control of banks and a low degree of capitalization have been shown to reduce the ability of the financial sector to perform its function to manage risk well (see Levine 2004). Foreign banks, in contrast, are associated with greater financial sector development and less risk (Claessens, Demirgüç-Kunt, and Huizinga, 2001).

There are many channels through which the deficiencies in the institutional framework may affect financial sector performance and stability. Poor regulation and supervision of the financial sector, as well as weak legal foundations – including poor

---

Box 6.6. Financial Safety Nets

Although banking has declined in relative importance in advanced countries, it remains significant. In developing countries, commercial banks still dominate financial intermediation. But banks are notoriously unstable, characterized by the possibility of contagious runs, in which a run on one bank leads to runs on other banks – possibly healthy ones. Rather than abandon the banking system, the tendency has been for depositors to seek redress from government. Historically, the creation of central banks was spawned by the instability of banks, dating back to the 17th century (Wisselbank, Bank of England), and to their adoption of lender of last resort facilities in the 19th century. Crises nevertheless persisted.

Governments have a variety of mechanisms that can be employed as part of a safety net for banks, such as the central bank discount window. Increasingly, deposit insurance schemes have become a key component. The United States adopted deposit insurance in the 1930s, but many countries resisted it. For example, Canada did not have a deposit insurance scheme until 1967. After the 1980s, the number of countries adopting deposit insurance schemes rose sharply – from 16 in 1980 to 68 in 1999, with two-thirds of the schemes adopted in the last 15 years. It does not take much knowledge of economics to observe that this increase in safety nets, especially in deposit insurance schemes, has not been matched by an equivalent increase in the countries' institutional capacity to supervise. As a consequence, the fiscal costs of financial crises have been enormous.

More generally, governments have provided banks with a safety net. The scope of the safety net will be defined by a combination of elements, including lender of last resort facilities, explicit or implicit deposit insurance schemes, the access of financial institutions to the payment system, the prevailing regulatory norms and their enforcement, and importantly, the rules for intervention in weak financial institutions, and the resolution processes for failed ones. Some form of safety net is unavoidable, and indeed can improve the functioning of the financial system as it avoids unnecessary deposit runs.

The experiences of many countries attest though that a wide scope can create large moral hazard: that is, financial institutions will take more risk at the final expense of the government, particularly through explicit and implicit deposit insurance. Cross-country experience shows that the expectation of ex-post recapitalization using government resources has induced imprudent behavior. Arrangements to reduce these include – most importantly – a proper regulatory and enforcement framework, especially regarding the capital adequacy of financial institutions. To ensure proper supervision and regulation, the supervisory authority should be free from political pressure. These arrangements can also include an explicit deposit insurance scheme. This needs to be complemented with specific actions, including clear exit rules and other design criteria (e.g., risk-sensitive premia).

Source: Adapted in part from World Bank (2002).

---

credit or and shareholder rights and a weak judiciary – have been found to undermine the development of the financial system, in terms of its size, efficiency, and stability. The quality of regulation and supervision, for example, affects the degree to which the financial sector can dampen or amplify volatility at the aggregate, country level.

James Barth, Gerard Caprio, and Ross Levine (2001 and 2003), after creating a database on specific features of bank regulation and supervision, show that the lack of some key regulation and supervision features can increase the risk of banking crises and volatility.

Another important weakness can be excessive deposit insurance, which blunts the incentives of banks to manage risk and can increase financial and economic volatility (for examples, see Box 6.6). Empirical work shows the impact of excessive deposit insurance and certain deposit insurance design features on increasing volatility (Cull, Senbet, and Sorge 2005). This evidence is corroborated at the level of individual financial institutions, where financial institutions in environments with worse regulation and supervision and more generous public safety nets engage in more risk taking (Laeven 1999). For a summary of this research, see Demirgüç-Kunt and Kane (2002).

The challenges for financial sector development is to distinguish these purely inefficient forms of government intervention from those interventions aimed to solve market failure (second best). Guidelines for directed credit or caps on interest rates are purely distortionary measures and indeed have been found to retard financial sector development. Deposit insurance or capital adequacy requirements, however, may be aimed to solve some underlying vulnerability and can in principle accelerate financial sector development, but create problems themselves. As such there is a trade-off to consider. James Barth, Gerard Caprio, and Ross Levine (2003) identified some of the more productive forms of regulations. Theirs and other work also highlighted, however, that the best forms of regulation can be institutional and country specific.

The Financial Sector and the Degree of Overall Risk Taking

The financial sector affects the degree of risk taking in the rest of the economy. Weak monitoring by banks can lead to excessive risk by firms – high leverage or mismatches in balance sheets – or poor performance. This weak monitoring may be induced by safety nets for banks that are too large, a perception that companies are "too big to fail," or political pressure. It can also be due to institutional weaknesses. To allow for monitoring by the financial sector, well-defined and enforced creditor and equity rights are necessary. Poor enforcement of creditor rights may mean that the level of nonperforming loans and general defaults in the country will be high. A poor corporate governance framework – weak minority shareholders rights, poor accounting standards, limited disclosure – can impede the ability or willingness of minority shareholders to appropriately monitor the behavior of insiders and firms' management. This, in turn, can lead firms to take on too much risk. And low accounting standards and low disclosure levels may mean less and more biased information on corporate and financial sectors' performance, making it harder for analysts to assess risk.

Rafael La Porta, Florencio Lopez-de-Silanes, Andrei Shleifer, and Robert Vishny (LLSV 1997) show that good creditor and equity rights help develop a country's banking system and capital markets and enhance the monitoring roles of the financial sector. Besides strong creditor and shareholders' rights that are enforced, good accounting standards and transparency have been shown to enhance financial sector development and improve overall risk taking in the economy. These and other relationships have been documented extensively in a number of papers (for a review, see Levine 2004).

Besides affecting overall risk sharing, deficiencies in institutional factors can be an important trigger for financial crises and affect the probability of and depth of a currency crisis. Simon Johnson, Peter Boone, Alasdair Breach, and Eric Friedman (2000) present country-level evidence that deficiencies in corporate governance standards were key factors in exacerbating the stock market declines in East Asian countries and elsewhere during the 1997 financial crisis. They find that in counties with weaker investor protection, net capital inflows were more sensitive to negative events that adversely affect investors' confidence. Their explanation is that in such countries, the risk of expropriation of minority shareholders increases during bad times, as the expected return of investment is lower and the safeguards to prevent this behavior by large controlling shareholders are limited. Controlling shareholders might, for example, siphon off funds ("tunnel") from a (near) bankrupt firm to another, but privately held corporation, and thereby expropriate minority shareholders. The (foreign) minority shareholders respond by taking their money out of the country. The country is therefore more likely to witness a collapse in currency and stock prices. Christian Mulder and Roberto Perrelli (2002) find that stronger creditors' rights and shareholders' rights reduce the likelihood of a crisis because domestic and international investors will be more confident to operate in those markets.

While the monitoring roles of the financial sector with respect to the rest of the economy has been increasingly recognized, there is not a standard list of indicators to check for real sector riskiness or institutional weaknesses. The degree of sustainable firm leverage (debt to equity ratio), for example, depends on the interplay between the features of the bankruptcy system, the rights of creditors, and the development of the banking system. In one country, high real sector leverage can be counterbalanced by a large role for banks in monitoring firms and strong creditor rights, and does not create risk. In another country, leverage would be lower as there is a large role for capital markets in combination with weaker creditor rights. While there will be large differences in measured real-sector leverage and other risk indicators as well as in institutional features between these two systems, there need not be a difference in effective risk taking or ability to absorb shocks. In the higher leverage system, banks may be willing to provide financing in case firms run into short-run liquidity problems. As such, the high leverage need not lead to risks, provided the banks are well capitalized. In the lower leverage system, shocks are less likely to affect firms as they are less exposed and can absorb more risks themselves. The worse creditor rights may not mean that risks are larger. As such, firm financial structure and leverage can not be evaluated independently of the institutional setup on whether a financial system absorbs shocks well.[4]

[4] Even when there are differences in the ability of a financial system to absorb risks, depending on its structure, there may be tradeoffs in other respects. A financial system that encourages more risk taking can help spur innovation and increase financing to new, risky projects, and thereby raise overall economic growth. A system with too much power for creditors, focusing too much on debt financing, may discourage entrepreneurial activity.

Another example is in respect to transparency. Some have argued that relationship-based financial systems – where loans are made on the basis of personal relationships rather than hard information, such as value of collateral or projected cash flows – create more financial risks. This need not always be the case; there may be tradeoffs. In environments with poor information, there may be no choice but to lend on the basis of softer information. Such systems work may well when contracts are poorly enforced, capital is scarce, and information asymmetries are large, as is the case in many developing countries. However, because of a lack of price signals and legal protection, investors will keep their contracts short-term. Thus such arrangements can work well for both investors and capital raisers during normal times, but may be vulnerable to shocks.

Financial Liberalization and Risks

The recent experiences with financial crises in emerging markets and elsewhere have highlighted the possibly of links between the speed and degree of financial sector liberalization and volatility. While the potentially perverse relationships between financial fragility and speed and scope of domestic deregulation are now accepted by many, the theory as to these links is just being developed and the exact tradeoffs are still unclear. The issue is *how* to move from the repressed, more tightly controlled systems that many developing countries once had to more liberal, market-oriented systems – for example, what aspects to liberalize first – and *what* the institutional setup during this transition should be. It is clear that the preferred approach of financial liberalization and forms of prudential regulation needs to vary with countries' degree of development. However, the exact tradeoffs – between encouraging institutional change, achieving the gains from a more reformed financial system, the possible accompanying risks and dynamic paths thereof, and their relationships with country circumstances – are not well known. This is especially the case as they relate to political economy factors. This in turn can create risks.

At the national level, there have been extensive studies on the effects of liberalization on financial sector development, examining such issues as the removal of interest controls, limits on lending, and entry restrictions. There have been fewer studies on the relationship between liberalization and volatility. Initial work in the area of financial structure and volatility found that volatility of financial markets did increase with opening up but that it had no effect on real sector variables (Greenwald 1998). A recent paper by Bekaert et al. (2002b) provides evidence that financial liberalization does not increase GDP volatility (it decreases it if the Asian crisis is excluded) and actually decreases consumption volatility. Gerard Caprio and Patrick Honohan (2002) also look at the regulation-volatility relationship and ask whether improving prudential quality can enhance financial sector stability in the short and long term, since neither markets nor officials will be able to forecast accurately which shocks are permanent and which are transitory. They show that by forcing greater adjustment to short-term changes, certain regulatory approaches, such as encouraging greater private monitoring, may be better at preventing the buildup of large vulnerabilities and (contingent) losses. Many of the regulatory characteristics that make financial systems more robust to large crises, however, appear to decrease the sector's ability to absorb short-term risk. In other words, a system might be less stable in the short term, but perform better in terms of insulating the macroeconomy from volatility in the long term, as it allows for more frequent adjustments. The result also suggests that political economy factors may be a key issue in explaining some of these choices, as political forces may repress short-term adjustments, thereby making the quest for early warning indicators even harder than appears at first sight.

For equity markets, liberalization has mostly involved opening up equity investment to foreign investors through the removal of ownership and investment restrictions, capital controls, and other restrictions.[5] For firms, evidence using stock prices and terms of corporate bonds generally shows that liberalization leads to lower cost of capital. These studies generally find positive effects of equity market liberalization on firm growth, through such channels as relaxing financing constraints, improving the efficiency of capital allocation, and spurring financial sector development (see, for example, Laeven 2003; Love 2003; and Henry 2003). The studies also report no obvious effects on volatility, besides increases in correlations with global markets as a consequence of increased financial integration (for reviews of this literature see Bekaert and Harvey 2003; and Karolyi and Stulz 2003). The fact that opening up does not lead to an increase in volatility is confirmed in most studies using microeconomic data on investor behavior. No evidence has been found, for example, that the behavior of foreign investors has had destabilizing effects on Korea's stock market (Choe, Kho, and Stulz 1999) or other emerging markets stock markets (Griffin, Nardari, and Stulz 2004). Others have investigated the role of mutual funds investing in emerging markets (Kaminsky, Lyons, and Schmukler 2001 review this literature). Here there are some mixed effects, as mutual funds managers sometimes aggravate the tendency of individual investors to follow trends by also rebalancing portfolios away from markets with recent declines (and toward markets with recent prices increases). Mutual funds managers thus seem to add to the volatility of asset prices and capital flows.

Some have found, however, that liberalization and a consequent greater role of foreign investors have led to increased asset price volatility (see Karolyi 2002). Effects seem to depend importantly on the institutional development of the country, with countries that were more developed before liberalization suffering less. In their review of this growing, individual firm-based literature, Bekaert and Harvey (2003) conclude that there are tradeoffs in opening up at the firm level. The "costs" of increased volatility appear to come with a permanent lower cost of capital and increased access to financing. The conclusions may thus be that there can be short-run costs to be balanced against longer-run gains.

Imperfections in International Financial Markets

In principle, international financial markets could serve to share risks among countries in the most optimal fashion. Many have highlighted the potential gains of risk sharing of international financial markets (Obstfeld 1994; Merton 2000; Shiller, 2003). In practice, however, these risk-reduction gains at the international level are

---

[5] This study does not review capital account liberalization. For such a review, there are many recent overviews, such as Eichengreen 2003.

limited, maybe even more so than in a domestic context. Obstfeld and Rogoff (2000) cite limited international financial integration as one of the main puzzles in international economics. As for domestic financial markets, risk sharing internationally is constrained by many market imperfections, distortions, and other barriers. Some are natural, while others are more policy-induced.

One policy imperfection at the international level is that there is no equivalent of a bankruptcy system or way to enforce collateral. Without an adequate mechanism to enforce claims internationally, developing countries, in particular, find it hard to attract finance when needed to smooth external shocks. With borrowing capacity limited because of the lack of valid collateral, countries must self-insure more than domestic firms by holding more foreign exchange reserves. This is costly, as these countries are in need of capital for investments. Failure to hold such reserves exposes themselves to more risk; this explains the more frequent liquidity crises. Either way, this inability to smooth shocks represents imperfect international risk sharing. The international imperfections can interact with the degree of local financial market development. An interaction can arise between an underdeveloped local financial market and weak international financial links in the incidence and size of crises (Caballero and Krishnamurty 2001). The basic idea of this literature is that in an underdeveloped local financial market, firms have too few incentives to hold international collateral, which is extremely valuable in the case of a crisis. This increases the probability of a crisis and the size of it once it occurs. This research also shows that the presence of financial intermediaries (banks) can make things worse, as they are usually subject to minimum capital requirements. A related study (Eichengreen and Hausmann, 2005) stresses the relationship between the local currency management and the unwillingness of foreigners to lend long and in local currency. Because government can dilute local currency denominated claims, through inflation or otherwise, and lack credibility or institutional framework (e.g., a way to enforce collateral) to convince (foreign) investors otherwise, many developing countries are forced to borrow short-term and in foreign currency, adding risks.

Another important dimension that can play a role in the ability of financial system to manage risk is size. Financial systems of many countries are simply too small to diversify risks. Of 106 developing countries, about three-quarters – 78 – had total bank deposits of less than $10 billion. Of those 78 countries, nearly half – 41 – had deposits under $1 billion (Bossone, Honohan, and Long 2001).[6] In terms of equity markets, only 60 of the 106 countries had stock exchanges. Of these, 40 had a market capitalization of less than $10 billion – a sum that would amount to a very small bank in most developed countries. Small financial systems are typically found in undiversified economies. The only way such economies can share risks meaningfully is by diversifying their financial system. This means inviting more foreign banks to enter their market, requiring domestic banks and other financial institutions to diversify their portfolios outside of the home markets, and perhaps

---

[6] The data exclude another 26 developing countries, all of which had deposits under $10 billion, and none of which had stock markets. These countries were excluded either because their data appear to reflect a role as an offshore financial center, or because they experienced large movements in offshore deposits during the period.

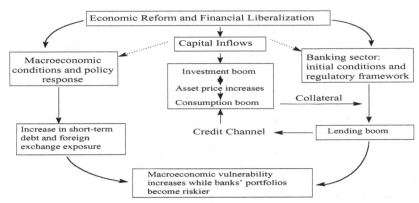

Figure 6.2. The Many Links between Capital Flows and Domestic Cycles. *Source*: Alba and others (1999).

by using risk-management tools that diversify risks internationally, such as commodity and currency hedges. In several countries, including Argentina, Estonia, Hungary, and Poland, the share of foreign banks in their banking systems already exceeds 50 percent (with gains in terms of financial volatility (Clarke, Cull, and Martinez-Peria 2001). The use of hedging as a risk-management tool remains more limited. For some commodity dependent countries, incentives to hedge are weak, as they already receive implicit insurance from their creditors (for example, in the form of Paris Club reschedulings, or new loans from international financial institutions).

International financial markets can even add to risk. Many countries have found that international capital flows can amplify a domestic cycle, a cycle that may be started by a process of financial liberalization or other economic reforms. The channels of amplification can run through the banking system, particularly when weakly regulated, through asset prices and through the overall macroeconomy (see Figure 6.2). Capital flows through the banking system can add directly to risk by creating currency mismatches in banks' balance sheets. Capital flows may add to risks indirectly by fueling a credit boom in the country, making banks portfolios more risky, and amplifying the business cycle. International financial integration can also amplify cycles in asset prices. Increased financial integration means asset prices will rise as assets become priced according to international norms. Since most emerging markets have a limited supply of savings and low covariances with global markets, required rates of return will typically drop and local asset prices rise as markets open. As local asset prices rise, a credit boom may start or grow. If the price rise is not sustainable, however, asset prices may follow a boom and bust cycle.

The movement and volatility in capital flows may be induced by distortions themselves, or by liberalization in the presence of some continued distortions or weaknesses. In the presence of overly generous implicit or explicit deposit insurance and weak governance structures, for example, banks may be inclined to take on extra risks – in the form of unmatched foreign exchange liabilities or more borrowing. This will increase the banks' vulnerabilities. Macroresponses can add to the buildup of risks, with the channels running more through the overall macroeconomy. Sterilization of inflows, for example, played a big role in encouraging capital flows in East Asia and elsewhere by keeping the interest differential high. Meanwhile, there were implicit exchange rate guarantees, as exchange rates were kept constant. This encouraged foreign exchange-denominated borrowings, thereby intensifying balance sheet mismatches of banks and firms. And at the international level, implicit guarantees in the form of possible international bailouts can add to the incentives of foreign investors to take on more risks and do less monitoring, as was the case for Argentina, Russia, and Turkey.

The difficulty for policymakers is that for some time, these cycles can display properties that look very desirable. A virtuous cycle may be apparent, with increased financial integration occurring along with increases in capital flows, higher asset prices, and booms in credit, consumption, and investment. Depending on policy responses and initial conditions, however, particularly in the banking system, excessive risks can arise, and vulnerabilities can build up. This can then be followed by a vicious cycle, perhaps triggered by a financial crisis. These cycles have a large domestic component, and have been seemingly unavoidable in even the most sophisticated markets. While the proximate causes of these cycles have been identified, many of the ultimate causes are still elusive. Nonetheless, it is clear the international dimension can be particularly important in developing countries, as rapid withdrawal of foreign capital flows often triggers the financial crisis or increases the depth of a crisis

In addition to increasing the amplitude of domestic cycles, there are also direct consequences of increased financial integration. With increased financial integration, asset prices will become more correlated with international factors. Over the past decade, correlations between equity prices in various markets have indeed risen. This means risks from other markets will be imported. The financial crises over the past decade have drawn attention to the issue of "contagion" or spillovers. Various forms of spillovers need to be distinguished. Dependencies among countries will cause shocks to an individual country (or group of countries) to affect other countries, often on a regional basis, as integration will typically be deeper regionally. A slowdown or a financial crisis in a major export market, for example, may have repercussions for the financial markets in the exporting countries, as in case of Uruguay following the onset of crisis in Argentina in 2000, or as a global slowdown hits all economies.

Many of these linkages are unavoidable shocks to the real sector, although they maybe transmitted through international financial markets. Economic fundamentals in weak countries, large similarities between countries, geographic proximity, and exposures to certain types of financial agents such as mutual funds, can increase the risk of these spillovers, however. Moreover, the state of the international financial system can play a role in increasing cross-market linkages. This was the case in the fall of 1998, when crises in East Asia, Russia, and Brazil coincided with turmoil in financial markets in developed countries, triggered by the collapse of LTCM, which had also invested in emerging markets. Such cross-market linkages put considerable stress on the financial systems of developed countries and also led to spillovers in many emerging markets. As such, international financial integration can be a mixed blessing.

To what extent these spillovers represent irrational behavior – that is, they ignore country fundamentals – is analytically unclear and being debated. The channels for contagion are not well understood, either. Some obvious channels, such as trade and regional links, have been identified (for a review of the contagion literature, see Dornbusch, Park, and Claessens 2000; for a collection of papers on international financial contagion, see Claessens and Forbes 2001).

A "common lender" channel has been identified (Kaminsky and Reinhart 1999). Countries may be infected because they source funds through a common financial center. The role of institutional investors has also been investigated. Many other channels are still obscure, however. For example, a rebalancing of portfolios by investors following a shock to one country, leading to capital outflows from many countries, could be rational behavior on the part of investors, as the shock may have provided information on the economic fundamentals of these other countries. Or it could be irrational behavior, as investors panic, following the actions of a few who are thought to have inside information, but do not necessarily have special information. In either case, it could be called financial contagion.

More generally, the functioning of the financial system is very dependent on the overall macroeconomy and macroeconomic policymaking. It is it in this respect that bad macropolicy can trump good financial sector regulation. No financial system can sustain the type of macroeconomic and legal shocks that Argentina underwent (see Chapter 10, this volume by Luis Servén and Guillermo Perry). Authorities can try to make the financial system so robust as to compensate for systemic events (and especially for events that one hopes are rare, such as deciding to apply different exchange rates to the two sides of banks' balance sheets, as in Argentina in the recent crisis). However, the result will be that financial intermediation will be killed off, which itself is not a tenable solution.

Furthermore, the "finger in the dike" approach to financial regulation must be avoided: that is, trying to reduce one apparent risk by putting more regulation in place. In case of Korea, banks were forced to apply stricter provisioning rules and had to reduce lending to weak firms. The problems of illiquid and insolvent *chaebols* (large Korean conglomerates) spilled over from the banking system into the nonbank financial institutions, as the *chaebols* started to issue commercial paper and bonds that were bought up by insurance companies and mutual funds. But these nonbank financial institutions were often controlled by the *chaebols*, allocated funds very poorly, and continued to support weak *chaebol* firms. As the nonbank financial institutions ran into liquidity problems themselves, banks were called in to provide support, thus triggering another round of necessary support for the banks as they acquired bad assets again.

FINANCIAL CRISES

Next, consider those types of crises where the financial sector plays a large role as a trigger or amplifier (for more general reviews of the causes and management of financial crises, see Tirole 2002; Frenkel 2000; Eichengreen 2003; Edwards and Frankel 2002; and Frankel and Dooley 2003; for a detailed review of the causes of banking and financial crises, see Appendix A). It is useful to distinguish the links between the financial sector and the macroeconomy in the lead-up to the financial crisis, where the issue is whether one can predict the crisis, from the links after the crisis, where the issue is crisis management.

In financial crisis management, especially in emerging markets, it is useful to think of three subphases. During the first phase, which can be called the containment phase, the financial crisis is still unfolding. Governments tend to implement policies aimed at restoring public confidence to minimize the repercussions on the real sector of the loss of confidence by depositors and other investors in the financial system. The second phase involves the actual financial restructuring of financial institutions and firms, and to a lesser extent an operational restructuring. The third phase involves structural reforms. The first two subphases are discussed below. Structural reforms, of which key examples are improvement of banking system regulation and supervision, improved accounting and disclosure rules for banks and corporates, better protection of property rights, and introducing more competition, as well privatization of any nationalized financial institutions and firms, are discussed elsewhere (see World Bank 2001).

Predicting Crises

The important point in terms of predicting crises is that success has been limited.[7] This has been the case for a number of reasons: poor data, especially in emerging markets; a limited number of crises, making it hard to predict what are rare events; and the difficulty in anticipating the behavior of market participants, as the same set of circumstances seems to appear to trigger different responses. There is also the difficulty of choosing the appropriate model, as exemplified in the proliferation of analytical models in response to crises in the late 1990s, the so-called third genera-tion balance-of-payments crisis models that stressed ever more and newer aspects, including balance sheets. Furthermore, much success with predicting crisis could imply some market inefficiency, as investors would not have used all information to predict events to maximize returns. Or, policymakers may be taking actions that reduce the chances of a current crisis on the basis of past events, thus making crises in general harder to predict. As a consequence, most Early Warning Systems (EWS) models do not achieve more than a marginal improvement over naïve forecasts. This does not make them irrelevant, but their importance should not be overstated.

A particularly difficult area is financial contagion. In a domestic context, this is reflected in a limited ability to anticipate and understand the interactions between banks in the interbank market in the face of some shocks. Banks have extensive relationships in the form of interbank claims, which can lead to shocks from one bank spilling over to another bank. Some attempts are underway to analyze the effects of these interrelations among banks.[8] The formal credit and debit relationships are, however, only one element of financial contagion. Especially in emerging markets, a small crisis can spill over not through formal credit relationships, but through

---

[7] It is important to differentiate between trying to explain the patterns typically encountered in a financial crisis after the fact and trying to predict whether a particular crisis will occur over a certain horizon – such as 12 to 24 months – in which action can be taken to avoid the crisis.

[8] The Bundesbank and Central Bank of Austria, for example, have developed approaches that look at a matrix of interbank relationships to check for the possibility of contagion.

such actions as reduction in liquidity, refusal to rollover claims, or deposits runs. For example, in late 1997 the announcement by the Government of Indonesia that it would close 16 banks triggered a depositor run because depositors were aware that some banks known to be insolvent, but politically connected, were still being kept open. This meant that in the eyes of investors, the uncertainty over the solvency of individual banks and which banks might be closed next was not resolved. This contagion triggered large-scale deposit movements from private banks to state-owned banks and foreign banks operating in Indonesia, as well as banks abroad, leading to a collapse of the Indonesian financial sector.

Although crises remain hard to predict, it might still be possible to assess risks better, to help trigger responses from policymakers and alert investors before the onset of a crisis, and thus avoid a crisis. Many analytical tools are now available for assessing risks in the financial sector, including those risks arising from interactions between the macroeconomy and the financial sector. The main approach of these tools is to conduct stress tests on the financial system under different macroeconomic assumptions, including exchange rates, interest rates, and economic growth. Appendix C provides a short overview of some of these tools, including stress tests conducted under the Financial Sector Assessment Program and tests using more market-based information. The tools represent a welcome improvement, particularly where they have been incorporated in the institutional context of the country and where results are made public. This is the case with the financial stability assessments many countries now do on a regular basis. Yet even these tools have limits. This is especially so in emerging markets given problems with data quality, the limited length of data series, and the difficulty of quantifying some of the behavioral relationships, such as between exchange rates, interest rates, and macroeconomic variables, such as output and industrial production. Thus crises are likely to remain a feature of the financial and economic landscape of many countries.

The Containment Phase

Policymakers often fail to respond effectively to evidence of an impending banking crisis, hoping that banks and corporations will grow out of their problems.[9] But intervening early with a comprehensive and credible plan can avoid a systemic crisis, minimize adverse effects, and limit overall losses. Early intervention appears to be especially important in stopping the flow of financing to loss-making financial institutions and corporations and in limiting moral hazard in financial institutions and corporations gambling for survival. Experience also suggests that the intervention and closing of weak financial institutions need to be properly managed. Uncertainty among depositors needs to be limited; otherwise the government may be forced to resolve a loss of confidence with an unlimited guarantee on the liabilities of banks and other financial institutions. But in practice, ad hoc closures of a few financial institutions without a comprehensive plan for the rest of the financial system are more the norm, and often add to uncertainty, triggering a systemic crisis. Similarly,

---

[9] The following section is based on Claessens, Klingebiel, and Laeven (2003a). There are many political economy reasons why policymakers may not wish to act – thereby giving rise to a crisis (see Haggard 2001).

the suspension of financial institutions for a long period can increase uncertainty among depositors as well as borrowers. This was shown in the case of Thailand where most finance companies were suspended. In the end, only a few finance companies survived and most were closed, but the lack of clarity made depositors run from the whole financial system.

Reviewing several cases, Herbert Baer and Daniela Klingebiel (1995) suggest that, to avoid uncertainty among depositors and limit their incentives to run, policymakers need to deal simultaneously with all insolvent and marginally solvent institutions. Intermittent regulatory intervention makes depositors more nervous and undermines regulatory credibility – especially if regulators had previously argued that the institutions involved were solvent.[10] Given the weaknesses of data on financial solvency in many emerging markets, however, bank supervisors in practice have problems in identifying those weak banks. Moreover, regulations and laws for intervening in banks are often weak, creating further uncertainty. The solutions are not obvious. Intervention tools may need to be fairly simple where institutions are weak. Even then, governments may not avoid mistakes in dealing with weak banks. Rather than focusing on which institutions to close, they may need to provide more support for those better-run financial institutions that can survive.[11] Even then, uncertainty will often remain and the government may need to respond. This response often takes the form of liquidity support or a guarantee on financial institutions' liabilities.

There are two schools of thoughts on whether to use liquidity support and unlimited guarantees during the containment phase.[12] Some argue that crisis conditions make it almost impossible to distinguish between solvent and insolvent institutions, leaving the authorities with little choice but to extend liquidity support. Moreover, it is argued that an unlimited guarantee preserves the payments system and helps stabilize institutions' financial claims while restructuring is being organized and carried out (Lindgren, Garcia, and Saal 1996). Others argue that open-ended liquidity support provides more time for insolvent institutions to gamble (unsuccessfully) on resurrection, facilitates continued financing of loss-making borrowers, and allows owners and managers to engage in looting. Supporters of this view also argue that a government guarantee on financial institutions' liabilities reduces the incentives of large creditors to monitor financial institutions, allowing bank managers and shareholders to continue gambling on their insolvent banks and increasing fiscal costs.

---

[10] Baer and Klingebiel also point out that a comprehensive approach places less demand on supervisory resources. Under a piecemeal approach, insolvent and marginally solvent institutions would continue to exist while other insolvent institutions were being closed or restructured. Marginally solvent institutions would be subject to moral hazard and fraud while being unable and unwilling to raise additional capital. Especially in an environment with weak supervision, comprehensive approaches are needed even more.

[11] For example, a rehabilitation program for undercapitalized financial institutions – which involves institutions indicating how they plan to meet capital adequacy requirements in the future – requires careful government oversight and good financial statements. But such features are often missing in developing countries. Instead of relying on rehabilitation that requires good oversight and data, regulators could apply a 100 percent (marginal) reserve requirement on deposit inflows and other new liabilities. That is, 100 percent of new deposits will be kept with the central bank or in government securities, limiting the ability of weak banks to reallocate resources in a detrimental way.

[12] A third school argues that the granting of government guarantees is the outcome of the circumstances of the political economy, and so is often a foregone conclusion. See Dooley and Verma (2003).

Adherents further point out that extensive guarantees limit government maneuver-ability in allocating losses, often with the end result that government incurs most of the cost of the systemic crisis (Sheng 1996).

In practice, the issue becomes at what price to restore stability. Evidence on the tradeoff between restoring confidence and containing fiscal costs comes from Patrick Honohan and Daniela Klingebiel (2003), who show that much of the variation in the fiscal cost of 40 crises in industrial and developing economies from 1980 to 1997 can be explained by government approaches to resolving liquidity crises. The authors find that governments that provided open-ended liquidity support and announced (new) blanket deposit guarantees to preempt a further bank run after a crisis had started incurred much higher costs in resolving financial crises. They also find that these costs are higher in countries with weak institutions. Most important, they find no obvious tradeoff between fiscal costs and subsequent economic growth (or overall output losses). Countries that used policies such as liquidity support, blanket guarantees, and particularly costly forbearance, that is, the relaxing of prudential standards – did not recover faster. Rather, liquidity support appears to make recovery from a crisis longer and output losses larger – a finding confirmed by Michael Bordo and others (2001). This work suggests that during the containment phase it is important to limit liquidity support and not to extend guarantees.

Restructuring Financial Institutions

Once financial markets have been stabilized, the second phase involves restructuring weak financial institutions and firms. Restructuring is complex because policymak-ers need to take into account many issues. Financial restructuring will depend on the speed at which macroeconomic stability can be achieved, because that determines the viability of firms, banks, and other financial institutions, and more generally the reduction in overall uncertainty. But macroeconomic stability often requires progress on financial and corporate restructuring, and so cannot be viewed independently of the restructuring process.

Restructuring refers to several related processes: recognizing and allocating financial losses; restructuring the financial claims of financial institutions and firms; and operational restructuring of financial institutions and firms. Recognition involves the allocation of losses and associated redistribution of wealth and control. Losses – that is, differences between the market value of assets and the nominal value of liabilities held by financial institutions and firms – can be allocated various ways: to shareholders (through dilution); to depositors and creditors (by reducing the present value of their claims); to employees (through reduced wages); to suppliers (through lower prices for inputs); and to the government or the public (through higher taxes, lower spending, or inflation).

To minimize moral hazard and strengthen financial discipline, governments can allocate losses not only to shareholders but also to creditors and large depositors who should have been monitoring the banks. Often, however, governments assume all losses through their guarantees. There are exceptions to the model of govern-ments guaranteeing all liabilities in an effort to restore confidence. In some crises – notably in the United States (1933), Japan (1946), Argentina (1980–82), and Estonia (1992) – governments have imposed losses on depositors, with little or no adverse

Finance and Volatility   243

macroeconomic consequences or flight from the currency (Baer and Klingebiel 1995). In these cases, economic recovery was rapid and financial intermediation, including household deposits, was soon restored. Thus allocating losses to creditors or depositors will not necessarily lead to runs on banks or end in contraction of aggregate money, credit, and output. In a related vein, a review of country cases by Gerard Caprio and Daniela Klingebiel (1997) indicates that financial discipline is further strengthened when bank management – often part of the problem – is changed and banks are operationally restructured.

Financial and corporate restructuring crucially depends on the incentives under which banks and firms operate. Successful debt workouts require proper incentives for banks and borrowers to come to the negotiating table. The incentive framework for banks includes accounting, classification, and provisioning rules: that is, financial institutions need to be asked to realistically mark their assets to market. The framework also includes laws and prudential regulations. Regulators should ensure that undercapitalized financial institutions are properly disciplined and closed. The bankruptcy system should enable financial institutions to enforce their claims on firms, allow for speedy financial restructuring of viable corporations, and provide for the efficient liquidation of enterprises that cannot be rehabilitated. Proper incentives also mean appropriate limits on ownership links between banks and corporations (since otherwise the same party could end up being both debtor and creditor). In Korea, for instance, as nonperforming loans migrated to nonbank financial institutions, conflicts arose as many of the nonbank financial institutions were controlled by the same *chaebols* that were in default. More generally, close banking–commerce connections can create risks, although many have more to do with the concentration of power rather than any poor allocation of resources or an increase in risks. Nevertheless, in countries where the quality of corporate governance and regulation and supervision is weak, there can be reasons not to allow for universal-type banks, which can undertake commercial, investment banking, and insurance activities. Such an arrangement would raise the scope of risk-taking activities. The better option might be for more narrow banks that are only allowed to invest in government securities and other, very safe assets.

Adequately capitalized financial institutions are a key component of a proper incentive framework. Financial institutions need to have sufficient loss absorption capacity to engage in sustainable corporate restructuring. In a systemic crisis, capital will often have to come from the government through recapitalization. But general experience – supported by events in East Asia, Turkey, and elsewhere – suggests that recapitalization of financial institutions needs to be carried out and managed to limit moral hazard. Repeated, incomplete recapitalizations tend to increase the fiscal costs of resolving a crisis, Honohan and Klingebiel (2003) find. One possible explanation is that marginally capitalized banks tend to engage in cosmetic corporate restructuring – such as maturity extensions or interest rate reductions on loans to nonviable firms – rather than writing off debts.

Banks' incentives to undertake corporate restructuring can be strengthened by linking government financing to the restructuring. For example, a capital support scheme in which additional fiscal resources are linked to corporate restructuring through loss-sharing arrangements can make banks more willing to write off bad loans and induce them to conduct deeper restructuring. Especially in weak institutional settings, limits on the actions of marginally capitalized banks will typically be necessary.

In principle, governments should capitalize or strengthen the capital base of only those financial institutions with franchise value (franchise value is the value of the institution derived from future net income streams). But once again, political economy problems make it difficult for governments to select only certain banks for assistance, and not others. More fundamentally, it is often difficult for governments to distinguish good banks from bad. Risk-sharing mechanisms with the private sector – such as cofinancing arrangements where infusions of government equity only take place when the private sector provides capital – can help identify the better banks. This setup still requires a decent institutional environment to avoid misuse of government funds (private agents, for example, may not bring in genuine new capital, but rather use borrowed funds). Especially in a weak institutional environment with limited private capital, governments may want to rely more on hard budget constraints on weak banks (such as a 100 percent marginal reserve requirement on new deposits) to prevent a large leakage of fiscal resources – including through excessive guarantees on financial institutions' liabilities. And good banks may need to be actively coerced to receive support – in the form of credit lines, capital support, or technical assistance – because they may resist government interference. But without some support, good banks may not be able to provide financial intermediation to firms, aggravating the crisis.

RESTRUCTURING FIRMS. The nature of a systemic crisis, and the already close links between the solvency and performance of the real and financial sectors in normal times, make it clear that bank restructuring needs to be complemented by corporate restructuring. Financial restructuring for firms takes many forms: reschedulings (extensions of maturities), lower interest rates, debt-for-equity swaps, debt forgiveness, indexing interest payments to earnings, and so on. Operational restructuring, an ongoing process, includes improvements in efficiency and management, reductions in staff and wages, asset sales (such as a reduction in subsidiaries), enhanced marketing efforts, and the like, with the expectation of increased profitability and higher cash flow. In a first best world, to start corporate restructuring, firms should quickly be triaged into three categories: operationally viable and not financially distressed firms; operationally viable but financially distressed firms; and financially and operationally unviable firms. The question is, who will do so? In a normal restructuring of an individual case of financial distress, private agents will make these decisions and start the operational and financial restructuring. But in a systemic crisis, case-by-case restructuring will be difficult because the incentives under which agents operate are likely not conducive, private capital is typically limited, and coordination problems are large.[13]

Nevertheless, the starting point is providing proper incentives for private agents to allow and encourage market-based, sustainable corporate restructuring. Given that the crisis was likely partly induced by weaknesses in the environment in which the real sector operated, the first step for government will have to be creating an

---

[13] For papers on systemic corporate restructuring, including specific case studies, see Claessens, Djankov, and Mody (2001).

enabling environment. Depending on country circumstances, this can imply undertaking corporate governance reforms, improving bankruptcy and other restructuring frameworks, making the judicial system more efficient, liberalizing entry by foreign investors, changing the competitive framework for the real sector, or introducing other supportive structural measures. In general, the political economy of reform suggests that a crisis can often be a time to get difficult structural reforms accepted or at least initiated.

Most crisis countries do reform the incentives for restructuring, though the strengths and depth of the reforms differ. For example, Indonesia adopted a new bankruptcy system to replace its pre-World War II Dutch code in August 1998, some 12 months after its crisis started. Similarly, Thailand's Senate approved the Act for the Establishment of and Procedure for Bankruptcy Court, intended to increase the efficiency of judicial procedures in bankruptcy cases, only in February 1999, 19 months after its crisis began. But despite the act's adoption, bankruptcies in Thailand remained few in number and fraught with difficulties for several years.

Beyond fixing the environment, it can be necessary to provide extra incentives for private agents to engage in speedy corporate restructuring. These incentives can involve tax, accounting, and other measures. Banks, for example, may be given more tax relief for provisioning or restructuring loans. Firms may be given more favorable accounting relief for recognizing foreign exchange losses. In the wake of its crisis, the Republic of Korea adopted more favorable tax rules for corporate restructuring, though they ended up being misused through cosmetic rather than real restructuring. Some countries have offered guarantees on exchange rate behavior, such as Indonesia's INDRA scheme and Mexico's FICORCA scheme, to induce firms and creditors to undertake restructuring. The efficiency of such measures should be evaluated from various perspectives, taking into account their benefits for restructuring and public finance, as well as their possible redistributive effects. But while such measures may speed recovery, they often do not contribute to fundamental reforms. In any case, the general opinion is that such measures should be temporary (that is, with sunset clauses).

Even when adequate for normal times, a revamped bankruptcy and restructuring framework might not be sufficient during a systemic crisis, given the coordination problems and weaknesses in other aspects of the institutional framework. Thus governments have created special frameworks for corporate restructuring, such as the "London Rules"[14] first used in Mexico, then in several East Asian countries (Indonesia, Korea, Malaysia, Thailand), and tried in Turkey. The London Rules involve an out-of-court accord, under regular contract or commercial law, that all or most creditor institutions are coerced to sign. With such an accord, agreements reached among most creditors can often be enforced on other creditors without formal judicial procedures.

Arbitration with specific deadlines – and penalties for failing to meet the deadlines – can also be part of the accord, avoiding a formal judicial process to

---

[14] The London Rules are principles for corporate reorganization first proposed in the United Kingdom in the early 1990s. Because the rules were not designed for systemic corporate distress, countries have tightened them in various ways.

resolve disputes.[15] The degree of such enhancements to the London Rules has varied among countries. In East Asia, the frameworks in Korea, Malaysia, and Thailand were the most conducive to out-of-court restructuring, while the framework in Indonesia was the least (Claessens, Djankov, and Klingebiel 1999). These differences appear to partly explain the variations in the speed of restructuring in these four countries.

The most far-reaching proposal for enhancing the restructuring framework is "super-bankruptcy" (or "super Chapter 11"), a temporary tool that allows corporate management to stay in place and forces debt-to-equity conversions (Stiglitz 2001a). This tool can preserve firms' value as going concerns by preventing too many liquidations and keeping in place existing managers, who arguably most often know best how to run the firms. An important issue is when to call for a super Chapter 11: that is, when is a crisis systemic, and who has the authority to call for such a suspension of payments? Political economy factors should be taken into account, because some debtors could gain disproportionately from a suspension of payments. To date, no country has taken this approach. It is useful to note, however, that, while bankruptcy laws differ considerably even among industrial countries, there has been a general move from more creditor-friendly regimes that are liquidation-oriented, to more debtor-friendly regimes that are more restructuring-oriented.

Even with a better enabling environment, agents will probably be unable to triage corporations quickly and proceed with restructuring. The resulting debt overhang or deadlock in claims can be especially risky when institutions are weak, and can greatly increase the final costs to the public sector of resolving the crisis. Weak banks may continue to lend to corporations that are "too big to fail," partly as a way of gambling for resurrection, and so delay sustainable corporate restructuring. Owners of defunct enterprises may strip assets, leaving only shells of liabilities for creditors. Even financially viable firms may stop paying promptly if faced with an insolvent banking system.

In such cases, it may be necessary in the short run to use hard budget constraints to limit the flow of resources to weak corporations from weak financial institutions or other sources. To increase credit to corporations that can actually repay and limit lending to weak firms, it may also be necessary to have temporary across-the-board mechanisms for certain types of borrowers (such as small and medium-size enterprises) or certain activities (such as trade financing). The need for such blunter tools will increase with a country's institutional weaknesses. Indonesia's market-based approach to corporate restructuring, where banks were asked to work out the distressed loans in exchange for capital support from the government, for example, seems to have had little impact and probably led only to further asset stripping.

As a next step, it is often necessary for government to support corporate restructuring more directly. As with support for the financial system, it is essential to

---

[15] Out-of-court negotiations and bankruptcy or other legal resolution techniques are not the only ways of dealing with financial distress. Economists have been proposing alternative procedures for some time, centering on versions of an asset sale or cash auction. Cash auctions are easy to administer and do not rely on the judicial system. While attractive from a theoretical perspective, these proposals have not had recent followers, except Mexico in 1998.

restructure strong and viable firms, and not weak ones. But all too often, unviable firms (such as those considered too big to fail) receive support instead of deserving, operationally viable firms. This was the case with two of Korea's largest *chaebols* and with Indonesia and Thailand's large family-controlled conglomerates. These firms ended up receiving disproportionately large financing during the first phase of the crisis, while smaller firms lacked even working capital (Domac and Ferri 1999). Thus it is crucial to choose a lead agent that ensures proper analysis of firms' prospects, as well as durable operational and financial restructurings.

CHOOSING THE LEAD AGENT FOR RESTRUCTURING. The main choice for the lead agent in restructuring is between the government and the private sector. Many approaches are possible. A centralized asset management corporation will put the government in charge. Recapitalization of private banks will put the banks in charge. Under other models, investors and firms can become the lead agent, with the government sharing the risks. Banks can work out nonperforming loans, for example, but with some stop-loss arrangements with the government. Or nonperforming loans can be transferred to a number of corporate restructuring vehicles that, though state-owned, can be privately run by asset managers with incentive stakes.

Most important is that the lead agent has the necessary capacity to absorb losses, as well as the institutional capacity, incentives, and external enforcement mechanisms to effect restructuring. Undercapitalized banks, for example, will not be very effective restructuring agents. And without a working bankruptcy regime, private agents will not be able to force recalcitrant debtors to the negotiating table – as in Indonesia, where restructuring are still ongoing from the 1997 crisis, and in Thailand, where the restructuring of Thai Petrochemical Industry took at least three years.

Countries often choose a mix of these approaches when dealing with a systemic crisis. In 1995 Mexico tried both an asset management corporation and a more decentralized approach. The four East Asian crisis countries (Indonesia, Korea, Malaysia, Thailand) all eventually used asset management corporations; all used out-of-court systems for corporate restructuring; and most used, after some initial period, fiscal stimulus and monetary policy to foster economic growth. In addition, all enhanced, to varying degrees, their basic frameworks for private sector operations, including bankruptcy and corporate governance frameworks, and liberalization of foreign entry in the financial and corporate sectors. But success has varied with the intensity of these measures (Claessens, Djankov, and Klingebiel 1999). In Argentina and Russia, more decentralized approaches have been used, whereas in Turkey, a more centralized approach has been used. Empirical evidence on these mechanisms is limited but tends to favor the decentralized model (see Box 6.7).

CHANGING OWNERSHIP STRUCTURES. Just as a crisis can offer a window to undertake structural reform, it can provide an opportunity to reform a country's ownership structures. As a direct party to the restructuring process, the state often becomes the owner of defunct financial institutions and corporations. This development severely complicates the resolution of the crisis because government may not have the right incentives or capacity to effect the needed operational and financial restructuring. At the same time, large indirect ownership by the state of the financial and real sectors

---

Box 6.7. Asset Management Companies

A study of seven centralized approaches using asset management companies found that most of the corporations did not achieve their stated objectives with corporate restructuring (Klingebiel 2001). The study distinguishes corporate restructuring asset management corporations from bank rehabilitation asset management companies. Two of the three corporate restructuring companies did not achieve their narrow goal of expediting restructuring. Only Sweden's asset management company successfully managed its portfolio, acting in some instances as the lead agent in restructuring. Rapid asset disposition vehicles fared somewhat better, with two of four – in Spain and the United States – achieving their objectives. These successes suggest that asset management corporations can be effective, but only for narrowly defined purposes of resolving insolvent and unviable financial institutions and selling their assets. But even achieving these objectives requires many ingredients: a type of asset that is easily liquidated (such as real estate), mostly professional management, political independence, a skilled human resource base, appropriate funding, adequate bankruptcy and foreclosure laws, good information and management systems, and transparent operations and processes.

The findings on asset management companies are corroborated by a review of three East Asian countries (Dado 2000). The centralized asset management companies in Indonesia and Korea did not appear likely to achieve their narrow goal of expediting bank or corporate restructuring, while Malaysia's was relatively successful, aided by that country's strong bankruptcy system. Success has also varied when a mix of approaches is tried. In Mexico neither the asset management company nor the enhanced restructuring framework was effective, possibly because fundamental reforms were lacking (Mexico's bankruptcy regime, for example, was not revamped until four years after its crisis). Export-led growth appears to have led Mexico's recovery after 1995 (though growth did not resolve banking problems).

Marinela Dado and Daniela Klingebiel (2002) analyze decentralized restructuring in seven countries: Argentina (in the 1980s), Chile, Hungary, Japan, Norway, Poland, and Thailand. They find that the success of this approach depended on the quality of the institutional framework, including accounting and legal rules, and on initial conditions, including the capital positions of banks and ownership links. In Norway the government built on favorable initial conditions to attain a solid overall framework for the decentralized approach. The biggest improvement to the overall framework was made in Chile, with favorable results. Poland and Hungary ranked behind Chile, though Poland improved its framework much faster than Hungary. Thailand made little progress on strengthening its framework. In Japan, despite many reforms to the overall framework, efforts remained blocked by large ownership links. Argentina relied solely on public debt relief programs where the government granted extensive debt service reduction to borrowers and did not change its overall framework for restructuring.

---

provides an opportunity to change ownership structures as part of restructuring. This move can have several benefits.

First, the changes can correct ownership structures that contributed to the crisis and so help prevent future crises. For example, to the extent that ownership concentrated in the hands of a few families contributed to the crisis – as argued by some for East Asia – government can try to widen ownership structures.

Second, government can try to obtain political support for restructuring by reallocating ownership.[16] One option is to reprivatize financial institutions or corporations in a way that redistributes ownership among the general public or employees of the restructured institution. Another option is to use some of the state ownership to endow previously unfunded pension obligations arising from a pay-as-you-go system. In this way, government can create ownership structures that will reinforce its reforms over time.

Third, changing ownership structures can introduce third parties that have better incentives and skills in restructuring individual corporations and determining financial relief. One option is to transfer nonperforming loans to a fund jointly owned by private and public shareholders, but with the private stake having lower seniority. Private shareholders in the fund would then have the right incentives when deciding on the financial viability of a corporation, but without having full formal ownership of the assets. Public resources would be provided only when all parties – creditor banks, other creditors, new private investors, the government, and the private shareholders in the fund – had reached agreement with the corporation.

PURSUING SUPPORTIVE MACROECONOMIC POLICIES. Another common theme in the literature is that corporate restructuring should occur in the context of supportive macroeconomic policies. The right macroeconomic policies (fiscal and monetary) can speed the recovery of overall economic activity. In the stabilization phase – that is, the phase following the immediate crisis – there will be many linkages between the financial sector and the macroeconomy, the most important being that the macropolicy response needs to be conditioned on the state of the financial system. In some way, a financial crisis means that the normal linkages between macropolicies and the overall real economy through the financial sector are even more pronounced. But there are some qualitative differences. In particular, there will be a link between the extent to which financial sector vulnerabilities have been allowed to build up, through mismatched financial or real sectors balance sheets, and the possible and preferred macropolicy mix during the early phases of a financial crisis.

The appropriate fiscal stance has been extensively reviewed, especially in the context of the East Asian crisis. A review by the International Monetary Fund suggests that East Asian countries' fiscal stance was too tight initially (Lane and others 1999). The appropriate monetary stance has been more controversial and is still being debated, but mainly in terms of defending the exchange rate. One dimension of this is the tradeoff between interest rate and exchange rate policies in stabilizing the economy. This is a complex topic. If public and private balance sheets are strong and there is a temporary confidence shock, then a high interest rate policy may be the best (temporary) way to defend or support the exchange rate. But if there is a problem with both public debt sustainability and balance sheet

[16] Regardless of the changes in ownership and the relationships between debtors and creditors, the government may want to create a special social safety net for laid-off workers to help sustain political support for restructuring over time.

currency mismatches in the context of an overvalued real exchange rate (as was the case with Argentina, for example), it is not obvious what the best macropolicy mix is. In such cases, raising interest rates to defend the currency will only make the public debt dynamics worse, while letting the exchange rate depreciate could lead to bankruptcies of banks and corporations, with adverse consequences on confidence, the overall economy, and public sector finances. In such cases, there may not be much scope for a tradeoff between interest-rate and exchange-rate adjustment. Some heterodox macroeconomic responses and measures may then be useful to regain stability in light of these imbalances, including some form of debt restructuring or capital controls. Capital controls were employed by Malaysia in the 1997 financial crisis and Indonesia, the Philippines, and Thailand imposed restrictions on the ability of speculators to short the local currency.

An important related aspect is the effect of tight monetary policy on the real sector through a possible credit crunch, which was an important issue of debate in the East Asian countries' financial crisis. Microeconomic-based empirical literature suggests evidence of a credit crunch early in the East Asian crisis. The crunch was likely the result of tighter capital adequacy requirements and the monetary policies being pursued. Given the unbalanced financial systems in East Asia – where banks dominate and little alternative financing was available, and many banks were fragile even before the crisis – it is likely that, at least initially, banking weaknesses and tighter regulation and supervision led to a credit crunch. The result was a reduction in working capital and trade finance for East Asian firms. Following this initial crunch, many firms ended up with solvency problems and a debt overhang, with a consequent need for financial restructuring.

Links with the overall macropolicies being pursued also arise from the degree of financial sector liquidity support, the recapitalization needs of weak banks, and the scope of necessary bank interventions. Many a financial crisis has been triggered by excessive liquidity support. In many financial crises, at first governments try to keep insolvent institutions afloat by injecting liquidity. In doing so, they incur large fiscal costs. The liquidity support restrains monetary policy, and the fiscal authority must step in to provide fiscal support. But this delayed and sometimes partial response of governments means further financial turbulence, and can lead to runs on financial institutions. Governments responded to the resulting crisis in public confidence (Argentina, Indonesia, Malaysia, Thailand, and Turkey) or foreign currency outflows (Korea and Mexico) by issuing unlimited guarantees on the liabilities of the financial system. These guarantees can stem the outflows; however, they weaken governments' need to act comprehensively and add to the fiscal costs.

Relatedly, there will be a link between the fiscal headroom the country has, and the resulting scope for financial sector support, and financial sector policies, with a possible perverse feedback. Specifically, countries that have a large amount of public debt outstanding going into a financial crisis, may be constrained in providing open financial support to recapitalize. Financial sector restructuring costs in the four East Asian crisis countries ranged from 15 to 50 percent of GDP – and sharply increased public debt. As financial restructuring costs were absorbed by the government, the ratio of public debt to GDP rose sharply in all the crisis countries: in Indonesia, to more than 90 percent from about 40 percent; and in Korea, Malaysia, and Thailand, to 37–48 percent from initial levels in the 15–30 percent range. Large increases in debt burdens may mean that a more gradual financial sector reform policy becomes necessary. An inability of the government to provide fiscal resources for quick recapitalization of the banking system can mean a protracted deadlock of claims. The intensity of financial-sector and corporate-sector restructuring will thus be linked through the fiscal headroom.

In the restructuring phase, the many normal linkages between the financial and corporate sectors will remain important, such as the viability of the financial sector depending on the speed and intensity of corporate sector restructuring. Of course, these linkages are critical, as no banking system can be solvent when a large part of the corporate sector is insolvent. There will also be links the other way around. The degree to which liquidity problems in the corporate sector will become solvency problems will depend on the ability of the banking system to provide new financing. If the banking system remains undercapitalized or is weakly governed, then a vicious cycle of less credit, more corporate sector insolvencies, and an even weaker banking system can result.

These links mean that the incentive structure under which the financial and corporate sector function, the degree of (re)capitalization of the banking system, and the extent to which nonperforming loans are removed from the banking system (to asset management companies or others), will have consequences for both sectors. As such, the speed and intensity of financial and corporate sector restructuring will have also direct macroeconomic implications. Recent financial crises suggest that recapitalization that is either too slow or too quick can affect macroeconomic performance and create risks (see Appendix D for some work on Korea). More generally, financial reform, or the announcement thereof, can strengthen the confidence of investors, domestic as well as foreign, in the financial system and thereby improve macroeconomic outcomes. These links were one of the main arguments, for example, for the IMF to include the financial sector in the reforms programs in East Asia and elsewhere (Fischer 2000).

AREAS OF LIMITED KNOWLEDGE

In many areas, the knowledge on the relationship between the financial sector and the volatility is still limited. A few specific areas are the following.

FINANCIAL STRUCTURE AND VOLATILITY. While there is no strong empirical evidence that financial structure matters in the transmission of shocks, many individual experiences suggest that there is such a link. The lack of well-developed domestic bond markets, for example, has been mentioned as reasons for the crises in East Asia, Russia, and Brazil. A high proportion of short-term debt tends to increase the probability of self-fulfilling crises, as investors might suddenly decide not to roll over maturing debt or increase required yields on new debt. Shallow domestic bond markets can make this problem worse. They not only limit the governments' capacity to lengthen debt profiles, but also decrease the ability of the government to roll over outstanding debt and investors' ability to liquidate positions. At the same time, many countries have difficulty issuing domestic currency claims of longer maturity, as they lack credit history and credibility. This is in part due to earlier "sins." As a consequence, they suffer adverse public debt dynamics, with high real interest rates leading to increasing debt stocks. Regardless, the exact contribution of the lack of bond markets to financial crises is not yet known.

Little is also known about how the forms of financing affect the vulnerabilities of national financial systems and real sectors, and how these relationships depend on macroeconomic policies. While mismatches in balance sheets and financial structures more generally have received much attention as possible factors in causing or triggering financial crises, including the type of capital flows, there are still many unknowns about the exact channels. For example, it is unclear to what extent commercial banks, mutual funds, or hedge funds have contributed to the volatility of capital flows and specific financial crises. It has become clear that the institutional context in which capital flows take place or financial structures arise has a clear effect on the degree to which they lead to vulnerabilities. Financial structures in more developed countries vary in many ways as well, yet these seem to have much less impact on the transmission of financial and economic shocks.

THE DYNAMICS OF FINANCIAL SECTOR DEVELOPMENT AND LIBERALIZATION. The relationships between financial system performance, access to financing, growth, and financial sector stability are complex – and even more so when considering issues of dynamics and liberalization. Some of the tradeoffs concerning financial sector stability and volatility center on franchise value: that is, the value of an institution, based on future projected income streams. This has both static and dynamic effects. Many have stressed the importance of franchise value for banks in maintaining incentives for prudent behavior. This in turn has led banking system regulators to carefully balance entry and exit, with a more concentrated system considered more stable, as it leads to a higher franchise value for banks and thus more prudent behavior. This is a static view, however. In a dynamic model, higher current concentration does not necessarily reduce risky lending. However, an expected increase in future market concentration can make banks choose safer lending today as they can retain access to future profit opportunities only by choosing a less risky portfolio today.

Another dynamic aspect is that market power in banking, perhaps associated with a more concentrated banking system, may be beneficial for access to financing. The greater its market power, the more likely a bank is to invest in information-gathering about firms, especially in firms for which information is difficult to obtain, as the bank will have a better chance to recoup its investments through a future lending relationship. With more market power, the bank will be more likely to provide credit to those borrowers in which it has invested in gathering information.

Vigorous rivalry may then not be the first best for financial sector performance or stability. But too little competition is not good either. Borrowers will be less willing to enter a relationship with a bank if they are subject to a holdup problem: that is, where the bank can extract excessively high payments from them, as it has more information on the borrowers than the rest of the market does. When the market for external financing is more competitive, a borrower will be more willing to enter a relationship with a bank, as it knows it will be less likely to be subject to holdup problems. Increased interbank competition may then induce banks to make not fewer relationship loans, but more of them, thereby improving financial sector performance, and possibly stability as well. Indeed, there is some recent evidence suggesting that a more concentrated banking sector hinders the entry of firms (Cetorelli 2001; Cetorelli and Strahan 2004).

These two examples, of stability and access, illustrate some of the complex dynamic relationships associated with the functioning of banks. Dynamics are also present in the functioning of a country's entire financial system. These relate to the incentives of financial institutions and markets to innovate and improve efficiency and performance. As in other industries, competition can matter for the quality of financial products and the degree of innovation in the sector. Competition in the financial sector will also matter for the efficiency of the production of financial services. But liberalization and reform aimed at increasing competition do not necessarily lead to these results. Financial institutions may engage in excessive competition or political economy factors undermine expected actions. Identifying the proper mix of regulatory instruments and reforms requires a dynamic analysis of the potential profitability of financial institutions under different regulatory paths and states of the economy, as Joseph Stiglitz (2001b) notes. The policy implication is that governments and others involved in the emerging markets' financial sector reform should consider a more general equilibrium, dynamic approach. Unfortunately, this has been rarely done, leading to volatility and even financial crises.

FINANCIAL SYSTEM REGULATION AND INTERNATIONAL FINANCIAL ARCHITEC-TURE. An important part of the efforts to reform the international financial architecture has been the promulgation of new standards to which a country can adhere. The financial sector is one area where the proliferation of global standards has been the most pronounced. There are, however, many other areas where new standards have been developed, including corporate governance, accounting, bankruptcy, social policies, fiscal management, and financial transparency. While there has been much attention to new standards, it is not clear what works bests in terms of bank regulations, supervisory practices, accounting system practices, laws, and so on, and how to adopt approaches and standards to country circumstances.

Clearly, public sector-driven regulation and supervision cannot solve all problems. As Barth, Caprio, and Levine (2003) show, one cannot put all one's faith in minimally paid supervisors in developing countries, since they are unlikely to be able to resist the temptation of corruption. Rule-based regulations, like the Basel II Capital Adequacy Accord under discussion, and strong supervisors are thus not necessarily the way to go. Indeed, strong supervisors in institutionally underdeveloped settings lead to worse outcomes unless they are independent and embrace market-based supervision strategies. Giving supervisors more powers without checks and balances may actually make things worse, as many countries also have discovered.

Additional analysis is needed to define solutions appropriate to country circumstances. Policies to analyze include the specific arrangements for deposit insurance and the strength of supervision and regulation policies. The balance between the risks of financial turmoil and the risks of misuse of an overly generous financial safety net must be addressed, as well as the balance between powers of regulators and supervisors and check and balances. The tradeoff between government oversight and market-based discipline needs to be considered, taking into account the limited ability in many developing countries of the private sector to monitor financial institutions adequately, given the poor quality of data. More generally, the role of political economy factors in financial reform and triggering institutional changes remains an area where more research is needed.

CONTAGION, ASSET MARKET LINKAGES, AND CRISES. Contagion remains a poorly understood concept. This is so in the domestic context, in terms of asset market linkages and interbank relationships, as well as in an international context, in terms of a crisis in one country affecting other countries. While some of the patterns have been documented, the channels through which the contagion occurs remain unclear. Although much concerning contagion need not represent irrational behavior of investors, it is still unknown what makes countries vulnerable to contagion and through which precise mechanisms and associated transmission channels contagion is being transmitted. What is clear is that volatility will remain a feature of the financial and economic landscape. Specific measures at the national level and the international financial architecture might be necessary to reduce risks, manage their impact, and recover as efficiently as possible. Which policy interventions are least intrusive – that is, which ones do not distort normal financial markets functioning – is not obvious.

As asset markets have grown in importance, their role in the spillovers among financial markets, both national and international, through prices and liquidity seems to have increased as well. Yet the mechanisms are not clear. To some extent, the procyclicality of financial markets is unavoidable, as decentralized, profit-oriented financial institutions are at work. The issue is how to engender more caution in good times and avoid excessive lending and asset prices increases during the upswing.

The procyclicality of asset markets and behavior of financial institutions seems to be not only – or no longer predominantly – a function of macropolicies. Yet the exact role of specific microeconomic factors that affect these cycles are not yet known. What types of policies (such as dynamic provisioning, fair value accounting, and loan-to-value ratios) can most effectively reduce the incidence of bubbles or other securities market failures is still being researched. Without knowing precisely what type of measures can counter the sources of procyclicality and financial vulnerability, rectifying microeconomic distortions and creating a robust financial and regulatory system may be the only and first best solution.

CONCLUSION

Some of the study's main conclusions are as follows:

- In theory, a well-developed financial system can yield many gains in risk sharing. Indeed, empirically it has been found that economic volatility is lower in more developed financial systems – for households, firms, and countries.
- There are, however, many reasons why any financial system does not provide perfect risk sharing at all times, even when there are no distortions. These have to do with information asymmetries, the nature of banks, and the decentralized functioning of financial markets.
  - Information asymmetries make lenders fear that they will end up lending to the riskiest borrowers. As a precaution, they may ration loans, and will

tighten credit even more when macroeconomic conditions worsen (and loosen credit when macroeconomic conditions improve). This can make the financial system amplify shocks, rather than smooth them.

- By nature, banks are high-leveraged institutions that borrow on a short-term basis and lend on a long-term basis. This makes them susceptible to bank runs and to shocks, whether due to tightened regulation or to economic shocks, such as weakening balance sheets or changes in asset prices. This susceptibility can make the curtailment or expansion of credit – including working capital and trade financing – more volatile, with effects on the real sector.

- Financial markets function in a decentralized manner: that is, with many participants. This can lead to excessive price volatility and the propagation of shocks, rather than their mitigation. Much of the (relative) movements in asset prices are not easily explained, even in mature markets. Thus expectations about well-developed financial system reducing financial and economic volatility must of necessity remain modest. While there is some scope in adopting measures to counter the sources of procyclicality and financial vulnerability, rectifying microeconomic distortions and creating a robust financial and regulatory system may be the only and first best solution.

- Risk sharing can also depend on the level of the country's overall institutional development and the role of government. Both can amount to distortions, aggravating the imperfect risk sharing already present because of the nature of financial intermediation.

  - Despite much liberalization, the role of government remains high in many financial sectors, with potential adverse consequences on risk. For example, state-owned banks are less likely to have the proper incentives to manage risk than privately owned banks. The state may continue to provide excessive deposit insurance, which blunts the incentives of banks to manage risk. Control of interest rates and credit allocation may persist, thwarting banks from considering (credit) risk and developing their own capacity to manage risks.

  - Poor macroeconomic fundamentals (such as unsustainable public debt dynamics, and inconsistencies between fiscal and exchange rate policy); poor and weakly enforced property rights; poor quality regulation and supervision; and other microeconomic distortions and weaknesses in the supporting infrastructure can impede the functioning of the financial sector. All this can further impede risk sharing and even lead to build up of risks in the financial and real sectors.

- Systemic crises generate additional links between the financial sector and the rest of the economy, with the possibility of further spillovers in terms of volatility. It is useful to distinguish between prefinancial crisis and postcrisis phases, with the latter subdivided into a stabilization phase and a financial restructuring phase.

  - Despite much progress, it remains difficult to predict financial crises – because of poor data, a limited number of crises, difficulties in choosing the appropriate analytical and empirical model, and varying behavior of market participants. Furthermore, the usefulness of Early Warning Systems based on statistical relationships observed in past crises may be limited in predicting future crises

if investors already use information to anticipate crises and/or modify their behavior in response to policy changes provoked by past crises.[17]
- When the financial crisis first unfolds, government will try restore confidence in the financial sector. In this containment phase, two policies are most important to limit fiscal costs and to allow for a speedy economic recovery: *not* to extend liquidity support to financial institutions; and *not* to extend government guarantees on those institutions' liabilities.
- In the restructuring phase after the crisis, especially in countries where institutions are weak, governments may need to use simple methods in dealing with weak banks and to restore confidence. This can help prevent higher fiscal cost, speed up the recovery, and avoid further risks. Governments should refrain from using forbearance: that is, waiving prudential regulations. Instead, governments should put in place the necessary institutional framework for the private sector to resolve the debt overhang.

APPENDIX A. PREDICTING FINANCIAL CRISES: THEORY AND EMPIRICAL RESULTS

There are two types of banking distress: individual bank distress and systemwide banking distress. The theory regarding causes of the first type of bank distress takes a more microview and has been extensively applied in the empirical models used mainly in developed countries to predict financial distress. This theory is relevant to review because individual banking distress can lead to systemic distress, depending upon various factors. Although the theory regarding the determinants of systemwide banking distress is somewhat similar to that regarding individual bank distress, there are some important differences and additions. A review of both types of situations follows.

Much of the literature on bank runs has modeled the phenomenon as an asymmetric information problem between depositors and banks. Some consider banking panics as random manifestations of mass hysteria or mob psychology, as discussed by Charles Kindleberger (1978). This "pure panic" or "sunspot" theory of a bank run is formalized in the 1983 study by Douglas Diamond and Philip Dybvig. They posit that the illiquidity of assets provides the rationale for a bank's vulnerability to runs. Multiple equilibria can exist where one of the equilibrium points is a bank run scenario arising from the panic of agents. They also show that a bank run can be self-fulfilling when depositors believe that other depositors are withdrawing their funds even without any initial deterioration of the bank's balance sheet.

The theory of banking system insolvency takes off from the theory of individual bank distress. Varadarajan Chari and Ravi Jagannathan (1988) provide an extension of the Diamond–Dybvig model to explain banking panics. They posit that banking panics result when uninformed depositors withdraw their own funds after misinterpreting liquidity withdrawal shocks as connoting pessimistic information about bank's assets. Charles Jacklin and Sudipto Bhattacharya (1988) further distinguish between pure panics and information-based bank runs by emphasizing the role of interim private information about bank loans and asset payoffs as the source of bank

---

[17] This is essentially the Lucas critique. See Lucas (1976).

runs. Both models can be interpreted to imply that a single banking run causes a system-wide banking crisis. Another version is that bank runs systematically relate to the occurrence of events that change the perception of depositors' risk, such as extreme seasonal fluctuations (Miron 1985), unexpected failure of a large (typically financial) corporation, and major cyclical downturns (Gorton 1988). Frederick Mishkin (1996) provides a broader framework on the role of asymmetric information in financial crises in developing countries.

Another propagation mechanism is contagion through interbank deposits. Spillovers of individual banking distress can affect the whole banking system through interbank lending. Factors like the size of the financial institution and the functioning of the interbank and other financial markets will determine the likelihood of contagion. In this respect, banks in emerging markets are more at risk. In term of theoretical models, Franklin Allen and Douglas Gale (2000b) show that, to protect themselves against liquidity preference shocks, banks hold interbank claims with each other, which are interregional in nature. However, this opens the possibility of a small liquidity preference shock in one bank or region to spread throughout the economy. Another propagation mechanism, suggested by Douglas Diamond and Raghurajan Rajan (2002), assumes that banks have a common pool of liquidity. Bank failures can cause aggregate liquidity shortages, which can lead to the failure of other banks, thus making a total meltdown possible, even without any informational or contractual links between banks.

The microfactors that can be important determinants for banking system distress refer to the quality of a country's whole institutional framework. Poor market discipline due to moral hazard or limited disclosure, a weak corporate governance framework, excessive deposit insurance, and poor supervision can determine the degree of information asymmetries, quality of bank management, and the buildup of vulnerabilities, which in turn can trigger banking system crises.

At the system-level, macroeconomic factors – such as shocks to interest rates, foreign exchange devaluations, commodity shocks, economic slowdowns, and capital outflows – can also be important determinants of crises. Banking crises can be triggered by sudden capital outflows (Calvo, Leiderman, and Reinhart 1994). Foreign currency exposures by banks and their subsequent issuance of foreign currency-denominated domestic loans can make banks vulnerable to external shocks (Chinn and Kletzer 2000). System-wide inherited problems can come into the open with or after financial liberalization. Finally, there are many cases when poor early intervention led a small degree of distress to become a major banking crisis. For example, ad hoc policy approaches can cause confusion among depositors, trigger further runs by depositors, and lead to a full-scale financial crisis. This has happened in Indonesia and Thailand in 1997, and in Argentina in 2001 when banks and nonbank financial institutions were closed without and adequate plan for the whole financial system. These causes have been reviewed by many papers, most notably World Bank (2001).

The Role of the Financial Sector in Triggering Crises

Financial crises can occur for many reasons. In terms of the role of the financial sector in triggering or propagating crises, one can distinguish macrobased aspects, channels, and dimensions, as well as microeconomic ones, although the distinction is somewhat arbitrary.

MACRODIMENSIONS. Several macrodimensions can be distinguished. First, the macroeconomic policy mix and management can lead to the buildup of financial and corporate sector vulnerabilities. These policies can include the monetary policy mix, exchange rates management, and fiscal management. There can be a relationship between the exchange rate management and maturity structure of the banking system, for example. Managed or pegged exchange rates have been argued to induce a greater share of short-term capital flows, as investors try to take advantage of the interest differential without taking too much risk.[18] This is the case especially for capital flows into the banking system, as was true of Korea, Thailand, and other East Asian countries, as well as Turkey, before their financial crises.

More generally, procyclical monetary and fiscal policy can exacerbate domestic credit cycles and induce greater variability in capital flows, thereby leading to greater vulnerabilities in the financial and corporate sectors and more ex post volatility. The buildup of financial vulnerabilities in East Asia in the 1990s was associated with reinforcing dynamics between capital flows, macropolicies, and weak financial and corporate sector institutions. In several East Asian countries, the 1990s were characterized by the adoption of a tight medium-term stance for fiscal policy. Although in surplus, short-run fiscal policy actually was not sufficiently contractionary – in view of the overheating – to result in a cyclically neutral position. Rather, in most East Asian countries it imparted a positive impulse, and as a result, added to the pressures on domestic interest rates and widened the differential between domestic and foreign rates. The macroeconomic policy responses to large capital inflows, the weaknesses in domestic financial intermediation, and poor corporate governance interacted with and exacerbated the risks associated with large inflows. Lack of due diligence by international investors facilitated the buildup of vulnerability in East Asian countries. Similar developments occurred in Turkey before its financial crisis.

These issues are analyzed in more detail elsewhere (see, for example, Alba and others 1999). The point here is not as much that the macroeconomic policy mix can affect the evolution (buildup) of vulnerabilities in the financial and corporate sectors – as that has been documented extensively – but rather that there can be feedbacks from these sectors to the macroeconomy policy mix. It is possible, for example, that an initial set of vulnerabilities in the financial sector induces policymakers to continue with a set of macroeconomic policies in order not to risk short-run instability. By pursuing such policies, however, they may be increasing the risk in the medium to longer term of a financial crisis. Arguably, for example, the existing vulnerabilities in the Thai financial sector, particularly the large foreign exchange exposures, led policymakers to continue with a closely managed exchange rate throughout 1996 and the first half of 1997. This only increased the vulnerabilities further, and required the central bank to support many financial institutions with large liquidity infusions. Similarly, in the case of Argentina, Mexico, Russia, and Turkey,

---

[18] As the risks of currency movements over the longer term is higher, creditors may not be willing to extend financing for longer maturity, as they realize that doing so may lead to adverse behavior and even more risk taking by the country.

large initial outstanding public debts – for some countries, mainly denominated in foreign exchange – and in some cases, weak financial sectors, made the governments pursue for a long time combinations of a pegged exchange rate regime and high domestic interest rates. These eventually collapsed and added to the severity of the overall financial crises.

At another macro level, one can search for the set of aggregate macrofinancial sector indicators that help predict financial crises. The role of financial sector conditions in causing or triggering crises has been studied empirically extensively, including in the twin crises literature. This has led to various types of econometric models aimed at predicting financial crises, so-called Early Warning Systems (EWS). The first empirical crisis paper using a probability model appeared in 1998. The authors, Aslï Demirgüç-Kunt and Enrica Detragiache (1998) identified a number of macro dimensions and anticipated future work on microissues such as regulation and deposit insurance. The typically "best" indicators found to predict systemic banking crises have been reviewed by Morris Goldstein, Graciela Kaminsky, and Carmen Reinhart (2000). Of the 15 monthly indicators they review, they find that six – an appreciation of the real exchange rate (relative to trend), a decline in equity prices, a rise in the money (M2) multiplier, a decline in real output, a fall in exports, and a rise in the real interest rate – have been good predictors of banking system crises. In terms of annual indicators, among eight indicators reviewed, two – a high ratio of short-term capital flows to GDP and a large current-account deficit relative to domestic investment – have been good predictors.

Generally, however, they note that the models still have a poor out-of-sample performance, in part due to poor timing, difficulties in dating of banking system crises, and limited availability of institutional variables. Besides these and many other macroeconomic indicators, some banking crisis EWS models have found a number of indicators specific to the financial sector to be useful in predicting financial crises. The ratio of foreign liabilities to foreign assets of the banking sector and a rise in the M2 multiplier have been found to be useful predictors of financial crises, especially currency crises (ADB 2002).

Yet the general success of using financial sector data to predict financial and banking crises has been limited. This is not surprising, as a high predictive power would be an indication of market inefficiency. After all, if predicting financial crisis were easy, much profit could be made from taking a short position in the local currency. But the limited success also reflects weaknesses of the data and distortions. Many of the traditional indicators of bank fragility relate to the CAMEL-framework (Capital, Asset, Management, Earnings, and Liquidity). Indicators related to a bank's CAMEL are then used to try to predict its financial distress. While these indicators, such as capital-to-assets ratios, net profits to income, operating costs to assets, and liquidity ratios, have had some success in developed countries, they are less useful in emerging markets. This includes market indicators (interest rate spreads, sovereign credit ratings) that do not rank high among a long list of early warning indicators of systemic banking crises (Goldstein, Kaminsky, and Reinhart 2000). The lack of success for emerging markets can in part be attributed to the poorer quality of accounting and financial data in many emerging markets, but also to issues such as large public safety nets for banking systems in emerging markets and international bailouts, which make markets signals less useful.

There have also been sets of so-called macroprudential indicators (MPI) and Financial Soundness Indicators (FSI) developed by the IMF, BIS, ECB, and others. These MPI and FSI are (rather long) list of indicators of the financial conditions and performance of financial sector, nonbank financial institutions, as well as real sector. Countries are encouraged to make these data available so investors and others can better evaluate risks. Some indicators are considered part of a core set. Others fall into an encouraged set, in part to differentiate the urgency for countries to compile these data. For emerging markets, the problems arise in the quality, timeliness, and periodicity of these data. Furthermore, while there may be empirical regularities between the data and in predicting financial crises, the analytical frameworks on how these factors relate to risks are not always clear. As a consequence, it is possible that the success of some of these variables in predicting financial crises reflects data sample selection. Even when the predictions are done out-of-sample, the "regularities" would have to be screened for data snooping: that is, the use of those data that provide the best fit. Another problem can be model back testing: that is, the tendency to update the use of explanatory data on the basis of the last financial crisis. Following the East Asian financial crisis, for example, real sector indicators have increasingly been used and found to be "effective" in predicting the crisis, even out-of-sample. Clearly, this success using real sector data is with the benefit of some hindsight and may not help predict the next financial crisis.

MICRODIMENSIONS. Much of the origin of financial exposures and their roles in triggering a financial crisis can be traced to preexisting, structural microweaknesses in the financial sector. These microdimensions relate not to the actual conditions of financial institutions, but rather to the framework under which financial institutions operate. Weaknesses include poor monitoring of the financial sector, a large degree of moral hazard from an overly wide government safety net, and poor corporate governance. As such, these conditions do not differ from the factors that determine the overall functioning of the financial sector. In terms of factors typically cited as affecting the risk of financial crises, a representative study is a survey of 29 cases by Gerard Caprio and Daniela Klingebiel (1997). Among microeconomic factors, poor supervision and regulation was mentioned 26 times, deficient bank management, 20 times; political interference, 11 times; connected lending, nine times; fraud, six times; legacies such as lending to state-owned enterprises, six times; a weak judiciary, twice; and the presence of bank runs, twice.

While this gives some indication of the factors deemed to have been important causes, many of them are not truly causal factors, but rather symptoms of a financial crisis. The literature on explaining systemic banking crises has, however, identified some microweaknesses that appear to have contributed especially to the risk of banking system crises and which are less subject to endogeneity issue. There is empirical work, for example, on the impact of excessive deposit insurance and certain deposit insurance design features on increasing the probability of a banking crisis (Demirgüç-Kunt and Detragiache 2003). Clearly, large implicit deposit insurance guarantees added to the occurrence of banking crises in East Asia and Turkey. As noted, weak creditor and shareholder rights and poor accounting data have also been identified as contributing to the risk of financial crises.

The structure of the banking system in combination with institutional factors can also affect the risk of a systemic banking crisis. Thorsten Beck, Aslï Demirgüç-Kunt, and Ross Levine (2003) study the impact of bank concentration, regulations, and national institutions on the likelihood of suffering a systemic banking crisis. Using data on 79 countries from 1980 to 1997, this study finds that crises are less likely in more concentrated banking systems; in countries with fewer regulatory restrictions on bank competition and activities; and in economies with better institutions: that is, institutions that encourage competition and support private property. (For a general review of the financial sector structure, competition policy and fragility, see Allen and Gale 2004.)

The quality of corporate governance can also affect firms' behavior in times of economic shocks and actually contribute to the occurrence of financial distress, with economywide impacts. It has been found that during the East Asian financial crisis, cumulative stock returns of firms in which managers have high levels of control rights, but have separated their control and cash flow ownership, are 10 to 20 percentage points lower than those of other firms (Lemmon and Lins 2003). This suggests that for these firms, inside owners took a higher share of firm cash flow during crisis periods, at the expenses of minority shareholder. As ownership structures are in part endogenous to the corporate governance framework, this shows that corporate governance can play an important role in determining individual firms' behavior, in particular the incentives of insiders to expropriate minority shareholders during times of distress. Todd Mitton (2002) examines the stock performance of listed companies from Indonesia, Korea, Malaysia, the Philippines, and Thailand during the East Asian financial crisis. He reports that performance is better in firms with higher accounting disclosure quality (proxied by the use of Big Six auditors) and higher outside ownership concentration, even when correcting for self-selection: that is, that firms with better fundamentals would be more willing to disclose information and would be more likely to attract outside shareholders.

This firm-level evidence is consistent with the view that corporate governance helps explain country performance during a financial crisis. Related is work that shows that hedging by firms in countries with weak corporate governance frameworks is less common (Lel 2003) and to the extent it happens, that it adds very little value (Allayannis, Lel, and Miller, 2003). The latter evidence suggests that in these environments, hedging is not necessarily for the benefit of outsiders, but more for insiders. There is also evidence that stock returns in emerging markets tend to be more positively skewed than in developed countries (Bae, Lim, and Wei 2003). This can be attributed to managers having more discretion in emerging markets over the disclosure of bad information, which imparts a positive skewness to stock returns, or that firms in these markets share risks through internal markets.

Data problems can make predicting financial distress more difficult not only at the country level but also at the individual financial institutions level. One recent study that analyzed banking problems in Mexico (1993–94), Venezuela (1993–94), Colombia (1991–98), and Thailand, Korea, and Malaysia (each in 1996–97) reported that traditional indicators of bank fragility, such as capital-to-assets ratios, net profits to income, operating costs to assets, and liquidity ratios, did a relatively poor job of picking out subsequent problem banks (Rojas-Suarez 2001). Since these traditional CAMEL-type ratios have some success in developed countries, the lack of success relates in part to the poor quality of accounting and financial data in many emerging markets. But more likely, the micro weaknesses that on one hand help predict systemic banking crisis in emerging economies, can actually make it more difficult to anticipate problems and failures at individual banks using traditional CAMEL-type indicators. With an extensive safety net, one may expect actual financial information not to be as useful for predicting distress for two reasons. The financial institution will tend to "cheat" on the information disclosed, so as to maintain its access to the safety net. Ultimately, the risks of the financial institutions matter less than the willingness and ability of the fiscal authority to provide the safety net. Intervention in banks in weak environments that experience financial distress is less likely to be transparent, at least one study has found (Bongini, Claessens, and Ferri 2001). Without a large safety net, other, more market-oriented data may be more useful than CAMEL-indicators to predict financial distress.

Studies on predicting the distress of individual banks in environments where the official safety net has been limited and when investors face a real prospect of losses, such as some countries in Latin America, suggest that bank deposit volumes and interest rates on bank deposits can provide useful information on banks' creditworthiness and on the ex post incidence of bank failures (Calomiris and Powell 2000; Peria and Schmukler 1999; Rojas-Suarez 2001). While these indicators work in some economies, they do not provide good signals when these same conditions are not fulfilled: that is, when safety nets are extensive. With an extensive safety net, a crisis may eventually occur – because at some point the fiscal costs become too high – but this can be preceded by a prolonged period where CAMEL indicators signal risks, but no crisis occurs.

Still, predicting financial distress is difficult; often even basic data are not available. Furthermore, for a given country, many of the micro weaknesses are highly correlated. A low level of judicial efficiency, poor equity and creditor rights, and weak accounting standards, among other factors, are commonly found together in many developing countries. As such, it is difficult to pinpoint the precise mechanisms through which risks in the financial sector are being built up. The recent financial crises in East Asia and elsewhere have yielded some specific lessons on how risks might be mitigated (for a recent review, see IMF 2003). Notably, in the early phases of financial liberalization, quantity-based constraints can be important, such as limits on portfolio composition (in real estate), limits of mismatches (in foreign exchange or maturity), and speed bumps (limits on the pace of credit growth). (See Appendix B on specific mechanisms to reduce volatility in foreign exchange and securities markets.)

APPENDIX B. POSSIBLE STRATEGIES TO REDUCE CURRENCY VOLATILITY AND TURMOIL

Even in well-developed market economies with robust financial markets, currency movements can be large and can exceed what would be suggested by relative fundamentals. In developing countries, currency swings can be even larger, given that their economies are more vulnerable to shocks, markets are thinner, and information asymmetries are greater. These large currency swings can be of policy concern when there are substantial risks of a downward spiral, with consequent social costs.

A number of medium-term actions can be used to reduce vulnerability, combined with short-term actions to curb foreign speculators. The efficacy and efficiency of these actions are the subject of some controversy, however, and these actions may not be appropriate for a specific country as either short-term or long-term solutions.

Actions to Reduce Medium-Term Vulnerability[19]

1. *Measures to regulate foreign exchange exposures of financial institutions.* All countries have prudential guidelines on financial institutions, which are often quite extensive. These include limits on the net open positions financial institutions can take in the foreign currency market. Sometimes, further precautionary measures can be useful to reduce vulnerabilities. For example, financial institutions can be required to hold more liquid foreign exchange assets relative to total foreign exchange liabilities than they are required to hold on domestic currency liabilities. Not only will this reduce indirect foreign exchange exposure, but it will also provide banks with a source of liquidity, which is less likely to dry up during period of stress in the domestic financial markets. Financial institutions can also be encouraged to ascertain that their borrowers have the capacity to repay foreign exchange loans or otherwise put in place a hedge.

2. *Measures to regulate other exposures of financial institutions.* Lending to real estate, for consumer finance, and for stock market-related transactions can be large in some countries and be sources of (perceived) vulnerability. Some measures to reduce real estate exposures and price increases can be put in place (such as a cap on the share of bank portfolios to real estate of say 20 percent, higher property taxes, and other limitation for purchases of houses). One other way to curb credit growth without adverse effects on the existing portfolio of banks is to set higher reserve requirements for incremental lending. Countries may wish to consider further limiting the growth in property exposures through more stringent maximum loan-to-value ratios, lower maximum individual loan sizes, prohibitions against certain forms of real estate lending, and imposing minimum requirements for the share of equity finance for developers. Some of these limits will already be in place, but several could be strengthened in the face of increased vulnerabilities, both in terms of the relative levels of the limits and in the degree of disclosure, and importantly in the implementation and monitoring of rules. In terms of securities markets, margin-lending, lending against stock and other tradable assets, consumer lending, and connected lending are other areas where lending limits, valuation rules (such as the frequency of marked-to-market of investments), and disclosure requirements could be tightened. These measures can be phased in by making them effective only for new lending. Over time, they can cover all outstanding loans.

3. *Measures to curtail excessive borrowing by corporations.* Corporate exposures to foreign exchange–denominated instruments will often rise (other than for direct trade financing) as part of an increase in financial vulnerabilities, especially through the issue of debt securities. Improvements in standards for the quality and disclosure of information will help domestic and foreign investors

[19] This section is based on Alba and others (1998).

make better risk assessment and lending decisions in the medium term. Better corporate governance more generally will help improve resource allocation, reduce risks, and thus limit vulnerabilities. One additional measure that could be considered involves reducing the tax-deductibility of offshore borrowings. This will raise the costs of funding offshore, and thus limit the amount of funds raised offshore. If desirable, this limited tax-deductibility can be further differentiated according to the type of offshore funding (such as short-term borrowing) and sector. In addition, minimum or maximum criteria can be suggested for the terms of offshore loans and securities.

4. *Broader measures to curb capital inflows.* In some cases, vulnerability can arise from the form in which capital has been and is being intermediated. Some countries such as Chile and Colombia have used broad-based measures to curb large capital inflows, with some effect on the composition of inflows. There may be a case for restrictions of foreign investment in money market instruments or flows to the banking system. However, a broad-based measure to restrict capital inflows could adversely affect foreign investment and have negative consequences for confidence more generally. Capital inflows in the form of foreign direct investment may also be less risky and not need to be restricted. Governments can explore the extent to which tax policy can be used to discourage specific forms of borrowing.

5. *Circuit breakers for equity markets.* Some countries have used a variety of "circuit-breaker" mechanisms that impose temporary trading restrictions, including the orderly shut down of markets, when there are large and rapid price declines. These mechanisms refer to restrictions for the market as a whole, and are over and above trading halts and other mechanisms that may be imposed on an individual stock when there is a large order imbalance for that stock.[20] These circuit-breaker mechanisms are designed to deal with the chaotic conditions of an extreme market correction, but not to negate a fundamental price adjustment. It is also important to note that it is difficult to open markets once they are closed. Such mechanisms may still be important at some times in bolstering confidence in markets.

6. *Circuit breakers in currency markets.* Circuit breakers are another option that has been suggested to reduce volatility in currency markets. In the Philippines, for example, the Bankers' Association introduced a band of 1.5 percent in 1997. Trading was suspended for a maximum of one hour when this band was reached. The band triggered frequent market closures, however, suggesting that it was too narrow. It was subsequently abandoned. There are additional complications when using trading restrictions in foreign exchange markets. First, the market for foreign exchange is more diffuse than that for equities, with substantial trading

---

[20] Two of the most common circuit-breaker mechanisms are price limits and trading halts. Price limits refer to a suspension of trading in stock index futures below a particular price. Trading halts involve a temporary stop to trading in all markets, including cash, stock index futures, and options. Typically, in industrial countries the time out imposed by circuit breakers is usually quite short, lasting from five minutes to one hour. Finally, stock markets have imposed some additional procedures to address potential problems with program trading (i.e., trading according to preset rules that may accentuate price changes) during sharp market swings (such as the October 1987 stock market crash in the United States).

taking place over the counter and in offshore markets. In these circumstances, circuit breaker mechanisms are likely to be ineffective. Second, restrictions would need to be set up and coordinated across both cash and futures markets. Still, there can be some value at times from guidance.

Specific Actions to Curb Speculative Activity

Arbitrage between domestic and foreign lending/credit markets is an essential ingredient for a well-functioning forward market. However, there may be a case to regulate certain types of speculative activity or to consider exceptional measures during periods of extreme pressure.

1. *Restricting access to credit.* Speculators can speculate against the local currency only if they have access to domestic credit. There are two ways to reduce access to such credit, especially during periods of speculative attack. First is to restrict access to domestic credit by nonresidents, on the assumption that the largest players who are taking a speculative position in the market are nonresidents. Any large-scale speculation by nonresidents therefore implies that the lending restrictions on financial institutions are not effective. If this is the case, the authorities need to improve the monitoring of lending to nonresidents and the capacity to investigate violations of such rules by financial institutions. The second is to reduce access to credit more generally for taking short forward positions on a temporary basis during a period of intense currency pressures. The efficacy of such a step, however, remains questionable, as the loopholes available to domestic players are more numerous and imposition of such a curb may be damaging to the development of forward markets.

2. *Improved information on foreign exchange markets.* With a limit or prohibition on the ability of nonresidents to access credit, a potential source of pressure on the exchange rate would be removed. To make this limit effective, however, authorities may need to improve their monitoring of individual transactions. This could involve a need to formalize the authorization of institutions involved in foreign exchange trading. In addition, authorities could require transactions above a certain amount to be reported and the source/beneficiary be identified to the authorities. The marginal cost of such disclosure would be smaller for exporters than for speculators, which is desirable. In cases of concern, authorities would need to have the ability to follow up on individual transactions to identify the ultimate source. The authorities would have to carefully consider the transaction costs of these measures for market players. Trading could move (further) offshore, with attendant loss of regulatory coverage and the possibility of dual exchange rates, with associated distortions.

APPENDIX C. TOOLKITS: MODELS TO MEASURE DEGREE OF RISK IN BANKS AND BANKING SYSTEMS

There are many approaches to measuring risk in banking systems, as developed in the Financial Sector Assessment Program (FSAP), in the financial stability assessments

Table C-1. *Inputs for a basic stress test*

Short-term risk factors	Balance sheet item affected	
Exchange rate shocks	FX-denominated loans both directly by currency and indirectly by changed loan-loss experience	Other FX-denominated (net) (affected mainly by translation)
Property shocks	Loans to real estate (net worth of borrowers affected)	Other loans secured on estate (value of collateral)
General shocks	Loan (net worth of borrowers affected)	Marketable (market values affected)
Problematic accounting	Government-related (unrecognized collection due to political influence)	Other (evergreening; over-collateral valuation)

done by many central banks, and by private sector participants.[21] First consider a basic approach for a stress test (as documented by Honohan 1999). Such models analyze the effects of exchange- and interest-rate changes and macroeconomic shocks (such as economic slowdown), given the maturity and currency composition of financial institutions' liabilities and given asset compositions (such as share of loans to the real sector). The model then applies a concept now commonly used in commercial banks to assess risks, the Value at Risk (VaR) approach, to the balance sheets, to see which shocks may significantly reduce or even wipe out the capital. By including all or at least most large banks, the model can try to cover the risk to the whole banking sector. By making assumptions as to what capital shortfall is the responsibility of the government, the model can also be used to assess the probability and the extent of fiscal contingencies arising from the banking sector due to changes in the macroenvironment.

Basic Stress Model

Using accounting data on the size and composition of the balance sheet of the banks, the model simulates a number of short-term risk factors that can adversely affect bank balance sheets. These risk factors are then used to estimate the risk of a capital shortfall. The approach is as follows (see Table C-1). First, the model specifies and quantifies possible economic shocks, such as changes in the exchange rate, changes in property market values, terms of trade, or a general economic downturn (Column 1). Using information from banks' balance sheets, it classifies various balance sheet items according to whether and to what extent they would be adversely affected by these economic shocks (Columns 2 and 3). The model then applies a multiplier to each group of balance sheet items based on the size of the assumed shock to the affected balance sheet category. Then the capital positions in the various banks are estimated after the effects of each shock and the systemwide capital deficiency are calculated.

---

[21] For another review of how risks can accumulate and be measured, see Draghi, Giavazzi, and Merton (2003).

The latter deficiency can be assumed to be met fully or partly by the government. The same exercise is repeated under different sizes of shocks: for example, different changes in the exchange rate, with probabilities assigned to each discrete macroshock. A matrix can be constructed for a given macro shock, indicating the potential size of the losses. For example, in a hypothetical country, the potential fiscal liabilities could amount to US$6.9 billion if the exchange rate depreciation is greater than 40 percent and loan losses are greater than 50 percent. As Patrick Honohan notes, with a 100 percent assumption by the government of the capital loss, the model assumes that banks will be made whole by the fiscal authority. The methodology thus also provides an estimate of maximum fiscal liability, although it would allow for loss absorption by other claimants.

Mario Blejer and Liliana Schumacher (2002) similarly employ a value-at-risk approach to appraising central bank solvency. They examine the factors possibly affecting solvency from traditional central bank operations and off-balance sheet positions, including foreign exchange and financial sector guarantees. While a central bank cannot commercially fail, it may behave equivalently if it has to forsake a commitment to an announced nominal regime (such as an exchange rate or inflation target) because its solvency has been threatened. If the probability of a central bank abandoning its commitments is linked to its vulnerability to solvency losses, measures such as VaR could be used as forward-looking indicators of credibility crises. This model might help in identifying the risk of a financial crisis.

Other Models and Their Assumptions

The same underlying fundamental structure is also used in more recent stress tests for banks. The newer models are more detailed, however, and many decision are to be made. The models can best be seen as a decision tree (for an overview of stress tests, see Blaschke and others 2001, upon which this section draws). Choices have to be made on the toolkit and methodology and the types of risks to be covered: *only market risk* (such as interest and exchange rates, and asset prices), *credit risks* (nonperforming loans), or *operational risks* (fraud, lack of internal controls). Then one can decide the type of data to be used. For commercial bank loans, typically only accounting data can be used. For securities markets claims held by banks, such as bonds or equities, market prices can be used. In term of risk-estimation techniques, several types of approaches are possible. One is a simple sensitivity test, where a single factor is perturbed. Another way is to look at possible scenarios using multiple factors, thus taking into account the correlation among the risks. This would also provide the whole distribution of outcomes. Another approach is to look only at so-called extreme value or maximum loss situations.

The same framework can be applied to shocks. The stress test can apply shocks to one individual (market) variable at a time, or more variables can be shocked at one time. Volatility can be assumed to be constant or to vary over time and circumstances. Similarly, the degree of correlation can be adjusted. An important example is whether interest and exchange rate shocks are positively or negatively correlated. While in normal times the correlation may be negative, it could become positive in a crisis period.

Finally, the way in which the analysis is done can vary. Scenarios can be constructed by drawing from historical distributions, performing hypothetical scenarios, or by doing Monte Carlo simulations. A number of decisions must be made. What type of assets classes should be shocked: only core assets, such as loans for commercial banks, or all assets, including the trading portfolios? The size of shocks and time horizon must be chosen: will the analysis cover risks in the next month, next year, or next five years? The model then needs to aggregate the results across financial products. Should repricing/mark-to-market be adopted for balance sheet calculations and capital shortfall? What are the risk-management techniques that are being considered: for example, can the bank hedge currency and interest risks fully or only in a limited way? And what are the benchmark comparisons to be used: for example, is the capital adequacy guideline to be used the international norm or a domestic norm? Thus many decisions greatly influence the outcomes and validity of the scenarios.

Other Approaches

Other approaches to measuring risks in the banking sector include the gross assets-at-risk approach used by the rating agency Standard and Poors (S&P 1999). As the label "gross banking assets-at-risk" suggests, the S&P approach tries to estimate the gross exposure of the economy to banking system distress. As such, it is close to a VaR-approach.

This is more of a cross-country approach to measuring risks. S&P estimates the gross banking assets-at-risk from a major economic downturn. The framework relies on a quality rating of countries, based on perceived vulnerability to asset quality pressure during a recession. The rating is subjective and provided by S&P staff, which also conducts ratings of countries. The model then applies a factor – between zero and one, depending on the rating – to the total assets of the financial system. The figure obtained through this exercise is called the "gross banking assets-at-risk" from a major economic downturn. The risk of a downturn occurring in the forecast horizon is then assessed in a separate exercise.

Finally, there are models that rely more on market-based prices. One is an implicit deposit insurance approach, using stock prices (Laeven 2000). The market value of the implicit government guarantee is calculated using financial institutions' specific stock price behavior and balance sheet information. This information is then used to estimate to what degree the government subsidizes the bank through deposit insurance, either implicit or explicit. This provides a measure of the degree of risk taking and can be applied to a whole banking system.

CROSS-COUNTRY–BASED APPROACHES. There are a number of studies using large samples of countries that try to document the relationships between institutional features and risks and fragility. Asli Demirgüç-Kunt, Thorsten Beck, and Ross Levine (2003), for example, study the impact of bank concentration, regulations, and national institutions on the likelihood of suffering a systemic banking crisis using data on 79 countries over the period 1980–97. The study finds that crises are less likely: in more concentrated banking systems; in countries with fewer regulatory restrictions on bank competition and activities; and in economies with better institutions, that is, those that encourage competition and support private property rights. Other institutional-based studies for large samples of countries include the 2003 work by James Barth, Gerard Caprio, and Ross Levine. They find that greater regulatory restrictions on the activities of commercial banks lead to a higher probability of crisis. They do a number of robustness tests and document that weaker systems do not use restrictions to compensate for risks, but instead to support political constituencies. They find that restricting bank activities is negatively associated with bank development, performance, and access to financing because restrictions are not designed so much to limit the risks of a financial crisis or enhance access, but to support political constituencies. The analysis comes with some caveats. Importantly, the analysis suggests that a contestable system – that is, proper entry and exit – is required, with the possibly of some tradeoffs between financial stability/access/concentration and growth/efficiency.

APPENDIX D. THE LINKS BETWEEN THE FINANCIAL SECTOR AND CORPORATE RESTRUCTURING

To illustrate the links between financial sector and real restructuring, one can do a simulation of future real financial positions, trace through the implications of firms' financial positions on the banking sector, and from this, estimate the fiscal outlays that would be necessary to raise banks' capital adequacy to the required ratios. This was applied to the case of Korea (this is from the 1999 Korea Country Economic Memorandum (CEM), see World Bank 1999).

The exercise used the first-half 1998 income, balance sheet, and cash flow statements of over 1,000 listed and registered Korean manufacturing companies, which represented about half the total real sector assets, and all the largest firms.[22] Feeding in the projected macroeconomic outlook over 1999–2003,[23] it simulated corporations' future cash flows. At the end of each year, corporations were categorized into seven categories (Table D-1).

Under the first scenario – designed to illustrate the potential costs of limited restructuring – only firms in categories 1–2 (those with less than 50 percent interest coverage) were assumed to go through a onetime restructuring at the beginning of 1999. The restructuring pattern was also assumed to be limited to interest exemptions and interest reductions, with very little (less than 10 percent of the restructured amounts) consisting of debt equity swaps or convertible bonds.

Corporations with less than 50 percent interest coverage were also assumed to have no further access to external financing, forcing them to reduce their investment, and resulting in a reduction in subsequent growth. Corporations with coverage between 50 percent and 100 percent, however, were assumed to continue to have access to outside financing, such that they could invest sufficiently to maintain their sales growth at the overall economywide projected growth rate.

---

[22] Financial firms were excluded, as were all firms that had been declared in default or that had negative equity before end-1998. Data used are nonconsolidated data and include state-owned enterprises. Data exclude the second half of 1998 to reduce the impact of already ongoing financial restructurings on firms' financial statements.

[23] The macroeconomic outlook involves simplified assumptions for sales growth, operating expense growth, and interest rates.

Table D-1. *Classification of corporations for scenarios*

Category	Definition	Bank classification[a]	Required provisions[b]
Default	Companies with negative equity	Loss	100%
0	Companies with negative coverage of interest expense	Loss	100%
1	Companies with interest coverage of 0–25%	Loss	100%
2	Companies with interest coverage of 25–50%	Doubtful	75%
3	Companies with interest coverage of 50–75%	Substandard	20%
4	Companies with interest coverage of 75–100%	Precautionary	2%
5	Companies with interest coverage of 100% or more	Normal	0.5%

Note: [a] Classification assumed to be applied by banks. The classification differs from that in place at the time, as the criteria used here consider the level of a corporation's ability to meet interest payments from current operating cash flow during the calendar year, while Korean regulations at the time classify corporations according to their payment record. Forward-looking classification requirements, which would among others consider these ratios, were expected to be in place by end-1999, although resulting provisioning requirements would be phased in.
[b] Required provisions indicate the percentage of provisioning under regulations at the time.
Source: World Bank 1999.

As in the case of the corporate sector block, banks' balance sheet and profit and loss statements were simulated over 1999–2004, based on end-1998 financial positions of banks and feeding in the projected macroeconomic outlook. At the end of each year, the implications of corporations' financial positions on banks' financial positions were traced. In particular, it was assumed that corporations with interest coverage of 100 percent or more would be classified as performing loans. At the other end of the scale, corporations with interest coverage ratios of negative to 25 percent were classified as "loss" (as shown in Table D-1), and banks' balance sheets and profit and loss statements were adjusted accordingly. The simulation also included the effects of the (onetime) corporate workouts on banks' profit and loss statements – through changes in provisioning and changes in their equity positions (for firms in categories with less than 25 percent coverage). Finally, the actual and planned purchases of nonperforming loans (NPLs) by the Korea Asset Management Company (KAMCO) in 1999 were also taken into account. (They were subtracted from the overall commercial banks' NPLs figures.)

The results from this analysis suggest that limited restructuring would lower the share of corporations in the group with less than 50 percent coverage (loss or doubtful loan category) only temporarily. The share of such corporations would rise again in the year 2000.[24] This is because many financially weak corporations would essentially have to continue to borrow from commercial banks and nonbank financial institutions to fill their operational financing needs. As a result, a large segment of firms (amounting to accounting for between 15 percent and 30 percent of all firm liabilities) would continue to be vulnerable, with rising, rather than declining,

[24] Nonperforming loans rise because the (limited) interest reductions and forgiveness only temporarily lowers the interest–coverage ratio.

Table D-2. *Nonperforming loans and fiscal outlays under different scenarios*
(percentage of 1997 GDP, unless noted otherwise)

	Already recognized	Future NPLs and additional costs	
		Scenario 1: Limited restructuring	Scenario 2: Deeper restructuring
Peak NPLs (as a percentage of bank loans) and year of peak	7.4 (in 1998)[a]	22.1 (in 2000)	21.0 (in 1998)
Past KAMCO & KDIC outlays	15.3	15.3	15.3
Committed future outlays	2.4	2.4	2.4
Additional expenditures needed to bring banks' CAR up to 8 percent	0	19.3	11.3
Total fiscal outlays for bank restructuring	17.7	37	29

[a] Based on backward looking criteria. This number does not include 44 trillion won (or 14.7 percent of financial system loans) already acquired by KAMCO.
Source: World Bank 1999.

debt-equity ratios. Only those firms that were able to fully cover interest payments from operating cash flow would be able to reduce their debt-to-equity ratio, although even their ratios would still not be below 200 percent. Figure D-1 shows the simulated leverage ratios of firms (by the classes of financial solvency) under this scenario of limited firm restructuring.

Continued fragility of firms would have adverse repercussions for the financial sector (Table D-2). NPLs would peak at about 22 percent of total loans, with corresponding implications for banks' capital adequacy ratios. Capital adequacy ratio would be a negative 10 percent or less. While the purchases of NPLs by KAMCO in 1999 and the temporary debt service relief for some corporations would lead to a modest reduction in NPLs in 1999, these effects would be short-lived. NPLs would

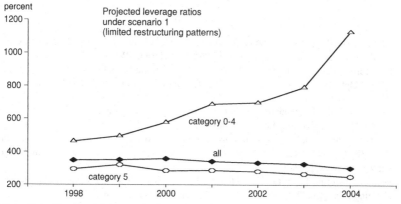

Figure D-1. Simulated Leverage Ratios under a Scenario of Limited Corporate Restructuring.
Source: World Bank 1999.

rise again significantly thereafter, reflecting the rising debt burdens and deteriorating situation of those corporations that need to continue to borrow to cover their interest expenses.

In turn, the resources needed to fully restore capital adequacy of commercial banks over the whole simulation period would amount to about 19 percent of 1997 GDP. This would be in addition to 17.7 percent of GDP[25] that the Government had already committed at that time to spending, even after taking into account already planned purchases of nonperforming loans by KAMCO. Experience suggested that the required recapitalization amounts would be difficult to raise from private sources, meaning that further fiscal outlays would arise.

Sensitivity analyses suggested that the corporate and banking sector would not grow out of their problems even if economic fundamentals were better than projected under the base case (which already assumed growth rates between 5.5 percent and 6.5 percent over the projection period). A 1 percentage-point gain in the economic growth rate over the whole period, for example, would lead to an average reduction in nonperforming loans in 2002 of only 0.7 percentage points. The effect of lower interest rates would also not be that significant. A two percentage point drop in interest rates (over the whole period) would lower nonperforming loans in 2001 by 1.0 percentage points, but the share of corporations with low interest coverage would still be more than 25 percent until the year 2002. Thus the scenario highlighted the need to ensure adequate restructuring. Relying on a strategy of "growing out" of corporate distress would be unlikely to be successful. Moreover, it would be fraught with risks that the favorable macroeconomic outlook itself would be jeopardized as corporations and the financial sector run into difficulties.

With the benefits of hindsight, it is evident that some of these scenarios materialized. The government was forced to allocate more public money to the recapitalization of banks, as the initial amounts were insufficient to restore their capital adequacy. Concerns about the fragility of the financial and corporate sectors persist, even today. At the same time, the economy performed better than expected for most of the period, due to a boom in consumer spending and generally favorable external conditions. This alleviated some of the impact of the still weak banking system.

REFERENCES

Agenor, Pierre-Richard, and Joshua Aizenman. 2002. "Financial Sector Inefficiencies and the Debt Laffer Curve." Working Paper 2842. World Bank, Washington, DC.

Alba, Pedro, Amar Bhattacharya, Stijn Claessens, Swati Ghosh, and Leonardo Hernandez. 1998. "Options to Respond to Currency Turbulence in Southeast Asia." World Bank, Washington, DC.

Alba, Pedro, Amar Bhattacharya, Stijn Claessens, Swati Ghosh, and Leonardo Hernandez. 1999. "The Role of Macro-Economic and Financial Sector Linkages in East Asia's Financial Crisis." In Pierre Richard Agenor, Marcus Miller, David Vines, and Axel Weber, eds., *The Asian Financial Crisis: Cause, Contagion, and Consequences*. Cambridge, UK: Cambridge University Press, pp. 9–64.

Allayannis, George, Ugur Lel, and Darius Miller. 2003. "Corporate Governance and the Hedging Premium." University of Virginia, Darden Business School.

---

[25] This figure includes KAMCO and KDIC outlays.

Allen, Franklin, and Douglas Gale. 2000a. *Comparing Financial Systems.* Cambridge and London: MIT Press.

———. 2000b. "Financial Contagion." *Journal of Political Economy* 108(1):1–33.

———. 2004. "Competition and Financial Stability." *Journal of Money, Credit and Banking,* 36(3) Pt. 2, 453–80.

Asian Development Bank (ADB). 1998. "Managing Global Integration in Asia: Emerging Lessons and Prospective Challenges." Manila. Processed.

———. 2005. *Early Warning System of Financial Crises: Applications to East Asia.* Palgrave MacMillan, Houndsmill, Basnigstoke and New York.

Bae, K. H., Chanwoo Lim, and K. C. John Wei. 2003. "Corporate Governance and Conditional Skewness in World's Stock Markets." Hong Kong University of Science and Technology.

Baer, Herbert, and Daniela Klingebiel. 1995. "Systemic Risk when Depositors Bear Losses: Five Case Studies." *Research in Financial Services Private and Public Policy* 7:195–302.

Barth, James R., Gerard Caprio Jr., and Ross Levine. 2001. "The Regulation and Supervision of Banks around the World: A New Database." In Robert E. Litan and Richard Herring, eds., *Integrating Emerging Market Countries into the Global Financial System.* Brookings–Wharton Papers on Financial Services. Washington, DC: Brookings Institution Press.

Barth, J. R., Gerard Caprio Jr., and Ross Levine. 2004. "Bank Supervision and Regulation: What Works Best?" *Journal of Financial Intermediation* 13(2):205–48.

Beck, Thorsten, Asli Demirgüç-Kunt, and Ross Levine. 2000. "A New Database on the Structure and Development of the Financial Sector." *World Bank Economic Review* 14:597–605.

———. 2003. "Bank Concentration and Crises." World Bank and University of Minnesota.

Beck, Thorsten, Asli Demirgüç-Kunt, and Vojislav Maksimovic. 2004. "Bank Competition, Financing Constraints and Access to Credit." *Journal of Money Credit and Banking* 36(3) Pt. 2, 627–48.

Beck, Thorsten, Mattias Lundberg, and Giovanni Majnoni. 2001. "Financial Development and Economic Volatility: Does Finance Dampen or Magnify Shocks?" Policy Research Working Paper 2707. World Bank, Washington, DC.

Bekaert, G., and C. R. Harvey. 2003. "Emerging Markets Finance." *Journal of Empirical Finance* 10(1–2):3–6.

Bekaert, G., C. Harvey, and Christian Lundblad. Forthcoming. "Does Financial Liberalization Spur Growth? *Journal of Financial Economics.*

Bekaert, G., C. Harvey, and C. Lundblad. 2004. "Growth Volatility and Equity Market Liberalization," NBER Working Paper 10560, Cambridge, MA.

Berg, Andrew, and Catherine Pattillo. 1999. "Are Currency Crises Predictable: A Test." *IMF Staff Papers* 46(2):107–38.

Bernanke, B., and C. Lown. 1991. "The Credit Crunch." *Brooking's Papers on Economic Activity,* 2:205–47.

Bernanke, Ben, and Mark Gertler. 1987. "Banking and Macroeconomic Equilibrium." In William Barnett and Ken Singleton, eds., *New Approaches to Monetary Economics.* Cambridge, UK: Cambridge University Press.

———. 1995. "Inside the Black Box: The Credit Channel of Monetary Policy Transmission." *Journal of Economic Perspectives* 9(4):27–28.

BIS (Bank for International Settlements). 1999. "Capital Requirement and Bank Behavior: The Impact of the Basel Accord." Basel Committee on Banking Supervision Working Papers, Basel, Switzerland.

Blaschke, Winfrid, Matthew T. Jones, Giovanni Majnoni, and Soledad Martinez Peria. 2001. "Stress Testing of Financial Systems: An Overview of Issues, Methodologies, and FSAP Experiences." IMF Working Paper 01/88. International Monetary Fund, Washington DC.

Bleijer, Mario, and Liliana Schumacher. 2002. "VAR for Central Banks' Risk." Volume 11. In Hana Polackova Brixi and Allen Schick, eds., *Government at Risk. Contingent Liabilities and Fiscal Risk.* New York: Oxford University Press for the World Bank.

Bongini, Poala, Stijn Claessens, and Giovanni Ferri. 2001. "The Political Economy of Bank Distress: Evidence from East Asia." *Journal of Financial Services Research* 19(1):5–25.

Bordo, Michael, Barry Eichengreen, Daniela Klingebiel, and Maria Soledad Martinez-Peria. 2001. "Is the Crisis Problem Growing More Severe?" *Economic Policy* 16(32):51–82.

Borio, Claudio, and Philip Lowe. 2002. "Asset Prices, Financial and Monetary Stability: Exploring the Nexus. BIS Working Paper 114 (July): 1–35. Bank for International Settlements.

Brock, Philip L., and Liliana Rojas Suárez. 2000. "Understanding the Behavior of Bank Spreads in Latin America." *Journal of Development Economics* (Netherlands) 63(1): 113–34.

Caballero, R. 2000. "Structural Volatility in Modern Latin America," mimeo, MIT, Cambridge, MA.

Caballero, R., and A. Krishnamurty. 2001. "International and Domestic Collateral Constraints in a Model of Emerging Market Crises." *Journal of Monetary Economics* 48(3):513–48.

Calomiris, Charles W., and Andrew Powell. 2000. "Can Emerging Market Bank Regulators Establish Credible Discipline? The Case of Argentina, 1992–1999." NBER Working Paper 7715: 1–45. National Bureau of Economic Research, Cambridge, MA.

Calvo, G., L. Leiderman, and C. Reinhart. 1994. "Capital Flows and Macroeconomic Management: Tequila Lessons." *International Journal of Finance and Economics* 1(3):207–24.

Caprio, Gerard, and Stijn Claessens. 1997. "Importance of the Financial System for Development." Background paper for World Bank Board Seminar on Financial Sector, April 1997. World Bank, Washington, DC.

Caprio, Gerard, and Patrick Honohan. 2002. *Banking Policy and Macroeconomic Stability: An Exploration.* Working Paper 2856. World Bank, Washington, DC.

Caprio, Gerard, Jr., and Daniela Klingebiel. 1997. "Bank Insolvency: Bad Luck, Bad Policy, or Bad Banking?" In Michael Bruno and Boris Pleskovic, eds., *Annual World Bank Conference on Development Economics.* Washington, DC: World Bank.

———. 2002. "Episodes of Systemic and Borderline Financial Crises." In Daniela Klingebiel and Luc Laeven, eds., *Managing the Real and Fiscal Effects of Banking Crises.* World Bank Discussion Paper 428. Washington, DC.

Cetorelli, N. 2001. "Does Bank Concentration Lead to Concentration in Industrial Sectors?" FRB Chicago WP 2001-01.

Cetorelli, N. and P. Strahan. 2004. "Finance as a Barrier to Entry. Bank Competition and Industry Structure in Local U.S. Markets." Federal Reserve Bank of Chicago WP 2004-04.

Chang, Roberto, and Andres Velasco. 2001. "A Model of Financial Crises in Emerging Markets." *Quarterly Journal of Economics* CXVI 2:489–517.

Chari, V., and R. Jagannathan. 1988. "Banking Panics, Information, and Rational Expectations Equilibrium." *Journal of Finance* 43(3):749–61.

Chinn, M., and K. Kletzer. 2000. "International Capital Inflows, Domestic Financial Intermediation and Financial Crises under Imperfect Information." NBER Working Paper 7902. National Bureau of Economic Research, Cambridge, MA.

Choe, H., B. Kho, and R. Stulz. 1999. "Do Foreign Investors Destabilize Stock Markets? The Korean Experience in 1997." *Journal of Financial Economics* 54(2):227–64.

Christiano, L., M. Eichenbaum, and C. Evans. 1999. "Monetary Policy Shocks: What Have We Learned and to What End?" In Michael Woodford and John Taylor, eds., *Handbook of Macroeconomics.* Amsterdam, NY: Elsevier.

Claessens, Stijn, Asli Demirgüç-Kunt and Harry Huizinga. 2001. "How Does Foreign Entry Affect Domestic Banking Markets?" *Journal of Banking and Finance* 25:891–911.

Claessens, Stijn, Simeon Djankov, and Giovanni Ferri. 1999. "Corporate Distress in East Asia: Assessing the Impact of Interest and Exchange Rates Shocks." *Emerging Markets Quarterly* 3(2):8–13.

Claessens, Stijn, Simeon Djankov, and Daniela Klingebiel. 1999. *Financial Restructuring in East Asia: Half Way There?* Financial Sector Discussion Paper 3. World Bank, Washington, DC.

Claessens, Stijn, Simeon Djankov, and Ashoka Mody, eds. 2001. *Resolution of Financial Distress.* Washington, DC: World Bank Institute.

Claessens, Stijn, Simeon Djankov, and Tatiana Nenova. 2001. "Corporate Risk around the World." In Reuven Glick, Ramon Moreno, and Mark Spiegel, eds., *Financial Crises in Emerging Markets.* Cambridge, UK: Cambridge University Press.

Claessens, Stijn, and Kristin Forbes, eds. 2001. *International Financial Contagion.* Boston: Kluwer Academic Press.

Claessens, Stijn, and Thomas Glaessner. 1997. "Are Financial Sector Weaknesses Undermining the East Asian Miracle?" *Directions in Development.* World Bank, Washington, DC.

Claessens, Stijn, and Daniela Klingebiel. 2002. "Fiscal Risks of the Banking System: Approaches to Measuring and Managing Contingent Government Liabilities in the Banking Sector." In Hana Polackova Brixi and Allen Schick, eds., *Government at Risk. Contingent Liabilities and Fiscal Risk.* New York: Oxford University Press for the World Bank, 311–34.

Claessens, Stijn, Daniela Klingebiel, and Luc Laeven. 2003a. "Financial Restructuring in Banking and Corporate Sector Crises, What Polices to Pursue?" In Michael Dooley and Jeffrey Frankel, eds., *Currency Crises Management.* Chicago: NBER/University of Chicago Press, 147–80.

———. Forthcoming. "Resolving Systemic Crises: Policies and Institutions," Chapter 6, forthcoming in Luc Laeven, ed., *Systemic Crises,* World Bank, Cambridge University Press.

Clarke, George, Robert Cull, and Marie Soledad Martinez Peria. 2001. "Does Foreign Bank Penetration Reduce Access to Credit in Developing Countries: Evidence from Asking Borrowers." Policy Research Working Paper 2716. World Bank, Washington, DC.

Colaco, Francis, Mary Hallward-Driemeier, and Dominique Dwor-Frecaut. 1999. "Asian Corporate Recovery: A Firm-Level Analysis." World Bank, Washington, DC.

Corsetti, Giancarlo, Paolo Pesenti, and Nouriel Roubini. 1999. "What Caused the Asian Currency and Financial Crisis?" *Japan and the World Economy* 3(September):305–73.

Cull, Robert, Lemma W. Senbet, and Marco Sorge. 2005. "Deposit Insurance and Financial Development." *Journal of Money Credit and Banking* 37(1):43–82.

Dado, Marinela. 2000. "Note on Centralized Asset Management Companies in Indonesia, Korea and Thailand." World Bank, Washington, DC.

Dado, Marinela, and Daniela Klingebiel. 2002. "Decentralized, Creditor-Led Corporate Restructuring: Cross-Country Experience." World Bank, Washington, DC. Policy Research Working Paper 2901.

Demirgüç-Kunt, Asli, and Enrica Detragiache. 1998. "The Determinants of Banking Crises in Developing and Developed Countries." *IMF Staff Papers* 45(1):81–109. International Monetary Fund, Washington, DC.

———. 1999. "Financial Liberalization and Financial Fragility." In B. Pleskovic and J. E. Stiglitz, eds., *Proceedings of the 1998 World Bank Conference on Development Economics.* Washington, DC: World Bank.

———. 2002. "Does Deposit Insurance Increase Banking System Stability? An Empirical Investigation." *Journal of Monetary Economics* 49:1373–406.

Demirgüç-Kunt, Asli, and Ross Levine, eds. 2001. *Financial Structure and Economic Growth: A Cross-Country Comparison of Banks, Markets, and Development.* Cambridge, MA: MIT Press.

Demirgüç-Kunt, Asli, and Edward Kane. 2002. "Deposit Insurance around the Globe: Where Does it Work?" *Journal of Economic Perspectives* 16(2):17–195.

Diamond, Douglas W., and Philip H. Dybvig. 1983. "Bank Runs, Deposit Insurance, and Liquidity." *Journal of Political Economy* 91(3):401–19.

Diamond, Douglas W., and Raghurajan Rajan. 2002. "Liquidity Shortages and Banking Crises." NBER Working Paper 8937. National Bureau of Economic Research, Cambridge, MA.

Ding, Wei, Ilker Domac, and Giovanni Ferri. 1998. "Is There a Credit Crunch in East Asia?" Policy Research Working Paper 1959. World Bank, Washington, DC.

Djankov, S., J. Jindra, and L. F. Klapper. 2000. "Resolution of Bank Insolvency and Borrower Valuation in East Asia." In *The Changing Financial Industry Structure and Regulation: Bridging States, Countries, and Industries.* Bank Structure Conference Proceedings. Chicago: Federal Reserve Bank of Chicago.

Dollar, David, and Mary Hallward-Driemeier. 1999. "Crisis, Adjustment, and Reform in Thailand's Industrial Firms." *World Bank Research Observer* 15(1):1–22.

Domac, Ilker, and Giovanni Ferri. 1999. "The Credit Crunch in East Asia: Evidence from Field Findings on Bank Behavior." World Bank, Washington, DC.

Dooley, Michael P. 2000. "A Model of Crises in Emerging Markets." *Economic Journal* 110:256–72.

Dooley, Michael, and Jeffrey Frankel, eds., 2003. *Managing Currency Crises in Emerging Markets.* Chicago: University of Chicago Press.

Dooley, Michael, and Sujata Verma. 2003. "Rescue Packages and Output Losses Following Crises." In Michael Dooley and Jeffrey Frankel, eds., *Managing Currency Crises in Emerging Markets.* Chicago: University of Chicago Press.

Dornbusch, Rudiger, Yung Chul Park, and Stijn Claessens. 2000. "Contagion: Understanding How It Spreads." *World Bank Research Observer* 15(2):177–97.

Draghi, Mario, Francesco Giavazzi, and Robert C. Merton. 2003. "Transparency, Risk Management and International Financial Fragility." Harvard Business School Working Paper 03-118; Harvard NOM Working Paper 03-41. Harvard University, Cambridge, MA.

Easterly, William, Roumeen Islam, and Joseph E. Stiglitz. 2000. "Shaken and Stirred: Explaining Growth Volatility." *Annual World Bank Conference on Development Economics* 191–211.

ECB (European Central Bank). 2002. *Report on Financial Structures.* Frankfurt am Main.

Edwards, Sebastian, and Jeffrey A. Frankel. 2002. *Preventing Currency Crises in Emerging Markets.* Chicago: University of Chicago Press.

Eichengreen, Barry. 2003. *Capital Flows and Crises.* Cambridge, MA.

Eichengreen, Barry, and Ricardo Hausmann, eds. 2005. *Other People's Money: Debt Denomination and Financial Instability in Emerging Market Economies.* Chicago: University of Chicago Press.

Ferri, G., T. S. Kang, and I. J. Kim. 2001. "The Value of Relationship Banking during Financial Crisis: Evidence from Republic of Korea." Working Paper 2553. World Bank, Washington, DC.

Fischer, Stanley. 1999. "On the Need for an International Lender of Last Resort." *Journal of Economic Perspectives* 13(4):85–104.

———. 2002. "Financial Crises and the Reform of the International Financial System." NBER Working Paper 9297. National Bureau of Economic Research, Cambridge, MA.

Flood, Robert P., and Peter M. Garber. 1984. "Collapsing Exchange-Rate Regimes: Some Linear Examples." *Journal of International Economics* 17:1–13.

Frankel, Jeffrey, and Michael Dooley, eds. 2003. *Managing Currency Crises in Emerging Markets.* NBER Conference Report. National Bureau of Economic Research, Cambridge, MA.

Frenkel. 2000. "No Single Currency Regime is Right for All Countries or at All Times," Graham Lecture, Princeton University. Essays in International Finance No. 215, Princeton University Press.

Furman, Jason, and Joseph Stiglitz. 1998. "Economic Crises: Evidence and Insights from East Asia." *Brooking's Papers on Economic Activity* 1:1–135. Washington, DC.

Gertler, M., and S. Gilchrist. 1994. "Monetary Policy, Business Cycles, and the Behavior of Small Manufacturing Firms." *Quarterly Journal of Economics*, May.

Ghosh, Swati, and Atish R. Ghosh. 1999. "East Asia in the Aftermath – Was There a Crunch?" IMF Working Paper 99/38. International Monetary Fund, Washington, DC.

Goldstein, Morris, Graciela L. Kaminski, and Carmen M. Reinhart. 2000. *Assessing Financial Vulnerabilities: An Early Warning System for Emerging Markets.* Washington, DC: Institute for International Economics.

Gorton, Gay. 1988. "Banking Panics and Business Cycles." *Oxford Economic Papers* 40(3):221–55.

Greenspan, Alan. 1999. "Lessons from the Global Crises." Speech at the World Bank-IMF Annual Meetings, Washington, DC. Available at http://www.bog.frb.fed.us/BoardDocs/speeches/1999/199909272.HTM.

Greenwald, Bruce. 1998. "International Adjustment in the Face of Imperfect Financial Markets." Paper prepared for the Tenth Annual Bank Conference on Development Economics, April 21, Washington, DC.

Griffin, John M., Federico Nardari, and René M. Stulz. 2004. "Daily Cross-Border Equity Flows: Pushed or Pulled? *Review of Economics and Statistics* 86(3):641–57.

Group of Ten. 2001. *Report on Consolidation in the Financial Sector.* Available at the Bank for International Settlements website. http://www.bis.org/publ/gten05.pdf.

———. 2002. *Turbulence in Asset Markets: The Role of Micro Policies Report of the Contact Group on Asset Prices.* Available at the Bank for International Settlements website. http://www.bis.org/publ/gten07.htm#pgtop.

Haggard, Stephan. 2001. "The Politics of Corporate and Financial Restructuring: A Comparison of Korea, Thailand and Indonesia." In Stijn Claessens, Simeon Djankov, and Ashoka Mody, eds., *Resolution of Financial Distress.* Washington, DC: World Bank Institute.

Hanson, James A., Patrick Honohan, and Giovanni Majnoni. 2003. "Globalization and National Financial Systems: Issues of Integration and Size." In James Hanson, Patrick Honohan, and Giovanni Majnoni, eds., *Globalization and National Financial Systems.* New York: Oxford University Press for the World Bank.

Harvey, Campbell, and Andrew H. Roper. 1999. "The Asian Bet." In Robert Litan, Michael Pomerleano, and Alison Harwood, eds., *Financial Markets and Development: Preventing Crises in Emerging Markets.* Washington, DC: Brookings Institution/World Bank.

Hellman, Thomas, Kevin Murdock, and Joseph Stiglitz. 2000. "Liberalization, Moral Hazard in Banking, and Prudential Regulation. Are Capital Requirements Enough?" *American Economic Review* 90:147–65.

Henry, Peter Blair. 2003. "Capital-Account Liberalization and the Cost of Capital, and Economic Growth. *American Economic Review, Papers and Proceedings* 93(2):91–96.

Hoelscher, David, and Marc Quintyn. 2003. "Managing Systemic Banking Crises." IMF (International Monetary Fund) Occasional Paper 224.

Honohan, Patrick. 1999. "Fiscal Contingency Planning for Banking Crises." Policy Research Working Paper 2228. World Bank, Washington, DC.

Honohan, Patrick, and Daniela Klingebiel. 2003. "The Fiscal Cost Implication of an Accommodating Approach to Banking Crises." *Journal of Banking and Finance* 27(8):1539–60.

Hoshi, T., and A. Kashyap. 2001. *Corporate Financing and Governance in Japan.* Cambridge, MA: MIT Press.

Jacklin, C., and S. Bhattacharya. 1988. "Distinguishing Panics and Information-Based Bank Runs: Welfare and Policy Implications." *Journal of Political Economy* 96(3):568–92.

Johnson, Simon, Peter Boone, Alasdair Breach, and Eric Friedman. 2000. "Corporate Governance in the Asian Financial Crisis." *Journal of Financial Economics* 58(4):141–86.

Kaminsky, Graciela L., and Carmen M. Reinhart. 1999. "The Twin Crises: The Causes of Banking and Balance-of-Payments Problems." *American Economic Review* 89(3):473–500.

Kaminsky, Graciela, Richard Lyons, and Sergio Schmukler. 2001. "Mutual Fund Investment in Emerging Markets – An Overview." *World Bank Economic Review* 15:315–40.

Karolyi, G. A. 2004. "The Role of ADRs in the Development and Integration of Emerging Equity Markets." *Review of Economics and Statistics* 86(3):670–90.

Karolyi, Andrew, and Rene Stulz. 2003. "Are Assets Priced Locally or Globally?" In George Constantinides, Milton Harris, and René Stulz, eds., *The Handbook of the Economics of Finance.* North Holland.

Kashyap, A., J. Stein, and D. Wilcox. 1993. "Monetary Policy and Credit Conditions: Evidence from the Composition of External Finance." *American Economic Review* 83(1):78–98.

Kashyap, Anil, and Jeremy Stein. 1994. "Monetary Policy and Bank Lending." In Gregory Mankiw, ed., *Monetary Policy.* Chicago: University of Chicago Press.

Kindleberger, Charles. 1978. *Manias, Panics, and Crashes: A History of Financial Crises.* New York: Basic Books.

Klingebiel, Daniela. 2001. "The Role of Asset Management Companies in the Resolution of Banking Crises." In Stijn Claessens, Simeon Djankov, and Ashoka Mody, eds., *Resolution of Financial Distress.* Washington, DC: World Bank Institute.

Krugman, Paul. 1979. "A Model of Balance-of-Payments Crises." *Journal of Money, Credit, and Banking* 11:311–25.

———. 1997. "Are Currency Crises Self-Fulfilling?" In *NBER Macroeconomics Annual.* Cambridge, MA: MIT Press.

———. 1999. "Balance Sheets, the Transfer Problem, and Financial Crises." In Peter Isard, Assaf Razin, and Andrew K. Rose, eds., *International Finance and Financial Crises: Essays in Honor of Robert P. Flood, Jr.* Boston: Kluwer Academic Publishers.

La Porta, Rafael, Florencio Lopez-de-Silanes, Andrei Shleifer, and Robert Vishny. 1997. "Legal Determinants of External Finance." *Journal of Finance* 52:1131–50.

———. 2002. "Government Ownership of Banks." *Journal of Finance* 57(1):265–302.

Laeven, Luc. 1999. "Risk and Efficiency in East Asian Banks." Policy Research Working Paper 2255. World Bank, Washington, DC.

———. 2002. *Pricing of Deposit Insurance.* Working Paper 2871. World Bank, Washington, DC.

———. 2003. "Does Financial Liberalization Reduce Financing Constraints?" *Financial Management* 32(1):5–34.

Lane, Timothy, Atish Ghosh, A. Javier Hamann, Steven Phillips, Marianne Schultze-Ghattas, and Tsidi Tsikata. 1999. IMF-Supported Programs in Indonesia, Korea, and Thailand, IMF Occasional Papers 178, IMF, Washington, DC.

Lel, Ulgur. 2003. "Currency Hedging, Corporate Governance and Financial Markets Development." Working Paper. Indiana University.

Lemmon, M. L., and K. V. Lins. 2003. "Ownership Structure, Corporate Governance, and Firm Value: Evidence from the East Asian Financial Crisis." *Journal of Finance* 58(4):1445–68.

Levine, Ross. 2005. "Finance and Growth: Theory, Evidence, and Mechanisms." In Phillipe Aghion and Steven Durlauf, eds., *Handbook of Economic Growth.* Amsterdam: North-Holland Elsevier Publishers, forthcoming.

Levine, Ross, and Sarah Zervos. 1998. "Stock Markets, Banks, and Economic Growth." *American Economic Review* 88:537–58.

Lindgren, Carl-Johan, Gillian Garcia, and Matthew I. Saal. 1996. *Bank Soundness, and Macroeconomic Policy*. Washington, DC: International Monetary Fund.

Love, Inessa. 2003. "Financial Development and Financing Constraints: International Evidence from the Structural Investment Model." *Review of Financial Studies* 16:765–91.

Lucas, R. E. 1976. "Econometric Policy Evaluation: A Critique." *Carnegie-Rochester Conference Series on Public Policy* 1:19–46.

Merton, Robert C. 2002. "Future Possibilities in Finance Theory and Finance Practice." In H. Geman, D. Madan, S. Pliska, and T. Vorst, eds., *Mathematical Finance: Bachelier Congress 2000*. Berlin, NY: Springer.

Miron, J. 1985. "Financial Panics, the Sensitivity of the Nominal Interest Rate, and the Founding of the Fed." *American Economic Review* 76(1):125–40.

Mishkin, F. 1996. "Understanding Financial Crises: A Developing Country Perspective." NBER Working Paper 5600. National Bureau of Economic Research, Cambridge, MA.

Mitton, Todd. 2002. "A Cross-Firm Analysis of the Impact of Corporate Governance on the East Asian Financial Crisis." *Journal of Financial Economics* 64:215–41.

Mulder, Christian, Roberto Perrelli, and Manuel Rocha. 2002. "The Role of Corporate, Legal, and Macroeconomic Balance Sheet Indicators in Crisis Detection and Prevention." IMF Working Paper 02/59. International Monetary Fund, Washington, DC.

Obstfeld, Maurice. 1986. "Rational and Self-Fulfilling Balance-of-Payments Crises." *American Economic Review* 76(1):72–81.

———. 1994. "Risk-Taking, Global Diversification, and Growth." *American Economic Review* 84(December):1310–29.

Obstfeld, Maurice, and Kenneth Rogoff. 2000. "The Six Major Puzzles in International Macroeconomics: Is There a Common Cause? NBER Working Paper 7,777: 1–64. National Bureau of Economic Research, Cambridge, MA.

Peria, Maria Soledad Martinez, and Sergio L. Schmukler. 2001. "Do Depositors Punish Banks for Bad Behavior? Market Discipline, Deposit Insurance, and Banking Crises." *Journal of Finance* 56(3):1029–51.

Pesenti, Paolo, and Cedric Till. 2000. "The Economics of Currency Crises and Contagion." Federal Reserve Bank of New York. *Economic Policy Review Bulletin* (September), 3–16.

Raddatz, Claudio. 2003. "Liquidity Needs and Vulnerability to Financial Underdevelopment." World Bank Policy Research Working Paper 3161.

Rajan, Raghuram, and Luigi Zingales. 1998. "Financial Dependence and Growth." *American Economic Review* 88(3):559–96.

Rodrik, Dani. 2000. "How Far Will International Economic Integration Go?" *Journal of Economic Perspectives* 14(1):177–86.

Rojas-Suarez, Liliana. 2001. "Rating Banks in Emerging Markets." Working Paper 01-6: May. Institute for International Economics, Washington, DC.

Sheng, Andrew, ed. 1996. *Bank Restructuring: Lessons from the 1980s*. Washington, DC: World Bank.

Shiller, Robert. 2003. *The New Financial Order: Risk in the 21st Century*. Princeton, NJ: Princeton University Press.

Standard & Poor's Sovereign Ratings Service. 1999. "Global Financial System Stress: 24 Show Adverse Trends in Credit Quality."

Stiglitz, Joseph E. 2001a. "Bankruptcy Laws: Basic Economic Principles." In Stijn Claessens, Simeon Djankov, and Ashoka Mody, eds., *Resolution of Financial Distress: An International Perspective on the Design of Bankruptcy Laws*. Washington, DC: World Bank Institute.

———. 2001b. "Principles of Financial Regulation: A Dynamic Portfolio Approach." *World Bank Research Observer* 16(1):1–18.

Stiglitz, Joseph E., and Amar Bhattacharya. 1999. "Underpinnings for a Stable and Equitable Global Financial System: From Old Debates to a New Paradigm." Paper prepared for the Eleventh Annual Bank Conference on Development Economics, April 28–30, Washington, DC.

Stiglitz, Joseph E., and Andrew Weiss. 1981. "Credit Rationing in Markets with Imperfect Information." *American Economic Review* 71(3):393–410.

Stulz, R. 1999. "International Portfolio Flows and Security Markets." In Martin Feldstein, ed., *International Capital Flows.* NBER Conference Report. Chicago: University of Chicago Press.

Tirole, Jean. 2002. *Financial Crises, Liquidity, and the International Monetary System.* Princeton, NJ: Princeton University Press.

Townsend, Robert M. 1981. "Resource Allocation under Asymmetric Information." *Econometrica* 49:33–64.

Vasquez, F. 2003. "Bank Lending and Monetary Conditions in Emerging Economies: International Evidence on the Lending Channel," mimeo IMF.

Vives, Xavier. 2001. "Competition in the Changing World of Banking." *Oxford Review of Economic Policy* 17:535–45.

World Bank. 1999. "Korea Country Economic Memorandum." Washington, DC.

_____. 2001. *Finance for Growth: Policy Choices in a Volatile World.* Washington, DC.

7. Evaluating Pricing Signals from the Bond Markets

John J. Merrick, Jr.[1]

ABSTRACT: This study analyzes emerging market yield spreads, utilizing a step-by-step approach designed to be accessible to a general audience including policy specialists, market practitioners, and debt market students. The discussion highlights the roles of investor perceptions regarding the probability of bond default and default-state recovery value in bond valuation. The core framework for interpreting yield spreads as signals of default probabilities is developed within a series of examples. These examples reflect the important effects of alternative recovery value assumptions on yield spreads. First, the standard sovereign spread computation is related to per period default probability under the special assumption of zero-percent recovery of face value in default. Next, the "stripped" sovereign spread concept – applicable to issues like Brady bonds that have 100 percent collateral against face value – is explained and related to the perceived default rate. Finally, the general case where recovery value is greater than 0 percent but less than 100 percent of par value is considered. In this case, yield spread determination is shown to be more complex.

This analysis provides a simple resolution to the puzzle of the gap in spreads between Brady bonds and eurobonds. In particular, the framework explains why stripped sovereign spreads from Brady issues *should* be larger than the calculated sovereign spreads from the same issuer's eurobonds. A divergence should occur between the two spreads even though both reflect an identical default probability. The analysis suggests the definition of a special "stripped-of-recovery-value" yield spread.

Finally, a more formal emerging market bond valuation model is applied to value a cross-section of U.S. dollar-denominated eurobonds issued by the Republic of Argentina in the midst of that country's 2001 debt market crisis. The results are contrasted with those from the standard yield-based sovereign spread analysis.

INTRODUCTION

The explosive growth in the issuance of sovereign emerging market foreign currency debt in the 1990s has generated substantial interest in the underpinnings of fair valuation for these bonds. Domestic and international investors, investment banks, securities dealing firms, the issuing governments themselves, and international financial institutions (IFIs) share an interest in understanding the forces governing value in these markets. Investors, investment banks, and dealing firms must decide upon proper debt security portfolio allocations. Issuing governments must

[1] I thank Brian Pinto and the referees, Ashoka Mody and Sergio Schmukler, for valuable comments on an earlier draft.

structure sustainable fiscal and debt management policies that permit continued access to international sources of funds. IFIs must develop policies that promote international capital market stability. In all cases, effective decision making necessitates a clear understanding of emerging market bond valuation.

In recent years, academic research has also expanded rapidly into emerging markets, especially those for foreign currency debt.[2] A number of studies have analyzed the structure of emerging market debt yields. Standard macroeconomic variables like economic growth rates, inflation rates, and budget and trade deficits – the "fundamentals" – explain the cross-section of sovereign spreads during normal periods quite well. However, one crucially important finding emerges from this work: *shifts* in such fundamental variables explain very little of the short-run variation in emerging market yield spreads during times of crisis (see, for example, Eichengreen and Mody 1998). Instead, unexplained variation in "market sentiment" – perhaps reflecting shifts in risk aversion or herd behavior on the part of investors or managers – accounts for a disproportionate component of the movement in emerging market yield spreads. This finding that yield spread fluctuations cannot be adequately explained by movements in the standard fundamental macroeconomic variables is disappointing. Moreover, this result clearly leads policymakers to begin focusing more attention toward acquiring a clear understanding of the "story" that bond yield spreads tell about the prospects of issuer default, as well as possible contagion effects.

Yield spreads on risky emerging market debt produce important signals regarding the market's consensus of prospective issuer probabilities of default. Policymakers may find such information extremely valuable in assessing the proper policy response to a crisis episode. However, these market-based signals are sometimes confusing and need to be interpreted with care. For example, the literature has identified one specific puzzle in sovereign yield spreads: the persistent gap between spreads on Brady bonds and eurobonds with equivalent sovereign risk. A number of studies have raised questions as to whether these securities are priced appropriately and why these differentials have not been arbitraged (see, for example, IMF 1997).

This chapter analyzes emerging market yield spreads, utilizing a step-by-step approach designed to be accessible to a general audience including policy specialists, market practitioners, and debt market students. The discussion highlights the roles of investor perceptions regarding the probability of bond default and default-state recovery value in bond valuation. The core framework for interpreting yield spreads as signals of default probabilities is developed within a series of examples. These examples reflect the important effects of alternative recovery value assumptions on yield spreads. First, the standard sovereign spread computation is related to per period default probability under the special assumption of zero-percent recovery of face value in default. Next, the "stripped" sovereign spread concept – applicable to 100 percent collateralized issues like Brady bonds[3] – is explained and related to the perceived default rate. Finally, the general case where recovery value is greater than

---

[2] For example, see Durbin and Ng (1999); Eichengreen and Mody (1998); Kamin and von Kleist (1999); Mauro, Sussman, and Yafeh (2002); and Sy (2001) for general studies of bond yields and spreads. See Merrick (2001) and Duffie, Pedersen, and Singleton (2003) for studies of individual markets.

[3] Brady issues were created in the 1990s as part of the debt restructurings of defaulted emerging market sovereign loans. A key component of the Brady bond structure was that each issue is partially

0 percent but less than 100 percent of par value is considered. In this case, yield spread determination is shown to be more complex.

Importantly, this analysis provides a simple resolution to the Brady bond-eurobond spread differential puzzle. In particular, the framework explains why stripped sovereign spreads from Brady issues *should* be larger than the calculated sovereign spreads from the same issuer's eurobonds. This is because the quoted eurobond spread "blends" the true sovereign yield used to discount the risky cash flows and the risk-free yield used to discount the bond's assumed recovery value. Thus a divergence should occur between eurobond and unblended ("stripped") Brady spreads, even though both reflect an identical default probability. The analysis here suggests the definition of a special "stripped-of-recovery-value" yield spread.

This chapter also applies a more formal emerging market bond valuation model to valuing U.S. dollar-denominated eurobonds issued by the Republic of Argentina. This model, based upon a discounted expected cash flow approach, is a variant of that presented in John Merrick's (2001) study of Russian and Argentine eurobond pricing during the Russian GKO default crisis of August 1998.[4] The model implemented here values a crosssection of 15 outstanding Republic of Argentina eurobonds in the midst of that country's 2001 debt market crisis. The results are contrasted with those from a standard yield-based sovereign spread analysis.

SOVEREIGN DEBT YIELD SPREADS: BASIC CONCEPTS AND HYPOTHESES

A bond's yield-to-maturity is defined as the internal rate of return computed from the bond's current market price using its promised future cash flows.[5] (For more definitions, see the glossary at the end of this chapter.) As such, a bond's yield is inversely related to its market value. A yield "spread" measures the difference in quoted yields on two bonds. An emerging market bond's yield does not represent a true expected return measure because the promised cash flows may never materialize; the issuer may default. Therefore, the (positive) yield spread of a U.S. dollar-denominated emerging market sovereign bond versus its U.S. Treasury counterpart reflects a valuation discount attributable to expected default losses.[6]

Market observers use the yield spread on an emerging market debt issue to summarize the state of pricing at any particular time. Expressing the valuation discount for an emerging market bond in terms of yield-to-maturity and yield spread follows standard market practice for quoting other bonds subject to default risk, such as U.S. corporate bonds, whether investment grade or high-yield. A bond's "initial offering spread" or "issuance spread" reflects its pricing at the time of issue. A

---

collateralized by zero-coupon U.S. Treasury bonds. Typically, the zero-coupon Treasury collateral covers the entire principal amount and a rolling portion of the remaining coupon interest.

[4] GKOs (Gosudarstvennye Kratkosrochnye Obyazatel'stva) are ruble-denominated Russian state treasury bills. The Russian Federation defaulted on its GKOs in the domestic debt-restructuring plan announced on August 17, 1998.

[5] By convention, this internal rate of return calculation assumes that all scheduled coupon and principal payments are paid in full to the investor and that the coupon payments are reinvested until the bond's maturity date at the same rate of return. Thus, as is well known, the conventional yield-to-maturity concept does not properly handle coupon reinvestment risk.

[6] A portion of the observed spread could also reflect a liquidity difference.

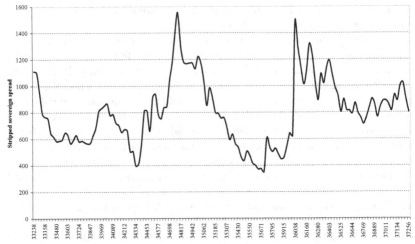

Figure 7.1. EMBI Stripped Sovereign Spreads, December 1990–December 2001. *Source*: J. P. Morgan Chase & Co.

"secondary market spread" reflects the state of the bond's pricing as a seasoned issue trading in the dealer market after issuance. The spread on a collateralized issue such as a Brady bond can be computed as a "stripped sovereign spread" by adjusting for the valuation impact of the bond's riskless collateral.

Figure 7.1 plots a monthly history of JP Morgan's Emerging Market Bond Index (EMBI) of stripped sovereign spreads on Brady bonds of various emerging market issuers versus U.S. Treasury bonds beginning December 1990 and ending December 2001. This spread index averaged about 800 basis points during this period. As the figure reveals, EMBI spreads were extremely volatile. The maximum observed spread was 1,555 basis points. The minimum spread was 350 basis points. The EMBI's standard deviation was about 250 basis points. Two yield spread "spikes" appear during this time period. The first, beginning in December 1994 and peaking in March 1995, represents the market sell-off in the Mexican credit crisis. The second, beginning in August 1998 and peaking in January 1999, portrays the sector's valuation collapse during the Russian GKO default crisis.

Understandably, the importance of emerging market debt valuation in a crisis-filled environment has led to a growing number of academic studies of yield and yield spread determination. Spreads can be thought of as depending on four types of variables: macroeconomic fundamentals; debt instrument and country characteristics; interest rates in the United States, Germany, and Japan; and market sentiment. Barry Eichengreen and Ashoka Mody (1998) conduct a broad examination of initial offering yield spreads on more than 1,000 new bond issues in 55 countries from 1991 to 1997.[7] These authors document significant inverse

---

[7] These authors calculate each bond's offering yield spread as the arithmetic difference between that bond's yield-to-maturity (derived from its issuance price) and the corresponding yield on a riskless sovereign issue of comparable maturity in the currency of issue (that is, for U.S. dollar issues, the corresponding U.S. Treasury yield). The *compound* spread definition discussed below is easier to apply consistently.

impacts of both issuance size and a credit rating variable on issuance yield spread levels, as well as mixed evidence for a positive relationship between issuance spreads and the level of U.S. interest rates.[8] Perhaps the most important conclusion of the Eichengreen and Mody study is that the short-run variation in spreads appears to be better explained by shifts in market sentiment than by shifts in economic fundamentals. For example, variation in standard macroeconomic variables explain very little of the short-run variation in spreads associated either with the Mexican crisis or the period of emerging market spread compression during the second half of 1996 and the first of 1997. Such shifts in market sentiment might be more easily understood as reflecting unobservable changes in investor risk aversion. Alternatively, such shifts might be evidence of herd behavior on the part of returns-chasing investors and investment managers.

Steven Kamin and Karsten von Kleist (1999) construct a coherent picture of issuance spread behavior over the decade after controlling for deal-specific factors such as issuer home region, creditworthiness, bond maturity, and currency denomination. They document sensible and important impacts on non-Brady bonds and loan issuance spreads of credit ratings, term-to-maturity, currency issue choice, and dummy variables interpreted as year-by-year sentiment shifts. Their regression results again reveal that the general fall in the spreads over the period were dominated by unexplained market sentiment shifts.

Kamin and von Kleist also address the possibility that interest rate policies in the major industrial countries – the United States, Germany, and Japan – significantly affect spreads. Under a view popularized by the financial press, emerging market spreads collapsed in late 1996 and early 1997 because the "appetite for risk" rose as interest rates in the major industrialized countries fell. Despite substantial effort, the authors find scant support for significant interest rate effects on their emerging market non-Brady bond and loan issuance spreads. Figure 7.2 below presents an updated scatter graph of the level of the EMBI sovereign stripped spread versus the coincident Treasury bill yield level from December 1990 to December 2001.[9] This figure evinces little support for the hypothesis that spread levels and Treasury bill yields have any correlation at all.[10]

Kamin and von Kleist argue that trends in the secondary spreads on Brady debt – the spread data most often previously employed to depict emerging market bond valuation – may not be representative of spread trends for a broader sample of non-Brady credits. Indeed, the authors document that the stripped sovereign spreads on Brady bonds, the primary type of long-term sovereign bond issued in the early 1990s, are significantly higher than the issuance spreads on non-Brady bonds and loans. In focusing on the large difference between spreads on Brady debt versus those on

---

[8] In an investigation of issuance decisions, the authors document a significant inverse relationship between the *volume* of new issues and the level of U.S. Treasury yield. Thus high U.S. interest rates depress new issuance of emerging market debt.

[9] In this "dynamic" scatter graph, a line that traces the period-by-period time path connects the data points.

[10] The popular conception reported by Kamin and von Kleist that spreads were interest rate-dependent no doubt reflects the experience of 1991, when spreads collapsed 500 basis points as short-term U.S. interest rates eased 350 basis points, combined with that of 1994, when spreads rose more than 1,100 basis points as U.S. interest rates tightened nearly 300 basis points.

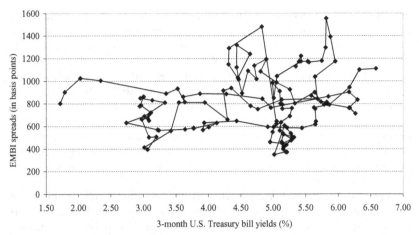

Figure 7.2. EMBI Stripped Spreads versus U.S. Treasury Bill Yields. *Source*: J. P. Morgan Chase & Co.

non-Brady debt, the authors echo analysis presented by the International Monetary Fund in their 1997 report (IMF 1997). In assessing market conditions during 1996, the IMF report (pp. 70 and 75) states: "[Y]ield spread differentials between the Brady and Eurobond sectors endured, suggesting continued market segmentations.... In particular, persistent spread differentials between Brady bonds and Eurobonds with equivalent sovereign risk have raised questions as to whether these securities are priced appropriately and why these differentials have not been arbitraged."[11] In the opinion of the IMF study, the suggested explanations for the continuing spread differential remain unconvincing.[12] Paolo Mauro, Nathan Sussman, and Yishay Yafeh (2002) also refer to the spread differential as an "anomaly" and concur that proffered explanations seem less than fully satisfying. However, the IMF study also points to certain buyback and/or debt exchange programs that particular emerging market issuers implemented beginning in 1996 to retire Brady debt in favor of newly issued eurobonds. Brazil, Ecuador, Mexico, Panama, the Philippines, and Poland all participated in such programs at that time, and Argentina later followed suit.

More recent research on emerging market bonds has moved on to analyze the valuation aspects of the restructuring process accompanying a potential default. The role of collective action clauses found in some bond indentures has received particular focus.[13] Collective action clauses enable a qualified majority of bondholders to modify key financial terms of the debt agreement and to make decisions binding on all other holders. Such clauses eliminate the risk that any individual investor

---

[11] See IMF (1997, pp. 70 and 75).

[12] Such explanations include a "stigma effect" on Brady bonds carried forth from their genesis out of loan restructuring; the implicit costs of "stripping" the collateral from Brady bonds to obtain a pure sovereign spread exposure; the unusual cash flow patterns of Brady bonds; the bearer form of some eurobonds; the lower volatility of eurobonds; the call features of Brady bonds; and repurchase agreement market costs inhibiting arbitrage between the Brady and eurobond markets.

[13] See, for example, IMF (2002a).

holds out from the majority's agreement in order to litigate separately to seek full repayment. Collective action clauses can facilitate sovereign restructurings either prior to or after a default. However, clauses designed to facilitate restructurings may also encourage moral hazard on the part of issuers leading to an increased frequency of default.

Eichengreen and Mody (2000) and Torbjrn Becker, Anthony Richards, and Yungyong Thaicharoen (2001) examine the empirical impact of collective action clauses on spread determination. In both studies, the empirical strategy exploits the strong correlation between the presence of collective action clauses in a bond indenture and that bond's governing law. Bonds governed under English law, such as eurobonds issued in London, typically incorporate collective action clauses. In contrast, bonds governed under New York law, such as Brady bonds, typically do not incorporate such clauses. In principle, this governing law/collective action clause effect could explain why New York-based Brady bond yield spreads are larger than London-based eurobond spreads. Unfortunately, the evidence on the valuation impact of governing law choice is mixed.[14]

A complementary research direction places more intense focus on investor perceptions regarding how much of a bond's value would be recovered in the event of default. Clearly, the relationship between the sovereign yield spread and issuer default probability entails understanding bond payoffs in the default state. A sovereign debt default event is couched under a forced "rescheduling" agreement that exchanges the originally promised cash flow stream for new, more lenient terms. From the investor's perspective, the value of the involuntarily exchanged new security is less than that of the original debt. The percentage of the value of the new security to the par value of the original security can be termed the bond's default recovery value.

Assumptions about the default recovery value crucially affect sovereign foreign currency debt valuation. For different classes of U.S. corporate debt, investors can utilize a well-documented default experience history to help predict potential default recovery rates. For example, Edward Altman and Allan Eberhart (1994) examine a sample of 91 U.S. firms that filed for and emerged from Chapter 11 bankruptcy between 1980 and 1992. The authors estimate bondholder recovery by measuring actual postbankruptcy bond values for individual firms.[15] That sample's average recovery rate is about 50 percent, with significant differences among seniority classes. Using a much larger sample over the 1978 to 1998 period, Altman, Diane

---

[14] Eichengreen and Mody (2000) report large and different impacts of the choice of governing law on issuance yield spreads for high-rated versus low-rated issuers. In line with the idea that collective action clauses add value, that study finds that the use of English law by issuers with high credit ratings reduces issuance yield spreads. In contrast, low-rated issuers adopting English law are penalized though higher issuance yield spreads, presumably because of increased moral hazard. In a more recent study incorporating both secondary and issuance spreads, Becker, Richards, and Thaicharoen (2001) find that use of English law adds value (spreads tend to be lower), but the effects are often statistically insignificant at standard significance levels. Moreover, they can find no evidence that the use of English law (and, therefore, the presence of collective action clauses) increases yields for low-rated issuers.

[15] Altman and Eberhart analyzed the price or payoff of the defaulted debt securities upon emergence from Chapter 11.

Cooke, and Vellore Kishore (1999) estimate the weighted average recovery rate of U.S. corporate debt defaults to be 40 percent of face value.

However, unlike the U.S. domestic corporate debt markets, the sovereign bonds in emerging markets offer no rich histories of default for reference. A large portion of such debt initially was issued under the Brady bond structure. A Brady bond's Treasury collateral ameliorates the investor's problem of reliably estimating a default recovery value.[16] However, uncollateralized eurobond issues have become more important sources of funding in the sovereign emerging markets. In the absence of Brady bond-like guarantees, a default crisis scenario for unsecured sovereign eurobond debt is destined to be a fluid situation.

Eurobonds are uncollateralized obligations. An emerging market investor discounting the expected cash flows of a eurobond must jointly estimate recovery value and payment probabilities. Merrick (2001) examined the role of revisions in *implied* recovery value in both Russian Federation and Republic of Argentina eurobond valuation during extraordinarily volatile Russian GKO default crisis of 1998. The empirical analysis led to a number of conclusions. First, recovery value estimates for Argentine debt embodied a "standard" assumption of 50 percent recovery value for U.S. corporate debt. In contrast, the precrisis implied recovery value for Russian eurobonds was much lower. Second, the implied Russian recovery value – reasonably stable prior to and just after the GKO default – fell sharply one week after the actual default announcement. Third, significant downward revisions in the implied recovery value of Russian eurobonds continued even after the default probability stabilized at its higher value.[17]

Finally, Brady bonds and eurobonds clearly differ along the recovery value dimension. A Brady bond's principal is fully collateralized by U.S. Treasury zero-coupon bonds of equal face value. Investors have a precise understanding of the market value of this underlying collateral. The impact of this differential recovery concept on quoted yield spreads for Brady bonds versus eurobonds is significant. The next section examines this impact within the context of a full analysis of the relation between recovery values and yield spreads.

INTERPRETING YIELD CURVES FOR RISKY SOVEREIGN DEBT: SOME SIMPLE ANALYTICS

This section develops some simple yield spread analytics for emerging market debt. One goal is to relate market yield spreads to investor perceptions regarding both default probability and default recovery value. Perceptions of the probability of issuer default play a central role in emerging market bond valuation. Many authors have interpreted the yield spread on an emerging market bond as a direct measure of the issuer's per period "default rate" after assuming that default-state recovery value is zero.

---

[16] See Claessens and Pennachi (1996) and Bhanot (1998) for empirical analysis of Brady bonds.

[17] The downward revision in implied recovery value occurred as investors digested relevant "news" – the contentious dealings of the Russian government and GKO investors in the aftermath of the GKO default. Russian did not default on its eurobond obligations.

In contrast, the analysis here will highlight the importance of the assumed default recovery value in determining yield spreads. When a more realistic recovery value is anticipated – that is, a positive one – the implied default probability consistent with a given observed yield spread can rise significantly. The important conclusion is that the observed yield spread does not directly measure the issuer's default rate. Thus recovery value assumptions matter.

This section's second goal is to distinguish between the yield spread concepts appropriate for uncollateralized debt (such as eurobonds) versus collateralized debt (such as Brady bonds). As discussed earlier, a number of studies have documented that stripped sovereign yield spreads quoted on Brady bonds exceed the yield spreads quoted on eurobonds of the same issuer. The literature interprets this difference either as an unexplained pricing anomaly or a product of the collective action clauses within the eurobond indenture. The analysis here offers an alternative explanation. While lacking explicit Brady-type collateralization, a given issuer's eurobond presumably has positive recovery value in default. Thus the conventional yield-to-maturity on a eurobond blends the high discount rates appropriate for the default-sensitive component of expected cash flow with the low discount rate appropriate for the perceived recovery value component. In contrast, the Brady bond's computed stripped sovereign spread is strictly appropriate for the uncollateralized coupon flows, where 0 percent recovery might more reasonably be assumed. Thus the stripped sovereign yield spreads quoted on Brady bonds *must* be higher than the yield spreads quoted on eurobonds of the same issuer if nonzero eurobond recovery value is assumed.[18]

All of the results will be demonstrated through a series of examples based upon two types of discounting analysis. The conventional method discounts the *promised* cash flows of a given bond and, given the bond's market value, generates the bond's quoted yield-to-maturity. This yield is the internal rate of return on the bond's promised cash flows. A second discounting method discounts the bond's *expected* cash flows based on a specific analysis of default prospects that incorporates particular assumptions about both the issuer's probability of making the scheduled payments and any recovery value should default occur. Side-by-side analysis of these two discounting methods reveals how a bond's quoted yield and spread reflect the key parameters determining expected default losses.

Yield Spreads on Uncollateralized Bonds Assuming Zero Recovery in Default

Consider a simple one-period example in the spirit of Kamin and von Kleist's analysis linking benchmark country (here, the United States) and emerging market country yields. Let V be the market value and let Y be the quoted yield-to-maturity on a one-period emerging market 10 percent coupon rate bond per $100 of the bond's par value. Then the quoted yield, defined as the internal rate of return on the investment when purchased at the current market value, is such that

$$V = \frac{10 + 100}{1 + Y}. \tag{1}$$

---

[18] Assuming some positive value for the Brady's uncollateralized cash flows would complicate the algebra, but not change the general thrust of the result.

Practitioners will use the spread between an emerging market debt issue's yield and that of the counterpart benchmark market issue to summarize current market conditions. Thus, practitioners will compare the yield-to-maturity on the emerging market bond (Y) to the yield on the U.S. Treasury issue of the same maturity (denoted here as y). The difference between Y and y reflects a valuation discount attributable to the emerging market issuer's default potential.

For example, suppose that a one-year U.S. Treasury 0 percent coupon rate bond was priced at $95.238 per $100 of par value to yield 5 percent on an annually compounded basis: ($100/$95.238 $= 1.0500 = 1 + y$; $y = 0.0500$). Furthermore, suppose that an emerging market issuer's one-year U.S. dollar-denominated 10 percent coupon rate bond was priced at $96.38 per $100 of par value to yield 14.13 percent on an annually compounded basis:

$$V = \frac{10 + 100}{1.1413} = 96.38. \tag{1''}$$

Market practitioners might define the emerging market bond's yield spread, s, via the compound form:[19]

$$(1 + Y) = (1 + y)(1 + s). \tag{2}$$

Thus,

$$s = \frac{(1 + Y)}{(1 + y)} - 1. \tag{3}$$

Here, the emerging market issuer's yield spread could be calculated as

$$s = 1.1413/1.0500 - 1 = 0.0870 \ (8.70\% \text{ or } 870 \text{ basis points}). \tag{4}$$

While the yield and spread computations above conveniently summarize current market quotations, they provide little insight. The financial logic behind the setting of V in the market is more usefully described through an equilibrium relationship to the probability of payment, p, and the appropriate discount rate. If the emerging market bond's $100 principal is repaid in full, the investor receives $110 (= $100 of principal plus $10 of coupon interest). However, if the issuer defaults, assume that the investor recovers only R dollars per $100 of par value. Assume that this specific recovery value, R, replaces all other cash flow claims. Then V can be expressed as the expected discounted value of the two possible end-of-period cash flow outcomes, where the outcomes occur with the assumed probabilities, p and $1 - p$. If investors are risk-neutral, then the risk-free one-period yield is properly used to discount both state-dependent cash flows:[20]

$$V = p\frac{110}{(1 + y)} + (1 - p)\frac{R}{(1 + y)}. \tag{5}$$

---

[19] This multiplicative form for the spread is more convenient than an additive form for compounding purposes.

[20] Alternatively, if investors are risk-averse, the payment probability can be thought of as an *adjusted* risk-neutral probability distribution, as in Harrison and Kreps (1979).

As in Kamin and von Kleist (1999), assume that the emerging market bond investor recovers nothing (that is, 0 percent of par value) in the default state. In this setting, $R = 0$ and the emerging market one-period zero-coupon bond is valued as

$$V = p\frac{110}{(1+y)} + (1-p)\frac{0}{(1+y)}. \tag{5'}$$

Substituting Equation 1 into Equation 5', the emerging market bond's quoted yield, Y, can be determined as

$$1 + Y = \frac{1+y}{p}. \tag{6}$$

Combining the expression above with the definition of the multiplicative yield spread produces a particularly convenient interpretation: $1 + s$ equals the inverse of the bond's payment probability. Thus,

$$1 + s = \frac{1+Y}{1+y} = \frac{1}{p} \tag{7}$$

and, finally,

$$s = \frac{1-p}{p}. \tag{8}$$

Thus under the above assumptions, s equals the ratio of the default probability $(1 - P)$ to the payment probability (p). The yield spread rises as default becomes more likely (that is, s rises as p falls).

The analysis extends naturally to the case of a two-period coupon-bearing bond paying a per period coupon of C per \$100 of par value. The bond's yield-to-maturity, Y, is defined as

$$V = \frac{C}{(1+Y)} + \frac{(C+100)}{(1+Y)^2}. \tag{9}$$

The companion risk-neutral valuation equation must account for all possible cash flow outcomes. For simplicity, assume that the benchmark term structure of zero-coupon yields is flat ($y_1 = y_2 = y$). The probability of being fully paid in both periods is p^2 and the associated discounted cash flow is $C/(1+y) + (100+C)/(1+y)^2$. The probability of being paid the coupon in period one, but experiencing a default in period two equals $p(1-p)$, and the associated discounted cash flow is $C/(1+y)$ (since a recovery value of $R = 0$ is assumed). Finally, the probability of experiencing default in period one is $1 - p$ and the associated discounted cash flow is zero. Thus, under the zero-percent recovery value assumption, the risk-neutral valuation equation simplifies to

$$V = p^2\left[\frac{C}{(1+y)} + \frac{C+100}{(1+y)^2}\right] + p(1-p)\frac{C}{1+y}. \tag{10}$$

This can be rearranged to derive

$$V = \frac{pC}{(1+y)} + \frac{p^2(C+100)}{(1+y)^2}. \tag{11}$$

Clearly, Equation 11 is consistent with Equation 9 above if

$$1 + Y = (1 + y)(1 + s) = \frac{1+y}{p}. \tag{12}$$

Hence, as with its one-period bond counterpart, the spread variable (s) is again determined as the ratio of the per period default probability ($1 - p$) to the payment probability (p):

$$s = \frac{1-p}{p}. \tag{13}$$

These relationships can also be reverse engineered to uncover implied market parameters from bond market prices. For example, suppose that a two-year 10 percent coupon rate bond of an emerging market issuer currently sells in the secondary market for $93.21 per $100 of par value. Assume a recovery value of $0. If the annually compounded yields on one-year and two-year zero-coupon U.S. Treasury are each 5 percent, what is the emerging market bond's yield spread?[21] Moreover, what per period default rate is the market using to price this emerging market issue?

At a market value of $93.21, the emerging market bond's yield-to-maturity (Y) equals 14.13 percent from Equation 9:

$$93.21 = \frac{10}{1.1413} + \frac{(10 + 100)}{(1.1413)^2}. \tag{9'}$$

Via Equation 3, the bond's yield spread equals

$$s = (1 + Y)/(1 + y) - 1 = (1.1413/1.05) - 1 = .0870 \text{ (or 8.70\%)}. \tag{3'}$$

Finally, this 870 basis point spread implies that the market is attributing the issuer a per period payment probability of 0.92. In particular,

$$s = (1 - p)/p = .0870 \tag{8'}$$

if and only if $p = .92$ and $(1 - p) = .08$. Thus at a price of $93.21, the bond market's *implied* default rate is 8 percent per period.

The analysis works for the simple cases of one-period and two-period bonds. However, assuming a 0 percent default recovery value, these results for yield spread and per period payment rates also hold for bonds with maturities extending beyond two periods.

The "Stripped Spread" Yield Concept for Brady Bonds

Brady bonds, created in the 1990s as part of the debt restructurings of defaulted emerging market sovereign loans, are an important class of emerging market debt. By the middle part of the decade, the Brady market stood as the largest and most liquid

---

[21] All of the examples of this section are based upon flat term structures of risk-free per period discount rates and payment probabilities. The introduction of more general curve shapes necessitates applying appropriate term rates for each payment date and permits a nontrivial analysis of the "forward" default rate curve.

emerging debt market sector.[22] The key component of the Brady bond structure is that each issue is partially collateralized by zero-coupon U.S. Treasury bonds. Typically, the zero-coupon Treasury collateral covers the entire principal amount and a rolling portion of the remaining coupon interest. A Brady issue's Treasury collateral is held by the Federal Reserve Bank of New York and provides important protection for investors should the issuing sovereign fail to make timely payment of coupon or principal. But for present purposes, the presence of the collateral complicates the calculation of the appropriate yield spread. The complication arises because all cash flows do not carry equivalent exposures to default. Clearly, the uncollateralized portion of the bond's cash flow stream should be discounted at a default-risk adjusted rate. Investors need to earn a premium on this portion of the bond's promised payment stream to compensate for expected default losses. However, the collateralized portion of the cash flow stream should be discounted at the risk-free rate. No default premium is required on this Treasury-backed portion. Practitioners who reference the standard yield-to-maturity calculation (that is, a single internal rate of return for all cash flows) for a Brady bond are careful to term the result the "blended yield," since this calculation improperly lumps together cash flows that differ in underlying risk. A yield spread derived from this blended yield would be artificially low and could not be directly used to accurately characterize sovereign default probabilities via Equation 13.

The discounting complications that Brady bonds present suggest an adjustment to the spread calculation methodology. Practitioners apply the standard spread calculation only after "stripping out" the present value of the collateralized cash flow component. The present value of the collateralized cash flow component is calculated using the risk-free discount rate. As a simple example, consider the definition of s^s, the "stripped spread" on a two-period, coupon-bearing Brady bond with full collateral against principal and no collateral against either coupon.[23] For the default-free collateralized principal amount, use $1 + y$ to discount this default-free cash flow. For the uncollateralized, default-exposed coupon amounts, use the spread-adjusted rate $Y = (1 + y)(1 + s^s) - 1$. The stripped spread term (s^s) in the discount factor for the uncollateralized coupons would define the "pure" sovereign yield spread.

In practice, this calculation is performed in two steps. First, subtract out the present value of the Treasury collateral from the Brady bond's market value and denote this "stripped value" of the bond as V^*:

$$V^* = V - \frac{100}{(1 + y)^2}. \tag{14}$$

---

[22] Beginning with Mexico in 1996, emerging market sovereigns have retired a significant portion of the outstanding Brady issues via buybacks and debt exchanges for newly issued uncollateralized sovereign eurobond market issues. For example, $1.8 billion of Brady issues were part of Argentina's June 2001 voluntary debt exchange. By September 2002, about half the original Brady issues had been retired. Moreover, during 2001, secondary market trading volume in eurobonds was more than double that of the remaining Brady bond sector. For details, see IMF (2002b).

[23] In practice, terms for coupon collateralization vary across specific issues. A common structure involves collateralization of the next three coupon payments (on a rolling basis).

Second, solve implicitly for Y, the sovereign yield, from the following definition, where C represents the promised (but uncollateralized) coupon payments:

$$V^* = \frac{C}{(1 + Y)} + \frac{C}{(1 + Y)^2}. \tag{15}$$

Given Y, solve for the stripped spread from the definition as before:

$$(1 + Y) = (1 + y)(1 + s^s). \tag{16}$$

Assuming 0 percent recovery for *coupon* payments in default, the risk-neutral valuation equation for this coupon-bearing two-period Brady bond extends to

$$V^* = \frac{pC + (1 - p)0}{(1 + y)} + \frac{p^2 C + p(1 - p)0}{(1 + y)^2}. \tag{17}$$

Furthermore, s^s, the "stripped spread," can be solved for directly by combining Equations 16 and 17:

$$s^s = \frac{1 - p}{p}. \tag{18}$$

Suppose that the same per period emerging market issuer payment probability used by the market for the uncollateralized bond ($p = 0.92$) is also used for a two-year, 10 percent coupon rate Brady bond. From Equation 18, the stripped yield spread on this bond (s^s) would be $0.0870 = (1 - 0.92)/(0.92)$. Thus, from Equation 16, the sovereign yield on this bond would be $Y = (1 + y)(1 + s^s) - 1$ or $Y = (1.05)(1.0870) - 1 = 0.1413$. At this sovereign yield, the fair value of the two 10 percent annual rate coupons is given by[24]

$$V^* = \frac{10}{1.1413} + \frac{10}{(1.1413)^2} = 16.439. \tag{19}$$

Next, solve for the fair market value of the collateralized principal. The value of the collateral is found by discounting the bond's par value by the risk-free rate of 5 percent. Thus, the collateral would be valued at \$90.703 ($= 100/(1.05)^2$). Finally, this two-year Brady bond's fair market value would be the sum of the two component values, or $V = 16.439 + 90.703 = 107.142$.

The solution for the "stripped spread" reduces to 870 basis points, the same ratio of default-to-payment probabilities as in the case of s, the spread on non-Brady bonds: $s^s = (1 - 0.92)/0.92 = 0.870$. But a conventionally calculated yield-to-maturity on this Brady bond at a price of \$107.142 is 6.099 percent via Equation 9:

$$107.142 = \frac{10}{1.06099} + \frac{(10 + 100)}{(1.06099)^2}. \tag{9''}$$

---

[24] The valuation for V^* could also have been computed through the risk-neutral discounted expected value of the coupons using $p = 0.92$:

$$V^* = \frac{0.92(10) + (0.80)0}{(1.05)} + \frac{(0.92)^2 10 + .92(0.08)0}{(1.05)^2} = 16.439.$$

Think of this calculated 6.099 percent as the "blended yield" on this collateralized bond. This blended yield – the bond's internal rate of return conditional on no default – provides little substantive information on the market's implied default probability rate, since it mixes the true sovereign yield (relevant to form the discount rate on the risky coupons) and the risk-free yield (relevant for the collateralized principal). Furthermore, the 105 basis point yield spread to Treasury bonds derived from this computed blended yield – 1.05 percent $= .0105 = (1.06099/1.05) -1$ – is a "blended spread" that offers a fuzzy picture of the market. Policymakers attempting a direct read on the market's implied default probability rate should track a Brady bond's 870 basis point stripped sovereign spread, not its 105 basis point blended spread. Only the 870 basis point stripped sovereign spread directly reveals the market's true 8 percent assessment of the issuer's per period default probability.

Positive Recovery Values Shift Yield Spreads

The yield spread analysis for non-Brady, uncollateralized emerging market debt discussed above invoked the most conservative possible recovery value assumption: 0 percent. Under this assumption, a bond's yield spread directly reflects the issuer's default probability. However, based upon previous experience with both corporate bond and sovereign loan defaults, investors may expect some positive recovery value to emerge in the default state. Ceteris paribus, these same investors would price emerging market bonds higher to reflect this perceived positive recovery value. As the analysis below will note in detail, the introduction of a positive recovery value shifts the relationship between the yield spread and the default rate.

Assume that a known specific recovery value, R, is paid to the bondholder upon the event of default and replaces all other cash flow claims. To simplify the analysis, assume that this recovery value is actually received only at the bond's maturity date, regardless of when default actually occurs. This substituting payment of R replaces any remaining cash flows (that is, the remaining coupons and principal) from the initially promised stream. In the discounting equation below, a default in period two generates a payment of R. However, a default in period one is attributed a payment of $R/(1 + y)$: that is, the period one present value of R actually received in period two. Given these assumptions about the bond's recovery value, the investor values the bond according to the following risk-neutral valuation equation:

$$V = \frac{pC + (1 - p)[R/(1 + y)]}{(1 + y)} + \frac{p^2(C + 100) + p(1 - p)R}{(1 + y)^2}. \qquad (20)$$

Typically, uncollateralized emerging market bonds (such as eurobonds) are quoted on a yield-to-maturity basis, as described by equation 9 and repeated here:

$$V = \frac{C}{(1 + Y)} + \frac{(C + 100)}{(1 + Y)^2}. \qquad (9)$$

Note that the multiplicative form of the yield spread will no longer reduce to the simple ratio of per period default-to-payment probabilities because of the extra R terms in Equation 20. The multiplicative yield spread concept will correspond to those previously examined only in two extreme cases. First, if the recovery value equals 0, the analysis reduces to the case initially studied in the opening of this section. Second, if $R = 100$, the analysis reduces to that for the "stripped spread" case of the Brady bond discussed above. Because neither of these two conditions is likely to hold in practice, yield spread determination is now more complex.

Consider once again U.S. dollar-denominated 10 percent coupon rate, one- and two-year maturity bonds of an emerging market issuer. However, instead of a recovery value of $0, assume that the market perceives default recovery value to be $50 per $100 of par ($R = 50$). Again, assume that the equivalent 1- and 2-year riskless benchmark zero-coupon yields are each 5 percent and that the issuer's per period payment probability is $p = 0.92$. Under these assumptions, the discounted expected cash flow valuation for the one-year bond follows from Equation 5″:

$$V = 0.92\frac{110}{1.05} + (1 - 0.92)\frac{50}{1.05} = 100.19. \tag{5″}$$

From Equation 1, the one-year bond's yield is 9.79 %:

$$100.19 = \frac{10 + 100}{1.0979}. \tag{1′}$$

Furthermore, from Equation 3, this bond's yield spread is 456 basis points:

$$s = \frac{1.0979}{1.05} - 1 = 0.0456. \tag{3′}$$

Now turn to the two-year bond. Assuming $R = 50$, the discounted expected cash flow valuation for the two-year bond follows from Equation (3.20):

$$V = \frac{0.92(10) + (1 - 0.92)[50/1.05]}{1.05} + \frac{(0.92)^2(10 + 100) + 0.92(1 - 0.92)50}{(1.05)^2}$$
$$V = 100.18. \tag{20′}$$

From Equation 9, this two-year bond's yield is 9.90 percent:

$$100.18 = \frac{10}{1.0990} + \frac{(10 + 100)}{(1.0990)^2}. \tag{9′}$$

Furthermore, from Equation 3, this bond's yield spread is 466 basis points:

$$s = \frac{1.099}{1.05} - 1 = 0.0466. \tag{3″}$$

These answers offer some surprises. With a positive recovery value ($R = 50$), the yields on the one- and two-year bonds are not equal, even though the benchmark risk-free yield structure reflects a "flat" 5 percent curve and the assumed per period payment probability is constant. Moreover, the computed yield spreads no longer equal the ratio of default to payment probabilities. as in the $R = 0$ case.

Table 7.1 compares bond values and associated yields for 10 percent coupon rate emerging market bonds from 1 to 10 years in maturity under alternative assumptions for both the level of R and the value of p. The upper panel of Table 7.1 uses a "normal" value for the payment probability: $p = 0.92$. Bond values and associated yields are computed for all 10 issues under three different recovery value assumptions: $R = 0$, 50, and 100. The $R = 0$ column reflects valuation as in the

Table 7.1. *Recovery value assumption effects on bond values and yields in "Normal"*
and "Crisis" periods

Panel 1: "Normal" market conditions: per period payment probability $p = 0.92$

Bond maturity	$R = 0$ Value	Yield	$R = 50$ Value	Yield	$R = 100$: "Brady-type" Value	Yield	Payment probability factors $p = 0.92$	Risk-free discount factors $y = 5\%$
1	96.38	14.13%	100.19	9.79%	104.00	5.77%	0.920	0.952
2	93.21	14.13%	100.18	9.90%	107.14	6.09%	0.846	0.907
3	90.43	14.13%	99.99	10.00%	109.55	6.40%	0.779	0.864
4	88.00	14.13%	99.66	10.11%	111.33	6.68%	0.716	0.823
5	85.86	14.13%	99.22	10.21%	112.58	6.94%	0.659	0.784
6	84.00	14.13%	98.68	10.30%	113.37	7.18%	0.606	0.746
7	82.36	14.13%	98.07	10.40%	113.78	7.40%	0.558	0.711
8	80.92	14.13%	97.40	10.50%	113.87	7.62%	0.513	0.677
9	79.67	14.13%	96.68	10.59%	113.69	7.82%	0.472	0.645
10	78.56	14.13%	95.93	10.68%	113.29	8.02%	0.434	0.614

Panel 2: "Crisis" market conditions: per period payment probability $p = .60$

Bond maturity	$R = 0$ Value	Yield	$R = 50$ Value	Yield	$R = 100$: "Brady-type" Value	Yield	Payment probability factors $p = 0.60$	Risk-free discount factors $y = 5\%$
1	62.86	75.00%	81.90	34.30%	100.95	8.96%	0.600	0.952
2	41.63	75.00%	70.66	32.08%	99.68	10.18%	0.360	0.907
3	29.50	75.00%	63.37	30.25%	97.23	11.14%	0.216	0.864
4	22.57	75.00%	58.38	28.85%	94.18	11.91%	0.130	0.823
5	18.61	75.00%	54.74	27.81%	90.87	12.57%	0.078	0.784
6	16.35	75.00%	51.92	27.08%	87.49	13.14%	0.047	0.746
7	15.06	75.00%	49.60	26.59%	84.14	13.66%	0.028	0.711
8	14.32	75.00%	47.59	26.30%	80.87	14.15%	0.017	0.677
9	13.90	75.00%	45.80	26.19%	77.71	14.61%	0.010	0.645
10	13.66	75.00%	44.17	26.22%	74.68	15.06%	0.006	0.614

Note: Computations based on a flat 5 percent benchmark risk-free yield curve. R assumed paid at bond's original maturity. Payment probability and discount factors reported for individual annual cash flow dates.
Source: Author's calculations.

examples discussed at the opening of this section. The $R = 100$ column reflects valuation as in the collateralized Brady bond examples discussed above. The $R = 50$ column reflects valuation as in the examples of the current section. The lower panel of Table 7.1 recalculates all bond values and yields under a much lower payment probability: $p = 0.60$. Interpret this $p = 0.60$ as a "crisis" value for the payment probability.

The impacts of assuming positive recovery value on bond values are easy to understand. Consider the two-year bond valued under normal market conditions ($p = 0.92$) at 93.21 if $R = 0$, and 100.18 if $R = 50$. Thus there is a difference in value of $+6.97$ moving from the $R = 0$ column to the $R = 50$ column in the upper panel of Table 7.1. This $+6.97$ change reflects the 15.4 percent probability that the bond defaults by the end of the two-year horizon ($0.154 = 1 - 0.846$ where, from the Table, $0.846 = 0.92^2$) multiplied by the discounted value (using the two-year risk-free discount factor $= 0.907$) of the assumed recovery value ($R = 50$). Thus, aside from rounding error, $+6.97 = (0.154)(0.907)(50)$. The bond values for all of the other positive recovery value cases (in either the upper or lower panels) versus an $R = 0$ benchmark can be computed in a similar fashion.

Table 7.1 reveals that yield levels and yield curve shapes are complex functions of payment probability and recovery value. The complexity reflects bond value impacts that depend on the assumed payment rate and the present value of the assumed recovery value, as well as on the differing sensitivities of the conventional value/yield translation for long versus short maturity bonds. For example, under the $R = 50$ assumption, the emerging market issuer's yield curve could be either upward or downward sloping depending upon whether the payment probability is high or low. Furthermore, the same bond value can result from markedly different parameter pairings. The value of the eight-year bond is essentially the same under "normal" conditions ($p = 0.92$) with 0 percent recovery as it would be under "crisis" conditions ($p = 0.60$) with 100 percent recovery (Brady-type collateralization). These examples show that bond price level and yield curve shape do not necessarily reveal market expectations regarding issuer default probability. A second key variable – default recovery value – must be simultaneously considered. In this light, emerging market bond yield spreads are quite complex signals of market sentiment.

Blended Yields and Blended Spreads

Positive recovery value complicates the interpretation of yield spreads as direct indicators of default prospects. One more example based upon the 10 percent coupon rate, two-year bond may help clarify the problem and suggest the appropriate adjustment. If recovery value is $50 per $100 of par value ($R = 50$), a bondholder is assured of at least $50 at maturity, even if default occurs in period one. Given an assumed per period payment probability value of 0.92, the market should be willing to pay $100.18 for this bond, as in Equation 20′ and Table 7.1. At this value, the bond's yield-to-maturity is 9.90 percent and the quoted yield spread is 466 basis points: $(1.0990/1.05) - 1 = 0.0466$. However, this 9.90 percent yield-to-maturity and this quoted spread of 466 basis points should be treated as a "blended yield" and a "blended spread," respectively. The blended nature of these yield and spread concepts becomes apparent when the valuation framework is recast in discounted cash flow terms. In particular, the yield and spread logic that flows from the risk-neutral valuation result is best seen after rewriting Equation 20 in the following forms:

$$V = \frac{pC}{(1+y)} + \frac{p^2(C+100)}{(1+y)^2} + \frac{[(1-p) + p(1-p)]R}{(1+y)^2}, \qquad (21)$$

and

$$V = \frac{pC}{(1+y)} + \frac{p^2(C+100-R)}{(1+y)^2} + \frac{R}{(1+y)^2}. \tag{22}$$

Note that while the first two terms of Equation 22 contain p – the key parameter of the payment probability distribution – the third term does not. Given this insight, it is useful to reexpress Equation 22 as a set of cash flows discounted by two different rates:

$$V = \frac{C}{(1+Y^R)} + \frac{(C+100-R)}{(1+Y^R)^2} + \frac{R}{(1+y)^2}. \tag{23}$$

An amount equal to the recovery value R should be discounted at the riskless rate, y. However, the coupons and the amount of the promised principal payment that exceeds the recovery value should be discounted at the spread-adjusted rate:

$$(1+Y^R) = (1+y)(1+s^R), \tag{24}$$

where

$$s^R = \frac{1-p}{p}. \tag{25}$$

In the example, the bond's *true* sovereign yield (Y^R) and sovereign spread (S^R) equal

$$s^R = \frac{1-p}{p} = \frac{0.08}{0.92} = 0.0870 \ (= 8.70\%), \tag{26}$$

and

$$Y^R = (1+y)(1+s^R) - 1 = (1.05)(1.0870) - 1 = 0.1413 \ (= 14.13\%). \tag{27}$$

The bond's true sovereign yield ($Y^R = 14.13$ percent) – as *used* by the market to discount the risky component of cash flow – is dramatically higher than the blended yield ($Y = 9.90$ percent) – as *quoted* by the market for daily business. Likewise, the bond's true sovereign spread (870 basis points) – as *used* by the market – is dramatically higher than the blended spread (466 basis points) that might be *quoted* by market participants. The sovereign spread, s^R, can be thought of as a special "stripped-of-recovery-value" spread that is comparable in nature to the stripped-of-collateral spread for a Brady bond.

The Positive Eurobond versus Brady Bond Spread Gap: No Anomaly

One interpretation in the literature for the substantial spread gap between Brady bonds and eurobonds has been a sustained valuation anomaly. The analysis above shows that this is not the case at all. Indeed, the stripped sovereign spread on an emerging market Brady bond *must* be higher than the quoted spread on the same issuer's eurobond in an efficiently priced market if a positive eurobond default recovery value is assumed. The quoted spread on a eurobond is based upon a "blended" yield derived as a single internal rate of return computed for a mix of a default risk-free cash flow (the assumed recovery value) and other risky cash flows (coupons and principal in excess of the assumed recovery value). In the framework used above, the "blend" in the quoted eurobond spread occurs because the market uses the true sovereign yield to discount the risky cash flows and the risk-free yield to discount the bond's assumed recovery value. A more accurate study of potential eurobond and Brady bond yield spread misalignment would compare "stripped-of-recovery-value" eurobond yield spreads with stripped sovereign spreads on Brady issues.

Risk-Aversion and Adjusted Risk-Neutral Payment Probabilities

If investors are risk-neutral, the risk-free rates used in the examples above are appropriate for expected bond cash flow discounting. However, most market observers would maintain that investors in emerging markets are risk-averse. In fact, many hold that shifts in market risk aversion were key factors in explaining observed emerging market price volatility and contagion effects. One way to handle risk aversion in discounted expected cash flow valuation is to substitute risk-adjusted discount rates for the risk-free rates used above. This substitution would require specifying a particular form of the appropriate risk premium.

An alternative approach would retain the use of risk-free rates and finesse the discounting problem posed by risk-averse investors by reinterpreting the nature of the payment probability distribution. In particular, this approach reinterprets the per period payment probability p used above as reflecting an *adjusted* risk-neutral probability distribution, as in Harrison and Kreps (1979). This adjusted distribution is sometimes referred to as the *equivalent Martingale measure*.[25] Alternatively stated, the adjusted distribution is that distribution that would result in the same market value (V) as the objective distribution in a risk-neutral world.

For current purposes, consider two alternative representations of the two-period bond. Let p now denote the adjusted risk-neutral payment probability. When paired with the risk-free discount rate, y, to value a one-period bond subject to default, the relevant discounted expected cash flow value is

$$V = \frac{p(C + 100)}{1 + y} + \frac{(1 - p)R}{1 + y}. \tag{32}$$

Let the *objective* (true) payment probability equal q and let the appropriate *risk-adjusted* discount rate equal λ. The corresponding discounted expected cash flow valuation equation would be

$$V = \frac{q(C + 100)}{1 + \lambda} + \frac{(1 - q)R}{1 + \lambda}. \tag{33}$$

Finally, denote the appropriate risk premium of the required expected return on the emerging market bond relative to the risk-free bond as $\pi = [(1 + \lambda)/(1 + y)] - 1$. Then, clearly, the adjusted risk-neutral payment probability p is a derived "mongrel"

---

[25] See Sundaram (1997) for an introduction to equivalent Martingale measures and risk-neutral pricing.

parameter determined by both the objective payment probability and the appropriate risk premium:

$$p = q/(1 + \pi). \tag{34}$$

If risk premiums do exist (that is, if $\pi > 0$), the implied risk-neutral payment probabilities estimated from observed bond price data would be smaller than the true payment probabilities. Thus any default probabilities estimated from market data will need to be interpreted with care. In particular, evidence of contagion based upon correlations of implied payment probabilities (p) between two emerging markets might reflect common movements in risk premiums (π) rather than objective payment probabilities (q).[26] However, casting the model in terms of adjusted risk-neutral probabilities permits simple, unbiased, preference-free estimation of the key recovery value parameter, even in a risk-averse world.

EMERGING MARKET BOND VALUATION: THE CASE OF ARGENTINA

This section applies an expected discounted cash flow model to value Republic of Argentina eurobonds during the midst of the market collapse before Argentina's default in December 2001. The analysis works backward from available market Argentine eurobond bond prices to extract measures of the market's implied recovery value and payment probabilities. Implementation requires decisions about both the appropriate recovery value assumption and the exact functional form for payment probabilities at alternative horizons.

Implied Recovery Values

The examples in the previous section treated the investor's expected recovery value as a known quantity. But how would a policymaker or any other market observer know what recovery value investors are using to value any particular issuer's bonds? As noted above, previously estimated average realized recovery rates on U.S. corporate debt defaults range between 40 and 50 percent of face value. However, unlike the U.S. domestic corporate debt markets, no rich histories of default experience exist for the sovereign foreign currency bond markets. Merrick (2001) addressed this issue in the context of both Russian Federation and Republic of Argentina Eurobond prices during the Russian GKO default crisis of 1998. That framework valued the available cross-section of bonds as a function of risk-free discount factors derived from the term structure of Treasury bond yields, a parsimonious function describing the term structure of bond cash flow payment probabilities, and the implied recovery value. In particular, the market's implied recovery value was *jointly* estimated on a daily basis, along with the parameters of the payment probability distribution. For the August to December 1998 period, estimated recovery values derived from Argentina's Eurobond prices were quite close to a standard assumption of 50 percent applied to U.S. corporate debt.

---

[26] See www.worldbank.org/contagion for links to papers and other resources related to the emerging markets contagion literature.

Joint Examination of Payment Distribution and Recovery Value Parameters

The discounted expected cash flow model has four components. The first is the bond's promised cash flow stream, consisting of coupons and principal value. Denote the date t coupon payment by C_t and the maturity date N principal repayment by F_N. The second component is an assumed recovery value, R, paid to the bondholder immediately upon the event of default.[27] In the event of default, this immediate substituting payment of R replaces any remaining cash flows (that is, the remaining coupons and principal) from the initially promised stream. This recovery value represents the default date present value of the bond's payment rescheduling. The third component is the set of discount factors. Let f_t denote the present value discount factor for a time t cash flow as generated from the risk-free rate of interest for a cash flow with horizon t. The discount factor for each futures horizon date will be interpolated from observed prices of U.S. Treasury zero-coupon bonds (that is, Treasury coupon strips). These risk-free present value discount factors can also be represented as a function of $y_{0,t}$, the set of initial date 0 risk-free zero-coupon bond yields applicable to any date t discounting horizon:

$$f_t = 1/(1 + y_{0,t})^t. \tag{35}$$

The final valuation component is the payments probability distribution.[28] To handle the possibility that per period payment probabilities (and therefore default rates) are not constant, the notation of the previous section must be altered. Let d_t denote the probability of *default* during the specific date $(t-1)$ to date t period. Next, denote the probability of a timely payment of the promised date t cash flow as P_t. Since each coupon payment has a "cross-default" provision with every subsequent coupon, P_t represents the *joint* probability of no default occurring from issue date through date t. Thus, P_t can be expressed as

$$P_t = 1 - \sum_{j=1}^{t} d_j. \tag{36}$$

Given these payment probabilities, d_t can also be written as the *difference* in the joint probabilities of no default occurring through dates $(t-1)$ and t:[29]

$$d_t = (P_{t-1} - P_t). \tag{37}$$

Hence, the probability of receiving the recovery value R on any particular date t equals d_t, the probability of default during the specific date $(t-1)$ to date t period, and the cash flow effect of recovery value spreads out across the event tree.

[27] This specific form for R differs from that utilized in the previous section. Here, regardless of when default occurs, the investor immediately recovers a cash flow of R. In the previous section, the recovery payment was delayed until bond maturity. The common immediate payment assumption of the current section makes more sense in a context examining multiple bonds of different maturities but equal seniority from the same issuer.

[28] As discussed in the previous section, when discounting at risk-free interest rates, this distribution may be interpreted either as the *objective* distribution if investors are risk-neutral or as an *adjusted risk-neutral* distribution if investors are truly risk-averse.

[29] By construction, $P_{t-1} \geq P_t$.

Equation 38 expresses the bond's current value, V_0, as the expected discounted cash flow relation:

$$V_0 = \sum_{t=1}^{N} P_t f_t C_t + P_N f_N F_N + \sum_{t=1}^{N} d_t f_t R. \tag{38}$$

Equation 38 views the bond's current value as a probability-weighted sum of three components: coupon flows, principal repayment and recovery value.[30] Finally, cross-default provisions with *other* coupon-paying bonds may also exist. In this case, recovery value realization on a particular bond may occur even on a date when none of its own coupon payments is scheduled. Careful treatment of recovery value as a separate flow component involves analyzing the specific institutional cross-default framework.

The Term Structure of Per Period Payment and Default Rates

Some valuation models for U.S. corporate bonds (such as Fons 1987) and emerging market Brady bonds such as Bhanot 1998) apply the assumption of constant per period payment and default rates over the promised cash flow life of the specific issues studied. However, there are good reasons to question such an assumption. Both Eichengreen and Mody (1998) and Kamin and von Kleist (1999) report significant maturity effects on offering yield spreads (upward sloping spread curves) for their samples of emerging market issues. Since yield spreads are determined at least in part by default rates, this evidence suggests that per period default rates themselves may exhibit a positively sloped structure. That is, perceived default probabilities for deferred periods may be higher than those for near-term periods. On the other hand, in the midst of a crisis, default rates for deferred periods – which apply to per period default probabilities in future periods conditional on the sovereign's ability to successfully avoid an earlier default – might be *lower* than near-term default rates.

It is useful to apply well-known bond market term structure formulations to the term structure of default rates. Denote the date 0 continuously compounded *term default probability rate* for a date t cash payment as δ_t. Define the probability of timely payment of a future date t cash flow following from this term rate as:[31]

$$P_t = \exp(-\delta_t t) \tag{39}$$

---

[30] As in Jonkhart (1979); Fons (1987); Hurley and Johnson (1996); Leland and Toft (1996); and Merrick (2001). Again, the specific form of the valuation equation need not correspond to Equation 37. For example, Hurley and Johnson (1996) assume that bond recovery in a default takes a special form: a known fraction of what the bond's value would be if no default had occurred. However, such a form would be hard to motivate in the current application. The Republic of Argentina's eurobonds contain cross-default provisions and maintain equal standing in default regardless of coupon or remaining term to maturity.

[31] Thus, suppose $t = 3$ and $\delta_3 = 0.10$. Then $P_t = \exp(-\delta_t t) = \exp(-[0.10][0.3]) = 0.741$. The probability that a default would have occurred by the end of period 3 = $1 - P_3 = 1 - 0.741 = 0.259 = d_1 + d_2 + d_3$.

For any t-period horizon, assume that the term default rate curve takes the following functional form:[32]

$$\delta_t = \alpha_0 + \alpha_1[1 - \exp(-t)]/t. \tag{40}$$

In Equation 40, α_0 is a parameter that reflects the "long-run" component of the default rate curve. The parameter α_1 reflects a corresponding "short-run" component. A "flat" default rate term structure ($\alpha_1 = 0$; $\delta_t = \alpha_0$) would imply identical forward default rates for all periods. A positive value for α_1, the short-run component, might be expected in the midst of a crisis. In that case, Equation 40 would generate an inverted term structure of default rates. The associated term structure of forward default rates would also be inverted, but would show a gradual decay back to its long-run level. Equations 39 and 40 close the model.

Estimation of Model Parameters

In sum, the framework incorporates three unknown parameters: R, α_0, and α_1. The risk-free discount factors and the bond's notional cash flows are known. Since $d_t = (P_{t-1} - P_t)$, Equation 41 embodies an estimable form of the bond valuation expression:

$$\begin{aligned}
V_0 = \sum_{t=1}^{N}\{-\alpha_0 t - \alpha_1[1 - \exp(-t)]\} f_t C_t \\
+ \exp\{-\alpha_0 N - \alpha_1[1 - \exp(-N)]\} f_N F_N \\
+ \sum_{t=1}^{N}(\exp[-\alpha_0(t-1) - \alpha_1\{1 - \exp[-(t-1)]\}] \\
- \exp\{-\alpha_0 t - \alpha_1[1 - \exp(-t)]\}) f_t R.
\end{aligned} \tag{41}$$

Estimates of the three implied model parameters for *any day* (date 0) can be derived by choosing the values for R, α_0, and α_1 that minimize the sum of squared residuals for the daily crosssection of individual bond values, while simultaneously constraining the average cross-sectional bond pricing residual to equal zero. For each issue in the cross-section, the residual is constructed as the difference between the bond's observed market value and the value generated by Equation 41 at the selected R, α_0, and α_1 parameter values.[33]

---

[32] Equation 40 is a special case of the functional form proposed by Nelson and Siegel (1987) for the term structure of default-free discount rates. Here, for any t-period horizon, Nelson and Siegel's expanded model would introduce two additional parameters, α_2 and α_3, and take the form:

$$\delta_t = \alpha_0 + (\alpha_1 + \alpha_2)[1 - \exp(-\alpha_3 t)]/(\alpha_3 t) - \alpha_2[\exp(-\alpha_3 t)].$$

Equation 37 is the special case of Nelson and Siegel's model where $\alpha_2 = 0$ and $\alpha_3 = 1$. This restricted version is used because the more general form fits the data "too well." In its attempt to explain what most likely are bond-specific value factors, the general form's parameters produce an oscillating forward default rate curve that takes on negative values. See Duffie, Pedersen, and Singleton (2003) for an example of the impact of bond-specific factors in the Russian debt market.

[33] The GRG2 (generalized reduced gradient) algorithm for nonlinear optimization subject to nonlinear constraints is used. This algorithm is generally available through the Solver function within Microsoft's Excel software package.

Figure 7.3. Price History of Argentina '27s (9.75%, 9/19/2027). *Source*: Bloomberg.

Application to Argentine Eurobond Pricing: October 3, 2001

Figure 7.3 reveals the depth of the Argentine bond market's sell-off in the second half of 2001 through a plot of the weekly price history (taken from Bloomberg) of the Republic of Argentina eurobond 9.75 percent 9/19/2027 (Argentina '27s). The Argentina '27s began the year priced about $85 per $100 of par value. However, the price deteriorated throughout the year as Argentina's prolonged economic recession continued unabated, violent demonstrations took place in the streets of Buenos Aires and other locales, and the country's political situation grew increasingly unstable. At year-end, Argentina defaulted on $141 billion of its public debt. On December 28, the last plotted point in Figure 7.3, the Argentina '27s were marked at $27.50 per $100 of par value.

The recovery value-enhanced model developed above can be applied and estimated to value the Argentine U.S. dollar eurobond market on any chosen day. This exercise studies the market at the close of trading on October 3, 2001, when the Argentina '27s were marked at $50.50 per $100 of par value. This particular day occurs during the bond market's price collapse before the Argentine government's default.

Table 7.2 lists the Argentine U.S. dollar eurobond market's 15 outstanding issues marked as of the close of trading on October 3, 2001.[34] Twelve of the fifteen issues are standard semiannual-pay, level coupon issues maturing at par. Three bonds – those issued in June 2001 as part of a voluntary debt exchange restructuring plan – have

---

[34] These market closes on these bonds were obtained from a large investment bank. Part of the expansion in the number of outstanding issues in the Argentine eurobond market (from only five in 1998) can be traced to a restructuring program that retired existing Brady bond debt in exchange for new eurobond issues. See the discussion at the end of the second section above, as well as IMF (1997).

Table 7.2. *Republic of Argentina U.S. dollar eurobonds*

Price date: October 3, 2001					Settlement date: October 9, 2001	
Coupon rate	Maturity date	Market price	Accrued interest	Total value	Yield	Sovereign spread
8.375	12/20/2003	69.50	2.54	72.04	27.80%	2,491
11.000	12/4/2005	64.50	3.82	68.32	25.26%	2,178
11.000	10/9/2006	62.50	0.00	62.50	24.38%	2,071
7.000^{a,c}	12/19/2008	55.63	2.14	57.76	24.96%	2,118
11.750	4/7/2009	55.50	0.07	55.57	25.26%	2,138
11.375	3/15/2010	52.75	0.76	53.51	25.09%	2,112
12.375	2/21/2012	55.25	1.65	56.90	24.37%	2,030
11.750	6/15/2015	54.00	3.72	57.72	22.79%	1,865
11.375	1/30/2017	54.00	2.18	56.18	21.85%	1,767
12.250^{b,c}	6/19/2018	49,00	1.83	50.83	19.57%	1,500
12.125	2/25/2019	53.50	1.48	54.98	23.10%	1,894
12.000	2/1/2020	53.50	2.27	55.77	22.79%	1,862
9.750	9/19/2027	50.50	0.54	51.04	19.45%	1,513
10.250	7/21/2030	50.50	2.22	52.72	20.35%	1,607
12.000^{b}	6/19/2031	50.75	1.86	52.61	18.17%	1,346

Note: ^{a} Coupon steps up to 15.5 percent on 6/19/2004.
^{b} Interest capitalizes until 12/19/2006.
^{c} Sinking fund provisions.
Source: Major Wall Street investment bank and author's calculations.

a more complex structure. The 7 percent 12/19/2008 (Argentina '08s) has a coupon rate of 7 percent until 2004, when the coupon rate "steps up" to 15.5 percent. This issue also has a sinking fund structure. Both the 12.25 percent 6/19/2018 (Argentina '18s) and 12 percent 6/19/2031 (Argentina '31s) capitalize interest payments until December 2006. The Argentina '18s also employ a sinking fund structure.[35]

To implement the model, the individual issue cash flow streams were generated and valuation equations of the form of Equation 41 were developed for each bond. Closing quotes from the U.S. Treasury coupon strips market for October 3 were interpolated to generate the risk-free U.S. dollar discount factors (taken from Lehman Brothers). Estimates of the three parameters – R, α_0, and α_1 – for this day's observations were selected to minimize the standard deviation of the zero-mean residuals (market value less model value) for the crosssection of 15 bonds. Table 7.2 presents the empirical results. These include estimates of the model's three parameters, as well as the fitted total value (price plus accrued interest) for each issue. The "Difference" column is the residual value for each bond constructed as the difference between the market and fitted values for each bond in this fifteen-issue crosssection.[36]

[35] In developing the individual issue cash flow stream, the two bonds with sinking fund provisions were assumed to sink at par.

[36] As in Merrick (2001) and Duffie, Pederson, and Singleton (2003), valuation models for emerging market debt tend to result in large residuals for individual issues. The interpretation of issue-specific value effects (perhaps due to repo market effects or market segmentation) is not pursued here.

Table 7.3. *Republic of Argentina eurobonds: Market versus model values*

Price date: October 3, 2001			Settlement date: October 9, 2001	
Coupon rate	Maturity date	Market value	Model value	Difference
8.375	12/20/2003	72.04	68.82	3.22
11.000	12/4/2005	68.32	65.19	3.13
11.000	10/9/2006	62.50	59.55	2.95
7.000	12/19/2008	57.76	58.37	−0.61
11.750	4/7/2009	55.57	57.65	−2.09
11.375	3/15/2010	53.51	56.89	−3.38
12.375	2/21/2012	56.90	58.87	−1.97
11.750	6/15/2015	57.72	59.11	−1.39
11.375	1/30/2017	56.18	56.75	−0.57
12.250	6/19/2018	50.83	48.09	2.74
12.125	2/25/2019	54.98	57.54	−2.56
12.000	2/1/2020	55.77	57.99	−2.22
9.750	9/19/2027	51.04	51.81	−0.77
10.250	7/21/2030	52.72	54.37	−1.65
12.000	6/19/2031	52.61	47.45	5.17
		Average difference:		0.00
		Standard deviation:		2.67
Model parameter estimates:				
R	34.33	Implied recovery ratio		
α_0	0.3108	Long-run forward rate		
α_1	0.3097	Short-run forward rate deviation		

Source: Author's calculations.

The implied recovery value is $34.3 per $100 of par value. This day's estimate is lower than the $50 per $100 reported by Merrick (2001), as the sample average implied recovery value for this market over the August 1998 to December 1998 period. The estimates of the two parameters of the default rate curve imply an instantaneous short rate of $\alpha_0 + \alpha_1 = 0.3108 + 0.3097 = 0.6205$ (62 percent) that decays to its estimated long-run forward rate level of .3108 (31 percent). These estimated parameters generate the entire payment probability schedule that supports the model bond values of Table 7.3.

The estimated term default rate curve is the empirical version of Equation 40 and is presented below as Equation 42.

$$\delta_t = 0.3108 + 0.3097\,[1 - \exp(-t)]/t. \tag{42}$$

This equation generates the market's implicit term default rate used to calculate expected payment probabilities for the cash flows (via Equation 39) due at alternative horizon dates. For example, a cash flow due in one year would have an estimated payment probability of 60 percent, calculated by applying a term default rate of 50.7 percent for the $t = 1$ year term:

$$\delta_1 = 0.3108 + 0.3097\,[1 - \exp(-1)]/1 = 0.507, \tag{43}$$

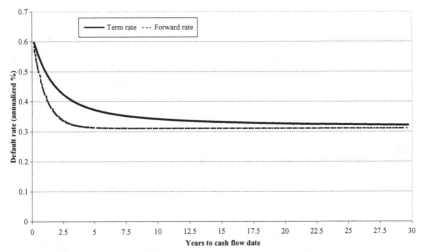

Figure 7.4. Implied Term and Forward Default Rates on Argentine Eurobond Cash Flows: Estimated from Recovery Value-Enhanced Model Price Date: October 3, 2001. *Source*: Author's calculations.

and

$$P_1 = \exp(-\delta_1 1) = \exp[(-.507)(1)] = 0.603. \tag{44}$$

Alternatively, a cash flow due in two years would have an estimated payment probability of 41%, calculated by applying a term default rate of 44.5% for the $t = 2$ year term:

$$\delta_2 = 0.3108 + 0.3097[1 - \exp(-2)]/2 = 0.445, \tag{45}$$

and

$$P_2 = \exp(-\delta_2 2) = \exp[(-0.445)(2)] = 0.411. \tag{46}$$

Note that the default rate for the two-year horizon is lower than that for the one-year horizon. Figure 7.4 plots the entire estimated term default rate curve. Initially, the term default rate curve slopes downward quite steeply; then it flattens out. Indeed, the initial instantaneous ($t = 0$) default rate is about double its long-run value.

Standard term structure analysis differentiates between *term* rates and *forward* rates. Forward rates are the elements of the specific path of short-term rates that, if rolled over, would just match the return of a single zero-coupon investment out to longer-dated horizons. Here, the one-year *forward* default rate priced on October 3, 2001 to apply to the one-year period from October 3, 2002 to October 3, 2003 is 38.3 percent. This result can be verified by showing the product of the two one-period discount factors (from δ_1, the initial one-year rate, and $\delta_{1,1}$, the one-year *forward*

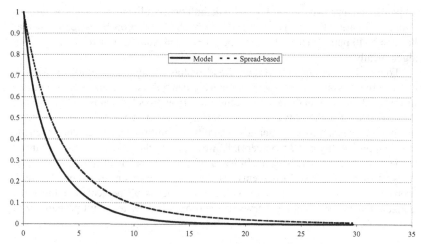

Figure 7.5. Argentine Eurobond Implied Cash Flow Payment Probabilities: Recovery Value-Enhanced Model versus Yield Spread-Based Approach Price date: 3, 2001. *Source*: Author's calculations.

rate beginning one year from now) equals the initial two-year discount factor:

$$\exp(-\delta_1 1)\exp(-\delta_{1,1}1) = P_2 = \exp(-\delta_2 2)$$
$$\exp[(-0.507)(1)]\exp[(-\mathbf{0.383})(1)] = 0.411 = \exp[(-0.445)(2)].$$

The one-year-ahead, one-year forward rate appears in bold and is easily solved for as the calculated rate that equates the returns of the "rollover" and "term investment" strategies.[37] Similar break-even rate calculations would produce the entire path of one-year forward default rates from the initial term default rates.[38]

The forward default rate of 38.3 percent calculated above applies to the one-year period beginning one year in the future. It is significantly lower than the initial one-year default rate of 50.7 percent. Within a crisis environment, such an inverted default rate structure makes perfect sense. The market imputes a lower future default rate for this forward period since actually surviving to this specific time interval is conditional on Argentina's ability to successfully avoid an earlier default. Escaping default through to October 3, 2002 (the start of the forward period) may mean some "good news" improving future payment prospects appeared along the way. Figure 7.4 plots the entire curve of sequential one-year forward default rates generated by the parameter estimates for this day's closing prices.

Figure 7.5 plots the estimated payment probability curve as a function of the cash flow payment date. For example, as of October 3, market prices imply a

---

[37] $\delta_{1,1} = -\ln[\exp(-\delta_2 2)/\exp(-\delta_1 1)] = -\ln[\exp(-[0.445][2])/\exp(-[0.507][1])] = .383.$

[38] For example, compare the discount factors on two- and three-year horizons to compute the one-year forward default rate beginning in two years:

$$\delta_{2,3} = -\ln[\exp(-\delta_3 3)/\exp(-\delta_2 2)]$$
$$= -\ln[\exp(-[0.409][3])/\exp(-[0.445][2])]$$
$$= 0.337, \text{ or } 33.7 \text{ percent.}$$

24 percent chance that Argentina would default on its obligations within six months (from the figure: $P[t = 0.5] = 0.76$). The implied default probability for a one-year horizon is 40 percent (from Figure 7.5: $P[t = 1] = 0.60$), as previously solved for algebraically).

For comparative purposes, Figure 7.5 also plots a *companion* default probability curve derived assuming zero-percent recovery using the sovereign spreads reported in Table 7.2.[39] Note that this zero-percent recovery approach severely underestimates the market's true probability of default. For instance, at the 2.5-year horizon, the zero-percent recovery approach generates a default probability of 42.5 percent (given the payment probability of 57.5 percent). However, using the recovery value-enhanced model, the implied default probability is 65 percent (payment probability at the 2.5-year horizon is just 35 percent). At the 10-year horizon, the implied default probability for the recovery value-enhanced model is 97 percent. For the same horizon, the zero-percent recovery value approach implies a default probability of just 85.2 percent.

SUMMARY

The explosive growth in the issuance of sovereign emerging market foreign currency debt issuance in the 1990s has generated substantial interest in the underpinnings of security valuation in these markets. Academic research indicates that shifts in standard macroeconomic variables – the "fundamentals" – explain very little of the short-run variation in emerging market yield spreads. Shifts in "market sentiment" account for a disproportionate share of emerging market yield spread movements. Thus, policymakers should focus more attention on the information that bond yield spreads contain about issuer default prospects.

Yield spreads on risky emerging market debt produce important signals regarding the market's consensus about the probability that an issuer will default. However, these market-based signals are sometimes confusing and need to be interpreted with care. This study highlights the importance of assumptions regarding default-state recovery value on attempts to interpret yield spreads as signals of the probability of issuer default. One byproduct of the analysis is an explanation of why stripped sovereign spreads from Brady issues should be larger than the calculated sovereign spreads from the same issuer's eurobonds (even though both spreads reflect identical default probabilities). The resolution of the apparent puzzle requires the definition of a special "stripped-of-recovery-value" spread.

The importance of default-state recovery value assumptions is stressed in the application of a discounted expected cash flow model to a cross-section of 15 outstanding U.S. dollar-denominated Republic of Argentina eurobond bonds in the midst of that country's 2001 debt market crisis. Estimates of the market's implied recovery value, along with implicit term and forward default rate curves, are

---

[39] The spread-based curve of Figure 7.5 was generated as follows. First, the sovereign spreads were converted to an annualized basis. Second, a quadratic function in years to maturity was fit via regression. Third, the parameters of the regression were used to generate a smooth set of fitted sovereign spreads for the plotted cash flow horizons. Finally, for each horizon, a payment rate was reverse engineered from Equation 8 and utilized to calculate a payment probability.

presented. The results are contrasted with the default probability signals from a standard yield-based sovereign spread analysis. The latter tends to be overly optimistic with regard to implied issuer prospects of avoiding default.

Yield spreads are traditional measures used by policymakers to assess emerging bond market conditions. In general, the relationships among yield spreads, default probability, and recovery value are quite complex. Bond valuation frameworks such as those examined here offer insight into the nature of these relationships, but, alas, no cures for crises. Nevertheless, policymakers need to understand the lessons of such models in order to accurately read the messages of the market.

GLOSSARY

A *blended spread* is a yield spread based upon a blended yield.

A bond's *blended yield* is the internal rate of return on the bond using cash flows with different default exposures.

A *bond indenture* is the legal agreement explaining the specific obligations of the issuer and the rights of the bondholder.

Brady bonds were created in the 1990s as part of the debt restructurings of defaulted emerging market sovereign loans. A key component of the Brady bond structure was that each issue is partially collateralized by zero-coupon U.S. Treasury bonds. Typically, the zero-coupon Treasury collateral covers the entire principal amount and a rolling portion of the remaining coupon interest.

Collective action clauses enable a qualified majority of bondholders to modify key financial terms of the bond indenture and to impose such decisions on all other holders.

A *cross-default* provision in an indenture places the bond in default if its issuer defaults on another linked issue.

The *default rate* expresses the default probability on a bond's cash flow t-periods in the future as a per period percentage rate.

The *equivalent martingale measure* is the adjusted probability distribution that, in a risk-neutral world, results in the same discounted expected cash flow value as the true objective probability distribution.

A *forward default rate* expresses the default probability on a bond's cash flow during a specific future time interval as a per period percentage rate.

Implied recovery value is the parameter from a specific discounted cash flow model estimated for a daily cross-section of an issuer's bonds that measures the recovery value investors are using to price the market.

The bond's *initial offering spread* or *issuance spread* reflects its yield spread at the time of issue.

A bond with *interest capitalization* pays no coupons for a set number of initial periods but instead increases the bond's par value by an amount equivalent to the interest otherwise earned.

Recovery value is the percentage of bond face value that an investor recoups after an issuer's default. A sovereign debt default event is couched under a forced "rescheduling" agreement that exchanges the originally promised cash flow stream for new, more lenient terms. From the investor's perspective, the recovery value is the ratio of the involuntarily exchanged new security's market value relative to the face value of the original debt.

Risk-neutral valuation implies that the term structure of risk-free interest rates was used to discount the expected value of a bond's future cash flows.

The bond's *secondary market spread* reflects its yield spread as it trades in the market any time after being issued.

A *sinking fund agreement* is the bond indenture mandates that the issuer retire the debt issue in scheduled stages prior to the actual maturity date.

The coupon rate on a *step-up bond* is scheduled to increase from an initial ("low") rate to a new higher level after a set number of periods.

The *stripped-of-recovery-value* spread is the yield spread on the default-exposed component of the issue's cash flow stream (computed after subtracting out the present value of the assumed recovery value).

A Brady bond's *stripped sovereign spread* is the yield spread on the uncollateralized component of the issue's cash flow stream (computed after subtracting out the value of the collateralized payments).

A *yield spread* measures the difference in quoted yields on two bonds. The spread can be used in either arithmetic form, $s = Y - y$, or multiplicative form, $1 + s = (1 + Y)/(1 + y)$.

A bond's *yield-to-maturity* is the investor's internal rate of return computed from the bond's current market value using its promised future cash flows.

REFERENCES

Altman, Edward I., and Allan C. Eberhart. 1994. "Do Seniority Provisions Protect Bondholders' Investments?" *Journal of Portfolio Management* 20(4):67–75.

Altman, Edward I., Diane Cooke, and Vellore Kishore. 1999. *Defaults and Returns on High Yield Bonds: Analysis through 1998 and Default Outlook for 1999–2001*. New York: New York University Salomon Center.

Becker, Torbjrn, Anthony Richards, and Yungyong Thaicharoen. 2001. "Bond Restructuring and Moral Hazard: Are Collective Action Clauses Costly?" IMF Working Paper 01/92. International Monetary Fund, Washington, DC.

Bhanot, Karan. 1998. "Recovery and Implied Default in Brady Bonds." *Journal of Fixed Income* 8(1):47–51.

Claessens, Stijn, and George Pennachi , 1996. "Estimating the Likelihood of Mexican Default from the Market Prices of Brady Bonds." *Journal of Financial and Quantitative Analysis* 31(1):109–26.

Duffie, Darrell, Lasse Pedersen, and Kenneth Singleton. 2003. "Modeling Sovereign Yield Spreads: A Case Study of Russian Debt." *Journal of Finance* 58(1):119–59.

Durbin, Erik and David Ng. 1999. "Uncovering Country Risk in Emerging Market Bond Prices." International Finance Discussion Paper 1999–639. Federal Reserve Board, Washington, DC.

Eichengreen, Barry, and Ashoka Mody. 1998. "What Explains Changing Spreads on Emerging Market Debt?" NBER Working Paper 6408. National Bureau of Economic Research, Cambridge, MA.

———. 2000. "Would Collective Action Clauses Raise Borrowing Costs? An Update and Additional Results." Research Paper C00-114. Center for International and Development Economics. University of California, Berkeley, CA.

Fons, Jerome. 1987. "The Default Premium and Corporate Bond Experience." *Journal of Finance* 42(1):81–97.

Harrison, J. Michael and David Kreps. 1979. "Martingales and Arbitrage in Multiperiod Securities Markets." *Journal of Economic Theory* 20(3):381–408.

Hurley, W. J., and Louis D. Johnson. 1996. "On the Pricing of Bond Default Risk." *Journal of Portfolio Management* 22(2)1:66–70.

IMF (International Monetary Fund). 1997. "International Capital Markets: Developments, Prospects, and Key Policy Issues." Washington, DC.

———. 2002a. "Collective Action Clauses in Sovereign Bond Contracts – Encouraging Greater Use." Washington, DC.

———. 2002b. "The Incredible Shrinking Brady Market." International Financial Research Note No. 19. Economic Policy and Prospects Group, Washington, DC.

Jonkhart, Marius. 1979. "On the Term Structure of Interest Rates and the Risk of Default: An Analytical Approach." *Journal of Banking and Finance* 3(3):253–62.

Kamin, Steven, and Karsten von Kleist. 1999. "The Evolution and Determinants of Emerging Market Credit Spreads in the 1990s." International Finance Discussion Paper 1999-653. Federal Reserve Board, Washington, DC.

Kharas, Homi, Brian Pinto, and Sergei Ulatov. 2001. "An Analysis of Russia's 1998 Meltdown: Fundamentals and Market Signals." *Brooking's Papers on Economic Activity* 1:1–50.

Leland, Hayne, and Klaus B. Toft. 1996. "Optimal Capital Structure, Endogenous Bankruptcy, and the Term Structure of Credit Spreads." *Journal of Finance* 51(3):987–1019.

Mauro, Paolo, Nathan Sussman, and Yishay Yafeh. 2002. "Emerging Market Spreads: Then and Now." *Quarterly Journal of Economics* 117(2):695–733.

Merrick, John. 2001. "Crisis Dynamics of Implied Default Recovery Rates: Evidence from Russia and Argentina." *Journal of Banking and Finance* 25(10):1921–39.

Nelson, Charles, and Andrew Siegel. 1987. "Parsimonious Modeling of Yield Curves." *Journal of Business* 60(4):473–89.

Sundaram, Rangarajan. 1997. "Equivalent Martingale Measures and Risk-Neutral Pricing: An Expository Note." *Journal of Derivatives* 5(1):85–98.

Sy, Amadou. 2001. "Emerging Market Bond Spreads and Sovereign Credit Ratings: Reconciling Market Views with Economic Fundamentals." IMF Working Paper 01/165. International Monetary Fund, Washington, DC.

8. Managing Macroeconomic Crises: Policy Lessons[1]

Jeffrey Frankel and Shang-Jin Wei

ABSTRACT: This study is an attempt to review broadly what the last decade reveals about which policies for crisis prevention or crisis management seem to work and which do not. The empirical investigation tries out a variety of methodological approaches: reasoning from examples of prominent crises of the last eight years, formal probit analysis, a regression tree analysis, conventional regression analysis, and a look at the typical profile of financing during the sudden stop preceding a crisis.

We seek to draw greater attention to policy decisions that are made *during the phase when capital inflows come to a sudden stop*. Procrastination – the period of financing a balance of payments deficit rather than adjusting – had serious consequences in some cases. Crises are more frequent and more severe when short-term borrowing and dollar denominated external debt are high, and foreign direct investment (FDI) and reserves are low, in large part because balance sheets are then very sensitive to increases in exchange rates and short-term interest rates.

Our point is that these compositional measures are affected by decisions made by policymakers in the period immediately *after* capital inflows have begun to dry up but *before* the speculative attack itself has hit. If countries that are faced with a fall in inflows adjusted more promptly, rather than stalling for time by running down reserves or shifting to loans that are shorter-termed and dollar-denominated, they might be able to adjust on more attractive terms.

In the last 30 years, emerging markets have experienced at least two complete boom-bust cycles. The last cycle was marked by rapid capital inflows from 1990 to 1996, followed by severe crises for some countries and scarce capital for all from 1997 to 2003. This cycle bore similarities to the preceding 14 years as well: large loans to developing countries from 1975 to 1981, followed by the international debt crisis of 1982–89. Despite this volatility, many developing countries – although certainly not all – have ended this 30-year period with a far higher level of per capita income than they began it.

TAKING STOCK OF RECENT HISTORY

It is a good time to take stock of what has been learned from recent experience about the determinants of economic performance in emerging market countries. Which policies seem to work and which do not? Scholarly research has not neglected the

---

[1] The authors wish to thank Harvard University students Yannis Itokatlidis, Evren Pacalioglu, Li Zeng, and especially Dora Douglass for very capable research assistance; and Joshua Aizenman and Brian Pinto for useful comments. Shang-Jin Wei contributed to this chapter before joining the staff of the International Monetary Fund (IMF). The views expressed do not necessarily reflect the views or policies of the IMF.

315

topic. (Much of the literature is summarized in Appendix A.) Indeed, it is striking how much emphasis has shifted within the field of international macroeconomics to the problems of developing countries. But most of the contributions to the subject focus on one particular model, or one particular empirical effect. While there are overviews of the late-1990s crises, there are not many that attempt to summarize and integrate what we have learned from the numbers. It would help if the lists of variables that are run through statistical predictors of crisis probabilities were more visibly tied to the various competing theoretical models of crises.

One lesson we are learning from the trend of recent research is that policymakers making decisions in real time are far more constrained in their options than we have pretended to believe. (The international financial institutions are of course one step further removed from the policy levers than the national authorities.) Committing to a noninflationary monetary policy with 100 percent credibility may simply not be an option in light of past history and current political structures, no matter how sincere the governor of the central bank. This is the case even in a proreform political environment, such as prevailed in many countries in the late 1980s and early 1990s, and even if an institutional commitment such as a currency board does happen to be an option politically. These policies can always be reversed later, as history has shown. Similarly, a decision to remove capital controls may not put a developing country in the same category of financial integration as an OECD country, because of the risk that capital controls will be reimposed in the future. Moreover, measures of the composition of capital inflows, such as the maturity structure or the share of foreign-denominated debt, may not be amenable to policy choice in any given year. Accordingly, the fourth section of this chapter will take a longer-run perspective. The data set will be constructed from country-averages over the period 1990–2002. The analysis focuses on whether countries that *on average* had a particular degree of exchange rate flexibility or financial openness over this period tended on average to have a high or low level of volatility over the period.

The study begins with a whirlwind summary of academic literature, emphasizing what is recent and what seems capable of producing a bottom line. Included are the theoretical models of speculative attacks, which come in three "generations." In addition, each of the major policy questions that a country must decide has produced its own body of literature: the choice of exchange rate regime; the choice of capital account regime; openness to trade; institutional issues such as the quality of financial regulation; the composition of capital inflows; and the management of "sudden stop" events once they occur.[2] Included in the empirical section of the literature review are studies of leading indicators or crisis warning signals, which seek to include many factors, but which are not designed specifically to look at a variety of policy variables. Given all the theories and claims that have been offered, this study seeks to ask what combinations of policy variables seem empirically to be the most important, and which policy choices seem to work.

---

[2] "Sudden stop" refers to any abrupt cut-off of foreign willingness to hold liabilities of the domestic country. The phrase originated with Rudiger Dornbusch (see, for example, Dornbusch, Goldfain, and Valdes 1995), but was further popularized by Guillermo Calvo (see, for example, Calvo and Reinhart 2001).

Methodologies

The study tries out a number of different methodologies to discern determinants of economic performance. An impressionistic consideration of the most visible crises of the 1994–2002 period (Mexico, Thailand, Korea, Indonesia, Malaysia, Russia, Brazil, Turkey, and Argentina) concludes that there are more variables and hypotheses that need to be evaluated than there are major-crisis data points. More systematic analysis requires turning to a larger set of developing countries. The study approaches this larger data set several ways.

First, a simple probit analysis looks to see which of the variables that are suggested by the literature are capable of helping forecast the increased likelihood of a currency crisis on an annual basis. Second, the technique of regression tree analysis allows the data to choose freely which variables seem to matter the most. The technique has been used in macroeconomics much less often than factor analysis. But it has the advantage that it does not impose a linear functional form on the relationship. It is a flexible way to look for robust statistical relationships including threshold and interactive effects. This will be particularly important when we consider some of the hypotheses that are on the research frontier. This includes the proposition that capital account liberalization is not helpful for all countries, but is helpful for those that have strong macroeconomic fundamentals, or those that have strong structural fundamentals, or those that have attained a threshold stage of financial or economic development. The study uses regression analysis on a broad sample of countries from the 1970s to the present to offer direction as to which directions our econometric energies may be best spent.

Third, the study applies conventional regression analysis to a cross-section of countries to explain performance during the most recent decade (taken to be 1990–2002, which includes both the boom and bust phase). Fourth, the analysis focuses on the timing of currency crises – in particular, looking at a typical month-by-month profile for reserves preceding crises – again to see which crisis management policies seem to help and which do not.

We use as our main criteria of economic performance the probability of having currency crises and the total output lost during crises. The crisis prevention policies that we examine include: macroeconomic discipline (as measured by inflation, debt, budget deficits, money creation); institutional quality (corruption); financial integration (freedom from capital controls); currency regime (hard pegs, intermediate, and floating); openness (trade/GDP ratio); composition of inflows (maturity, share of FDI, currency mismatch); and reserves. The crisis management policies that we examine include: promptness versus delay of adjustment (measured either as the length of the lag after reserves peak, or the amount of reserve loss during this period); changes in composition (again, maturity and currency); and the mix of policies during the adjustment period (expenditure reduction versus devaluation).

Measures of Performance

Before going further, it is important to be explicit about the objective function. What is meant by "economic performance"? The econometrics undertaken for this study included, among the performance measures, growth in real income over the sample period, or real income per capita, as in the standard growth literature. However, the chapter places more emphasis on economic volatility than on the average growth rate. The second measure of performance examined was the standard deviation of real growth. The third measure was the number of financial crises, where each crisis is defined as a sharp drop in reserves or in the foreign exchange value of the currency (with the choice between the two presumed to be a matter of crisis management, rather than of the magnitude of the sudden stop of international investment). The fourth measure was the average severity of the crises that do occur, measured by the depth of the output loss. The fifth measure was the cumulation of output lost in financial crises. This is a direct aggregation of Measures 3 and 4, but is also intended to be correlated with Measures 1 and 2. While this fifth composite measure, called "crisis loss," has no precise economic interpretation – the study does not attempt to guess what potential output might be during the crisis, for example – it is intended to be a good single heuristic to capture overall economic performance in a study on volatility. This composite measure is the one that is emphasized in the reported results.

In firmly grounded theoretical models, the key variable to use in evaluating economic performance is not real income, but consumption. In theory, fluctuations in income (for example, as a result of exogenous fluctuations in the terms of trade) are not damaging for a small country integrated into world financial markets, because the country can sustain a smooth path for consumption by borrowing and lending. Indeed, this is one of several important arguments in favor of open capital markets. The study does not look at consumption data, for three reasons. First, during any given sample period, even one as long as several decades, consumption could grow unusually rapidly (as in Mexico in the early 1990s) or unusually slowly (as in Romania in the 1980s) because of expansionary or contractionary expenditure policies that will have to be reversed in the future. A country with a spending boom that ends the sample period with correspondingly high levels of debt and inflation should not count as high-performing. GDP is less vulnerable to this problem.

Second, there is by now a rough consensus that international financial markets do not in fact work in the perfect textbook fashion. International investors are not willing to lend more to countries undergoing recession to smooth consumption; if anything, the reverse is true. Third, as imperfect as are the data on GDP and the other variables in the analysis, the data on consumption are worse. For all three reasons, the study uses GDP to calculate the measures of economic performance: average growth, variability, and output lost to crises.

LITERATURE REVIEW AND HYPOTHESES TO BE TESTED

Theories of Speculative Attacks

Economists' theories of speculative attacks have organized themselves into three "generations." Each generation of models was launched by a seminal article or articles, of which a key feature was an attempt to answer the timing question, "What determines precisely *when* crises occur?" Each relied on the assumption that speculators think ahead and form their expectations rationally. Before considering the question of timing, it may be useful to explain the distinction among the three categories in terms of their attempts to answer the less technical and more inflammatory question of *why* they occur: Whose fault is the crisis? The first generation says domestic macroeconomic policy, the second generation says volatile financial markets, and the third generation says financial structure. In neutral language, the explanations are, respectively, excessive macroeconomic expansion, "multiple equilibria," and moral hazard. In finger-pointing language, the respective culprits are undisciplined domestic policymakers, crazy international investors, and "crony capitalists."[3]

FIRST GENERATION: OVERLY EXPANSIONARY MACROECONOMIC POLICY. The first generation of speculative attack models attributes balance of payments crises ultimately to overly expansionary macroeconomic policies. Most textbook analysis falls into this category. Budget deficits must be financed by borrowing or monetary expansion. Either way, the result is a current account deficit. If nothing is done to adjust in the face of what has become an overvalued currency, eventually the country will run out of reserves. Macroeconomic overexpansion and overvaluation were the standard diagnoses of balance of payments crises in developing countries before 1995, and were the basis of most adjustment programs administered by the International Monetary Fund. The international debt crisis of the 1980s is an important example.[4]

What determines the timing of the attack? This was the insight of the seminal article in the first generation approach by Paul Krugman (1979), the more intuitively accessible version of the model produced by Robert Flood and Peter Garber (1984), and the progenitor written by Stephen Salant and Dale Henderson (1978).

Consider a country in which the balance of payments deficit is a steady $1 billion a year, because of ongoing monetary and fiscal expansion. If the country has reserves of $5 billion, then apparently it can hold out for five years. Absent some change, it will run out of reserves at the end of that time and will be forced to devalue or depreciate, by enough to eliminate the deficit. Krugman's contribution was to identify the time at which the attack will come, in a country that will eventually run out of reserves. It will be sooner than five years. If speculators are rational, they will not wait until then. To do so would mean holding an asset – domestic currency – while knowing that it will suffer a discrete loss in value in the immediate future. Any self-respecting speculator would instead shift his or her money out of the country at an earlier date. When speculators all do this, they move the date of the crisis forward.

One might then try to take this logic to the other limit, reasoning that the attack must take place much earlier: at the moment when the pattern of overexpansion and eventual devaluation first become clear. But this also is not the right solution.

---

[3] A note on semantics. The distinction between the first and second generation models of speculative attacks is widely agreed. See, for example, Flood and Marion (1999), which is a survey of the literature; Flood and Marion (1996); or Jeanne (2000). But there is less of a consensus as to what constitutes the third generation. This chapter uses the distinction that seems the most useful (multiple equilibria versus structural flaws).

[4] Even after 1995, some economists continued to attribute currency crises to macroeconomic fundamentals. See Bordo and Schwartz (1997) or Mishkin (2001).

As long as the central bank has plenty of reserves to defend the exchange rate, speculators will be happy to wait. There is an intermediate date, when the remaining stock of reserves has been run down to just the right level: still high enough that the speculators can get their money out, but no higher than that. That is the date when the attack occurs. The remainder of the reserves is then suddenly depleted in a single day. This theory helps explain why the level of reserves is statistically a useful predictor – a low level of reserves signaling danger of crisis. More precisely, the most useful prediction is that, under the particular assumptions of the Krugman–Flood–Garber model, the speculative attack will occur when the level of reserves has fallen to a level equal to the semielasticity of money demand times the postcrisis rate of inflation. The latter variable is determined by the rate of expansion of domestic credit (assumed the same either precrisis or postcrisis).

There have been many extensions and elaborations of the approach. The original Krugman model emphasized certainty and assumed that the authorities would defend the parity until reserves declined to zero, giving the unrealistic implication that everyone could predict the date of the crisis with certainty. Incorporating uncertainty has been one of the more important extensions.[5]

SECOND GENERATION: MULTIPLE EQUILIBRIA. The second generation of models argues that there is more than one possible outcome – crisis and no-crisis – that can be consistent with equilibrium, even if there has been no change in true fundamentals.[6] The multiple equilibrium approach originally took its inspiration from the crises in the European Exchange Rate Mechanism (ERM) of 1992–93.

There had always been some who claimed that financial markets were excessively volatile, alternating between waves of optimism and pessimism. But the usual view among academic economists, as well as the international financial establishment, had been that markets are based on economic fundamentals, and that declining market prices or flows are merely the messenger or symptom of underlying problems. This view became harder to maintain as a sequence of European currencies succumbed to attack. The attack on France in 1993 was particularly puzzling, because the government had over the preceding years succeeded in attaining a level of macroeconomic discipline that by most indicators looked at least as great as that of Germany, its partner in the ERM. Moreover, after the bands were widened, the crisis passed without a substantial further depreciation of the franc, even though there had been no tightening of macroeconomic policy in the meantime. How then could the fundamentals have been responsible for the earlier speculative pressure? Also puzzling were the cases of Sweden and the United Kingdom. Both had shown a willingness to raise interest rates to extremely high levels to defend the krona and the pound in 1992. Yet speculators were unimpressed, and nonetheless persisted in attacks against those currencies. Such a policy response, known as the *interest rate defense*, could apparently no longer be relied upon to work.

The second generation point is most easily understood as a game played among speculators, along the lines of the classic "prisoners' dilemma." Consider two speculators. Each realizes that if the other sells, the resulting depreciation will reduce the

[5] Flood and Garber (1984); Flood and Marion (2002); Morris and Shin (1998, 2001).
[6] Obstfeld (1994).

value of his holdings of domestic currency. Neither wants to stand pat if the other might sell. Thus, the prisoners' dilemma equilibrium might entail both selling, even though everyone may be worse off after the devaluation.

Can one say anything about what conditions will make a country vulnerable to such an attack? If the fundamentals are particularly weak, both speculators will sell. If the central bank holds a sufficiently low level of reserves, then each speculator knows that if he chooses to sell his domestic currency, he will deplete the central banks' holdings of foreign reserves, and thereby force a devaluation. Each knows this, and so will sell to avoid being the one left "holding the bag." If the fundamentals are particularly strong, there will be no attack. For example, if the level of reserves is sufficiently high that both speculators know they cannot break the bank even acting together, they have no reason to attack. The interesting case comes in the intermediate range. If the fundamentals are bad but not terrible, then the country is vulnerable to an attack. But the game theory cannot predict what the outcome will be in this case. The attack and no-attack outcomes are equally valid equilibria. This is what is meant by multiple equilibria.

One variant is an international version of a standard model of domestic bank runs. Each bank depositor is motivated to take his money out of the bank only if he thinks others might do the same, so that there might not be enough cash to go around. The recommended solution is deposit insurance and adequate reserve holdings by the banks.[7]

Another variant treats monetary policy as endogenous. After all, why should governments decide to embark on a dangerous path of excessive money growth that they stubbornly maintain regardless of adverse developments, as the first-generation models assumed? The ultimate fundamentals are not macroeconomic policies, but rather the political conditions that might make the benefits of devaluation and monetary expansion more likely to outweigh the costs, from the viewpoint of the monetary authorities. Some models suggest that a key fundamental variable, determining whether a country is in the intermediate range where speculative attacks are a danger, is the level of unemployment; some say it is the level of debt.[8] If these indicators are at particularly high levels, then the tight monetary policy necessary to fight a speculative attack will involve particularly high costs relative to benefits. This is because the high interest rates may spark banking failures or social unrest. Speculators know that the high interest rates are not politically sustainable, which makes an attack more likely even if the policymakers sincerely do their best to hold the line.

THIRD GENERATION: "CRONY CAPITALISM" AND MORAL HAZARD. If crises of the 1970s and 1980s are represented by the first-generation approach, and if the 1992–93 ERM crises inspired the second-generation models, then the East Asian crises of 1997–98 motivated the third-generation models.

Unlike Latin America and other parts of the world with a history of large budget deficits, high inflation monetary policies, and overvalued currencies, East Asia in

---

[7] Diamond and Dybvig (1983). An international version is Chang and Velasco (2000a, b) and Velasco (1996).

[8] Obstfeld (1996, 1998).

the latter third of the 20th century earned a relatively good reputation for fiscal discipline and monetary stability. This record was largely maintained right up until the crisis. True, Thailand and Korea clung to overvalued currencies in the sense that they depleted their net reserves in futile attempts to defend the exchange rate, before trying something else. But there had been limited evidence of profligate monetary and fiscal policy on the part of these governments, or of currencies that were overvalued in real terms. Indeed, Westerners had argued earlier that such high-growth countries should experience real appreciations, reasoning according to the Balassa–Samuelson effect.

In light of the judgment that most of these countries had relatively good macroeconomic policies, diagnoses have placed new emphasis on a different sort of fundamentals: structural distortions in the financial structures of emerging economies. "Crony capitalism," defined more formally as implicit government guarantees for poorly regulated banks and corporate debtors, has been the inspiration behind a "third-generation" approach to currency crises.[9] (For some, the phrase "third generation" refers to the problems of balance sheet mismatch, particularly among banks. The two sets of issues are closely related.)

The third-generation models interpret recent crises as illustrations of the perils of moral hazard. Borrowers and lenders are less likely to be careful evaluating the true profitability of investment opportunities if they believe they will be bailed out in the event that the project goes badly.

Some believe that international bailouts by the IMF and G-7 create the moral hazard problem. But in the third-generation models, the root cause of moral hazard is at the national level rather than the international level. If moral hazard at the international level were the original and only root of the problem, then it would follow that the amount of capital flowing from rich to poor countries overall would be greater than socially optimal. But instead, the amount of capital flowing, on average, is *less* than predicted by neoclassical economic models. In other words, the large existing differences across countries in capital/labor ratios, and therefore in the rate of return to capital predict that capital flow, should be larger than what is observed, not smaller.

The phrase "crony capitalism" suddenly became popular in 1997, to describe newly evident flaws in the structure of Asian financial systems. In fairness, some of these same characteristics had been seen as strengths of Asian economies a short time earlier. Business deals are said to be dominated by personal connections (*guan xi*, in China), large family-run conglomerates (*chaebol*, in Korea), comprehensive clusters of allied firms (*keiretsu*, in Japan), or insider links to the government (charges of corruption, collusion, and nepotism in Indonesia, regarding President Suharto). Firms may fund investments by borrowing from bankers with whom they have close personal or political ties. The loans may come from a bank to which the firm is

---

[9] Even before the East Asia crises, this diagnosis was offered by a precious few far-sighted economists: Diaz-Alejandro (1985); McKinnon and Pill (1997); and Dooley (1997/2000). As usual, Krugman (1998a, b) produced an influential analysis. Those writing after the crisis began also include Corsetti, Pesenti, and Roubini (1999a, b); Chinn, Dooley, and Shrestha (1999); and Burnside, Eichenbaum, and Rebelo (1998, 1999).

affiliated, in which case they are called connected lending, or may come under guidance from the government, in which case they are called directed lending. In some countries, corruption pervades the system.

An idealized version of American capitalism is held up as a contrasting example (or was, until the Enron scandals): transactions among corporations are said to be made at arms' length, based on explicit contracts enforced under a transparent legal system. Corporations rely heavily on securities markets to fund investment, where rules require accounting by recognized standards, and public disclosure of information. The Asian system is termed "relationship-based," and the American system, "market-based."

The insurance model of Michael Dooley (1997/2000) starts from the assumption that government officials have a pot of resources that can be used to bail out political cronies if they get into financial difficulty. This pot is mainly identified with the central banks' holdings of foreign exchange reserves, but it could also include whatever sources of hard currency the government can lay its hands on in the event of a crisis, whether funds that the country can borrow from the IMF, the government's claim on revenue from export taxes, or any profitable state-owned enterprises or other holdings that the government could sell off. Well-connected banks and businessmen are able to borrow from abroad to finance risky projects, such as real estate development or a new factory in the already-glutted steel industry. They are aware of the risk. But they believe that they will be bailed out by the government if things go badly. In the worst countries, they have been explicitly promised that they will be bailed out. In other cases, the government may have tried to declare in advance that it will not be responsible for private debts, but this disclaimer is not believed.[10]

Asian countries did not suddenly develop critical structural flaws in their financial systems for the first time in 1997. Why does the crisis occur when it does? The timing of the attack again comes out of the calculations of speculators who worry that if they wait too long, there will not be enough foreign exchange reserves to go around. But there is a key difference from the first-generation models, which watched reserves decline steadily over time, and identified the timing of the attack as the point at which reserves sank to a particular critical level. The third-generation models watch liabilities rise steadily over time, artificially encouraged by moral hazard. They identify the timing of the attack with the point at which the liabilities have climbed to the critical level given by the level of reserves. At that point, speculators suddenly cash in their investments. If they wait any longer, they might not be able to get their money out. The speculative attack, as usual, then forces the central bank to abandon the exchange rate.

EMPIRICAL IMPLICATIONS OF SPECULATIVE ATTACK MODELS. Much of the theoretical literature on speculative attacks does not lead directly to empirical

---

[10] Diaz-Alejandro (1985). A "no bailout" declaration lacks credibility, particularly in the case of domestic banks. When the crisis comes, the pressure for the government to rescue insolvent banks will be irresistible for two reasons. First, most depositors are small savers, not sophisticated investors. Second, bank failures can have a devastating effect on the rest of the economy, particularly because banks constitute the payments system.

324 *Jeffrey Frankel and Shang-Jin Wei*

predictions. There exists a small empirical literature.[11] It is for the most part not designed to distinguish among the competing models of speculative attack.

One testable implication is the importance of the level of reserves, which features prominently in all three generations of models. The first-generation models suggest looking at the level of reserves relative to macroeconomic fundamentals such as the inflation rate and the rate of growth of domestic credit, or the budget deficit viewed as a key determinant of the rate of growth of domestic credit. The second generation agrees that reserves are important; but if there are other empirical measures that matter, they are more likely to concern unemployment, elections, and other political variables. The role of reserves in the third generation is less clear-cut. The Dooley version says, surprisingly, that a high level of reserves actually makes a speculative attack *more* likely – because there is a bigger pot of money to be exploited through shady connections – conditioned on the other variable the model considers to be most important: corruption. Important counterexamples to this prediction would seem to be the success of China and Taiwan, Province of China, each with very high levels of reserves, in weathering the volatility of 1997 and subsequently. One cannot claim that a higher quality of regulation is the explanation. Directed lending, connected lending, corruption, and bad loans are at least as important in these countries as in the rest of Asia.

When Korea rebounded strongly from the recession of 1998, recovering as quickly as had Mexico in 1995, some critics proclaimed that the V-pattern disproved the view on the parts of the international financial institutions and the U.S. Treasury that the cause of the crisis was crony capitalism: what is here termed the third-generation approach. They argued that, just as institutions go bad only slowly over time, they do not improve suddenly. Therefore the crisis must have been due to something else, such as an unfounded speculative attack (second generation) or IMF malfeasance.

The counterargument is that the Korean government did undertake fundamental economic reforms pursuant to the late-December 1997 agreement with the IMF, for the first time challenging the power of both the *chaebols* and the labor unions. The combination of an evident national economic emergency and the election of a new president with traditional antiestablishment support (Kim Dae Jung) allowed measures to be put through that had previously been impossible politically. Although the reform process may not have progressed very far by the time that Korean economic growth was fully restored (1999), the shift in approach worked to restore investor confidence from early 1998, and is sufficient to explain the turnaround. Indeed, some Korean economists argue that the country was better off, in light of the reforms, than it was before the crisis, and even that the country might have been better off if the recovery had come later, to keep up pressure for reform (although one need not go that far). Similarly, although the Russian devaluation and default of 1998 appeared at the time to augur disaster, in retrospect the crisis helped politically to bring about reforms that had previously been viewed as impossible, such as effective collection of taxes and hardening of firms' budget constraints (see Chapter 10, this volume).

---

[11] Empirical tests include Blanco and Garber (1986) and Prati and Sbracia (2002).

Early Warning Indicators

We now turn from theory without numbers, to numbers without theory. Everyone would like to be able to predict ahead of time when a crisis will happen. This is not easy to do. Even private "rating services," professionals who make their living by evaluating the risk of bonds from various issuers, have a poor track record. Indeed, if it were easy to predict the date of a crisis, according to the theory of efficient markets, investors would not have their money in the country at that date in the first place. But there are certain warning indicators that may signal that a country is at increased risk.

Traditional indicators are measures of aggregate indebtedness, such as the ratio of the current account deficit to GDP, the ratio of debt to GDP, or the ratio of external debt service to exports. One rule of thumb is that current account deficits in excess of 4 percent of GDP enter a danger zone. Such predictors are of limited use, however, and not just because they have little basis in theory.[12] Some countries repeatedly get into trouble at debt/GDP ratios as low as 15 percent, whereas that level would be considered safe for others.[13] Many countries are observed to run large current account deficits for years, and yet are able to finance them without getting into trouble. It depends, at least, on how the funds are used.

Periodically, someone will assert that a given country need not worry about a current account deficit, because the government budget is in balance, and thus it is only the private sector that is borrowing from abroad. There is a certain logic to the argument that decisions made freely by consenting adults who face explicit price signals are less likely to get into trouble than governments spending somebody else's money. Nevertheless, this principle has gone wrong frequently enough to earn the name "Lawson Fallacy" (after the British finance minister who downplayed fears regarding his country's current account deficit in the late 1980s). Examples of countries that borrowed to finance private deficits rather than public deficits and yet experienced crises include Chile in 1981 and Mexico in 1994.

Out of those experiences, a new guideline emerged: a country is more likely to get into trouble if an inflow goes to finance consumption, instead of investment. After all, the key to sustainable borrowing is to use the funds to build up a productive capital stock, so that the country will be able tomorrow to produce, export, and earn the foreign exchange that it will need to pay back the debt incurred today. East Asian countries in the 1990s, with their high rates of saving and investment, seemed by this criterion unimpeachable, despite their large current account deficits. Only when they too were hit by crises in 1997–98 did the flaw in this logic become clear. Much of the finance had gone to investment in unprofitable heavy manufacturing and real estate. A Korean firm that borrows heavily in order to invest in auto or steel factories may have trouble paying the money back if those sectors already have excess capacity.

Another set of indicators that appear statistically useful at predicting whether a given size current account deficit or external debt is likely to lead to crisis concerns

---

[12] For example, Edwards (1999) found that current account ratios are of little use in predicting crisis.

[13] Reinhart, Rogoff, and Savastano (2003) call these "debt intolerant" countries, and attribute the problem to histories of default and inflation.

the composition of the capital inflow. Relevant dimensions of the composition of inflows include maturity, currency of denomination, bank lending versus securities – and policy regarding reserves.[14] These variables are discussed below. A conclusion to emerge from many of the studies is that the single most useful indicator may be the ratio of short-term external debt to reserves.

Sachs, Tornell, and Velasco (1996) found that a combination of weak fundamentals (changes in real exchange rate or credit/GDP) and low reserves (relative to M2) made countries vulnerable to tequila contagion in 1995. Kaminsky, Lizondo, and Reinhart (1998) found that the best predictors are the real exchange rate, the ratio of M2 to reserves, GDP, and equity prices. Milesi-Ferretti and Razin (1998/2000) found that reserves, openness, current account balance, terms of trade, and world interest rates are among the indicators triggering crises and/or sharp reversals of the current account.[15]

Crisis Prevention Policies

Background on many of the variables to be considered in the quantitative analysis appears in Appendix A, which presents a brief review of other literature relevant to crisis prevention policies. The list includes the following topics: deep determinants that come originally from the growth literature (such as institutions/governance), the choice of exchange rate regime, the choice of capital account regime, the choice of trade openness, and the composition and use of capital inflows.

Crisis Management Policies

Once a country is hit by an abrupt cut-off in foreign willingness to lend, it hardly matters what was the cause. The urgent question becomes what is the appropriate policy response. Often the loss in foreign financing must be taken as given. Thus, there must be a reduction of the same magnitude in the previous trade deficit. How can the adjustment be accomplished? Is a sharp increase in interest rates (to reduce overall spending, and increase the attractiveness of much-needed capital inflow) preferable to a sharp devaluation (to switch expenditure away from the consumption of internationally traded goods, and to switch production toward them)?[16] Many victims of crises in the late 1990s had to experience both. Regardless what mix of policies has been chosen, recessions have been severe.[17] Is the output loss smaller if the country goes to the IMF?

[14] Frankel and Rose (1996), writing before the East Asia crisis, found that the composition of capital inflow matters for currency crashes (more than the total). Short-term bank debt raises the probability of crash; FDI and reserves lower the probability.

[15] Other important contributions include Rodrik and Velasco (2000); Edison (2000); Goldstein, Kaminsky, and Reinhart (2000); and Roubini, Manasse, Hemming, and Schimmelpfennig (2003). In the calculations of Berg and others (1999), the studies done before the Asian crisis did not perform very well postsample. Flood and Coke (2000) criticize the exercise as inherently flawed.

[16] Lahiri and Végh (2000); Christiano, Gust, and Roldos (2002); Caballero and Krishnamurthy (2001); Drazen (2003); Eichengreen and Rose (2003).

[17] Barro (2001) estimates that the combined currency and banking crises in East Asia in 1997–98 reduced economic growth in the affected countries over a five-year period by 3 percent per year, compared to 2 percent per year for more typical crises.

It would be particularly useful if we could sort out the problem of what is the desirable policy mix once the decision has been made to adjust a trade deficit, rather than to continue trying to finance it. This has been a subject of great controversy. The textbook framework of adjusting to an external imbalance via some combination of expenditure reduction and real devaluation, and the specific formulation in terms of traded and nontraded goods, remain among the most useful models for developing countries.[18] One of the most popular critiques of the management of the 1990s crises by national authorities and the IMF – that there was too much contractionary monetary and fiscal policy, imposing needlessly severe recessions – can best be interpreted in this framework as the proposition that the countries should have followed a different policy mix, one with less contraction and more devaluation.[19] (This logic takes the external financing constraint as given, i.e., it assumes that in the face of a sudden stop, the country must improve the trade balance one way or another. It is also quite possible, however, that these critics are really saying that the international financial community should come up with more funds so the country does not face so sharp an adjustment.) Others note that the devaluations were in most cases very large as it was; and that devaluation can be at least as bad for the balance sheets of debtor banks and corporations, and just as contractionary, as increases in the interest rate. Indeed, an increase in the interest rate at least has the virtue, with respect to balance sheets, that if things go well it will come back down over the subsequent months, whereas this seldom is true of the nominal exchange rate.[20] It is possible a country that finds itself with short-term dollar-denominated debt, unwillingness by its creditors to roll over, and low reserves has few policy options left other than a sharp and painful output contraction.[21]

Appendix B elaborates on the possibility that, for a country that has waited until very late in the day to adjust, there may in fact be no optimal combination of devaluation and expenditure-reducing policies that satisfy the external financing constraint and yet avoids a recession.

VARIABLES TO BE EXAMINED

This section begins by establishing a statistical criterion for what is to be considered a currency crisis. Then the study specifies policy variables and measures of economic performance. Appendix C contains details of definitions and data sources for the variables. Appendix D lists the countries constituting the data sample for each of our tests.

Criterion to Define a Crisis

Not all speculative attacks succeed. If there is a very sharp fall in the demand for a country's assets, that can be considered a crisis even if the authorities tighten monetary policy sufficiently to avoid a devaluation (perhaps automatically, in a currency board, for example). The approach here is generally to follow Eichengreen, Rose,

---

[18] Salter (1959); Swan (1963); Dornbusch (1973); Corden (1994).
[19] For example, Furman and Stiglitz (1998) and Sachs (1998).
[20] Fischer (2004b).
[21] Krugman (1998b); Frankel (2001).

and Wyplosz (1995) and Frankel and Rose (1996)[22] in using a foreign exchange market pressure index.[23] This index is defined as the percentage fall in reserves plus the percentage fall in the foreign exchange value of the currency. The idea is that this index measures the fall in demand for the country's currency; it is then up to the monetary authorities to determine whether to accommodate, by letting the money supply fall, or to depreciate. To avoid treating every year of a multiyear high-inflation period as a separate crisis, this study requires that the increase in exchange market pressure represent an acceleration of at least an additional 10 percent over the preceding period; and we also adopt an exclusion window of three years.

We define a crisis event at annual frequency in four steps:

1. Starting with monthly data, we compute the crisis index (IND) = percentage nominal exchange rate depreciation + percentage loss in foreign reserves.
2. A month m for country k is labeled as a "crisis month" if IND$(k, m) \geq 25$ percent, and IND(k, m) − IND$(k, m-1) \geq 10$ percent.
3. We next create a VCRISIS(k, t) variable at the annual frequency for country k and year t. VCRISIS$(k, t) = 1$ if year t for country k contains a crisis month, and 0 otherwise.
4. We define a crisis event variable at the annual frequency, ECRISIS(k, t), using the value of VCRISIS(k, t) plus a three-year window. The three-year window rule specifies that there can be no more than one crisis in any three-year period. For example, if there is a string of six years in which VCRISIS = 1, we define only the first and fourth years as crises, and disregard the other years from the probit estimation. The three-year window, used also in Frankel and Rose (1996), is designed to avoid the situation in which a multiyear crisis is labeled as several different crises. At the same time, if a country is in crisis year after year for nine years, counting them as one crisis would probably be insufficient. The three-year-window rule would assign (somewhat arbitrarily) three crises to the period as a compromise.

As a robustness check, we also experimented with higher and lower thresholds. The probit analysis seeks to predict these events.

Measures of Economic Performance

In the regression section, we considered five measures of economic performance for the crosssection of currencies during the sample period, 1990–2002.

1. The number of crises experienced during this period
2. The average depth of a country's crises, measured as the loss of GDP relative to the beginning of the crisis, up until the date when GDP reattains its precrisis level
3. A composite measure, consisting of total output lost in crises: the number of years that the country was in crisis times the average depth of its crises
4. The average rate of growth during the sample period
5. The standard deviation of the growth rate during the sample period.

[22] Who sought to explain, respectively, currency crises in European countries and in developing countries.
[23] Wyplosz (2001), rather than simply adding the two components of this "exchange market pressure" index, assigns weights to their movements according to their inverse variability.

Crisis Prevention Policies

We examined a number of key regressors. These variables are chosen to correspond to those identified by recent theories as potentially important for currency crises in developing countries. The objective is to check which of these are associated with crisis events, and with good economic performance more generally, when they are put to compete with one another other in a unified regression framework. The list of key regressors includes:

1. Trade openness, as measured by the ratio of total trade to GDP
2. Financial openness, measured either de jure by the Klein–Quinn rating of openness, or de facto by the ratio of gross foreign assets plus liabilities to GDP
3. Institutional quality, as measured by control of corruption (ICRG) or constraints on executive branch of the government (Polity IV)
4. The ratio of external debt to GDP
5. Reserves/GDP
6. Measures of composition, such as the ratio of the sum of FDI and equity inflows to gross foreign liabilities; and the ratio of short-term debt to GDP, to FDI plus equity, or to reserves
7. Expansionary monetary policies, as measured by the inflation rate and, in the regression section, its determinants, the rate of domestic credit creation and the budget deficit as a share of GDP
8. Exchange rate regimes, as captured by a time-weighted measure of flexibility, or by a dummy for fixed exchange regime and another dummy for intermediate exchange rate regimes
9. "Original sin," another composition variable that measures the currency mismatch arising from foreign liabilities denominated in dollars or other foreign currencies.

Crisis Management Policies

One important question is whether the country adjusts promptly when faced with balance of payments difficulties, or postpones the adjustment. We will look at the length of time that passes after reserves peak, before there is a devaluation, and how much reserves are lost during that time. We also consider the hypothesis that changes in the composition of liabilities during the period of sudden stop – toward shorter-term and toward dollar-denominated liabilities – are another method of stalling for time, in addition to running down reserves. We will also look at whether the country signed a program with the IMF.

Another interesting proposition to be tested may be that, when the day of adjustment comes, the mix of policies can make a difference. We will assume that net additional international financing is not possible during a financial crisis and therefore take as given the increase in the trade balance (typically eliminating a previous deficit). The question is whether this adjustment is achieved through contractionary monetary policies, which can be measured by the increase in the real interest rate; by contractionary fiscal policies, which can be measured by the increase in the budget surplus; or by real devaluation, which switches the composition of spending, and also encourages greater supply of tradable goods.

Keeping in mind the identity that output $Y \equiv A + TB$, where A is spending, there are three categories that a country could fall into, when it adjusts so as to improve the trade balance, TB:

(i) It could achieve an expansion, through trade-boosting policies such as devaluation or other expenditure-switching policies, without expenditure-reduction: $\Delta Y > \Delta A > 0$

(ii) It could achieve the improvement in the trade balance partly through expenditure reduction policies, but with no loss in overall output: $\Delta A < 0$, but $\Delta Y > 0$

(iii) It could achieve adjustment solely through expenditure-reduction, resulting in a contraction in output: $\Delta Y < 0$.

A simple way of parameterizing the policy mix is to compute the adjustment mix coefficient

$$\mu \equiv \Delta Y / \Delta TB.$$

We then identify the three cases by:

(i) $\mu > 1 = >$ expansion,
(ii) $\mu < 1 = >$ expenditure-reduction, and
(iii) $\mu < 0 = >$ contraction.

This calculation, across the set of crises that were followed by improvements in the trade balance, shows that all three cases occurred, but by far the most common was the first case. But the calculation measures income relative to the precrisis level. It thus misses cases of contraction relative to some other counterfactual, for countries with high trend growth in potential output.

We will express the relative importance of monetary contraction by the change in the real interest rate relative to the change in the real exchange rate. We will express the relative importance of fiscal contraction by the change in the budget surplus relative to the change in the trade balance. The interesting question is whether there exists some combination of these policies that puts the country in Category (ii) or even (i). Perhaps the country is doomed to Category (iii) if the period of sudden stop has already been spent running down reserves to low levels and switching the composition of liabilities toward short-term dollar loans.

How Exogenous Are the Policy Variables?

One more methodological point is necessary before beginning. When we draw our variables from the list of candidates that are prominent in discussions of policy determinants of financial crises, many of them are clearly endogenous. This is especially the case with the literature on early warning indicators. Examples include the inflation rate, growth rate, overvaluation relative to purchasing power parity (PPP), and fraction of short-term debt. These variables are so important that they cannot be left out of the analysis, but it is important to bear in mind the endogeneity point throughout.

At the next level of exogeneity are those that are traditionally thought of as macroeconomic policy variables, such as budget deficit, money growth, and choice of exchange rate regime. Even these variables, however, are now often viewed as the endogenous outcome of deeper structural or institutional factors, such as the rule of law. As explained in Appendix A, some authors argue that macroeconomic policies in developing countries are often the manifestation of deeper institutions and interest groups, so that an IMF requirement that a country devalue in order to raise the domestic price of export commodities may simply be offset by some other policy, such as a change in pricing by a marketing board, in order to restore the preceding political equilibrium. Accordingly, this study will give appropriate attention to such structural determinants. At the same time, we must recognize that even the so-called structural or institutional factors are endogenous; there is a fourth level of exogeneity consisting of geographic and historical factors.

EXPLORATORY EMPIRICAL ANALYSIS OF CURRENCY CRISES

The main goal is to see which of the competing claims regarding desirable policies for crisis prevention and crisis management are supported by the data. But there are too many possible effects and combinations of effects to construct a neatly nested theoretically grounded framework within which to carry out the tests. We begin, in this section, by exploring the data in various preliminary ways, to help point to the directions in which we should concentrate our energies.

Do the Most Visible Recent Crises Help Distinguish among Hypotheses?

Relative to other developing countries, a very large fraction of public attention and analysis has gone to fewer than a dozen emerging markets, particularly those experiencing dramatic currency crises and considered of systemic importance. ("Systemic importance" generally means countries that are large in the financial system, although the euphemism sometimes extends to geopolitical significance.) We, too, begin by considering these countries, before undertaking a broader and more systematic econometric analysis in subsequent sections. The analysis in this section will not be formal, but rather will take the approach that one clear data point (or counterexample) might be sufficient to reject the strong form of the hypothesis that any single factor is of overwhelming importance in determining which countries experience crises and which do not.[24]

---

[24] Some citation of background and evidence beyond an appeal to Table 8.1 and the authors' perceptions, is desirable. Overviews of the recent crises in emerging markets include Blustein (2002); Calvo, Leiderman, and Reinhart (1996); Desai (2003); Eichengreen (1999); Ito (2002); Radelet and Sachs (1998); and Willett (2000). Two retrospective exercises have been designed to shed light on competing propositions regarding the roles played by policy decisions. The *Report on Capital Account Crises of the IMF Independent Evaluations Office* (IMF 2003) sought to evaluate the many claims of errors on the part of the IMF, including claims of errors in the policies imposed on client countries, such as the critiques collected in McQuillan and Montgomery (1999). The *NBER Project on Exchange Rate Crises in Emerging Market Countries* covered the roles of national policy makers and other players (http://www.nber.org/crisis/); it included eight meetings on the specifics of crises in eight of these countries. Both informed this section of this study. Selected further references to some individual country cases are given below.

It does not seem possible to categorize the country experiences into first-generation, second-generation, and third-generation type crises. In each historical episode, some observers blame macroeconomic fundamentals, some volatile financial markets, and some structural flaws. In truth, all these factors play a role.

One can find examples to illustrate one's favorite hypothesis regarding policies to prevent crises; but counterexamples abound as well. Consider exchange rate regimes. The crises of 1994–2000 involved countries with intermediate regimes (bands, crawls, baskets, and adjustable pegs), which is why many observers considered them the root of the problem. But a free float did not save Brazil from a crisis in the run-up to the presidential election of 2002, a currency board did not save Argentina from disaster in 2001, and intermediate exchange rate regimes such as those pursued by Thailand and Korea certainly did not save them from becoming crisis victims of 1997–99.[25]

Or consider crisis management. On the one hand, the currency crises in Mexico (1994)[26] and Thailand (1997)[27] came nine months or more after investors had started pulling out of the country (as reflected in reserves or stock market prices). These cases support the hypothesis that early adjustment is critical, and that if a country waits until it has lost most of its reserves before going to the IMF and devaluing – assuming that is what it is going to have to do eventually anyway – the crisis will be much worse. Exchange rate based stabilizations fail, according to the conventional wisdom, because of the absence of an exit strategy. On the other hand, Russia engaged in the same procrastination in the first half of 1998,[28] as did Brazil later in the fall of 1998.[29] Yet in neither case were the predictions of disaster that accompanied the devaluations in August 1998 and January 1999, respectively, borne out. Ecuador lost 66 percent of its reserves before its currency crisis of early 2000, and suffered a correspondingly large output loss subsequently, while Brazil lost almost as much (52 percent of its reserves) and yet suffered no loss in output. Turkey followed the advice of building in an explicit exit strategy into its exchange-rate based stabilization plan – an accelerated rate of crawl prescheduled for July 2001 – and yet that did not help at all avoid speculative attack in February. (Nor, interestingly, does it appear to have hurt, in that participants did not cite the "exit clause" as one of the reasons behind pressure on the balance of payments.)[30]

Table 8.1 reports the base-case variables of interest for a set of countries that had the most visible crises during the 1994–2002 period (Argentina, Brazil, Ecuador, Indonesia, Korea, Mexico, Pakistan, Russia, Thailand, and Turkey). Also reported are four noncrisis "control cases" (Chile, China, Hong Kong SAR, and Taiwan,

---

[25] In Table 8.1, the column showing exchange rate flexibility offers some support for the hypothesis that exchange rate flexibility is useful. Taiwan, Province of China, was able largely to avoid the East Asian crisis by devaluing at the first sign of trouble in 1997, while Argentina, the most firmly fixed of the group, again had the worst recession. Thus in a later section, this study tests the effect of exchange rate flexibility as one of the base-case hypotheses.

[26] Dornbusch and Werner (1994); Sachs, Tornell, and Velasco (1996).

[27] Rajan (2001).

[28] Kharas, Pinto, and Ulatov (2001). See also Chapter 10 of this volume (Pinto, Gurvich, and Ulatov).

[29] Cardoso and Helwege (1999).

[30] Üçer and Van Rijckeghem (2004) and http://www.nber.org/crisis/turkey_report.html.

Table 8.1. *The base-case variables for the sample's dozen crisis countries*

	Policy Variables										Other Variables			Performance Measures				
	Non-corruptness	(qka) Absence capital controls	(share9295) Absence capital controls	Inflation	Short-term debt/ reserves	Short-term debt/ total debt	External debt/GDP	Exchange rate regime (flexibility)	Budget deficit/ GDP	Rate of increase domestic credit	Proportion time at war	GDP per capita (1990)	Original sin	Mean growth real income	Std. dev. real income	No. of crises	Average depth of crises	Composite crisis measure
Argentina	2.79	1.00	0.75	0.37	1.36	0.19	0.41	1.23	1.17	0.15	0.01	8.66	0.69	0.02	0.07	3.00	0.08	0.23
Brazil	3.29	1.50	0.00	1.13	1.21	0.17	0.32	2.62	5.79	1.05	0.00	8.31	0.63	0.02	0.02	1.00	0.01	0.01
Chile	3.53	1.83	0.00	0.09	0.24	0.11	0.45	2.23	-1.17	0.09	0.00	8.10	0.78	0.06	0.04	0.00	0.00	0.00
China	3.00	0.00	0.00	0.06	0.29	0.17	0.16	1.62	2.03	0.13	0.00	5.86	0.40	0.09	0.02	0.00	0.00	0.00
Hong Kong SAR	4.33	4.00	1.00	0.04				1.62	0.00	0.05	0.00	9.84	0.87	0.04	0.04	0.00	0.00	0.00
Colombia	2.13	1.50	0.00	0.17	0.47	0.15	0.36	2.31	1.93	0.16	0.07	7.66	0.80	0.02	0.03	0.00	0.00	0.00
Ecuador	3.08	2.33	0.50	0.04	1.64	0.15		1.77	-1.11	0.14	0.01	7.30	0.75	0.02	0.03	2.00	0.03	0.06
Indonesia	2.01	2.50	1.00	0.12	1.40	0.18	0.79	2.31	0.06	0.12	0.01	6.66	0.62	0.04	0.06	1.00	0.10	0.10
Korea	3.99	1.67	0.00	0.05	0.99	0.35	0.23	2.46	0.34	0.09	0.00	8.98	0.37	0.06	0.05	0.00	0.00	0.00
Malaysia	3.81	0.00	0.00	0.03	0.28	0.19	0.43	1.46	-1.15	0.10	0.00	8.04	0.37	0.06	0.05	0.00	0.00	0.00
Mexico	3.00	2.00	0.00	0.16	1.59	0.19	0.37	2.62	0.09	0.12	0.00	8.07	0.64	0.03	0.04	1.00	0.02	0.02
Pakistan	2.46	1.17	0.00	0.08	3.10	0.10	0.52	2.00	6.92	0.09	0.01	6.11	0.80	0.04	0.01	0.00	0.00	0.00
Russia	2.37			0.79	1.69	0.11	0.39	2.36	2.31	0.00	0.02	8.21	0.73	-0.03	0.09	1.00	0.03	0.03
South Africa	4.62	1.17	0.00	0.09	23.37	0.40	0.18	3.00	4.38	0.00	0.03	8.32	0.83	0.05	0.02	1.00	0.02	0.02
Taiwan, Prov. of China	3.55			0.02				3.00	0.00	0.00	0.00		0.43	0.05	0.03	0.00	0.00	0.00
Thailand	2.61	1.50	0.00	0.04	2.78	0.33	0.58	1.77	0.39	0.10	0.00	7.60	0.33	0.04	0.06	1.00	0.01	0.01
Turkey	2.64	1.17	0.00	0.54	1.82	0.21	0.47	2.23	8.03	0.41	0.05	7.85	0.87	0.03	0.06	2.00	0.06	0.13
Mean (above countries)	3.13	1.56	0.22	0.22	2.82	0.20	0.40	2.15	1.76	0.16	0.01	7.85	0.64	0.04	0.04	0.76	0.02	0.04

Note: qka Average of Klein's interpretation of Quinn's variable qka for the years 1973, 1982, and 1988, gauging capital account openess (higher value = more open). *share9295*: Proportion of period 1992–95 that country had open capital accounts or undertook financial liberalization.
Source: Authors' calculations.

Province of China) and three others of special interest (Colombia, Malaysia, and South Africa).

The column showing freedom from corruptness offers a possible illustration of the hypothesis that institutional quality is critical: Indonesia scores even more poorly than most developing countries, and suffered a correspondingly severe crisis in 1997–98. Yet Argentina is a counterexample, having a noncorruptness score that is no worse than the average,[31] but suffering the most severe output loss of any country in the sample. That Argentina had enacted most of the recommended institutional fixes (encouraging foreign-owned bank subsidiaries, taking out a contingent credit line, smoothing the term structure of obligations, and so forth) and yet experienced such a collapse is particularly discouraging.[32] Brazil, Pakistan, South Africa, and Turkey show up with egregious budget deficits; Turkey, Russia, and Brazil with the highest inflation records; Indonesia with the highest debt; Brazil with the highest credit creation; and Turkey with the worst currency mismatch.

The view that wins the most support from Table 8.1 is that countries that are not open to capital flows are more likely to have stable economies. It should perhaps not be surprising that countries that do not incur debt in the first place do not have debt crises. Still, it should be disturbing, from the viewpoint of proglobalizers, that the two countries that show up as most closed to capital flows, China and Malaysia,[33] are also the two with the fastest average growth over the period since 1990.

The answer in life is almost always that more than one factor is important in determining performance. A systematic analysis, to evaluate any one effect, must control for others. The strongest message to emerge from Table 8.1 is that a dozen highly visible cases is not a large enough sample to answer most of the questions we wish to answer. As soon as we start considering alternative variables, or hypotheses regarding nonlinearities, or interaction terms, we have used up our degrees of freedom, to say nothing of significance levels. Accordingly, the remainder of this study turns to econometrics on larger samples, generally consisting of all developing countries for which sufficient data are available. (Most of the members on the former Soviet Union and other transition economies are excluded, mostly for lack of data and noncomparability before and after the fall of the Soviet Union.) We turn now to probit models to search for robust correlates of crises.

Probit Analysis of Crisis Probability

In this section of the chapter, we describe possible correlates of currency crisis using standard probit models on a panel data set for the set of developing economies in

---

[31] 2.8 for Argentina, as compared to 3.1 for the countries in the table or 3.0 for the full sample.

[32] Mussa (2002); De la Torre, Levy Yeyati, and Schmukler (2003). See also Chapter 11 of this volume (Servén and Perry).

[33] There is only one data point representing an important case that responded to a sudden stop by clearly opting to thumb its nose at the IMF and put on capital controls: Malaysia. As noted above, the case is controversial. Malaysia's economic performance by the various measures was quite good (it does not even show up in Table 8.1 as having experienced a crisis). At the very least, the prediction that this choice would spell doom for Malaysia can be ruled out. Nevertheless, this case cannot be ruled as a definitive demonstration of the advantages of capital controls, in part because they were imposed after the worst of the Asian crisis had passed.

Table 8.2. *Summary of the probit regressions*

Variable	Sample regressions (1)	(2)	Pos significant 10% (3)	20% (4)	Neg significant 10% (5)	20% (6)	Contributor to crisis? (7)
Trade openness	0.006 (0.006)	−0.003 (0.009)	1/48	5/48	2/48	4/48	Not important
Financial openness	0.001 (0.003)	−0.029 (0.019)	3/48	5/48	2/48	6/48	Not important
Low corruption	0.056 (0.103)		0/24	0/24	0/24	0/24	Not important
Constraint on executives		−0.005 (0.093)	0/24	0/24	1/24	2/24	Not important
STdebt/Reserve	0.539 (0.796)	1.913 (1.91)	23/48	37/48	0/48	0/48	Very likely +
Debt/GDP	−2.52E-04 (0.001)	0.008 (0.004)	9/48	10/48	0/48	0/48	Not important
(FDI + ptf)/ Gross liability	−0.008 (0.003)	−0.010 (0.005)	0/24	0/24	9/24	13/24	Likely −
inflation	2.06E-04 (1.57E-04)	3.01E-04 (1.88E-04)	15/48	28/48	0/48	0/48	Very likely +
Fixed exchange rate regime	−0.246 (0.256)	0.350 (0.421)	0/48	1/48	1/48	4/48	Not important
Intermediate ex. rate regime	−0.377 (0.223)	−0.188 (0.344)	0/48	1/48	13/48	16/48	Likely −
Country dummy	yes	yes					
Year dummy	yes	yes					
No. observations	635	269					

Source: Authors' calculations.

the sample from 1974–2001. In the subsequent section, we use a regression tree technique to search for possible nonlinear threshold effects and interactive effects.

We try a large number of different probit specifications. The variations are: (a) including the year dummies, or not; (b) including the country fixed effects, or not; (c) measuring institutional quality by control of corruption versus constraint on executive branch of the government; (d) including the ratio of short-term external debt to reserve ratio, or not (since this variable is not available for a number of countries/years, its exclusion enlarges the sample size); and (e) defining currency crisis using three different thresholds for a "crisis month": 15 percent, 25 percent, and 35 percent. This gives a total of 48 regressions ($2^4 \times 3 = 48$).

To simplify the presentation, Table 8.2 reports a summary of these 48 regressions. Column 1 reports a sample regression with all the regressors, plus year and country fixed effects. Column 2 is a similar regression, this time replacing the variable "control of corruption" by "constraint on executive branch of the government." (Other individual Probit regression results are reported in Appendix E.)

Column 3 of Table 8.2 reports, for each regressor, in how many cases the coefficient is positive and statistically significant at the 10 percent level, relative to the total number of regressions in which the variable appears. For example, the first number in Column 3, 1/48, means that the regressor, "trade openness," appears in 48 Probit regressions, out of which, one is positive and statistically significantly different from zero at the 10 percent level. Column 4 reports, for each regressor, how many times it is positive and significant at the 20 percent level, relative to the total number of regressions it appears. Similarly, Columns 5 and 6 report, for each regressor, how many cases it is negative and significant at the 10 percent and 20 percent levels, respectively, relative to the total number of regressions it appears.

The last column in Table 8.2 presents our judgment on how likely a given variable is associated with a currency crisis. We label a variable as a "very likely" contributor to crisis if it is statistically significant at the 20 percent level more than half of the time and has a consistent sign in most regressions. We label a variable as a "likely" contributor to crisis if it is statistically significant at the 20 percent-level for between 20 percent and 50 percent of the regressions and have a consistent sign in most cases. We label a variable as "not important" for crisis in all other cases.

The labels of "very likely" and "likely" contributors to crisis are generous, not only because of the definition used above but also because we look only at correlates within the sample (that is, no cross-sample validation is used to further reduce significant variables). Even so, only two variables qualify as "very likely" contributors to crisis. They are the ratio of short-term external debt to foreign exchange reserve, and expansionary monetary policy (inflation). Both of them are likely to be positively related to the probability of crisis.

Two variables satisfy the generous definition for a "likely" contributor to crisis. The first is the ratio of FDI and equity inflows to gross foreign liabilities. This is likely to decrease the chance of a crisis. The second is the intermediate exchange rate regime. This is less likely to be associated with crisis than the floating exchange rate regime.

According to these results, the remaining variables are not likely to be important for currency crises – even judged by the generous criteria above. It may be particularly worth highlighting two such variables. First, financial openness is not robustly associated with crisis, one way or the other. Second, a fixed exchange rate regime is no more likely to be in crisis than a flexible exchange rate regime.

The recent literature on financial crisis has proposed a number of possible nonlinear "threshold" effects. For example, the financial openness on crisis probability may be hump-shaped. Some intermediate range of financial openness may be more crisis-prone than either low or high levels of financial openness. As another example, a combination of fixed exchange rate and high financial openness may be particularly prone to currency crisis. Or a combination of weak institutions (high corruption) and financial openness may make a country particularly vulnerable to speculative attacks on its currency. One could add quadratic terms or interactive terms to the above probit specification to capture some of these "threshold" effects. However, such terms are likely to be arbitrary and inflexible. The discussion that follows turns to the technique of regression tree analysis. This approach potentially can nest all such threshold and interactive effects and identify them in a relatively flexible way.

The Use of Regression Tree Analysis of Crisis Probability to Search for Threshold/Interactive Relationships

A regression tree is a data classification tool that performs a function analogous to factor analysis, but in a much more flexible way. While it is less familiar to economists, it has been used in statistical analysis of medical data to identify non-linear, interactive, or threshold patterns. We first illustrate the basic idea with an example, and then explain how we can apply the technique to our context.

The regression tree technique has three main advantages over linear regression that makes it suitable for our purpose. First, the same regressor does not have to have the same effect on the dependent variable in different ranges of value. In particular, the regression tree technique permits one or multiple threshold effects for any given regressor. Second, it identifies complex interactive relationships – how different combinations of variables in different data ranges could affect the dependent variable – in a relatively flexible way. Third, the classification result by the regression tree technique is invariant to monotonic transformations (such as logarithmic or quadratic transformations) of the explanatory variables.

Illustration of the basic idea. To illustrate the idea, we use a simplified version of a real-world medical example reported by Leo Breiman and his colleagues (Breiman and others 1984): how to classify heart attack patients into a high-risk group (those who would not survive in the next 30 days after testing) and a low-risk group (those who would live longer), using a small number of variables, so that they can be treated accordingly. The medical study has collected information on 19 different potentially relevant variables from a sample of patients. The regression tree technique searches for a data classification rule (splitting data into different branches and nodes) so that the difference between the predicted and actual values (sum of residuals squared) are sufficiently small. The classification also identifies which subset of explanatory variables is most important, and how they can be used to classify the data into different terminal nodes.

In this example, the final classification rule identified three variables as most important: minimum systolic blood pressure over the initial 24-hour period, age, and presence of sinus tachycardia. But they exhibit thresholds and interact with one another nonlinearly. More precisely, if a single variable – minimum systolic blood pressure – exceeds a threshold (91), then the patient should be in the high-risk group. No need to look at other variables. Otherwise, it depends on the interaction of two other variables. In particular, a combination of high age (>62.5 years) and presence of sinus tachycardia would again classify the patient in the high-risk group. In all other cases, the patient should be classified into the low-risk group. This statistical result can be described by a tree-like graph; hence the name of the statistical technique (see Figure 8.1.)

If the number and nature of thresholds, the needed transformation of the variables, and the pattern of variable interactions are known, one can modify a linear regression specification by adding suitably transformed variables, higher-order polynomial terms, interactive terms, and the like, to capture these relationships. If they

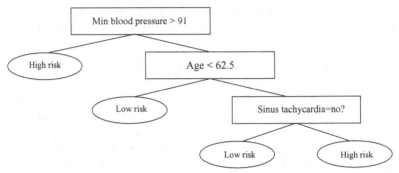

Figure 8.1. Example of Regression Tree Analysis on Heart Attack Patients. *Source*: Breiman et al. (1984).

are not known, then the regression tree is a more flexible approach to identify data patterns.

Applying the technique to the problem of currency crises. To implement the regression tree technique, one must decide on three parameters (similar to deciding on the size of a *t*-test or *F*-test, or choosing the convergence criteria in a maximum likelihood estimation of a regression). In addition, one must choose a list of candidate explanatory variables. The first parameter is mincut, the minimum number of observations needed before a first cut on a variable. The second parameter is minsize, the minimum number of observations before the last split. The statistical package we use (S-plus) requires minsize to be equal to at least twice the value of mincut. The third parameter is deviance, the tolerable level of sum of the square of the residuals for the variables at a given node. It is the amount of heterogeneity that can be tolerated without further splitting. Each of the three parameters could be a sufficient condition to stop splitting the data further.

The statistical literature does not provide definite guidance on how to choose these parameters. If one picks numbers for these parameters that are too small, then the sample may be split into too many branches and terminal nodes. In this case, sample variations and noise would clutter the reported data pattern. If one picks too big values for these parameters, the sample classification may be too coarse to be useful.

In the context of the currency crisis data, we have experimented with various possible values and discovered the following regularities. To err on the side of too fine a classification, we choose mincut = 1 percent of the sample, minsize = 2 × mincut, and deviance = 0.01. In this case, there would be a large number of combinations of variables that would generate a high crisis probability. These cases are not easily ranked in terms of the values of variables, reflecting in part the noise created by sample variation. This set of values (mincut = 1 percent of the sample) can be regarded as the lower bound for the three parameters that we wish to consider.

On the other end, we choose mincut = 5 percent of the sample, minsize = 2 × mincut, and deviance = 0.01. In this case, there will often be only one combination of variables that will generate a crisis probability of 50 percent or higher. Any higher values for mincut or minsize would typically not generate any combination of explanatory variables that are associated with a crisis probability of 50 percent or higher. This set of values therefore may be the upper bound of the parameters that we wish to consider.

Deviance $= 0.01$ is small enough that it is almost never used as a stopping rule. Thus how fine the sample/"tree" is split is essentially determined by the choice of mincut (and minsize).

The results of the regression tree analysis. We now turn to the actual statistical results. The list of the potential explanatory variables is similar to before, including:

(1) Trade openness, as measured by the ratio of total trade to GDP;
(2) De facto financial openness, as measured by the ratio of gross foreign assets plus liabilities to GDP;
(3) Institutional quality, as measured by constraint on executive branch of the government;
(4) Ratio of short-term debt to GDP;
(5) Ratio of external debt to GDP;
(6) Ratio of the sum of FDI and equity inflows to gross foreign liabilities;
(7) Expansionary monetary policies, as measured by inflation rate;
(8) Exchange rate regimes, as captured by a dummy for fixed exchange rate regime and another dummy for intermediate exchange rate regimes.

In addition, we also add decade dummies to allow for the possibility that crises are more frequent in one decade than in another, even if the values of other variables are held constant.

In the first case, there are 456 observations in total. We choose mincut $=$ 5 percent of the sample size, minsize $= 10$ percent of the sample size, and deviance $= 0.01$. The results can be reported in two ways: a visually intuitive tree-graph (with less information); and a somewhat cumbersome long form of description (with more information). In this case, we report both in the upper and lower panels of Figure 8.2, respectively. Out of the long list of possible variables, two variables are determined by the regression tree technique to be most important: ratio of short-term external debt to foreign reserves, and rate of inflation. When the ratio of short-term debt to reserves exceeds 157 percent and rate of inflation exceeds 17.2 percent, then there is a 50 percent probability of a crisis. (The long description in the lower panel of Figure 8.2 reveals that 26 country-years fall into the bin in which short-term debt to reserve ratio exceeds 157 percent and inflation exceeds 17.2 percent. Of the 26 cases, half of them are crisis episodes.) Other than this combination of variables, there does not exist any other combination of variables (from the universe of all variables specified above) that would generate a crisis probability of 50 percent or higher (for any subsample of observations that satisfy the parameters specified).[34] Therefore, the regression tree analysis suggests the combination of a high short-term debt to reserve ratio and a high inflation rate is likely to be lethal in terms of a proclivity for a currency crisis.

---

[34] The regression tree also generates branches that have no terminal nodes with crisis probability of 50 percent or higher. This study "prunes" the tree to leave out these branches, so the presentation is cleaner and more manageable.

Panel 1. Regression Tree Graph

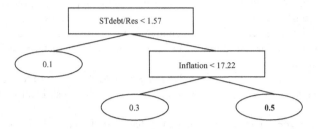

Panel 2. Long Description

Total number of observations = 456

Mincut = 5% of sample size, minsize = 10% of sample, deviance = 0.01

Pseudo R-squared = 1-51/441 = 88%

Average crisis probability = 20%

Reporting convention:

Split rule, #observation, deviance (X100), crisis probability

STdebt/RES < 1.57 347 30 0.10

STdebt/RES > 1.57 109 20 0.30

inflation < 17.2% 83 20 0.30

inflation > 17.2% 26 7 **0.50** *

Figure 8.2. Crisis Classification, Relatively Broad Cuts. *Source*: Authors' calculations.

In the second case, we have the same list of variables and the same sample, but choose smaller values for the key parameters. In particular, we let mincut = 3 percent of the sample size, minsize = twice of the mincut, and deviance = 0.01. The results (both the tree-graph and long descriptive form) are reported in Figure 8.3. When the minimum permissible node size is made smaller, more nodes (and more tree branches) would be generated. As before, a combination of high short-term debt to reserve ratio (exceeding 157 percent) and a high inflation rate (exceeding 17.2 percent) would still generate a high crisis probability. In addition, even in scenarios in which short-term debt to reserve ratio is below the threshold of 157 percent, a combination of a high inflation rate (exceeding 24.5 percent per year) and a high ratio of external debt to GDP (exceeding 80.1 percent) would also land a country into a situation of high crisis probability. (The long form reveals that 15 observations are in that bin, of which nine are crisis episodes.)

Other than these two combinations of variables, there does not exist any other combination of variables in the sample that could generate a crisis probability of 50 percent or higher (for any subset of observations that satisfy the parameters specified). Therefore, the regression tree analysis identifies three variables – ratio of external debt to GDP, in addition to ratio of short-term external debt to reserve

Panel 1. Regression Tree Graph

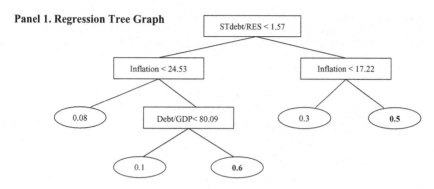

Panel 2. Long description

Total number of observations = 456
Mincut = 3% of sample size, minsize = 6% of sample, deviance = 0.01
Pseudo R-squared = 1-48/436 = 89%
Average crisis probability = 20%

Reporting convention:
Split rule, #observation, deviance(X100), crisis probability

STdebt/RES < 1.57 347 30.0 0.10

    Inflation < 24.5% 268 20.0 0.08
    Inflation > 24.5% 79 10.0 0.20

        External Debt/GDP < 80.1% 64 7.0 0.10
        External Debt/GDP > 80.1% 15 4.0 **0.60 ***

STdebt/RES > 1.57 109 20.0 0.30

    inflation < 17.2% 83 20.0 0.30
    inflation > 17.2% 26 7.0 **0.50 ***

Figure 8.3. Crisis Classification, Intermediate Cuts. *Source*: Authors' calculations.

and inflation – as the most important variables that can help classify country-years into high versus low probabilities of crisis. Note that the effect of these variables on the crisis probability is not linear, and depends on how they are combined.

Perhaps as telling as what has been chosen by the regression tree is what has *not* been chosen. For example, financial openness and institutional quality are not chosen. If there is a hump-shaped relationship between financial openness and currency crisis, or if there is a particular combination of weak institutions and high financial openness that would make a country vulnerable to crisis, the analysis suggests that these relationships are either not robust or are quantitatively unimportant (assuming that these variables are well-measured in the sample). Similarly, no decade dummies are selected by the regression tree, implying a lack of strong evidence that one decade is more crisis-prone than any other, once one takes into account the values of the other variables.

Long Description
Total number of observations=456,
Mincut = 1% of sample size, minsize = 2% of sample, deviance = 0.01
Pseudo R-squared=1-32/415 = 92%
Average crisis probability = 20%

Reporting convention: Split rule, #observation, deviance(X100), crisis probability

1)Root
2)STdebt/RES<157% 347 30.0 0.10
   4) inflation<24.5% 268 20.0 0.08
      8) cfdiequ<73% 17 4.0 0.30
        16) cfdiequ<46% 11 0.9 0.09
        17) cfdiequ>46% 6 1.0 **0.70** *
      9) cfdiequ>74% 251 20.0 0.07
        18) debt/gdp<240% 6 1.0 0.30 *
        19) debt/gdp>240% 245 10.0 0.06
           38) tradeopen<50% 131 10.0 0.09
              76) tradeopen<49% 125 7.0 0.06
              77) tradeopen>49% 6 1.0 **0.70** *
           39) tradeopen>50% 114 3.0 0.03
   5) inflation>24.5% 79 10.0 0.20
      10) tradeopen<74% 67 8.0 0.10
        20) debtgdp<86% 62 5.0 0.10
        21) debtgdp>86% 5 1.0 **0.60** *
      11) tradeopen>74% 12 3.0 0.70
        22) tradeopen<101% 5 0.0 **1.00** *
        23) tradeopen>101% 7 2.0 0.40 *
3)STdebtRES>157% 109 20.0 0.30
   6) inflation<17% 83 20.0 0.30
      12) finopen<6.84 40 9.0 0.30
        24) debt/gdp<28.5% 8 0.0 0.00 *
        25) debt/gdp>28.5% 32 8.0 0.40
           50) cfdiequ<8% 7 1.0 **0.70** *
           51) cfdiequ>8% 25 6.0 0.40
              102) STdebt/RES<250% 6 1.0 **0.70** *
              103) STdebt/RES>250% 19 4.0 0.30
      13) finopen>6.84 43 6.0 0.20
        26) debt/gdp<368% 38 4.0 0.10
        27) debt/gdp>368% 5 1.0 **0.60** *
   7) inflation>17.2222 26 7.0 0.50
      14) inflation<28.0874 6 0.0 1.00 *
      15) inflation>28.0874 20 5.0 0.30
        30) STdebtRES<0.0235644 11 3.0 0.50
           60) cfdiequ<18.2002 5 0.8 **0.80** *
           61) cfdiequ>18.2002 6 1.0 0.30 *
        31) STdebt/RES>0.0235644 9 0.9 0.10 *

Figure 8.4. Crisis Classification, Relatively Fine Cuts. *Source*: Authors' calculations.

We could generate even finer classifications by letting mincut = 1 percent of the sample, minsize = 2 percent of the sample, and deviance = 0.01. This would naturally generate even more tree branches and even more cases of high crisis probability (with fewer observations in each of the node). Because the tree-graph becomes too messy, we choose to report only the long descriptive form in Figure 8.4.

While the result is reported for completeness, we think that the increase in the number of variable combinations that can generate crisis involves terminal nodes with too few observations. The influence of sample variation (noise) is likely to have increased in this case. So the resulting classification is likely much less robust to out-of-sample validation than the previous two cases. Consequently, we would not wish to generalize too much from this particular result.

As a robustness check, we have also varied the crisis definition using the 35 percent (and 15 percent) threshold to identify crisis month (and hence the crisis year). The results are not reported to save space. The qualitative results are broadly similar to what is described above.

We have also conducted similar regression tree analyses using control of corruption instead of constraint on executives as a measure of institutional quality. The results are similar in spirit; to save space, these results are not reported.

Next Steps

The findings of this section are consistent with the previous literature on leading indicators of currency crises: high levels of external debt do not necessarily lead to crises on their own, but they do significantly raise the probability of crisis if capital inflow is tilted to the and is not used (in part) to build up reserves. Accordingly, we will want to pay special attention to the composition of capital and use of inflows in the next section of the study. At the same time, we must recognize that identifying a variable such as the ratio of short-term debt to reserves as a significant predictor of currency crises does not mean that we can necessarily distinguish among competing theories or choose the best policies for crisis prevention or crisis management. Debt and inflation are certainly endogenous, with respect to fiscal and monetary policy.

The composition of capital inflows can be endogenous, as well. It is not necessarily a deliberate policy decision to borrow short term, to borrow in dollars, or to borrow through bank loans rather than FDI. It may be the result of some deep structural cause, such as crony capitalism[35] or original sin.[36] Or a shift in composition could be a consequence of suddenly reduced foreign willingness to hold domestic assets, together with the authorities' determination not to devalue. That is, it could be a symptom of the sudden stop, rather than a cause.

The procrastination interpretation, for example, fits the shift in capital flows to Mexico during the course of 1994 toward the short term and toward the dollar-denominated, as the government substituted *tesobonos* (short-term dollar-linked bonds) for *Cetes* (peso bonds) as a stop-gap measure. The aim was to delay a painful choice between devaluing and continuing to lose reserves. In other words, the change in composition was a stalling tactic, analogous to a financially troubled household that starts charging its mortgage payments on its credit card.

Delayed adjustment – the lag from the date that reserves peak after a sudden stop to the date of a devaluation, restructuring, or an IMF program – may raise the ratio of short-term debt to reserves so much that an eventual crisis becomes more likely. Furthermore, if, as a result of delayed adjustment, the country goes

---

[35] For example, Wei and Wu (2002).
[36] For example, Eichengreen and Hausmann (1999).

into the crisis with a high proportion of dollar-denominated and short-term debt, then it may be more likely that the subsequent recession will be steep, whatever changes in macropolicies are then adopted. At that point, there may be no optimal combination of expenditure reduction and devaluation that avoids a sharp loss in output.[37] The lesson would be a more subtle story than simple admonitions to developing country policymakers to avoid borrowing short-term. The crisis Probit models cannot answer such questions, because they are not designed to do so, either with respect to their explanatory variables or with respect to what is being explained. Clearly more hypothesis testing is required.

TESTING HYPOTHESES REGARDING ECONOMIC PERFORMANCE

We test, first, if there are any policies of crisis prevention that seem consistently to have given countries better economic performance on average since 1990. Subsequently, we look at crisis-management policies.

Seven Measures of Crisis Prevention Policies

As noted, this study constructed a measure of output lost in crisis – *crisisloss* (or *Compcrisis*) – intended to be a composite measure of a country's proneness to severe crises. To see the effects of the seven "crisis prevention" policy variables, our first base-case regression, is Equation 1. We condition on initial income per capita, and also include a variable for war (with the scored severity of each conflict weighted by the number of years).[38] The two macroeconomic variables are taken to be debt/GDP and inflation, in light of the empirical success of the latter in the preceding section.

$$\text{Crisisloss} = a + b1 \text{ Noncorruptness} + b2 \text{ opencapital} + b3 \text{ gdpcap90}$$
$$+ b4 \text{ inflatn} + b5 \text{ externaldebt/gdp} + b6 \text{ compshort}$$
$$+ b7 \text{ origsin} + b8 \text{ war} + b9 \text{ exrateflex} + u \qquad (1)$$

The results are reported in Table 8.3. Neither of the macroeconomic variables is highly significant. But the composition of capital inflows is more important. The coefficient of original sin (that is, the currency mismatch) is significant at low levels, with the hypothesized sign. Noncorruptness has the expected effect, and is significant. The open capital markets variable has a negative sign, suggesting that liberalization actually reduces the frequency or severity of crises. This is the same result found, for example, by Reuven Glick and Michael Hutchison (2002). The effect appears to be significant at the 95 percent level when we use the Klein (2003) measure of capital account liberalization (which is based on data for 1973–85), though not when the updated Quinn (1997) measure is used (1992–95). Exchange

---

[37] Krugman (1998b); Frankel (2001).

[38] The War variable is in the equation largely to take into account the experience of many African countries. Easterly and Levine (1997), for example, find a large role for ethnic conflict. Aizenman and Glick (2003) point out that one needs to control for both military spending and threats.

Table 8.3. *Explaining output lost in crises: base case regression*

Variable	Using qka[a] Coefficient (Std. error)	Using qka[a] Number of obs = 67 F(10,56) = 1.02 Prob>F = 0.4370 R-squared = 0.1977	Using share[b] Coefficient (Std. error)	Using share[b] Number of obs = 68 F(10,57) = 0.72 Prob>F = 0.7048 R-squared = 0.1620
Noncorruptness	−0.049*		−0.044#	
	(0.029)		(0.029)	
Absence of capital	−0.038**		−0.010	
controls	(0.018)		(0.038)	
Inflation	0.141		0.160#	
	(0.114)		(0.120)	
External debt/GDP	0.002		−0.010	
	(0.017)		(0.019)	
Short-term debt/	−0.138		−0.166	
Total debt	(0.202)		(0.199)	
FDI/GDP	−0.008		−0.005	
	(0.008)		(0.008)	
Currency mismatch	0.093		0.146#	
	(0.088)		(0.098)	
War	0.277		0.318	
	(0.372)		(0.395)	
GDP per capita (1990)	0.023#		0.007	
	(0.017)		(0.013)	
Exchange rate	0.052		0.037	
regime (flexibility)	(0.058)		(0.054)	
Constant	−0.104		−0.049	
	(0.137)		(0.123)	

Note: Macro variables are inflation and external debt.
[a] Regression uses average of Klein's interpretation of Quinn's variables qka73, qka82, qka85 as gauge for "absence of capital controls."
[b] Regression uses Klein's "share9295" variable as gauge for "absence of capital controls."
Source: Authors' calculations.

rate flexibility – if anything – appears to make crises worse, rather than better. Fans of currency boards and other institutional fixes should like this result, but the effect is not statistically significant. War and initial income have no discernible effect.

Equation 2 replaces debt/GDP and inflation, which seem too endogenous to call policy variables, with budget deficit/GDP and the rate of credit creation (growth in net domestic assets). At the same time, it drops the war variable. Credit creation shows up with the right sign, but not with statistical significance. One possible interpretation of its weak effect is that, while the first-generation speculative attack models give it a starring role as villain, the growth literature considers it just the opposite, viewing increases in the ratio of domestic credit to GDP a reflection of financial development – and thus beneficial.[39] The budget deficit effect shows up better (particularly in those regressions where the 1990s measure of capital account liberalization is used in place of the 1980s measure). Two other variables do show up (at moderate levels of statistical significance): noncorruptness and original sin (currency mismatch). Countries tend to have fewer crises or less severe ones if they are free from corruption, and tilt the composition of their capital inflows away from dollar-denomination. Open capital markets are again marginally significant, and in a direction that suggests that liberalization actually reduces the frequency or severity of crises.

$$\text{Crisisloss} = a + b1 \text{ Noncorruptness} + b2 \text{ opencapital} + b3 \text{ gdpcap90}$$
$$+ b4 \text{ credit} + b5 \text{ bdgdp} + b6 \text{ compshort}$$
$$+ b7 \text{ origsin} + b8 \text{ war} + b9 \text{ exrateflex} + u \qquad (2)$$

There are two obvious problems with the specification for the exchange rate regime variable. One is that the move from a fixed exchange rate regime to a flexible one sometime during the decade may be the *result* of a currency crisis, rather than the cause. This is an argument for being more precise about the timing. The other possible objection would come from proponents of either the hard peg school of thought, or the corners hypothesis: that the exchange rate flexibility variable does not allow a test of their point of view.

Accordingly, we tested for each of these hypotheses. For the hard peg option, we defined a dummy variable that is equal to 1 only for currency boards, dollarization, and monetary unions – not for conventional pegs. The sign is as often negative as positive, and is not at all significant. Thus there is no evidence to support the claims for the hard peg. The estimated coefficient on the hard peg dummy points to amelioration of crises, but it is not at all statistically significant.

Next, we tested the corners hypothesis, with a dummy variable that is equal to 1 for *either* a hard peg or a float. In both cases, the dummy variable countries that had a corner regime during only part of the sample period receive the corresponding proportional weight on that regime. The results are not reported, to save space. The coefficient on the corner regimes – either hard peg or float – often attains low or moderate levels of significance. But it is of the opposite sign from the corners hypothesis. In other words, it rejects the popular hypothesis that the corner regimes are less crisis-prone than the intermediate regimes. This is consistent with the results regarding intermediate regimes in the probit analysis above. Perhaps intermediate regimes are better, after all.[40]

Before testing for some other combinations of policy variables, we checked the effects of the base-case list of variables on other more familiar measures of country performance. We tried defining the dependent variable, the measure of performance, to be the standard deviation of growth. This measure of performance is correlated with the crisis measure, as one would expect. (The correlation is 0.2101.) We add

---

[39] Those carrying on the tradition of Goldsmith include Bencivenga and Smith (1991), De Gregorio and Guidotti (1995), and King and Levine (1993), among many others.

[40] The intermediate regimes still have their supporters, such as Williamson (2001). Frankel (2004) includes a skeptical account of the "rise and fall of the corners hypothesis."

the standard deviation of the terms of trade as an obvious, and largely exogenous, determinant of volatility. It rarely shows significance, however (as is also true when the dependent variable is one of the crisis measures, in results not reported). The only variable to show even marginal levels of significance in determining volatility is noncorruptness, which reduces the standard deviation of growth, as one would hope.

Next we tried the average growth rate over the 1990–2002 period as the dependent variable. This equation is intended as a bridge to the large literature on the determinants of economic growth. Drawing on some of the conclusions from that literature, the list of variables include initial income, size of the country (population), tropical location, and two measures of factor accumulation: investment/GDP and a measure of education or human capital. The coefficient on education is of only marginal significance, and that on investment is of no significance. Other authors have found measurement problems as being very important in the performance of these variables. Population is highly significant, confirming that larger countries have an advantage. A high ratio of short-term debt to equity and FDI shows a negative effect on growth that is statistically significant. The same is true of exchange rate flexibility. Noncorruptness also shows a beneficial effect on growth, if again ·of marginal significance. This estimation could be refined by use of some of the measures that the most recent growth research has found to be relatively less prone to error.[41]

Interactive Effects

Many of the interesting claims in the recent literature concern the effects of combinations of our variables. To test for interaction effects, we return to the composite crisis variable (total output lost in crises) as the measure of performance.

The proposed hypotheses of interactive effects involving capital account openness did not receive much support here. When the capital account variables is interacted with noncorruptness, or with the measure of monetary policy (domestic credit creation, NDA), the estimates are insignificant. In the case of fiscal policy, the finding is worse: We can reject, at least at low significance levels, the hypothesis that the combination of open capital markets and a high budget deficit worsens the crisis problem. This does not mean that the two variables considered individually do not increase the frequency or severity of crises in an additive way; it is just that we have found nothing particularly noteworthy about the combination of the two.

In the cases regarding the composition of capital inflows, the answer is worse still: the coefficient appears to be statistically significant, but again of a sign that is the opposite of the proposed direction. We reject the hypothesized deadliness of the combination of open capital markets and short-tilted composition, and also reject the hypothesis regarding the deadliness of the combination of open capital markets and currency mismatch. The view that the combination of open capital markets and fixed

---

[41] For example, as surveyed in Bosworth and Collins (2003). Investment turns out to be an unreliable measure of additions to the capital stock, and the quantity of education turns out to be much less powerful than the quality. (This study also tried literacy, but it performed worse than years of secondary schooling.)

Table 8.4a. *Explaining output lost in crises: interaction of absence of*
capital controls and 1990 per capita GDP

	Using qka	
Variable	Coefficient (std. error)	Number of obs = 67 F(10,56) = 0.85 Prob>F = 0.5854 R-squared = 0.1675
Noncorruptness	−0.055# (0.034)	
Absence of capital controls	−0.184* (0.098)	
Growth of domestic credit	0.042 (0.104)	
Budget deficit/GDP	0.005 (0.004)	
Short-term debt/Total debt	−0.132 (0.192)	
FDI/GDP	−0.012# (0.009)	
Currency mismatch	0.145# (0.104)	
GDP per capita (1990)	0.001 (0.013)	
Exchange rate (flexibility)	0.048 (0.053)	
Absence of capital controls × GDP per capita (1990)	0.022* (0.012)	
Constant	0.051 (0.125)	

Source: Authors' calculations.

exchange rates causes crises also receives no support. This is not an encouraging result for most of the interaction effects.

The one interactive effect that shows up highly significant is reported in Tables 8.4a and 8.4b. The variable that interacts open capital markets and income shows a positive sign and is significant at the 95 percent level. This is the opposite of the finding of Javier Gomez Biscarri, Sebastian Edwards, and Fernando Perez de Gracia (2003). It might be rationalized by a Kuznets-style U-shaped relationship: open capital markets can lead to heavy borrowing and thereby to crises in middle-income countries, but are less dangerous in poor countries and rich (the latter are not present in our sample).

A few other variables here are statistically significant, as well. Countries with more open capital markets again show up here as having reduced frequency or severity of crises, now significant at the 95 percent level. An increase in the ratio of short-term debt to reserves increases the frequency or severity of crises. Non-corruptness and currency mismatch have the hypothesized effects, but at fairly low

Table 8.4b. *Explaining output lost in crises: interaction of absence of
capital controls and 1990 per capita GDP*

	Using qka	
Variable	Coefficient (std. error)	Number of obs = 66 F(8,57) = 0.86 Prob>F = 0.5513 R-squared = 0.1387
Noncorruptness	−0.056#	
	(0.039)	
Absence of capital controls	−0.287**	
	(0.134)	
Growth of domestic credit	0.044	
	(0.113)	
Budget deficit/GDP	0.005	
	(0.004)	
Short-term debt/Reserves	0.284*	
	(0.166)	
Currency mismatch	0.168#	
	(0.110)	
GDP per capita (1990)	−0.007	
	(0.015)	
Exchange rate (flexibility)	0.054	
	(0.054)	
Absence of capital controls × GDP per capita (1990)	0.035**	
	(0.017)	
Constant	0.036	
	(0.122)	

Source: Authors' calculations.

levels of significance. In this regression, the rate of growth of domestic credit, the budget deficit, and the exchange rate regime variable do not attain statistical significance.

Crisis Management Policies

We now turn to the merits of differing approaches to managing crises *after* they happen. This is rather different from analyzing policies to prevent crises – notwithstanding the importance of realizing that crisis *prevention* policies carry important implications for crisis *management* policies, particularly in the form of moral hazard generated by bailouts.

The approach begins by looking at the month-by-month statistical profile of reserves in crisis episodes. We retain our previous definition of what constitutes a crisis: an increase in exchange market pressure that exceeds the threshold in absolute terms (although to focus on the larger crises, we raise the threshold in this section to 45 percent) and also exceeds a threshold for acceleration relative to the preceding month (still 10 percent).

The period of sudden stop: From reserve peak to crisis. We define the period of sudden stop as the span of time that ends with the crisis itself and begins with the preceding peak in reserves. It marks the end of a period of inflow, and the beginning of the period of outflow. We use a seven-month centered moving average of reserves to identify the peak that precedes each crisis. In our calculations, the average length of the period of sudden stop is 6.3 months. Much of the literature, both theoretical and academic, essentially assumes that this period is collapsed to a single instance, thereby losing sight of some important questions.

Figures 8.5a–8.5e are bar graphs showing the time-profile of reserves for some prominent crises of the last eight years (Mexico, 1994; Indonesia, 1998; Russia, 1998; Brazil, 1999, Turkey, 2001). Dark bars indicate the date of the crisis (by the exchange market pressure index) and the date that adjustment began (devaluation or IMF program). The average reserve loss, across countries, during the period of sudden stop, is 35 percent (computed relative to the peak, not logarithmically). This does not count the reserves lost in the month of speculative attack, which we have identified as the month when the overall exchange market pressure index exceeds its threshold.

Figure 8.6 shows the average experience, over the last 12 years, among 87 country crises. Here, each country's reserves are expressed as a ratio to the level in the peak month, and the moving average is computed over three months. The peak of the average comes about 13 months before the crisis.

Delaying Adjustment

One key question is whether delaying adjustment, after the sudden stop has begun, makes crises more severe, or more likely to happen at all. The answer may well be "No," since the correct economics is to "finance" a deficit – provided it is temporary – by drawing down reserves, rather than necessarily to "adjust."

We could define the month when adjustment begins as the month of devaluation or of a substantial fiscal contraction, or as the month that an agreement on an IMF program is signed. But here we simply assume that adjustment begins at the same time as the crisis itself. A relevant metric for measuring the length of delay is what percentage of reserves the country has lost by the time of the crisis, relative to the peak. Does it affect the severity of the crisis?

We regressed output loss in the year of a crisis against a number of our "crisis management" policy variables: change in maturity composition during the sudden stop period, a dummy representing whether the country signed an agreement with the IMF, and a measure of the mix of adjustment policies. The fraction of reserves lost (during the interval from reserve peak to crisis) enters with the hypothesized positive sign, but is not significant at the 80 percent- or 90 percent-level of significance.

Shifting Composition of Debt During the Sudden Stop Period

The exploration in previous sections of the importance of the composition of inward foreign investment, and the realization that the composition changes substantially over time, inspire us to consider a new hypothesis. That is, that during the period of sudden stop, the authorities sometimes delay adjustment, not just by drawing down

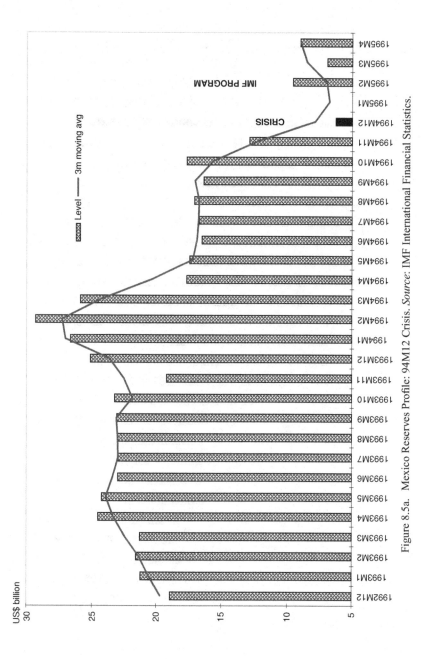

Figure 8.5a. Mexico Reserves Profile: 94M12 Crisis. *Source:* IMF International Financial Statistics.

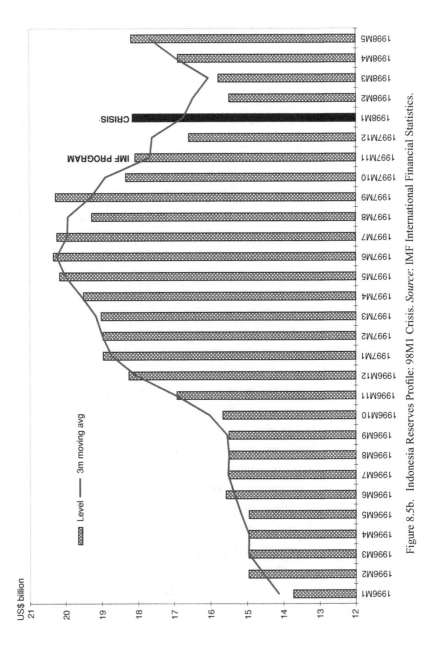

Figure 8.5b. Indonesia Reserves Profile: 98M1 Crisis. *Source*: IMF International Financial Statistics.

352

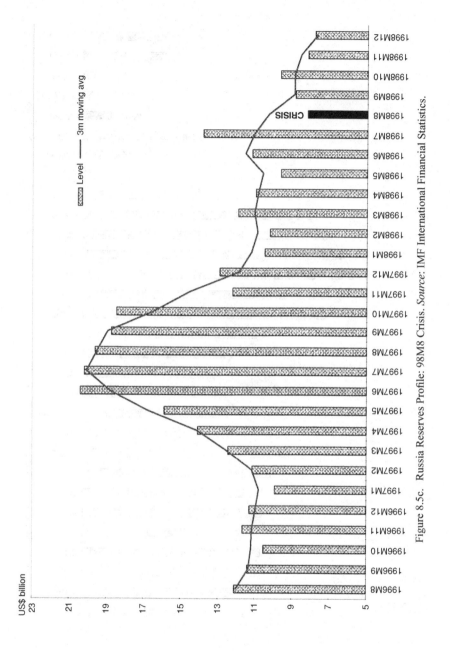

US$ billion

Level — 3m moving avg

CRISIS

Figure 8.5c. Russia Reserves Profile: 98M8 Crisis. *Source*: IMF International Financial Statistics.

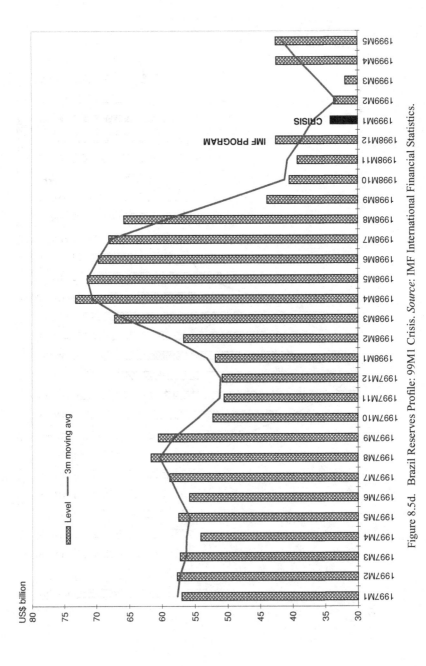

Figure 8.5d. Brazil Reserves Profile: 99M1 Crisis. *Source:* IMF International Financial Statistics.

354

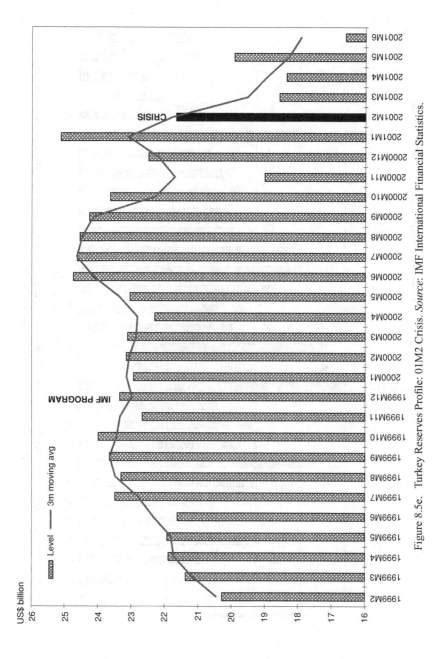

Figure 8.5e. Turkey Reserves Profile: 01M2 Crisis. *Source*: IMF International Financial Statistics.

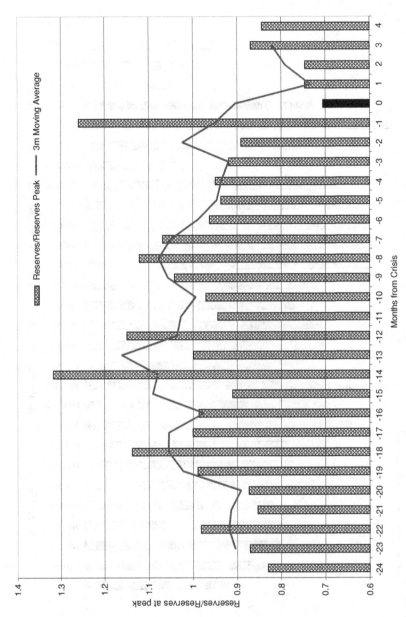

Figure 8.6. Average Precrisis Reserves Profile. *Note*: Reserves level is normalized against each country's precrisis peak before averaging for all crises. *Source*: IMF International Financial Statistics.

reserves, but also by shifting the composition of capital inflows toward short-term and dollar-denominated debt. This strategy helps sustain the willingness of foreign residents to continue lending, in the short term, but magnifies the fragility of the economy rapidly over time. In particular, the strategy worsens the balance sheet problems that have been identified in the literature as the major explanation for the severe losses in output that have followed recent crises (an identification that is consistent with our own results and beliefs). Whatever the composition of the capital inflows a year or two earlier, if on the day when the crisis occurs the debt is substantially dollar-denominated and short-term, then the country is in trouble – regardless of what mix of policies it chooses as the means of adjustment. Either a short-term increase in interest rates or a devaluation, or any combination of the two, will sharply worsen the balance sheets of debtor firms and banks, and thereby contribute to bankruptcies and contraction in output and employment.

A prime example is Mexico during the course of 1994. International enthusiasm for investing in Mexico began to decline after the beginning of the year, due to some combination of the uprising in Chiapas, the assassination of presidential candidate Colosio, a new upward trend in U.S. interest rates, and the sexennial fiscal laxity of the Mexican election year. The authorities clung to the exchange rate target and delayed adjustment, in the hopes circumstances would turn around. Most obviously, during much of the year they ran down reserves. But an important alternative mechanism of delay was to placate nervous investors by offering them *tesobonos* (short-term dollar linked bonds) in place of the peso bonds (*Cetes*) that they had previously held. Between the first and second halves of the year, the share of foreign borrowing that was of maturity less than 1 year rose from 0.48 to 0.55, an increase of 7 percentage points.[42] Figure 8.7a shows the dramatic increase in dollar-linked debt during the year leading up to the peso crisis of December 1994, and Figure 8.7b shows the shift toward shorter maturities. It seems likely that the magnitude of the Mexican recession in 1995 stemmed in part not just from the adverse balance sheet effects that have been so frequently noted since then, but particularly from the adverse *shift* in balance sheets that took place during the course of 1994.

Brazil may offer a more positive example: the exception that proves the rule.[43] Reserves peaked in May 1998. Subsequently, contagion from the Russian devaluation and default leapt across the Atlantic to Brazil. As in Mexico in 1994 (or Korea in 1997), Brazil faced an important presidential election toward the end of the year, which added to the authorities' incentives to delay adjustment and to rely instead on hopes that capital inflows would resume on their own. When Brazil was finally forced to devalue in January 1999, some observers predicted disaster, based on the analogies of recessions in Mexico in 1995 and East Asia in 1998. Indeed, reserves had been run down to similarly low levels. Yet Brazil suffered no output loss in 1999. What explains the difference? The most common answer from

---

[42] The data are from the BIS and refer only to bank loans. Nothing is available at higher frequency than annual.

[43] The expression "proves the rule" is used in its original and proper meaning of "puts the rule to a difficult test," rather than the common modern usage of "seems to violate the rule, but we don't know why."

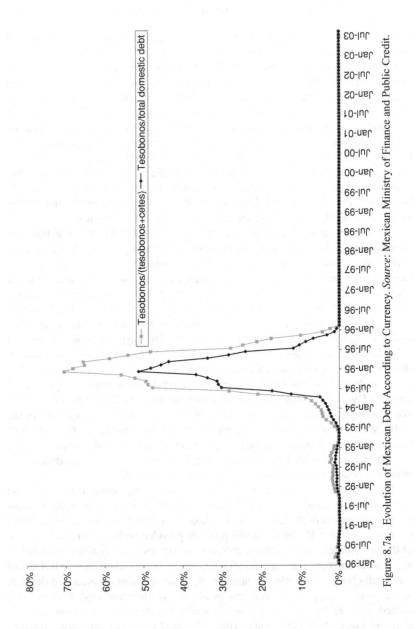

Figure 8.7a. Evolution of Mexican Debt According to Currency. *Source:* Mexican Ministry of Finance and Public Credit.

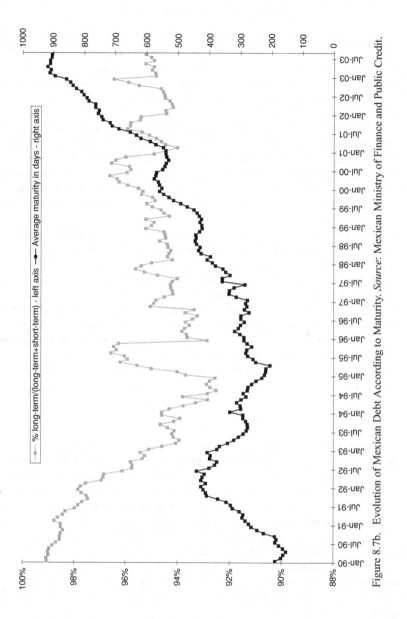

Figure 8.7b. Evolution of Mexican Debt According to Maturity. *Source*: Mexican Ministry of Finance and Public Credit.

knowledgeable participants and observers is that during the intervening eight months, the authorities had used their reserves to allow the private sector to hedge or unwind short-term dollar liabilities.[44] According to our data, the share of foreign borrowing that was short-term fell during the second half of the year from 0.68 to 0.62 or by 6 percentage points. By the end of the year, just before the devaluation, balance sheets were stronger, not weaker.[45]

Is the shift toward dollar-denominated debt during the period of sudden stop a general phenomenon? Many countries were never able to borrow much in domestic currency in the first place, so that there is little scope for shifting the composition to dollars. But are there more Mexico's than Brazil's? Unfortunately, data on the currency composition of debt are not available at a sufficiently high frequency to do the test. The "original sin" data on currency mismatch that we have been using are available only on an annual basis.

It is more feasible to test the proposition that the composition shifts in an undesirable direction with respect to the maturity structure, than it is to test with respect to currency denomination. Data on the maturity of bank loans are available from the BIS on a quarterly basis for the period since 2000, and on a biannual basis before that. Table 8.5 reports the change during the period of sudden stop for 74 crises. On average, the fraction of loans that were short-term increased by 0.6 percentage points after the peak in reserves (over a period of one or two quarters, depending on data availability). When we ran regressions of the subsequent output loss against our various crisis-management-policy measures, changes in maturity composition and the loss in reserves were both of the hypothesized sign, although not statistically significant.

Going to the IMF

Whether IMF programs help or hurt, relative to the relevant alternative, is an important and controversial question. Of course one does not necessarily want to blame the surgeon because his patients die more often than do the chiropractor's; the former is likely to get the more serious cases. Even those studies that have tried to do a careful job of constructing the relevant counterfactual have had a difficult time of it.[46] One of the problems for statistical differentiation is that so few countries choose the Malaysian option of *not* going to the Fund. But, for what it is worth, we looked for a statistical relationship between a country's signing a program with the IMF and the magnitude of the output loss in the year of the crisis. We found no relationship, whether conditioning on other policy variables or not. (We tried counting only countries that had gone to the Fund within a six-month period, or within a 12-month period.)

---

[44] For example, comments by Arminio Fraga and Ilan Goldfajn at a NBER conference in 2000 on Brazil (http://www.nber.org/crisis/brazil_report.html) covered the roles of national policymakers and other players (http://www.nber.org/crisis/).
[45] Other factors may also help explain why the Brazilian economy exceeded expectations after the devaluation, including worldwide reductions in interest rates in the interim, and the confidence-boosting appointment of Arminio Fraga as central bank governor.
[46] Hutchison (2003) finds no difference.

Table 8.5. *Shift toward short-term debt during period of sudden stop, 74 crises, 1990–2002*

Crisis	Date of reserve peak	ST/total in quarter of crisis	ST/total in comparison quarter[a]	Change	Crisis	Date of reserve peak	ST/total in quarter of crisis	ST/total in comparison quarter[a]	Change
ALG90M7	90M3	0.395	0.369	0.026	MAUR93M1	92M9	0.771	0.736	0.035
ALG94M3	93M10	0.351	0.399	−0.048	MEX94M12	93M12	0.554	0.485	0.069
ANG02M12	02M5	0.460	0.475	−0.016	MOLD98M11	97M10	0.543	0.438	0.106
ANG99M5	97M10	0.491	0.499	−0.009	MYAN96M6	95M7	0.945	0.629	0.316
AZER95M9	95M6	0.667	0.643	−0.024	NIC92M10	92M6	0.814	0.801	0.013
BEL99M2	99M1	0.267	0.192	0.076	NIGA92M3	91M11	0.381	0.347	0.034
BRAZ99M1	98M5	0.623	0.680	−0.057	NIGA99M1	98M5	0.550	0.531	0.019
CAM93M4	93M3	0.482	0.431	0.052	NIGR94M1	92M11	0.407	0.500	−0.093
CAM97M11	97M10	0.650	0.522	0.128	NIGR98M8	97M6	0.262	0.538	−0.277
CHIN92M7	92M3	0.402	0.446	−0.043	PAK90M10	90M3	0.710	0.675	0.036
CONG01M5	01M1	0.606	0.447	0.159	PAK96M10	96M3	0.488	0.658	−0.170
CONG90M6	90M4	0.576	0.671	0.095	PAN97M6	97M5	0.439	0.416	−0.023
CONG94M1	93M3	0.522	0.591	−0.069	ROM97M1	96M9	0.395	0.495	−0.100
CONG97M8	97M6	0.372	0.380	0.008	RUSS98M8	98M4	0.476	0.470	0.006
COT90M5	90M1	0.678	0.641	0.037	RWA90M11	90M10	0.667	0.706	−0.039
COT93M11	93M4	0.797	0.830	−0.033	SEN93M11	93M11	0.843	0.876	−0.033
DOM90M12	90M1	0.440	0.405	0.034	SOAF94M3	94M1	0.564	0.598	−0.034
DOM94M8	93M10	0.530	0.523	0.007	SRI98M7	97M11	0.541	0.542	−0.001
ECU92M5	92M1	0.518	0.475	0.044	SUD90M5	90M1	0.837	0.791	0.047
ETH92M10	91M9	0.187	0.261	−0.074	TANZ97M7	97M3	0.864	0.777	0.087
GAB01M9	01M1	0.593	0.622	−0.029	TOGO94M1	92M6	0.733	0.607	0.127
GAB97M2	96M6	0.454	0.583	−0.130	TT92M1	91M3	0.301	0.292	0.008

(*continued*)

Table 8.5 (*continued*)

Crisis	Date of reserve peak	ST/total in quarter of crisis	ST/total in comparison quarter[a]	Change	Crisis	Date of reserve peak	ST/total in quarter of crisis	ST/total in comparison quarter[a]	Change
GHA00M7	00M2	0.613	0.552	0.061	TUN91M4	90M9	0.563	0.519	0.044
GHA90M10	90M6	0.749	0.636	−0.114	TURK01M2	00M10	0.676	0.664	0.012
GUI97M6	97M2	0.849	0.794	0.055	TURK94M3	93M8	0.626	0.554	0.073
INDI91M4	90M3	0.297	0.305	−0.007	UAE95M9	95M7	0.920	0.886	0.034
INDO98M1	97M6	0.626	0.628	−0.002	UGA90M5	90M4	0.861	0.785	0.076
JAM91M9	91M2	0.374	0.379	−0.006	UKR98M9	97M9	0.489	0.427	0.062
JOR91M8	91M7	0.414	0.456	−0.042	URG02M7	01M9	0.605	0.652	−0.047
KEN94M11	94M7	0.619	0.597	0.022	VENZ02M2	00M11	0.341	0.387	−0.046
KOR97M12	97M7	0.728	0.775	−0.047	VENZ94M5	93M9	0.297	0.315	−0.018
LEB90M8	90M7	0.813	0.823	−0.010	ZAMB01M12	01M8	0.908	0.938	−0.030
LIBR93M3	93M1	0.405	0.397	0.007	ZAMB91M4	90M12	0.654	0.661	−0.007
LIBR96M12	96M10	0.362	0.396	−0.034	ZAMB94M11	94M11	0.542	0.577	−0.035
LIBY02M1	01M12	0.966	0.952	−0.015	ZIMB90M11	90M11	0.715	0.574	0.141
MALAW92M3	91M10	0.393	0.371	0.022	ZIMB97M9	96M8	0.740	0.753	−0.013
AVERAGE ACROSS CRISES									**0.006**

Note:

[a] Quarter of preceding reserve peak is used in comparison to crisis quarter. In cases where reserve peak and crisis fall in same quarter, that quarter is compared against the following quarter if crisis and/or reserve peak fall in June or December. If crisis and/or reserve peak fall in any other month, that quarter is compared against the preceding quarter. Data are available from BIS in semiannual frequency (Q2 and Q4). In cases where reserve peak or crisis fall in Q1 or Q3, the preceding quarter's data are used. For data after 2000, quarterly data is available. If crisis or reserve peak falls in first month of quarter, the preceding quarter's data are used; otherwise, that quarter's data are used.

For expansion of country abbreviations, see Table D-1, Appendix D to this chapter.

Source: World Bank *World Development Indicators*; IMF *World Economic Outlook*; and *International Financial Statistics*.

Table 8.6. *Crisis management policies*

					Number of obs = 7	
					F(4,2) = 12.48	
					Prob>F 0.0756	
					R-squared 0.9244	
Regressions with Roubst standard errors					Root MSE 0.90388	
Outputloss	Coeff.	Robust std. err.	T	P > |t|	[95% Confidence interval]	
resloss	1.140.57	1.176052	0.97	0.435	−3.919787	6.2005
composition	2.050635	3.989811	0.51	0.658	−15.11614	19.21741
imf6m	−0.6449699	0.8878959	−0.73	0.543	−4.465278	3.175338
rmindelrer	1.166299	0.190995	6.11	0.026	0.344514	1.988085
constant	0.0068248	0.270099	0.03	0.982	−1.155317	1.168967

Source: Authors' calculations.

The Mix: Spending Contraction versus Devaluation

Perhaps the most interesting question of crisis management is the question of the mix between adjustment by real devaluation versus expenditure reduction – assuming a fixed quantity of adjustment given by the balance of payments constraint. When we think of expenditure reduction as fiscal policy, our measure is the change in the budget relative to the increase in the trade balance. We found that countries where the fall in government consumption constituted a large share of the adjustment in the trade balance suffered a smaller output loss, other things being equal. The effect, however, was not generally significant at the 95 percent level.

When we think of expenditure reduction as monetary policy, our measure of the mix is the increase in the real interest rate relative to the increase in the real exchange rate. We found that countries that relied heavily on high interest real rates (either absolutely or relatively to the preceding year) suffered larger output losses than those that relied on big real depreciation of the currency. The difference was very significant statistically, as reported in Table 8.6.

It is useful to note that the regressions reported here do not include initial economywide corporate or bank balance sheet information due to lack of data. Those economies that started with a more serious currency-mismatch in their balance sheets before the crisis could fare less well with a depreciation approach as a crisis-management tool.

SUMMARY OF CONCLUSIONS

Our results are consistent with much of the previous empirical literature in that we do not find that crises are necessarily the outcome of high current account deficits or high indebtedness per se, nor even of domestic credit creation. Nor does exchange rate flexibility necessarily mean that crises will be avoided. There is stronger evidence that poor institutional quality (corruption) is a fundamental problem.

But some of the new conventional wisdoms do not appear to be borne out by our tests. The corner exchange rate regimes are, if anything, more prone to serious crises, not less. If emerging market countries liberalize their capital controls, they are less prone to crises, not more. An extensive search for interactive effects that have been claimed by others does not uncover much evidence that capital account openness is particularly dangerous in combination with low income, expansionary policies, or corruption.

Countries are likely to have more frequent and more severe crises if their capital inflows are tilted toward short-term dollar borrowing and away from FDI and equity inflows, and if they hold a low level of reserves. The ratio of short-term debt to reserves is a particularly important indicator. We find evidence with the regression tree technique that high levels of inflation significantly raise the probability of crisis when coming in combination with a low level of reserves and a composition of capital inflow that is tilted to the short-term.

This chapter has sought to draw greater attention to policy decisions that are made *during the phase when capital inflows come to a sudden stop.* All of the theoretical literature, and most of the empirical literature, treats the "sudden stop" phase as taking place in a single instant: The country goes directly from a period of capital inflows and strong reserves to a crisis of capital outflows and plunging reserves. In reality there is often an interim period, when international investors have begun to lose enthusiasm, but the crisis has not yet hit. Think of the lag between the beginning of 1994, when investors began to pull out of Mexico, and the December peso crisis. (It does not matter for our purposes why investors pulled out, whether it was U.S. interest rates, domestic instability, election year macroeconomics, or even investor fickleness.) We find, across a broad sample of developing countries (1990–2002), that the typical lag between the peak in reserves and a currency crisis was six months to a year, depending on the calculation. The average loss in reserves during the sudden stop phase was 35 percent. Some countries had lost almost all of their reserves by the time they decided to abandon the exchange rate target.

Procrastination – the period of "financing a balance of payments deficit rather than adjusting" – had serious consequences in some cases. Typically, by the time the crisis hit, the level of reserves was so low that confidence could not be restored without beginning to rebuild them. As a result, reserves could not play their designated role of cushioning the contraction. In addition, the composition of liabilities tended to shift adversely during the period of sudden stop.

In the example of Mexico during the course of 1994, when the authorities were not stalling for time by running down reserves, they were instead placating nervous investors by offering them *tesobonos* (short-term dollar linked bonds) in place of the peso bonds (*Cetes*) that they had previously held. We find that on average across country crises, the fraction of loans that were short-term increased by 0.6 percentage points after the peak in reserves (over a period of one or two quarters, depending on data availability).

Others have correctly pointed out that crises are more frequent and more severe when short-term borrowing is high, dollar denomination is high, FDI is low, and reserves are low – in large part because balance sheets are then very sensitive to increases in exchange rates and short-term interest rates. Our point is that these compositional measures are strongly affected by decisions made by policymakers in the period immediately *after* capital inflows have begun to dry up but before the speculative attack itself has hit. These crisis management policies merit more attention. If countries that are faced with a fall in inflows had adjusted more promptly, rather than stalling for time by running down reserves or shifting to loans that are shorter-termed and dollar-denominated, they might be able to adjust on more attractive terms.

Our conclusions can be succinctly summarized in 10 points.

1. There is as yet no clear evidence of a general tendency for the removal of capital controls to be harmful. If anything, in our results, financial liberalization appears to reduce crises.
2. There is also no evidence in favor of the conventional wisdom of the corners hypothesis: that the superior exchange rate regimes are hard pegs and floating. If anything, in our results, intermediate regimes seem to do better.
3. Our results regarding corruption are consistent with the trend in recent emphasis on issues of governance, the rule of law, and institutions, as key determinants of economic performance in developing countries. Indonesia is an example where corruption must be listed as an important contributing cause of the crisis.
4. Our probit model found inflation to be an important predictor of currency crises, as in the first-generation models of speculative attack. But inflation is endogenous, and we did not have any success tracing the problem back to domestic credit creation. We had slightly more success in identifying high budget deficits as a root cause, as in Brazil and Turkey.
5. Consistent with earlier research, the *level* of current account deficits or debt is not as useful a predictor as the *composition* of capital inflows. If inflows take the form of short-term dollar-denominated debt, they are more likely to lead to trouble. If the flows take the form of foreign direct investment or equity, crises are less likely. These composition variables are relevant not just for the probability of crisis, but also the severity. As the balance sheet literature points out, a country that suffers from maturity and currency mismatch is likely to experience bankruptcies and sharp contraction when a crisis comes.
6. The level of reserves plays a key role as well, as in all three generations of models of speculative attacks. The ratio of short-term debt to reserves is a particularly useful indicator. High levels of reserves helped China, Taiwan, Province of China, and Hong Kong SAR ride out the 1997–98 crises, and the otherwise puzzling propensity of these economies to continue running up ever-higher levels of reserves subsequently makes some sense in this light.
7. This study has sought to draw added attention to some aspects of the management of crises, particularly policy during the period that begins when capital flows turn around and reserves peak and that ends with the outright speculative attack and devaluation (or, in the case of a successfully defended hard peg, that ends with a discrete large loss of reserves). Across the average of the sample, this period lasts 6 to 13 months, depending on the method of estimation. In other words, the "sudden stop" typically lasts for the better part of a year; it is not the same as the speculative attack. Our claim is that delaying adjustment during this sudden stop period can have severe consequences when the attack finally comes, even when the shock appears to be temporary – and thus to merit financing under the usual textbook rules.

8. The significance of indicators such as reserves and the composition of debt may lie less in long-term tendencies that vary across countries than as key aspects of crisis management that vary over time within the same country Mexico in 1994 and Thailand and Korea in 1997 had run down the level of reserves sharply by the time they went to the IMF and began adjustment programs. In the months leading up to the Mexican attack, the composition of the debt had shifted from peso-denominated to dollar-linked, and from longer-term to shorter. These were decisions by the policymakers to delay adjustment. The pattern is typical.

9. We were unable to find evidence of a significant relationship between the severity of crises and whether the country had an IMF program or whether adjustment took the form of devaluation rather than fiscal contraction.

10. It is instructive to combine the balance sheet effects – wherein a country that enters a crisis with short-term dollar-denominated debt is likely to suffer a more severe crisis – with the tendency of countries to experience an adverse shift in composition during the period of sudden stop, as captured by an increase in the ratio of short-term debt to reserves. The implication is that it is precisely the decision to delay adjustment that leaves crisis victims with few good options, because balance sheets have deteriorated in the meantime. It is possible that, at this point, no combination of expenditure-reduction and expenditure-switching policies will, without a recession, satisfy the new external financing constraint.

APPENDIX A. BRIEF REVIEW OF LITERATURE RELEVANT TO CRISIS PREVENTION POLICIES

Deep Determinants from the Growth Literature

Recent research recognizes that macroeconomic and trade policies, although important influences on economic performance, may themselves reflect deeper determinants. The growth literature now emphasizes three big influences: openness to trade,[47] tropical geography,[48] and especially, the quality of a country's institutions, such as protection of property rights, efficacy of the legal system, and absence of corruption.[49] Financial market institutions, such as protection of shareholder rights and the quality of regulation, receive particular emphasis.[50] When a country is considered corrupt, foreign investors are skittish, for example.[51]

[47] For example, Sachs and Warner (1995), Frankel and Romer (1999), and Noguer and Siscart (2002). With a critique by Rodriguez and Rodrik (2001).

[48] Diamond (1997); Gallup, Sachs, and Messenger (1998); Hall and Jones (1999); Sachs (2003).

[49] Among the most important recent contributions are Acemoglu, Johnson, and Robinson (2001); Barro (1991); Easterly and Levine (2002); Engerman and Sokoloff, (1997); and Rodrik, Subramanian, and Trebbi (2002).

[50] Johnson, McMillan, and Woodruff (2002). Examples for equity markets include La Porta, Lopez-de-Silanes, and Shleifer (2003); Shleifer and Wolfenson (2000); and La Porta, Lopez-de-Silanes, Shleifer, and Vishny (1999).

[51] Wei (2000a, b, c) and Gelos and Wei (2002) find that investors respond negatively to corruption. Du and Wei (2003) find that countries with more insider trading have more variable stock markets. Alfaro, Kalemli-Ozcan, and Volosovych (2003) find that the explanation for the Lucas paradox – why so little capital flowed to "developing" countries during the period 1978–98 – is low institutional

This research ties in with some current trends in the practice of aid and development policy in Washington. The current trend is to say, not that such policies as macroeconomic discipline and openness are unimportant, but that countries cannot be artificially forced from the outside to agree to such policies, as under typical IMF or World Bank programs. Instead the country needs to "take ownership" of the reforms. If the political economy dictates transfers from rural farmers to urban workers, or if a federalist constitution gives provinces claim to income tax revenue, an agreement on paper with the IMF or World Bank to devalue the currency or reduce the budget deficit may be doomed to fail. This is the argument of a recent paper by Acemoglu, Johnson, Robinson, and Thaichaeron (2003). They find econometrically that institutions offer more explanatory power than policies. They also use the case study of Ghana to illustrate how an IMF-encouraged devaluation, with the aim of raising the real price of traded goods such as cocoa, can soon be offset by the governing elite, for example because the cocoa marketing board controls the price paid to the small inland farmers for cocoa.

Choice of Exchange Rate Regime

One major question remains what currency regime a country should choose: a fixed exchange rate, a floating exchange rate, or a regime with an intermediate degree of flexibility, such as a managed float, target zone, crawl, or adjustable peg. The debate is an old one, but it acquired some new features in the late 1990s.[52]

One new development has been the decision of some countries to abandon their independent currency for a device to fix its value firmly, such as a currency board[53] or dollarization.[54] The motivation, to promote credibility, was similar to the motivation of those who had based stabilization programs on exchange targets in the preceding decade, but the logic was that the revealed impermanence of these targets in the 1990s argued for a firmer commitment device.[55]

One of the arguments for a firm fix was that it would force domestic institutions to evolve in a favorable way, and would help prevent the chronic monetization of fiscal deficits that had undone so many previous attempts at macroeconomic stabilization.[56] Argentina's currency board, for example, appeared to work very well during most of the decade. It was believed that this "convertibility plan" had also encouraged reforms that by the late 1990s had turned Argentina's banking system

---

quality, specifically weak protection of property rights, rather than low human capital. Johnson, Boone, Breach, and Friedman (2000) find that those East Asian countries with the least protection for investor rights suffered the greatest declines in currency values and stock markets in the crises of 1997–98.

[52] Reviews of issues concerning the choice of currency regime, particularly for developing countries, include Edwards (2003); Frankel (1999a, 2004); Larrain and Velasco (2001); and Edwards and Savastano (1999).

[53] Ghosh, Gulde, and Wolf (2000) find that currency board countries outperform others. Such findings have generally changed, however, with the collapse of Argentina's convertibility arrangement in 2002.

[54] Edwards and Magendzo (2003a, 2003b) find that dollarization and currency unions have delivered lower inflation, as promised, but with higher income volatility.

[55] Guillermo Calvo and Carlos Vegh (1994) show that the end of stabilizations that rely on a pegged exchange rate has often led subsequently to dramatic balance of payments crises.

[56] Mendoza (2002).

into one of the best among all emerging markets.[57] But when the crisis came in 2001, neither the supposedly deep pockets of foreign parents that had been allowed local bank subsidiaries, nor any of the country's other innovative reforms, was able to protect its banking system. This outcome cannot but have had a dampening effect on international enthusiasm for currency boards.[58]

Another new argument for monetary union has been empirical findings by Andrew Rose and coauthors that the boost to bilateral trade is significant, and larger than had been previously assumed, as large as a threefold increase.[59] While many others have advanced critiques of the Rose research, the basic finding has withstood perturbations and replications remarkably well, even if the estimated magnitudes are sometimes smaller.[60] Most Central and Eastern Europeans now aspire to join the European Monetary Union. Some developing countries seeking enhanced regional integration – in South America, Africa, the Persian Gulf, or Southeast Asia – may try to follow Europe's lead.[61]

There are plenty of advantages to floating exchange rates as well, and most of the victims of crises in emerging markets over the last eight years have responded by increasing flexibility. One advantage that is beginning to receive renewed emphasis is that floaters are partially insulated against fluctuations in the world market for their exports.[62]

Another new proposition of the 1990s was that countries are, or should be, moving away from the intermediate regimes, in favor of one corner or another (hard peg or float).[63] Also relatively new is the realization that attempts in practice to categorize countries' choice of regime (into fixed, floating, and intermediate) differ from the official categorization.[64] Countries that say they are floating, for example, often in reality are not.[65] Countries that say they are fixing often in reality are not.[66] Indeed neat categorization may not be possible at all. While there are by now a number of attempts at de facto classification, the answers they yield show a surprisingly low correlation, not only with the de jure classification, but also with one another. This is probably the major reason why different attempts to measure economic performance by exchange rate regime give different answers.[67]

---

[57] Alston and Gallo (2000); Calomiris and Powell (2000).
[58] Edwards (2002).
[59] Rose (2000); Glick and Rose (2001); Frankel and Rose (2002).
[60] Tenreyro and Barro (2003); Anderson and van Wincoop (2003).
[61] Monetary unions are more often adopted for political reasons than economic reasons, as Eichengreen and Taylor (2003) point out.
[62] Among peggers, terms of trade shocks are amplified and long-run growth is reduced, as compared to flexible-rate countries, according to Edwards and Levy-Yeyati (2003).
[63] Fischer (2001).
[64] Reinhart and Rogoff (2002); Levy-Yeyati and Sturzenegger (2003)
[65] Calvo and Reinhart (2002).
[66] Obstfeld and Rogoff (1995) report that only six major economies with open capital markets, in addition to a number of very small economies, had maintained a fixed exchange rate for five years or more, as of 1995. Klein and Marion (1997) report that the mean duration of pegs among Western Hemisphere countries is about 10 months.
[67] To oversimplify a bit, Levy-Yeyati and Sturzenegger (2003) show floaters outperforming their competitors. Ghosh, Gulde, and Wolf (2000) show hard peggers performing the best. Reinhart and Rogoff (2002) show intermediate regimes in the lead.

That Argentina was in the end forced to abandon its currency board, in 2001, also dramatizes the lesson that the choice of exchange rate regime, including even the supposedly firm institutional fixes, is not so permanent or deep as had previously been thought.[68] Even full monetary union need not be a truly permanent choice, as the Czech-Slovak divorce illustrated. The choice of exchange rate regime is more likely endogenous with respect to institutions, rather than the other way around.[69] Furthermore, it may even be *desirable* that exchange rate regimes change along with circumstances. It has long been recognized, in the optimum currency area literature, that a single exchange rate regime does not suit all countries. (Fixed rates are more suitable for countries that are small and open to trade, for example.) It may also be true that, even for a given country, a single regime does not necessarily suit it at all points in its history. Criteria such as patterns of trade themselves evolve over time.

By now, all regimes – institutional fix, float, and intermediate regimes – have proven themselves to be something of a mirage.[70] That is, when a country officially opts for one regime, first of all, it may not in fact be following it. Second, it may be impossible to verify quickly what regime it is indeed following. Third, different attempts at de facto classification may give different answers. Finally, the regime may change in the subsequent year.[71] It may be more useful to think of what percentage of the time countries spend at various ends of the spectrum, rather than treating each new regime choice as a long-lasting one. The "corners hypothesis" is another possible casualty of the realization that no regime choice is in reality permanent, and that investors know that.[72]

Choice of Capital Account Regime

The literature on capital controls and capital account liberalization is also very large.[73]

REVIEW OF ARGUMENTS ON EFFICIENCY OF FINANCIAL MARKETS. Financial integration between an emerging market country and the rest of the world has many advantages. Some of the potential gains from international trade in financial assets are analogous to the gains from international trade in goods. First, for a successfully developing country – that is, one that has not just a low capital labor ratio but also sound fundamentals – the rate of return to domestic capital is sufficiently high that investment can be financed more cheaply by borrowing from abroad than out

---

[68] All these issues are reviewed in Frankel (2004).
[69] Alesina and Wagner (2003); Calvo and Mishkin (2003).
[70] The reference is to the 1995 study by Obstfeld and Rogoff, "The Mirage of Fixed Exchange Rates." But Calvo and Reinhart's "Fear of Floating" (2002) has done the same for floating, and the corners hypothesis did the same for the intermediate regimes (see, for example, Fischer 2001).
[71] Masson (2001) shows that the corners are not in fact "absorbing states."
[72] Reinhart and Reinhart (2003)
[73] Overviews include Dooley (1996); Edison, Klein, Ricci, and Sloek (2002); Eichengreen and Mussa (1998); Fischer (2004a); Frankel (1999b); Eichengreen and Leblang (2003); Rodrik (1998); and Prasad, Rogoff, Wei, and Kose (2003).

of domestic saving alone. Second, investors in richer countries can earn a higher rate of return on their savings by investing in the emerging market than they could domestically. Third, everyone benefits from the opportunity to diversify away risks and smooth disturbances. Fourth, letting foreign financial institutions into the country can improve the efficiency of domestic financial markets. Overregulated and potentially inefficient domestic institutions are subject to the harsh discipline of competition and the demonstration effect of having examples to emulate. At the same time, governments face the discipline of the international capital markets in the event they make policy mistakes (for example, in their domestic regulatory duties). The capital account liberalization can be a useful signal of commitment to market reform.[74]

Recent crises, however, suggest that financial markets do not always work quite as perfectly as the happy view of the economic theorist suggests. It is difficult to argue that investors have punished countries when and only when the governments are following bad policies. First, large inflows often give way suddenly to large outflows, with little news appearing in between that might explain the change in sentiment. Second, contagion sometimes spreads to countries where fundamentals appear strong. Third, the recessions that have hit emerging market countries have been of such magnitude that it is difficult to argue that the system is working well. Beyond the specific issue of crises in emerging markets, international capital inflows do not appear to increase during temporary downturns nor fall during booms, as the smoothing theory says they should.

EVIDENCE ON LIBERALIZATION. Do the advantages of open financial markets outweigh the disadvantages? Peter Henry and Anusha Chari, for example, have shown that when countries open up their stock markets, the cost of capital facing domestic firms falls (stock prices rise), with a positive effect on their investment and on economic growth.[75] Some researchers, such as Reuven Glick and Michael Hutchison (2002), have found that countries that liberalize restrictions on capital flows are less prone to speculative attacks. But the evidence is mixed.[76]

Capital account liberalization has often been implicated in the crises experienced by emerging markets over the last 10 years. Certainly a country that does not borrow from abroad in the first place cannot have an international debt crisis. It has been widely alleged that developing countries in Asia and elsewhere were pressured to liberalize their financial markets prematurely, in the interest of U.S. banks but to the detriment of the countries.[77]

Either a blanket indictment or a blanket vindication of capital controls would be too simplistic. One important point is that capital account liberalization may be good under some conditions and in some countries, and bad in other circumstances, much

---

[74] Bartolini and Drazen (1997).

[75] Chari and Henry (2002a, 2002b); Henry (2003). Gourinchas and Jeanne (2003) estimate the gains from financial integration at about 1 percent (of consumption), which they consider small.

[76] Prasad and others (2003) marks an important acknowledgment by the IMF that evidence on this question is mixed.

[77] Among many such critiques are Bhagwati (1998), Furman and Stiglitz (1998), and Sachs (1998).

as is the case with the choice of exchange rate regime. A second important point is that both the proponents of controls and their opponents tend indiscriminately to lump together Chile-style controls on inflows, Malaysia-style control on outflows, a Tobin tax on all foreign exchange transactions,[78] and other kinds of taxes and restrictions. But the precise nature of the restrictions matters a lot. Each of these two points is considered in turn below.

Some of the most interesting research examines under what circumstances capital account liberalization is more likely to be good or bad for economic performance. One claim is that only for rich countries does financial opening lower volatility[79] and raise growth;[80] capital account liberalization is more likely to lead to market crashes in lower-income countries.[81] A second claim is that capital account liberalization raises growth only in the absence of macroeconomic imbalances, such as overly expansionary monetary and fiscal policy.[82] A third important finding is that institutions such as shareholder protection and accounting standards determine whether liberalization leads to development of the financial sector,[83] and in turn to long-run growth.[84] A related finding is that corruption tilts the composition of capital inflows toward the form of banking flows, and toward dollar denomination, both of which have been associated with crises.[85] The implication is that capital account liberalization can help if institutions are strong and other fundamentals are favorable, but can hurt if they are not.

All these findings are consistent with a conventional lesson regarding the sequencing of reforms: that countries will do better in the development process if they postpone opening of the capital account until after other institutional reforms.[86] Of course, the observed positive correlation between the opening of capital markets and growth could be attributable to reverse causation – rich countries liberalize as a result of having developed, not as a cause. Hali Edison and colleagues (2002) conclude from their own tests that this is not the case.

---

[78] Some have sought to apply the Tobin tax idea to currency crises in developing countries, although it is not what Tobin had in mind. The chapters in ul Haq, Kaul, and Grunberg (1996) are among the few serious attempts to address the specific Tobin tax proposal.

[79] Biscarri, Edwards, and Perez de Gracia (2003). Kose, Prasad, and Terrones (2002) find that increasing financial openness is associated with rising volatility, and that the smoothing benefits of financial integration begin to kick in only after a certain threshold is reached.

[80] Klein and Olivei (2000); Edwards (2001).

[81] Martin and Rey (2002).

[82] Arteta, Eichengreen, and Wyplosz (2003). They reject the claim that it is the level of development per se that matters for the usefulness of financial opening. Wyplosz (2001) concludes that the reason financial liberalization seems to work for developed countries and not developing countries is that the latter are more likely to suffer from excessive growth of domestic credit.

[83] Chinn and Ito (2002); La Porta, Lopes-de-Silanes, Shleifer, and Vishny (1998).

[84] Klein's (2003) finding that financial liberalization is more successful in countries with good institutions is not necessarily corroborated by others such as Arteta, Eichengreen, and Wyplosz (2003) and Edison et al. (2002).

[85] Wei and Wu (2002).

[86] Edwards (1984) and McKinnon (1991), or, more recently, Kaminsky and Schmukler (2003). Indonesia tried early liberalization of international flows (see Cole and Slade 1992). The subsequent crisis is probably a good vindication of the early conventional wisdom.

MALAYSIA-STYLE RESTRICTIONS AND OTHER CONTROLS ON OUTFLOWS. Controls on capital outflows have been common in the past. This alternative is often proposed by those who observe that modern financial markets do not seem to work as smoothly as the theory predicts. Many developing countries – most importantly, China and India – had not made much progress at removing them by 1997. When the East Asia crisis hit, many in these countries felt vindicated.

Reimposing capital controls that had earlier been removed is one policy option for coping with a crisis, though not likely to be sanctioned by the IMF. The goal is often to allow a lower domestic interest, and sustain growth, without accelerating a capital outflow that would threaten the currency. One disadvantage is that reimposed controls may not be very effective. Once markets have developed and have become familiar with derivatives and offshore banks, it may be difficult to turn the clock back, and attempts to do so are likely to have negative repercussions in a democratic society. Malaysia adopted controls to prevent investors from taking money offshore in 1998. Tight administrative control made this strategy more effective than it might have been in a more open society. Dani Rodrik and Ethan Kaplan (2002) find evidence that Malaysia's decision to impose controls on outflows in 1998 helped it weather the Asia crisis.

Even when such controls are enforceable, a second disadvantage is that controls on outflows can weaken the discipline that international financial markets place on the quality of macroeconomic policy. Governments have all too often used controls to shield themselves temporarily from the implications of bad policies.[87] A third disadvantage is that they are likely to scare investors away from the country in the future.

CHILE-STYLE PENALTIES AND OTHER CONTROLS ON INFLOWS. The usual motivation for controls on inflows is to prevent overvaluation and overindebtedness, and thereby prevent a crisis from occurring in the first place. The enforcement problem is not as great as with outflows: it is easier to keep capital out than to keep it in. Some countries appear to have had some success discouraging inflow, so as to limit real appreciation and aggregate debt. At times in the early 1990s, Chile, Colombia, Thailand, and Malaysia each imposed controls to discourage capital inflows.

The clearest disadvantage to controls on capital inflows is that the country passes up an opportunity to finance its development by borrowing abroad at a relatively lower interest rate. Instead, it has to finance investment out of higher-cost domestic funds. Controls designed to moderate capital inflows may impact small firms in particular.[88]

Chile's controls have attracted the most attention, in part because they had the effect (if not the intention) of shifting the composition of capital inflows away from

---

[87] Johnson and Mitton (2003) find that Malaysian capital controls mainly worked to provide a screen behind which politically favored firms could be supported.

[88] Forbes (2003) finds that Chile's famous controls on capital inflows raised the cost of capital for small firms, in particular. Levine and Schmukler (2003) find, for 55 countries, that when some firms are able to raise equity capital abroad, the remaining firms *lose* liquidity. For Reinhart and Smith (2001), the main problem is being able to remove the controls at the right time.

the short end of the maturity spectrum, and in part because Chile's overall economic record has been so successful. As Sebastian Edwards (1999, 2000) has pointed out, the reforms undertaken by Chile were far too numerous and varied to allow one to attribute its overall economic performance specifically to those controls in place during the 1990s.[89] But there is a more persuasive argument related to the composition of capital inflows.

This study emphasizes that the composition of inflow is statistically a leading indicator of the probability that severe currency crashes will occur. The higher the reliance on foreign-currency borrowing that is short-term or intermediated through banks, the higher the probability of crisis. Although statistical correlation need not imply causality, this conclusion is consistent with proposals for controls that would seek to change the composition of capital inflows, as opposed to the total magnitude. Taxes or restrictions on short-term inflows may shift the composition toward longer maturities.

Chile imposed its famous tax on inflows in 1991. It took the form of a requirement that a percentage of any foreign borrowing be left in a noninterest bearing deposit maintained at the central bank for up to one year. In addition, there was a long-standing requirement that all FDI stay in the country for at least one year. These controls apparently succeeded in changing the composition of the capital inflow to Chile in the 1990s, in the direction of longer-term maturities, even if having little effect on the total magnitude.[90]

Some countries aim their restrictions specifically at banks. High reserve require-ments on banks' foreign borrowing fall well within the kind of enhanced prudential banking regulation that is widely recommended for emerging markets.

Chile removed its inflow penalties at the end of the decade. Some commentators saw this as a rejection of the usefulness of controls, or at least as confirmation that liberalization is appropriate as a country reaches a certain stage of development. But this move came during a period of capital drought for developing countries worldwide.

An alternative to the view that the immediate goal should be permanent liber-alization deserves more consideration. That alternative is the view that Chile-style controls will remain as one possibly useful tool to be applied during a particular stage of the cycle. If one closes the umbrella when it stops raining, that does not mean one has changed one's mind about the usefulness of umbrellas. Controls may have a role to play as a temporary measure when a country faces a large upsurge of inflows. They might help a government "play for time" until it can determine whether the funds are going to useful investments, which will generate the foreign exchange earnings needed in the future to service the debt, or whether they are instead going, for example, to consumption. After several years, policymakers may

---

[89] See also Sebastian Edwards, "Capital Controls Are Not the Reason for Chile's Success." *Wall Street Journal*, April 3, 1998, p. A19.

[90] Chucamaro, Laban, and Larrain (1996); Valdes-Prieto and Soto (1996). A more recent study finds effects on both the level of net inflows and the currency composition (Gallego, Hernandez, and Schmidt-Hebbel 1999). Also, for the case of Colombia, see Cardenas and Barrera (1997).

have a better idea whether their country is the next tiger, justifying the inflows, or merely the subject of a speculative bubble.[91]

Choice of Trade Openness

The case in favor of free trade in goods and services is generally considered more certain than the case in favor of free trade in assets, at least when it comes to influencing the average rate of growth. There is no necessary reason why openness to trade should reduce the volatility of real income, however. Indeed, for a country facing high variability in its terms of trade on world markets, it is entirely possible that higher levels of openness lead to larger cyclical swings. On the other hand, it has been observed that countries with a high ratio of trade to GDP, such as the East Asian tigers, tend to have an easier time adjusting to sudden stops, while those with a low ratio, like Argentina and other Latin American countries, tend to have a harder time.

One interpretation is that a higher ratio of trade to GDP (for a given debt/GDP ratio) means that in the aftermath of a cut-off of capital inflow of a given size, a smaller percentage increase in the output of traded goods is required to fill the gap (which in turn calls for a smaller devaluation or contraction in output). Another interpretation is that for countries that are highly dependent on trade, a cut-off of trade credit would be very costly. If the threatened loss of trade is the answer to the question why troubled debtors tend to pay their debts,[92] and thus the explanation as to why creditors are willing to lend to them, then a higher ratio of trade is a form of "giving hostages" that makes a cut off of lending less likely.[93] The implication is that openness to trade and openness to capital together is a good combination (analogously to the optimum currency area conclusion that openness to trade suits a country for a fixed exchange rate).

Composition and Use of Capital Inflows

As noted above, indicators that concern the composition of capital inflow, rather than the total amount, appear to be statistically useful at predicting the probability of currency crashes.

BANK LOANS VERSUS OTHER MODES OF FINANCE. Banks, in particular, have been implicated in most crises.[94] Foreign Direct Investment (FDI) is a less risky source of capital inflow than bank loans.[95] The same is true of equity flows.[96] FDI is thought

[91] That capital controls may come and go could as easily be the outcome of undesirable political constraints as of intelligent policymaking. Much as the choice of exchange rate regime, the choice of capital account regime is less permanent and more endogenous than economists usually consider.

[92] Rose (2002) offers evidence in support of this proposition.

[93] Sachs (1986). Many have argued that Argentina's low trade/GDP ratio helps explain why it was such a victim of the global sudden stop after 1998. See, for example, Calvo, Izquierdo, and Talvi 2003. For an instrumental variables study of the effect of openness on sudden stops, see Calvo and Frankel (2004).

[94] Among many other references, see Agenor and Aizenman (1998); Dekle and Kletzer (2001); Chinn and Kletzer (2000); Diamond and Rajan (2000); Aizenman and Powell (2003).

[95] Lipsey (2001).

[96] Razin, Sadka, and Yuen (2001).

to be relatively more stable. One theory is that bank flows in particular are more vulnerable to moral hazard problems created by the prospect of government bailouts than are other modes of finance. Another theory is that equities and FDI allow more efficient risk sharing: In the event of adverse developments, the price of the asset falls automatically, without the need for the costly and protracted negotiations and restructuring of bank loans or bonds. Indexation of debt to variables such as the commodity export price would accomplish much of the same purpose, but for some reason this is rarely done.

THE FRACTION OF CAPITAL INFLOW THAT IS SHORT-TERM (THE PROBLEM OF MATURITY MISMATCH). Countries that borrow funds short term are more likely to get into trouble, especially if those funds are intermediated through the banking system and denominated in dollars or other foreign currencies. Countries that borrow long term are less likely to get into trouble, especially if the inflow takes the form of foreign direct investment rather than bank loans. A mismatch of short-term bank liabilities with longer-term bank assets (such as real estate) leaves a country vulnerable. One possibility is that a run-up of short-term bank credit is a *symptom* of coming problems, rather than the fundamental cause, much as an individual who tries to charge his mortgage payments on his credit card reveals that he is overextended. Either way, a concentration of short-term debt, especially relative to reserves, is a danger signal.[97]

THE FRACTION OF DEBT THAT IS DOLLAR-DENOMINATED (THE PROBLEM OF CURRENCY MISMATCH). One prime culprit in explaining the apparent curse that follows developing countries in international financial markets is their inability to borrow internationally in their own currency. Ricardo Hausmann has called the problem "original sin," by which he means that it is the fundamental root of the problem. If countries incur foreign liabilities despite the inability to borrow in their own currency – that is, if they borrow in foreign currency on net – that is the problem of "currency mismatch."[98]

We are not interested solely in predicting *whether or not* a crisis will occur. Another important question is *why* were the crises so severe – inflicting recession and bankruptcy on much of the economy – once they occurred. The composition of capital inflows is also relevant for the magnitude of output loss if there is a crisis. Firms or banks that incur liabilities in dollars (or other foreign currencies) while their revenues are primarily in domestic currency face the problem of currency mismatch. This, in turn, can lead to insolvency and contraction when the domestic currency devalues sharply.[99] If most of the debt is denominated in dollars or other foreign

---

[97] Eichengreen and Mody (1999); Chang and Velasco (2000a, b).
[98] For example, Eichengreen and Hausmann (1999). Hausmann's terminology may overstate the degree of exogeneity of currency denomination, however. (As Tom Lehrer sang, "[only] the man who's got religion'll tell you if your sin's original.") Goldstein and Turner (2004), for example, argue that "national macroeconomic policies ... matter a lot for generating and managing currency mismatches." They also strongly criticize the measure of mismatch that Eichengreen and Hausmann have constructed, and that this study tries out in the econometrics.
[99] Schneider and Tornell (2000); Céspedes, Chang, and Velasco (2002); Cavallo, Kisselev, Perri, and Roubini (2002).

currencies, as is the case for most developing countries, then a devaluation can be contractionary, as the adverse balance sheet effect renders otherwise-solvent debtor corporations and banks insolvent, and leads to plant closings and recession. These balance sheet effects are at the center of many analyses of why emerging markets seem prone to severe crises.[100] (The balance sheet effect is only one of many ways in which devaluation can be contractionary.)[101]

RESERVES. The view that countries do not need reserves, because they can borrow them, has been thoroughly discredited. Reserves are important precisely because, in the event of a sudden stop, countries cannot borrow, at least not at regular world interest rates. And it may be that floating countries need reserves, not just countries with exchange rate targets as standard models imply.

Countries that accumulate a high level of international reserves are less likely to have problems. How high a level of reserves is enough? The traditional rule of thumb was phrased in terms of trade: A country needs a minimum level of reserves that is enough to pay for three months of imports. As the source of balance of payments crises has shifted from the trade account to the capital account, a new rule of thumb has been proposed, attributed to Pablo Guidotti (2003): A country should try to have enough reserves so that it could cover all debt coming due over the next year (short-term debt, as well as maturing longer-term debt), in the event that creditors suddenly lose willingness to roll it over or extend new loans. As already noted, one of the most useful summary indicators of danger is the ratio of short-term debt to reserves. The Guidotti rule says that as this ratio rises above 1, the danger of a crisis rises with it.

APPENDIX B. THE INTERNAL/EXTERNAL BALANCE FRAMEWORK WHEN DEVALUATION IS CONTRACTIONARY

In the traditional framework, there are two classes of policy instruments: expenditure-reducing policies, such as monetary contraction; and expenditure-switching policies, such as devaluation. The pair matches up nicely with the existence of two policy targets: internal balance and external balance.

Consider a graphical representation with the interest rate and exchange rate (price of foreign currency) on the axes. To satisfy external balance, there is an inverse tradeoff between the two instruments. A devaluation and an increase in the interest rate are each ways of improving the trade balance – the latter by reducing expenditure. Thus, the more you have of one, the less you need of the other. (If external balance is defined as equilibrium in the overall balance of payments, including the capital account along with the trade balance, the relationship is still downward-sloping, since a devaluation and an increase in the interest rate are both ways of making domestic assets more attractive to global investors.)

---

[100] Krugman (1999), Chang and Velasco (2000a,b; 2001), and Dornbusch (2002) are some of those who have emphasized the post-devaluation burden of short-term dollar-denominated debt.

[101] For the full list of 10 contractionary effects, see Caves, Frankel, and Jones (2002). See also Lizondo and Montiel (1989). The empirical verdict of Edwards (1986) that devaluations on net may be contractionary at first, but turn expansionary after a couple of years, is probably still true today.

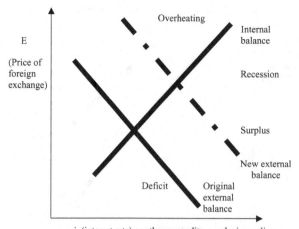

i (interest rate) or other expenditure-reducing policy

Figure 8.B-1. Attaining Internal and External Balance: Traditional Version. *Source*: Authors' calculations.

To satisfy *internal* balance, the tradeoff is traditionally considered to be upward-sloping. An increase in the interest rate reduces the domestic demand for domestic goods, while a devaluation increases the net foreign demand for domestic goods; if you have more of one, you also need more of the other, to prevent excess supply or excess demand for domestic goods. The existence of two independent instruments implies the possibility of attaining both targets simultaneously, at the intersection of the internal and external balance schedule. In the aftermath of an adverse shock in the foreign sector, for example, the right new combination of devaluation and monetary contraction will restore balance of payments equilibrium while maintaining real economic growth (as illustrated in Figure 8.B-1).

This is not the way things actually work.[102] By now we have had enough experience with crises in emerging markets that the traditional framework needs to be modified. The simple generalization seems to be that most developing countries that are hit by financial crises go into recession. The reduction in income is the only way of quickly generating the improvement in the trade balance that is the necessary counterpart to the increased reluctance of international investors to lend. External balance is a jealous mistress that can be satisfied only if internal balance is left to go wanting.

Some critics of the IMF say that the recessions are the result of Fund policies, specifically the insistence on monetary contraction. The argument is that the mix of a lower interest rate combined with a devaluation would successfully maintain internal balance. They often make the point that high interest rates are not in practice especially attractive to foreign investors when they carry increased probability of default (and associated recession). This is true. But in our view, it is not the most important correction in the traditional framework. Even if interest rates do not have as big a positive effect on the capital account as earlier models of high financial

[102] Krugman (1998b).

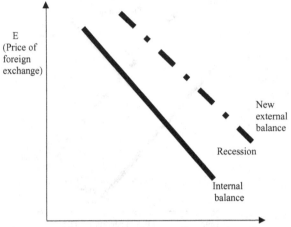

Figure 8.B-2. Attaining Internal and External Balance: When Devaluation Is Contractionary.
Source: Authors' calculations.

integration suggested – so that the graphical relationship may be flatter – we believe
that the sign of the effect is still the same. One cannot normally attract many investors
by *lowering* interest rates. Therefore the external balance line still slopes downward.
Claims that high rates are damaging to the real economy willfully ignore the lack
of an alternative, if the external balance constraint is to be met.

Where the traditional framework needs most to be modified is the relationship
giving *internal* balance – not external balance. By now the evidence seems strong
that devaluation is contractionary, at least in the first year, and perhaps in the second
as well. We have long been aware of various potential contractionary effects of
devaluation in developing countries. A total of 10 such effects are identified in
textbooks,[103] of which the difficulty of servicing dollar debts has turned out to be by
far the most important in recent crises (the balance sheet effect). But a mainstream
view has been that any negative effects from a devaluation were eventually offset by
the positive effect of stimulus to net exports, so that by the second year, when the
latter had gathered strength, the overall effect on output had turned positive.[104] Now
however, one must judge the negative effects stronger than had been thought, and
the positive effects weaker. Imports fall sharply; indeed crisis-impacted countries
have for this reason experienced sharp increases in their trade balances beginning
as soon as two or three months after the crisis. But this is clearly a response to the
unavailability of finance and collapse of income and spending, not to relative prices.
In other words, it is expenditure-reduction, not expenditure switching.

If devaluation is contractionary, then the internal balance line slopes down, not
up (as illustrated in Figure 8.B-2). Moreover the slope is disturbingly similar to the
slope of the external balance line. It is hard to see where the two intersect, if indeed

[103] Caves, Frankel, and Jones (2002). For further exposition, see Corden (1993).
[104] Edwards (1986) and Kamin (1988).

they intersect at all. This means that it is hard to see what combination of policy instruments, if any, can simultaneously satisfy both internal and external balance, after an adverse shock has shifted the latter outward. The depressing conclusion is that there is no escape from recession. All policy instruments work through reduction in income in the short run: devaluation, fiscal contraction, and monetary contraction. Even structural policy reform, such as insisting that bad banks go under, is likely to have a negative effect on economic activity in the short run.

Is the financing-versus-adjustment framework then no longer useful? The framework may still be relevant during the (relatively brief) period after a terms-of-trade or other shock arises, but before the financial or currency crisis hits. It is hard to identify and date the former, even with the benefit of hindsight. But consider the interval of one to two years preceding December 2001 in Argentina, preceding July 1997 in East Asia, preceding December 1994 in Mexico, and preceding July 1982 in Latin America. In each case, policymakers responded to deterioration in their trade or capital accounts by running down foreign exchange reserves or shifting to short-term borrowing. They succeeded in this way in postponing macroeconomic adjustment and in postponing crisis. But when the crisis came, it was that much worse, requiring at that point the unfortunate response of turning all dials to contractionary settings – as the only way of satisfying the constraints imposed by finicky international investors.

It would have been better in these cases if the countries had spent these short intervals adjusting rather than financing, at a time when there was still a meaningful tradeoff between the two and the choice set had not yet been narrowed in such an unattractively constrained manner. The trick is thus having the economic acumen and political will to recognize that an adverse shock has occurred and to enact prompt adjustment. This element is even more crucial than calculating the right amount of adjustment or choosing among the available instruments to carry it out.

APPENDIX C. DATA APPENDIX: DEFINITIONS AND SOURCES OF VARIABLES

"Crisis Prevention" Policy Variables and Related Control Variables

Governance/Structure (*noncorrupt*). *Source*: ICRG, *Corruption in Government*. Scale ranges from 0 to 6; lower point totals indicate higher risk. Averaged over the period of 1990 to 2002.

Openness (*opentrade*). *Source*: IMF, *International Financial Statistics*. Ratio of (Exports + Imports)/GDP.

Capital Controls (*qka*). *Source*: From Klein's (2003) interpretation of Quinn (1997) data; appropriating *qka*7388*r*, which is mean of *qka*73, *qka*82, *qka*88 using rmean where *qka* is Capital Account Liberalism for years 1973, 1982, and 1988, respectively; range is 0–5, with higher values indicating less restrictive.

Capital Controls (*share9295*). *Source*: Klein's (2003) *share9295* variable Proportion of period 1992–95 that country had open capital accounts or undertook financial liberalization.

Inflation (*inflat*). *Source*: IMF, *World Economic Outlook*. Annual inflation rates calculated from annual CPI data as [(CPIyear-CPIyear-1)/CPIyear-1]. Mean inflation levels determined for each country for period of 1990 through 2002.

Log of Mean Inflation (*loginflat*). *Source*: Natural log of mean inflation levels calculated above.

Short-term Debt/Total Debt (*shortotaldebt*). *Source*: *World bank, World Development Indicators* (WDI). Average for annual data for period 1990–2001. Short-term debt includes all debt having an original maturity of one year or less and interest in arrears on long-term debt.

FDI (net inflows)/GDP (*fdigdp*). *Source*: World Bank, WDI. Foreign direct investment, net inflows (percentage of GDP).

External Debt/GDP (*debtgdp*). *Source*: World Bank, *WDI*. Ratio of total external debt to GDP, expressed as decimal. Averaged over the period 1990 to 2002.

Exchange Rate Regime (Flexibility) (*exrateflex*). *Source*: IMF, *Annual Report on Exchange Arrangements and Exchange Restrictions*. Calculated as 1*(% time on regime 1) + 2*(% time on regime 2) + 3*(% time on regime 3); 1 = hard peg; 2 = intermed; 3 = float.

Short-Term Debt/Reserves (*stdebtres*). *Source*: World Bank, *WDI*; IMF, *World Economic Outlook*. Calculated as annual ratio of short-term debt outstanding to stock of reserves at year-end. Short-term debt includes all debt having an original maturity of one year or less and interest in arrears on long-term debt. Variable represents mean of ratio for each country during the period 1990 to 2002, divided by 1000.

Reserves/GDP (*resgdp*). *Source*: World Bank, *WDI*. Ratio of reserves to GDP, expressed as decimal. Averaged over the period 1990 to 2002.

Budget Deficit/GDP (*bdgdp*). *Source*: World Bank, *WDI*. Overall budget balance is current and capital revenue and official grants received, less total expenditure and lending minus repayments. Data are shown for central government only. Mean of annual data for the period 1990 to 2002.

Expansion of Domestic Credit (*ndagrowth*). *Source*: World Bank, *WDI*. Calculated using "Net domestic credit (current LCU)," which the World Bank defines as "The sum of net credit to the nonfinancial public sector, credit to the private sector, and other accounts. Data are in current local currency." The variable calculated as the mean of the series of values of ln(nda in year *m*) less ln(nda in 1990) for each year *m*, where 1990 < *m* < = 2002.

Standard Deviation of Terms of Trade (*sdTOT*). *Source*: World Bank, *WDI*. Standard deviation of annual Net Barter Terms of Trade data for the period 1990 to 2002. Net barter terms of trade (1995 = 100). Net barter terms of trade is the ratio of the export price index to the corresponding import price index measured relative to the base year 1995.

FSU (*fsu*). Dummy variable registering 1 if country is Former Soviet Republic, 0 otherwise.

Population (*pop*). Source: University of Pennsylvania, *Penn World Tables*, in thousands. Mean of annual data for the period 1990 to 2002.

War (*war*). (Intensity Level/pop) * Fraction of Period at War, summed over the period 1990 to 2002. *Source*: War data from Gleditsch and others (2002).

Concessional Borrower (*conces*). Countries eligible for IMF Poverty Reduction and Growth Facility (PRFG) as of April 2003. Dummy variable for 1 if eligible, 0 if not. *Source*: http://www.imf.org/external/np/exr/facts/prgf.htm.

Tropical (*tropical*). *Source*: "tropical" variable from Gallup, Sachs, and Messenger (1998). The proportion of the country's land area within the geographical tropics. Originally sourced from ArcWorld Supplement database (ESRI 1996).

GDP PPP-adjusted 1990 (*gdp90*). *Source*: World Bank, *WDI*. GDP, PPP current international US$, averaged over the period 1990 to 2002. This variable represents the natural log of that figure.

GDP Per Capita 1990 (*gdpcap90*). GDP per capita is gross domestic product divided by midyear population. Data sourced from World Bank *WDI*. GDP is the sum of gross value added by all resident producers in the economy plus any product taxes and minus any subsidies not included in the value of the products. It is calculated without making deductions for depreciation of fabricated assets or for depletion and degradation of natural resources. The data are in constant 1995 U.S. dollars, and this variable is constructed by taking the natural log of that figure.

Investment (*invest*). Mean of annual values of ratio of Investment (current prices, billions of local currency) to GDP (current prices, billions of local currency) for the period 1990 to 2002. *Source*: Variable constructed from *Penn World Tables* data.

Illiteracy (*illiter*). *Source*: World Bank, *WDI*. Illiteracy rate, adult total (percentage of people ages 15 and above).

Original Sin (*osin*). *Source*: IADBtotloan, methodology adopted from Eichengreen, Hausmann, and Panizza (2003). This variable is constructed employing Eichengreen, Hausmann, and Panizza's methodology for INDEXA, which is the ratio of securities plus loans in major currencies to total securities plus loans issued by the government. Mean of annual data for the period 1990 to 2002. See Goldstein and Turner (2004) for a critique.

Secondary Education, Percentage Completed (*seced*). *Source*: Data taken from Barro and Lee (2000). Average of lsc90, lsc95, and lsc99 which are percentage of "secondary school complete in the total population" for the years 1990, 1995, and 1999, respectively.

Hard Peg, Variation 1 (*hardpeg 1*). *Source*: Data from IMF's *Annual Report on Exchange Arrangements and Exchange Restrictions*. Hardpeg generates a value between 0 and 1: 0 if the country never had a hard peg (that is, institutionally fixed by means of a currency board, dollarization, or monetary union); 1 if it did the entire period; and a fraction of that if it did so for only a portion of the period, where the time range extends from 1990 to 2002.

Hard Peg, Variation 2 (*hardpeg* 2). *Source*: Data taken from Rose (2001). This variable is a dummy registering 1 for a country if it was classified by Rose as belonging to a common currency area, and 0 otherwise. Data extend only to 1996.

Corners, Variation 1 (*corners*1). *Source*: Data from *IMF's Annual Report on Exchange Arrangements and Exchange Restrictions*. Corners generates a value between 0 and 1: 0 if the country always had an intermediate regime; 1 if it always had floating or fixed; and a fraction of that equal to the fraction of the period it spent on floating and/or fixed, where the time range extends from 1990 to 2002.

Corners, Variation 2 (*corners*2). *Source*: Data appropriated from Rose (2001). This variable is a dummy registering a 1 if hardpeg = 1, a value between 0 and 1 for the fraction of the period the country had floating rates, and 0 if the country had an intermediate regime the entire period. Data extend only to 1996.

Interactive Variables

(Absence of Capital Controls) × [(GDP per capita (1990)]. opencapital × gdp-cap90

(Absence of Capital Controls) × (Noncorruptness). opencapital × noncorrupt

(Absence of Capital Controls) × (Rate of Increase in Domestic Credit). opencapital × ndagrowth

(Absence of Capital Controls) × (Budget Deficit/GDP). opencapital × bdgdp

(Absence of Capital Controls) × (Short-term Debt/FDI + Equity). opencapital × composition

Performance Variables

Number of Crises (*crises*). Number of crises determined where:

For annual determination of crises, a year registers as a crisis if $INDEX_{month}$ is greater than 0.25 and $INDEX_{month} - INDEX_{month-12m}$ is greater than 0.10, where INDEX is the month-on-month change in the natural log of the exchange rate less the month-on-month change in the natural log of reserves. In the case where a year registers as a crisis year, and the subsequent year(s) do so as well, a single crisis is counted as beginning in the initial crisis year and continuing up to three years after that. Therefore, in the case of four consecutive years registering as crises, only the first and fourth years will be noted as discrete incidents of crisis, with the first crisis lasting three years.

For monthly determination of crises, a month registers as a crisis if is greater than 0.45 and $INDEX_{month} - INDEX_{month-12m}$ is greater than 0.10. Similar to the methodology applied above, in the case of consecutive months registering as crises, a single crisis can extend up to 36 months. Therefore, in the case of 38 consecutive months registering as crisis, in actuality we will count two crisis: the first extending from month one through 36, the second occurring in months 37 and 38.

In both of the above cases, the period examined extends from January 1990 to December 2002. Exchange Rate and Reserves Level data are sourced from the IMF's *International Financial Statistics* database employing Exchange Rate (line AE.ZF) for the former and Total Reserves minus Gold (line 1L.DZF) for the latter.

Mean Growth Real Income (*avgrowth*). *Source*: World Bank *WDI*, calculated for each country over period 1990 to 2002 as mean difference of annual values of ln(gdpr), where gdpr is Gross Domestic Product, constant prices in billions of local currency.

Standard Deviation of Growth Real Income (*sdgrowth*). *Source*: World Bank *WDI*, calculated for each country over the period 1990 to 2002 as standard deviation of annual difference of ln(gdpr), where gdpr is Gross Domestic Product, constant prices in billions of local currency.

Output Loss in Crises (*crisisloss* [or *compcris*]). The sum of output lost during crises, excluding from that summation cases where crises were associated with output gain. Source: GDP, constant prices for each country from the World Bank's *World Economic Outlook*.

Depth of Crises (*depthofcrises*). The average loss to crises, essentially calculated as Output Loss to Crises over Number of Crises (*crisisloss/crises*).

For Monthly Analysis

Length of "Sudden Stop" Interval (*lag*) is determined as the number of months between a crisis month and the preceding reserve peak.

Reserve Peaks (*respeak*) are determined using seven-month moving average. Monthly reserves data used are from IMF's *International Financial Statistics*.

"Crisis Management Policy" Variables

Reserves Loss, percentage (*resloss*). Determined as the loss in reserves over the lag or length of sudden stop interval, as defined above. Source: Monthly reserves data used are from *IMF's International Financial Statistics*. Calculated as the difference of the reserves level at the peak and the reserves level at crisis month, expressed as a ratio to the reserves level at peak.

First IMF Program Dummy (*Imf6m*). A dummy variable registering one if the lag in months between the crisis month and preceding institution of an IMF program is equal to or less than six months.

Second IMF Program Dummy (*Imf12m*). A dummy variable registering one if the lag in months between the crisis month and preceding institution of an IMF program is equal to or less than 12 months.

Adjustment Policy Mix. Fiscal contraction vs. expenditure-switching. (Δ Govt Cons/Δ TB), over the period (Crisis Yr + 1) − (Crisis Yr): Monthly data sourced from IMF's *International Financial Statistics*. Line 91F used for Government Consumption and Trade Balance is constructed as Exports (line 98C) less Imports (line 90C). Calculated as difference in each variable from (Crisis + 1 year) versus (Crisis − 2 years).

Adjustment Policy Mix. Outcome of contraction vs expenditure-switching. (Δ GDP / Δ TB), Crisis Yr + 1 versus Crisis Yr: Monthly data sourced from IMF's *International Financial Statistics*, line 99B used for GDP and Trade Balance is constructed as Exports (line 98C) less Imports (line 90C). Calculated as difference in each variable from Crisis + 1 year versus Crisis − 2 years.

CPI. sourced from IMF's *International Financial Statistics*, "Consumer Prices."

RER. sourced from IMF's *International Financial Statistics*, "REER BASED ON REL.CP."

Real interest rate (r). Determined from monthly money market rates sourced from IMF's *International Financial Statistics*. Calculated as the current month's nominal interest rate, divided by 100, less the average of: the difference in the natural log of current CPI less the natural log of CPI for one year prior and the difference in the natural log of the CPI one year forward less the natural log of the current month's CPI.

Adjustment Policy Mix. Monetary contraction (level) versus devaluation (*Rmindelrer*). Calculated as r minus the difference in the natural log of that month's RER less the natural log of the RER for one year prior.

Adjustment Policy Mix. Monetary contraction (change) versus devaluation (*delrmindelrer*). Calculated as the difference in r for that month less r for one year prior minus the difference in the natural log of that month's RER less the natural log of the RER for one year prior.

Change in Maturity Composition. Data are available from BIS in semiannual frequency (Q2 and Q4) and constructed as ratio of short-term bank debt (maturity up to one-year) to bank debt of all maturities of consolidated claims of reporting banks on individual countries. Calculated as difference of this ratio; quarter of preceding reserve peak is used in comparison to crisis quarter. In cases where reserve peak and crisis fall in same quarter, that quarter is compared against following quarter if crisis and/or reserve peak fall in June or December. If crisis and/or reserve peak falls in any other month, that quarter is compared against preceding quarter. In cases where reserve peak or crisis falls in Q1 or Q3, preceding quarter's data are used. For data after 2000, quarterly data are available. If crisis or reserve peak falls in first month of quarter, preceding quarter's data are used; otherwise, that quarter's data are used.

Change in Currency Mismatch. Difference in *osin* ratio over time. Currency mismatch variable constructed from annual Q4 data. In cases where crisis occurred in the first six months of the calendar year, data were used from the preceding Q4. In cases where crisis occurred in the latter six months of the calendar year, data were used from the following Q4.

APPENDIX D. DATASET COUNTRY LIST

Table D-1. *Country coverage of data sets used in the 3 econometric approaches*

Country	Probit analysis (panel)	Regression trees (panel)	Linear regression analysis of crisis prevention and management (cross-section)
Albania			*
Algeria	*		*
Angola			*
Argentina	*	*	*
Armenia			*
Azerbaijan			*
Bangladesh	*		*
Belarus			*
Benin	*	*	*
Bhutan			*
Bolivia			*
Botswana	*		*
Brazil	*	*	*
Bulgaria			*
Burkina Faso			*
Burundi			*
Cambodia			*
Cameroon	*		*
Central African Rep.			*
Chad			*
China, P.R.: Mainland	*	*	*
Chile	*	*	*
China, P.R.: Hong Kong			*
Colombia	*	*	*
Congo, Republic of			*
Costa Rica	*		*
Cote d'Ivoire	*		*
Croatia			*
Czech Republic			*
Dominican Republic	*	*	*
Ecuador	*	*	*
Egypt	*	*	*
El Salvador			*
Eritrea			*
Estonia			*
Ethiopia			*
Gabon			*
Gambia, The	*		*

(continued)

Table D-1 (*continued*)

Country	Probit analysis (panel)	Regression trees (panel)	Linear regression analysis of crisis prevention and management (cross-section)
Georgia			*
Ghana	*	*	*
Guatemala	*		*
Guinea	*		*
Guinea-Bissau			*
Haiti	*		*
Honduras	*		*
Hungary			*
India	*	*	*
Indonesia	*		*
Iran, I.R. of	*	*	*
Jamaica	*	*	*
Jordan	*	*	*
Kazakhistan			*
Kenya	*	*	*
Korea			*
Kuwait	*		*
Kyrgyz Republic			*
Laos	*	*	*
Latvia			*
Lebanon			*
Lesotho			*
Liberia			*
Libya	*		*
Lithuania			*
Macedonia, FYR			*
Madagascar	*		*
Malawi			*
Malaysia	*		*
Mali	*	*	*
Mauritania			*
Mauritius			*
Mexico	*	*	*
Moldova			*
Mongolia			*
Morocco	*		*
Mozambique			*
Myanmar	*		*
Namibia	*	*	*
Nepal			*
Nicaragua	*	*	*
Niger			*
Nigeria	*		*

Country	Probit analysis (panel)	Regression trees (panel)	Linear regression analysis of crisis prevention and management (cross-section)
Oman	*		*
Pakistan	*	*	*
Panama	*	*	*
Paraguay			*
Peru	*	*	*
Philippines	*		*
Poland			*
Romania			*
Russia			*
Rwanda			*
Saudi Arabia	*	*	*
Senegal	*	*	*
Sierra Leone	*		*
Singapore			*
Sri Lanka	*		*
Sudan			*
Syria	*	*	*
Taiwan Prov. of China			*
Tajikistan			*
Tanzania	*		*
Thailand			*
Togo	*		*
Trinidad and Tobago	*		*
Tunisia	*	*	*
Turkey	*	*	*
Turkmenistan			*
Uganda	*	*	*
Ukraine			*
United Arab Emirates	*		*
Uruguay	*		*
Venezuela, Rep. Bol.	*	*	*
Vietnam	*		*
Zambia	*		*
Zimbabwe	*		*

Source: Authors' compilations.

APPENDIX E. RESULTS OF PROBIT REGRESSIONS, DIFFERENT THRESHOLDS FOR CRISIS

Table E-1. *Results of probit regressions (15%)*

Variable	(1)	(2)	(3)	(4)
Trade openness	0.003	0.005	0.007	−0.001
	(0.003)	(0.004)	(0.005)	(0.008)
Financial openness	0.001	−0.002	3.89E-04	−0.004
	(0.001)	(0.007)	(0.002)	(0.007)
Constraint on executives	−0.005	0.04	−0.082	−0.01
	(0.036)	(0.047)	(0.059)	(0.08)
STdebt/Reserve	1.986	1.977	2.179	2.475
	(1.067)	(1.24)	(1.429)	(1.646)
Debt/GDP	0.001	0.001	0.003	0.005
	(0.001)	(0.001)	(0.002)	(0.003)
(FDI + ptf)/Gross liability	−0.003	−0.004	−0.002	−0.003
	(0.003)	(0.004)	(0.003)	(0.005)
Inflation	1.61E-04	1.57E-04	3.00E-04	3.11E-04
	1.20E-04	1.24E-04	1.59E-04	1.59E-04
Fixed ex. rate regime	−0.032	−0.078	0.315	0.248
	(0.205)	(0.257)	(0.278)	(0.391)
Intermediate ex. rate regime	−0.087	−0.194	0.065	−0.029
	(0.194)	(0.229)	(0.246)	(0.309)
Country dummy	No	No	Yes	Yes
Year dummy	No	Yes	No	Yes
No. observations	456	325	439	293

Source: Authors' calculations.

Table E-2. *Results of probit regressions (15%)*

Variable	(1)	(2)	(3)	(4)
Trade openness	0.002	0.005	0.004	0.004
	(0.002)	(0.004)	(0.004)	(0.007)
Financial openness	0.001	0.007	1.12E-03	0.005
	(0.001)	(0.006)	(0.002)	(0.006)
Constraint on executives	0.012	0.034	−0.046	0.01
	(0.029)	(0.041)	(0.05)	(0.075)
STdebt/Reserve	0.988	1.3	1.936	2.407
	(0.678)	(0.842)	(0.935)	(1.215)
Debt/GDP	1.09E-04	−0.001	0.002	0.001
	(0.001)	(0.001)	(0.001)	(0.002)
Inflation	1.62E-05	−1.58E-05	−1.66E-07	−3.76E-05
	(7.91E-05)	(8.12E-05)	(9.57E-05)	(9.58E-05)
Fixed ex. rate regime	0.069	−0.05	0.315	0.264
	(0.172)	(0.214)	(0.225)	(0.33)
Intermediate ex. rate regime	−0.133	−0.217	0.065	−0.004
	(0.177)	(0.207)	(0.215)	(0.28)
Country dummy	No	No	Yes	Yes
Year dummy	No	Yes	No	Yes
No. observations	640	401	629	374

Source: Authors' calculations.

Table E-3. *Results of probit regressions (15%)*

Variable	(1)	(2)	(3)	(4)
Trade openness	−0.001	−0.001	0.001	0.001
	(0.002)	(0.002)	(0.004)	(0.005)
Financial openness	0.001	0.001	2.01E-03	0.003
	(0.002)	(0.003)	(0.002)	(0.003)
Low corruption	−3.77E-04	0.016	0.051	0.058
	(0.056)	(0.058)	(0.088)	(0.097)
STdebt/Reserve	1.176	1.157	1.038	1.014
	(0.498)	(0.523)	(0.676)	(0.727)
Debt/GDP	1.57E-04	3.07E-04	−4.15E-04	−0.001
	(4.68E-04)	(0.001)	(0.001)	(0.001)
(FDI + ptf)/Gross liability	−0.001	0.001	−0.004	−0.001
	(0.002)	(0.002)	(0.003)	(0.003)
Inflation	1.48E-04	1.58E-04	2.30E-04	2.49E-04
	(1.13E-04)	(1.15E-04)	(1.52E-04)	(1.55E-04)
Fixed ex. rate regime	−0.149	−0.171	0.007	−0.143
	(0.132)	(0.139)	(0.208)	(0.228)
Intermediate ex. rate regime	−0.253	−0.289	−0.225	−0.358
	(0.134)	(0.141)	(0.174)	(0.19)
Country dummy	No	No	Yes	Yes
Year dummy	No	Yes	No	Yes
No. observations	810	751	741	673

Source: Authors' calculations.

Table E-4. *Results of probit regressions (15%)*

Variable	(1)	(2)	(3)	(4)
Trade openness	−0.002	−0.001	−0.001	0.004
	(0.002)	(0.002)	(0.004)	(0.005)
Financial openness	0.002	0.002	0.003	0.005
	(0.001)	(0.002)	(0.002)	(0.002)
Low corruption	−3.40E-02	−0.01	−0.004	2.28E-04
	(0.05)	(0.052)	(0.081)	(0.088)
STdebt/Reserve	1.031	1.047	1.199	1.116
	(0.394)	(0.446)	(0.601)	(0.665)
Debt/GDP	−4.96E-05	−7.84E-05	−7.07E-04	−0.001
	(4.05E-04)	(4.58E-04)	(0.001)	(0.001)
Inflation	1.35E-05	−6.31E-06	1.92E-06	−1.83E-05
	(7.46E-05)	(7.73E-05)	(9.55E-04)	(9.62E-04)
Fixed ex. rate regime	−0.098	−0.154	0.047	−0.133
	(0.119)	(0.127)	(0.182)	(0.202)
Intermediate ex. rate regime	−0.27	−0.32	−0.2	−0.36
	(0.125)	(0.132)	(0.167)	(0.183)
Country dummy	No	No	Yes	Yes
Year dummy	No	Yes	No	Yes
No. observations	959	865	906	817

Source: Authors' calculations.

Table E-5. *Results of probit regressions (25%)*

Variable	(1)	(2)	(3)	(4)
Trade openness	0.002	0.003	−0.001	−0.003
	(0.003)	(0.005)	(0.005)	(0.009)
Financial openness	0.001	−0.009	4.20E-04	−0.029
	(0.001)	(0.013)	(0.002)	(0.019)
Constraint on executives	−0.005	0.002	−0.062	−0.005
	(0.038)	(0.051)	(0.067)	(0.093)
STdebt/Reserve	1.476	0.946	1.011	1.913
	(1.114)	(1.418)	(1.363)	(1.91)
Debt/GDP	1.87E-04	0.001	0.006	0.008
	(9.27E-04)	(0.002)	(0.002)	(0.004)
(FDI + ptf)/Gross liability	−0.004	−0.005	−0.005	−0.01
	(0.003)	(0.004)	(0.003)	(0.005)
Inflation	1.94E-04	1.54E-04	3.30E-04	3.01E-04
	(1.18E-04)	(1.34E-04)	(1.59E-04)	(1.88E-04)
Fixed ex. rate regime	0.01	−0.016	0.3	0.35
	(0.215)	(0.283)	(0.292)	(0.421)
Intermediate ex. rate regime	−0.174	−0.231	−0.081	−0.188
	(0.206)	(0.249)	(0.267)	(0.344)
Country dummy	No	No	Yes	Yes
Year dummy	No	Yes	No	Yes
No. observations	456	287	426	269

Source: Authors' calculations.

Table E-6. *Results of probit regressions (25%)*

Variable	(1)	(2)	(3)	(4)
Trade openness	0.001	0.002	−0.001	−0.004
	(0.002)	(0.004)	(0.004)	(0.008)
Financial openness	0.002	0.007	0.001	−0.002
	(0.001)	(0.005)	(0.002)	(0.012)
Constraint on executives	0.002	0.007	−0.04	0.022
	(0.032)	(0.045)	(0.051)	(0.084)
STdebt/Reserve	1.234	1.352	1.51	2.426
	(0.704)	(0.937)	(1.029)	(1.33)
Debt/GDP	−1.48E-04	−0.001	0.003	0.002
	(9.27E-04)	(0.001)	(0.002)	(0.002)
Inflation	1.50E-04	8.05E-05	1.58E-04	7.22E-05
	(7.26E-05)	(7.76E-05)	(9.19E-05)	(9.32E-05)
Fixed ex. rate regime	0.074	0.033	0.236	0.222
	(0.184)	(0.24)	(0.242)	(0.376)
Intermediate ex. rate regime	−0.169	−0.274	−0.026	−0.155
	(0.191)	(0.229)	(0.227)	(0.309)
Country dummy	No	No	Yes	Yes
Year dummy	No	Yes	No	Yes
No. observations	640	373	572	332

Source: Authors' calculations.

Table E-7. *Results of probit regressions (25%)*

Variable	(1)	(2)	(3)	(4)
Trade openness	−0.003	−0.003	0.002	0.006
	(0.002)	(0.002)	(0.005)	(0.006)
Financial openness	0.001	−3.85E-04	0.001	0.001
	(0.002)	(0.003)	(0.002)	(0.003)
Low corruption	0.016	0.03	0.06	0.056
	(0.058)	(0.06)	(0.091)	(0.103)
STdebt/Reserve	1.061	1.092	0.525	0.539
	(0.481)	(0.556)	(0.671)	(0.796)
Debt/GDP	3.90E-05	4.25E-04	−5.49E-04	−2.52E-04
	(4.92E-04)	(0.001)	(0.001)	(0.001)
(FDI + ptf)/Gross liability	−0.004	−0.003	−0.01	−0.008
	(0.002)	(0.002)	(0.003)	(0.003)
Inflation	1.53E-04	1.44E-04	2.24E-04	2.06E-04
	(1.12E-04)	(1.16E-04)	−0.000	(1.57E-04)
Fixed ex. rate regime	−0.166	−0.196	−0.101	−0.246
	(0.141)	(0.149)	(0.225)	(0.256)
Intermediate ex. rate regime	−0.373	−0.363	−0.347	−0.377
	(0.144)	(0.15)	(0.192)	(0.223)
Country dummy	No	No	Yes	Yes
Year dummy	No	Yes	No	Yes
No. observations	810	751	688	635

Source: Authors' calculations.

Table E-8. *Results of probit regressions (25%)*

Variable	(1)	(2)	(3)	(4)
Trade openness	−0.003	−0.003	−0.003	0.004
	(0.002)	(0.002)	(0.005)	(0.006)
Financial openness	0.001	6.89E-04	0.002	0.001
	(0.001)	(0.002)	(0.001)	(0.002)
Low corruption	−0.025	0.004	0.001	−0.014
	(0.052)	(0.052)	(0.084)	(0.094)
STdebt/Reserve	1.051	0.995	0.832	0.817
	(0.396)	(0.491)	(0.608)	(0.746)
Debt/GDP	−2.13E-05	1.46E-04	−5.91E-04	−2.75E-04
	(4.03E-04)	(0.001)	(0.001)	(0.001)
Inflation	1.30E-04	8.56E-05	1.58E-04	1.08E-04
	(6.43E-05)	(6.53E-05)	(8.51E-05)	(8.23E-05)
Fixed ex. rate regime	−0.184	−0.243	−0.192	−0.374
	(0.127)	(0.137)	(0.194)	(0.228)
Intermediate ex. rate regime	−0.375	−0.383	−0.293	−0.37
	(0.134)	(0.141)	(0.181)	(0.213)
Country dummy	No	No	Yes	Yes
Year dummy	No	Yes	No	Yes
No. observations	959	865	839	758

Source: Authors' calculations.

Jeffrey Frankel and Shang-Jin Wei

Table E-9. *Results of probit regressions (35%)*

Variable	(1)	(2)	(3)	(4)
Trade openness	0.004	0.009	−0.003	0.002
	(0.003)	(0.005)	(0.006)	(0.011)
Financial openness	−0.001	−0.031	−0.003	−0.084
	(0.001)	(0.013)	(0.002)	(0.025)
Constraint on executives	−0.002	0.051	−0.075	0.108
	(0.041)	(0.051)	(0.074)	(0.094)
STdebt/Reserve	1.642	1.748	0.95	3.197
	(1.17)	(1.576)	(1.517)	(2.314)
Debt/GDP	−3.24E-04	0.003	0.005	0.017
	(0.001)	(0.002)	(0.002)	(0.005)
(FDI + ptf)/Gross liability	−0.006	−0.006	−0.007	−0.013
	(0.003)	(0.005)	(0.004)	(0.007)
Inflation	3.23E-04	2.41E-04	5.64E-04	6.30E-04
	(1.43E-04)	(1.58E-04)	(2.33E-04)	(2.72E-04)
Fixed ex. rate regime	0.055	−0.066	0.123	0.074
	(0.236)	(0.313)	(0.303)	(0.464)
Intermediate ex. rate regime	0.106	−0.118	0.342	0.508
	(0.217)	(0.258)	(0.273)	(0.388)
Country dummy	No	No	Yes	Yes
Year dummy	No	Yes	No	Yes
No. observations	456	298	401	254

Source: Authors' calculations.

Table E-10. *Results of probit regressions (35%)*

Variable	(1)	(2)	(3)	(4)
Trade openness	0.003	0.007	1.77E-05	0.003
	(0.002)	(0.004)	(0.005)	(0.009)
Financial openness	−3.97E-05	−0.002	−0.003	−0.023
	(0.001)	(0.006)	(0.002)	(0.018)
Constraint on executives	−0.004	0.051	−0.097	0.101
	(0.033)	(0.045)	(0.059)	(0.088)
STdebt/Reserve	0.974	0.85	0.655	1.599
	(0.746)	(0.955)	(1.044)	(1.518)
Debt/GDP	−3.50E-04	−2.24E-04	0.003	0.005
	(0.001)	(0.001)	(0.001)	(0.003)
Inflation	1.09E-04	7.24E-06	7.95E-05	−3.56E-05
	(8.12E-05)	(7.56E-05)	(9.71E-05)	(8.29E-05)
Fixed ex. rate regime	0.027	0.047	0.101	0.016
	(0.195)	(0.255)	(0.259)	(0.412)
Intermediate ex. rate regime	0.006	−0.131	0.294	0.313
	(0.2)	(0.239)	(0.236)	(0.338)
Country dummy	No	No	Yes	Yes
Year dummy	No	Yes	No	Yes
No. observations	640	365	540	294

Source: Authors' calculations.

Table E-11. *Results of probit regressions (35%)*

Variable	(1)	(2)	(3)	(4)
Trade openness	−0.001	−0.001	3.31E-04	0.005
	(0.002)	(0.002)	(0.006)	(0.007)
Financial openness	−0.004	−0.002	−2.00E-03	−0.001
	(0.004)	(0.005)	(0.004)	(0.005)
Low corruption	−4.70E-02	−0.035	−0.042	−0.035
	(0.068)	(0.07)	(0.101)	(0.117)
STdebt/Reserve	1.471	1.557	1.6	1.744
	(0.51)	(0.544)	(0.726)	(0.736)
Debt/GDP	0.001	9.13E-04	7.22E-04	8.19E-04
	(4.92E-04)	(0.001)	(0.001)	(0.002)
(FDI + ptf)/Gross liability	−0.005	−0.002	−0.011	−0.006
	(0.002)	(0.003)	(0.004)	(0.004)
Inflation	3.09E-04	2.48E-04	4.66E-04	3.58E-04
	(1.33E-04)	(1.20E-04)	(2.04E-04)	(1.70E-04)
Fixed ex. rate regime	−0.105	−0.11	−0.096	−0.233
	(0.156)	(0.165)	(0.245)	(0.268)
Intermediate ex. rate regime	−0.152	−0.133	−0.019	−0.079
	(0.153)	(0.165)	(0.204)	(0.243)
Country dummy	No	No	Yes	Yes
Year dummy	No	Yes	No	Yes
No. observations	810	751	665	612

Source: Authors' calculations.

Table E-12. *Results of probit regressions (35%)*

Variable	(1)	(2)	(3)	(4)
Trade openness	−0.002	−0.001	−0.003	0.006
	(0.002)	(0.002)	(0.005)	(0.006)
Financial openness	−0.002	−4.88E-04	−0.001	−4.40E-04
	(0.002)	(0.003)	(0.003)	(0.003)
Low corruption	−0.069	−0.041	−0.1	−0.118
	(0.059)	(0.061)	(0.096)	(0.114)
STdebt/Reserve	1.117	1.092	1.639	1.787
	(0.423)	(0.504)	(0.646)	(0.689)
Debt/GDP	0.001	3.90E-04	5.77E-04	6.79E-04
	(5.83E-04)	(0.001)	(0.001)	(0.001)
Inflation	7.95E-05	2.52E-05	6.84E-05	3.17E-06
	(7.79E-05)	(6.85E-05)	(9.42E-05)	(7.88E-05)
Fixed ex. rate regime	−0.158	−0.181	−0.172	−0.287
	(0.139)	(0.15)	(0.209)	(0.24)
Intermediate ex. rate regime	−0.199	−0.18	−0.04	−0.068
	(0.142)	(0.155)	(0.188)	(0.229)
Country dummy	No	No	Yes	Yes
Year dummy	No	Yes	No	Yes
No. observations	959	865	797	716

Source: Authors' calculations.

REFERENCES

Acemoglu, Daron, Simon Johnson, and James Robinson. 2001. "The Colonial Origins of Comparative Development: An Empirical Investigation." *American Economic Review* 91(5):1369–401.

Acemoglu, Daron, Simon Johnson, James Robinson, and Yunyong Thaicharoen. 2003. "Institutional Causes, Macroeconomic Symptoms: Volatility, Crises and Growth." *Journal of Monetary Economics* 50:49–123.

Agenor, Pierre Richard, and Joshua Aizenman. 1998. "Contagion and Volatility with Imperfect Credit Markets." *IMF Staff Papers* 45(2):207–35.

Aizenman, Joshua, and Reuven Glick. 2003. "Military Expenditure, Threats and Growth." Federal Reserve Bank of San Francisco.

Aizenman, Joshua, and Andrew Powell. 2003. "Volatility and Financial Intermediation." *Journal of International Money and Finance* 22(5):657–79.

Alesina, Alberto, and Alexander Wagner. 2003. "Choosing (and Reneging on) Exchange Rate Regimes." NBER Working Paper 9809. National Bureau of Economics Research, Cambridge, MA.

Alfaro, Laura, Sebnem Kalemli-Ozcan, and Vadym Volosovych. 2003. "Why Doesn't Capital Flow from Rich Countries to Poor Countries? An Empirical Investigation." Harvard Business School and University of Houston.

Alston, Lee J., and Andres Gallo. 2000. "Evolution and Revolution in the Argentine Banking System under Convertibility: The Roles of Crises and Path Dependence." NBER Working Paper 8008. National Bureau of Economic Research, Cambridge, MA.

Anderson, James, and Eric van Wincoop. 2003. "Gravity with Gravitas: A Solution to the Border Puzzle." *American Economic Review* 93(1):170–92.

Arteta, Carlos, Barry Eichengreen, and Charles Wyplosz. 2003. "When Does Capital Account Liberalization Help More than It Hurts?" In Elhanan Helpman and Efraim Sadka, eds., *Economic Policy in the International Economy*. New York: Cambridge University Press.

Barro, Robert. 1991. "Economic Growth in a Cross Section of Countries." *Quarterly Journal of Economics* CVI (May):407–44.

———. 2001. "Economic Growth in East Asia Before and After the Financial Crisis." NBER Working Paper 8330. National Bureau of Economic Research, Cambridge, MA.

Barro, Robert, and Jong Wha Lee. 1993. "International Comparisons of Educational Attainment." *Journal of Monetary Economics* 32(3):363–94.

———. 2000. "International Data on Educational Attainment: Updates and Implications." Harvard University.

Bartolini, Leonardo, and Allan Drazen. 1997. "Capital Account Liberalization as a Signal." *American Economic Review* 87(1):138–54.

Berg, Andrew, Eduardo Borensztein, Gian Maria Milesi-Ferreti, and Catherine Pattillo. 1999. "Anticipating Balance of Payments Crises: The Role of Early Warning Systems." Occasional Paper 186. International Monetary Fund, Washington, DC.

Bencivenga, Valerie, and Bruce Smith. 1991. "Financial Intermediation and Endogenous Growth." *Review of Economic Studies* 58(April):195–209.

Bhagwati, Jagdish. 1998. "The Capital Myth." *Foreign Affairs* 77(3):7–12. Reprinted in Jagdish Bhagwati, 2002. *The Wind of the Hundred Days: How Washington Mismanaged Globalization*. Cambridge, MA: MIT Press.

Biscarri, Javier Gomez, Sebastian Edwards, and Fernando Perez de Gracia. 2003. "Stock Market Cycles, Liberalization, and Volatility." NBER Working Paper 9817. National Bureau of Economic Research, Cambridge, MA.

Blanco, Herminio, and Peter Garber. 1986. "Recurrent Devaluations and Speculative Attacks on the Mexico Peso." *Journal of Political Economy* 94:148–66.

Blustein, Paul. 2002. *The Chastening: Inside the Crisis That Rocked the Global Financial System and Humbled the IMF.* New York: Public Affairs.

Bordo, Michael D., and Anna J. Schwartz. 1997. "Why Clashes Between Internal and External Stability Goals End in Currency Crises, 1797–1994." NBER Working Paper 5710. National Bureau of Economic Research, Cambridge, MA.

Bosworth, Barry, and Susan Collins. 2003. "The Empirics of Growth: An Update." *Brooking's Papers on Economic Activity* 2:113–79.

Breiman, Leo, Jerome H. Friedman, Richard A. Olshen, and Charles J. Stone. 1984. *Classification and Regression Trees.* New York: Chapman & Hall/CRC.

Burnside, Craig, Martin Eichenbaum, and Sergio Rebelo. 1998. "Prospective Deficits and the Asian Currency Crisis." NBER Working Paper 6758. National Bureau of Economic Research, Cambridge, MA.

———. 1999. "Hedging and Financial Fragility in Fixed Exchange Rate Regimes." NBER Working Paper 7143. National Bureau of Economic Research, Cambridge, MA.

Caballero, Ricardo, and Arvind Krishnamurthy. 2001. "A 'Vertical' Analysis of Crises and Intervention: Fear of Floating and Ex Ante Problems." NBER Working Paper 8428. National Bureau of Economic Research, Cambridge, MA.

Calomiris, Charles W., and Andrew Powell. 2000. "Can Emerging Market Bank Regulators Establish Credible Discipline? The Case of Argentina, 1992–1999." NBER Working Paper 7715. National Bureau of Economic Research, Cambridge, MA.

Calvo, Guillermo A., and Frederic Mishkin. 2003. "The Mirage of Exchange Rate Regimes for Emerging Market Countries." NBER Working Paper 9808. National Bureau of Economic Research, Cambridge, MA.

Calvo, Guillermo A., and Carmen Reinhart. 2001. "When Capital Inflows Come to a Sudden Stop: Consequences and Policy Options." In Peter Kenen and Alexander Swoboda, eds., *Key Issues in Reform of the International Monetary System.* Washington, DC: International Monetary Fund.

———. 2002. "Fear of Floating." *Quarterly Journal of Economics* 117(2):379–408.

Calvo, Guillermo A., and Carlos Vegh. 1994. "Inflation Stabilization and Nominal Anchors." *Contemporary Economic Policy* XII (April):35–45. Reprinted in R. Barth and C. H. Wong, eds., 1994, *Approaches to Exchange Rate Policy.* Washington, DC: International Monetary Fund.

Calvo, Guillermo, Alejandro Izquierdo, and Ernesto Talvi. 2003. "Sudden Stops, the Real Exchange Rate, and Fiscal Sustainability: Argentina's Lessons." NBER Working Paper 9828. National Bureau of Economic Research, Cambridge, MA.

Calvo, Guillermo, Leo Leiderman, and Carmen Reinhart. 1996. "Inflows of Capital to Developing Countries in the 1990s." *Journal of Economic Perspectives* 10(2):123–39.

Cardenas, Mauricio, and Felipe Barrera. 1997. "On the Effectiveness of Capital Controls: The Experience of Colombia During the 1990s." *Journal of Development Economics* 54(1): 27–57.

Cardoso, Eliana, and Ann Helwege. 1999. "Currency Crisis in the 1990s: The Case of Brazil." World Bank, Washington, DC.

Cavallo, Eduardo, and Frankel Jeffrey. 2004. "Does Openness to Trade Make Countries Less Vulnerable to Sudden Stops? Using Gravity to Establish Causality." Working Paper No. 10957. National Bureau of Economic Research, Cambridge, MA.

Cavallo, Michele, Kate Schneider Kisselev, Fabrizio Perri, and Nouriel Roubini. 2002. Overshooting of Exchange Rates in Currency Crises: A Theoretical and Empirical Analysis. New York: New York University.

Caves, Richard, Jeffrey Frankel, and Ronald Jones. 2002. *World Trade and Payments: An Introduction.* Boston: Addison Wesley Longman (ninth edition).

Céspedes, Luis Felipe, Roberto Chang, and Andrés Velasco. 2002. "Dollarization of Liabilities, Net Worth Effects and Optimal Monetary Policy." In J. Frankel and S. Edwards, eds., *Preventing Crises in Emerging Markets*. Chicago: University of Chicago Press.

Chang, Roberto, and Andres Velasco. 2000a. "Liquidity Crises in Emerging Markets: Theory and Policy." In Ben S. Bernanke and Julio Rotemberg, eds., *NBER Macroeconomics Annual, 1999*. Cambridge, MA: MIT Press.

————. 2000b. "Banks, Debt Maturity and Crises." *Journal of International Economics* 51(1):169–94.

————. 2001. "A Model of Financial Crises in Emerging Markets." *Quarterly Journal of Economics* 2(116):489–517. From NBER Working Paper 6606 (1998). National Bureau of Economic Research, Inc., Cambridge, MA.

Chari, Anusha, and Peter Blair Henry. 2002a. "Capital Account Liberalization: Allocative Efficiency or Animal Spirits." NBER Working Paper 8908. National Bureau of Economic Research, Cambridge, MA.

————. 2002b. "Risk Sharing and Asset Prices: Evidence from a Natural Experiment." NBER Working Paper 8988. National Bureau of Economic Research, Cambridge, MA.

Chinn, Menzie, and Hiro Ito. 2002. "Capital Account Liberalization, Institutions, and Financial Development: Cross-Country Evidence." NBER Working Paper 8967. National Bureau of Economic Research, Cambridge, MA.

Chinn, Menzie, and Kenneth Kletzer. 2000. "International Capital Inflows, Domestic Financial Intermediation and Financial Crises under Imperfect Information." NBER Working Paper 7902. National Bureau of Economic Research, Cambridge, MA.

Chinn, Menzie, Michael Dooley, and Sona Shrestha. 1999. "Latin America and East Asia in the Context of an Insurance Model of Currency Crises." NBER Working Paper 7091. National Bureau of Economic Research, Cambridge, MA.

Christiano, Lawrence J., Christopher Gust, and Jorge Roldos. 2002. "Monetary Policy in a Financial Crisis." NBER Working Paper 9005. National Bureau of Economic Research, Cambridge, MA.

Chucamaro, R., R. Laban, and F. Larrain. 1996. "What Determines Capital Inflows: An Empirical Analysis for Chile." Catholic University of Chile, Santiago.

Cole, David, and Betty Slade. 1992. "Indonesian Financial Development: A Different Sequencing?" In D. Vittas, ed., *Financial Regulation: Changing the Rules of the Game*. EDI Development Studies. Washington, DC: World Bank.

Corden, W. Max. 1993. "Absorption, the Budget, and Debt: The Wonderland of Possibilities." In Horse Herberg and Ngo Van Long, eds., *Trade, Welfare, and Economic Policies: Essays in Honor of Murray C. Kemp*. Ann Arbor: University of Michigan Press.

————. 1994. "A Model of Balance of Payments Policy." In Max Corden, *Economic Policy, Exchange Rates, and the International Monetary System*. Oxford: Oxford University Press.

Corsetti, Giancarlo, Paolo Pesenti, and Nouriel Roubini. 1999a. "Paper Tigers? A Model of the Asian Crisis," NBER Working Paper 6783. Also in *European Economic Review* 43(7):1211–36.

————. 1999b. "What Caused the Asian Currency and Financial Crisis?" *Japan and the World Economy* 11(September):305–73.

De Gregorio, Jose, and Pablo Guidotti. 1995. "Financial Development and Economic Growth." *World Development* 23(September):443–48.

De la Torre, Augusto, Eduardo Levy Yeyati, and Sergio Schmukler. 2003. "Living and Dying with Hard Pegs: The Rise and Fall of Argentina's Currency Board." *Economia* (Spring):43–107. Reprinted in V. Alexander, J. Mélitz, and G. von Furstenberg, eds., *Monetary Unions and Hard Pegs: Effects on Trade, Financial Development, and Stability*. Oxford: Oxford University Press.

Dekle, Robert, and Kenneth Kletzer. 2001. "Domestic Bank Regulation and Financial Crises: Theory and Empirical Evidence from East Asia." NBER Working Paper 8322. National Bureau of Economic Research, Cambridge, MA. In Sebastian Edwards and Jeffrey Frankel, eds., 2002, *Preventing Currency Crises in Emerging Markets*. Chicago: University of Chicago Press.

Desai, Padma. 2003. *Financial Crisis, Contagion, and Containment: From Asia to Argentina*. Princeton: Princeton University Press.

Diamond, Jared. 1997. *Guns, Germs, and Steel*. New York: W. W. Norton and Co.

Diamond, Douglas, and Philip Dybvig. 1983. "Bank Runs, Deposit Insurance, and Liquidity." *Journal of Political Economy* 91(June):401–19.

Diamond, Douglas, and Raghuram Rajan. 2000. "Banks, Short-Term Debt and Financial Crises: Theory, Policy Implications, and Applications." NBER Working Paper 7764. National Bureau of Economic Research, Cambridge, MA.

Diaz-Alejandro, Carlos. 1985. "Good-bye Financial Repression; Hello Financial Crash." *Journal of Development Economics* 19(September):1–24.

Dooley, Michael. 1996. "A Survey of Literature on Controls over International Capital Transactions." *IMF Staff Papers* 43(4):639–87.

————. 1997. "A Model of Crises in Emerging Markets." NBER Working Paper 6300. National Bureau of Economic Research, Cambridge. Also in *Economic Journal* 110 (460) (January 2000):256–72.

Dornbusch, Rudiger. 1973. "Devaluation, Money and Nontraded Goods." *American Economic Review* 63(December):871–80.

————. 2002. "Crises in Emerging Markets: A Primer." In Sebastian Edwards and Jeffrey Frankel, eds., *Preventing Currency Crises in Emerging Markets*. Chicago: University of Chicago Press.

Dornbusch, Rudiger, and Alejandro Werner. 1994. "Mexico: Stabilization, Reform and No Growth." *Brookings Papers on Economic Activity* 1:253–97.

Dornbusch, Rudiger, Ilan Goldfajn, and Rodrigo Valdes. 1995. "Currency Crises and Collapses." *Brookings Papers on Economic Activity* 2:219–93.

Drazen, Allan. 2003. "Interest Rate Defense against Speculative Attack as a Signal: A Primer." In Michael Dooley and Jeffrey Frankel, eds., *Managing Currency Crises in Emerging Markets*. Chicago: University of Chicago Press.

Du Julan, and Shang-Jin Wei. 2003. "Does Insider Trading Raise Market Volatility?" NBER Working Paper 9541. National Bureau of Economic Research, Cambridge, MA. *Economic Journal* 114:927–56, October 2004.

Easterly, William, and Ross Levine.1997. "Africa's Growth Tragedy: Policies and Ethnic Divisions." *Quarterly Journal of Economics* CXII(4):1203–50.

Easterly, William, and Ross Levine. 2002. "Tropics, Germs, and Crops: How Endowments Influence Economic Development," Center for Global Development Working Paper No. 15, Washington, DC. In *Carnegie-Rochester Conference Series on Public Policy. Journal of Monetary Economics* 51, Jan. 2003.

Easterly, William, and Sergio Rebelo. 1994. "Fiscal Policy and Economic Growth: An Empirical Investigation." Working Paper 885. Centre for Economic Policy Research, London.

Edison, Hali. 2000. "Do Indicators of Financial Crises Work? An Evaluation of an Early Warning System." International Finance Discussion Papers No. 675. Federal Reserve Board, Washington, DC.

Edison, Hali, Michael Klein, Luca Ricci, and Torsten Sloek. 2002. "Capital Account Liberalization and Economic Peformance: Survey and Synthesis." NBER Working Paper 9100. National Bureau of Economic Research, Cambridge, MA.

Edwards, Sebastian. 1984. "The Order of Liberalization of the External Sector in Developing Countries." In *Essays in International Finance*, No. 156. Princeton University.

—————. 1986. "Are Devaluations Contractionary?" *Review of Economics and Statistics* 68(3):501–08.

—————. 1999. "Crisis Prevention: Lessons from Mexico and East Asia." NBER Working Paper 7233. National Bureau of Economic Research, Cambridge, MA.

—————. 2000. "Capital Flows, Real Exchange Rates, and Capital Controls: Some Latin American Experiences." In Sebastian Edwards, ed., *Capital Flows and the Emerging Economies*. Chicago: University of Chicago Press.

—————. 2001. "Capital Mobility and Economic Performance: Are Emerging Economies Different?" NBER Working Paper 8076. National Bureau of Economic Research, Cambridge, MA.

—————. 2002. "The Great Exchange Rate Debate after Argentina." NBER Working Paper 9257. National Bureau of Economic Research, Cambridge, MA.

—————. 2003. "Exchange Rate Regimes." In Martin Feldstein, ed., *Economic and Financial Crises in Emerging Market Economies*. Chicago: University of Chicago Press.

Edwards, Sebastian, and Jeffrey Frankel. 2002. *Preventing Currency Crises in Emerging Markets*. Chicago: University of Chicago Press.

Edwards, Sebastian, and Eduardo Levy-Yeyati. 2003. "Flexible Exchange Rates as Shock Absorbers." NBER Working Papers 9867. National Bureau of Economic Research, Cambridge, MA.

Edwards, Sebastian, and Igal Magendzo. 2003a. "A Currency of One's Own? An Empirical Investigation of Dollarization and Independent Currency Unions." NBER Working Paper 9514. National Bureau of Economic Research, Cambridge, MA.

—————. 2003b. "Strict Dollarization and Economic Peformance: An Empirical Investigation." NBER Working Paper 9820. National Bureau of Economic Research, Cambridge, MA.

Edwards, Sebastian, and Miguel A. Savastano. 1999. "Exchange Rates in Emerging Economies: What Do We Know? What Do We Need to Know?" NBER Working Paper 7228. National Bureau of Economic Research, Cambridge, MA.

Eichengreen, Barry. 1999. *Toward a New International Financial Architecture: A Practical Post-Asia Agenda*. Institute for International Economics, Washington, DC.

Eichengreen, Barry, and Tamim Bayoumi. 1999. "Is Asia an Optimum Currency Area? Can It Become One?" In Stefan Collignon, Jean Pisani-Ferry, and Yung Chul Park, eds., *Exchange Rate Policies in Emerging Asian Countries*. London: Routledge.

Eichengreen, Barry, and David Leblang. 2003. "Capital Account Liberalization and Growth: Was Mr. Mahatir Right?" NBER Working Paper 9427. National Bureau of Economic Research, Cambridge, MA.

Eichengreen, Barry, and Ricardo Hausmann. 1999. "Exchange Rates and Financial Fragility." NBER Working Paper 7418. National Bureau of Economic Research, Cambridge, MA.

Eichengreen, Barry, and Ashoka Mody. 1999. "Lending Booms, Reserves, and the Sustainability of Short-Term Debt: Inferences from the Pricing of Syndicated Bank Loans." NBER Working Paper 7113. National Bureau of Economic Research, Cambridge, MA.

Eichengreen, Barry, and Michael Mussa. 1998. "Capital Account Liberalization: Theoretical and Practical Aspects." Occasional Paper No. 172, International Monetary Fund, Washington, DC.

Eichengreen, Barry, and Andy Rose. 2003. "Does It Pay to Defend against a Speculative Attack?" In Michael Dooley and Jeffrey Frankel, eds., *Managing Currency Crises in Emerging Markets*. Chicago: University of Chicago Press.

Eichengreen, Barry, and Alan Taylor. 2003. "The Monetary Consequences of a Free Trade Area of the Americas." NBER Working Paper 9666. National Bureau of Economic Research, Cambridge, MA.

Eichengreen, Barry, Ricardo Hausmann, and Ugo Panizza. 2003. "The Pain of Original Sin." Inter-American Development Bank, Washington, DC.

Eichengreen, Barry, Andy Rose, and Charles Wyplosz. 1995. "Exchange Market Mayhem: The Antecedents and Aftermath of Speculative Attacks." *Economic Policy* 21: 249–96.

Engerman, Stanley, and Kenneth Sokoloff. 1997. "Factor Endowments, Institutions, and Differential Paths of Growth among New World Economies: A View from Economic Historians of the United States." In Stephen Haber, ed., *How Latin America Fell Behind*. Stanford, CA: Stanford University Press.

ESRI (Environmental Systems Research Institute Inc.) 1996. *ArcWorld Supplement Database*. Redlands, CA.

Fischer, Stanley. 2001. "Exchange Rate Regimes: Is the Bipolar View Correct?" *Journal of Economic Perspectives* 15(2):3–24.

———. 2004a. "Capital Account Liberalization and the Role of the IMF." In Stanley Fischer, *IMF Essays from a Time of Crisis: The International Financial System, Stabilization, and Development*. Cambridge, MA: MIT Press.

———. 2004b. *IMF Essays*. Cambridge, MA: MIT Press.

Flood, Robert, and Rebecca Coke. 2000. "Is 'Predicted Currency Crisis' an Oxymoron?" International Monetary Fund, Washington, DC.

Flood, Robert, and Peter Garber. 1984. "Collapsing Exchange Rate Regimes: Some Linear Examples." *Journal of International Economics* 17(August):1–14.

Flood, Robert, and Nancy Marion. 1996. "Speculative Attacks: Fundamentals and Self-Fulfilling Prophecies." NBER Working Paper 5789. National Bureau of Economic Research, Cambridge, MA.

———. 1999. "Perspectives on the Recent Currency Crisis Literature." IMF Working Paper 98/130. In *International Journal of Finance and Economics* 4(1):1–26. Also in Guillermo Calvo, Rudiger Dornbusch, and Maurice Obstfeld, eds., 2001. *Money, Capital Mobility, and Trade: Essays in Honor of Robert Mundell*. Cambridge, MA: MIT Press.

———. 2002. "A Model of the Joint Distribution of Banking and Currency Crises." International Monetary Fund, Washington, DC.

Forbes, Kristin. 2003. "One Cost of the Chilean Capital Controls: Increased Financial Constraints for Smaller Firms," NBER Working Paper 9777. National Bureau of Economic Research, Cambridge, MA.

Frankel, Jeffrey. 1999a. "No Single Exchange Rate Regime Is Right for All Countries or at All Times." *Essays in International Finance*, No. 215. Princeton University.

———. 1999b. "Proposals Regarding Restrictions on Capital Flows." *African Finance Journal* 1(1):92–104.

———. 2001. "The Balance between Adjustment and Financing." In P. Kenen and A. Swoboda, eds., *Key Issues in Reform of the International Monetary System*. Washington, DC: International Monetary Fund.

———. 2004. "Experience of and Lessons from Exchange Rate Regimes in Emerging Economies." In Asian Development Bank, ed., *Monetary and Financial Cooperation in East Asia: The Way Ahead*, Volume 2. New York: Palgrave Macmillan Press.

Frankel, Jeffrey, and David Romer. 1999. "Does Trade Cause Growth?" *American Economic Review* 89(3):379–99.

Frankel, Jeffrey, and Andrew Rose. 1996. "Currency Crashes in Emerging Markets: An Empirical Treatment." *Journal of International Economics* 41(3/4):351–66.

———. 2002. "Estimating the Effects of Currency Unions on Trade and Output." *Quarterly Journal of Economics* CXVII(2):437–66.

Furman, Jason, and Joseph Stiglitz. 1998. "Economic Crisis: Evidence and Insights from East Asia." *Brooking's Papers on Economic Activity* 2:1–135.

Gallego, Francisco, Leonardo Hernandez, and Klaus Schmidt-Hebbel. 1999. "Capital Controls in Chile: Effective? Efficient?" Working Paper 59. Central Bank of Chile, Santiago.

Gallup, John, Jeffrey Sachs, and Andrew Messenger. 1998. "Geography and Economic Development." NBER Working Paper 6849. National Bureau of Economic Research, Cambridge, MA. In *International Science Review* 22(2) (August 1999):179–232.

Gelos, R. Gaston, and Shang-Jin Wei. 2002. "Transparency and International Investor Behavior." NBER Working Paper 9260. National Bureau of Economic Research, Cambridge, MA. Forthcoming in *Journal of Finance*.

Ghosh, Atish, Anne-Marie Gulde, and Holger Wolf. 2000. "Currency Boards: More Than a Quick Fix?" *Economic Policy* 31(October):270–335.

Gleditsch, Nil Peter, Peter Wallensteen, Mikael Eriksson, Margareta Sollenberg, and Håvard Strand. 2002. "Armed Conflict 1946–2001: A New Dataset." *Journal of Peace Research* 39(5):615–37.

Glick, Reuven, and Michael Hutchison. 2002. "Capital Controls and Exchange Rate Instability in Developing Economies." Federal Reserve Bank of San Francisco, Center for Pacific Basin Monetary and Economic Studies Working Paper PB–05 (revised December 2002).

Glick, Reuven, and Andrew Rose. 2001. "Does a Currency Union Affect Trade? The Time Series Evidence." NBER Working Paper 8396. National Bureau of Economic Research, Cambridge, MA. In *European Economic Review* 46(6)(June 2002):1125–51.

Goldstein, Morris, and Philip Turner. 2004. *Controlling Currency Mismatches in Emerging Economies: An Alternative to the Original Sin Hypothesis.* Washington, DC: Institute for International Economics.

Goldstein, Morris, Graciela Kaminsky, and Carmen Reinhart. 2000. *Assessing Financial Vulnerability: An Early Warning System for Emerging Economies.* Washington, DC: Institute for International Economics.

Gourinchas, Pierre-Olivier, and Olivier Jeanne. 2003. "The Elusive Gains from International Financial Integration." NBER Working Paper 9684. National Bureau of Economic Research, Cambridge, MA.

Guidotti, Pablo. 2003. In Jose Antonio Gonzalez, Vittorio Corbo, Anne Krueger, and Aaron Tornell, eds., *Latin American Macroeconomic Reforms: The Second Stage.* Chicago: University of Chicago Press.

Hall, Robert, and Chad Jones. 1999. "Why Do Some Countries Produce So Much More Output per Worker Than Others?" *Quarterly Journal of Economics* 114(1):83–116.

Hausmann, Ricardo, Michael Gavin, Carmen Pages-Serra, and Ernesto Stein. 1999. "Why Do Countries Float the Way They Do?" Presented at conference on New Initiatives to Tackle International Financial Turmoil. Inter-American Development Bank Annual Meetings of the Board of Governors, Paris.

Henry, Peter Blair. 2003. "Capital Account Liberalization, the Cost of Capital, and Economic Growth," NBER Working Paper 9488. National Bureau of Economic Research, Cambridge, MA.

Hutchison, Michael M. 2003. "A Cure Worse Than the Disease? Currency Crises and the Output Costs of IMF-Supported Stabilization Programs." In Michael Dooley and Jeffrey Frankel, eds., *Managing Currency Crises in Emerging Markets.* Chicago: University of Chicago Press.

IMF (International Monetary Fund). 2003. *Report on Capital Account Crises of the IMF Independent Evaluations Office.* Washington, DC: IMF.

International Country Risk Group (ICRG). 1994–2003. *Corruption Ratings.* Available at http://www.icrgonline.com/page.aspx?page=icrgmethods.

Ito, Takatoshi. 2002. "Asian Currency Crises, Five Years Later: Retrospect of Thailand, Malaysia, Indonesia, Philippines and Korea." Presented at conference on Financial Sector Reform Across Asia, Center for Business and Government, December, Harvard University.

Jeanne, Olivier. 2000. "Currency Crises: A Perspective on Recent Theoretical Developments." Special Papers in International Economics, No. 20. Princeton University.

Johnson, Simon, and Todd Mitton. 2003. "Cronyism and Capital Controls: Evidence from Malaysia." *Journal of Financial Economics* 67(2):351–82.

Johnson, Simon, John McMillan, and Christopher Woodruff. 2002. "Property Rights and Finance." *American Economic Review* 92(5):1335–56.

Johnson, Simon, Peter Boone, Alasdair Breach, and Eric Friedman. 2000. "Corporate Governance in the Asian Financial Crisis." *Journal of Financial Economics* 58(1): 141–84.

Kamin, Steven. 1988. "Devaluation, External Balance, and Macroeconomic Performance: A Look at the Numbers." Studies in International Finance, No. 62. Princeton University.

Kaminsky, Graciela, and Sergio Schmukler. 2003. "Short-Run Pain, Long-Run Gain: The Effects of Financial Liberalization." NBER Working Paper 9787. National Bureau of Economic Research, Cambridge, MA.

Kaminsky, Graciela, S. Lizondo, and C. Reinhart. 1998. "Leading Indicators of Currency Crises." *IMF Staff Papers* 5(1):1–48.

Kharas, Homi, Brian Pinto, and Sergei Ulatov. 2001. "An Analysis of Russia's 1998 Meltdown: Fundamentals and Market Signals." *Brookings Papers on Economic Activity* 1:1–68.

King Robert, and Ross Levine. 1993. "Finance and Growth: Schumpeter Might be Right." *Quarterly Journal of Economics* 108(3):717–37.

Klein, Michael. 2003. "Capital Account Openness and the Variety of Growth Experience." NBER Working Paper 9500. National Bureau of Economic Research, Cambridge, MA.

Klein, Michael, and Nancy Marion. 1997. "Explaining the Duration of Exchange-Rate Pegs." *Journal of Development Economics* 54(2):387–404.

Klein, Michael, and Giovanni Olivei. 2000. "Capital Account Liberalization, Financial Development, and Economic Growth." NBER Working Paper 7384. National Bureau of Economic Research, Cambridge, MA.

Kose, M. Ayhan, Eswar Prasad, and Marco Terrones. 2002. "Financial Integration and Macroeconomic Volatility." Paper prepared for Annual Research Conference, International Monetary Fund.

Krugman, Paul. 1979. "A Model of Balance-of-Payments Crises." *Journal of Money, Credit and Banking* 11(3):311–25. Reprinted in Paul Krugman, ed., 1992, *Currencies and Crises.* Cambridge, MA and London: MIT Press.

———. 1998a. "What Happened to Asia?" Available at http://web.mit.edu/krugman/www/DISINTER.html.

———. 1998b. "Latin America's Swan Song." Available at http://web.mit.edu/krugman/www/swansong.html.

———. 1999. "Balance Sheets, the Transfer Problem and Financial Crises." In P. Isard, A. Razin, and A. Rose, eds., *International Finance and Financial Crises: Essays in Honor of Robert Flood.* Boston: Kluwer Academic Publishers.

Lahiri, Amartya, and Carlos A. Végh. 2000. "Delaying the Inevitable: Optimal Interest Rate Policy and BOP Crises." NBER Working Paper 7734. National Bureau of Economic Research, Cambridge, MA.

La Porta, Rafael, Florencio Lopez-de-Silanes, and Andrei Shleifer. 2003. "What Works in Securities Markets?" NBER Working Paper 9882. National Bureau of Economic Research, Cambridge, MA.

402   *Jeffrey Frankel and Shang-Jin Wei*

La Porta, Rafael, Florencio Lopez-de-Silanes, Andrei Shleifer, and Robert Vishny. 1998. "Law and Finance." *Journal of Political Economy* 106(6):1113–55.

―――. 1999. "Investor Protection: Origins, Consequences, and Reform." NBER Working Paper 7428. National Bureau of Economic Research, Cambridge, MA. In *Journal of Financial Economics* 58(12) (October 2000):3–27.

Larrain, Felipe, and Andres Velasco. 2001. "Exchange Rate Policy in Emerging Markets: The Case for Floating." Studies in International Finance No. 224. Princeton University.

Levine, Ross, and Sergio Schmukler. 2003. "Migration, Spillovers and Diversion: Impact of Internationalization on Stock Market Liquidity." NBER Working Paper 9614. National Bureau of Economic Research, Cambridge, MA.

Levy-Yeyati, Eduardo, and Federico Sturzenegger. 2003. "To Float or to Trail: Evidence on the Impact of Exchange Rate Regimes." *American Economic Review* 93(4):41173–93.

Lipsey, Robert E. 2001. "Foreign Direct Investors in Three Financial Crises." Working Paper 8084. National Bureau of Economic Research, Cambridge, MA.

Lizondo, Saul, and Peter Montiel. 1989. "Contractionary Devaluation in Developing Countries: An Analytical Survey." *IMF Staff Papers* 36(March):182–227.

Manasse, Paolo, Nouriel Roubini, and Axel Schimmelpfennig. 2003. "Predicting Sovereign Debt Crises." IMF Working Paper 03/221. International Monetary Fund, Washington, DC.

Martin, Philippe, and Helene Rey. 2002. "Financial Globalization and Emerging Markets: With or Without Crash?" NBER Working Paper 9288. National Bureau of Economic Research, Cambridge, MA.

Masson, Paul. 2001. "Exchange Rate Regime Transitions." *Journal of Development Economics* 64(2):571–86.

McKinnon, Ronald. 1991. *The Order of Economic Liberalization: Financial Control in the Transition to a Market Economy.* Baltimore: Johns Hopkins University Press.

McKinnon, Ronald, and Huw Pill. 1997. "Credible Economic Liberalizations and Overborrowing." *American Economic Review* 87(2):189–93.

McQuillan, Lawrence, and Peter Montgomery, eds. 1999. *The International Monetary Fund: Financial Medic to the World?* Stanford, CA: Hoover Institution Press.

Milesi-Ferretti, Gian Maria, and Assaf Razin. 1997. "Sharp Reductions in Current Account Deficits: An Empirical Analysis." NBER Working Paper 6310. National Bureau of Economic Research, Cambridge, MA. Also in *European Economic Review* 42(3–5) (May 1998):897–908.

―――. 1998. "Current Account Reversals and Currency Crises: Empirical Regularities." NBER Working Paper 6620. National Bureau of Economic Research, Cambridge, MA. Reprinted in Paul Krugman, ed., 2000, *Currency Crises*. Chicago: University of Chicago Press.

Mendoza, Enrique. 2002. "Why Should Emerging Economies Give up National Currencies: A Case for 'Institutions Substitution.'" NBER Working Paper 8950. National Bureau of Economic Research, Cambridge, MA.

Mishkin, Frederic S. 2001. "Financial Policies and the Prevention of Financial Crises in Emerging Market Countries." NBER Working Paper 8087. National Bureau of Economic Research, Cambridge, MA. In Margin Feldstein, ed., *Economic and Financial Crises in Emerging Market Countries*. Chicago: University of Chicago Press, 2003.

Morris, Stephen, and Hyun Song Shin. 1998. "Unique Equilibrium in a Model of Self-Fulfilling Crises." *American Economic Review* 88(3):587–97.

Morris, Stephen, and Hyun Song Shin. 2001. "Rethinking Multiple Equilibria in Macroeconomic Modeling." In Ben S. Bernanke and Kenneth Rogoff, eds., *NBER Macroeconomics Annual, 2000.* Cambridge, MA: MIT Press.

Mssa, Michael. 2002. *Argentina and the Fund: From Triumph to Tragedy.* Washington, DC: Institute for International Economics.

Noguer, Marta, and Marc Siscart. 2002. "Trade Raises Income: A Precise and Robust Result." Department of Economics, New York University.

Obstfeld, Maurice. "The Logic of Currency Crises." 1994. *Cahiers Economiques et Monetaires* 43:189–213.

———. 1996. "Models of Currency Crises with Self-Fulfilling Features." *European Economic Review* 40(April):1037–47.

———. 1998. "Destabilizing Effects of Exchange-Rate Escape Clauses." NBER Working Paper National Bureau of Economic Research, Cambridge, MA. In *Journal of International Economics* 43(Aug 1997):61–77.

Obstfeld, Maurice, and Kenneth Rogoff. 1995. "The Mirage of Fixed Exchange Rates." *Journal of Economic Perspectives* 9(Fall):73–96.

Pinto, Brian, Evsey Gurvich, and Sergei Ulatov. 2004. "Lessons from the Russian Crisis of 1998 and Recovery" (Chapter 10, this volume).

Prasad, Eswar, Kenneth Rogoff, Shang-Jin Wei, and M. Ayhan Kose. 2003. "Effects of Financial Globalization on Developing Countries: Some Empirical Evidence." Occasional paper No. 220, International Monetary Fund, Washington, DC. Available at http://www.imf.org/external/pubs/nft/op/220/index.htm.

Prati, Alessandro, and Massimo Sbracia. 2002. "Currency Crises and Uncertainty About Fundamentals." International Monetary Fund, Washington, DC.

Quinn, Dennis. 1997. "The Correlates of Change in International Financial Regulation," *American Political Science Review* 91(September):531–51.

Radelet, Steven, and Jeffrey Sachs. 1998. "The East Asian Financial Crisis: Diagnosis, Remedies, Prospects." *Brookings Papers on Economic Activity* 1:1–74 and 88–90.

Rajan, Ramkishen. 2001. "(Ir)relevance of Currency-Crisis Theory to the Devaluation and Collapse of the Thai Baht." Princeton Studies in International Economics, No. 88. Princeton University.

Razin, Assaf, Efraim Sadka, Chi-Wa Yuen. 2001. "Why International Equity Flows to Emerging Markets Are Inefficient and Small Relative to International Debt Flows." NBER Working Paper 8659. National Bureau of Economic Research, Cambridge, MA.

Reinhart, Carmen, and Vincent Reinhart. 2003. "Twin Fallacies about Exchange Rate Policy in Emerging Markets." NBER Working Paper 9670. National Bureau of Economic Research, Cambridge, MA.

Reinhart, Carmen M., and Kenneth S. Rogoff. 2002. "The Modern History of Exchange Rate Arrangements: A Reinterpretation." NBER Working Paper 8963. National Bureau of Economic Research, Cambridge, MA. *Quarterly Journal of Economics* CXIX (1) (February, 2004):1–48.

Reinhart, Carmen M., and R. Todd Smith. 2001. "Temporary Controls on Capital Inflows." NBER Working Paper 8422. National Bureau of Economic Research, Cambridge, MA.

Reinhart, Carmen, Kenneth Rogoff, and Miguel Savastano. 2003. "Debt Intolerance." NBER Working Paper 9908. National Bureau of Economic Research, Cambridge, MA.

Rodríguez, Francisco, and Dani Rodrik. 2001. "Trade Policy and Economic Growth: A Skeptic's Guide to the Cross-National Evidence." In Ben Bernanke and Kenneth Rogoff, eds., *NBER Macroeconomics Annual 2001*. Cambridge, MA: MIT Press.

Rodrik, Dani. 1998. "Who Needs Capital-Account Convertibility?" Essays in International Finance, No. 207. Princeton University.

Rodrik, Dani, and Ethan Kaplan. 2002. "Did the Malaysian Capital Controls Work?" In Sebastian Edwards and Jeffrey Frankel, eds., *Preventing Currency Crises in Emerging Markets*. Chicago: University of Chicago Press.

Rodrik, Dani, and Andres Velasco. 2000. "Short-Term Capital Flows." In *Annual World Bank Conference on Development Economics 1999*. Washington, DC: World Bank.

Rodrik, Dani, Arvind Subramanian, and Francesco Trebbi. 2002. "Institutions Rule: The Primacy of Institutions over Geography and Integration in Economic Development." NBER Working Paper 9305. National Bureau of Economic Research, Cambridge, MA.

Rose, Andrew. 2000. "One Money, One Market: Estimating the Effect of Common Currencies on Trade." *Economic Policy* 30(April):9–45.

———. 2001. "Common Currency Areas in Practice." In *Revisiting the Case for Flexible Exchange Rates*. Ottawa: Bank of Canada.

———. 2002. "One Reason Countries Pay Their Debts: Renegotiation and International Trade." NBER Working Paper 8853. National Bureau of Economic Research, Cambridge, MA.

Roubini, Nouriel, Paolo Manasse, Richard Hemming, and Axel Schimmelpfennig. 2003. "An Early Warnings Model of Sovereign Debt Crises: A Panel Data Econometric Estimation for the 1970–2000 Period." International Monetary Fund, Washington, DC.

Sachs, Jeffrey. 1986. "Managing the LDC Debt Crisis." *Brooking's Papers on Economic Activity* 2:397–432.

———. 1998. "THE IMF and the Asian Flu." *American Prospect* 37(March–April): 16–21.

———. 2003. "Institutions Don't Rule: Direct Effects of Geography on Per Capita Income." NBER Working Paper 9490. National Bureau of Economic Research, Cambridge, MA.

Sachs, Jeffrey, and Andrew Warner. 1995. "Economic Reform and the Process of Global Integration." *Brookings Papers on Economic Activity* 1:1–95.

Sachs, Jeffrey, Aaron Tornell, and Andres Velasco. 1996. "Financial Crises in Emerging Markets: The Lessons from 1995." *Brookings Papers on Economic Activity* 1: 147–216.

———. 1996. "The Collapse of the Mexican Peso: What Have We Learned?" *Economic Policy* 22(April):13–63.

Salant, Stephen, and Dale Henderson. 1978. "Market Anticipation of Government Policies and the Price of Gold." *Journal of Political Economy* 86(4):627–48.

Salter, W. E. G. 1959. "Internal and External Balance – The Role of Price and Expenditure Effects." *Economic Record* (August):226–38 (Australia).

Schneider, Martin, and Aaron Tornell. 2000. "Balance Sheet Effects, Bailout Guarantees and Financial Crises." NBER Working Paper 8060. National Bureau of Economic Research, Cambridge, MA.

Servén, Luis, and Guillermo Perry. 2004. "Argentina's Macroeconomic Collapse: Causes and Lessons" (Chapter 11, this volume).

Shleifer, Andrei, and Daniel Wolfenson. 2000. "Investor Protection and Equity Markets." NBER Working Paper 7974. National Bureau of Economic Research, Cambridge, MA.

Swan, Trevor. 1963. "Longer Run Problems of the Balance of Payments." In H. W. Arndt and W. M. Corden, eds., *The Australian Economy*. Melbourne: Cheshire.

Temple, Jonathan. 1999. "The New Growth Evidence." *Journal of Economic Literature* 37(1):112–56.

Tenreyro, Silvana, and Robert J. Barro. 2003. "Economic Effects of Currency Unions." NBER Working Paper 9435. National Bureau of Economic Research, Cambridge, MA.

Ücer, Murat, and Caroline Van Rijckeghem. 2004. *Murder on the Orient Express: The Turkish Currency Crises of 2000–01*. Revised as *A Chronicle of Sudden Death: The Turkish Financial Crises of 2000–01*. Istanbul: Bogazici University Press.

Ul Haq, Mahbub, Inge Kaul, and Isabelle Grunberg, eds. 1996. *The Tobin Tax: Coping with Financial Volatility*. New York: Oxford University Press.

Valdes-Prieto, S., and M. Soto. 1996. "New Selective Capital Controls in Chile: Are They Efficient?" Catholic University of Chile, Santiago.

Velasco, Andres. 1996. "When Are Fixed Exchange Rates Really Fixed?" NBER Working Paper 5842. National Bureau of Economic Research, Cambridge, MA. Also in *Journal of Development Economics* 54(1) (1997):5–25.

Wei, Shang-Jin, 2000a. "How Taxing Is Corruption on International Investors?" *Review of Economics and Statistics* 82(1):1–11. Available at www.nber.org/~wei.

———. 2000b. "Domestic Crony Capitalism and International Fickle Capital: Is There a Connection?" World Bank–Country Economics Department Paper 2429. In *International Finance* 4 (Spring) (2001):15–46. Available at http://www.brook.edu/dybdocroot/views/articles/wei/20010409.pdf.

———. 2000c. "Local Corruption and Global Capital Flows." *Brooking's Papers on Economic Activity* 2:303–54. Available at www.nber.org/~wei.

Wei, Shang-Jin, and Yi Wu. 2002. "Negative Alchemy: Corruption, Composition of Capital Flows, and Currency Crises." In Sebastian Edwards and Jeffrey Frankel, eds., *Preventing Currency Crises in Emerging Markets*. Chicago: University of Chicago Press.

Willett, Thomas. 2000. "International Financial Markets as Sources of Crises or Discipline: The Too Much, Too Late Hypothesis." Essays in International Finance, No. 218. Princeton University.

Williamson, John. 2001. "The Case for a Basket, Band and Crawl (BBC) Regime for East Asia." In David Gruen and John Simon, eds., *Future Directions for Monetary Policies in East Asia*. Sydney: Reserve Bank of Australia.

Wyplosz, Charles. 2001. "How Risky Is Financial Liberalization in the Developing Countries?" *G-24 Discussion Paper Series*, No. 14, United Nations, New York and Geneva.

9. Lessons from the Russian Crisis of 1998 and Recovery[1]

Brian Pinto, Evsey Gurvich, and Sergei Ulatov

ABSTRACT: This case study covers events from mid-1995, when Russia's quest for single-digit inflation began, to the end of 2002. The focus is on Russia's 1998 crisis and subsequent recovery. These events offer valuable lessons for countries facing simultaneous problems of unsustainable public debt dynamics and low international liquidity – a list that in recent years has included Argentina, Brazil, and Turkey. Lessons include implications for the appropriate design of rescue packages, moral hazard, and factors driving postcrisis recovery. This study presents a framework that may make it possible to distinguish between a first-generation and second-generation crisis by juxtaposing economic fundamentals and market signals. This could help in making the judgment about whether a soft landing scenario supported by the announcement of a fiscal-structural reforms package and liquidity injections from the international financial institutions (IFIs) is feasible, or whether the abandonment of the exchange rate target and even a possible debt restructuring may be unavoidable.

THE RUSSIAN MELTDOWN: IMPLICATIONS FOR OTHER CRISIS EPISODES

In February 1998, Russia attained its goal of single-digit inflation set under the stabilization program that began in mid-1995. Only six months later, it experienced a comprehensive macroeconomic collapse, involving its exchange rate, the banking system, and public debt. This occurred soon after a large rescue plan put together by the international financial institutions (IFIs) took effect. In addition to a program of fiscal and structural reforms, a unique feature of the plan was an upfront liquidity injection from the IFIs prior to any exchange rate adjustment and a debt swap out of short-term ruble treasury bills (GKOs) into long-term dollar Eurobonds in an attempt to boost market confidence and avoid a devaluation.[2] Preserving the fixed exchange rate band was seen as vital for credibility and retaining what were regarded as hard-won stabilization gains. As it turned out, only about a quarter of the envisaged

---

[1] The authors gratefully acknowledge insightful comments from the chapter reviewers, Robert J. Anderson and Sergei Vasiliev, as well as from participants in a seminar held at the World Bank on May 1, 2003, notably Robert Flood and Michael Mussa.

[2] The Central Bank of Russia announced at the end of 1997 that it would target a central rate of 6.2 rubles per dollar, with a +/− 15 percent band. However, it also announced its aim of a constant bilateral real exchange rate with the dollar for 1998. Given an 8 percent inflation target and assuming 2 percent U.S. inflation, this meant a nominal devaluation target of 6 percent for 1998.

financing package of $22.6 billion was disbursed before the rescue plan was abandoned with the government's announcement of emergency measures on August 17, 1998. These measures included an immediate devaluation, with a forced restructuring of ruble-denominated public debt maturing up to the end of 1999. The suspension of the rescue might have surprised those who believed Russia was "too big to fail" and that a bailout would proceed regardless. In another notable development, the Russian economy recovered much faster after the crisis than anyone expected.

The crisis was costly. GDP shrank by 4.9 percent in 1998, compared to initial expectations of slight growth. By December that year, 12-month inflation reached 84 percent, compared to a target of 8 percent. Some $30 billion in total foreign exchange – equivalent to one-sixth of 1999 GDP – was used to defend the fixed exchange rate between late October 1997 and the decision to float on September 2, 1998. Of this, $16 billion was incurred in the last 10 weeks before the meltdown. Most of the big Moscow-based banks failed, while retail depositors took a big hit. The reformist government headed by Prime Minister Sergei Kirienko was dismissed. The crisis also had social costs.[3] It produced reverberations felt across the financial world, developed as well as emerging. In the United States, it precipitated the bailout of Long-Term Capital Management, a heavily leveraged hedge fund with systemic links to large banks.[4]

Surprising everyone, the crisis became a positive turning point in Russia's transition to a market economy.[5] Macroeconomic policy and government behavior changed radically. Budget constraints started hardening for all levels of the government and for enterprises. As a direct result, dismantling of the costly nonpayments system began (see discussion below).[6] Most significantly, the Russians at last assumed "ownership" of their reforms.[7]

In spite of these features, the Russian crisis has not received as much attention as the recent Argentine crisis, perhaps because of the belief that Russia is a "special" case and its postcrisis recovery an "oil play," a fortuitous product of the rise in oil prices after mid-1999. To the contrary, a timely review of the Russian experience might well have impacted the way in which the IFIs approached Argentina.[8]

Notably, a debate often rages in the run-up to a crisis about whether a country is in a first-generation or second-generation world. *First-generation* models emphasize fiscal fundamentals, credit rationing, and inconsistencies between fiscal and exchange rate policies.[9] *Second-generation* models emphasize market sentiment,

---

[3] For an analysis, see Lokshin and Ravallion (2000). See also World Bank (2001).

[4] See Dungey and others (2002).

[5] For accounts of events leading to the Russian crisis, see Gaidar (2002); Granville (2001); Kharas, Pinto, and Ulatov (2001). This study borrows considerably from Kharas, Pinto, and Ulatov (2001).

[6] Gaddy and Ickes (1998) painted the nonpayments system as an incorrigible antimarket and cultural choice by the Russians, while Pinto, Drebentsov, and Morozov (2000a, b) described it as a rational outcome to incentives generated by an inconsistent policy mix and exceptionally high real interest rates.

[7] In July 2000, the Russian government adopted a 10-year strategic program, described in Government of the Russian Federation (2000).

[8] In a frank and critical paper, Mussa (2002) describes developments in the lead-up to Argentina's 2001 crisis. Aizenman, Kletzer, and Pinto (2005) note the remarkable similarities between the fundamentals in Argentina and those preceding the Russian crisis.

[9] Krugman (1979); Flood and Garber (1984); Sargent and Wallace (1981).

confidence and liquidity, and the presence of multiple equilibria.[10] The desirable features of a rescue plan would critically depend upon a determination of which set of factors is predominant, as aspects of both models are usually present in the real world.

This study argues that it may be possible to distinguish between a first- and second-generation crisis by juxtaposing economic fundamentals and market signals. This could help in making the judgment about whether a soft landing scenario based on liquidity injections from the IFIs is feasible, or not. Alternatively, an orderly debt write-down may be inevitable, and could also make both private creditors and governments better off relative to a crisis and a forced, chaotic restructuring. However, politics and the inadequacies of international law pose impediments. As a result, Kenneth Rogoff (2003) notes:

> [The] official lending community, typically led by the IMF, is often unwilling to force the issue and sometimes finds itself trying to keep a country afloat far beyond the point of no return. In Russia in 1998, for example, the official community threw money behind a fixed exchange-rate regime that was patently doomed. Eventually, the Fund cut the cord and allowed a default, proving wrong those many private investors who thought Russia was "too nuclear to fail." But if the Fund had allowed the default to take place at an earlier stage, Russia might well have come out of its subsequent downturn at least as quickly and with less official debt.

Moreover, moral hazard stemming from an IFI bailout is likely to be much more costly in a first-generation crisis. This is especially the case when unsustainable public debt dynamics are present alongside low international liquidity, as discussed later.

It is now accepted that Russia's 1998 crisis occurred as a result of unsustainable public debt dynamics and an overvalued real exchange rate, and was not therefore primarily a matter of confidence and liquidity.[11] Moreover, Russia recovered from the crisis faster than anyone expected. While there are always lessons to be learned from an ex post review, it is also useful to ask whether the nature of the public debt dynamics and the real appreciation could have been detected ex ante. What sorts of analysis can be done to form a better picture in the run up to a crisis? This is the approach taken here. The lessons from Russia would apply to any country simultaneously facing unsustainable public debt dynamics and low international liquidity, and either a fixed exchange rate or a flexible one with an inflation target – a list that has recently included Argentina, Brazil, and Turkey. This study presents an easily replicable framework consisting of four parts.

The first and most basic is an analysis of macroeconomic fundamentals, especially fiscal and growth. Potential balance sheet problems or contingent fiscal liabilities such as bank bailouts are also relevant, as are trends in international liquidity, measured as the ratio of various claims to foreign exchange reserves.[12]

---

[10] Obstfeld (1996); Furman and Stiglitz (1998).

[11] IMF (1999, 2000a, 2003); GAO (2000); Kharas, Pinto, and Ulatov (2001).

[12] IMF (2000b) finds the ratio of short-term external debt to reserves to be a crucial predictor of vulnerability. Chang and Velasco (1998) identify low international liquidity as key in the East Asian crisis.

The second is an assessment of market signals. Unlike the 1980s, when secondary markets for emerging market sovereign debt were either nonexistent or limited, most sovereign debt is continuously repriced in secondary markets today. This study describes a simple approach to extracting interest rate premia demanded by investors for bearing perceived default and devaluation risk based on secondary market prices.

Third, the framework examines potential crisis triggers. These could be a ratings downgrade, a political crisis, contagion or spillovers from other crises, *or even the design of the rescue package*. Finally, the analysis turns to moral hazard. The expectation of an IFI-led bailout may influence investor behavior in a way that turns out to be costly for the country. The study concludes by summarizing the lessons.

A BRIEF TIMELINE[13]

Russia launched its quest for macroeconomic stabilization in July 1995, supported by a three-year Extended Fund Facility (EFF) IMF credit, which specified inflation and fiscal deficit targets for 1996–98. The targets for 1995 had been set earlier in the context of an IMF Stand-By Arrangement (SBA). The plan was to fix the exchange rate, replace money printing with ruble treasury bills (GKOs) and bonds (OFZ) and other market borrowings, and implement fiscal and structural reforms. But political uncertainty and opposition to reform hurt credibility and kept real interest rates on GKOs and OFZs at crippling levels for the real sector. In July 1996, President Boris Yeltsin was reelected following a tense second round run-off against the Communist Party leader, Gennady Zyuganov. The preelection period was marred by controversy over the now infamous "loans-for-shares" privatization auctions, whereby lending by Russian commercial banks to the government was collateralized with the shares of valuable companies in the oil, metals, and telecommunications industries.[14]

By 1997, nonresident access to the ruble treasury bill/bond GKO/OFZ market – which had been restricted directly and indirectly with dollar returns capped through compulsory purchases of forward currency contracts at preset prices – was substantially liberalized. This, together with reduced political uncertainty and the appointment of an economic "dream team" in the spring of 1997, led to falling interest rates. Inflation also came down over the first 10 months of 1997, and Russia was about to register its first positive growth since the start of transition. Portfolio investment in equities and government debt had driven up reserves to a record level of $25 billion by August.

But Russia faced a chronic shortfall in cash tax collection. Although this was commonly interpreted as a lack of political will to crack down on tax cheats, in reality the tax shortfall was symptomatic of deeper economic problems. It was the counterpart of large implicit subsidies transferred by the biggest tax delinquents, the energy monopolies, to manufacturing firms as part of a system of soft budget

---

[13] For detailed discussions of Russia's reforms, politics, and especially developments in the mid- to late-1990s, see Aslund (1995); Gaidar (2002); IMF (1999); Shleifer and Treisman (2000); and GAO (2000).

[14] The size of the loans was determined in auctions that were not transparent and were suspected to be rigged. See Lieberman and Veimetra (1996); Black, Kraakman, and Tarassova (2000). See also Blasi and others (1997).

constraints embodied in the so-called nonpayments system.[15] The energy monopolies in effect reimbursed themselves by not paying their own assessed taxes. The manufacturing companies followed suit.

As a result of the tax problem, the IMF decided to hold up disbursements of its loans at the end of October 1997. This coincided with the first bout of instability as Korean and Brazilian investors, facing liquidity pressures at home, began exiting the GKO market in early November. This marked the start of speculative attacks on the ruble, and culminated in the emergency measures of August 17, 1998.

The emergency measures included a devaluation; the announcement that all the government's ruble debt obligations falling due to the end of 1999 would be restructured; and a 90-day moratorium on private external principal payments, settlement of currency forwards, and repos to protect Russia's commercial banks and corporate sector.[16] Only a few weeks earlier, on July 13, 1998, an emergency package had been announced in the hopes of avoiding a devaluation and giving a new boost to reforms. It did not work. However, 1999 witnessed an unexpectedly strong rebound: real GDP grew by 5.3 percent and inflation fell to less than 40 percent. This study will attempt to explain this sequence of events, using the four-part framework described above.

ECONOMIC FUNDAMENTALS

This section analyzes the basic determinants of public debt dynamics and tries to answer the question of why expectations regarding economic growth were consistently belied.

Public Debt Sustainability (PDS)

The size of the primary fiscal surplus[17] required to keep the ratio of public debt to GDP constant is given by the formula, $[(r - g)/(1 + g)]d$, where d is the ratio of public debt to GDP in a given year, r is the real interest rate, and g is the growth rate of real GDP. This discrete-time formula is based on the difference equation for d, shown as Equation 1 below, of which a detailed derivation is contained in Section VII.A. of the Technical Appendix. While this debt-to-GDP stabilizing primary fiscal surplus provides a useful benchmark that is commonly used in World Bank and IMF documents, there may be situations where a *reduction* in the debt/GDP ratio is called for. The acid test is how much debt the market is willing to tolerate in a world of mobile capital. Moreover, debt dynamics may not be as transparent as Equation 1 suggests, a point also discussed in the Technical Appendix.

$$d_t - d_{t-1} = (pd_t - ndfs_t) + \frac{(r_t - g_t)}{1 + g_t}d_{t-1}. \tag{1}$$

---

[15] Pinto, Drebentsov, and Morozov (2000a, b). See also Gaddy and Ickes (1998); Woodruff (1999).

[16] As President Yeltsin had asserted only the previous Friday that a devaluation would never occur, the devaluation was achieved by widening the exchange rate band to 6–9.5 rubles per dollar, compared to a level of 6.29 the previous trading day. By September 2, the ruble had broken through the upper end of the band and a float was announced.

[17] Defined as tax plus nontax revenues minus noninterest spending. Central bank profits (seignorage) are included in nontax revenues.

Table 9.1. *Public finances and economic growth, 1995–1998*

Year	Primary deficit (percent of GDP)	Interest payments Percent of GDP	Interest payments Percent of revenues[a]	Government debt[b] US$ billion	Government debt[b] Percent of GDP	Real GDP growth (percent per year)
1995	2.2	3.6	28	170	50	−4.0
1996	2.5	5.9	47	201	48	−3.4
1997	2.4	4.6	38	218	50	0.9
1998	1.3	4.6	43	242	75	−4.9

[a] Cash plus noncash basis.
[b] Domestic plus foreign, end of period.
Source: Ministry of Finance, Goskomstat, and internal IMF reports.

In addition to the variables defined above, *pd* is the ratio of the primary fiscal deficit to GDP, and *ndfs* refers to nondebt financing sources such as privatization proceeds and seignorage. The latter is incorporated into the primary deficit *pd* when central bank profits are counted as part of fiscal revenues (the case here). Alternatively, it can be measured as the change in base (reserve) money divided by GDP. The time subscript is *t*. This equation provides an organizing framework for presenting data on public finances and growth in Table 9.1 for 1995–98.[18] Over this period, revenues from privatizations were negligible.[19]

From 1995 to 1997, the debt/GDP ratio was roughly constant in spite of primary deficits, significant interest payments, and negative or negligible growth – in apparent violation of Equation 1. With public debt at 50 percent of GDP at the end of 1995 and fiscal deficits (primary deficit plus interest payments; see Table 9.1) on the order of 7 percent of GDP in 1996 and 1997, public debt should have climbed to approximately 64 percent of GDP.

As Table 9.2 shows, while the original inflation targets were largely met for 1996 and 1997, actual fiscal deficits far exceeded their original targets. This explains why nominal debt levels rose in Table 9.1, but the riddle of the constant debt/GDP ratio remains, especially as growth was either negative or negligible.

To solve this, consider another equation, which decomposes the real interest rate, *r*, into its component parts:

$$r = wr_d + (1 - w)(r_f - \rho). \tag{2}$$

This equation, derived in the technical appendix, shows that the real interest rate, *r*, is a weighted sum of the real interest rate on domestic debt, r_d, and that on foreign debt, r_f, minus the percentage change in the dollar/ruble real exchange rate, ρ, defined so

[18] Tables 9.1 and 9.2 present data only for the federal (central) government, where most of the fiscal problem lay and for which targets were defined.
[19] Note from Equation 1 that it makes no difference to public debt dynamics whether privatization proceeds are classified as a financing source (*ndfs*) or revenues (incorporated into *pd*). As Mussa (2002) discusses in the Argentine context, if they are classified as revenues and are not likely to last, this may give the misleading impression that primary fiscal balances are much stronger than they actually are.

Table 9.2. *Targeted and actual inflation and fiscal deficit, 1995–1998*

Year	12-month inflation rate (percent per year)		Fiscal deficit (percent of GDP)[a]	
	Target[b]	Actual	Target[b]	Actual
1995	63	131	6.0	5.7
1996	25	22	4.2	8.4
1997	9	11	3.2	7.0
1998	6	84	2.2	5.9[c]

[a] Of the federal government before rescheduling of external debt service.
[b] Targets for 1995 were set by the Stand-By-Arrangement with the IMF. Targets for 1996–98 were set as part of a three-year Extended Fund Facility credit. (These were the original program targets, which were later revised.)
[c] Excludes overdue interest on GKOs and OFZs.
Source: Ministry of Finance and internal IMF reports.

that a real appreciation means $\rho > 0$, with weights equal to w, the share of domestic currency debt in total public debt, and $(1 - w)$ respectively.

Equation 2 shows that if the share of foreign currency debt in total debt is high and the real exchange rate is appreciating sizably, this could dominate the effect of both a high domestic real interest rate and poor growth. For example, if the ratio of foreign currency debt to GDP is 60 percent, then a 15 percent real appreciation will act to lower the ratio of public debt to GDP by 9 percentage points and could disguise the effects of a large fiscal deficit. This was the case in Russia. Its real exchange rate appreciated sizably between mid-1995 and mid-1997 – a common feature of exchange rate-based stabilizations. In 1996 alone, the effect of real appreciation was to lower the ratio of public debt to GDP by 8 percent, according to Kharas, Pinto, and Ulatov (2001).

The problem is that high rates of real appreciation are unlikely to be sustainable and could eventually produce a crash. For Russia, the stability in the public debt/GDP outcomes between 1995 and 1997 was not due to sound fundamentals, but to one-shot gains from a real appreciation that could not be expected to continue, and that disguised the rise in nominal debt. By the beginning of 1998, with inflation approaching single-digit levels and the real exchange rate flattening out, public debt dynamics began reflecting their true determinants: namely, high primary deficits and real interest rates, and weak economic growth. By mid-May 1998, the marginal real interest rate was 27 percent under the macroeconomic program assumptions, compared to zero growth expectations, and public debt was on an explosive path.

Growth

One can always live in the hope that a country will grow out of its debt problem; indeed, growth is almost always crucial for public debt sustainability. This may have been a reasonable hope for Russia, as transition economies could be expected to benefit from higher efficiency in asset use in a market regime. Moreover, greater

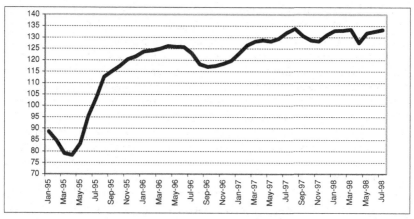

Figure 9.1. Real Effective Exchange Rate Index, 1995–mid-1998, 1995=100. *Source*: IMF.

foreign direct investment could have been expected, contingent upon a better invest-ment climate related to stabilization and structural reforms. Following the reelection of President Yeltsin in 1996, it was expected that growth would resume and reach sustainable growth rates of 5–7 percent per year by 1997.[20]

However, growth expectations in Russia were consistently belied. Why? First, real interest rates soared as a result of the credit squeeze and large public borrowing associated with the stabilization program, averaging 56 percent a year based on the average GKO yield between May 1995 and July 1997.[21] This was accompanied by a sizable real appreciation, hitting enterprises with a "double whammy."

Second, there were serious structural problems, manifested in the so-called non-payments problem. These are discussed in turn. Precrisis movements in the real exchange rate (dollar/ruble), which appreciated 55 percent between May 1995 and July 1997, are shown in Figure 9.1. Some analysts have argued that this was an equilibrium phenomenon reflecting the Balassa–Samuelson effect, or the potential for rising productivity in the traded goods sector as transition economies open up; they noted that Russia never had a serious current account gap. However, the real appreciation from 1995 to 1997 had already been preceded by substantial real appre-ciation during the first few years of transition and was not accompanied by rising productivity and restructuring in the enterprise sector. To the contrary, 1995–97 was a period during which nonpayments proliferated and asset stripping became the norm.[22] Moreover, real appreciation masked the increasingly unsustainable public debt dynamics, as noted above, while the high real interest rates probably con-tributed to current account balance by stifling private demand. Interest rates fell through October 1997, and the real exchange rate flattened after July, but interest rates were raised to defend the ruble after the East Asian crisis spilled over at the end of October.

---

[20] Buckberg and Pinto (1997).

[21] See Kharas, Pinto, and Ulatov (2001). On the credit squeeze for enterprises, see Commander and Mumssen (1999) and OECD (1997).

[22] For a discussion of real appreciation in the Mexican context, see Dornbusch and Werner (1994).

One can think of the Russian real exchange rate over the three precrisis years as having been influenced by oil prices, capital flows, and the stabilization program. According to KPU (2001), oil prices did not play a big role in the precrisis real appreciation of the ruble. Even though nominal oil prices rose by 25 percent in 1996, the terms of trade improved by a much smaller 8 percent.

Moreover, the usual transmission channels one associates with an oil price rise translating into a real appreciation were weak for two reasons. First, because many of the oil taxes were specific in nature, the oil price elasticity of fiscal revenues was low, so that higher oil revenues did not automatically feed into higher public spending. Second, capital flight would have diluted the "spending effect" or even the monetary expansion effect of increased current account surpluses, a point discussed further below. However, the sharp decline in oil prices in 1998, leading to a 13 percent drop in the terms of trade, should have led to a real depreciation – although the real exchange rate remained flat after July 1997 and right up to the crisis. The reluctance of the Central Bank to let the ruble depreciate resulted in a build-up of expectations of depreciation and a return to persistently high real interest rates, after they had fallen during the first 10 months of 1997 following President Yeltsin's reelection and liberalized access to the GKO market.[23]

The net effect of capital flows is ambiguous, because chronic capital flight occurred side-by-side with large surpluses on the capital account. Thus gross capital outflows for 1996 were estimated at $26.7 billion, or 7.3 percent of GDP. Outflows of such large magnitude should normally put downward pressure on the real exchange rate – not upward pressure. But the net impact on reserves was much smaller, as much of the capital flight was financed by the current account surplus, official borrowings, and inflows into the equity and treasury bill markets, so that foreign exchange reserves fell by only $1.9 billion.

This suggests that the stabilization program itself was the main factor underlying the ruble's real appreciation. As has been observed in several stabilization episodes, when the nominal exchange is fixed or managed within a narrow range to bring inflation down, the real exchange rate tends to appreciate because inflation comes down much more slowly.[24] For example, end-year inflation in 1995 was 131 percent, far less than the 200 percent in 1994, but much more than the 31 percent nominal depreciation of the ruble/dollar exchange rate over the same period. Moreover, the interest rate defense of the ruble, which was implemented starting in late 1997 to preserve stabilization gains, then propped up the real exchange rate until the emergency measures of August 17, 1998.

This interest rate defense in combination with increasingly unsustainable public debt dynamics suggests that the biggest threat to the real exchange rate by 1998 was the risk that public debt may have had to be monetized or repudiated. This is what the market appeared to be signaling by May 1998, as discussed below. By then, the Sargent–Wallace (1981) conditions were satisfied. That is, real interest rates far exceeded the growth rate; the government was rolling over its debt,

[23] Gurvich and Andryakov (2002) discuss the implications of the Central Bank's reluctance to let the ruble depreciate.
[24] Dornbusch and Werner (1994); Dornbusch, Goldfajn, and Valdes (1995).

creating a pyramid as interest rates rose; and Russia appeared to have hit a credit ceiling, judging by the persistent rise in eurobond spreads and real yields on GKOs.

The preceding analysis applies to any country with fiscal problems, a fixed exchange rate, and capital mobility. Next, add on a feature peculiar to Russia at the time: the nonpayments problem. Nonpayments acted to kill growth and locked in the fiscal deficit. However, the problem did not move to the top of the policy agenda until June 1998, when discussions began on the emergency rescue package.[25]

The main reason for not dealing with nonpayments much earlier was the belief that it was an idiosyncratic, elaborate tax evasion scheme that reflected a lack of political will. To the contrary, it had a sound economic explanation and reflected rational economic behavior. It was a product of the punishing macroeconomic environment, combined with a deliberate policy of bailing out enterprises.[26]

Nonpayments developed into a system enveloping all levels of government, the energy monopolies, and manufacturing enterprises. It consisted of two parts. First were arrears, or overdue payments, which grew from 15 percent of GDP at end-1994 to an estimated 40 percent of GDP at end-1998. Second was the growing use of nonmonetary exchange. The system of nonpayments got entrenched because manufacturing enterprises were allowed to fall farther and farther into arrears on tax and energy payments with impunity. At the same time, the persistently high interest rates accompanying the stabilization program fueled a desire to economize on cash.

In other words, nonpayments grew because of a policy inconsistency: the macroeconomic object of squeezing inflation out of the system, coupled with the contradictory microeconomic object of bailing out enterprises with implicit subsidies. While the bailout might have been motivated by the fear that many enterprises did not stand a chance in a market economy, it was reinforced by the punishing macroeconomic environment that accompanied stabilization, characterized by exceptionally high real interest rates and the large real appreciation between 1995 and 1997. Not surprisingly, enterprises and the government economized on cash and ran arrears whenever they could. By the summer of 1998, cash collections were as low as 12–13 percent on domestic sales for the gas and electricity monopolies, and about 30 percent for the railways. By 1998, the share of noncash settlements in enterprise sales had increased to 50–70 percent, with the largest enterprises at the high end of

---

[25] Prior to June 1998, the tendency was to treat nonpayments mainly as an aspect of the reform of the infrastructure monopoly, where most of the problem seemed to lie (primarily the gas monopoly, Gazprom, the electricity monopoly RAO UES, and the railways) – not as the systemic growth-strangling issue it was.

[26] This argument is developed in Pinto, Drebentsov, and Morozov (2000a, b). The first to link macroeconomic policy and nonpayments were Commander and Mumssen (1999). Tax evasion figured prominently in Hendley, Ickes, and Ryterman (1998). IMF (1999, annex II) argued that there was no obvious link between nonpayments and interest rates. In personal communication, Michael Mussa has argued that focusing on cash fiscal deficit targets provided an impetus to budgetary arrears. Pinto, Drebentsov, and Morozov (2000a, p. 9) note that, "The government's own arrears stemming from unrealistic budgeting and general fiscal management contributed to nonpayments." They also note on the same page that, "The practice of offsetting budget expenditures and tax arrears quickly became an intrinsic element of budgeting, despite pressure from IFIs."

416   *Brian Pinto, Evsey Gurvich, and Sergei Ulatov*

Table 9.3. *Yield spreads on Russian Eurobonds upon issue,*
1997–1998

Date of Issue	Maturity	Spread (bps)	Face Value ($ billion)
June 1997	2007	375	1.00
June 4, 1998	2003	650	1.25
June 18, 1998	2008/2028[a]	753	2.50
July 20, 1998	2005/2018[b]	940	6.44

[a] 30-year bond with put-at-par after 10 years.
[b] As part of GKO-Eurobond exchange in conjunction with July package.
Source: KPU (2001).

this range. During the 1995 to mid-1998 period of disinflation, noncash settlements accounted for as much as half of spending by regional governments, while money surrogates and offsets averaged more than a fifth of federal government noninterest spending.

Nonpayments eventually fed into the accumulation of public debt. The implicit subsidies transferred by the infrastructure monopolies (gas and electricity primarily, and the railways to some extent) to manufacturing enterprises got passed on to the fiscal accounts, as these monopolies became delinquent on their own tax payments. This led to a chronic tax shortfall relative to targets, and hence rising borrowing requirements.

At the same time, the manufacturing sector ran its own tax arrears. About 65 percent of the net new borrowing at the federal government level for 1996 and 1997 could be attributed to these two factors, Pinto, Drebentsov, and Morozov (2000b) estimate. The link to growth was straightforward: the soft budgets in nonpayments destroyed incentives for enterprise restructuring – and with it, the microfoundations for the resumption of economic growth.

MARKET SIGNALS

How did the market price Russian government dollar- and ruble-denominated debt instruments against the above background of deteriorating fiscal and growth fundamentals?

Foreign Currency Debt

The marginal cost of foreign currency debt was high and rising in the period running up to the crisis, as Table 9.3 shows. By July 24, 1998, the spread for long-term dollar borrowings over U.S. treasuries was 940 basis points. An idea of the market's perception of Russian sovereign (default) risk can be obtained by comparing spreads on 10-year bonds with Indonesia, noting that after mid-May 1998, Indonesia was in the throes of a political and financial meltdown. On June 10, the spread on the Russian Eurobond was 100 basis points lower; by June 25, it had pulled even; by July 24, upon completion of the GKO-Eurobond swap, it was 160 basis points higher.

Ruble Debt

To examine how the domestic interest rate can be decomposed to give estimates of default risk and devaluation risk, consider Equation 3. It is an expanded form of the familiar interest parity equation[27]

$$i^d = i_r^f + SRP + (dx/x)^* + DRP. \tag{3}$$

In the equation, i^d is the domestic interest rate and i_r^f is a base risk-free rate, such as the yield on one-year U.S. Treasury bills; SRP is the sovereign risk premium and captures default risk; $(dx/x)^*$ is the target rate of devaluation of the currency against the U.S. dollar; and DRP is the devaluation risk premium, or the compensation for the risk that actual devaluation exceeds the target rate, $(dx/x)^*$. The decomposition in Equation 3 was effected as follows: For i^d, the market yield on one-year GKOs (ruble treasury bill) was used. The yield on the one-year U.S. Treasury bill was used for i_r^f. As this was fairly steady at about 5.5 percent over the period of interest, it was assumed fixed at 5.5 percent.[28]

SRP was proxied by the spread of the market yield of the Russian 2001/9.25 percent coupon dollar Eurobond over the comparable 2001/6.25 coupon percent U.S. Treasury note.[29] The target devaluation rate $(dx/x)^*$ was obtained as follows: For 1997, the starting exchange rate was 5.55 rub/\$ and it was anticipated that the exchange rate at the end of the year was going to be at the mid-point of the announced 5.75–6.35 rub/\$ band for the end of the year, giving a target devaluation rate of 9 percent. For 1998, CBR announced a constant ruble/\$ real exchange rate. With an 8 percent inflation target for Russia and with U.S. inflation at about 2 percent, this gives a target nominal devaluation rate of 6 percent for 1998. Lastly, DRP was obtained as a residual.

DRP and SRP started rising in November 1997, as the Thai crisis spread to Korea and other Asian markets. There was another increase in SRP in January/February 1998. The situation appeared to calm down until mid-May, when the final speculative attack began. Table 9.4 gives the SRP and DRP for key dates between May 15 and the meltdown. It shows that the devaluation risk had become acute by July 13. Even though DRP more than halved after the announcement of the international package on that day, it was nevertheless much higher than its level on May 15, when the speculative attack started. Default risk barely budged, indicating market skepticism about the package and concern about the total volume of debt. Both DRP and SRP jumped on July 24, when the GKO-Eurobond swap was settled, and continued rising as the speculative attack intensified, leading to the events of August 17, 1998. This was surprising, as the debt swap was expected to improve short-run debt dynamics, a point discussed further in the next section.

---

[27] This is a variant of a decomposition originally made by Frankel and MacArthur (1988).

[28] The volatility and level of the yield on the one-year U.S. Treasury bill were so low in comparison to the one-year GKO that assuming the former fixed is a mild assumption.

[29] An implicit assumption is that GKOs and the 2001 dollar Eurobond (the closest in maturity to the one-year GKO) had the same default risk. Postcrisis, Eurobonds were treated as senior to GKOs, which means that part of what is measured as devaluation risk premium in Equation 3 is the wedge between default risk on the 2001 Eurobond and GKOs. If this is treated as a constant, then Equation 3 still gives a good idea of the trend.

Table 9.4. *GKO yield, SRP, and DRP for key dates,*
May–August 1998 (percent per year)

	GKO yield	SRP	DRP
May 15	39.3	4.8	23.0
July 13	102.3	8.5	82.3
July 14	58.2	8.1	38.6
July 24	66.4	10.0	44.9
August 10	99.0	20.0	67.5
August 14	144.9	23.8	109.5

Source: Brunswick–Warburg, Moscow; authors' calculations.

CRISIS TRIGGERS

At least three factors played a role in triggering the crisis: international liquidity; balance and off-balance sheet exposures of banks; and the GKO-Eurobond swap. A fourth factor may have also played a role: failure by the Russian Duma to approve the full fiscal package developed as part of the rescue plan during a special legislative session held between the rescue plan's announcement on July 13, 1998 and its approval by the IMF Board on July 20, 1998. As a result, the IMF reduced the first tranche of its funding from $5.6 billion to $4.8 billion. Both actions signaled potential difficulty in full implementation of the package.

Liquidity

There is no hard and fast rule on how to measure liquidity. Two indices for Russia are presented in Table 9.5: a comprehensive liquidity index (CLI), and a limited liquidity index (LLI). The first is based on the idea that when a speculative attack begins, there is likely to be a comprehensive exit from domestic currency assets: in the case of Russia, whether they are ruble treasury bills, ruble currency notes (in view of widespread currency substitution), or even ruble bank deposits. At the same time, if bank solvency becomes an issue, as it often does during a crisis, people could start withdrawing their bank deposits, be they domestic- or foreign-currency denominated, in order to flee into hard currency. The CLI was therefore defined as broad money (including foreign exchange deposits in banks) plus the market value of ruble treasury bills divided by CBR's gross foreign exchange reserves, including gold. LLI was defined simply as the ratio of the market value of GKOs held by nonresidents to reserves. It was assumed that nonresidents were the most likely to flee the market.

　　Liquidity deteriorated throughout 1996, and again in the fourth quarter of 1997 as the ruble came under attack (see Table 9.5). By May 1998, a portfolio shift of less than 12 percent out of domestic assets broadly defined would have exhausted reserves. The June 4 and 18 Eurobonds, the IFI liquidity injection, and the debt swap all temporarily improved liquidity (see CLI and LLI for July 24). But fiscal dynamics were quick to assert their dominance. Only the devaluation and debt restructuring brought liquidity down to manageable levels, as will be seen in the next section.

Table 9.5. *Liquidity measures, 1996:1–August 14, 1998*

End of quarter/period	Comprehensive liquidity index^a	Limited liquidity index^{a,b}
1996:1	4.1	0.28
1996:2	5.7	0.50
1996:3	6.4	0.65
1996:4	6.9	0.77
1997:1	6.8	0.80
1997:2	5.2	0.62
1997:3	5.9	0.76
1997:4	7.5	0.95
1998:1	7.8	1.07
end-May	8.6	1.08
end-June	7.6	0.94
July 17	9.3	1.19
July 24	6.2	0.72
August 14	7.2	0.73

^{a} For definitions, see text.
^{b} Based on the assumption that 30 percent of GKO/OFZs were held by foreigners.
Source: Authors' calculations.

Vulnerable Banks

Banks in Russia, unlike those in East Asia or Argentina, were small and had limited links with the real sector. Total household deposits just before the crisis were of the order of 7 percent of GDP, compared to over 30 percent for East Asia. Credit to the private sector was under 4 percent of GDP, compared to 30 percent for Central and Eastern Europe.[30] Moreover, over 75 percent of household deposits were held in the state-owned savings bank, Sberbank, under an implicit deposit guarantee.

The main feature of the banking system was that, apart from Sberbank, it was dominated by a few large private Moscow-based banks. These were politically well connected and part of so-called Financial Industrial Groups built around natural resource exporters that engaged in connected lending and had heavily invested in government securities. For this reason, the banks were vulnerable to devaluation and default risk and were effectively sovereign risk.[31] Most of these banks had made their money through their designation as "authorized banks" for treasury operations. These operations amounted to interest-free loans at a time of high inflation and devaluation – and subsequently, high real interest rates. The banks perpetuated their wealth through the notorious "shares-for-loans" privatization auctions in 1995–96.[32]

---

[30] Figures for household deposits from Sinegubko (1998). Central and Eastern Europe includes Bulgaria, the Czech Republic, Hungary, Poland, Romania, and Slovenia. See IMF (2003, Table 6.2).
[31] CA IB (1997).
[32] For one account of how the large Moscow banks made their money, see Black, Kraakman, and Tarassova (2000). In the "loans-for-shares" scheme carried out in late 1995, Russian banks lent the government money collateralized with the shares of valuable companies in the oil, metals, and

Precrisis assessments of bank portfolios were made difficult because of unreliable data.[33] Nevertheless, the banks' vulnerability to a deteriorating macroeconomic environment became obvious after the first contagion episode in late 1997. The interest rate defense of the ruble and increasing concerns about default toward the end of 1997 reduced the market value of their portfolios. This made them vulnerable to rising margin calls on repo operations collateralized with their holdings of MinFin bonds,[34] and potential refusals by foreign banks to rollover syndicated loans. Either or both would have forced Russian banks to sell liquid assets – their holdings of government debt – at a loss, further depressing the price of government debt and possibly setting off a downward spiral. The need to raise dollars to meet margin calls and repay syndicated loans in part or full would have depleted CBR reserves.

Would a bank bailout have contributed to crisis?[35] Given the small size of the banking system and high proportion of household deposits held in Sberbank, the amount spent to prop up banks, including emergency loans to large banks before the meltdown, has been estimated at no more than 2 percent of 1998 GDP. This compares with public bailouts of over 10 percent in Hungary in the early 1990s, and a multiple of that figure in the 1997–98 Asian crisis countries.

A last point relates to the banks' exposure to currency forwards, or dollars sold forward to nonresident ruble-denominated GKO holders hedging their currency risk. While the precise volume was not known, it was believed to be substantial enough to cause a banking crisis in the event of devaluation. For this reason, and in view of the banks' political clout, it was believed that any devaluation would be postponed until at least November 15, because most of the currency forwards of the influential Moscow banks would have matured by then. The main factor that brought the crisis forward to August 17 was the GKO-Eurobond swap in conjunction with the substantial exposures of the Moscow banks to exchange rate and interest rate risk.[36]

GKO-Eurobond Swap

The swap out of GKOs into dollar-denominated long-term Eurobonds was conceived as a masterstroke to save on interest costs and bolster liquidity. With a large volume

telecom sectors, with the proviso that if the loans were not repaid, the banks would acquire the shares. The loan size was determined through auctions that were suspected to be rigged (see Lieberman and Veimetra 1996). An excellent analysis of the weakness of the banking system appears in Sinegubko (1998), which also contains an early quantification of balance sheet and off-balance sheet losses. The results of a postcrash audit of 18 large banks based on international accounting standards are reported in van Schaik (1999). Tompson (1997) describes how the role of Russian banks, once regarded as in the vanguard of the movement toward markets, differed little from their Soviet-era counterparts.

[33] See Sinegubko (1998). van Schaik (1999) quotes an auditor as saying that some banks inflated their capital by 50 to 80 percent.

[34] Dollar-denominated MinFin bonds, totaling $11 billion, were issued after the collapse of the Soviet Union to compensate holders of foreign currency accounts with the state-owned Vneshekonombank, a Soviet-era bank charged with managing external debt of the government. Five tranches were issued in 1993 (Soviet-era debt) and an additional two tranches were issued in 1996 (debt of the Russian Federation).

[35] The moral hazard argument of Dooley (1998); Burnside, Eichenbaum, and Rebelo (2001); and Kharas and Mishra (2001) explores the role of prospective fiscal deficits caused by implicit bailout guarantees to banks in the context of the Asian crisis.

[36] Details may be found in Kharas, Pinto, and Ulatov (2001) and references therein.

of GKOs yielding upward of 50 percent maturing every week, it was anticipated the benefits would be sizable. For example, a $20 billion-equivalent swap would mean interest savings of at least $7.5 billion a year, given the interest differential of 35 percentage points or more, or about 2 percent of precrisis GDP – while lengthening maturities. The logic and benefits seemed irresistible.

But the market was unenthusiastic. Of a total of $32 billion of GKOs by market value at prevailing exchange rates that were eligible under the swap, only $4.4 billion was actually swapped, even though the offered spread of 940 basis points implied a much higher yield than that in secondary markets for outstanding eurobonds. At the margin, the increased supply of dollar-denominated debt in a market close to saturation led to a fall in the price of MinFin bonds and other dollar-denominated debt instruments, triggering margin calls from banks on repos and raising bond spreads. This coincided with August being a peak month for bank syndicated loan rollovers. With their liquidity squeezed, banks were forced to sell GKOs in order to raise dollars, which depleted reserves and further hiked ruble interest rates. All this combined to hasten exit from the GKO market, leading to the emergency measures of August 17.

There are good reasons to expect that such swaps will not work when the market is concerned about public debt sustainability. First, the swap implicitly assumes that the country can borrow as much dollar-denominated debt as it wants at the going interest rate. This is unlikely to be true; spreads are bound to rise as more eurobonds are issued, as shown vividly in Table 9.3.

Second, the Russian swap was an attempt by the government to arbitrage the difference between ruble and dollar debt yields; but if an arbitrage is available, why would the private sector not exploit it? On the other hand, if investors are pricing default and devaluation risks consistently, the arbitrage is illusory.

Third, interactions with existing investor portfolios (as with the margin calls triggered from Russian banks) could lead to unintended and unanticipated outcomes. Fourth, swaps could trigger shifts in seniority that lead to an exit from less senior debt instruments. Thus if ruble GKOs are considered less senior to the Eurobonds they are replaced with, and if an IFI loan is provided at the same time, this could trigger exit from the remaining GKOs.

Fifth and most importantly, if the swap is market-based, it by definition does not lower the debt burden of the country. Indeed, it would make matters worse if a devaluation is eventually needed to restore balance to the government's intertemporal budget constraint. The size of the needed devaluation will *increase* because the ruble-denominated debt base (on which the devaluation acts as a capital tax) is lowered by the swap.[37] In short, in a situation where the private sector believes there is a fundamental problem with public debt sustainability and is pricing assets to reflect potential losses associated with devaluation and default, debt swaps and IFI liquidity injections could actually end up accelerating crisis.[38]

[37] For a formal statement, see Aizenman, Kletzer, and Pinto (2005).
[38] If fiscal fundamentals are strong and public debt sustainability is not an issue, a debt exchange that lengthens maturity can be beneficial, as Korea's experience showed. In March 1998, Korea managed to lengthen its banks' foreign debt maturity, supported by a government guarantee. But the guarantee

MORAL HAZARD

By May 1998, Russia's report card on fundamentals, international liquidity, and market signals portended crisis. The tax collection problem had become acute, and nonpayments dominated the economy. With oil prices falling, the government was openly talking about "combating the crisis." The Kirienko government issued its anticrisis plan on June 19, attributing Russia's problems to fiscal deficits, too much high-yielding short-term ruble debt (GKOs), contagion effects from Asia, and falling oil and gas prices. It singled out two corrective measures: raising the primary fiscal surplus in 1999 and resolving the nonpayments crisis.[39] In spite of the crisis atmosphere, Russia was able to increase its foreign currency public debt by $16 billion or 8 percent of 1999 GDP between June 1 and the August 17 meltdown. This analysis suggests that this increase was driven by moral hazard generated by expectations of a large IFI rescue package.[40]

Moral hazard is relevant in a potential sovereign debt crisis because the behavior of private portfolio investors could be influenced by the chances of an IFI-led rescue package. This could have implications for private sector involvement (PSI), as well as the level and creditor and currency composition of public debt that needs to be dealt with in the aftermath of a crisis. Steven Kamin (2001) defines moral hazard in terms of access to the international bond market, and argues that the IMF-led bailout of Mexico did not increase such access. In contrast, Giovanni Dell'Ariccia, Isabel Godde, and Jeromin Zettelmeyer (2000) look at the relationship between country spreads and fundamentals and find evidence of moral hazard in the context of the 1998 Russian crisis.

This study examines how the behavior of investors might have been influenced by the prospects of an IFI-led rescue package after mid-May 1998 and before the August collapse. This ex ante approach better captures the "insurance" nature of moral hazard than the analysis of ex post outcomes.[41] The evidence is based on news accounts of the time. To start with, after mid-May, Russia was in the middle of a speculative attack based on fundamentals. The news excerpts below show that investors were concerned about both liquidity and economic fundamentals, and attached more importance to fundamentals than politics.

May 18: "It has been a sell-off," said Yuri Plechko, a trader at Deutsche Morgan Grenfell in Moscow. "A lot of clients are taking money out. No bottom has been seen so far."   (Reuters, May 18, 1998)

---

was credible precisely because fiscal and debt fundamentals were strong. The exchange is described in Kim and Byeon (2001). Its impact is explored in Chopra and others (2002, Box 2).

[39] The anticrisis package was outlined in two documents (Government of the Russian Federation 1998a, b).

[40] Michael Mussa has argued that if a moral hazard problem existed, it did so before May 1998, because after that the risks of lending to Russia were well-known. He also notes that since IFI loans are senior and fully repaid, lending at a time of impending crisis amounts to a redistribution between private investors who exit and those who stay (robbing Peter to pay Paul); in this sense, there is no "subsidy" from the IFIs. While these points are well-taken, it could be that at the margin the prospect of an IFI bailout leads to private investors lending larger amounts or staying in for a longer time than they would without any chance of a bailout. Further, the chances of an IFI loan could affect the probability of being Peter rather than Paul, and thereby also affect investor behavior.

[41] Dell'Ariccia, Godde, and Zettelmeyer (2000) look at bond spreads after the rescue package collapsed.

May 19: Russia's central bank said on Tuesday it had spent $500 million propping up the ruble in the past week against "speculative attacks" and said the government should consider action against the Western firms involved. . . . Bearish British investors prefer to take their lead from Russia's economic problems rather than recent signs of political progress, investment strategists said on Tuesday. "The political situation has improved in Russia," said Oliver Fratzscher, chief economist, emerging markets at ABN AMRO Bank. "But it has $32 billion of short-term debt compared to forex reserves of less than $16 billion including gold and $11.5 billion excluding gold," he added. "That's a 200 percent ratio of short-term debt over reserves. That ratio was 50 percent a year ago," he said. Investors were largely unmoved by the Russian central bank's decision to hike its key refinancing rate to 50 percent from 30 percent overnight. . . . "There has been a lot of disappointment," [Radhika Atmerja] added. Very high real interest rates might have supported the ruble but they had hampered economic growth and equity earnings had been "dismal." These factors and current account and fiscal deficits were more significant to investors than the new government's chance of achieving political and structural reforms before the parliamentary elections due at the end of 1999, [investors] said.

(Excerpts from Reuters, May 19, 1998)

By the end of May, a collapse appeared imminent. The market was waiting for a bailout.

May 26: The benchmark RTS shares index retreated to its lowest since 1996, treasury bill yields were at 18 month highs and the ruble leapt past the weak end of the central bank's daily quotation band, completing a grim picture. Share dealers blamed the government for not initiating discussion of new aid from the International Monetary Fund, whose mission left Russia at the weekend without having taken a decision to disburse a $670 million loan tranche. Government officials have said they expect the IMF board to approve the tranche at a meeting next week, but markets are looking for further support to back the central bank and government in its fight to shore up the ruble and the budget . . . Russia's leading business dailies raised hopes on Tuesday that the International Monetary Fund might step in to prop up the shaky government securities market, but Russian and IMF officials were quick to dampen speculation. Kommersant Daily and Russky Telegraf ran front-page stories quoting Prime Minister Sergei Kirienko as saying Russia was discussing the possibility of a special multi-billion-dollar IMF credit to buy back short-term government debt.

(Excerpts from Reuters, May 26, 1998)

As hope of a rescue package rose, market indicators improved:

May 28: Hopes for fast approval of the next tranche [of IMF lending] and speculation about additional support helped battered Russian markets up in early trade on Thursday, but dealers said the tranche would bring only temporary relief and more substantial aid was needed . . . Fitch IBCA, the international rating agency, believes that the ruble is not fundamentally over-valued, and bold action from the Russian authorities' and financial support from the IMF and international financial community can avoid a damaging devaluation. . . . The international community, and the IMF, must also play their part in ensuring that the hard-won stabilization gains of recent years are not lost through a forced but avoidable devaluation of the ruble.

(Excerpts from Reuters, May 28, 1998)

June 3: The Russian central bank said the annualized average yield on a new 343-day tranche of Russian GKO treasury bills was 54.02 percent at an auction on Wednesday.

Dealers had forecast the average yield would be in the 57.53–69.16 percent range. Following is a list of analysts' comments. Vlad Sobell, analyst, Daiwa Europe in London – "This is good news. It looks like the crisis is over, but everyone is still waiting for news of financial support.[42] But I would anticipate further instability if there are any problems on this front. I do expect these negotiations to be successful." ... David Lubin, economist at HSBC, London – "It's obviously good news. I think the market is still working on the assumption that a multilateral financing package will become available and in that context the rally makes sense. The danger is that the IMF and the G7 might take the rally as evidence that their support is not needed. That would be a big mistake."   (Excerpts from Reuters, June 3, 1998)

> June 4: Emerging signs of confidence in Russian markets and the economy on Thursday appear to have calmed fears of a ruble meltdown, at least for now. Treasury bill yields fell almost 20 percentage points without budging the ruble from well within the central bank's target range, and shares inched up, bringing this week's gains to about 25 percent. None of 13 analysts surveyed in a Reuters poll believed the ruble would be devalued and all predicted a cut in interest rates, which the central bank has consistently hiked when the ruble was in danger. Traders and analysts pointed to a widespread belief that international help was on the way for Russia, buttressing the central bank's resolve, and reserves, to hold the ruble.   (Reuters, June 4, 1998)

In fact, things looked so good that on June 4, Russia launched a surprise eurobond for $1.25 billion, but at a spread of 613 basis points compared to only 347 basis points a year earlier. However, as the discussions between the IMF and Russia slowed, market indicators worsened once again.

> June 10: Leading Russian shares nose-dived in early trade on Wednesday as nerves wore thin ahead of crucial government debt auctions later in the day and hopes faded for an announcement of concrete foreign support for markets.... "We are in a potential meltdown situation at present ... there is simply no confidence whatsoever," said Regent European Securities' chief strategist Eric Kraus. "The market is profoundly disappointed by the failure of (German Chancellor Helmut) Kohl, the G7 or the IMF to provide any kind of support."   (Excerpts from Reuters, June 10, 1998)

> June 15: Russia's central bank faced a new threat to its interest rate policy on Monday as Asia's problems infected Moscow again and investors asked if the West would ever send help ... Western allies have kept investors on edge and markets volatile on promises of new aid – but only if the need arises.... "People are looking for at least some announcement from the IMF. On the other hand, there is Asia, which is becoming the major problem once again." ... Markets have swung wildly, and Monday's moves raised the prospect of the central bank being forced to review interest rates, which were cut to 60 percent from 150 percent on June 5.
> (Excerpts from Reuters, June 15, 1998)

But news of a visit by an IMF mission once again buoyed markets and Russia actually issued a second Eurobond:

> June 16: Russian markets rose on Tuesday, helped by an expected visit next week by an International Monetary Fund delegation to discuss extra financial support, but sentiment was still mixed, dealers said.   (Reuters, June 16, 1998)

---

[42] It is ironic that an interest rate of 54 percent with an inflation target of 8 percent would be considered "good news." But perhaps from the perspective of GKO holders it was, because they could still get over 50 percent with reduced devaluation risk, preserving their one-way bet because of the prospect of an IMF loan.

June 17: Russia's Finance Ministry is considering one or more dollar-denominated Eurobonds by the end of June . . . Russia [had earlier] launched a surprise $1.25 billion Eurobond on June 3. The paper, led by Goldman Sachs, was well received amid widespread anticipation of extra international support to help Russia out of its financial crisis.
(Excerpts from Reuters, June 17, 1998. Material in square brackets added by authors.)

On June 18, Russia issued a second eurobond, but a costly one. It was a 30-year Eurobond with a put at par after 10 years and issued at a spread of 753 basis points, Russia's most expensive up to that point. It was so well-received that the size was increased from a planned $1.5 billion to $2.5 billion. However, in a remarkably candid assessment, an investment analyst noted that, "Readers should recognize that this issue was sold – as all Russian debt has been in the past several months – essentially because investors believe that Russia will not be allowed to fail, rather than because its fundamentals are encouraging."[43] A few days later, it was announced that negotiations would begin on an emergency package.

June 24: The Russian president's special liaison to international financial institutions, Anatoly Chubais, said Wednesday he hopes that the IMF board's meeting in Washington, D.C. Thursday will approve a $670-million tranche of the Extended Fund Facility to Russia. . . . The money will pave the way for the beginning of talks on a large package of assistance the IMF may provide to Russia, he said. "In fact, starting from tomorrow, we will begin talks with the IMF on provision of a large credit package to Russia," Chubais said.   (Excerpts from Interfax, June 24, 1998)

"We believe that Russian debt is oversold and should rally in the next week," Morgan Stanley said in a research note published on Wednesday . . . Morgan Stanley's recommendations are based on a belief that the Russian government has no desire to see a ruble devaluation and that the International Monetary Fund and the Group of Seven industrialized nations have sufficient reserves to meet the country's desired $10–$15 billion loan. "We continue to believe that Russia will get an IMF agreement," the statement said.   (Excerpts from Reuters, June 24, 1998)

When and why should one care about moral hazard? The Russian experience suggests that moral hazard is a particularly serious issue when a country faces a combination of high public debt and low liquidity. IFI loans in these circumstances might merely facilitate private exit. In addition, private loans that would not normally be forthcoming would materialize.

In Russia's case, there was a conscious plan to replace "expensive" GKO debt with "cheap" dollar-denominated debt, resulting in a $16 billion build-up in hard currency debt between June 1 and the meltdown of August 17. As reserves continued to get depleted, the dollar debt build-up was matched by exit from ruble debt – which means that GKO investors who waited for their treasury bills to mature and exited through the spot market did in fact earn dollar-equivalent rates of more than 50 percent. Consider two other pieces of evidence. First, dollar Eurobond spreads remained high throughout. Even after GKO yields halved to 55 percent on July 14, the day after the rescue package was announced, bond spreads did not fall, indicating unchanged concern about default. Second, the response to the GKO-Eurobond exchange was weak. Only $4.4 billion at market prices were tendered, showing that investors did not want to go long on Russia.

[43] Mutkin (1998).

Taken together, this means that from the market's perspective the main feature of a bailout would be its alleviation of short-term liquidity problems. While fiscal and structural reforms could in principle lower default risk, these would take much more time to become credible and have a visible impact. Thus, the best time to exit would be soon after the IFI loans came in. In this sense, a large IFI package in the context of public debt unsustainability and low liquidity can actually trigger a collapse: the IFI loan increases short-run liquidity with a matching increase in senior public debt. It becomes the perfect time for more junior bondholders to exit.

For the borrowing country, the implications are serious. First, the external borrowing headroom is used up in defense of an unsustainable peg rather than to support basic reform or alleviate the social impact of a crisis. Second, the debt burden becomes even more severe when the real exchange rate depreciates to restore fiscal and balance of payments solvency. Indeed, a much bigger devaluation is then needed to restore balance because there is more external and dollar-denominated debt.[44]

POSTCRISIS DEVELOPMENTS

Following the 1998 crisis, Russia experienced a dramatic recovery. The crucial underlying factors were hard budgets, for government and enterprises alike, and a shift in the macropolicy stance toward the twin goals of maintaining a competitive real exchange rate and achieving public debt sustainability. Facilitating this shift was the seemingly disastrous decision to devalue and seek debt restructuring in August 1998. This stimulated a profound change in government behavior, subsequently reinforced by President Yeltsin's decision to step down in favor of then-Prime Minister Putin on December 31, 1999. While discussing this political change is beyond the scope of this case study, there is little doubt that the new leadership and strategic shift it sponsored in economic policy was also a critical factor in Russia's rebound.[45]

Criticality of Hard Budgets and Real Exchange Rates

Ironically, the decision to "devalue and default" in August 1998 proved critical to the subsequent recovery, even though it might have been seen at the time as just the first step in a severe setback to the transition. The expectation was that this would be followed by a suspension even of internal convertibility, the large-scale printing of money to bail out banks and enterprises, and the reimposition of trade barriers, internationally and among regions in Russia. The replacement of the reformist Kirienko government with the Primakov government might reasonably have been interpreted as supporting such a move.

But two factors intervened. The government realized that suspending convertibility and hyperinflation would be unpopular; and buoyed by the devaluation, a recovery in industrial output appeared as early as October 1998, with industrial production growing by 5 percent in October relative to September and by 2.2 percent in November relative to October.[46] This combination of events might

---

[44] This is argued in Aizenman, Kletzer, and Pinto (2005).
[45] IMF (2003, Chapter 1), stresses the "relative political stability" and "well thought-out and ambitious program of structural reforms" that have been facilitated by the Putin presidency.
[46] Seasonally adjusted and reflecting differences in working time.

Table 9.6. *Swing in combined foreign asset position of CBR and GOR 1999–2002 (US$ billion)*

	1999	2000	2001	2002	1999–2002
Change in CBR reserves	+0.2	+15.5	+6.6	+13.3	+35.6
Change in external public debt	+1.0	−15.1[a]	−11.3	−8.5	−33.9

[a] Incorporates agreement with London Club. See below.
Source: Ministry of Finance; CBR; authors' calculation.

well have led to a decision on the part of the government to let matters take their course.

The default acted to shut Russia out of the capital markets. This provided a powerful incentive for the Russian government to begin translating its own "hard budget constraint" into similar constraints on the energy monopolies – a process that had ripple effects throughout the economy and initiated the dismantling of the costly nonpayments system. This was facilitated by the large devaluation, which almost shut down imports and switched domestic demand across the board toward Russian-made goods, starting with the cash-rich, fast-moving consumer goods sector.

As a result, the profitability of the Russian enterprise sector improved, as did its liquidity, which was also aided by the reduction in real wages and the decision to let energy tariffs decline in real terms. A World Bank survey of three regions in late 2000 and early 2001 to assess the social consequences of hardening enterprise budgets found that the tangible improvement in enterprises persuaded regional and local authorities to insist that enterprises make more prompt tax payments in cash, so that they in turn could meet the payments pressure from the gas and electricity monopolies, Gazprom and RAO UES, to pay local utility bills on time or face disconnection.[47] It had been argued before the crisis that disconnection was illegal under the existing provisions of the civil code! Gazprom and UES were in turn pressured by the government of the Russian Federation (GOR) to increase the share of cash in their sales and pay their taxes on time and in cash. GOR's leverage was facilitated by its controlling ownership in both monopolies. The combination of the real depreciation and the hardening of budgets thus played a critical role in the dismantling of nonpayments and gave a new impetus to market reforms.[48]

Liquidity and Debt Dynamics

Postcrisis, there was a big swing in the combined foreign asset position of the Central Bank of Russia and the Government of Russia, measured as the sum of the increase in CBR reserves and the reduction in GOR's foreign currency debt. The cumulative increase from 1999 to 2002 was $70 billion, or 20 percent of 2002 GDP (see Table 9.6).

---

[47] World Bank (2001).

[48] Goskomstat data show that noncash settlements (including barter, offsets, and promissory notes) declined from over 50 percent of sales in 1999 to 18 percent in 2002 for enterprises in the five main sectors of the economy.

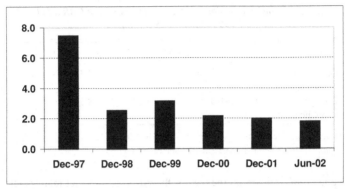

Figure 9.2. Comprehensive Liquidity Index, 1997–2002. *Source*: Authors' calculations.

Second, international liquidity improved dramatically, as measured by the comprehensive liquidity index defined above (CLI) (see Figure 9.2). Compared to 7.4 at the end of 1997 and an average of 7.9 during the first eight months of 1998, the CLI stood at 1.8 at the end of the first half of 2002.

This improvement is attributable to three factors: devaluation and domestic debt restructuring, which lowered the market value of GKOs/OFZs to about $6 billion on June 30, 2002, compared to $60 billion at the end of the first quarter of 1998; limited issuance of new debt as fiscal surpluses grew; and accumulation of reserves facilitated by the oil/gas boom.

Third, public debt dynamics became much more favorable, as indicated in Table 9.7. Primary fiscal balances moved from deficit to surplus, interest payments fell, and growth picked up. Averages for 1995–98 are presented as a benchmark.

Change in Macropolicy Stance

The government's macropolicy stance changed from its seemingly lexicographic precrisis pursuit of low inflation to the twin goals of maintaining a competitive real exchange rate (to help enterprises and improve the trade balance) and placing public debt on a stable trajectory through fiscal restraint.[49] The results, as noted above, were remarkable. No less remarkable is the process by which this change occurred. As discussed earlier, an element of serendipity was involved. The tangible positive effects of the real depreciation on Russian enterprises, a recognition that hyperinflation and a reversal of reforms would be unpopular, and the hard budget imposed on GOR as a result of the default all interacted to sow the seeds of recovery and therefore a new commitment to completing market reforms.

The depreciation in the real exchange rate, which collapsed in September 1998 as a result of the crisis, relative to the precrisis level is evident in Figure 9.3.

---

[49] While summing up lessons from exchange rate-based stabilizations, Dornbusch and Werner (1994) note that Chile, learning from its unsuccessful experience in the 1970s, "never made inflation the absolute and exclusive target" in the 1980s.

Table 9.7. *Postcrisis public debt dynamics of the general government,*
1995–2002[a] (percentages)

	Avg. 1995–98	1999	2000	2001	2002
Primary fiscal balance/GDP	−2.7	3.0	6.9	5.8	3.4[b]
Interest on public debt/GDP	4.4	4.0	3.8	2.7	2.2
Real GDP growth	−2.9	5.4	9.0	5.0	4.3
Public debt/GDP	75[c]	94	65	48	42

[a] "General government" includes federal and regional governments plus extra-budgetary funds.
[b] Preliminary estimate.
[c] For 1998.
Source: Ministry of Finance; Goskomstat.

It appreciated subsequently, as might be expected, because of the doubling of the oil price after 2000 relative to 1998, and the increase in the current account balance from zero in 1998 to 9.1 percent of GDP by 2002 (see Table 9.8). Nevertheless, in November 2002, the real exchange rate was some 20 percent less than its level in July 1998.

Two factors helped restrain real appreciation postcrisis. The first was the budgetary decision in 1999 to reintroduce price-related export taxes on oil and gas while strengthening control over expenditure at all levels of the government, with the federal government leading by example. As a result, fiscal surpluses were generated, which helped to "sterilize" the monetary effects of the current account boom and which were used to lower public debt.

Second, the Central Bank made a conscious decision to build-up reserves rather than let the nominal exchange rate appreciate. Indeed, the nominal ruble/dollar rate depreciated by 7 percent in 2001 and 5.4 percent in 2002. Nevertheless, 12-month inflation declined steadily from 37 percent in 1999 to an estimated 14 percent in 2002. A faster decline in inflation would doubtless have been secured had the nominal exchange rate been allowed to float upward; however, the chance to improve the joint net foreign assets position of the Central Bank of Russia and the Russian government

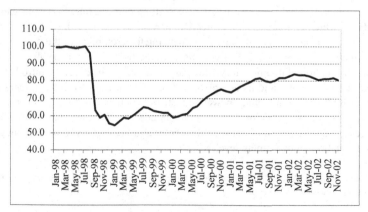

Figure 9.3. Post-Crisis Real Effective Exchange Rate, July 1998=100. *Source*: IMF.

Table 9.8. *Real exchange rate, oil price, and current account surplus, 1998–2002*

	1998	1999	2000	2001	2002[a]
REER Index, July 98=100 (e-o-p)	55.2	61.7	74.4	81.8	80.9
Urals oil price ($/bbl, pd. avg.)	10.2	15.2	24.0	20.9	21.4
CA balance – $ billion	0.7	24.7	46.4	34.8	31.7[b]
– % of GDP	0.2	12.8	18.5	11.8	9.1

[a] REER is at the end of November.
[b] Preliminary CBR estimates.
Source: IMF; Goskomstat; CBR.

would have been foregone. The conscious decision to accumulate reserves and pay down public debt greatly improved the profile for future inflation, creating a long-term basis for stabilization because of the accompanying improvement in public debt dynamics.

The fiscal adjustment at the general government level is examined in Table 9.9. Comparing outcomes in 2001 with the average over 1995–97, there has been a remarkable fiscal adjustment, the bulk of it explicable by expenditure reduction. However, some caution is advised in interpreting the numbers, because of the high-level of noncash shares in both expenditures and revenues in the precrisis period.[50] To the extent that these were recorded at inflated prices – the counterpart of implicit subsidies – expenditures and revenues were both overestimated. Thus, the subsequent expenditure reduction was probably smaller and the rise in revenues larger than portrayed by a superficial comparison of the numbers for 1995–97 and 2001 in Table 9.9.

Another important factor has been the large increase in oil-related revenues. While the perception that Russia's postcrisis rebound is "just an oil play" is unjustified in view of the change in government behavior and change in macropolicy stance noted at the start of this section, some estimates suggest that 4 of the 5 percentage points of GDP rise in revenues between 1998 and 2001 (Table 9.9) came from the oil sector.[51]

Equally important is the quality of fiscal adjustment, as the 2001 outcome was achieved with a virtual elimination of noncash settlements and mutual arrears leading to offsets, which characterized the precrisis period. In this regard, several reforms and institutional changes contributed to enhancing the credibility of the fiscal effort. These included the elimination of tax offsets at the federal level in 1999, followed by full elimination of nonmonetary budgetary transactions in 2001; the introduction of the treasury system and its completion at the federal level by 2001; integration of extra-budgetary funds and "power ministries" (defense and security) into the treasury system; the adoption of a new budget code in 2000; and tax reforms and changes in tax-sharing rules between the center and the regions to harden budgets at the subnational government level.

---

[50] We are grateful to Michael Mussa for raising this point and suggesting that greater emphasis be placed on the oil price increase.
[51] Kwon (2003).

Table 9.9. *Fiscal adjustment of the general government, 1995–2001 (percentages)*

	Avg. 1995–97	1998	1999	2000	2001
Expenditure/GDP	43.0	37.7	35.4	33.9	34.0
noncash exp./total exp.	17.3	22.6	13.3	4.0	0
Revenues/GDP	35.3	32.5	34.3	37.0	37.2
noncash rev./total rev.	21.1	26.2	13.7	3.7	0
Fiscal balance/GDP	−8.3	−5.9	−0.6	3.1	3.2

Source: Ministry of Finance; authors' calculations.

Debt Restructuring[52]

Two components of public debt accounted for the bulk of losses borne by creditors: the ruble treasury bills and bonds (GKOs/OFZs); and Soviet-era commercial debt (debt incurred by the Soviet Union before January 1, 1992, which Russia inherited) under the auspices of the London Club (LC). The face value of GKOs/OFZs (excluding OFZ coupons) subject to restructuring was about $45 billion at the immediate precrisis exchange rate. This debt was held in almost equal amounts by Russian commercial banks, the Central Bank of Russia, and nonresidents. Under the restructuring terms, Russian commercial banks and nonresidents are estimated to have suffered losses estimated at 70 percent of the face value, a substantial fraction of this owing to the devaluation. Russian banks were able to pass through some of their losses to depositors, while another part was borne by CBR, which attempted to bail out some banks soon after the crisis.

An important facilitating factor is that GKOs/OFZs were subject to Russian law. Another factor that might have helped was that Russian commercial banks were known to have made their money in less than transparent ways, by acting as "authorized banks" for treasury operations, which amounted to getting interest-free loans when inflation was high and devaluation rapid, or, after 1995, when real interest rates were high; and subsequently, through the loans-for-shares privatization auctions conducted in 1995 and 1996.[53] The debt restructuring thus amounted to a belated tax payment. Lastly, the banks had limited links to the real sector. In cases where substantial retail deposits were held, arrangements were made to transfer these to the state-owned savings bank, Sberbank. Nevertheless, significant losses were borne by small depositors, estimated at between 37 and 58 percent for ruble deposits and between 49 and 64 percent for dollar deposits.[54]

London Club (LC) debt had three components: Prins, or principal, ($22.2 billion); IANs, or interest arrears notes, ($6.8 billion); and past-due interest on the first two components ($2.8 billion). The agreement reached with the London

---

[52] Details of restructuring for the various components of public debt are available in IMF (2003, Chapter 7). The goal here is to concentrate on a few of the insights.

[53] See Lieberman and Veimetra (1996); Tompson (1997); and Black, Kraakman, and Tarassova (2000). See also Kharas, Pinto, and Ulatov (2001) and the references therein. In any event, there were concerted attempts to "help" the Russian banks in the months following August 1998, including on the settlement of their off-balance sheet exposures to currency forwards.

[54] IET (2000).

Club in August 2000 involved a write-down of $10.6 billion on Prins and IANs and
the replacement of all three components by long-term eurobonds of the Russian
Federation. The package resulted in a debt reduction estimated in present value
terms of 50 percent. Two factors facilitated the conclusion of this deal: Prins and
IANs were the obligations of Vneshekonombank, and not a sovereign liability.[55]
Had Vneshekonombank been allowed to go bankrupt, this would have created a
legal nightmare for the holders of the debt, which meant that the offer to issue
sovereign bonds in exchange was difficult to refuse. Moreover, the market value of
Prins and IANs was a paltry $1.8 billion in October 1998, compared to $14.2 billion
in July 2000 just before the exchange.

Social Impact

Any crisis is bound to have negative social consequences, and Russia's was no
exception. Studies show that poverty rates increased after the 1998 crisis and as a
result of the inflationary burst in 1999.[56] While these findings are to be expected,
interpreting the social impact of the crisis is complicated by two factors. First, if the
standard of living enjoyed before the crisis was being supported by an unsustainable
accumulation of public debt, then one could question if precrisis living standards
were a reasonable benchmark. Second, while nominal wage and other social payments precrisis may have appeared high, large arrears in actual payment existed. In
fact, these arrears existed alongside the hidden subsidies transferred to enterprises
as part of the precrisis nonpayments system. One study estimates the total amount
of subsidies being received by enterprises (the sum of explicit budgetary subsidies
and those implicit in nonpayments) as between 15 and 20 percent of GDP per year
during the three years before the crisis.[57]

The large magnitude of the subsidies fueled corruption and delayed enterprise
restructuring, keeping unviable enterprises in business. While it may have been
politically convenient to argue that keeping such enterprises going was necessary
to avert a crisis, the survey evidence in World Bank (2001) suggests that the social
consequences of doing so were negative. Workers were laid off anyway and new,
worthwhile jobs that might have been created by restructuring firms did not materialize because managers were busy stripping assets instead.

Two lessons emerge. Keeping unviable firms in business as a way of helping
workers is ineffective and eventually unaffordable. Furthermore, the cost of maintaining these firms diverts resources from the truly needy. Indeed, a better designed
and targeted social safety net for needy individuals (as opposed to hefty explicit and
implicit subsidies to unviable enterprises) would have been both more effective and
less costly.

---

[55] As noted above, Vneshekonombank managed government external debt during the Soviet era, a role it
continued after the dissolution of the Soviet Union. In this capacity, it and not the Russian government
was the official holder of commercial debts owed to the London Club, all of which pertained to the
Soviet era.
[56] Lokshin and Ravallion (2000); IMF (2003, Chapter 2).
[57] Pinto, Drebentsov, and Morozov (2000b, Table A1, p. 324).

LESSONS

Contrary to the view that the Russian situation was unique, it contains useful lessons for all countries facing simultaneous problems of public debt sustainability and low international liquidity – a list that has included Argentina, Brazil, and Turkey in recent years.

General Lessons

First, crises, in spite of the visual image of a sudden, sharp dislocation, can develop over a period of two or three years or more.[58] Second, countries that make squeezing out inflation the centerpiece of their economic program at the expense of fiscal and growth fundamentals can end up paying a heavy price for it. Third, emerging policy inconsistencies need to be taken seriously and nipped in the bud; prevention is less painful than cure. Fourth, if fiscal and growth fundamentals are shown to be problematic based on economic analysis, then market signals on devaluation, and especially default, risk, need to be taken seriously. This will also help in the judgment of whether an economy is in a "first-generation" or "second-generation" world and therefore aid in the appropriate design of a rescue package.

Crisis Management

There are two lessons. First, it is difficult to design a package to deal with confidence (liquidity) and fundamentals at the same time, especially in the context of a fixed exchange rate. If public debt is on an unsustainable course and the market is signaling high levels of default risk, attempts to bolster liquidity with loans from the IFIs could actually trigger a crisis. Payments to IFIs are typically perceived to be senior claims. Additional infusions of senior debt at a time of fiscal constraints lowers the chances that more junior debt will be serviced. Therefore, more junior debt holders (such as GKO holders, in the case of Russia) could seize the opportunity to exit – and the temporarily increase in liquidity as the result of the IFI loan provides the exit opportunity.

The second lesson is that it is important to understand the payoffs of the various agents involved, especially creditors. Russia was able to secure good terms from GKO holders and the London Club. This was partly because high rates of default had been priced into these instruments. It was also because of special circumstances whereby GKOs were governed by domestic law; and the debt owed to the London Club was not a sovereign liability but a liability of Vneshekonombank, which put the Russian government in a strong bargaining position.

Stabilization

The lesson is that inflation reduction should be viewed with suspicion if it is achieved in an environment of weak growth prospects, an appreciating real exchange rate, and stubbornly large fiscal deficits. This combination can only mean that public debt

---

[58] The same observation could be made of Turkey. Perry and Serven (2003) note that Argentina's real exchange rate was significantly overvalued by the end of 1999; its crisis occurred at the end of 2001.

　　　Brian Pinto, Evsey Gurvich, and Sergei Ulatov

is either on an obvious or latent explosive trajectory and will eventually lead to a collapse in stabilization. Indeed, if a country is squeezing inflation out but running large fiscal deficits, this should be taken as an immediate red flag.

Microeconomic Hard Budgets

Russia's seemingly idiosyncratic problem with nonpayments also has lessons for other economies: that macroeconomic stabilization is eventually unsustainable without hard budgets for enterprises. Conversely, the effects of macroeconomic policy are eventually transmitted to the real sector through real exchange rates and real interest rates. These constitute the "macro–micro" links. A punishing macroeconomic environment of tight money with contradictory loose fiscal policy (explicitly, or implicitly as with nonpayments) will eventually derail stabilization.

Real Exchange Rate Sustainability

It has been commonplace in recent crisis episodes to agonize over whether the real exchange rate is in equilibrium or not. Three lessons emerge in this connection. First, the nominal exchange rate can play a major role in real exchange rate movements, especially when stabilization relies on fixing the nominal exchange rate and public debt levels are low to begin with. Second, it should not be taken as an article of faith that the real exchange rate is in equilibrium just because the current account is in good shape. Equally critical are public debt dynamics, growth prospects, and enterprise productivity. If real appreciation occurs alongside deteriorating enterprise performance and worsening public debt dynamics, it should be viewed with suspicion. Third, long periods of high real interest rates should also raise concerns about the sustainability of the real exchange rate.

Liquidity Monitoring

Tracking liquidity trends in the lead-up to a crisis can be valuable. But the liquidity indices must be carefully interpreted. For example, a large IFI loan will improve the index, but with a matching increase in public debt. Raising interest rates to defend the exchange rate will lower the market value of domestic currency treasury bills, improving liquidity but also increasing fiscal costs. And continued exit from the market will worsen liquidity. In a situation of fixed exchange rates, currency substitution, and full convertibility, the most appropriate liquidity index may be a comprehensive one that considers all potential claims on reserves – not just short-term external debt.

Financial Engineering

In a situation of unsustainable public debt dynamics and low liquidity, financial engineering – in the form of market-based debt swaps to lower nominal interest payments and lengthen maturities by altering currency composition in favor of dollars[59] – is likely to accelerate a crisis. This is the case even if the interest

---

[59] Indeed, the presumption given Hausmann's "original sin" is that any lengthening of maturities and lowering of coupons is going to involve a shift to dollar debt.

differential between domestic currency-denominated debt and foreign currency-denominated debt is temptingly high. The experience with Russia's GKO-Eurobond swap illustrates the point about the unavailability of arbitrage opportunities. On July 24, $3 billion of 20-year bonds were issued in connection with the GKO-eurobond swap at a price of 74 percent, with a coupon of 11 percent, giving a yield-to-maturity of 15.2 percent in dollar terms. If one takes the ruble/dollar rate to be 24.2 by the time of the first coupon payment (July 1999), and assumes a nominal devaluation of 8 percent/year up to 2008 and 5 percent/year after that to maturity, the internal rate of return (yield) of the ruble-equivalent cash flow stream is 65.6 percent/year for 20 years! This compares with a one-year GKO yield of 66 percent on July 24, the date the swap was settled.

Social Costs of Crisis

Another lesson from Russia is that the social costs of crisis must be carefully interpreted. In Russia's case, bailing out unviable enterprises through the nonpayments system in turn fed into unsustainable public debt accumulation. This was the wrong way to go, as it wasted resources and fueled crisis without helping those in social need. Hard budgets for enterprises, accompanied by a conducive macroeconomic framework in terms of a competitive real exchange rate and reasonable real interest rates (which would have been facilitated by the fiscal savings from large explicit and implicit subsidies), would have been preferable. A more effective safety net for needy individuals could have been designed, while also creating better jobs through enterprise restructuring.

A last point: it is difficult to think of a successful "escape" without crisis from the "unsustainable debt/low liquidity" case exemplified by Russia. Theoretically, if credible commitments and upfront actions to address fiscal fundamentals have possible – backed by liquidity support/financial engineering – a crisis might be avoided. On the other hand, if the corrective actions are perceived to be difficult, liquidity support might be seen as an excuse for postponing difficult decisions, while also propping up an overvalued real exchange rate. In this case, a crisis might act to propel the government to action. This seems to have been the case in Russia.

REFERENCES

Aizenman, Joshua, Kenneth M. Kletzer, and Brian Pinto. 2005. "Sargent–Wallace Meets Krugman–Flood–Garber, Or: Why Sovereign Debt Swaps Don't Avert Macroeconomic Crises." *Economic Journal* 115:343–67.

Aslund, Anders. 1995. *How Russia Became A Market Economy*. Washington, DC: Brookings Institution Press.

Black, Bernard S., Reinier Kraakman, and Anna Tarassova. 2000. "Russian Privatization and Corporate Governance: What Went Wrong?" *Stanford Law Review* 52:1731–808.

Blasi, Joseph, Maya Kroumova, and Douglas Kruse. 1997. *Kremlin Capitalism*. Ithaca and London: Cornell University Press.

Brixi, Hana Polackova, and Allen Schick. 2002. *Government at Risk: Contingent Liabilities and Fiscal Risk*. Oxford: Oxford University Press for the World Bank.

Buckberg, Elaine, and Brian Pinto. 1997. "How Russia Is Becoming a Market Economy: A Policy Maker's Checklist." International Finance Corporation, Washington, DC.

Burnside, Craig, Martin Eichenbaum, and Sergio Rebelo. 2001. "Prospective Deficits and the Asian Currency Crisis." *Journal of Political Economy* 109(6):1155–97.

CA IB Investment Bank. 1997. "Riding Out the Storm." Sector Report: Banking Update, Russia, December.

Chang, Roberto, and Andres Velasco. 1998. "The Asian Liquidity Crisis." NBER Working Paper 6796. National Bureau of Economic Research, Cambridge, MA.

Chopra, Ajai, Kenneth Kang, Meral Karasulu, Hong Liang, Henry Ma, and Anthony Richards. 2002. "From Crisis to Recovery in Korea: Strategy, Achievements and Lessons." In David T. Coe and Se-Jik Kim, eds., *Korean Crisis and Recovery*. Washington, DC: International Monetary Fund and Korean Institute for International Economic Policy.

Commander, Simon, and Christian Mumssen. 1999. "Understanding Barter in Russia." Working Paper 37. EBRD, London.

Dell'Ariccia, Giovanni, Isabel Godde, and Jeromin Zettelmeyer. 2000. "Moral Hazard and International Crisis Lending: A Test." IMF, Washington, DC.

Dooley, Michael. 1998. *A Model of Crises in Emerging Markets*. International Finance Discussion Papers No. 630. Board of Governors of the Federal Reserve System, Washington, DC.

Dornbusch, Rudiger, and Alejandro Werner. 1994. "Mexico: Stabilization, Reform, and No Growth." *Brookings Papers on Economic Activity* 1:253–315.

Dornbusch, Rudiger, Ilan Goldfajn, and Rodrigo Valdes. 1995. "Currency Crises and Collapses." *Brookings Papers on Economic Activity* 2:219–93.

Dungey, Mardi, Renee Fry, Brenda Gonzalez-Hermosillo, and Vance Martin. 2002. "International Contagion Effects from the Russia Crisis and the LTCM Near-Collapse." IMF Working Paper. Washington, DC.

Flood, Robert, and Peter Garber. 1984. "Collapsing Exchange Rate Regimes: Some Linear Examples." *Journal of International Economics* 17(1–2):1–13.

Frankel, Jeffrey, and Alan MacArthur. 1988. "Political vs. Currency Premia in International Real Interest Differentials: A Study of Forward Rates for 24 Countries." *European Economic Review* 32(5):1083–121.

Furman, Jason, and Joseph Stiglitz. 1998. "Economic Crises: Evidence and Insights from East Asia." *Brooking's Papers on Economic Activity* 2:1–115.

Gaddy, Clifford G., and Barry W. Ickes. 1998. "Russia's Virtual Economy." *Foreign Affairs* 77(5):53–67.

Gaidar, Yegor. 2002. *The Economics of Russian Transition*. Cambridge, MA: MIT Press.

GAO (General Accounting Office). 2000. *Foreign Assistance. International Efforts to Aid Russia's Transition Have Had Mixed Results*. Washington, DC.

Government of The Russian Federation. 1998a. "Stabilization Measures Plan." June 19, 1998.

———. 1998b. "Stabilization of the Economy and Finance Program." June 19, 1998.

———. 2000. "Basic Trends in Social and Economic Policy of the Government of the Russian Federation over the Long Term."

Granville, Brigitte. 2001. "The Problem of Monetary Stabilization." In Brigitte Granville and Peter Oppenheimer, eds., *Russia's Post-Communist Economy*. Oxford University Press.

Gurvich, Evsey, and Alexander Andryakov. 2002. "A Model of the Russian Crisis Development." EERC WP 02/03. Moscow.

Hendley, Kathryn, Barry Ickes, and Randi Ryterman. 1998. "Remonetizing the Russian Economy." In H. G. Broadman, ed., *Russian Enterprise Reform: Policies to Further the Transition*. World Bank Discussion Paper 400. Washington, DC.

IET (Institute for Economies in Transition). 2000. "Banking Crisis in Russia and Its Consequences. The Problem of Post-Crisis Adaptation of the Banking System." Moscow.

IMF (International Monetary Fund). 1999. *Russian Federation – Recent Economic Developments*. Washington, DC.

———. 2000a. *Russian Federation. Staff Report for the 2000 Article IV Consultation and Public Information Notice Following Consultation.* IMF Staff Country Report No. 00/145. Washington, DC.

———. 2000b. *Debt- and Reserve-Related Indicators of External Vulnerability.* March 23, 2000. Available at http://www.imf.org/external/np/pdr/debtres/debtres.pdf.

———. 2003. "Russia Rebounds."

Kamin, Steven B. 2001. "Identifying the Role of Moral Hazard in International Financial Markets." Federal Reserve Board, International Finance Division, Washington, DC. Draft.

Kharas, Homi, and Deepak Mishra. 2001. "Fiscal Policy, Hidden Deficits and Currency Crisis." In S. Devarajan, F. Halsey Rogers and L. Squire, eds., *World Bank Economists Forum.* Washington, DC: World Bank.

Kharas, Homi J., Brian Pinto, and Ulatov, Sergei. 2001. "An Analysis of Russia's 1998 Meltdown: Fundamentals and Market Signals." *Brookings Papers on Economic Activity* 1:1–68.

Kim, Woochan, and Yangho Byeon. 2001. "Restructuring Korean Banks' Short-Term Debts in 1998." Seoul.

Krugman, Paul. 1979. "A Model of Balance-of-Payments Crises." *Journal of Money, Credit, and Banking* 11(3):311–25.

Kwon, Goohoon. 2003. "Post-Crisis Revenue Developments in Russia from an Oil Perspective." International Monetary Fund, Washington, DC. Draft.

Lieberman, Ira W., and Rogi Veimetra. 1996. "The Rush for State Shares in the 'Klondyke' of Wild East Capitalism: Loans-for-Shares Transactions in Russia." *George Washington Journal of International Law and Economics* 29(3):737–68.

Lokshin, Michael, and Martin Ravallion. 2000. "Welfare Impacts of the 1998 Financial Crisis in Russia and the Response of the Public Safety Net." *The Economics of Transition* 8(2):269–95.

Mussa, Michael. 2002. "Argentina and the Fund: From Triumph to Tragedy." Institute for International Economics, Washington, DC.

Mutkin, Lawrence. 1998. "Actually, Russia *Can* Fail." Market Commentary, Tokai Bank Europe, June 19.

Obstfeld, Maurice. 1996. "Models of Currency Crises with Self-Fulfilling Features." *European Economic Review* (April):1037–47.

OECD (Organisation for Economic Co-operation and Development). 1997. *Economic Surveys-Russian Federation.* Paris.

Perry, Guillermo, and Luis Servén. 2003. "The Anatomy of a Multiple Crisis: Why Was Argentina Special and What Can We Learn from It?" In George M. Von Furstenberg, Volbert Alexander, and Jacques Melitz, eds., *Monetary Union and Hard Peg: Effects on Trade, Financial Development, and Stability.* New York: Oxford University Press.

Pinto, Brian. 1996. "Russia after Yeltsin's Re-election: An Economic Report." International Finance Corporation, Washington, DC.

Pinto, Brian, Vladimir Drebentsov, and Alexander Morozov. 2000a. "Dismantling Russia's Nonpayments System: Creating Conditions for Growth." World Bank Technical Paper No. 471. Washington, DC.

———. 2000b. "Give Macroeconomic Stability and Growth in Russia a Chance: Harden Budgets by Eliminating Non-Payments." *Economics of Transition* 8(2):297–324.

Rogoff, Kenneth. 2003. "The IMF Strikes Back." *Foreign Policy* (January). Available at http://www.foreignpolicy.com/issue_janfeb_2003/rogoff.html.

Sargent, Thomas J., and Neil Wallace. 1981. "Some Unpleasant Monetaristic Arithmetic." *Federal Reserve Bank of Minneapolis Quarterly Review* 5(3):1–17.

Shleifer, Andrei, and Daniel Treisman. 2000. *Without a Map: Political Tactics and Economic Reform in Russia.* Cambridge, MA: MIT Press.

Sinegubko, Boris. 1998. "A Chance to Start Over? Sacrificing Banks May Be the Lowest Cost of Structural Adjustment." Brunswick Warburg, Moscow (August 21).

Tompson, William. 1997. "Old Habits Die Hard: Fiscal Imperatives, State Regulation and the Role of Russia's Banks." *Europe-Asia Studies* 49(7):1159–85.

van Schaik, John. 1999. "Russia: The Newly Wed and the Nearly Dead." *Euromoney* (June):254–63.

Woodruff, David M. 1999. "Money Unmade. Barter and the Fate of Russian Capitalism." Ithaca and London: Cornell University Press.

World Bank. 2001. *The Russian Federation after the 1998 Crisis: Towards "Win-Win" Strategies for Growth and Social Protection.* Washington, DC.

10. Argentina's Macroeconomic Collapse: Causes and Lessons[1]

Luis Servén and Guillermo Perry

ABSTRACT: The Argentine crisis of 2002 has been variously blamed on fiscal imbalances, real overvaluation, and self-fulfilling investor pessimism triggering a capital flow reversal. This chapter provides an encompassing assessment of the role of these and other ingredients in the gestation of the crisis. Conceptually, the macroeconomic collapse must have resulted from much greater shocks than those hitting other countries, or from a weaker and more vulnerable policy framework, or both. In this framework, the chapter shows that in the final years of Convertibility, Argentina was not hit harder than other emerging markets by global terms-of-trade and financial disturbances. Hence the crisis primarily reflects the high vulnerability to shocks built into Argentina's policy framework. Three key sources of vulnerability are examined: the hard peg adopted against Optimal Currency Area considerations in a context of wage and price inflexibility; the fragile fiscal position resulting from an expansionary stance during the boom; and the pervasive mismatches in the portfolios of banks' borrowers. These vulnerabilities were mutually reinforcing, and severely constrained the room for maneuver available to the authorities – who failed to use it effectively while there was still time to avert the collapse.

WHAT CAUSED THE CRISIS

In the early 1990s, Argentina appeared to resurface from decades of instability and declining per capita income. Throughout much of the 1990s, under the one-peso–one-dollar rule of the Convertibility regime, the economy outperformed most other emerging markets, and Argentina managed to escape the aftershocks of Mexico's Tequila Crisis of 1994 relatively unscathed. Following the Russian crisis of 1998 and the ensuing turmoil in world financial markets, other Latin American countries underwent a temporary growth slowdown followed by a modest recovery. Meanwhile, Argentina plunged into a deepening recession that ultimately led to the collapse of Convertibility in the midst of a severe economic and social disruption (see Figure 10.1).

[1] Office of the Chief Economist for Latin America, the World Bank. This study draws from previous work developed in collaboration with Augusto de la Torre, Humberto López, Norbert Fiess, Rodrigo Suescún, and Sergio Schmukler. However, the authors of this study are solely responsible for any errors and for the views expressed here. The authors gratefully acknowledge valuable comments and suggestions from Mauricio Carrizosa, Robert Flood, Michael Mussa, Brian Pinto, and John Williamson. Patricia Macchi provided excellent research assistance.

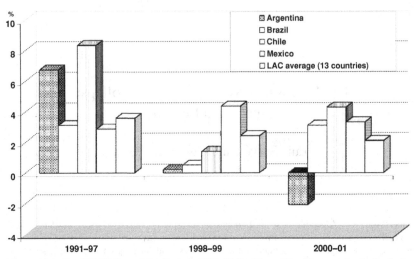

Figure 10.1. Real GDP Growth by Period, 1991–2001. *Note*: The 13 countries in the Latin America average are: Argentina, the Bahamas, Barbados, Belize, Bolivia, Brazil, Chile, Colombia, Costa Rica, Ecuador, Mexico, Peru, and Venezuela. *Source*: *World Development Indicators*, World Bank.

The huge proportions of the Argentine crisis – which involved a decline in real GDP of close to 20 percent from 1999 to 2002 – have prompted a booming literature searching for the causes of such a cataclysmic collapse and the lessons to be drawn from it. The majority of analyses concur that the exchange rate had become significantly overvalued at the end of the 1990s, and stress the fact that the Convertibility regime was ill suited to deliver the real depreciation that was required to realign the exchange rate.[2] According to this view, the overvaluation resulted from various ingredients, most notably the appreciation of the U.S. dollar and the depreciation of the Brazilian real, as well as global financial shocks.[3] The threat of a major real depreciation was particularly disruptive because of the large currency mismatches in the financial system.

Many observers have also identified fiscal policy as a key factor in the crisis. Some of them have blamed the collapse squarely on Argentina's persistent fiscal imbalances throughout the 1990s. But the magnitude of the these imbalances was not extraordinary by international standards – although Mario Teijeiro (2001) has documented how published deficit data grossly understated the true accumulation of public liabilities over the period, and Michael Mussa (2002) has argued that such standards are not applicable to Argentina because its degree of vulnerability was well above the international norm.

Other authors point to the procyclicality of fiscal policy, and in particular the failure to put public finances on firm footing in the boom years, which forced a procyclical contraction in the recession. They argue that this created uncertainty

---

[2] This view is stated, for example, by Corden (2002); Calvo, Izquierdo, and Talvi (2002); Hausmann and Velasco (2002); Rodrik (2002). See also Joseph Stiglitz, "Argentina Shortchanged." *Washington Post*, May 12, 2002.

[3] This latter ingredient is emphasized by Calvo, Izquierdo, and Talvi (2002).

about future growth and political stability, which markets perceived as an increase in default risk, and which eventually triggered the reversal of capital flows and the actual collapse.[4]

Yet another group of authors conclude that the role of fiscal imbalances was much more limited and find the roots of the crisis in other factors: real misalignment (as already noted); political shocks, which turned a mild fiscal adjustment problem into a major collapse (Powell 2002); and investors' self-fulfilling expectations of default (Sachs 2002), which led to a vicious circle of rising interest rates, weakening solvency, and increased default perceptions.

This chapter provides an encompassing assessment of the role of all these ingredients, and especially the interactions among the peg, fiscal factors, financial factors, and external shocks in the gestation of the crisis. The objective is to arrive at a better understanding of the roots of the crisis, as well as its policy lessons.

Argentina's meltdown must have resulted either from much greater shocks than those felt elsewhere, or from a much weaker and more vulnerable policy framework, or both. The distinction between these ingredients – bad luck and bad policies – is essential for drawing lessons from the crisis. The rest of the chapter is guided by this consideration. The chapter first offers a comparative international perspective on the major external shocks suffered by Argentina and other Latin American countries in the second part of the 1990s. The next three sections examine in depth Argentina's three key sources of vulnerability: the straitjacket imposed by the hard peg, the destabilizing fiscal policy stance, and the fragilities hidden in the financial system. The chapter closes by outlining the main policy lessons to be drawn from the crisis.

BAD LUCK

In the second half of the 1990s and early years of the new century, Argentina, like other emerging economies, had to cope with shocks in terms of trade, the fallout from the East Asia and Russia financial crises of 1997–98, and the global slowdown that started in late 2000. This section first assesses whether these textbook shocks were more severe for Argentina than for other countries. It then turns to reviewing other shocks specific to Argentina.

Real Shocks

Consider first the terms of trade. After rising in 1996, Argentina's terms of trade declined through 1999 by a cumulative 10 percent, and then returned close to their previous levels. The decline, while significant, was much more modest than that suffered by other countries, particularly oil exporters like Venezuela and Ecuador.

Moreover, the economic dimension of the temporary loss in terms of trade was quite modest relative to other countries because of Argentina's low degree of trade openness. This is seen in Figure 10.2, which depicts terms of trade changes scaled by the degree of openness in several Latin American countries, as defined by the ratios of imports and exports to GDP. Such a measure provides a rough quantification of the income effect of changes in export and import prices (see Appendix A for the specifics of the underlying calculation). It shows that the decline in Argentina's

---

[4] See Corden (2002); Mussa (2002); and Perry and Servén (2003).

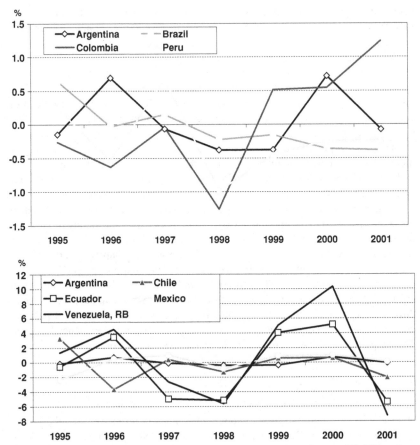

Figure 10.2. Terms of Trade Shocks, 1995–2001 (percent of GDP). *Source*: *World Development Indicators*, World Bank.

terms of trade from the peaks of 1996 involved a real income loss of up to 1 percent of GDP relative to that year. However, the income loss was recouped in 2000. Yet the graph also shows that the income effects of the changes in Argentina's terms of trade were among the smallest in the region.

The other global real shock was the U.S. and worldwide growth slowdown, which started in late 2000. Relative to 2000, real GDP growth in 2001 declined by over 3 percent in the United States, and by almost as much in the rest of the OECD. As a result, the rate of expansion of world demand for exports from emerging market, including Argentina's, also declined. As with the terms of trade, however, the impact on Argentina's aggregate demand was much smaller than in most other Latin American countries, because of its lower degree of openness. The aggregate demand decline resulting from the global slowdown is estimated to have amounted to 0.25 percent of GDP in Argentina (Perry and Servén 2003). In other major Latin American countries, the impact was much more severe, ranging from 0.40 percent of GDP in Brazil to 1.9 percent of GDP in Mexico.

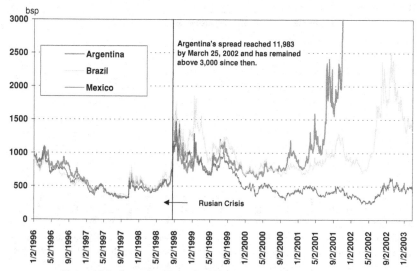

Figure 10.3. Sovereign Spreads, 1996–2003. *Source*: J. P. Morgan.

Financial Shocks

Major global financial shocks also occurred in the late 1990s, and some observers have attributed the key role in the Argentine crisis to them.[5] The Russian default of August 1998 led to a sharp increase in emerging market sovereign spreads as capital inflows dried up. Figure 10.3 depicts the trajectory of sovereign spreads for Argentina, Brazil, and Mexico. While the generalized rise starting in late 1998 is apparent, Argentina's spreads remained below Brazil's from 1998 to 1999, and even below Mexico's until mid-1999. It was only in late 2000 that Argentina's spread started drifting above Brazil's.

The trajectory of capital inflows over this period was the mirror image of that of spreads. The sudden stop of mid-1998 affected all countries shown, but the drop in capital flows was, if anything, more abrupt in Brazil and Mexico than it was in Argentina. As with spreads, the collapse of capital flows to Argentina took hold only in late 2000. Until then, Argentina was able to keep financing large current account deficits, in the range of 4–5 percent of GDP (Figure 10.4). After that, however, Argentina, unlike other countries, ran into increasing difficulties in securing external financing.[6]

The conclusion that the impact of these global shocks was milder in Argentina than in other emerging markets is also confirmed by an assessment of the role of global forces in the observed behavior of spreads and capital flows across countries during the late 1990s. This type of assessment has been developed by Norbert Fiess (2003), using an approach based on the identification of the common and

---

[5] See Calvo, Izquierdo, and Talvi (2003).

[6] The average current account balance shown in Figure 10.4 shows a pattern similar to that in Figure 10.4 if Argentina is excluded from the calculation. The evolution of capital flows to Argentina and other Latin American countries is documented in more detail by Perry and Servén (2003).

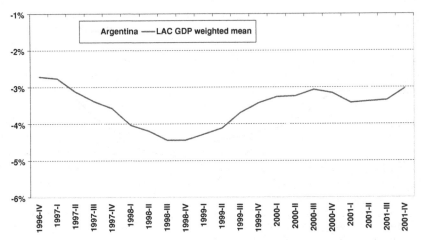

Figure 10.4. Current Account Balance, 1996:IV–2001:IV (percent of GDP, four-quarter moving average). *Note*: Latin America average includes Argentina, Brazil, Chile, Colombia, Mexico, and Peru. *Source*: Balance of Payments from domestic sources via HAVER.

idiosyncratic factors underlying the performance of individual countries. Using a principal components procedure, that analysis yields an estimated "global factor," which provides a summary indicator of the global conditions (world discount rates, international investors' appetite for risk, and so on) affecting capital flows to emerging markets.[7]

Figure 10.5 depicts the contribution of the global factor described above to the evolution of spreads in Argentina, Brazil, and Mexico. For each of these countries, the figure shows the fraction of the total variation in its spread attributable to the global factor. In all three countries, the global factor accounts for the bulk of the variation of spreads during 1997–98, but its contribution declines after the Russia crisis of 1998. The extent of the decline, however, differs sharply across countries. In the case of Argentina, it is much more marked, and accelerates noticeably in the second half of 2000. After that time, global factors account for less than half the observed variation in Argentina's spreads. The conclusion is that after 1998 (and especially from 2000 onward) such variation increasingly reflects country-specific factors – most likely, investors' rising concern with the exchange rate and the fiscal situation.[8]

In summary, the evidence strongly indicates that Argentina was not affected more severely than other emerging markets by the global financial shocks of the late

---

[7] The full details are spelled out in Fiess (2003). The principal component analysis constructs the global factor using end-of-the-month EMBI spreads data for Argentina, Brazil, Mexico, Venezuela, and the non-Latin EMBI index over the period from January 1991 to March 2002. The global factor is given by the first principal component. The fraction of the variance in each country's spreads explained by the global factor is computed over a rolling window of 48 months, and the resulting series is smoothed by averaging the values obtained for each data point over the 48 windows in which it appears. A number of robustness checks lead to results qualitatively similar to those shown in Figure 10.5.

[8] The same result is found if the analysis is applied to capital flows rather than spreads. See Perry and Servén (2003).

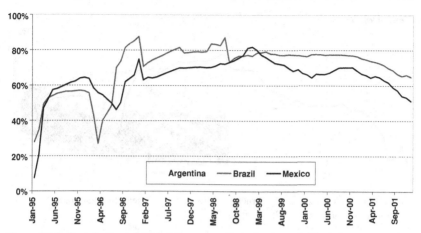

Figure 10.5. Contribution of Global Factors to Variation in Individual Country Spreads, 1995–2001. *Source*: Fless (2003).

1990s. The collapse in capital inflows to Argentina and the steep rise in spreads in late 2000 and 2001 appear to reflect mainly factors that are specific to Argentina, rather than the action of worldwide shocks. This suggests that they reflect ongoing developments in the country, and likely contributed to amplify the crisis, rather than being its primary, exogenous cause.

The Other Shocks

The discussion above implies that Argentina was not hit harder than other countries by the global shocks of the late 1990s: the terms of trade shocks after the East Asian crisis of 1997, the global slowdown of 2001, and the capital flow reversal that followed the Russian crisis.

But in those years, Argentina did suffer two real shocks specific to Argentina. These stemmed from changes in the exchange rates of major trading partners relative to the U.S. dollar. The first was the appreciation of the U.S. dollar relative to other major currencies (including, most importantly, the euro) from 1996 on. The second was the devaluation of the Brazilian *real* in 1999.

These were significant developments, in light of the geographic composition of Argentina's trade. This is shown in Figure 10.6, which highlights the percentage composition of Argentina's combined imports and exports from 1998 to 2000. Brazil was the leading trading partner, with 30 percent of total flows, followed by the euro area, with 23 percent.

These cross-exchange-rate changes amounted to true real shocks for Argentina only to the extent that its nominal exchange rate was firmly pegged to the U.S. dollar under the Convertibility Law. As a result, the appreciation of the dollar relative to Argentina's trading partners was automatically passed on to the Argentine peso. Moreover, the currency board left no scope for rapidly correcting the appreciation through a nominal devaluation.

How much of a real appreciation was caused by these exchange rate changes? To answer this question, it is useful to focus on the real effective (that is, trade-weighted)

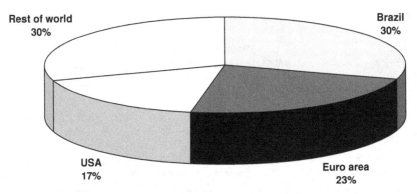

Rest of world 30%

Brazil 30%

USA 17%

Euro area 23%

Figure 10.6. Argentina's Trade Structure, 1998–2000 (percent of total trade). *Source:* Alberola, López, and Servén (2004).

exchange rate (henceforth REER). Any country's (log) REER can be expressed as the difference between its bilateral real exchange rate vis-à-vis the numeraire and a trade-weighted sum of the bilateral real exchange rates of its trading partners vis-à-vis the same numeraire (see Appendix B for derivations). Thus, in the case of Argentina, using the dollar as numeraire reveals that the change in the REER is equal to the change in the bilateral peso-dollar REER minus the weighted sum of the changes in the dollar real exchange rates of its trading partners. A depreciation (appreciation) of the currency of a trading partner against the dollar leads ceteris paribus to an appreciation (depreciation) of the REER, by a magnitude proportional to the trade share of the partner in question.

Using these trade weights, Figure 10.7 illustrates the impact of the changes in the bilateral exchange rates of trading partners' currencies on Argentina's REER.[9] The figure shows the trajectory of their dollar real exchange rates after 1996. In the figure, an increase denotes an appreciation, and a decrease a depreciation. From 1996 to 2001 the euro depreciated by close to 30 percent in real terms against the dollar, while the Brazilian *real* depreciated by almost 50 percent in real terms. In turn, the Argentine peso also depreciated steadily vis-à-vis the dollar, although at a modest 2 percent per year, for a total of some 12 percent from 1996 to 2001. As a result, over this period the peso appreciated considerably against both currencies.

Figure 10.8 shows the cumulative contribution of the movement in each bilateral real exchange rate to the observed trajectory of the peso REER. The latter appreciated by 20 percent from 1996 to 2001. This total resulted from two opposing forces. On the one hand, the real depreciation of the euro against the dollar accounted for an 8 percent appreciation of the peso REER, while that of the Brazilian real accounted for another 19 percent and that of all other trading partner currencies added a further 6 percent.[10] The combined result, other things equal, was a 33 percent real

---

[9] The figure uses the GDP deflator as the relevant price index. Using the CPI leads to very similar results.

[10] This third effect reflects primarily the real depreciation of Asian currencies against the dollar following the East Asia and Russia crises of 1997–98.

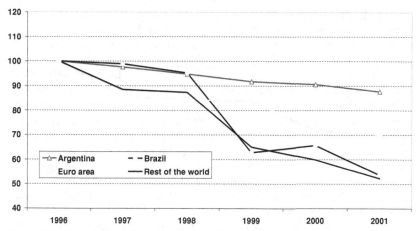

Figure 10.7. Argentina's Trading Partners: Bilateral Real Exchange Rates against the United States, 1996–2001 (GDP-based, 1996 = 100). *Sources*: *World Development Indicators*, World Bank; *International Financial Statistics*, International Monetary Fund; and Alberola, López, and Servén (2004).

appreciation. On the other hand, the real depreciation of the peso against the U.S. dollar helped offset in part the appreciation, contributing ceteris paribus a 13 percent depreciation of the REER. The combined result of all these ingredients was the above-mentioned 20 percent REER appreciation.

Thus, the impact on Argentina's REER of the changes in the real exchanges rates of its trading partners against the dollar was quite significant. One may view such changes as major exogenous disturbances. But the country's vulnerability to these shocks was largely a result of its policy choices, relating particularly to the exchange

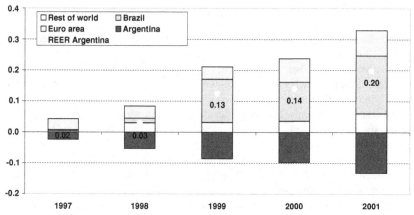

Figure 10.8. Cumulative Contribution of Bilateral RER Changes to the Trajectory of the Peso REER, 1997–2001 (GDP-based, logs). *Sources: World Development Indicators*, World Bank; *International Financial Statistics*, International Monetary Fund; and Alberola, López, and Servén (2004).

rate regime. Rather than bad luck, in this case the main problem was the straitjacket imposed by the hard peg, an issue that will be examined in the next section.

Finally, mention should be made also of what some observers have labeled "political shocks" that took place in the final years of Convertibility.[11] These relate to the increasing weakness of the De la Rua administration, which took office in late 1999, and most importantly its repeated failures to bring public finances under control. As the recession deepened and political infighting escalated, the administration's support was gradually eroded, prompting the resignation of the Vice President in late 2000 and Minister of Economy Jose Luis Machinea in early 2001, as well as that of his successor, Ricardo Lopez-Murphy, shortly thereafter. The appointment of Domingo Cavallo as Minister of Economy in March 2001, with emergency powers to undertake fiscal correction measures, failed to yield the resumption of growth that had been hoped for. Credibility was further weakened as Mr. Cavallo amended the Convertibility Law, forced central bank governor Pedro Pou out of office, and embarked on a last-ditch attempt to avoid default through a "mega-swap" of public debt to lengthen its maturity and the announcement of a zero-deficit policy in July 2001. In all likelihood, these did more harm than good to investor expectations.

There is no question that these political developments contributed to shape international investors' perceptions about Argentina's prospects, and probably also to accelerate the collapse. Yet one should not overstate their role as independent determinants of the crisis itself. First, to a large extent these political events were themselves the reflection, rather than the cause, of an increasingly difficult economic situation, magnified by the weak institutional framework (particularly fiscal) underlying Argentina's policies. Second, these events had only temporary effects on risk perceptions. Following each one of them, sovereign spreads rose but then returned to their previous level.[12] It was only in July 2001 that the increases in the spread started to become irreversible, without any obvious political development to account for this change.

THE HARD PEG: A SUBOPTIMAL CURRENCY AREA

It is difficult to dispute the view that the hard dollar peg adopted at the beginning of the 1990s was the wrong monetary regime from the perspective of Argentina's productive and trade structure. Optimal Currency Area (OCA) theory suggests that an irrevocable peg, such as Argentina's under the Convertibility Law, is more likely to be beneficial for the client country if it trades a lot with the anchor, and if client and anchor are not exposed to significant asymmetric shocks that would demand monetary policy responses of different signs in the two countries. If the scope for asymmetric shocks is substantial, the peg might still make sense if the client country can easily adjust to real shocks through nominal price and wage flexibility, or through other mechanisms such as a system of fiscal transfers and/or unrestricted labor mobility with the anchor.

It is obvious that Argentina failed to meet these conditions for an OCA with the U.S. dollar. As already shown, the United States accounted for less than one-fifth

---

[11] See Powell (2002) and Cline (2003).
[12] See for example Schmukler and Servén (2002); and De la Torre, Levy-Yeyati, and Schmukler (2003).

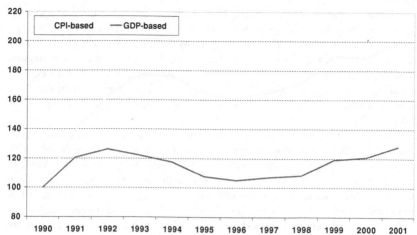

Figure 10.9. Real Effective Exchange Rate of the Peso, 1990–2001 (1990 = 100). *Source*: Alberola, López, and Servén (2004).

of the country's total trade (some 3 percent of GDP), leaving a very large scope for asymmetric shocks – as the events would eventually prove. Wage and price flexibility were limited, making adjustment to real shocks difficult, and the scope for fiscal transfers or unrestricted labor mobility was remote.

All this is unsurprising, however, because the adoption of Convertibility was not guided by OCA arguments, but by two other considerations. First, it was viewed as an expeditious shortcut to monetary credibility, after many years of acute instability largely due to the persistent monetization of runaway fiscal deficits. Indeed, it was hoped that Convertibility would enforce a hard budget constraint on the public sector, and even shelter the financial system from the dangers of arbitrary manipulation of the value of the currency.

The second consideration was the high degree of de facto financial dollarization, reflecting the preference of Argentine investors for dollar-denominated instruments after years of high and volatile inflation. Convertibility sanctioned this status quo and, as will be shown later, encouraged further dollarization, under the implicit guarantee that the one-peso–one-dollar parity was unbreakable.

Overvaluation and Its Causes

During the Convertibility years, the peso appreciated significantly in real terms. The precise extent of the real appreciation varies depending on the measure used. The CPI-based REER rose by almost 100 percent between 1990 and 2001, while its GDP-based counterpart rose by a more modest 30 percent over the same period (Figure 10.9). Much of the real appreciation developed in the early years of Convertibility, in accordance with the international experience regarding exchange rate – based stabilization. The initial appreciation was followed by a partial reversal until 1996, after which time the REER again began to appreciate, largely driven by the changes in cross-exchange rates as described earlier.

While supporters of the Convertibility regime argued that the real appreciation of the early 1990s was an equilibrium phenomenon, driven by the efficiency-
enhancing reforms undertaken in those years, by the late 1990s most observers con-
curred that the peso had become overvalued. The precise extent of the overvaluation
was disputed, depending on the real exchange rate measure used and the equilibrium benchmark against which it was compared.[13] The later was typically some
historical value, under the implicit view that the equilibrium real exchange rate is
constant.[14]

In reality, however, there are well-known theoretical reasons why the equilibrium real exchange rate may change over time. First, productivity does not march
in lockstep across sectors and countries. Other things being equal, an increase in
productivity in the traded goods sector relative to that of the nontraded goods sector
in a given country above that experienced by its trading partners should lead to an
appreciation of the equilibrium real exchange rate, the so-called Balassa–Samuelson
effect. Second, the equilibrium real exchange rate must be consistent with a sustainable long-run net foreign asset position, without leading to explosive accumulation
of external assets or liabilities over the long run, the "external equilibrium" view of
the real exchange rate.[15]

An empirical assessment of the trajectory of Argentina's REER using an equilibrium benchmark incorporating the two factors just summarized yields the results
shown in Figure 10.10. The empirical framework, which is sketched in Appendix
C, incorporates the effects on the equilibrium real exchange rate of changes over
time in both relative sector productivity and net foreign assets.[16] The figure depicts
the percentage deviation[17] of the actual REER from its estimated equilibrium value,
along with 95 percent confidence bands. A positive value indicates overvaluation,
and a negative one means undervaluation.

The graph reveals two stages of real misalignment. Between 1991 and 1998,
the REER was close to its equilibrium value. From 1998 on, however, the REER
exceeded its equilibrium counterpart by a widening margin, resulting in an increasing
overvaluation. By 2001, the log REER exceeded its equilibrium value by 37 percent. Equivalently, the ratio of the observed REER to its equilibrium value was
145 percent.[18]

The framework underlying these empirical results allows further analysis of the
causes of the misalignment. Enrique Alberola, Humberto López, and Luis Servén
(2004) show that over the second half of the 1990s, the *equilibrium* REER followed
a depreciating trend, which was particularly steep after 1997.[19] As shown above,

---

[13] Cline (2003) argues that a consensus estimate would place the overvaluation around 30 percent in
2001.

[14] This is just the standard *purchasing power parity* (PPP) view. See Balassa (1964).

[15] See, for example, Mussa (1984).

[16] Full details are given in Alberola, López, and Servén (2004).

[17] More precisely, the graph shows logarithmic deviations. These are approximately equal to percentage
deviations for small values, but not for large ones.

[18] These results pertain to the GDP-based measure of the real exchange rate. If the CPI-based measure
is used instead, the estimated overvaluation is even larger: more than 50 percent. In independent
work using an approach very similar to that employed here, but using a different measure of relative
productivity, Gay and Pellegrini (2003) estimate the degree of misalignment of the GDP-based REER
at 43 percent (in terms of log-deviations) in 2001.

[19] The same result is found by Gay and Pellegrini (2003).

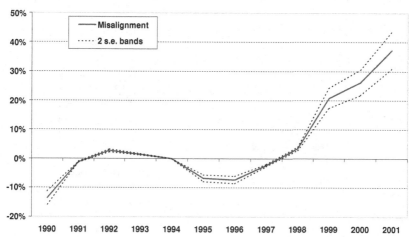

Figure 10.10. Estimated Real Misalignment of the Peso, 1990–2001. *Source*: Alberola, López, and Servén (2004).

during these years the *actual* REER was appreciating due to the effect of the changing dollar exchange rates of Argentina's trading partners. Hence, the increasing misalignment reflected the opposing trends of the actual and equilibrium exchange rates. Digging one level deeper, it is possible to see that the main driving force behind the equilibrium real depreciation of the late 1990s was the rapid increase in Argentina's net foreign liabilities relative to GDP. This resulted from the combination of substantial current account deficits – particularly in 1997–99 (as shown in Figure 10.4)[20] – and a persistent deterioration in growth in the late 1990s.[21]

Was the misalignment of the peso at the end of the 1990s a result of the wrong choice of peg under Convertibility? In other words, did it arise because Argentina failed to meet the conditions for an OCA with the U.S. dollar, or was it due to the failure to support the peg with the right macroeconomic policies? To answer this question, it is useful to break down the misalignment of the peso into three parts (see Appendix D). The first is due to the divergence in fundamentals (productivity differentials and foreign asset ratios) between Argentina and the United States. This causes the equilibrium REERs of the dollar and the peso to diverge, and reflects the pursuance of policies inconsistent with the dollar peg. This must eventually lead to misalignment even if the peg were otherwise "right" for the Argentinean economy.

The other two components reflect the inadequacy of the dollar peg itself. One is the overvaluation of the dollar, which is automatically translated to the peso. The other results from changes in the real exchange rates of third currencies whose weight in Argentina's total trade is different from their weight in the U.S. total trade. Clearly, this is the case of the Brazilian *real*. Note that, in the case of Argentina,

---

[20] Large current account deficits were incurred over 1995–96 as well, but during those years the Argentine economy was still growing at a rapid pace, which helped contain the impact of such deficits on the ratio of foreign liabilities to GDP.

[21] It is worth noting that Argentina's external deficits were being incurred in the midst of a severe recession with escalating unemployment. The full-employment current account deficit would have been much bigger than that actually observed, a point underscored by Roubini (2001).

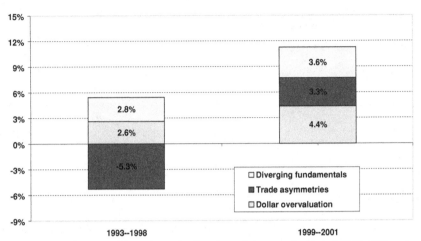

Figure 10.11. Sources of Peso Overvaluation–Annual Averages by Period, 1993–1998 and 1999–2001. *Source*: Alberola, López, and Servén (2004).

misalignment results from pegging to a misaligned anchor currency, while in the case of Brazil, it results from asymmetries in the trade structure of the client and anchor countries.

The decomposition is shown in Figure 10.11, taken from Alberola, López, and Servén (2004), which shows the sources of the cumulative misalignment of the peso over 1993–98 and 1999–2001. As noted earlier, over the first of these two periods the REER was close to its equilibrium value, while over the latter it developed a large overvaluation. The figure reveals a contrasting pattern between both periods. In 1993–98, trade structure asymmetries worked toward *undervaluation* of the peso – basically because of the appreciation of the *real*, which rose by more than 30 percent against the dollar in 1993–98. Indeed, this was sufficient to offset almost exactly the effects of diverging fundamentals and the initial stages of the overvaluation of the dollar (after 1995), that pushed toward overvaluation of the peso.

After 1998, however, trade asymmetries started working in the opposite direction. The devaluation of the *real* and the euro added to the increasing overvaluation of the dollar and the continuing divergence in fundamentals – itself reflective of Argentina's wide current account imbalances and declining growth in those years. Thus both the wrong choice of peg and inconsistent fundamentals lay behind the mounting overvaluation of the peso in the final years of Convertibility – although to different extents. The appreciating U.S. dollar and the depreciating Brazilian *real* accounted directly for over two-thirds of the overvaluation: 23 of the 34 percentage points of overvaluation that occurred between 1998 and 2001. The remaining 11 percentage points can be attributed to the divergence in fundamentals between Argentina and the United States, itself a reflection of the external imbalances that Argentina incurred throughout the decade under the pressure of persistent public deficits.[22]

---

[22] It is important to note that these calculations may understate the true contribution of the dollar overvaluation and the depreciation of the *real* to the misalignment of the peso. To the extent that the overvaluation due to these two factors widened Argentina's current account deficits over time,

Adjustment under the Hard Peg

Real misalignments occur under both fixed and flexible exchange rate regimes. But large and persistent overvaluations are much less frequent under floating regimes than under fixed regimes (Goldfajn and Valdes 1999). The reason is that under a floating regime, an overvaluation can be eliminated quickly through a nominal devaluation. By contrast, in a pegged regime the real exchange rate adjustment must occur through changes in the domestic price level relative to the price level of trading partners. If trading partner inflation is low, domestic prices need to fall in *absolute* terms. Since downward flexibility of nominal prices and wages is usually limited, this in turn requires a recession, making the adjustment process slow and costly in terms of output and employment. Under appropriate conditions – such as a big overvaluation and a high degree of price rigidity – the magnitude of these costs can be so large as to force the abandonment of the peg.

Indeed, the international evidence from a sample of 93 countries from 1960 to 1994 analyzed by Iian Goldfajn and Rodrigo Valdes (1999) shows that once a currency appreciates significantly, a smooth return to equilibrium becomes highly unlikely. In their sample, 85 percent of the cases in which currencies reached an overvaluation of 25 percent or more ended abruptly with a collapse of the nominal exchange rate.

These empirical results are consistent with Argentina's experience. Under the hard peg, real exchange rate adjustment was hampered by the rigidity of nominal wages and key prices.[23] Domestic prices did fall in absolute terms, but by a very modest magnitude – a total around 3 percent between 1998 and 2001 – which was insufficient to have any significant effect on the misalignment of the REER. Arguably, Argentina's fragile institutional framework would have made a faster deflation politically very difficult. It would have required an even deeper recession and higher unemployment than actually witnessed in 1999–2001, which would have put the country's social and political institutions under severe stress.

THE DESTABILIZING POWER OF PRO-CYCLICAL FISCAL POLICY

Fiscal Trends

As already noted, lack of fiscal discipline has been singled out by many observers as the primary cause of the Argentine crisis.[24] Both the federal and provincial governments ran persistent deficits throughout the decade, and the overall balance of the consolidated government deteriorated steadily after 1994, and especially after 1998 (Figure 10.12).[25] The widening public deficit was the driving force behind

---

and hence led to declining net foreign assets and a falling equilibrium REER, such factors would be indirectly responsible for additional peso overvaluation. This suggests that the role of the "wrong peg" component in the overvaluation of the peso is even larger than shown in the figures.

[23] For example, utility prices were contractually set in dollars and indexed to U.S. inflation.

[24] See in particular Mussa (2002) and Teijeiro (2001).

[25] The contribution to the public imbalance of the 1994 Social Security reform has attracted some controversy (Hausmann and Velasco 2002; Teijeiro 2001). The reform added about 1 percent of GDP to the measured public sector deficit between 1994 and 2000–2001. See Perry and Servén (2003) for a discussion of this point.

454   *Luis Servén and Guillermo Perry*

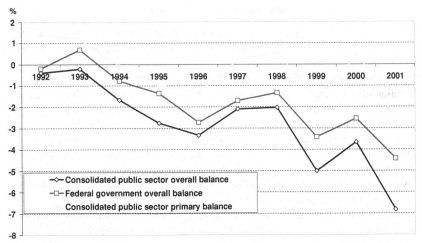

Figure 10.12. Fiscal Balance Excluding Privatization Revenues, 1992–2001 (percent of GDP). *Source*: Ministerio de Economía de la República Argentina and World Bank.

the large current account deficits of the 1990s, which led to the steady erosion of Argentina's foreign asset position and – as argued in the previous section – to a depreciating equilibrium real exchange rate.

Public debt indicators also rose, from some 25 percent of GDP in 1992 to over 60 percent in 2001 (Figure 10.13). Despite the significant privatization proceeds collected over the 1990s, the increase in public debt outpaced the cumulative fiscal deficit, because of the recognition of a variety of hidden liabilities at various times during the decade (Teijeiro 2001).

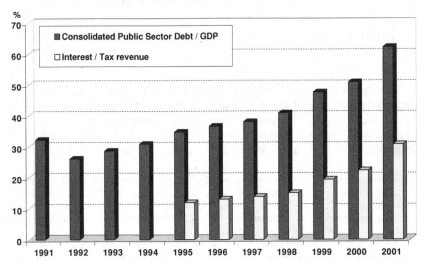

Figure 10.13. Consolidated Public Debt and Service, 1991–2001 (percent). *Source*: International Monetary Fund.

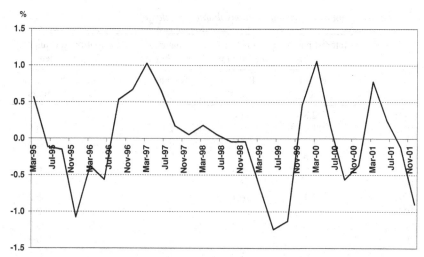

Figure 10.14. Blanchard's Indicator of Fiscal Impulse, Mid-1995 to Late 2001 (percent of GDP). *Source*: Ministerio de Economía de la República Argentina.

However, the trajectory of Argentina's fiscal balance was also affected by developments beyond direct control of the authorities. In particular, the sharp fiscal deterioration in the final years of the decade is partly the result of the decline in growth, and thus in tax collection, as well as rising interest rates and debt service.[26]

The sign of fiscal policy can be better gauged with the help of Figure 10.14, which shows a measure of the cyclically adjusted change in the fiscal stance of the federal government (unfortunately, the data do not allow a similar calculation for the provinces). The figure is based on a comparison of the actual primary balance with the one that would have happened if the "economic environment" (as described by unemployment and trend output) had been the same as in the previous year. The details of the calculation are given in the Technical Appendix, section viii.[27] The figure describes the fiscal impulse: that is, the change in the adjusted fiscal stance, with a positive value denoting an expansion and a negative one a contraction. The figure shows a major expansionary change in fiscal policy during the boom years from mid–1996 to late 1998, a then a reversal, and brief interruptions at the end of 1999 (in the run up to the presidential election) and 2001. Thus, the misguided fiscal expansion in the midst of the boom left no alternative but a contraction in the downturn, which added to the recession and severely damage growth expectations and investors' confidence.

Apart from the recession, the rise in interest rates on public debt also added to the fiscal problems in the late 1990s. Implicit interest rates on public debt were on the

---

[26] This is underscored by Hausmann and Velasco (2002).
[27] Unlike conventional cyclical corrections, this measure (based on Blanchard 1993) avoids taking a stand on the nature of business fluctuations or on trend-cycle decomposition techniques. However, other cyclical corrections yield similar qualitative results; see Perry and Servén (2003).

Table 10.1. *Interest payments on consolidated public debt, Argentina, 1991–2001*

	Interest payment on debt	Implicit interest rate	Change interest burden	Contribution to change in interest burden	
	Percent GDP	Percent GDP	Percent GDP	Debt volume effect	Interest rate effect
1991	2.8	8.6			
1992	1.6	6.2	−1.1	−0.4	−0.8
1993	1.4	5.0	−0.2	0.1	−0.3
1994	1.6	5.1	0.1	0.1	0.0
1995	1.9	5.4	0.3	0.2	0.1
1996	2.1	5.6	0.2	0.1	0.1
1997	2.3	6.1	0.3	0.1	0.2
1998	2.6	6.4	0.3	0.2	0.1
1999	3.4	7.2	0.8	0.5	0.3
2000	4.1	8.0	0.7	0.3	0.4
2001	5.4	8.0	1.3	1.0	0.3
Total Changes					
1991–2001	–	–	2.6	2.2	0.5
1993–2001	–	–	3.9	2.4	1.5

Source: Ministerio de Economia de la Republica Argentina and International Monetary Fund.

rise, especially after the Russian crisis, reflecting investors' perceptions of increased riskiness. Interest payments rose from around 2 percent of GDP in 1995–96 to 4.1 percent in 2000 and 5.4 percent in 2001. But as Table 10.1 shows, the rise in interest rates accounted for less than half the increase in the interest bill between 1995 and 2001. The rest was due to the steady growth in the stock of outstanding debt.

The Arithmetic of Solvency

While Argentina's public debt ratios had been rising steadily, at the end of the decade they did not look worse than in other emerging markets. Yet the rise in interest rates, and especially the decline in growth, increasingly threatened solvency. Moreover, the anticipation of a protracted deflationary adjustment under the hard peg likely had a major adverse effect on perceptions of debt sustainability – making further fiscal adjustment more difficult and painful, as the ratio of revenues to GDP collapsed – and lowering expectations of future growth and hence of the government's repayment capacity.

To illustrate the point, Table 10.2 reports conventional solvency calculations based on growth expectations formed using the information available in each year (see Technical Appendix, section viii, for details). Assuming that markets assessed long-term growth potential based on a (3- or 5-year) moving average of past growth, the simulations indicate that by the year 2000, and certainly by 2001, debt sustainability was clearly open to question. The third and fourth columns in the table show that the primary balance of the consolidated government required for solvency

Table 10.2. Indicators of fiscal sustainability, Argentina, 1991–2001

	Consolidated gov. primary balance	At the observed RER			At the equilibrium RER	
		Debt output ratio	Sustainable balance		Debt output ratio adjusted for RER misalignment	Sustainable balance adjusted for RER misalignment
	Percent of GDP	Percent	3-year[a] Percent of GDP	5-year[b] Percent of GDP	Percent	3-year[c] Percent of GDP
1991	−0.4	32.3	2.7	2.8	31.9	2.37
1992	1.4	26.1	0.1	1.4	26.8	0.15
1993	1.2	28.7	n.s.p.	0.5	29.1	n.s.p.
1994	−0.1	30.9	n.s.p.	n.s.p.	30.9	n.s.p.
1995	−1.0	34.8	0.8	0.1	32.5	0.83
1996	−1.3	36.6	0.9	0.4	34.0	0.88
1997	0.2	38.1	0.9	0.6	37.2	0.83
1998	0.6	40.9	0.2	0.9	42.3	0.21
1999	−1.6	47.6	1.7	2.0	58.6	1.77
2000	0.3	50.9	3.9	2.5	66.2	4.74
2001	−1.4	62.2	6.0	4.0	90.2	7.84

Note: n.s.p. means no sustainability problem.

[a] 3-year moving average (growth rate based on last 3 observations).
[b] 5-year moving average (growth rate based on last 5 observations).
[c] 3-year moving average (growth rate based on last 3 observations).

Source: Estimates based on International Monetary Fund, Ministerio de Economía de la República Argentina data; and Alberola, López, and Servén (2004).

457

approached or even exceeded 4 percent of GDP – a figure that looked unlikely given Argentine fiscal record and institutions.

But in reality the situation was even worse. The overvaluation implied that measures of sustainability based on the observed ratio of public debt to GDP – valued at the *observed* real exchange rate – understated by a considerable margin the public sector's difficulties. Most public debt was denominated in dollars, while government assets (in particular its capacity to tax) were not. Thus a real depreciation restoring real exchange rate equilibrium would have raised public debt ratios by a large amount – up to 20 to 30 percentage points of GDP in 2000–01, as shown in the fifth column of Table 10.2 (which shows debt ratios adjusted for the RER misalignment depicted in Figure 10.10). This would have occurred irrespective of whether the real depreciation was achieved under Convertibility through nominal deflation or through a nominal devaluation and thus a collapse of the peg.[28] In either case, the real depreciation would have eventually revealed the reduced capacity of the government to pay back its debt. The sixth column of Table 10.2 shows that once this is factored into the analysis, by 2001 government solvency would have required an *additional* primary surplus of about 2 percent of GDP annually.[29]

In this manner, the peg played a subtle destabilizing role. It hid from public view the increasing precariousness of the fiscal situation, and thus made it more difficult to elicit political support for an adjustment while there was still time for an orderly correction.

FINANCIAL FRAGILITY

Convertibility allowed a clean break with Argentina's past of acute monetary instability, which had wiped out confidence in the peso and domestic financial intermediation. The hard peg quickly restored the function of local currency as a store of value and enabled a rapid regeneration of financial intermediation, as reflected by the rapid rise in loan and deposit ratios to GDP over the 1990s (Figure 10.15).

The authorities undertook ambitious prudential and regulatory reforms to build a resilient financial sector based mostly on dollar-denominated deposits and loans. Absent a lender of last resort (which was ruled out by the currency board), large prudential liquidity buffers were built into the system, sufficient to withstand sizeable liquidity and solvency shocks – including a flight of more than one-third of the system's deposits, as well as a sudden and complete default in up to 10 percent of the loan portfolio – without endangering Convertibility.

By the late 1990s, Argentina's banking system appeared to be in a very solid position, and the quality of its regulatory environment was widely praised. However, the exchange rate guarantee under Convertibility had encouraged large mismatches in asset holders' balance sheets. Debtors without dollar-related incomes had large dollar denominated liabilities, issued mostly to the banking system. Figures 10.16–10.18, taken from De la Torre, Levy-Yeyati, and Schmukler (2003), illustrate the

---

[28] This is underscored by Roubini (2001).
[29] This calculation only takes into account the government's explicit liabilities. The real depreciation would have also brought into insolvency many households and firms in the nontraded-goods sector. This would have had a major adverse impact on banks' portfolios, raising potentially huge fiscal contingencies. This issue is examined below.

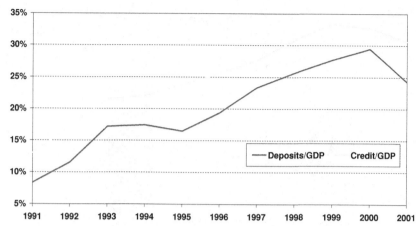

Figure 10.15. Financial Deepening, 1991–2001. *Note*: Credit includes loans to private sector, loans to public sector, loans to residents abroad, and private and public securities held by the financial system. Deposits include demand deposits, savings deposits, time deposits, and other deposits, by private sector, public sector, and residents abroad. Figures correspond to end-of-year values. *Source*: Banco Central de la República Argentina and World Bank.

steady increase in financial dollarization. By the late 1990s, 70 percent or more of firms' outstanding debt was dollar denominated, and the degree of dollarization was particularly high for firms in the nontraded sector. Nearly 80 percent of outstanding mortgage credit was dollar denominated as well. Time and saving deposits showed also a high (and increasing) degree of dollarization.

These large mismatches in the balance sheets of banks' debtors – dollar debts of households and nontraded-sector firms – meant that a breakdown of the rule of

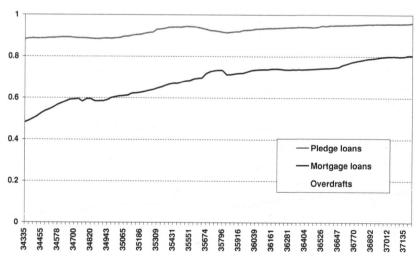

Figure 10.16. Private Sector Dollarization by Type of Credit, 1994–Mid-2001 (credit in U.S. dollars over total credit). *Source*: De la Torre, Levy-Yeyati, and Schmukler (2003).

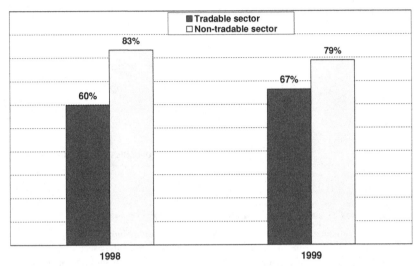

Figure 10.17. Firm's Balance Sheet Dollarization, 1998–1999 (average share of U.S. dollar debt across firms). *Source*: De la Torre, Levy-Yeyati, and Schmukler (2003).

one-peso–one-dollar would have rendered many debtors insolvent and thus wrecked the banking system. While this was obvious to all observers, the authorities could not signal the possibility of a nominal devaluation through prudential norms without undermining their own quest to raise the credibility of Convertibility above all doubts.

In hindsight, however, the failure of the prudential framework to recognize the risks posed by a real depreciation was a major weakness that made the seemingly strong banking system highly fragile, regardless of whether Convertibility was

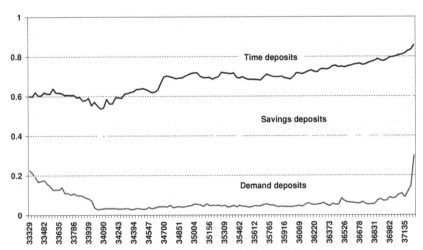

Figure 10.18. Dollarization by Type of Deposit, 1991–2001 (dollar deposit over total deposits). *Source*: De la Torre, Levy-Yeyati, and Schmukler (2003).

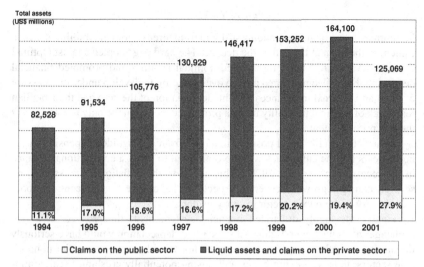

Figure 10.19. Financial System: Exposure to Public Sector, 1994–2001. *Source*: Banco Central de la República Argentina.

maintained. The reason lies in the credit risk raised by a large overvaluation of the real exchange rate, such as Argentina's around 2000–01. Even if the adjustment of the real exchange rate toward its equilibrium value had been achieved through nominal deflation under Convertibility, the protracted and painful recession that would have been required would have seriously hampered the repayment capacity of those debtors whose earnings came from the nontradable sector.

Hence, the prudential shortcoming was the failure to recognize the special risk posed by loans to debtors in the nontradable sector – a credit risk that would materialize in the event of significant adverse shocks that led to a deflationary adjustment. It would have been advisable for the authorities to require tougher loan classification criteria (higher loan–loss provisions or a higher weight for the purposes of measuring capital requirements, or both) in the case of loans to the nontradable sector, regardless of whether the loans were peso-denominated or dollar-denominated.

In the final years of Convertibility, a second vulnerability developed. As the government ran into growing difficulties in financing its deficit through market borrowing, it resorted increasingly to placing its debt with the financial system. Thus instead of accepting the need for an orderly debt reduction, the authorities opted for draining the liquidity of banks and pension funds. As a result, total banking system claims on the government rose from under 18 percent of total assets in 1998 to over 26 percent in mid-2001 (Figure 10.19). In this way, the solvency of the banking system became tightly linked to that of the government: a large public debt write-down was almost assured to bring down the banks because of their large exposure to government risk. This was in effect the reverse of what had been expected from Convertibility: namely, that it would help insulate the stability of the banking system from the vagaries of the fiscal process, including an event of government debt default.

POLICY LESSONS

In summary, the Argentine economy suffered from three major vulnerabilities, which came into the open at the end of the decade. The hard peg adopted against Optimal Currency Area (OCA) criteria allowed nominal stability and promoted financial deepening, but it also permitted a large overvaluation to develop under the pressure of fiscal and external imbalances and the depreciation of the euro and the Brazilian real. Lack of nominal flexibility made a protracted recession the only way to correct the real misalignment.

In turn, the fragile fiscal position inherited from a misguided expansion in the boom years left the authorities with no option but to adopt a contractionary stance in the recession of the late 1990s. This added to the deflationary pressures and severely damaged growth recovery prospects and hence investors' perceptions about the capacity of the public sector to repay its debt.

Finally, the highly dollarized financial system made the prospect of a real exchange rate adjustment highly risky, as a real depreciation would have seriously threatened the debt repayment capacity of households and firms in the nontradable sectors, thus weakening banks and raising potentially crushing fiscal contingencies.

These vulnerabilities were mutually reinforcing in such a way that left the authorities with very little room for maneuver. The real depreciation was assured to hit public finances hard, as most of the government debt was denominated in dollars while public revenues were not. Banks' high exposure to government risk made the option of debt restructuring potentially costly in terms of their financial health. As time went on without decisive action on the part of the authorities, their options continued to narrow. The peg itself helped postpone decisions, as it hid from public view the impending solvency problems of public and private debtors. As the peso became increasingly overvalued, nontraded-sector debtors and the government (and thus banks) edged closer to insolvency at the *equilibrium* real exchange rate, while their debts still appeared manageable at the *observed* real exchange rate.

Missed Opportunities in the Boom

In hindsight, it is clear that the authorities repeatedly missed the opportunity to mitigate Argentina's vulnerability by acting decisively in the boom years up to 1998. At that point, a choice should have been made between staying with the hard peg and exiting it. Either option would have required deep reforms.

Staying with the hard peg, or hardening it further through dollarization, while minimizing the risks associated with adverse shocks, would have required three supporting ingredients. First and foremost would have been significant fiscal strengthening – not only to protect solvency, but with the broader objective of providing some room for countercyclical fiscal policy. This meant achieving fiscal surpluses in the boom years, instead of the expansionary stance that was actually followed. The second ingredient would have been considerable flexibilization of labor and other domestic markets (including utility prices). Third, even stricter prudential regulation of banks would have been required than was actually adopted (in spite of the significant progress achieved in this field). This would have included harder provisioning and/or capital requirements for loans to households and firms in nontradable sectors, and suitable regulations to limit banks' exposure to government risk.

Alternatively, an orderly exit from the peg toward a successful flexible exchange rate regime with a monetary anchor (such as an inflation target) would have also required significant structural reforms and institution building. Fiscal strengthening would have been a basic ingredient to help build up credibility in monetary institutions, and market flexibilization would have been required as well to remove any inflationary biases in the price and wage setting system. Moreover, regulatory steps would have been needed to encourage gradual dedollarization and reduce the cost of exchange rate changes in the presence of portfolio mismatches.

But the opportunity to act was missed. Instead the boom was a period of inaction and laxity on many fronts. There are good political-economy reasons why radical reform rarely occurs in good times. Thus in accordance with Latin American tradition, the seeds of the crisis were planted in the boom years by imprudent behavior and lack of precautionary action. The consequences were revealed only when bad times arrived.

Tough Choices in the Downswing

In contrast, in 1999 and later the authorities faced much harder choices in a context of recession, mounting overvaluation, and increasing difficulties to finance the large fiscal deficit. Keeping the hard peg would have required a protracted deflationary adjustment to bring the real exchange rate back to equilibrium.[30] This would have added to the growth decline and reduced further the repayment capacity of private debtors, especially those in the nontradable sectors, and the government. A harsh fiscal adjustment would have had to be imposed to restore solvency, adding further to the recession and the deterioration of debtors' solvency, as well as that of their banks. Furthermore, the output and employment cost of such process would have put Argentina's institutions under major stress.

A second alternative was to accept the need for a protracted deflationary adjustment and adopt full dollarization. This might have been the option with lower short-term costs. It would have eliminated currency risk and – under unchanged perceptions of default risk – achieved some reduction in interest rates. This would have somewhat limited the duration of the recession and alleviated the required fiscal adjustment. Eventually, however, debtors would still have had to cope with the adverse impact of the deflation on their repayment capacity.

Under either of these options, prospects for success were uncertain, as the large costs of the impending deflation could have become socially and politically intolerable. Furthermore, Argentina would have remained vulnerable to similar episodes in the future, and to prevent this the authorities would have had to tackle the above-mentioned reform agenda that they had failed to implement in the good years.

A third alternative was a large nominal devaluation to speed up the adjustment and shortcut the painful deflationary adjustment. This, however, would have induced immediate bankruptcy in a large number of households and firms in the nontradable

---

[30] Unless, of course, the external environment had unexpectedly taken a turn for the better, with a significant real depreciation of the U.S. dollar against the euro and/or the Brazilian *real*.

sector with dollar-denominated debts, probably leading to a banking crisis. More-over, the ratio of public debt to GDP would have ballooned, likely forcing the gov-ernment to seek a rescheduling. Admittedly, all this would have happened grad-ually anyhow under the hard peg, but the abruptness of the balance sheet effects might have precipitated an even larger wave of bankruptcies than in the alternative scenario – and, as a consequence, triggered the insolvency of the banking system and a deposit run.

The last alternative was to decree a *pesification* of all domestic contracts before devaluing. This would have contained the adverse balance sheet effects of the deval-uation, helping protect the financial sector. But forcefully breaking dollar deposit contracts would in all probability have led to a major bank run and forced a deposit freeze in order to protect the payments system.[31]

Faced with these difficult dilemmas, the authorities did not use their limited margin of maneuver well. They postponed the needed public debt restructuring too long and sent mixed signals on the ultimate choice of exchange rate regime – thus further undermining the already deteriorating confidence. In the end, the author-ities were forced out of the peg in the midst of a major financial and payments crisis. This was compounded by an arbitrary asymmetric *pesification* of assets and liabilities, which involved a widespread violation of property rights and led to a highly disruptive deposit freeze (the *corralito*). Such chaotic exit from Convertibil-ity entailed huge economic and political disruption. High exit costs were supposed to be the main advantage of the hard peg. They proved to be very high indeed.

Four Lessons

The Argentine crisis carries valuable lessons for other emerging markets. Four will be highlighted here. The first is that the hard realities of OCA criteria cannot be ignored in the choice of currency regime. The dollar peg might have seemed a logical choice given the deep distrust of the local currency by Argentine asset holders, but it was ill-suited to the country's productive and trade structure. This conflict, combined with the above-mentioned nominal rigidities, was instrumental in the overvaluation of the peso in the late 1990s, which proved impossible to resolve within the straitjacket of Convertibility.

Second, procyclical fiscal policy can be disastrous. Following the Latin Amer-ican tradition, Argentina's mismanagement of the boom was the root of the col-lapse. Instead of taking advantage of the good times to build a solid fiscal position, the misguided expansion forced a self-destructive contraction in the recession. For Argentina and other emerging markets, this failure underscores the critical need to

[31] One variant of this exit option would have imposed *pesification at the margin* after full dollarization. In other words, the one-peso, one-dollar parity would have been respected for all *existing* financial contracts, but the authorities would have started issuing a new domestic currency. Its exchange rate to the dollar would have been left to float, and the government would have used it to make payments to private agents (instead of the disorderly emergence of provincial quasimonies that actually took place). On paper at least, this might have been the best exit option at the time the crisis erupted. But forging the necessary consensus and implementing it smoothly – in particular, allaying fears that the *pesification* could eventually extend to existing contracts – would have been no easy matter under the circumstances. See De la Torre, Levy-Yeyati, and Schmukler (2003).

develop an institutional framework with strong incentives for the achievement of surpluses in good times that create room for maneuver in bad times.

Third, even with an apparently strong banking system, a real exchange rate adjustment can degenerate into a major financial crisis. In the Argentine case, this became clear enough with the collapse of the peg. But even if the overvaluation of the peso could have been undone through nominal deflation and recession, the solvency of many nontraded-sector borrowers (and thus banks, as well) would have been threatened by old-fashioned debt deflation. This means that prudential regulation must explicitly face the risks posed by loans to those borrowers.

The fourth lesson is perhaps the broadest and, like the first, is about exchange rate regimes. A hard peg is not a shortcut to credibility and macroeconomic stability. Convertibility offered a seemingly quick escape from decades of monetary misman-agement – quicker, it was hoped, than a gradual rebuilding of confidence in the peso. However, it was not accompanied by the development of a supportive institutional framework upholding a sound policy regime – which should have included strong fiscal institutions, labor market reform, and nominal price flexibility. The Argentine experience shows that the naïve presumption that a hard peg would somehow result in fiscal orthodoxy, flexible prices, and crash-proof banks was clearly unfounded. Ultimately, hard pegs are no substitute for institution building. Indeed, their institu-tional requirements may be as stringent as, or even more stringent than, those posed by credible floats.

APPENDIX A. MEASURING TERMS OF TRADE SHOCKS

Terms of trade changes fail to capture the economic impact of changing import and export prices because they do not take into account the degree of openness of the economy. To remedy this, the terms of trade *shocks* reported in Figure 10.2 are based on the following calculation:

$$
ToT\ Shock_t
$$

$$
= 100^* \left\{ \frac{\left[(Px_t - Px_{t-1})^* \left(\frac{X_t + X_{t-1}}{2} \right) \right] - \left[(Pm_t - Pm_{t-1})^* \left(\frac{M_t + M_{t-1}}{2} \right) \right]}{GDP_t} \right\},
$$

where

GDP = GDP (current US$)
X = Exports of goods and services (current US$)
M = Imports of goods and services (current US$)
Px = Export price
Pm = Import price

APPENDIX B. BILATERAL AND MULTILATERAL REAL EXCHANGE RATES

The decomposition in Figure 10.8 is constructed as follows. Let q_i denote the (log) real effective exchange rate of country i, defined so that an increase represents an appreciation. It can be expressed as a weighted sum of its bilateral real exchange rates vis-à-vis trading partners:

$$q_i = \sum_{j \neq i} \alpha_{ij}(p_i - e_{ij} - p_j), \quad \text{where} \sum_{j \neq i} \alpha_{ij} = 1; \quad j = 1, \ldots, N.$$

Here e_{ij} denotes the (log) nominal exchange rate, expressed as number of units of currency i per unit of currency j, and the p_j are the (log) price levels. Let $\rho_{ij} \equiv (p_i - e_{ij} - p_j)$ denote the bilateral RER between i and j. Note that an increase in ρ_{ij} is a real appreciation of the exchange rate of i. Take the N-th currency (for example, the U.S. dollar) as the numeraire. This implies $e_{NN} = \rho_{NN} = 0$. Observe that $e_{iN} - e_{ij} = e_{jN}$; hence $\rho_{ij} = \rho_{iN} - \rho_{jN}$. Then the REER of currency i can be rewritten:

$$q_i = \rho_{iN} - \sum_{j \neq i} \alpha_{ij}\rho_{jN}$$

or, in terms of rates of change,

$$\Delta q_i = \Delta\rho_{iN} - \sum_{j \neq i} \alpha_{ij}\Delta\rho_{jN}.$$

Thus, the change in country i's real effective exchange rate equals the change in the bilateral rate vis-à-vis the numeraire minus a weighted sum of the changes in the bilateral real exchange rates of its trading partners vis-à-vis the numeraire currency. Hence, a depreciation (appreciation) of the currencies of trading partners against the numeraire leads ceteris paribus to an appreciation (depreciation) of the REER. This is the decomposition used in the figure.

APPENDIX C. THE EQUILIBRIUM REER MODEL

The model employed to assess the equilibrium exchange rate is described in detail in Alberola, López, and Servén (2004). A brief summary is as follows: Consider two economies, each producing two goods: one tradable (denoted by the subscript T in what follows) and one nontradable (N). The (log) real exchange rate (q) is defined as the relative price of two consumption baskets at home and abroad:

$$q = p - (e + p^*), \tag{C.1}$$

where e is the (log) nominal exchange rate, defined as the price of foreign currency in terms of domestic currency, and p and p^* are the (log) domestic and foreign price indices respectively. Throughout, asterisks denote foreign variables. An increase in q represents an appreciation of the real exchange rate. Each country's consumer price index (CPI) is a weighted-average of exportable, nontradable, and importable prices, all expressed in the currency of the respective country:

$$p = (1 - \alpha_N - \alpha_T)p_T + \alpha_N p_N + \alpha_T(e + p_T^*) \tag{C.2}$$
$$p^* = (1 - \alpha_N^* - \alpha_T^*)p_T^* + \alpha_N^* p_N^* + \alpha_T^*(p_T^{-e}),$$

where the αs are the weights of the respective goods in the consumer basket. Substituting these expressions in equation C.1, assuming that $\alpha_N = \alpha_N^*$, and rearranging terms yields

$$q = (1 - \alpha_T - \alpha_T^*)q_X + \alpha_N q_I, \qquad (C.3)$$

where $q_X = p_T - (e + p_T^*)$ is the relative price of domestic tradables in terms of foreign tradables, and $q_I = (p_N - p_T) - (p_N^* - p_T^*)$ is the price of nontradables relative to tradables across countries. Here q_X captures the competitiveness of the economy, which will be related below to the evolution of the foreign asset position. Since sustainable capital flows eventually lead to the desired stocks of assets and liabilities across countries, the equilibrium level of q_X is associated with the external equilibrium of the economy. On the other hand, the cross-country differential in relative tradable-nontradable prices q_I is related to productivity differentials. Since these prices determine the allocation of resources across sectors in a given country, the equilibrium level of q_I can be associated to the internal equilibrium of the economy.

The equilibrium exchange rate is attained when both q_X and q_I are at their equilibrium values, and thus follows from internal and external equilibrium:

$$\bar{q} = (1 - \alpha_T - \alpha_T^*)\bar{q}_X + \alpha_N \bar{q}_I \qquad (C.4)$$

with the bars denoting equilibrium values. Next, consider the internal and external equilibrium of the economy.

The internal equilibrium refers to the allocation of resources across sectors, which can be shown to depend on the evolution of their relative productivity. Letting n denote the difference between relative tradable/nontradable productivity at home and abroad, the internal equilibrium exchange rate is:

$$\bar{q}_I = \bar{n}, \qquad (C.5)$$

In turn, external equilibrium is defined by the attainment of investors' desired foreign asset stock, in the spirit of portfolio models of real exchange-rate determination (Mussa 1984). Over time, the accumulation of net foreign assets relative to GDP (f) is given by the current account balance ratio (ca), which equals the trade balance (xn) plus the income that residents receive (or pay) on f, adjusted for the economy's growth rate:

$$\Delta f = ca = xn + (i^* - g)f, \qquad (C.6)$$

where i^* is the international interest rate, assumed given. Assume that the trade balance improves with a real depreciation: that is, $xn = -\gamma q_x$, where $\gamma > 0$. In turn, the capital account deficit reflects the rate of accumulation of net foreign assets by the home country. This is assumed to depend on the divergence between the current net foreign asset ratio and its desired equilibrium level ($\bar{f}$) – itself determined by exogenous factors such as saving preferences and demographics not modelled here:

$$\Delta f = a(\bar{f} - f) \quad a > 0. \qquad (C.7)$$

Combining these expressions and defining the equilibrium external real exchange rate $\overline{q}_X$ as that consistent with $f = \overline{f}$ (that is, consistent with asset holdings at their equilibrium level) it follows that

$$\overline{q}_X = [(i^* - g)/\gamma]\overline{f}. \qquad (C.8)$$

The equilibrium exchange rate obtains when both internal and external equilibrium hold:

$$\overline{q} = [(1 - \alpha_T - \alpha_T^*)(i^* - g)/\gamma]\overline{f} + \alpha_N \overline{n}. \qquad (C.9)$$

In principle, both $(1 - \alpha_T - \alpha_T^*)(i^* - g)/\gamma$ and α_N should be positive. Indeed, empirical implementations of this framework confirm this assertion. Thus, the equilibrium real exchange rate appreciates in response to a higher long-run asset stock and/or a higher relative productivity differential.

The equilibrium real exchange rate can be estimated empirically using data on foreign assets and relative productivity. However, the estimation has to deal with the fact that the *equilibrium* values of foreign assets and productivity are not directly observable (see Alberola, López, and Servén 2004). Real misalignment is given by the difference between the observed and the equilibrium real exchange rates.

APPENDIX D. THE COMPONENTS OF REAL MISALIGNMENT

The decomposition in Figure 10.11 is based on the following identity, taken from Alberola, López, and Servén (2004):

$$\hat{q}_A = \underbrace{(\overline{q}_\$ - \overline{q}_A)}_{\substack{\text{diverging} \\ \text{fundamentals}}} + \underbrace{(q_A - q_\$)}_{\text{inadequate peg}} + \hat{q}_\$,$$

where the subscripts A and $\$$ denote the Argentine peso and the U.S. dollar, respectively, and a hat over a variable is used to denote its deviation from the equilibrium value.

This is a decomposition of peso misalignment into three terms. The first one captures the divergence between the equilibrium REERs of the dollar and the peso. In the context of Argentina's peg to the dollar, a nonzero value for this term implies a long-term divergence between the fundamentals of the anchor and client countries. To the extent that in the model above the fundamental determinants of the real exchange rate – the foreign asset position and relative productivity growth – can be affected by macroeconomic policies and structural reforms, this component of peso misalignment can be associated with persistent policy divergences between Argentina and the United States, which in the long run are inconsistent with Argentina's dollar peg.

The other two terms in the right-hand side of the equation capture the peso misalignment occurring even in the absence of policies inconsistent with the peg. Thus such misalignment may be viewed as reflecting the inadequacy of the peg itself. It combines two items. One is the divergence between the actual REERs of the peso and the U.S. dollar. Since, as shown earlier, the REER can be expressed as a weighted sum of the bilateral real exchange rates of trading partners (where the weights are their respective trade shares), this term basically arises from differences between the trade structures of the United States and Argentina.

In practice, the key difference in their trade structures concerns Brazil, which is a major trading partner for Argentina but not for the United States.[32] Hence, the time path of $(q_A - q_\$)$ is dominated by the real exchange rate of the Brazilian real. The rest of the misalignment attributable to inadequacy of the peg is just the misalignment of the REER of the U.S. dollar, which the peso inherits through the peg. The logic of this term is quite simple: absent policy divergences and asymmetries in trade structure (already captured by the first two terms in the right-hand side of the above expression), pegging to a misaligned anchor currency necessarily leads to misalignment.

REFERENCES

Alberola Enrique, Humberto López, and Luis Servén. 2004. "Tango with the Gringo: The Hard Peg and Real Misalignment in Argentina." Policy Research Working Paper Series 3322. The World Bank, Washington, DC.

Alesina, Alberto, Robert Barro, and Silvana Tenreyro. 2002. "Optimal Currency Areas." Discussion Paper 1958. Harvard University, Institute of Economic Research, Cambridge, MA.

Balassa, Bela. 1964. "The Purchasing Power Parity Doctrine: A Reappraisal." *Journal of Political Economy* 72(6):584–96.

Blanchard, Olivier. 1993. "Suggestions for a New Set of Fiscal Indicators." In H. A. A. Verbon and F. A. A. M. Van Vinden, eds., *The Political Economy of Government Debt*. Amsterdam: North Holland.

Calvo, Gilberto, Alejandro Izquierdo, and Ernesto Talvi. 2003. "Sudden Stops, the Real Exchange Rate and Fiscal Sustainability: Argentina's Lessons." NBER Working Paper 9828.

Cline, William. 2003. "Restoring Economic Growth in Argentina." Policy Research Working Paper Series 3158. The World Bank, Washington, DC.

Corden, W. Max. 2002. *Too Sensational: On the Choice of Exchange Rate Regimes*. Cambridge, MA: MIT Press.

De la Torre, Augusto, Eduardo Levy-Yeyati, and Sergio L. Schmukler. 2003. "Living and Dying with Hard Pegs: The Rise and Fall of Argentina's Currency Board." Policy Research Working Paper Series 2980. The World Bank, Washington, DC.

Fiess, Norbert. 2003. "Capital Flows, Country Risk and Contagion." Policy Research Working Paper Series 2943. The World Bank, Washington, DC.

Gay, Alejandro, and Santiago Pellegrini. 2003. "The Equilibrium Real Exchange Rate of Argentina." Manuscript. Instituto de Economéa, Universidad de la Republica, Uruguay.

Goldfajn, Iian, and Rodrigo Valdés. 1999. "The Aftermath of Appreciations." *Quarterly Journal of Economics* 114(1):229–62.

Hausmann Ricardo, and Andrés Velasco. 2002. "The Argentine Collapse: Hard Money's Soft Underbelly." Harvard University, Kennedy School of Government, Cambridge, MA.

Mussa, Michael. 1984. "The Theory of Exchange Rate Determination." In *National Bureau of Economic Research Conference Report*. Chicago and London: University of Chicago Press.

———. 2002. *Argentina and the Fund: From Triumph to Tragedy*. Institute for International Economics, Washington, DC.

---

[32] Brazil accounts for 30 percent of Argentina's trade, but for only 2 percent of U.S. trade.

Perry, Guillermo, and Luis Servén. 2003. "Anatomy of a Multiple Crisis: Why Was Argentina Special and What Can We Learn from It?" In George M. Von Furstenberg, Volbert Alexander, and Jacques Melitz, eds., *Monetary Union and Hard Peg: Effects on Trade, Financial Development, and Stability*. New York: Oxford University Press.

Powell, Andrew. 2002. "Argentina's Avoidable Crisis: Band Luck, Bad Economist, Bad Politics, Bad Advice." Paper prepared for Brookings Trade Conference, May 2, Washington, DC.

Rodrik, Dani. 2002. "Argentina: A Case of Globalization Gone Too Far or not Far Enough." *New Republic*, January. http://ksghome.harvard.edu/ndrodrik/argentina%2g(tnr)%20final. doc, MA.

Roubini, Nouriel. 2001. "Should Argentina Dollarize or Float? The Pros and Cons of Alternative Exchange Rate Regimes and Their Implications for Domestic and Foreign Debt Restructuring/Reduction." Manuscript. New York University, Stern School of Business, NY.

Sachs, Jeffrey. 2002. "Understanding and Responding to Argentina's Economic Crisis." Manuscript. Harvard University, Center for International Development, Cambridge, MA.

Schmukler, Sergio, and Luis Servén. 2002. "Pricing Currency Risk under Currency Boards." *Journal of Development Economics* 69(2):367–91.

Stiglitz, Joseph. 2002. "Argentina, Short Changed: Why the Nation That Followed the Rules Fell to Preles." *Washington Post*, May 12, DC.

Teijeiro, Mario. 2001. "Una Vez Más, La Política Fiscal . . ." Manuscript. Centro de Estudios Públicos, Buenos Aires.

11. Default Episodes in the 1980s and 1990s: What Have We Learned?

Punam Chuhan and Federico Sturzenegger[1]

ABSTRACT: This chapter reviews the approaches to resolving sovereign defaults on external debt to private creditors in the 1980s and 1990s. Approaches to dealing with debt crises have changed quite radically during this period; the formal mechanisms of the 1980s that were designed to facilitate cooperation among debtors and creditors have given way to the more recent market-based debt workouts. The focus is on assessing the effectiveness of the various approaches to dealing with market inefficiencies, and offering some lessons for debt workout mechanisms for the future.

DEBT CRISES CAN BE COSTLY

External financing can help a country grow faster by financing productive investment and by minimizing the impact of shocks on economic activity. Excessive debt flows, however, can be a problem for emerging market countries. As debt burden rises, a country becomes more vulnerable to stoppages or reversals of such flows and to debt crises. Historical evidence from the 19th and 20th centuries suggests that cross-border lending to sovereigns has generally been characterized by cycles of boom and bust, and associated debt crises. Historically, foreign lending has been characterized by recurrent debt crises: in the 1820s, 1870s, 1890s, 1930s, and 1980s (Lindert and Morton 1989). These debt crisis episodes usually followed a wave of international lending, such as the British lending spurt of the 1850s and 1860s to finance railroads in Latin America, the wave of European financing to Argentina in the 1880s, the U.S.-led bond financing boom of the late 1920s, and the bank lending spurt of the 1970s that recycled petro-dollars from the first oil price shock of 1973 to developing countries. However, the severity of crises and the response of creditors and borrowers to the crises have varied.[2]

Not surprisingly, recent day debtor countries are encountering debt problems, just like their historical counterparts. What is surprising is that the frequency – and perhaps intensity – of these crises seems to have risen. Since the early 1980s, groups of emerging market economies have experienced many episodes of international

---

[1] World Bank and Business School, Universidad Torcuato Di Tella. The authors wish to thank Paul Beckerman, Craig Burnside, Thomas Laursen, and Brian Pinto for helpful comments, and Nevin Fahmy for insights and data on recent bond defaults.

[2] See also Eichengreen and Fishlow (1996).

capital market closure, as investors have been unwilling to roll over amounts coming due or to provide additional financing. Standard and Poor's survey of default episodes finds 84 events of sovereign default on private-source debt between 1975 and 2002 (Appendix A).[3] This contrasts with the experience of the 19th century, where debt difficulties were confined to relatively few countries. Indeed, Michael Bordo and Barry Eichengreen (1999) estimate that for a randomly selected country the probability of experiencing a crisis in a post-1973 year is twice as high as in a pre-1914 year. The largest incidence of defaults, however, occurred in the 1930s, following the lending boom of the 1920s.[4]

Debt crises can have potentially substantial costs to the economy in terms of large output losses, higher unemployment, and slippage on poverty alleviation. Using data from 1975 to 1997 for 24 emerging market economies, Michael Hutchinson and Ilan Neuberger (2002) find that currency and balance of payment crises on average reduce output in crisis countries by an estimated 5–8 percent over a two- to three-year period. Using cross-country data, Robert Barro (2001) finds that for a currency-cum-banking crisis real per capita GDP growth is lower than trend by an average of 2 percent a year over five years.[5] Federico Sturzenegger (2002a) obtains similar results when looking at the output costs of defaults in the 1980s. Controlling for other factors that may explain growth performance in the aftermath of a default, he estimates the average cumulative drop in output that can be associated with the default decision to be 4 percent over the four years immediately following a default. This number is larger with successive defaults or if defaults are responsible for either currency or banking crises.

These costs arise because of several factors. Important among these is the macroeconomic adjustment in response to the lower availability of financial resources, and therefore larger net transfers to creditors. Also important is the potential for default to severely disrupt the domestic financial system. Before default, there may be an effect on the financial sector, as agents become aware of the risks of maintaining their deposits in a system highly exposed to government bonds. This can lead to bank runs at the time of the default decision. After default, difficult and lengthy debt negotiations between debtors and creditors also hinder the recovery of the financial sector, especially where financial systems are weak, impairing overall confidence in the financial system and the government.[6] The potential for default to adversely affect other international arrangements such as trade relations is another source of economic costs.

Given the fact that debt payment problems are far from uncommon in emerging market economies, and the associated costs of debt crises can be so high, an orderly

---

[3] The increase in frequency of defaults beginning in the 1980s may have to do with the fact that there was a new wave of lending from 1974 to 1981, whereas there was a near hiatus in foreign lending to developing countries from 1930 to 1973.

[4] See Bordo and Eichengreen (1999); Eichengreen (1989); and Eichengreen and Fishlow (1996).

[5] The reduction in economic growth was more severe for the crisis countries of the East Asia crisis during 1997–98.

[6] Debt negotiations can be protracted. It typically took five years of negotiations (and sometimes over 10 years) to reach a debt restructuring agreement on defaulted bonds in the 1930s (Fernandez-Ansola and Laursen 1995). More recently, such protracted negotiations have also been common: it took almost 10 years for the debt crisis of the 1980s to be resolved.

and quick resolution of crises is desirable. Recognizing the market inefficiency arising from the collective action problem of private creditors[7] and the systemic risk posed to the international financial system by banks' exposure to defaulting countries, the debt resolution frameworks of the 1980s and early 1990s involved official intervention either by multilateral agencies like the International Monetary Fund (IMF) or creditor countries.[8] This type of "three-party" involvement contrasts sharply with the earlier periods, where there was little or no creditor government intervention in debt resolutions.[9] While the focus in the 1980s and early 1990s remained on addressing the collective action problem of creditors, the approaches to dealing with debt crises have changed quite radically. The approach in the 1980s was a formal framework that essentially involved a reprofiling of debt service to provide cashflow relief to the debtor and ensure availability of new money from creditor banks. This approach was designed to address a liquidity problem, as opposed to resolving a sustainability issue. The recognition that persistently high or rising debt burdens in the 1980s were indicative of solvency problems rather than illiquidity called for a paradigm shift in the response to crises and in crisis resolution. By 1990, market-based approaches to resolving debt crisis had gained favor. Thus the Brady Plan provided a formal mechanism for restructuring loans. The Brady Plan recognized the reduced value of nonperforming debt, as well as the issue of sustainability of debt and the need to provide an exit strategy for countries from a debt trap. The Brady Plan was generally viewed as a success, as restructuring countries were able to return to capital markets.

The dramatic shift from bank lending to bond financing in the 1990s altered the international financial structure. The default episodes in the second half of the 1990s increasingly involved bonds, as opposed to loans. The latter part of the 1990s witnessed several bond workouts.[10] Unlike loan restructurings, no formal mechanisms for sovereign bond workouts were established. This is most likely because the risks posed by the underlying credit events were not viewed as posing a systemic risk to the international financial system. Instead, markets have addressed the issues of bond workouts on a case-by-case basis, and essentially without intervention by creditor countries or multilateral institutions. Two approaches to sovereign bond

---

[7] The collective action problem among creditors arises when the potential return for one investor (that is, the holdout investor) is larger than that of other investors.

[8] See Rogoff and Zettelmeyer (2002) for a review of sovereign bankruptcy proposals.

[9] See Eichengreen and Portes (1995) and Eichengreen and Fishlow (1996). In the 1800s and 1900s, bondholders responded to debt crises by forming committees to represent them in negotiations with sovereign debtors. Initially, these committees were set up in an ad hoc manner to negotiate individual sovereign defaults. Once an agreement was negotiated and approved by bondholders, the committee was liquidated. Often, more than one committee was set up to negotiate restructurings, leading to competition among committees. This system suffered from problems of high administrative costs and the scope for debtors to play one committee against another. This system was replaced by the establishment of the Corporation of Foreign bondholders in the United Kingdom in 1868. In the mid-1930s, the United States established the Foreign bondholders Protective Council. Although creditor governments created formal entities to facilitate sovereign debt renegotiations, they were usually not active participants in the negotiations.

[10] The Mexican Tesebono crisis of 1994–95 was the first big debt crisis of the bond-financing era. As bondholders refused to rollover maturing tesobonos, a large financing package ($49 billion) involving the U.S. Treasury, the IMF, and other bilateral creditors was cobbled together to assist the country to avert a debt default.

Box 11.1. Collective Action Clauses Approach

What is it?
Changing majority action clauses in debt instruments.

Objective
To facilitate negotiations between debtors and creditors so as to improve the debt restructuring process. Address the problem of coordination among bondholders.

Features
CACs apply to individual bond issues.
A supermajority of bondholders (usually 75 percent) can agree to changing payment terms of the bond. The new terms would be binding for all holders of the bond.

Drawbacks
Inclusion of CACs in bond agreements could raise borrowing costs for this class of instruments.
CACs do not facilitate cross-issue creditor coordination (the aggregation problem). Existing debt not affected by this (the transition problem), as it would affect new issues only.

---

workouts have been followed: voluntary and involuntary or concerted. Voluntary exchanges involve debt that is being serviced, although default could occur, while involuntary exchanges involve defaulted debt. Voluntary exchanges typically repro-file debt service, but do not lower the nominal value of debt, and when they impose present-value (PV) reductions, they usually do so by a small amount. A concerted approach, by contrast, will likely involve a haircut – a reduction in nominal value – either in capital or in interest for investors, and a subsequent debt reduction for the debtor.

The current framework can best be described as one of muddling through. While the beginning of the 1990s saw a radical change in the approach to dealing with debt crises, the more recent debt crises have not evoked a similar response. In moving forward on approaches to debt restructuring, there appears to be broad support for solutions involving incremental change as opposed to sweeping solutions that radically overhaul the international financial architecture. Moreover, market participants are seemingly relying on market solutions to cope with the difficulties introduced by newer financial structures. Thus voluntary, market-friendly approaches to debt restructuring – such as the inclusion of collective action clauses (CACs) in sovereign bond contracts – are increasingly being viewed as a step forward in improving the current debt restructuring process.[11,12] (For more on collective action clauses, see Box 11.1 and Appendix B.) This is happening despite the concern that CACs would

---

[11] Collective action clauses are provisions in bond contracts that facilitate restructuring of bonds. CACs work primarily by allowing a qualified majority of bondholders to amend key financial terms of a bond contract, and these amendments are binding on the remaining bondholders.

[12] In a Plenary Statement at the 2003 Annual Meeting of the World Bank and the IMF, U.S. Treasury Secretary John W. Snow noted that, "We have been making great progress in strengthening the international financial system. Collective action clauses in sovereign debt are now the market standard. . . ."

likely impose higher borrowing costs (especially on weaker credits) and lower over-all financial flows to emerging markets. The inclusion of collective action clauses, which began appearing in bond issues in early 2003, has grown rapidly. By contrast, the IMF's sovereign debt restructuring mechanism (SDRM), which embodies an international bankruptcy procedure to facilitate debt workouts and calls for chang-ing IMF Articles to override some aspects of domestic law, might be perceived by the international community as a less viable option at this time. While CACs address the creditor coordination problem for individual bond issues, they do not solve the problem of such coordination across bond issues (the so-called aggrega-tion problem) or the problem of creditor coordination for an existing stock of debt (the so-called transition problem), as CACs apply only to new bond issues. Thus it remains to be seen whether CACs will be enough to resolve debt crises or whether additional mechanisms will be needed.

The principal focus of this chapter is on sovereign defaults on external debt in the 1980s and 1990s and the lessons that have been learned. The rest of the chapter is organized as follows: The next section explains the meaning of debt default, why countries default on their debt obligations, and the benefits of restructuring debt. The chapter then examines the debt restructuring mechanisms of the 1980s, and compares these to the approaches to resolving sovereign debt crises in the 1990s. The final section offers some lessons for the future.

THE THEORY OF DEBT DEFAULT AND DEBT RESTRUCTURING

What Is Debt Default and Why Do Countries Default?

DEBT DEFAULT. Debt default occurs when a borrower does not meet a debt payment obligation – that is, the borrower fails to meet the terms of a contractual agreement. Thus nonpayment of principal or principal and interest, as well as outright debt repudiation, qualify as a default. This definition is useful for comparisons of default episodes across different time periods.

Although the focus of this chapter is on sovereign defaults on external debt to private creditors, public and private sector defaults that shift liabilities onto the government's balance sheet are also included. Sovereign defaults on external official debt – whether bilateral or multilateral – are not addressed here.

WHY DO COUNTRIES DEFAULT? Sovereigns default because they cannot meet their contractual obligations or because they do not want to meet their contractual obli-gations. Among those debtors that cannot pay their obligations are those that cannot pay now, and those that cannot pay over any reasonable time period. Understanding sovereign debt defaults is complex. Issues of liquidity, solvency, and willingness to pay need to be addressed when evaluating the incentive for sovereigns to default.

- *Liquidity problem.* An economy faces a liquidity problem when its debt liabilities coming due in a given period exceed its liquid foreign currency assets, including funds that it has or can borrow. That is, an economy faces a cash flow problem, although it might be solvent in the long run. Liquidity problems generally emerge when there is a sudden change in investor sentiment that results in a sharp stop or reversal of capital flows by nonresidents or in capital flight by residents. Consequently, the economy is unable to meet its immediate external obligations.

• *Sustainability problem.* A solvency problem, by contrast, occurs when the economy may never be able to service its debt out of its own resources. Thus, the maximum discounted sum of current and future trade balances is less than its current outstanding debt. A solvency problem implies that the balance of payments is unsustainable over the medium- to long-term horizon. While a solvency problem implies a liquidity problem, it is possible for a liquidity problem to arise independently of a solvency problem. Distinguishing a liquidity problem from a solvency problem is not necessarily easy. While it is possible to draw a distinction between illiquidity and solvency in theory, it is difficult to distinguish between these two phenomena on the basis of observable consequences.

• *Willingness to pay.* A country may decide to stop servicing its debt well before it becomes insolvent. Since external debt service payments reduce current income and reduce welfare, a country may think it can improve welfare by repudiating (not servicing) its debt. The chosen decision not to pay is highly controversial. While debt payments fall, at least in the short run, there are other effects that make the welfare decision highly problematic, including output contraction and financial crises.

Does It Matter Whether the Nonperforming Debts of Sovereigns Are Restructured?

WHY DO COUNTRIES REPAY DEBT? The economic literature on debt recognizes the inherent problem of moral hazard in uncollateralized borrowing arrangements by debtor countries. This lack of collateral suggests that there must be some alternative incentive that prompts sovereigns to repay obligations. The question that researchers have asked is, why do sovereigns ever repay their debt?[13] Jonathan Eaton and Mark Gersovitz (1981) argue that sovereigns repay debt because future lending to the sovereign is dependent upon good repayment reputation. Jeremy Bulow and Kenneth Rogoff (1989) argue that good reputation is not enough to explain lending to sovereigns. They believe that lending is possible because of direct sanctions that creditors can impose on sovereigns. The importance of reputation versus direct sanctions has implications for debt contracts and debt forgiveness. Bulow and Rogoff conclude that if reputation does not matter, then debts that are forgiven will be forgotten by the market, and a debtor country should try to negotiate as large a debt reduction as possible.[14]

---

[13] See also Eaton and Fernandez (1995) and Friedman (2000) for a comprehensive review of the literature on this issue.

[14] Thus Lindert (1989) and Eichengreen (1989) find that historical evidence does not show that countries that defaulted were shut out of capital markets (for several years in the future) to any greater extent than countries that continued to pay their debts. Indeed, in the 1930s both good and bad creditors were unable to borrow. However, there is some recent evidence by Reinhart, Rogoff, and Savastano (2003) suggesting that a borrower's history matters. The study finds that countries that have experienced serial default might be more vulnerable to a debt crisis as debt burden ratios rise. Thus, "debt intolerant" countries have lower "safe" debt burden thresholds than countries with no history of debt defaults. Weak internal institutions – namely, financial systems and fiscal structure – are behind the

Harold Cole and Patrick Kehoe (1992) extend Bulow and Rogoff's model to assume that at any moment, a country enjoys many kinds of relationships involving trust such as trade, and that a country's debt relationships have implications for these other relationships. It then follows that a breakdown in a debt relationship will have negative outcomes for other relationships. Cole and Kehoe use this model to explain why countries repay debt, even when there are no direct sanctions.[15]

The one observed economic cost of default is protracted loss in output in defaulting countries. Michael Dooley (2000) suggests that the potential for crises and output losses provide an incentive for sovereign borrowers to repay.[16] It is this element of the international financial system that makes international lending possible. Without the threat of output losses, international lending might not be possible. Thus creditors have an interest in structuring contracts so that creditor coordination is difficult. Therefore, renegotiating contracts is difficult, making it less easy for the borrower to default. This is accomplished through equal sharing clauses, whereby creditors who are not being paid can make claims on payments made to any one creditor. Unanimous or near unanimous approval for changing payment terms on a contract are another means by which contract renegotiation are made costly.

RESCHEDULING AND RESTRUCTURING SOVEREIGN DEBT. Although sovereigns have incentives to repay, debt defaults do occur. The resolution of debt crises has involved debt relief ranging from a mere rescheduling of debt service payments to conversion of nonperforming debt into new debt with a lower debt service burden to debt write-downs. The incentives for lenders and borrowers to reschedule or restructure obligations are quite different. The incentive for lenders to negotiate debt restructurings is a wish to recover as much as possible of the value of defaulted debt. Since the unilateral penalty, in terms of seizure of assets, that a lender can impose on the debtor is usually much smaller than the contractual value of the debt, there is an incentive to negotiate. The debtor has the option to repudiate debt, but the potential output costs plus the direct costs in terms of seizure of assets by creditors are likely to outweigh the benefits of not paying. Thus, the debtor can benefit from negotiating, as well. Through negotiation, both lenders and borrowers can improve upon the outcome associated with their unilateral positions. It is these potential mutual gains that motivate debt renegotiations.

Even among creditors, banks behave differently from bondholders.[17] This is because banks have relationships with lenders, and this relationship is valued because

---

debt intolerance. The study finds that while countries can graduate from debt intolerance, the process is slow and involves strong adherence to structural reforms and to keeping low debt ratios low over a long period. Countries with serial defaults thus face higher borrowing costs than those without. Similar results are obtained by Özler (1992, 1993).

[15] See also Rose (2002) for an empirical analysis of this issue.

[16] Dooley distinguishes between strategic default and unavoidable defaults: that is, defaults that are a result of bad luck. His view is that if the IMF can distinguish between strategic and bad luck defaults, and support countries in their negotiations with private creditors in the event of bad luck defaults, this will be beneficial in terms of reducing the dead weight loss associated with such a default. Eichengreen and Portes (1995) also recommend that the IMF provide assistance in the case of self-fulfilling crises as opposed to crises originating from weak fundamentals. Both studies acknowledge the difficulty of distinguishing between these two types of crises, however.

[17] Friedman (2000).

it assists in better evaluating borrowers' credit risk. A better understanding of risks means that banks may be more willing to restructure debt than bondholders. Also, banks may not immediately mark to market. They have more control over the value they can assign a nonperforming or potentially nonperforming asset than do bondholders, who are required to mark to market on a daily basis. Since bank balance sheets are not immediately affected by nonperforming loans, bank lenders may have more of an incentive to try to restructure debt than do bondholders.

There is also the issue of a collective action problem among creditors. The free rider behavior problem and the possibility of litigation by holdout creditors give rise to coordination difficulties among creditors. Even if all creditors are better off working together, individual creditors might be convinced that they can do better by not participating in the debt negotiations, and holding out for a better individual outcome. Thus holdout creditors could reject a restructuring and take legal action to obtain better terms. They may also bet on a successful conclusion of the restructuring, because this reduces the relative importance of their claims and increases the likelihood of a favorable settlement. This is the mechanics by which so-called vulture funds operate.[18] However, while sovereigns can now be held legally accountable for their commercial contracts with foreign counter parties in the same manner as private parties,[19] accessing assets that can be attached is difficult.[20,21]

The incentives for borrowers to reschedule or restructure are to minimize the output and other economic costs of a default and to reduce the country's debt burden. Borrowers benefit from restructuring because it helps them regain access to markets for financing trade and investment, as well as to lower their cost of funds. The costs of a default are likely to be lower, the more orderly and quick is the restructuring.

---

[18] Contrary to what is sometimes believed, vulture funds generate strong stabilization forces by buying a country's debt when it is very cheap. While the U.S. courts do not allow the purchasing of bond issues for the sole purpose of suing the creditors, this objective is unverifiable and thus its usefulness as a deterrent for vulture funds rather limited.

[19] See Buchheit (1995, 1997).

[20] The authors of this study believe the threat of litigation has been grossly overstated. Roubini (2002) considers a number of reasons for why the risk of litigation is less than what has usually been considered. The most important are: unilateral exchange offers have turned out to be very successful, with large participation; exit consents dilute the benefit of holdouts; sweeteners associated with the exchange can be used to entice all bondholders; it is not clear that a holdout will be able to recover the full nominal value of its liabilities; the risk of the new instruments may be lower, increasing the perceived value of the newly issued instruments and providing an incentive for participation; large financial institutions and large players have an incentive to keep a good working relation with the government and thus avoid litigation; the court decision in the Elliott case (with regard to Peru), allowing Elliott Associates to attach bond coupons, will probably not hold if challenged in court; and the introduction of CACs in bond contracts can reduce the benefits of litigation.

[21] Sovereign immunity historically prevented bondholders from suing sovereign debtors. The origin of this principle was an attempt to foster the well-being between nations, by protecting a country from being sued in potentially biased foreign courts. With the years, and with many national companies (that is, those owned by the sovereign) conducting business in other countries, the absolute version of the sovereign immunity was left aside. The United States started to use a more restrictive approach in 1952 that was codified in 1976 in the Foreign Sovereign Immunities Act. The United Kingdom adopted similar legislation in 1978. This limited version allows suing sovereigns if they are engaged in commercial activities.

Of course, any improvement in country creditworthiness assumes that there will be no repetition of the default. For a debtor country, the main objectives of any debt operation are to:

   i. Achieve cash flow relief, that is, reprofile debt payments to avoid short-run financing needs;
  ii. Achieve debt relief, that is, to reduce the debt burden;
 iii. Avoid holdouts and litigation in the restructuring process; and
  iv. Normalize access to global financial markets.

Cash flow relief. In order to obtain cash flow relief, it is not necessary to default on the debt, as there is always a price at which the payment profile can be adjusted in a voluntary manner.[22] The most straightforward mechanism is a voluntary debt swap, by which a maturing debt instrument is exchanged for another debt instrument with similar market value, but a different payment stream. In the case of bonds, bondholders have several reasons to participate in a bond swap. First, the new issues will be more liquid; holdouts from the exchange risk being stuck with an illiquid instrument after the exchange.[23] Second, the creditor may fear a default if the bond exchange is unsuccessful. Having said that, voluntary debt exchanges may be more feasible when fewer creditors are involved and free rider incentives are weakened.

In addition, the new bonds may include a wide range of benefits, generally referred to as sweeteners. These can be cash payouts, interest increases, or the offering of collateral or guarantees. They could also arise from regulatory and tax prerogatives, such as tax exemptions, tax-canceling properties, and rediscount window privileges. Finally, sweeteners can include a number of warrants: such as exchange warrants, which give the option to increase participation in the exchange in a given time period; and extension warrants, which allow bondholders to exchange some bonds for longer maturity instruments. Pakistan's 1999 debt exchange, for example, included no debt relief and substantial upgrades in the interest payment stream.

Cash flow relief or voluntary debt refinancing can also be obtained by changes in regulation that increase the demand for government debt. One example is to allow banks to use government bonds to fulfill reserve requirements. Argentina, Russia, and Ukraine used this mechanism to prop up demand for their debt prior to default. Governments also offered to retire debt at face value if debt is used to pay taxes or to purchase equity (for example, in privatization offers). While this implies a one-to-one reduction in tax collection, if concentrated in short-term instruments, it may create demand for short-term bond instruments, facilitating the rollover of public debt. If it includes longer maturity bonds, it can actually aggravate the short-run cash-flow problem if it reduces tax collection.

For a country that does not expect to default, allowing firms to pay taxes with bonds allows for a substantial tax break for local corporations at the expense of bondholders (some of whom may be foreigners). If the government expects to honor its debt, this means that for debt traded at heavy discounts, there will be sizable capital

---

[22] See also Sturzenegger (2002a).
[23] If the new instruments provide improved liquidity, they may be issued at a lower return than previous instruments, yielding a debt reduction in net present value terms.

gains when it is realized that the government will pay. By allowing local corporations to pay taxes at nominal value with debt instruments, the government reduces the risks of holding such instrument, thus giving an advantage to local firms. When a bondholder takes a loss by selling a debt instrument to the local entrepreneur at a deep discount, this effectively reduces the tax liability of the local firm at the expense of the capital loss to the bondholder.[24]

Debt reduction. The theoretical arguments for debt reduction are the debt overhang issue and the debt Laffer curve.[25] A country with a given amount of external debt has to make a choice between how much to consume and invest. Investing today will increase future output. However, some of this increased output will go toward repaying debt. If claims on future output are large, the incentive to pursue proinvestment policies may not be strong. The debt overhang problem can be easily explained using a two-period model. In Period 1 the economy has debt obligations that it must repay in Period 2. In Period 1 the economy must decide how much to invest so as to get a return in Period 2. The larger the debt in Period 1, the greater will be the amount that will have to be paid out of investment returns in Period 2. Thus, debt represents a tax on the resources of the economy.

The investment disincentive effect of a large debt burden are used to obtain a debt Laffer curve. The debt Laffer curve relates the levels of expected debt repayment with debt levels. The slope of the Laffer curve is the change in expected repayment with a change in initial debt stock. For low initial levels of debt, the expected repayment increases by the same amount as the change in initial debt, and the slope of the Laffer curve is 45 degrees. For higher levels of initial debt, the increase in expected repayment is less than the increase in debt stock. At some size of initial debt, the change in expected repayment associated with an increase in initial debt stock is zero. Beyond this point, the expected repayment falls with larger debt stocks. It follows from the above that there is a maximum amount of debt beyond which payments on debt decline. The concepts of debt overhang and the debt Laffer curve suggest that creditors are thus better off canceling any debt (and in turn, debt service) above the level of maximum repayment.

In order to achieve debt reduction, a country must convince creditors that it cannot pay – that is, that the market value or present value of debt is less than the face value. While creditors and debtors may have a common understanding of the sustainability of debt and the ability of a country to pay, agreeing on the appropriate market price of impaired debt may be more contentious. Also problematic is avoiding litigation and holdouts from those creditors that choose not to participate.

To secure creditor participation, debt reduction deals usually include some short-run sweetener. Typical sweeteners are cash payouts and increases in the interest rates. Creditor upgrades are also possible incentives. Payment guarantees by third parties and collateralization provide incentives to creditors as they reduce credit risk. If neither guarantees nor an upgrade in the quality of the lender are possible, an alternative is to upgrade the instrument – that is, offer a more liquid instrument, a more

---

[24] However, a secondary market for these instruments could develop, which may allow for a sharing of the benefits.

[25] Sachs (1988).

reliable jurisdiction, better terms in the covenants of the issue, or instruments with tax or accounting advantages. Indexation and growth clauses, also known as value recovery rights or economic and credit-linked warrants, allow some bondholders or creditors to share in the benefits of their effort in granting debt relief. The mechanism is a clause in which the payment is associated with some macroeconomic factor, such as the price of an export commodity or output growth. While these factors have not been common in recent defaults, value recovery rights remain an interesting option as they align the interests of the countries and bondholders. In some cases – for example, linking the recovery value to GDP – performance may carry moral hazard risks if it is the country itself that produces the national statistics. Linking the performance to commodity prices or some other well-defined asset price reduces this risk significantly. The relatively modest use of this instrument remains an open question. Puts and acceleration clauses are other ways of enhancing instruments.[26]

Avoiding litigation and holdouts. The third objective is that of avoiding holdouts and litigation. One mechanism by which a country can minimize litigation risk is through the introduction of collective action clauses, CACs (Appendix B). By allowing a supermajority of creditors to change payment terms, CACs make the restructuring process easier and reduce the incentives for maverick litigation.[27] CACs are more easily introduced in issues under London law than New York law. London law allows for changes in the conditions of the bonds under majority ruling, whereas New York law does not allow changing payment conditions of a bond except with unanimity, although amendment to nonpayment terms can be made. Recently, CACs have been introduced in bonds issued under New York law.

While the literature has focused on international litigation, domestic litigation should not be disregarded. If a country defaults on its own citizens, these citizens have the right to pursue the case in domestic courts. Barring the case of a completely corrupt judicial system, they may have certain power to obtain favorable court rulings. Notably, attachments may be much more feasible. For example, Argentina has faced a number of legal actions called *amparos* (protection of constitutional rights) when the government attempted to change the terms of the domestic bond exchange by changing their currency of denomination from dollars to pesos at the conversion rate of 1.4 pesos per dollar (when the market rate was closer to 3 pesos per dollar). The government used an economic emergency law to justify the swap, but the Supreme Court, in a related recent ruling regarding the deposit freeze, stated that the emergency law cannot be used to wipe out property rights.[28] Whether the Supreme Court would take a similar stance regarding the resolution of the *amparos* relating to the domestic bond exchange is still unclear at this time. In the Argentine default, the government is facing massive litigation in local courts, while foreign

---

[26] A put option on a bond gives the bondholder an option to sell the bond at a preagreed price and protects the bondholder against a fall in price. An acceleration clause is a provision in a bond contract that allows the bondholder, in the event of a default, to demand immediate or faster payment on the bond.

[27] See Becker, Richards, and Thaicharoen (2001).

[28] The case is *Smith contra Poder Ejecutivo Nacional*.

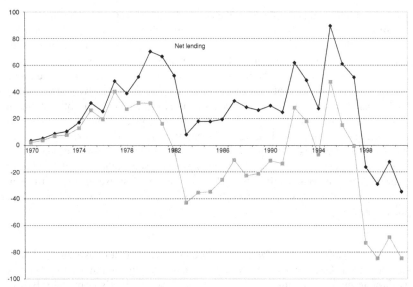

Figure 11.1. Net Flows and Transfers on Commercial Bank and Trade Finance to Developing
Countries.
Note: Net flows are disbursements on loans less loan repayments (i.e., net lending). Net trans-
fers are net flows minus interest payments. *Source*: *Global Development Finance* database.

bondholders have been extremely cautious and have presented only a few litigation
cases so far.

Clearly, both lenders and borrowers can potentially benefit when defaulted debt
is rescheduled or restructured. The issue is whether markets are efficient and can
yield orderly workouts – particularly whether markets can overcome collective action
problems among creditors. While debt rescheduling and restructuring can ameliorate
payment difficulties and make both creditors and debtors better off than under a
default, Benjamin Friedman (2000) argues that some nonperforming debts should
not be restructured. Some amount of defaults should be allowed as a market process,
so that investors can better price borrower risks – that is, promote ex ante market
efficiency. By forcing defaults to be at artificially low levels, cross-border flows
are higher than they would be in an environment of higher defaults. Thus, the aim
of debt markets should not be merely to maximize debt flows; rather, it should
also be to appropriately evaluate risk. This suggests the need for balance between
appropriately pricing risk and determining investment levels (ex ante efficiency) and
reducing debt burdens (ex post efficiency).

APPROACHES TO RESOLVING DEBT DEFAULTS
IN THE 1980s AND 1990s

Like their historical counterparts, recent-day debtor countries have experienced
booms and reversals in cross-border lending and debt problems associated with
such lending cycles. Thus the 1980s debt crisis followed on the heels of a bank
lending boom that began after the first oil shock of 1973 (Figure 11.1). In 1982,

in response to a substantial hike in interest rates in the United States, and as new money from banks dried up, Mexico declared a moratorium on its debt, triggering the beginning of a debt crisis that lasted through the early 1990s.[29] Once the default in Mexico occurred, banks withdrew from other emerging markets, leading to a domino effect that triggered defaults in a large number of developing economies. The debt crises lasted for nearly a decade as successive approaches were adopted in resolving the crises.

In the 1990s, lending to emerging markets was characterized by booms followed by sharp contractions or reversals of these flows. In the early 1990s, private lending resumed, led by bond investors. Debt flows nearly tripled between 1991 and 1993, before collapsing in the wake of the Mexican Tequila crisis at the end of 1994. Flows resumed in 1995, reaching a peak of $110 billion in 1996. Again, debt flows collapsed in the midst of the East Asian crisis of 1997 and were further affected by the debt crisis in Russia in 1998.[30] The crises in Korea and Indonesia led to debt rescheduling arrangements backed by sovereign guarantees for these countries (Appendix D). The crisis in Russia led to a default on domestic currency debt, one-third of which was held by nonresidents. This marked the beginning of a string of new restructuring experiences. In the following four years, Ukraine, Pakistan, Ecuador, Argentina, and Uruguay all defaulted or had to restructure under the threat of default.

Standard and Poor's survey of default episodes finds 84 events of sovereign default on private-source debt between 1975 and 2002 (Appendix A), with many countries experiencing serial default. S&P's definition of default is somewhat broad, ranging from missed principal and or interest payments to outright repudiation. There is thus considerable variation in the severity of default episodes. Nevertheless, the relatively large incidence of payment difficulties demonstrates the fact that debt difficulties are far from uncommon in emerging market economies. Both rated and nonrated sovereign issuers have experienced defaults on private debt. The survey includes both external and local-currency debt defaults, although the frequency of external debt default is much higher – at a ratio of 10 to 1.

Approaches to Resolving Debt Defaults in the 1980s

DEALING WITH THE 1980S DEBT CRISIS. The debt crisis of the early 1980s resulted from a combination of factors. Unrealistic positive expectations in debtor countries led to significant increases in domestic absorption. These, in turn, produced large current account deficits financed by external borrowing. When this large increase in debt faced a negative international environment, solvency problems became immediately obvious. The two main negative developments in the international environment were the productivity slowdown and the world economy recessions of the

---

[29] The 1980s debt crisis resulted from a combination of factors: namely, weak economic policies in several countries in the period preceding the crisis; a bank lending boom that began after the 1973 oil shock and that was especially strong from 1979 to 1981; and adverse global macroeconomic shocks, specifically in interest rates and commodity terms of trade.

[30] These crises were mostly associated with collapsing pegged exchange rate regimes.

mid-1970s and early 1980s, as well as the hike in interest rates that was the result of the disinflation program in the United States.

When the debt crisis erupted in 1982, policymakers and market participants were acutely concerned over the potential systemic risk that it posed to the international financial system and the associated disruption of international trade and finance.[31] There was a realization that creditors and debtors needed to cooperate so as to allow countries to grow out of their debt problems and reaccess capital markets.[32] A formal framework was initiated to facilitate debt agreements.[33] The key market failure that the framework was addressing was that of coordination among creditors – that is, collective action problems among creditors. Consequently, banks gathered in a consortium – the London Club – with the purpose of conducting debt renegotiations. The strategy that was adopted can be thought of as having had three phases.[34] The common elements of the three phases were rescheduling of debt maturities to provide front-loaded cash flow relief to debtors, along with provision of new money by creditor banks (Table 11.3). The incentives for banks to participate were that this strategy maintained the face value of developing country claims on their books, and it also meant that they would benefit from any future improvement in countries' ability to service debt. For debtor countries, the incentives were that it provided them with near-term cash flow relief and new money. The 1980s new money approach was designed to address a liquidity problem, as opposed to resolving a sustainability issue.[35]

NEW MONEY APPROACH: FIRST PHASE. The first phase was an immediate response to the Mexico crisis, and it emphasized adjustment and austerity. Under this approach, which was supported by the U.S. administration, countries adopted IMF approved adjustment programs and commercial banks rescheduled debt obligations maturing over a short period – usually one to two years – and debt in arrears. Banks also maintained short-term credit lines and provided new money commitments, which partially covered interest payments. This so-called concerted lending – new money packages – was designed to fill a country's financing gap.[36] The feature of new money by banks did not represent voluntary lending, however. Countries were also able to access short-term bridge financing from major creditor governments. Mexico was the test case for this approach. In August 1983, the country reached agreement with its creditor banks to reschedule $23.3 billion of maturing debt, and

---

[31] Clark (1994) shows that the high exposure of banks to developing country debt was behind the concern over the vulnerability of the international financial system. The exposure of U.S. money center banks to developing countries restructuring their debt at end-1982 was 215 percent of banks' capital and 260 percent of banks' equity. The exposures of UK and Canadian banks at the end-1984 were about 275 percent and 195 percent of equity, respectively.

[32] As noted earlier, intervention by officials – creditor governments or multilateral institutions – in resolving debt crises was a new phenomenon.

[33] The framework for negotiating bank debt developed in line with the Paris Club framework for official debt.

[34] See Brainard (1985).

[35] As we noted in the previous section, problems of illiquidity and solvency are observationally equivalent, which makes it difficult to distinguish between these two types of problems.

[36] Until 1988, IMF disbursements were conditional upon a country reaching agreement with its creditor banks on debt restructuring and new financing.

during 1983–84 Mexico also obtained two new money agreements totaling $8.9 billion. In turn, the austerity measures adopted by the government shifted the current account from a deficit to a surplus. During 1983–84, 47 rescheduling agreements were negotiated, covering $130 billion. Principal coming due over one to two years was rescheduled. The typical terms on rescheduled debt were eight-year maturity and four-year grace, with an interest margin of $1\frac{7}{8}$ percentage points over Libor. A major limitation of the first phase was the focus on the near-term and lack of a framework for promoting medium-term growth in crisis countries.

NEW MONEY APPROACH: SECOND PHASE. The shift to a second phase began in 1984, and represented an improvement over the first phase. Now, the approach to managing the debt crisis moved from a near-term to a longer-term focus, with a view to normalizing bank lending to developing countries. Instead of rescheduling maturities on a year-to-year basis, the new approach advocated multiyear rescheduling agreements (MYRAs). Under this approach, banks agreed to reschedule debt maturing within three to five years. The terms on rescheduled debt were also more favorable, at maturities of 9 to 14 years. Banks provided concessions in terms of narrower interest rate spreads on rescheduled debt and elimination of rescheduling fees. In turn, banks were not required to pledge new money – that is, there was no forced lending. The obvious benefit to debtor countries was that it lowered debt servicing amounts over a longer period, providing significant cash flow relief. While IMF conditionality was still an important aspect of this approach, the economic adjustment that was required under IMF programs was less severe. Eight countries (two agreements for Mexico) rescheduled their debt using the MYRA framework. Like the first phase, this approach lacked a focus on promoting medium-term growth.

NEW MONEY APPROACH: THE BAKER PLAN. In October 1985, the United States unveiled the Baker Plan. The third phase of handling the debt crisis marked an important departure from the two earlier approaches in that it recognized the need for fostering economic growth. The Baker Plan advocated structural adjustment and market-oriented policies for generating growth. Another key element of the plan was increased lending by commercial banks. In association with an IMF program, participation of multilateral organizations such as the World Bank was also greatly enhanced. The Plan envisaged net commercial bank lending of $20 billion from 1986 to 1988 and multilateral development bank net lending of $9 billion.

A fundamental premise of the debt resolution of the 1980s, including the Baker Plan, was that all similarly situated commercial creditor banks should be treated equally, both in terms of rescheduling of their existing exposure and as to their proportional participation in new credit facilities. From a legal standpoint, this equal treatment was ensured through a series of contractual provisions in the rescheduling deals, such as sharing clauses, mandatory prepayment provisions, negative pledge clauses, and pari-passu covenants. However, syndication of all loans could not be compelled legally so some degree of moral suasion remained necessary. This monolithic approach implied complete ignorance on the specifics of each bank, however. This, in the end, was responsible for some delays and difficulties in reaching agreements. Thus, over the years, new flexibility had to be introduced to suit the differences both of different creditors and debtors. In all cases, however, debt forgiveness was off the table as an alternative.[37] To solve the free rider problem among commercial banks, several sweeteners were offered to those participating in the rescheduling.

Although 10 countries negotiated debt agreements with commercial banks, the level of net bank lending fell far short of the Baker Plan targets. Indeed, public sector borrowers received only $4 billion in net bank flows. However, several middle-income countries were able to negotiate better terms on their debt obligations.

FAILURE TO RESOLVE THE 1980s DEBT CRISIS. The success of the new money approach in managing the debt crisis was rather uneven (Tables 11.1 and 11.2). While systemic risk to the international financial system was contained, the goals of lowering the indebtedness of crisis countries and normalizing their access to financial markets was not achieved. Indeed, the main failure of this approach was that debtor countries were unable to exit from the cycle of debt rescheduling. There are several reasons for this. First, rescheduling of maturities provided cash flow relief for a relatively short period. New money packages only partially covered interest payments on existing debt. Thus, if crisis countries' payment capacity did not improve quickly, they would need additional rescheduling or new money. Second, new money packages combined with rescheduling increased the stock of debt and contributed to a debt overhang problem. Crisis countries had little incentive to grow in the face of mounting debt and debt service. Third, a continuous cycle of rescheduling deterred normalization of bank lending. Thus, external finance for new investment and growth was not forthcoming. Also, by the mid-1980s, new money packages became increasingly difficult to negotiate, as smaller banks were looking to reduce exposure to developing country debt. Lastly, debt rescheduling negotiations were usually drawn out and costly. Banks had diverse business objectives, and getting all creditor banks to sign on to what was agreed by the banks' advisory committee was time-consuming. For small banks there was also a free rider problem, as these banks could potentially benefit, at no cost, from the efforts of the larger banks. Small banks could share in interest payments facilitated by new money, without contributing to it.

Approaches to Resolving Debt Defaults in the 1990s

DEALING WITH THE 1990s DEBT CRISES. The 1990s defaults were characterized by the resolution of the loan defaults of the 1980s during the early part of the 1990s and bond defaults toward the end of the decade (also included are defaults through 2002). At the start of the decade, there was a growing recognition that persistently high or rising debt burdens were indicative of insolvency problems rather than illiquidity problems. This called for a paradigm shift in the response to crises and in crisis resolution. By 1990, market-based approaches to resolving debt crisis had gained favor. These approaches recognized the loss of value of nonperforming debt, as well as the issue of sustainability of debt and the need to provide an exit strategy for countries from a debt trap. A new formal mechanism for restructuring defaulted loans was introduced, the so-called Brady Plan. The Brady Plan was generally viewed as a success, as major restructuring countries were able to reenter international capital markets.

[37] However, banks were slowly building provisions to exit from developing country risk exposure.

Table 11.1. *Characteristics of the new money approach and the performance of GDP growth and net debt transfers in default countries*

New money approach	Formal mechanism to facilitate cooperation among debtors and creditor banks. Three-party involvement: creditor banks, sovereign borrowers, and multilateral institutions and/or creditor countries. Phase 1: 1982–84 Phase 2: 1984–85 Phase 3: 1985–89 (Baker Plan)
Goal	Address collective action problem among private creditors: free rider problem and litigation. Avert a systemic disruption of international finance and trade. Gain time for debtor countries to improve their debt-servicing capacity. Get debtor countries back on a sustainable growth path. Restore debtor countries' access to international capital markets.
Features	Countries remain current on interest payments and adjust aggregate consumption and investment. In later periods, the emphasis was on structural reform. No menu of options for banks. Banks reschedule amortization payments falling due and in arrears. Phase 1: Maturities falling due in 1 to 2 years were rescheduled at average terms of 8 years maturity and 4 years grace, and 1 7/8% interest spread. Phase 2. MYRAs: Maturities falling due in 3 to 5 years were rescheduled at terms of 9 to 14 years maturity and 1 3/8% interest spread. Phase 3. Baker Plan: Better terms on rescheduled debt. Up to 20 years maturity and interest spreads as low as 13/16%. Banks maintain short-term credit lines, and extend new loans to partially refinance interest obligations. Multilateral creditors increased lending; initially IMF and then World Bank (under the Baker Plan). Addresses a liquidity problem, not a solvency problem.
Rescheduling episodes	47 rescheduling agreements (for 26 countries) during 1982–84, covering $130 billion of debt. 8 MYRAs during 1985–86, covering $81 billion of debt. 10 Baker Plan rescheduling agreements during 1985–88, covering $165 billion of debt.
Impact on debtors	Performance of 26 countries that rescheduled in 1982–84: GDP average annual growth rate in 1970–80 = 5.8%, and in 1982–84 = 0.57%. Debt/exports in 1981 = 212% and in 1984 = 258% Debt/GDP in 1981 = 40% and in 1984 = 63% Transfer private external debt obligations to the public sector.

(continued)

Punam Chuhan and Federico Sturzenegger

Table 11.1 (continued)

Impact on creditors and/ or creditor countries	Concerted lending – new money packages – by creditor banks, and multilaterals. Banks provided trade credits and bank lines. IMF lending conditional upon agreement with banks on debt rescheduling and new financing.
Results	Systemic risks to banks contained.
	Repeated rescheduling by debtor countries and no exit from debt trap.
	Banks reluctant to extend new money because of risk of repeated rescheduling.
	The coordination problem among banks was resolved, but it did not address the problem of new financing effectively.

Source: Data are from *Global Development Finance*, various issues.

At the private sector level, the shift in policy favoring debt reduction had been in the making for some time. During the later part of the 1980s, a secondary debt market had appeared for developing country debt, with this debt trading at sizable discounts. The realization that losses had already been incurred pushed debtor countries to try to share the benefits from honoring their commitments. On the other hand, the development of the secondary market put pressure on banks that had not sold off their loans, as they feared that at some point they would be called to mark to market the

Table 11.2. *Performance of 26 countries that rescheduled their debt in 1982–1984[a]*

	Average 1970–80	Average 1981–82	Average 1983–84	Average 1983–86			
Net resource transfers in billions of US$ (on medium- and long-term debt)	8.0	9.6	−12.7	−16.1			
Debt/GDP (in %)	26.3	44.5	61.3	63.2			
Per capita GDP growth (in %) (annual change)	3.2	−2.9	−1.2	0.4			
	1980	1981	1982	1983	1984	1985	1986
Net resource transfers in billions of US$ (on medium- and long-term debt)	7.2	16.2	3.0	−10.4	−15.1	−21.1	−18.0
Debt/GDP (in %)	36.9	40.5	48.6	59.6	63.1	64.0	66.2
Per capita GDP growth (in %) (annual change)	4.5	−2.7	−3.1	−4.2	1.8	0.8	3.2

[a] Data for Bulgaria are from 1980.
Source: *Global Development Finance* database.

value of such loans. In fact, Citibank started along this path in May 1987 by posting loan loss provisions against its developing country debt. Thus, toward the later part of the 1980s, the new money approach became unstable and started veering naturally toward some kind of debt reduction. For the banks, this was further enhanced by the fact that tax benefits for writing down debt would accrue only upon the granting of the debt relief.

Indeed, Mexico offered a preview of the Brady deal in late 1987 by offering an exchange of bank loans for a new Mexican bond with a 20-year maturity and with principal collateralized with U.S. Treasury zero-coupon bonds. The reception to this instrument, without interest collateral, was muted. Discounts offered on principal were in the order of 30 percent, but only a fraction of the amount Mexico was prepared to exchange was subscribed. Obviously, more resources had to be put on the table to provide additional enhancements to switch out of the original debt instruments.

In spite of having only partial success initially, the program moved ahead swiftly in the following years, with committed support from creditor countries and multilaterals. The debt situation of many countries was quickly normalized. The return of emerging market countries to the global capital market in 1991 started a new lending boom. Private debt flows in the form of bond financing to these countries surged.

Beginning in the latter part of the decade, however, there were several episodes of bond defaults and distress bond exchanges. Most of these credit events were resolved through market-based informal mechanisms, which represent a muddling through approach. What is remarkable about these debt exchanges is that the speed with which these cases were resolved contrasts strongly with the view that sovereign bond exchanges were extremely difficult to undertake. There are several reasons behind the perceived difficulty of such bond operations, including coordinating negotiations with an increasingly large number of diverse and anonymous investors that hold bonds and the potential for hold-out investors to disrupt negotiations.

LOAN DEFAULTS OF THE EARLY 1990s AND THE BRADY PLAN. In a bid to overcome the shortcomings of the new money approach of the 1980s, the United States introduced the Brady Plan in March 1989.[38] This plan signaled a major shift in the official position to managing the debt crisis. Under the new approach, there was official support and encouragement of debt reduction packages that could resolve pending debt problems and reopen market access for many of these economies. In fact, the Brady Plan mandated multilaterals to increase lending in support of these debt operations.

The major distinguishing elements of the Brady Plan were debt relief through a menu of market-based options ranging from debt stock reduction to rescheduling of principal and interest, and new money (Table 11.3). The menu approach addressed the issue of increasingly divergent business goals of banks with exposure to developing countries. Banks could chose the option that best suited their business interests. If banks wished to exit from the country, they could chose the debt reduction option.

---

[38] The plan is named after U.S. Secretary of the Treasury Nicholas Brady, who succeeded Secretary James Baker.

Table 11.3. *Characteristics of the Brady Plan and the performance of GDP growth and net transfers on debt in default countries*

Brady Plan	Introduced in March 1989.
	Formal mechanism to facilitate more efficient cooperation among debtors and creditor banks.
	Three-party involvement: creditor banks, sovereign borrowers, and multilateral institutions and/or creditor countries.
Goal	Address collective action problem among private creditors: free rider problem and litigation.
	Address the shortcomings of the Baker Plan.
	Address the diverse business interests of creditor banks. Some banks wanted to exit emerging markets, while others did not.
	Break the cycle of continuous debt renegotiations.
	Improve countries debt-servicing capacity through debt and debt-service reduction.
	Get debtor countries back on a sustainable growth path.
	Restore debtor countries' access to international capital markets.
Features	Market-based approach recognizing the market value of impaired debt.
	Reduction in PV of debt through debt and debt-service reduction.
	Menu of options for banks, recognizing the diversity of banks' business interests.
	The choice of either debt reduction or new concerted lending limited the free rider problem.
	Addresses a debt solvency problem.
Instruments	Debt reduction: • discount bonds • buybacks
	Debt-service reduction: • interest reduction bonds or par bonds • front loaded interest reduction bonds • new money with or without conversion bonds.
Results	18 countries have had Brady operations, restructuring $200 billion of bank claims for $154 billion of bonds.
Impact on debtors	Performance of 17 countries with Brady deals:
	Debt/exports in 1990 = 263% and in 1996 = 188%
	Debt/GDP in 1990 = 47% and in 1996 = 39%
	Up-front cash requirement for DDSR operations: buybacks, purchase of collateral for bond exchanges, payments on arrears.
Impact on creditors	IMF lending into arrears.
Results	Renewed access to global capital markets for restructuring countries.
	Exit from the continuous cycle of restructuring.
	The coordination problem among creditors was resolved, as was the problem of new financing.

Source: Data are from *Global Development Finance*, various issues.

Those wishing to stay on and benefit from the resulting improved debt burden of the country were expected to provide new money. The benefit to debtor countries was lower debt burden through debt reduction, debt service reduction, and/or substantial extension of the time horizon of contractual relief. Lower debt burdens improved countries' prospects of exiting from the cycle of debt renegotiations. Along with a reduction in countries' debt burden, implementation of a strong, growth-oriented policy framework was critical to resolving the debt situation.

Menu approach. The menu approach addressed the issue of increasingly divergent business goals of banks. It provided these banks with a market-based menu of options from which banks could choose. The Brady deals included a number of relatively standard instruments.

Par or discount bonds. Pars were loans exchanged for fixed rate bonds issued at par with below-market interest rates. Discounts were floating rate bonds issued with market interest rates, but with a capital write-off. Both types of bonds had principal collateralized by U.S. Treasury zero-coupon bonds. Par and discount bonds had long-term maturities, were expected to be very liquid, and had a long average life and bullet amortization (or lump sum payment). They represent the most common Brady bonds outstanding.

Front-loaded interest reduction bonds (FLIRBs). In this case, loans were exchanged for medium-term step-up bonds at below-market interest rates for the initial five to seven years, and then stepping up to at a market-based floating rate for the remainder of the term. These bonds provided partial interest collateral in the form of cash, with collateral rolled over for subsequent periods upon timely interest payments. While these were less liquid than the par/discounts, they had a much shorter average life, as amortization payments ordinarily began after 5–7 years.

Interest arrears capitalization. Commercial banks had rescheduled interest in arrears on Argentine, Brazilian, and Ecuadorian debt, capitalizing the interest into new short-term floating rate bonds, called interest due or unpaid bonds, as in Brazil's IDU and Ecuador's PDI. These bonds had been issued prior to the rescheduling of principal into the Brady format.

Debt conversion bonds or new money bonds. In some cases, countries were believed to have the ability to pay their foreign loans, but had so far been unwilling to service the debt. The initiation of a Brady deal was a sign of a new willingness to repay foreign debt, augmenting the creditworthiness of the countries. Thus, creditors exchanged loans for bonds at par, and even provided additional funds to the Brady issuing nation, at a floating rate of interest through the so-called new money bonds. They included short-term floating rate bonds as issued by the Philippines, Uruguay, and Venezuela, and carried no collateral.

The menu approach advocated by the Brady Plan allowed banks to choose the options that were most appropriate to their particular situation – their external situation in terms of the accounting and regulatory environment, as well as their internal situation in terms of banks' policies. The possibility that one option might be picked

Table 11.4. *Performance of 17 Brady bond countries*[a]

	Average 1983–89	1990	1991	1992	1993	1994	1995	1996
Net resource transfers in billions of $US (on medium- and long-term debt)	−19.7	−10.6	−10.2	−11.1	3.3	−6.3	1.3	1.4
Debt/GDP (in %)	54.0	47.1	46.8	42.9	42.7	39.6	41.2	38.6
Per capita GDP growth	−1.9	−2.3	1.1	1.1	2.0	3.2	−0.4	2.0

[a] Data for Poland are from 1990 and data for Vietnam are from 1984.
Source: *Global Development Finance* database.

more often than another, thereby undermining the menu approach, was an issue. The menu approach, however, encouraged wide participation by banks in restructuring agreements.

Another perceived favorable aspect of the Brady bonds was that they were believed to have been structured as an inviolable set of instruments. Not only were they issued according to New York law, which does not allow bondholders to change the payment conditions of the bonds unless there is unanimity, but also they included a series of provisions that made them practically default-risk free. Among these provisions were mandatory prepayment clauses that restrict not ratable prepayments (that is, preferential repayment) to others; turnover clauses that require creditors receiving preferential prepayments to turn these payments over to others; the sharing clause, which requires a creditor to share what it receives with others; the negative pledge clause, which requires other lenders are not to be given a preference by having assets pledged to them; and the acceleration clause, wherein a creditor that holds defaulted debt can ask for all the debt to be paid immediately.

The Brady Plan was designed to reduce countries' debt and debt-service burdens. This improvement was achieved through permanent cash flow relief resulting from debt stock reduction and lower interest rates.[39] Thus, Brady-style debt restructurings lowered the present value of debt relative to the face value of the original debt. Since net transfers under the Brady Plan were not much different from those in the pre-Brady period, debt burdens improved overall (Table 11.4). There was considerable variation among countries, however. Countries like Argentina and Brazil that were in nonpayment status experienced an increase in debt service payments as relations with creditors were normalized. By contrast, countries that were already paying their creditor banks found that their debt service was reduced. While the cash flow relief in the near term was about the same as under the Baker Plan, it was the longer-term improvement in sustainability of debt that was critical.

[39] The debt restructuring operations required up-front financing for purchasing collateral for bonds, repaying arrears, and buybacks. A large amount of the financing was provided by official sources, with debtor countries also making a significant contribution. Brady agreements also continued to support debt conversion schemes as a way to reduce debt burden. Under these agreements, countries typically agreed to convert a minimum level of debt into equity, among other mechanisms. Although several conversions took place at the beginning of the decade, and were important in countries like Argentina and Chile, the overall size of conversions was low.

The Brady deal was considered a success. It normalized the relations between creditors and debtors and opened up a new era of resumed lending to emerging economies. While there were many factors behind the surge in financial flows to emerging markets, the resolution of the countries' debt problems was an important contributing factor to renewed flows. However, some of the characteristics of the deal, particularly the stepped up characteristic of the interest payments included in some bonds, would impose an unsustainable burden on some debtors 10 years later. In addition, the belief that the restructuring had produced default-free instruments would later also be found to have been wrong (as first evidenced by the 1999 debt default by Ecuador).

BOND DEFAULTS OF THE LATE 1990s AND A MUDDLING THROUGH APPROACH. During the later part of the 1990s, several countries faced a combination of debt, currency, and banking crises that led to debt restructurings. In most of these cases, unsustainable fixed exchange rate regimes and large current account deficits, along with fiscal problems and liability dollarization, combined to induce significant uncertainties regarding the solvency of the banking system and the government. This eventually led to sharp contractions in capital flows, and thus to an inability to roll over government debt. As a result, the past several years have seen a spate of both large and small sovereign bond exchange operations, many of them of "distressed" debt. What is remarkable about these bond operations is that there has been no formal mechanism for resolving debt problems. Moreover, the approach has varied from case to case. The overall situation can best be described as one of muddling through.

Until fairly recently, the popular view was that sovereign bond exchanges were extremely difficult to undertake. There are several reasons behind the perceived difficulty of such bond operations. First is an increasingly large number of diverse and anonymous investors that hold bonds. The diverse goals of private bondholders and their large numbers pose difficulties of coordination (compare this to a handful of creditor banks under the loan restructurings of the 1980s). Second is the legal recourse available to bondholders, who can disrupt bond restructuring negotiations as hold-out investors seek repayment through national courts.[40] Indeed, the threat of such a disruption may actually deter a country from seeking a necessary restructuring.[41]

Recent sovereign bond exchanges like those of Pakistan, Ukraine, Ecuador, Argentina (June 2001), and Uruguay (May 2003) demonstrated that bond exchange operations may be relatively easy to implement and can be completed in a short period.[42] The experience from these bond exchanges also suggests that high investor participation may be achieved without the use of collective action clauses.[43]

---

[40] Holdout creditors are those creditors that are unwilling to accept a bond restructuring by the sovereign. These creditors are usually small in number, but can exhibit opportunistic behavior that can derail a bond restructuring.

[41] See Krueger (2001, 2002).

[42] See Chuhan (2002).

[43] Inclusion of collective action clauses or CACs in bond contracts is viewed as being potentially helpful in bond restructurings because they allow for collective representation of bondholders and for qualified majority voting to change payment terms on bonds. Cram-down clauses force holdout investors to join the majority of investors. See Appendix B.

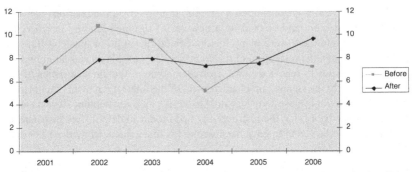

Figure 11.2. Argentina: Impact of the June 2001 Bond Exchange on Debt Service Profile.
Source: National data, World Bank's Debtor Reporting System, and authors' estimates.

Moreover, the fears that litigation would disrupt some of these bond operations were not realized. With over $500 billion in emerging market bonds – about $400 billion of which are public and publicly guaranteed – the recent bond exchanges are significant as they provide a precedent for future sovereign bond exchanges of distressed debt.

A bond exchange operation can be voluntary or involuntary (concerted). Voluntary exchanges involve debt that is being serviced, although default could occur. In a voluntary operation the market price of the exchange is expected to be higher than the preexchange price, with the investor likely to get all the benefit of the price increase. Voluntary exchanges are also likely to include sweeteners in terms of higher interest rates and more liquid or tradable bonds to attract investor participation. The benefit to the debtor is to achieve a reprofiling of its debt service, so as to reduce rollover risk in the near and medium-term. For example, Argentina's "mega" bond exchange lowered debt service payments in 2001–2003 (Figure 11.2). Uruguay's bond exchange reprofiled maturities yielding a nominal saving of $0.45 billion in amortization in 2003 and $2.4 billion between 2003 and 2010 (Figure 11.3).[44,45] Voluntary exchanges typically do not lower the value of debt relative to its face value, but may include a reduction in present value in some cases. Involuntary exchanges involve defaulted debt. Such exchanges will likely involve a haircut for investors and a subsequent debt reduction for the debtor. (A default may also have other costs, such as loss of reputation and market access, as well as domestic output losses for the debtor.) Thus, the present value of the debt after the exchange is likely to be less than the face value of the defaulted debt. (See Table 11.5 for a list of voluntary and concerted bond exchanges.)

A recent example of a voluntary bond exchange of "distressed" debt was Pakistan in late 1999 (Appendix C). Argentina's mega bond exchange of June 2001 was viewed by the market as a voluntary exchange during a period of heightened

---

[44] Domestic bonds account for a larger share of the reduction in amortization in 2003–04, while international bonds dominate the savings in amortization in 2005–10.

[45] A novel feature of the Uruguayan restructuring has been the use of collective action clauses in its Samurai bond to avoid holdouts, and the issue of new bonds with collective action clauses.

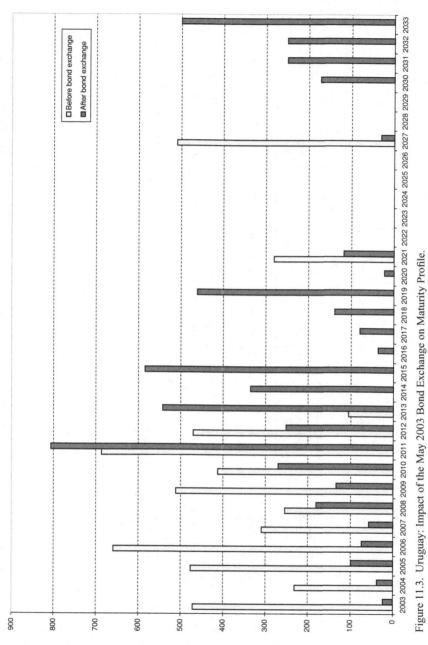

Figure 11.3. Uruguay: Impact of the May 2003 Bond Exchange on Maturity Profile.
Note: Includes both international and domestic bonds. *Source*: National data, World Bank's Debtor Reporting System, and authors' estimates.

Table 11.5. *External bond exchanges*

EXTERNAL BOND EXCHANGES

	Voluntary approach				Concerted Approach	
	Argentina[a] June-01	Pakistan Nov-99	Uruguay[b] May-03	Ukraine Feb-00	Ecuador Aug-00	Russia Aug-00
Debt Eligible	$29.5 billion	$0.61 billion	$5.4 billion	$2.7 billion	$6.7 billion	$31.8 billion
Debt Reduction	No debt reduction	No debt reduction	No debt reduction	No debt reduction	Average of 40%	Average of 36.5%
Amounts Exchanged	$29.5 billion	$0.61 billion	$5.1 billion	$2.3 billion	$6.6 billion	$31.8 billion
Exchange Bonds issue	$30.4 billion	$0.62 billion	$5.1 billion	$2.3 billion	$3.95 billion	$21.14 billion
	5-year local bond; 7-year, 17-year, and 30-year global bonds	5-year Eurobond	Benchmark bonds: 8-year, 12-year, 30-year; Extension bonds: 5 to 14 years	7-year Eurobond in US$ and euro	30-year and 12-year Eurobonds	30-year and 10-year Eurobonds

[a] Exchange includes $2.1 billion of local bonds eligible for exchange.
[b] Includes $1.6 billion of foreign-currency denominated domestic bonds eligible for exchange.

Source: National data; *Global Development Finance*, various issues; and World Bank's Debtor Reporting System.

credit risk for the country.[46] Uruguay's bond exchange was also undertaken in the face of financing difficulties. The amount of bonds exchanged by Pakistan totaled $0.6 billion, while the Argentine mega bond exchange involved $29.5 billion. Both these countries provided some form of sweetener to enhance investor participation. For example, the terms offered by Pakistan on the new bond provided a sweetener relative to the prevailing market price of the bond, and the size and structure of the new bond implied that this instrument would be more liquid than the original bonds. These factors, along with a relatively narrow and small investor base – mostly institutional investors – yielded a high investor participation rate – nearly 99 percent. The high investor participation rate meant that collective action clauses did not need to be invoked in the Pakistan bond exchange. The new bonds issued under Argentina's bond exchange operation had a higher average yield than the old bonds, and because of their size were potentially more liquid than the old bonds. By extending maturities without affecting nominal debt stocks, Uruguay's $5.1 billion bond exchange achieved some reduction in debt in present value terms. However, the exchange did provide $107 million in up-front cash payments of principal and interest.

Two recent examples of involuntary bond exchanges were the bond restructurings by Ecuador and Russia (notes for bonds).[47] Both these bond operations involved debt reduction; the amounts of bonds exchanged were $38.4 billion, with Russia accounting for $31.8 billion. Ecuador's bond exchange operation, involving defaulted Brady bonds and Eurobonds, resulted in a 41 percent reduction in principal for bondholders (overall). Investor participation in the deal was about 97 percent; well over the 85 percent acceptance level. One factor that encouraged participation was the government's offer to pay bondholders $140 million of past-due principal and interest on defaulted bonds. Exit amendments to cross default and negative pledge clauses in the old bonds, by investors who were tendering their old bonds for new bonds, and an amendment to delist the bonds pushed up the investor participation rate as well (Bucheit and Gulati 2000).[48] Ecuador's bond restructuring (from default to bond exchange) was completed in about one year – a relatively short time period compared to the loan restructuring episodes of the 1980s. Although Ecuador's bond exchange offer involved a haircut for creditors, the country did not engage in formal negotiation with its bondholders. A Consultative Group comprising large institutional investors was set up, but the function of this group was to provide a medium for communication between the government and the creditor community and not to negotiate the terms of the offer.

Russia's debt operation exchanged Vneshekonombank's $31.8 billion of Prins (restructured loans of Vneshekonombank and due 2002 to 2020) and IANs (interest notes issued by Vneshekonombank and due 2002 to 2015) for $21 billion of

---

[46] See IMF (2001).

[47] Argentina defaulted on its debt is 2002 and this default has not been resolved yet.

[48] Cross default provisions in debt agreements place a debtor, who has defaulted on one obligation, in default on other obligations as well. Negative pledge clause in a debt agreement binds the debtor to agree not to pledge any assets to other creditors that would undermine the ability of the debtor to repay one set of creditors over others.

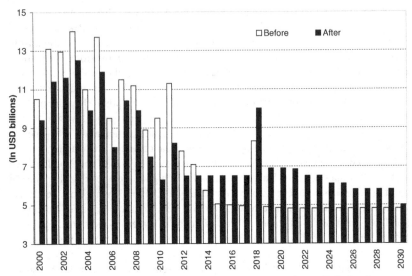

Figure 11.4. Russia: Impact of the August 2000 Bond Restructuring on Debt Service.
Source: National data.

new instruments – Eurobonds of the Russian Federation due in 2010 and 2030. The restructuring carried a substantial principal reduction – 37.5 percent for Prins and 33 percent for IANs (Figure 11.4). The deal had many interesting features (J. P. Morgan 1997 and 2000). Among these:

- There was an upgrade in the obligor. Creditors had had relatively limited legal recourse after the December 1998 default on the Prins and IANs because Russia did not guarantee the debt incurred by Vneshekonombank. Now, it assumed that debt Directly.
- Cross-acceleration clauses were expanded. In any new issues, Russia committed to include clauses to ensure equal status in the event of default or acceleration of the new bonds maturing in 2010 and 2030. The clauses would be symmetric, tying default on the 2010 bonds and 2030 bonds to new issues of sovereign eurobonds.
- In order to have these bonds rank pari passu with other Eurobonds, holders of existing and other new issues of the Russian Federation would have the right to put back those bonds at par to Russia, in the event of acceleration of the 2010s and 2030s. This repurchase right would expire once Russia issued at least $1 billion of new Eurobonds, as Russia committed to include expanded cross-acceleration clauses tied to 2010 and 2030 in new issues.
- MinFins as domestic debt remained subordinated.
- Initially, a minimum threshold of 75 percent of bondholders was needed to consummate the exchange if less than $19 billion was tendered. However, if this happened and Russia wanted to go ahead with the exchange, it had the option open upon requesting consent from creditors to do so.

- Russia retained the right to re-tap both the 2010s and 2030s without prior notice. This was included to allow for additional restructuring of FTO paper, and did not work against the deal.[49]

Ukraine's bond operation in early 2000 could be viewed as a concerted bond exchange, as the country was not current on its bond payments. Ukraine provided a $220 million payout of accrued interest and also used collective action clauses in three of its bonds to boost investor participation.

The experience from the six bond exchanges discussed above suggests that these operations may be relatively easy to implement and can be completed in a short period, despite the lack of a formal mechanism for bond workouts. These bond exchanges were also successful in achieving high investor participation without the use of collective action clauses. The six bond workouts demonstrate that markets appear to be responding fairly well to the financial structures in which they are operating, and that creditor coordination issues have not undermined the debt resolution process.

The discussion leaves out Argentina's December 2001 default, where a resolution of the debt crisis is still in process. Two years into the Argentine default, and with many uncertainties to be resolved, a couple of distinctive features are already clear. First, this will be a longer and less friendly restructuring when compared to other bond workouts since 1998. Second, a substantial haircut is likely. Third, the power of litigation is extremely minor. So far, the few cases brought to the New York courts have faced a clear resistance to impose attachments that may derail the restructuring process. More so, plaintiffs had difficulties in specifying potentially attachable assets to the judge.[50] As of this writing, bondholders had offered the government maturity extensions and substantial interest rate reduction, equivalent to an estimated present value reduction of about 60 percent. At the same time, the government was demanding a present value reduction of about 92 percent. As the economy recovers, it is likely that the final agreement will imply a larger return to the shareholders.*

SOME COMPLEXITIES REGARDING BOND DEFAULTS. In contrast to the mechanics of the 1980s, in which a sudden stop in financing prompted a default, the experiences in the late 1990s left open many more dimensions on which the country had to make decisions. First of all, countries had to decide which instruments they would default upon or exchange – and, therefore, which broad group of creditors would be affected. The countries also had to decide if the default would be focused on local creditors or on foreign creditors. This distinction can be difficult to make; some instruments are clearly segmented in terms of their bearers, so that segmentation is at least partially feasible. While in general, policymakers would prefer to go harder on foreign creditors, the reputation and international implications of such decision may make

---

* Postscript: Argentina eventually concluded its debt restructuring at 34 cents on the doller (*Financial Times*, 3 June 2005, "Argentina closes door on Dollars 100 bn. debt exchange," by Adam Thomson).
[49] FTO paper corresponds to unsecured and uninsured foreign exchange assets of Foreign Trading Organizations held as FX-denominated deposits at Vnesheconombank and hence originally London Club-eligible.
[50] German courts have attached payments to diplomatic employees. The Argentine government moved such payment to Switzerland.

this alternative unfeasible. Thus one thing is what policymakers would prefer to do, and another is what they may be able to.[51] For example, in 2002, Ecuador and Argentina chose to default on all debt instruments. By contrast, Russia, Ukraine, and Uruguay chose a limited default or exchange that covered just a few types of instruments. When Ecuador decided initially to exclude Eurobonds from its default, it met criticism from the international financial community, which invoked a pari-passu clause among bondholders that obliged the Ecuadorian government to backtrack and include Eurobonds. However, it did manage to limit the discount on PDI bonds, which were mostly held by local bondholders. On the other hand, Russia initially defaulted mostly on local bondholders (holder of GKOs and OFZs).[52] Argentina implemented a local exchange in November 2001 in anticipation of a harsher restructuring of external debt.[53]

Similarly, governments had to decide whether to implement the default in several successive steps or in one step. The initial defaults (Russia and Ukraine) proceeded in a stepwise fashion, with the country denying default to the last minute, only to restrict the default to specific instruments and those strictly necessary. The most recent two defaults, Ecuador and Argentina, were broader and simultaneous. To a great extent, how the default is implemented is closely related to the motives underlying the default. A country facing a liquidity or credibility problem may choose to default selectively, to obtain the necessary relief to go through a particularly difficult moment in terms of financing needs. A country with a solvency problem or an unwillingness to pay may be more inclined to broad-based default.

LESSONS FOR THE FUTURE

Does the debt default experience of the 1990s have applicability for the future? The basic issue is whether a formal international mechanism for debt workouts is needed or whether markets are addressing these issues adequately. The current approach to resolving debt crisis is informal and has a precedent in recent bond operations. While it represents a market-based approach, it is clearly a process of muddling through.

---

[51] Similarly, a decision must be made regarding debts with international financial institutions and bilateral lending. Here there appears to be a clear pattern. IFI lending is seen as senior to everything else, with only a few cases of default to multilaterals. This seniority may be a way of buying the seal of approval that only IFIs can provide to a country, as well as the direct link that multilaterals open with the countries that "own" these organizations. In many cases, it is the private creditors themselves that want the country to agree with the multilaterals first, as they consider that these institutions' job is to go through a "due diligence" process with the country, which the creditors cannot do themselves. Thus the seniority of IFIs lending is a market-accepted and encouraged outcome. On the other hand, bilateral lending and concessional official lending is usually considered junior to other lending. For example, Pakistan built up substantial arrears with the Paris Club, while never entering into default with private bondholders. Ecuador was in arrears with the Paris Club and still was able to issue a Eurobond in 1997.

[52] However, there were sizable holdings of these instruments by nonresidents.

[53] This debt was later pesified – that is, forcibly redenominated in pesos. Many local pension funds did not accept this pesification and sued the government. In response, the authorities moved them back to the pool of defaulted debt. Furthermore, the government barred the possibility of switching these obligations to indexed pesos, an alternative that should have been attractive both to government and pension funds. As a result of a public outcry, the government allowed for this swap in the current restructuring proposal, where it is expected local pension funds will obtain a better deal.

Better debt workout mechanisms might be possible – namely, mechanisms that would correct for (or reduce the inefficiency from) perceived collective action failures on the creditor side. These include market-based approaches, such as the inclusion of collective action clauses in new bond contracts and the establishment of formal bondholder councils, and more comprehensive and sweeping approaches, such as an international bankruptcy procedure like the IMF's Sovereign Debt Restructuring Mechanism (SDRM).

Following the Mexican Tesobono crisis of 1994–95, analysts such as Jeffrey Sachs (1995) emphasized the need for new institutional arrangements to deal with debt crises resulting from investor overreaction and crises of confidence. Sachs advocated an international bankruptcy mechanism to counter this type of market inefficiency and to achieve orderly debt workouts. Such a procedure would call for a payment standstill by the debtor country during debt renegotiations. While the international bankruptcy mechanism advocated by Sachs would streamline debt workouts, it would not address the important issue of moral hazard for debtors.

The Sovereign Debt Restructuring Mechanism or SDRM has been proposed as part of the IMF's effort to improve crisis management and the international financial architecture.[54] The SDRM aims to address the problems of creditor coordination in debt workouts by proposing a statutory approach that borrows some of the principles of U.S. domestic corporate bankruptcy and collective action clauses.[55] The key elements of the international bankruptcy procedure are: provision allowing an insolvent country to activate the SDRM on request; aggregation of all external debt owed to private creditors; provision allowing a supermajority of creditors to negotiate a debt restructuring that would be binding for all creditors; sharing of proceeds from litigation; and provision permitting disputes to be adjudicated by independent bankruptcy tribunals. Thus, the SDRM would make it easier for a country to reach an agreement with a supermajority of its creditors, while avoiding a creditor holdout problem.

By providing a predictable environment for restructuring, the SDRM would in principle facilitate an orderly debt workout and avoid prolonged and costly debt renegotiations. Reducing transactions costs in this way enhances efficiency and stability of the international financial system. The SDRM has some potential disadvantages, however. Notably, it does not eliminate the moral hazard problem for debtors. By lowering the costs of crises, debtors might be more likely to overborrow and ignore fiscal discipline. If this mechanism does not address moral hazard problems, it will be unable to avoid excessive delays in debt resolution as countries struggle to avoid falling into an SDRM restructuring process. Implementation issues also complicate the viability of the SDRM. The SDRM calls for changing IMF Articles to override some aspects of domestic law, and these changes may not survive legal challenges.

A proposal for a voluntary code of conduct, advocated by Jean Claude Trichet (2001), calls for the uniform adoption of best practices in sovereign debt restructuring so as to speed up resolution of debt crises.[56] The code defines nine principles

---

[54] See Boorman (2002); Krueger (2001, 2002); and Rogoff and Zettelmeyer (2001).

[55] There is some similarity with corporate debt reorganization under Chapter 11 of the United States Bankruptcy Code.

[56] See also Couillault and Weber (2003).

that should be agreed by both creditors and debtors: early engagement with creditors before and after debt servicing problems arise, fair information sharing, fair representation of creditors, an expeditious and cooperative process, comparable treatment among creditors, fair burden-sharing, good faith negotiation, preserving of debtors' financial situation, and a quick restoration of debt sustainability. The weakness of the proposal relies on the fact that, while everybody may agree ex ante to comply with these principles, the power to enforce them once a default has occurred appears rather limited.[57]

In moving forward on approaches to debt restructuring, there appears to be broad support in the international community for solutions involving incremental change, as opposed to solutions that radically overhaul the international financial architecture. Thus voluntary, market-friendly approaches to debt restructuring – such as the inclusion of CACs in sovereign bond contracts – are increasingly being viewed as a step forward in improving the current debt restructuring process. This – despite the concern that CACs could impose higher borrowing costs and lower overall financial flows to emerging markets. By facilitating coordination among creditors and lowering the cost of restructuring, CACs could contribute to a moral hazard problem for debtors.[58]

Barry Eichengreen and Richard Portes (1995) first introduced the concept of using contractual innovations such as collective action clauses so as to overcome creditors' collective action problems. They argued against a statutory approach on the grounds that it would be difficult to implement and, more importantly, because of the moral hazard problem for debtors that such an approach would create. They also see some merit in having an informal bondholders' organization that would function like the London Club.

Using a model of sovereign debt, Kenneth Kletzer (2003) argues that CACs are more efficient than the commonly used unanimity clauses in bond contracts because unanimity clauses can promote rent-seeking behavior in creditors and this can give rise to inefficient outcomes for lending and repayment.[59] He further concludes that if all sovereign bonds have CACs, then there is no added benefit of establishing a formal international bankruptcy procedure, such as the SDRM. However, renegotiation costs may invalidate the welfare equivalence of CACs and the SDRM-type statutory approach. Thus, if the formation of bondholder renegotiation committees is costly because of a large number of different bonds issued in different legal jurisdictions, then the SDRM might be more efficient because it aggregates debt. Also, while the CAC approach is useful in a forward-looking sense, it does not effectively address the issue of default on existing bonds (the so-called transition problem), most of which do not have CACs.

Collective action clauses have begun appearing in several recent sovereign bond issues. For example, in February 2003, Mexico became the first major emerging

---

[57] Argentina, however, has claimed its willingness to comply with this code of conduct. It remains to be seen how this will develop.

[58] Eichengreen and Mody (2000) find that for creditworthy borrowers, the inclusion of CACs lowers bond spreads in primary issues, but less creditworthy borrowers are likely to experience higher spreads on bond issues.

[59] Kletzer obtains these results by making the assumption that the transaction costs of renegotiations are either zero or lower under contracts with CACs than those with unanimity clauses.

market borrower to issue a bond with CACs under New York law, and Uruguay issued all of its bonds created during the recent bond restructuring with CACs, also under New York law. These developments suggest a growing market support for the CAC approach, and the inclusion of CACs in bond contracts is progressing rapidly. Again, while CACs address the creditor coordination problem for individual bond issues, they do not solve the problem of cross-issue creditor coordination (the so-called aggregation problem) or the problem of creditor coordination for the existing stock of debt (the so-called transition problem).

Thus, there is a recognition that CACs may not go far enough to smoothing the debt restructuring process, and that additional mechanisms will be needed. Barry Eichengreen, Kenneth Kletzer, and Ashoka Mody (2003) suggest that supercollective action clauses, bondholder committees, and code of creditor conduct might be such additional mechanisms. For example, supercollective action clauses in bond contracts would overcome the cross-issue coordination problem by allowing a qualified majority of bondholders to vote on bond restructuring terms. By facilitating creditor coordination, bondholder committees would likewise enhance the debt workout process. However, bondholder committees may provide only limited benefits because they would not overcome the problem of lawsuits from holdout creditors (Mauro and Yafeh 2003). The debate on the usefulness of these and other additional mechanisms is evolving, and there is no consensus yet on the next set of innovations that will be needed to improve debt crises resolution.

As we move ahead in the Argentine restructuring, some lessons are clear. On the one hand, bond restructurings are feasible and can be implemented relatively quickly. On the other hand, such debt restructurings are extremely costly to both creditors and debtors. Such costly events may be necessary for sovereign debt to exist. But to the extent that such large crises impose deadweight costs and *do occur* (as opposed to being some off-equilibrium outcome used for deterrence), there is still much to be improved upon, as market players, international financial institutions, and creditor countries continue struggling in the common objective of building a smoother and safer global capital market.

APPENDIX A. SOVEREIGN DEFAULTS ON DEBT
TO PRIVATE CREDITORS

Table A-1. *Rated issuers: years in default, 1975–2002*

Rated issuers: years in default, 1975–2002			
Issuer	Local currency debt	Foreign currency bond debt	Foreign currency bank debt
Argentina	1982, 1989–90, 2002	1989, 2001–02	1982–93
Bolivia		1989–97	1980–84, 1986–93
Brazil	1986–87, 1990		1983–94
Bulgaria			1990–94
Chile			1983–90
Cook Islands			1995–98

(*continued*)

Punam Chuhan and Federico Sturzenegger

Table A-1 (*continued*)

	Rated issuers: years in default, 1975–2002		
Issuer	Local currency debt	Foreign currency bond debt	Foreign currency bank debt
Costa Rica		1984–85	1981–90
Croatia	1993–96		1992–96
Dominican Republic	1981–2001		1982–94
Ecuador	1999	1999–2000	1982–95
Egypt			1984
El Salvador	1981–96		
Guatemala		1989	1986
Indonesia			1998–89, 2000, 2002
Jamaica			1978–79, 1981–85, 1987–93
Jordan			1989–93
Kuwait	1990–91		
Mexico			1982–90
Mongolia	1997–2000		
Morocco			1983, 1986–90
Pakistan		1999	1998–99
Panama		1987–94	1983–96
Paraguay			1986–92
Peru			1976, 1978, 1980, 1983–97
Philippines			1983–92
Poland			1981–94
Romania			1981–83, 1986
Russia	1998–99	1998–2000	1991–97
Senegal			1981–85, 1990, 1992–96
Slovenia			1992–96
South Africa			1985–87, 1989, 1993
Trinidad & Tobago			1988–89
Turkey			1978–79, 1982
Ukraine	1998–2000		1998–2000
Uruguay			1983–85, 1987, 1990–91
Venezuela	1995–97, 1998	1995–97	1983–88, 1990
Vietnam	1975		1985–98

Source: Standard and Poors (2002) *Sovereign Defaults: Moving Higher Again in 2003.*

Table A-2. *Unrated issuers: years in default, 1975–2002*

Issuer	Local currency debt	Foreign currency bond debt	Foreign currency bank debt
Albania			1991–95
Algeria			1991–96
Angola	1992–2002		1985–2002
Antigua & Barbuda			1996–2002
Bosnia & Herzegovina			1992–97
Burkina Faso			1983–96
Cameroon			1985–2002
Cape Verde			1981–96
Central African Republic			1981, 1983–2002
Congo (Brazzaville)			1983–2002
Congo (Kinshasa)			1976–2002
Cuba			1982–2002
Ethiopia			1991–99
Gabon			1986–94, 1999, 2002
Gambia			1986–90
Ghana	1979		1987
Guinea			1986–88, 1991–98
Guinea-Bissau			1983–96
Guyana			1976, 1982–99
Haiti			1982–94
Honduras			1981–2002
Iran			1978–95
Iraq			1987–2002
Ivory Coast		2000–02	1983–98
Kenya			1994–2002
North Korea			1975–2002*
Liberia			1987–2002
Macedonia			1992–97
Madagascar	2002		1981–84, 1986–2002
Malawi			1982, 1988
Mauritania			1992–96
Moldova		1998, 2002	
Mozambique			1983–92
Myanmar (Burma)	1984		1998–2002
Nauru			2002
Nicaragua			1979–2002
Niger			1983–91
Nigeria		1986–88, 1992	1982–92
Sao Tome & Principe			1987–94
Serbia & Montenegro			1992–2002
Seychelles			2000–02
Sierra Leone	1997–98		1983–84, 1986–95
Solomon Islands	1995–2002		

(continued)

Table A-2 (*continued*)

Issuer	Local currency debt	Foreign currency bond debt	Foreign currency bank debt
Unrated issuers: years in default, 1975–2002			
Sri Lanka	1996		
Sudan			1979–2002
Tanzania			1984–2002
Togo			1979–80, 1982–84, 1988, 1991–97
Uganda			1980–93
Yemen			1985–2001
Former Yugoslavia		1992–2002	1983–91
Zambia			1983–94
Zimbabwe		1975–80**	2000–02

* Debt initially defaulted on in 1974.
** Bonds initially defaulted on 1965.
Source: Standard and Poor's (2002) *Sovereign Defaults: Moving Higher Again in 2003*.

APPENDIX B. COLLECTIVE ACTION CLAUSES

Collective action clauses include three types of clauses: the sharing clause, the collective representation clause, and the majority clause.[†]

SHARING CLAUSE. The sharing clause states that any payments received by one bondholder must be shared with other bondholders. Sharing clauses were introduced as part of syndicated loan restructuring deals of the 1980s. The aim was to protect banks with little relation with a given debtor country and that feared that they could be defaulted upon if the debtor made it a priority to stay current with those banks with which it had stronger commercial ties. In addition, sharing clauses are an important deterrent to litigation, as any proceeds obtained from litigation must be shared with other bondholders.[60] There are two ways in which the sharing clause can be effected. In the English-style sharing clause, the excess payment is handed to a fiscal agent for ratable distribution. In the American-style clause, the original recipient purchases subparticipations in other creditors' debt.[61]

[†] This appendix draws on Sturzenegger (2002b).

[60] Buchheit (1998b, p.19) proposes a sharing clause to read as follows: "Each bondholder agrees that if it shall obtain (whether by way of payment from the Issuer or following the exercise of set-off rights, litigation or otherwise) any payment in respect of the Bonds held by the bondholder that is proportionally greater than the payment received by any other bondholder in respect of the Bonds held by that other bondholder, then: (i) the bondholder receiving such excess amount shall pay such excess amount to the Fiscal Agent; (ii) the Fiscal Agent shall treat such amount as if it were a payment received from the Issuer in respect of the Bonds and shall distribute it accordingly; and (iii) as between the Issuer and the bondholder originally receiving the excess amount, such excess amount shall be treated as not having been paid; provided, however, that no bondholder shall be required by this Section to share any amount recovered by it as a result of litigation against the Issuer if bondholder holding at least 90% of the outstanding amount of the Bonds shall have previously consented in writing to the commencement of that litigation."

[61] See Buchheit (1998b).

MAJORITY ACTION CLAUSES. While New York law does not allow for changes in the payment conditions without the consent of all bondholders, London law allows changes in payment terms with a quorum of 75 percent.[62] The rules that allow the change in the terms of the bonds with a qualified majority are dubbed majority action clauses. In the case of Ukraine, the tendering of the bonds in the exchange was automatically a proxy vote to apply the majority action clause. Thus, any bondholder that remained with the original bond risked the terms being changed in such a way that would render the original instrument worth less in both characteristics and payment conditions. As the threshold participation rates assigned for the transaction were larger than those required to change the conditions of the bonds, bondholders had a large incentive to participate in the transaction. This type of clauses can be complemented with cram-down clauses. *Cram-down clauses* force an agreement reached with a majority of bondholders to be binding on holdouts. For example, to protect sovereign debtors from disruptive lawsuits, majority action clauses prevent a small number of creditors from blocking an attempt to renegotiate the terms of the bonds. This clause makes litigation feasible only if a majority of bondholders vote in favor of pursuing litigation.

COLLECTIVE REPRESENTATION CLAUSES. Once a country decides to default, it needs to establish a counterpart. The experience in recent debt restructurings has been varied. Pakistan established direct contact with major bondholders in order to gauge possible acceptable settlements. Russia negotiated with the London Club. Ecuador, on the other hand, called for a creditors committee as a consulting group (this turned ineffectual, as creditors chose to present their demands in a private manner). Legally, the question is whether a debt renegotiation counterpart can be established in the legal framework. One possible candidate to take up such a role is the fiscal agent(s) under whom the bonds were originally issued. This would probably meet with strong resistance both from the fiscal agent(s), who may not wish to be involved in a problem between third parties, and from bondholders who could have doubts as to whether the fiscal agent(s) would necessarily defend their interests in a renegotiation. Lead managers of the outstanding bonds would be another candidate. But they will probably be equally disinclined to participate because of reluctance to accept any coresponsibility in the default. A third option is a group of bondholders. As long as this group is not enshrined in the covenants of the bond, there is no formal obligation to do the negotiations through such a group. However, even in those cases, these groups have remained an informal and valid counterpart.

---

[62] Buchheit (1998a) proposes a majority action clause as follows: "Modifications and amendment to the Fiscal Agency Agreement or the Bonds requiring bondholder consent of the issuer and the holder of at least a majority of aggregate principal amount of the Bonds at the time outstanding, provided that no such modification, amendment or waiver of the Fiscal Agency Agreement or any Bond may, without the consent of holders of at least 90% of aggregate outstanding principal amount of the Bonds voting at the bondholders meeting convened for this purpose (i) change the stated maturity of the principal of or interest on any such Bond; (ii) reduce the principal of or interest on any such Bond; (iii) change the currency of payment of the principal of or interest on any such Bond; or (iv) reduce the above stated percentage of aggregate principal amounts of Bonds outstanding or reduce the quorum requirements or the percentage of voters required for the taking of any action."

Their nonbinding recommendations, are usually useful to individual bondholders to decide whether to follow suit (see Buchheit 1998c).

In some cases, the debt renegotiation cannot appeal to the majority clause. An example is bonds issued under New York law. A way around this is known as *exit consent*. This consists of changing the conditions of other characteristics of the bond, in particular nonpayment conditions, which can be changed by a qualified majority even under New York law. This methodology was used in the Ecuador restructuring. As bondholders exited from the original instruments, they voted for changes in other conditions on the original Brady bonds. Among these, they removed provisions that would have interfered with Ecuador's ability to close the exchange offer at a time when the country was in payment default. They removed the so-called exit covenants by which Ecuador had promised never to seek a further restructuring of the Brady bonds. They deleted the cross default clauses; the requirement that all payment defaults be cured as a condition to any rescission of acceleration; the negative pledge covenant; and the covenant to maintain the listing of the defaulted instruments on the Luxembourg Stock Exchange.

APPENDIX C. BOND RESTRUCTURINGS IN ARGENTINA, RUSSIA, ECUADOR, PAKISTAN, UKRAINE, AND URUGUAY

Argentine Government Bond Exchange of June 2001

Between June 1 and 4, 2001 Argentina conducted a "mega" bond exchange operation to extend bond maturities. The government received exchange offers worth $33.3 billion from bondholders and swapped existing bonds with an original value of $29.5 billion for $31.04 billion of new instruments. The bond exchange was voluntary and was the biggest exchange of its kind.

Under the bond exchange, existing bonds, including Brady bonds, Eurobonds, and local securities, were exchanged for five types of new instruments. Three of the new bonds have an interest capitalization feature (up to five years of interest capitalization), and the other two bonds have step-up coupon rates. The five new bonds are:

- A $11.5 billion, seven-year global bond with a 7 percent coupon for the first three years and 15.5 percent from the fourth year till maturity. Amortization is in six semiannual equal payments from June 2006 until December 2008.
- A $0.9 billion, 7-year global bond with a 10 percent coupon for the first three years and 12.4 percent from the fourth year till maturity. Amortization is in the form of a bullet payment in December 2008.
- A $7.5 billion, 17-year global with a 12.25 percent coupon and interest capitalization of five years. Amortization is in five semiannual equal payments from June 2016 to June 2018.
- A $8.5 billion, 30-year global with a 12 percent coupon and interest capitalization of five years. Amortization is in the form of a bullet payment in June 2031.
- A $2.1 billion, five-year local bond at floating interest rates and interest capitalization of two years.

Table C-1. *Argentina: Mega bond exchange, June 2001*

New bonds	Pagare 2006	Global $/US$ 2008	Global 2008	Global 2018	Global 2031	Total exchange
Nominal value of new issues (US$millions)	2,060	931	11,716	7,812	8,521	31,040
Maturity date	June-06	Sep-08	Dec-08	June-18	June-31	
Coupon	BALDAR (local) + 150 bp	10% from first to third year, 12% from fourth year to maturity	7% from first to third year, 15.5% from fourth year to maturity	12.25%	12%	
Interest capitalization	2 years	No	No	5 years	5 years	
Amortization	6 equal semiannual payments	Bullet	6 equal semiannual payments	5 equal semiannual payments	Bullet	
Average maturity (years)	3.75	7.25	6.3	16	30	
Schedule of payments	12/19/03 16.66% 6/19/04 16.66% 12/19/04 16.66% 6/19/05 16.66% 12/19/05 16.66% 6/19/06 16.7%	9/19/2008	6/19/06 16.66% 12/19/06 16.66% 12/19/07 16.66% 12/19/08 16.66% 6/19/08 16.66% 12/19/08 16.7%	6/19/16 20% 6/19/17 20% 6/19/17 20% 12/19/17 20% 6/19/18 20%	6/19/2031	
Issue price	100%	78%	79%	73%	71%	
Old nominal value (US$millions)	2,028	1,215	11,093	7,123	8,034	29,493
Old market price (US$millions)	2,030	729	8,999	5,467	6,024	23,249
Clearing price	100%	60%	81%	77%	75%	

Source: Adapted from Ministry of Economy website.

Russian Bond Restructuring of 1998

On July 18, 1998, Russia launched an exchange offer for its defaulted Prins and IANs, former Soviet Union debt assumed by the Vneshekonombank. The exchange was completed on August 25, 2000 and involved the swap of US$22.2 billion Prins and US$6.8 billion IANs and overdue interest for two new 2030 and 2010 Eurobonds. The new bonds covered interest arrears from December 2, 1998 on Prins and from June 2, 1999 for IANs until March 31, 2000. Interest on the new bonds would accrue from March 31, 2000.

The 10-year bond was offered to cover overdue coupon payments. This bond issue totaled US$2.8 million (9.5 percent of which was paid in cash at the moment of the offer) and was given in exchange of:

- US$368 million on Prins due on December 2, 1998 (the amount that should have been paid in cash).[63]
- US$1.337 million on Prins due on June 2, 1999 and December 2, 1999 (this included the amount that should have been paid in cash plus the part that should have capitalized).
- US$512 million on Prins accrued from December 2, 1999 until March 31, 2000 (this included the amount that should have been paid in cash plus the part that should have capitalized).
- US$414 million on IANs due on June 2, 1999 and December 2, 1999.
- US$158 million on IANs accrued from December 2, 1999 until March 31, 2000.

The 30-year bond was offered in exchange of Prins and IANs with an important write-off of 37.5 percent of nominal value on Prins and 33 percent of nominal value on IANs.

In September 2000, Russia announced that over 99 percent in aggregate amount of Prins and 98 percent in aggregate amount of IANs were tendered in its exchange offer.

This exchange implied an upgrade in the obligor, as the responsibility switched from Vneshekonombank to the Russian government.

Ecuador Bond Restructuring of 2000

In August 2000, Ecuador completed a bond exchange operation involving defaulted Brady bonds and Eurobonds. Some $5.9 billion of defaulted Brady bonds and $465 million of eurobonds were swapped for two global bonds with a face value of $3.9 billion. The global bonds comprised a $2.7 billion, 30-year multicoupon bond and a $1.25 billion, 12-year fixed-rate bond. All bondholders were first offered the 30-year bond, which could (simultaneously) be exchanged for the 12-year bond at an additional 35 percent discount on the principal of the 30-year bond. Ecuador's bond offer resulted in a 41 percent reduction in principal for bondholders.

---

[63] A distinguishing feature of Prins was that a varying portion (ranging from 15 to 60 percent) of its coupon payments until 2002 were capitalized in the form of IANs. The rest of the coupon was to be paid in cash.

Table C-2. *Russia: bond exchange of 2000*

Agreement date	2000 July
Debt eligible	$ 22.2 billion in defaulted Restructured Principal Bonds (Prins)
	$ 6.8 billion in defaulted Interest Arrear Notes (IANs)
Discount rate	37.5% on Prins
	33.0% on IANs
Amounts exchanged	$28.6 billion
New bonds issued	$21.2 billion
2030 Eurobond	In exchange for principal on Prins and IANs:
Term	A sinkable bond repaying its principal in 47 semi-annual installments, with date of issue March 31, 2000.
Amount	$18.4 billion
Interest rate	Initial coupon rate of 2.25% for the first interest period, rising to 2.5% in the second interest period, 5% from year 2 to year 7 (inclusive), and 7.5% thereafter.
2010 Eurobond	In exchange for overdue interest on Prins and IANs:
Term	9.5% paid in cash on issue date. Nine equal semiannual amortization payments commencing March 31, 2006.
Amount	$2.8 billion
Interest rate	8.25%

Source: National sources.

Investor participation in the deal was about 97 percent, well above the over 85 percent participation acceptance level that had been set. One factor that encouraged participation was the government's offer to pay bondholders $140 million of past-due principal and interest on defaulted bonds. Exit amendments to cross-default and negative pledge clauses in the old bonds, by investors who were tendering their old bonds for new bonds, and an amendment to delist the bonds pushed up the investor participation rate as well. The government's pledge to repurchase at least 3 percent of the 30-years bonds each year, starting in 2013, and at least 10 percent of the 12-year bonds beginning in 2006, was also a factor.

Ecuador's bond restructuring (from default to bond exchange) was completed in about one year, a relatively short time compared to the loan restructuring episodes of the 1980s. Although Ecuador's bond exchange offer involved a haircut for creditors, the country did not engage in formal negotiation with its bondholders. A Consultative Group comprising large institutional investors was set up, but the function of this group was to provide a medium for communication between the government and the creditor community and not to negotiate the terms of the offer.

Pakistan Eurobond Exchange of 1999

The January 1999 agreement with Paris Club creditors required Pakistan to obtain comparable treatment of its debt due to all its external public and private creditors, including to bondholders. This meant that the government had to seek from its bondholders a reorganization of its bonds on terms comparable to those on bilateral debt.

On November 15, 1999, Pakistan launched a "voluntary" bond exchange involving three dollar-denominated Eurobonds with a face value of $610 million. The

Table C-3. *Ecuador: bond exchange of 2000*

Agreement date	2000 August
debt eligible	(a) $5.9 billions in defaulted Brady bonds
	$1.6 billion of PAR Bonds
	$1.4 billion of discount bonds
	$2.2 billion of PDIs
	$181 million of IEs
	(b) $465 million in 12- and 30-year Eurobounds
	$322 million of 11.25% fixed-rate Eurobond
	$143 million of floating-rate Eurobond
Discount rate	41%
Amounts exchanged	$6.7 billion
New bonds issued	$3.95 billion
30-year multicoupon bond–first phase	All investors were offered the 30-year bonds, which can be exchanged for the 12-year bonds for an additional 35% discount
Term	Bullet payment in 2030
Interest rate	Initial coupon rate of 4% until August 2001, reset annually at 5%, 6%, 7%, 8%, 9%, thereafter 10%.
12-year bond – second phase	
Term	Bullet payment in 2012
Interest rates	12% fixed interest rate
	With the released collateral, the government offered to pay bondholders $140 million of past-due principal and interest in defaulted debt.
	The government pledged to repurchase at least 3% of the 30-year bond, starting in 2013 and at least 10% of the 12-year bond beginning in 2006

PDIs: Past-due interest bond
IEs: Interest equalization bond
Source: National sources.

Table C-4. *Pakistan bond exchange of 1999*

Agreement date	1999 November
Debt eligible	(a) $150 million, 11.5% Eurobond due in December 1999
	(b) $300 million floating rate note due in May 2000
	(c) $160 million, 6% convertible due in February 2002
Discount	No debt forgiveness
Amounts exchanged	$610 million
New bonds issued	
Eurobond 2005	
Term	Matures 2005
Amount	$623 million
Interest rate	10%; semiannual payments in May and November

Source: National sources.

Table C-5. *Ukraine: bond exchange of 2000*

Agreement date	2000 February
Debt eligible	About $2.7 billion
	(a) 500 million Pounds Sterling Eurobond due in 2000/03
	(b) $258 million Zero coupon paper due in 2000/09
	(c) DM 1.5 billion Eurobond due in 2001/02
	(d) $ 76 million Eurobond due in 2000/10
	(e) $ 280 million of Gaxprom bonds due in 2000 and 2001
	(f) $ 735 million of Gaxprom bonds due in 2002–2006
Discount	No debt forgiveness
Amounts exchanged	$ 2.3 billion
New bonds issued	
7-year Eurobond either	
(a) denominated in euros	
Term	Semiannual amorization payments with 6-month grace period (schedule)
Amount	1.13 billion euro
interest rate	10%
(b) denominated in US$	
Term	Semiannual amortization payments with 6-month grace period (schedule)
Amount	$1.13 billion
interest rate	11%

Notes: This agreement not to be confused with
(a) Sept. 1998 $590 million exchange of short-term domastic T-bills held by nonresident for dollar-denominated 2-year Eurobond, or
(b) July 1999 $163 million Eurobond swap to 3-year D-Mark-denominated Eurobond (80%) and payment 20%.
Source: National sources.

three bonds were: a $150 million, 11.5 percent Eurobond due in December 1999; a $300 million floating rate note due in May 2000; and a $160 million, 6 percent convertible bond due in February 2002 and with a put in February 2000. Under the bond operation, the three Eurobonds were swapped for a six-year, $623 million Eurobond with a 10 percent coupon.

The bond operation was viewed as a success because of the very high investor participation rate: nearly 99 percent. A relatively narrow investor base – a limited number of mostly institutional investors – and the possibility of a default on the original bonds are believed to have contributed to the high participation rate. Investor participation was also boosted by the terms on the new bond, which provided a sweetener relative to the prevailing market price. The size and structure of the new bond implied that this instrument would be more liquid than the original bonds, thereby adding to the attractiveness of the offer. Because of these and other factors, majority or collective action clauses in the old bonds did not need to be invoked to achieve high investor participation.

Ukraine Bond Exchange of 2000

On February 4, 2000, Ukraine presented an offer to exchange its Eurobonds for new bonds. The exchange involved four Eurobonds and all Gazprom bonds. The Eurobonds comprised a 500 million pound sterling, 14.75 percent Eurobond due March 2000, a $258 million zero-coupon Eurobond due September 2000, a $75 million, 16.75 percent Eurobond due October 2000, and a DM 1.5 billion, 16 percent Eurobond due February 2001. The $280 million of Gazprom bonds falling due in 2000–01 were included in the exchange. Later, $735 million of Gazprom bonds maturing between 2002–06 were added to the offer.

Of the $2.7 billion of debt eligible under the offer, $2.3 billion was exchanged for two new bonds: a $1.13 billion, 7-year Eurobond with an 11 percent coupon; and a 1.13 billion euro-denominated, 7-year Eurobond with a 10 percent coupon. The investor participation rate exceeded the minimum 85 percent participation acceptance level that had been set for Eurobonds and bonds falling due in 2000–01. This is noteworthy, because 40 to 50 percent of the investor base was comprised of retail investors. A sweetener to investors in the form of a $220 million payout of accrued interest helped boost investor participation. The use of collective action clauses in three of the bonds (the DM 1.5 billion bond did not have CACs) may also have exerted a favorable affect on participation.

Uruguay Bond Exchange of May 2003

In May 2003, Uruguay conducted a voluntary bond exchange operation to reprofile debt maturities. Under the debt operation, existing bonds, including Bradys, Eurobonds, Samurai bonds, and domestic securities were exchanged for several types of new instruments. Of the $5.4 billion of foreign-currency denominated international and domestic securities eligible for the exchange, $5.1 billion were swapped.

The exchange had an international component and a domestic component. The international exchange offer covered $3.8 billion of foreign securities, including $400 million of Brady bonds and $250 million of Samurai bonds. The holders of the bonds were offered two types of swap options:

A liquidity option – Old bonds would be exchanged for new U.S. dollar – denominated fixed rate bonds that are expected to be traded in the secondary debt market and that would provide a benchmark for future issues.

A maturity extension option – Old bonds would be exchanged for new bonds, generally at par value and at the same coupon rate, for new bonds with deferred maturities. The option maintained the currency and the coupon of issuance. Samurai bonds would be amended so as to extend the maturity from 2006 to 2011, and to raise the interest rate from 2.2 to 2.5 percent.

The new instruments included collective action clauses, which would allow a supermajority (75 percent) of bondholders to modify bond repayment terms. Also, there was a sweetener – upfront cash payment – for securities maturing in the near to medium term, 2003–07.

Table C-6. *Uruguay bond exchange of 2003 (in million US$)*

Agreement date	2003 May
Debt eligible	5,390
International exchange offer	3,771
of which Brady bonds	401
Samurai bonds	250
Domestic exchange offer	1,619
Amounts exchanged	5,055
International exchange offer	3,455
of which Brady bonds	239
of which Samurai bonds	250
Domestic exchange offer	1,600
Discount	none
Cash payment	107
New external bonds issued	3,426
Benchmark Bonds:	2,614
7.25% bond maturing in 2011 in US$	500
7.50% bond maturing in 2015 in US$	1,059
7.875% bond maturing in 2033 in US$ (PIK)	1,055
Extension Bonds	812
7.875% bond maturing in 2008 in US$	84
8.375% bond maturing in 2011 in US$	61
7.0% bond maturing in 2013 in US$	64
7.25% bond maturing in 2014 in US$	32
7.875% bond maturing in 2014 in US$	20
8.75% bond maturing in 2015 in US$	51
7.625% bond maturing in 2017 in US$	41
FRN bond maturing in 2009 in US$	2
FRN bond maturing in 2010 in US$	5
CLP bond maturing in 2016 in CLP	2
EUR bond 7% maturing in 2012 in EUR	110
EUR bond 7% maturing in 2019 in EUR	139
SAMU bond 2.5% maturing in 2011 in JPY	203

Source: Central Bank of Uruguay.

The domestic exchange offer covered $1.6 billion of bills and longer-term instruments. Like the foreign bonds, the new domestic bonds included CACs. In addition, cash incentives were applicable to debt maturing in the short term – that is, in 2003.

The investor participation rate – at 90 percent for the international offer and 98 percent for the domestic offer – met the target rate of at least 90 percent set by the authorities. Investors appeared to favor the liquidity option: the new benchmark bonds account for 73 percent (or $2.6 billion) of the new external bonds, while the maturity extension bonds account for 28 percent (or $0.8 billion).

APPENDIX D. EAST ASIA CRISIS AND DEBT WORKOUTS

In the wake of the East Asia crisis of 1997, domestic financial institutions in Korea and Indonesia faced severe payment difficulties on their external debts. These countries were forced to reschedule their debt obligations with the help of government guarantees.

In March 1998, the Korean government signed an agreement with foreign creditor banks on rescheduling short-term foreign debt of domestic financial institutions. The agreement scheduled $24 billion of short-term foreign debt into long-term debt: loans with one to three years maturity and interest rate spreads over Libor of 225 basis points (bp) for one-year loans, 250 bp for two-year loans, and 275 bp for three-year loans. Some $20 billion of the new debt carried government guarantees.

In June 1998, Indonesia reached an agreement (the Frankfurt Agreement) with a group of 13 foreign creditor banks on a framework for rescheduling private sector debt ($80 billion). The categories of debt covered were interbank debt, trade finance, and corporate debt. Indonesian commercial banks were able to exchange their foreign currency obligations to foreign banks for new loans with government guarantees. The new loans ranged in maturity from one to four years, and were at interest rate spreads of 275 bp, 300 bp, 325 bp, and 350 bp over Libor. About $7 billion of the $9.2 billion of short-term interbank debt was rescheduled. The framework for corporate debt restructuring allowed Indonesian companies to reschedule their loans with a three-year grace period and an eight-year maturity and a real interest rate of 5.59 percent. The creation of the Indonesian Debt Restructuring Agency (INDRA) was to provide foreign exchange cover for Indonesian corporations with foreign currency debt, once they have reached debt rescheduling agreements.

REFERENCES

Barro, Robert J. 2001. "Economic Growth in East Asia Before and After the Financial Crisis." NBER Working Paper 8330. National Bureau of Economic Research, Cambridge, MA.

Becker, Torbjorn, Anthony Richards, and Yungyong Thaicharoen. 2001. "Bond Restructuring and Moral Hazard: Are Collective Action Clauses Costly?" IMF Working Paper 01/92. International Monetary Fund, Washington, DC.

Boorman, Jack. 2002. "Sovereign Debt Restructuring: Where Stands the Debate?" Presentation at conference sponsored by the CATO Institute and *The Economist*, October 17, New York. Available at http://www.imf.org/external/np/speeches/2001/sp01ind.htm.

Bordo, Michael, and Barry Eichengreen. 1999. "Is Our International Economic Environment Unusually Crisis Prone?" Reserve Bank of Australia Annual Conference Volume (199–03): 18–74.

Brainard, Lawrence J. 1985. "Managing the International Debt Crisis: The Future of the Baker Plan." *Contemporary Policy Issues* 5(3):66–75.

Buchheit, L. 1995. "The Sovereign Client." *Journal of International Affairs* 48:527–40.

———. 1997. "US Cases Put Immunity of Second Tier State Entities in Doubt." *International Financial Law Review* 16(30).

———. 1998a. "Majority Action Clauses May Help Resolve Debt Crises." *International Financial Law Review* 17(8):17–18.

———. 1998b. "Changing Bond Documentation: The Sharing Clause." *International Financial Law Review* 17(7):17–19.

———. 1998c. "The Collective Representation Clause." *International Financial Law Review* 17(9):19–21.

Buchheit, L., and G. Mitu Gulati. 2000. "Exit Consents in Sovereign Bond Exchanges." *UCLA Law Review* 48(1):59–84.

Bulow, Jeremy, and Kenneth S. Rogoff. 1989. "Sovereign Debt: Is to Forgive to Forget?" *American Economic Review* 79(March):43–50.

Chuhan, Punam. 2002. "Recent Experience with Bond Exchanges." World Bank, Washington, DC. Processed.

Clark, John. 1994. "Debt Reduction and Market Reentry under the Brady Plan." *FRBNY Quarterly Review Winter* 1993–1994, pp. 38–62.

Cline, William R. 1983. International Debt and the Stability of the World Economy. Cambridge, MA: MIT Press.

Cole, Harold L., and Patrick J. Kehoe. 1992. "Reputation Spillover Across Relationships with Enduring Transient Benefits: Reviving Reputation Models of Debt." Working Paper 534. Research Department, Federal Reserve Bank of Minneapolis.

Couillault, Bertrand, and Pierre-Francois Weber. 2003. "Towards a Voluntary Code of Good Conduct for Sovereign Debt Restructuring" *Financial Stability Review* (Banque de France)(2):154–62.

Dooley, Michael P. 2000. "Can Output Losses Following International Financial Crises be Avoided?" NBER Working Paper 7531. National Bureau of Economic Research, Cambridge, MA.

Eaton, Jonathan, and Raquel Fernandez. 1995. "Sovereign Debt." NBER Working Paper 5131. National Bureau of Economic Research, Cambridge, MA.

Eaton, Jonathan, and Mark Gersovitz. 1981. "Debt with Potential Repudiation: Theoretical and Empirical Analysis." *Review of Economic Studies* 48(April):289–309.

Dornbusch, Rudiger. 2002. "A Primer on Emerging Market Crises." In Sebastian Edwards and Jeffrey Frankel, eds., *Preventing Currency Crises in Emerging Markets*. Chicago: University of Chicago Press, pp. 743–54.

Eichengreen, Barry. 1989. 'The U.S. Capital Market and Foreign Lending, 1920–1955." In Jeffrey D. Sachs, ed., *Developing Country Debt and Economic Performance*. Vol. 1, *The International Financial System*. Cambridge, MA: National Bureau of Economic Research.

Eichengreen, Barry, and Albert Fishlow. 1996. "Contending with Capital Flows: What Is Different About the 1990s?" In Miles Kahler, ed., *Capital Flows and Financial Crises*. Ithaca: Cornell University Press, 1998.

Eichengreen, Barry, and Ashoka Mody. 2000. "Would Collective Action Clauses Raise Borrowing Costs?" NBER Working Paper 7458. National Bureau of Economic Research, Cambridge, MA.

Eichengreen, Barry, and Richard Portes. 1986. "Debt and Default in the 1930s: Causes and Consequences." *European Economic Review* 30:481–513.

———. 1989. "Dealing with Debt: The 1930s and the 1980s." In Ishrat Husain and Ishac Diwan, eds., *Dealing with the Debt Crisis, A World Bank Symposium*. Washington, DC: World Bank.

———. 1995. *Crisis? What Crisis? Orderly Workouts for Sovereign Debtors*. London: Centre for Economic Policy Research.

Eichengreen, Barry, Kenneth Kletzer, and Ashoka Mody. 2003. "Crisis Resolution: Next Steps." UC Santa Cruz Economics Working Paper 03–11. University of California at Santa Cruz.

Fernandez-Ansola, Juan Jose, and Thomas Laursen. 1995. "Historical Experience with Bond Financing." IMF Working Paper 95/27. International Monetary Fund, Washington, DC.

Friedman, Benjamin M. May 2000. "Debt Restructuring." NBER Working Paper 7722. National Bureau of Economic Research, Cambridge, MA.

Hutchison, Michael M., and Ilan Neugerger. 2002. "Output Costs of Currency and Balance of Payments Crises in Emerging Markets." *Comparative Economic Studies* XLIV, (2)(Summer):15–45.

IMF (International Monetary Fund). 2001. *Emerging Market Financing. A Quarterly Report on Development and Prospects,* 2(3).

J. P. Morgan. 1997. "Russia: Vnesh Now Expected Mid-November." J. P. Morgan, London.

——. 2000. *A Rough Guide to the Prin/IAN Exchange for 2010 and 2030 Eurobonds.* London: J .P. Morgan.

Kletzer, Kenneth M. 2003. "Sovereign Bond Restructuring: Collective Action Clauses and Official Crisis Intervention." IMF Working Paper 03/134. International Monetary Fund, Washington, DC.

Klingen, Christoph, Beatrice Weder, and Jeromin Zettelmeyer. 2004. "Estimating Private Returns to Emerging Market Lending, 1970–2000." IMF Working Paper 04/13. International Monetary Fund, Washington, DC.

Krueger, Anne. 2001. "International Financial Architecture for 2002: A New Approach to Sovereign Debt Restructuring." Address given at the National Economists' Club Annual Members' Dinner, November 26, American Enterprise Institute, Washington, DC. Available at http://www.imf.org/external/np/speeches/2001/sp01ind.htm.

——. 2002. "New Approaches to Sovereign Debt Restructuring: An Update on Our Thinking." Conference on Sovereign Debt Workouts: Hopes and Hazards, Institute of International Economics, April 1, Washington, DC. Available at http://www.imf.org/external/np/speeches/2002/040102.htm.

Lindert, Peter H. 1989. "How Sovereign Debt Has Worked." In Jeffrey D. Sachs, ed., *Developing Country Debt and Economic Performance Vol. 1. The International Financial System.* Cambridge, MA: National Bureau of Economic Research.

Lipworth, Gabrielle and Jens Nystedt. 2001. "Crisis Resolution and Private Sector Adaptation." *IMF Staff Papers* 47 (Special Issue):188–214.

Mauro, Paolo, and Yishay Yafeh. 2003. "The Corporation of Foreign bondholders." IMF Working Paper 03/107. International Monetary Fund, Washington, DC.

Özler, S. 1992. "The Evolution of Credit Terms: An Empirical Study of Commercial Bank Lending to Developing Countries." *Journal of Development Economics* 38(1):79–97.

——. 1993. "Have Commercial Banks Ignored History?" *American Economic Review* 83(3):608–20.

Reinhart, Carmen M., Kenneth S. Rogoff, and Miguel A Savastano. 2003. "Debt Intolerance." *Brookings Papers on Economic Activity* 1:1–74.

Rogoff, Kenneth S. and Jeromin Zettelmeyer. 2002. "Bankruptcy Procedures for Sovereigns: A History of Ideas 1976–2001." IMF Working Paper 02/133. International Monetary Fund, Washington, DC.

Rose, Andrew. 2002. "One Reason Countries Pay Their Debts: Renegotiation and International Trade." NBER Working Paper 8853. National Bureau of Economic Research, Cambridge, MA.

Roubini, N. 2002. "Do We Need a New International Bankruptcy Regime? Comments on Bulow, Sachs, and White." *Brookings Papers on Economic Activity* 1:321–33.

Sachs, Jeffrey D. 1988. "The Debt Overhang of Developing Countries." In Jorge B. de Macedo and Ronald Findlay, eds., *Debt Growth and Stabilization: Essays in Memory of Carlos F. Diaz Alejandro.* Oxford: Blackwell.

——. 1995. "Do We Need an International Lender of Last Resort?" Frank D. Graham Lecture, Princeton University, Princeton, April 20.

Snow, John W. 2003. "Plenary Statement 2003 IMF/WB Annual Meeting." Dubai, UAE, September 23.

Standard and Poor's. 2002. *Sovereign Defaults: Moving Higher Again in 2003?* New York: Standard and Poor's.

Sturzenegger, Federico. 2002a. "Toolkit for the Analysis of Debt Problems." *Journal of Restructuring Finance.*

———. 2002b. "Default Episodes of the 90s: Fact Book and Preliminary Lessons." Universidad Torcuato Di Tella, Buenos Aires.

Trichet, Jean Claude. 2001. "Preserving Financial Stability in an Increasingly Globalized World" Keynote speech at the European Financial Markets Convention, Paris, June 15.

World Bank. *Global Development Finance*. Various issues. Washington, DC.

Technical Appendix

Viktoria Hnatkovska

This appendix provides a basic set of derivations and the intuition underlying the technical concepts in selected chapters. The audience we have in mind is the busy, and possibly impatient, practitioner who will want guidance on how to interpret the various analytical approaches without necessarily acquiring a textbook level of knowledge. The more sophisticated reader is likely to want more. In anticipation of this need, we have a list of references to supplement the material presented here.

The appendix is divided into three main parts. Each part is in turn divided into a few sections, which are serially numbered throughout the appendix. Part I is devoted to the basics of volatility, including definitions and measurement, as well as trend-cycle decomposition methods. Part II discusses commodity price volatility and the basics of hedging techniques. Part III contains an overview of macroeconomic vulnerability assessment and the basic concepts of public debt sustainability, while also deriving related equations.

PART I. BASICS OF VOLATILITY

I. Definition and Measurement of Volatility

A. DEFINITION OF VOLATILITY. Intuitively, volatility can be thought of as the step-size of a random variable: the amount by which it is likely to change, or its step-size up or down, during a given time interval, usually, a year. More volatile variables have larger step-sizes, that is, are liable to vary more up or down. For convenience of presentation, two types of volatility can be distinguished: "Crisis or Boom" and "Trend or Structural" volatility. Crisis/boom volatility is characterized by large, one-time swings in an economic variable, for example, a large swing in output growth simulated in Figure I-1a. Trend volatility is characterized by recurrent and moderate, albeit unpredictable, oscillations around a deterministic or stochastic trend over a longer period of time (Figure I-1b).

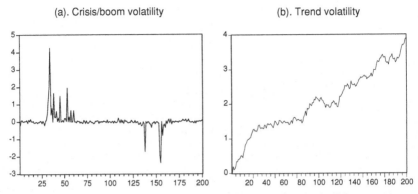

Figure I-1. Variables Exhibiting Crisis/boom and Trend volatilities.

B. MEASUREMENT OF VOLATILITY. Most economic variables are nonstationary in levels.[1] This means that they tend to fluctuate around a changing mean with the size of the fluctuation potentially changing over time, for example, national output fluctuating around a rising trend. The first step in computing volatility is to make the series stationary. This typically involves separating the permanent component (trend) from the transitory component (cycle) in the data. Common ways of carrying out such trend-cycle decomposition in modern empirical macroeconomics include:

- First differencing
- Application of Hodrick–Prescott filter (Hodrick and Prescott 1980, 1997)
- Application of Band-pass filter (Baxter and King 1995)
- Moving Average
- Beveridge–Nelson decomposition (Beveridge and Nelson 1981)

The *first-difference filter* obtains the cyclical component X_t^c from the series X_t, where X_t is usually in natural logarithms, as follows – recall that the first difference of a variable expressed in natural logarithms approximates a growth rate:

$$X_t^c = X_t - X_{t-1}.$$

Obtaining the first difference (or growth rate) of the series removes the permanent component from the data and a stationary time series is obtained. As we will discuss in Section IV of this appendix, first-differencing may not always be sufficient to obtain stationarity. Often a second and, occasionally, a third difference may be necessary. One should also note several potential problems that the first-difference filter presents. Understanding these problems and comparing the filters listed above requires some knowledge of frequency-domain or spectral analysis, which we will not cover here; the interested reader is referred to Chapter 6 in Hamilton (1994).

The *Hodrick–Prescott* (HP) *filter* and *Band-Pass* (BP) *filter* belong to the family of filters used in real business cycle research, which focuses on analyzing

---

[1] Nonstationarity generally refers to the series that are drifting up or down and therefore, can not be characterized well by their average value. We discuss this in more detail in Section 3 of this appendix.

short-run fluctuations and changes in economic variables in response to macroe-conomic policies. Chapter 3 of this book uses these detrending procedures in an empirical study. The two filters are similar and are designed to produce stationary series, even when applied to data exhibiting time trends ("trending data").

The idea behind *Hodrick–Prescott technique* (Hodrick and Prescott 1980, 1997) is to find a smooth path $\{s_t\}$ for the series of interest $\{X_t\}$ (in logs), such that the path $\{s_t\}$ tracks the original series as closely as possible. The following function is minimized with respect to $\{s_t\}$:

$$min_{\{s_t\}_{t=1}^{T}} \sum_{t=1}^{T}(X_t - s_t)^2 + \lambda \sum_{t=2}^{T-1}[(s_{t+1} - s_t) - (s_t - s_{t-1})]^2.$$

The first term in the expression above is the penalty associated with the deviation of the desired path s_t from the actual series $\{X_t\}$. The second term is the smoothing term. It penalizes the path $\{s_t\}$ if its growth over a period is very different from its growth in the previous one. The weight attached to this second term is λ, which is a smoothing parameter, with higher values resulting in more smoothness. λ depends on the frequency of the data with the standard measures being $\lambda = 100$ for annual data; $\lambda = 1,600$ for quarterly data and $\lambda = 14,400$ for monthly data. With s_t referred to as a *trend or long-run* component, while the residual $X_t - s_t = X_t^c$ as the *business cycle or cyclical* component, Hodrick and Prescott showed that under some conditions, the optimal choice of λ is given by the ratio of the variances of the cyclical X_t^c and the second difference of the trend s_t components.

The *Band-Pass filter* is an alternative technique developed by Baxter and King (1995) and based on the decomposition of the data into three components: low frequency, business cycle, and high frequency components. It extracts the cycli-cal (business cycle) component by eliminating the components outside a range of frequencies specified by the researcher and dependent on the characteristics of the business cycles in the particular economy under study. Baxter and King (1995) defined the business cycle to be no less than six quarters in duration and last fewer than 32 quarters. In annual data, this corresponds to a cycle of 2–8 years. In theory, the removal of the components of the data at higher and lower frequencies than those within six-year periods produces a two-sided moving average of an infinite order. This requires more data points than most macroeconomic series have and, therefore, some approximation is needed. Baxter and King (1995) suggest using a moving average based on seven years of data (three years of past data and three years of future data as well as the current year) to approximate the optimal (ideal) band-pass filter. This moving average represents the trend, while the difference between the actual current observation and the moving average represents the cyclical com-ponent. Though the ideal band-pass filter can be approximated better with longer moving averages, it is undesirable since this would result in losing some observations at the beginning and at the end of the sample.

As an illustration, Figure I-2 presents the trend component, Figure I-3 the cyclical component, and Table I-1 the related moments of real GDP for Argentina obtained from the three procedures discussed above.

The dynamics of the cyclical component produced by the first difference filter are quite different from those produced by the HP and BP filters. In particular, using

524   *Viktoria Hnatkovska*

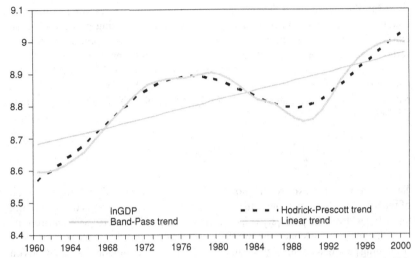

Figure I-2. Trend Component of Real GDP, Argentina (1960–2000). *Source*: Author's Calculations Based on WDI (2003) Data.

annual data, volatility given by the standard deviation of the cyclical component from the HP or BP filters will, generally, tend to be lower in many cases. This result is often reversed for the quarterly data series (Baxter and King 1995). With the HP and BP filters, researchers will tend to find similar characteristics of the business cycle. Some distinctions, however, exist. In particular, the BP filter tends to perform better than the HP filter at the tails of the distribution. For the analytical details, see Baxter and King (1995).

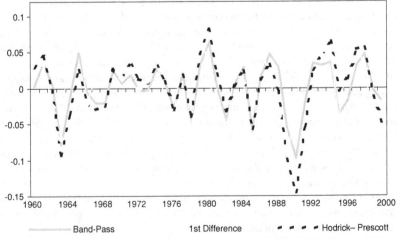

Figure I-3. Cyclical Component of Real GDP, Argentina (1960–2000). *Source*: Author's Calculations Based on WDI (2003) Data.

Table I-1. *Moments of the Cyclical Component of Real GDP Argentina (1960–2000)*

Variable	Mean	Std. dev.	Min	Max
First Difference	0.00947170	0.05412	−0.09397	0.10607
Hodrick–prescott	−0.00000007	0.04672	−0.14498	0.08201
Band–pass	0.00047120	0.03629	−0.09812	0.06336

Source: Author's calculations

Another widely used detrending method for macroeconomic time series is based on *moving averages*. In particular, the trend component is defined as a centered moving average, while the cyclical component is defined simply as the deviation of the original series from the trend so computed. The trend component is defined as:

$$s_t = \frac{1}{2K+1} \sum_{j=-K}^{K} X_{t+j}$$

and the cyclical component as $X_t^c = X_t - s_t$. Yet another common method of extracting the cyclical component is the *Beveridge–Nelson decomposition*. In order to discuss it, we first need to develop a set of tools used in time-series analysis, so we return to this decomposition in Section IV.B. of this appendix.

After decomposing the economic time series into permanent s_t and business cycle X_t^c components using the procedures above, we can calculate volatility. There are numerous measures of volatility, with the most conventional being the standard deviation. Different measures include:

Mean Absolute Deviation	$(1/N) \sum |X_t^c - \text{Mean}(X^c)|$
Variance (Std. dev.)	$(1/N) \sum (X_t^c - \text{Mean}(X^c))^2$
Variance (Std. dev.) using Median	$(1/N) \sum (X_t^c - \text{Median}(X^c))^2$
Coefficient of Variation	$\sqrt{Var(X_t^c)}/\text{Mean}(X^c)$

There is no universal volatility measure. The standard practice should be to do some robustness checks by applying the volatility formulas to the cyclical components of the data obtained through the various decomposition methods described above.

C. VARIABLES OF INTEREST. The variables of interest from the standpoint of volatility are summarized in Table III-1 at the end of Section III. These variables may be classified as:

• *Exogenous factors*: terms of trade (TOT), world interest rate, international commodity prices, diversified portfolio of world stock market returns.
• *Endogenous factors*: GDP, consumption, investment.
• *Policy factors*:
  (a) Government consumption/expenditure, fiscal balance;
  (b) Base Money, Broad Money or M2, interest rate.
• *Prices*: Real exchange rate, consumer and producer price indices.

As noted in Chapter 1 of this volume, one needs to be careful when classifying volatility as exogenous. The time dimension plays a crucial role. Consider, for instance, TOT volatility. Trade openness and sectoral concentration of trade might be exogenous in the short run, but becomes endogenous in the long run. An extreme example is provided by oil exporting countries, which often become increasingly dependent upon oil over time as a result of Dutch Disease. Dutch Disease itself is often reinforced and propagated by how government spending and other macroeconomic policies respond to oil price boom–bust cycles. Thus, over the long run, oil dependence is endogenous to the conduct of macroeconomic policies, even though it may appear exogenous in the short run.

D. MEASUREMENT OF UNCERTAINTY. An alternative to calculating volatility from the observed or realized variability in an economic variable is to recognize that part of this variability may have been predictable. In order to isolate the pure risk or uncertainty component in the series of interest, one could use the Generalized Autoregressive Conditional Heteroskedasticity (GARCH) technique proposed by Bollerslev (1986). This method is standard in analyzing time series which exhibit nonstationarity in the variance, such as financial series that tend to have highly volatile periods, followed by relatively calm periods.[2]

The GARCH procedure involves estimation of the system of equations. For our purposes, GARCH (1,1) is usually a sufficient specification and we characterize it below. The system of equations includes the process for Y_t in Equation (I.1a) and a process for the variance in Equation (I.2):

$$Y_t = c + \varphi Y_{t-1} + u_t, \qquad (\text{I.1a})$$

$$\text{where } E(u_t) = 0 \text{ and } E(u_t \, u_\tau) = \begin{cases} \sigma^2, & t = \tau \\ 0, & t \neq \tau \end{cases}. \qquad (\text{I.1b})$$

Note that (I.1b) only implies that the unconditional variance of u_t is constant, the conditional variance (conditional on the past realizations of u_t^2), on the other hand, can change over time. One approach would be for the variance to follow an autoregressive process, say AR(1), as well:

$$u_t^2 = \eta + \alpha u_{t-1}^2 + w_t,$$

where w_t is a new white noise process. A process for u_t that satisfies the equation above is an autoregressive conditional heteroskedastic (ARCH) process of order 1, $u_t \sim \text{ARCH}(1)$, introduced by Engle (1982).

Alternatively, GARCH model assumes a specific serial correlation pattern of residuals u_t in (I.1a). In particular, suppose $u_t = \sqrt{h_t} \upsilon_t$, where $\upsilon_t \sim iid \ Normal$, $E(\upsilon_t) = 0$ and $E(\upsilon_t^2) = 1$, and h_t evolves according to:

$$h_t = \kappa + \delta h_{t-1} + \alpha u_{t-1}{}^2, \qquad (\text{I.2})$$

where $\kappa = 1 - \delta$

---

[2] See Section IV of this appendix for a discussion of the main time-series concepts and nonstationarity.

Note that the conditional variance of u_t is time varying and is equal to h_t (hence the term GAR Conditional Heteroskedasticity):

$$E\lfloor u_t^2 \mid u_{t-1}^2 \rfloor = E\lfloor h_t v_t^2 \mid u_{t-1}^2 \rfloor = h_t E\lfloor v_t^2 \mid u_{t-1}^2 \rfloor = h_t.$$

To accomplish the second step, we used the fact that h_t only depends on h_{t-1} and u_{t-1}^2, and thus can be factored out of the expectations operator. In the last step the assumption $E(v_t^2) = 1$ was used. Therefore, h_t here denotes conditional variance of u_t and can be interpreted as the forecast of u_t^2 based on its own past values. To show this more formally, consider the following transformations. First, add u_t^2 on both sides of Equation (I.2). Second, add and subtract δu_{t-1}^2 to the right-hand side of Equation (I.2) to obtain:

$$h_t + u_t^2 = \kappa + \delta u_{t-1}^2 + \alpha u_{t-1}^2 - \delta \left(u_{t-1}^2 - h_{t-1} \right) + u_t^2.$$

Collect the terms:

$$u_t^2 = \kappa + (\delta + \alpha) u_{t-1}^2 + \omega_t - \delta \omega_{t-1}, \qquad (\text{I.2}')$$

where $\omega_t = u_t^2 - h_t$.

We showed that formulation in Equation (I.2) is equivalent to the formulation in Equation (I.2') and therefore, the fitted values $\hat{u}_t^2$ from the Equation (I.2') could be used to measure uncertainty in Y_t. Maximum likelihood methods (MLMs) are necessary to obtain the set of parameters characterizing the system above. At the same time, it can be shown that the unconditional variance of u_t remains constant at σ^2. For more details on time-series models with heteroskedasticity, see Hamilton (1994), Chapter 21.

Possible candidates for Y_t include:[3]

a. Inflation – a generalized measure of stability of economic environment;
b. Terms of trade;
c. GDP growth;
d. Real exchange rate.

II. Poverty and Volatility

A. POVERTY AND INCOME DISTRIBUTION DEFINITIONS/MEASUREMENT. While one would ideally want to focus on the broadest possible measures of poverty (the welfare of the poor, their consumption, and nonincome dimensions of poverty), data limitations restrict us to look primarily at income measures (as has been the case for most other studies of poverty, at least cross-country).[4]

There is an important distinction between absolute and relative income poverty measures. The former include the poverty headcount (share of population below a defined threshold, such as a dollar per day) and the poverty gap (which measures the depth of poverty), while the latter typically includes the income share of the

---

[3] For the relation between uncertainty based on some of these variables and investment, see Serven (1999).

[4] The UNDP has tried to develop a measure of wellbeing, the Human Development Index, which one could alternatively use.

bottom quintile or the average income of the lowest quintile relative to the average income of the country, or the ratio of income share of the richest group of the income distribution to the poorest group of that distribution. The Gini coefficient provides a more general representation of income distribution. Table III-2 contains a description of different poverty measures and their data sources.

B. MICRO- AND MACRO-ECONOMIC TOOLS DESIGNED TO ASSESS THE EFFECT OF ECONOMIC POLICIES ON POVERTY. A set of tools and methodologies developed by the World Bank to assess the impact of the economic policies on poverty can be found at: http://www.worldbank.org/psia.

III. Growth and Volatility

A. EMPIRICAL ENDOGENEITY. The model of interest for Chapter 2 is:

$$y = \beta_0 + \beta_1 x_1 + \beta_2 x_2 + \cdots + \beta_K x_K + u$$

where $y, x_1, x_2, \ldots, x_K$ are observable random scalars, u is the unobservable random disturbance term, and $\beta_0, \beta_1, \beta_2, \ldots, \beta_K$ are the parameters of interest. This is a structural model in a sense that it represents a causal relationship, rather than just reflecting linear associations among the variables.

One of the key assumptions of the classical linear model necessary for obtaining consistent estimators with ordinary least squares (OLS) is that the regressors X_is not be correlated with the error term, u. We define variable X to be endogenous if this assumption is violated. If X_j is not correlated with u, then X_j is said to be exogenous. There are several sources of endogeneity in applied econometric work.

1. **Omitted variable.** Omitted variable problem arises when some important explanatory variable that should be included in the model is omitted on account of data unavailability or specification error. For instance, a person's ability is not directly observable but is an important determinant of the returns to her education. As a result, the effect of ability is captured by the error term, and if the included explanatory variable, say number of years of education, is correlated with ability (which is usually the case), it will also be correlated with the error term, leading to the endogeneity of education in this model.
2. **Simultaneity.** When one of the explanatory variables is determined simultaneously with the dependent variable, y, it gives rise to the simultaneity problem. A practical illustration of such a problem in the growth regression and the solution to it are discussed in Chapter 2, "Volatility and Growth," in this volume.
3. **Measurement error.** This problem arises when the explanatory variable of interest is not directly observable; however, some imperfect measure for it is available. When such a proxy is used instead of the actual regressor, a measurement error results that is captured by the error term u.

Under any individual or combination of scenarios described above, OLS estimates are inconsistent and an instrumental variable (IV) technique must be used. A Hausman–Wu test which is the modification of the Hausman test could be used to test for endogeneity.

Table III-1. *Sources of volatility*

Sources of volatility	Measurement	Underlying determinants of volatility
Endogenous:		
Real GDP	Std. dev. of Growth Rate of variable or Std. Dev. of filtered log variable in constant local currency units	Significantly correlated with TOT and M2/GDP volatility, and is affected by political instability, strength of the financial system, and trade openness.
Private Consumption	Std. dev. of Growth Rate of variable or Std. dev. of filtered log variable in constant local currency units	
Domestic Investment	Std. dev. of Growth Rate of variable or Std. dev. of filtered log variable in constant local currency units	
Total Factor Productivity	TFP is measured as a Solow residual from i.e., Cobb–Douglas production function. Volatility is calculated as std. dev. of TFP growth or std. dev. of filtered log TFP series.	
Terms of Trade	Std. dev. of the variable Growth Rate or Std. dev. of filtered log variable, weighted (multiplied) by Trade Volume/GDP	This interactive measure of volatility adjusts the strength of the exogenous price shocks (volatility of TOT) by vulnerability of the country to those shocks (openness/GDP).
International Capital Flows/GDP	Std. dev. of Change in variable or Std. dev. of filtered log variable	
World Interest Rate	Std. dev. of the variable or Std. dev. of filtered log variable, weighted by Capital Flows Volume/GDP	External shock from the world interest rate changes is weighted by the exposure of the country to that shock (volume of its capital flows).
Prices:		
Annual Inflation Rate	Std. dev. of Growth Rate of price index (i.e. CPI) or Std. dev. of filtered log variable	Inflation could serve as an indicator of uncertainty that households face.

(continued)

Viktoria Hnatkovska

Table III-1 *(continued)*

Sources of volatility	Measurement	Underlying determinants of volatility
Real Effective Exchange Rate	Std. dev. of the variable or Std. dev. of filtered log variable	REER could be used as an indicator of the relative price changes. REER volatility is highly correlated with volatility of domestic inflation. Fiscal policy and especially monetary policy are crucial determinants of REER volatility. Political instability and capital flows tend to play role as well.
Policy:		
Fiscal Balance/GDP	Std. dev. of Change in variable or Std. dev. of filtered log variable	This indicator is used to measure the effect of fiscal policy volatility.
Government Consumption/GDP	Std. dev. of Change in variable or Std. dev. of filtered log variable	Tends to be procyclical thus amplifying shocks. Is influenced by TOT volatility and political instability.
Money/GDP	Money Base or M2 could be used. Volatility is measured as Std. dev. of Change in variable or Std. dev. of filtered log variable	This indicator is used to measure the effect of monetary policy volatility.
Domestic Interest Rate	Std. dev. of the variable or Std. dev. of filtered log variable	

Table III-2. *Measures of poverty and income inequality*

Indicator	Definition	Data sources
Human Development Index (UNDP)	A composite index measuring average achievement in three basic dimensions of human development – a long and healthy life, knowledge and a decent standard of living. The HDI is calculated as the arithmetic average of life expectancy index, education index and GDP per capita index.	http://www.undp.org/hdr2003/ pdf/hdr0 3_backmatter_2.pdf for the HD indicator calculation http://www.undp.org/hdr2003/ indicator/index_indicators.html for the HD indicator data and trends
A. Absolute Measures		
Poverty Headcount	Percentage of the population living below the national poverty line. National estimates are based on population-weighted subgroup estimates from household surveys.	World Development Indicators, various years
Poverty Gap at $1 a day,%	The average percentage difference between actual spendings and the poverty line (counting the nonpoor as having zero shortfall). This measure reflects the depth of poverty as well as its incidence.	World Development Indicators, various years
Population below $1 a day, %	Percentage of population living below $1 a day	World Development Indicators, various years
B. Relative Measures		
1st quintile	Share of overall income that accrues to the individuals whose per-capita income is in the lowest 20% of income distribution	World Development Indicators, various years; Deininger and Squire (1996) dataset; Dollar D. and A. Kraay (2002) dataset on www.worldbank.org/research/ growth
2nd quintile	Share of overall income that accrues to the individuals whose per-capita income is ranked between 20% and 40% of income distribution	World Development Indicators, various years; Deininger and Squire (1996) dataset; Dollar D. and A. Kraay (2002) dataset on www.worldbank.org/research/ growth

(continued)

Table III-2 *(continued)*

Indicator	Definition	Data sources
3rd quintile	Share of overall income that accrues to the individuals whose per-capita income is ranked between 40% and 60% of income distribution	World Development Indicators, various years; Deininger and Squire (1996) dataset; Dollar D. and A. Kraay (2002) dataset on www.worldbank.org/research/growth
4th quintile	Share of overall income that accrues to the individuals whose per-capita income is ranked between 60% and 80% of income distribution	World Development Indicators, various years; Deininger and Squire (1996) dataset; Dollar D. and A. Kraay (2002) dataset on www.worldbank.org/research/growth
5th quintile	Share of overall income that accrues to the individuals whose per-capita income is in the highest 20% of income distribution	World Development Indicators, various years; Deininger and Squire (1996) dataset; Dollar D. and A. Kraay (2002) dataset on www.worldbank.org/research/growth
Gini index	Gini index measures the extent to which the distribution of income (or, in some cases, consumption expenditure) among individuals or households within an economy deviates from a perfectly equal distribution. A Lorenz curve plots the cumulative percentages of total income received against the cumulative number of recipients, starting with the poorest individual or household. The Gini index measures the area between the Lorenz curve and a hypothetical line of absolute equality, expressed as a percentage of the maximum area under the line. Thus, a Gini index of zero represents perfect equality, while an index of 100 implies perfect inequality.	World Development Indicators, various years; Deininger and Squire (1996) dataset; Dollar D. and A. Kraay (2002) dataset on www.worldbank.org/research/growth
Transition Matrix	Takes into account the income mobility – movement of the families up and down the ranking within the income distribution in a given country for a given time period	For references, see Glewwe, Gragnolati, and Zaman (2002); Auffret (2003)

PART II. COMMODITY PRICES: TREND-CYCLE
DECOMPOSITIONS AND HEDGING

IV. Commodity Price Volatility

Commodity prices are often analyzed using time-series methods. This section summarizes the main concepts and techniques used in Chapter 4 of the book. The notation
is used: $\{x_1, x_2, \ldots, x_T\} = \{x_t\}$ represents a sequence of realizations of a random
variable X_t over time periods $1, 2, \ldots, T$. $\varepsilon_t \sim {}^{iid} N(\mu, \sigma^2)$ means that random
variable ε_t is independently and identically normally distributed variable with mean
μ and variance σ^2. We use Δ to denote the first difference of the variable.

A. MAIN TIME-SERIES CONCEPTS

1. Stationarity

- The time-series $\{x_t\}$ is *weak-* or *covariance-stationary* if its first and second
  moments are finite and time-invariant: $E[x_t] = \mu, E[x_{t_1} - \mu) * (x_{t_2} - \mu)] = \gamma_{t_2 - t_1}$,
  $\forall t_1, t_2$. These conditions imply that a covariance stationary process must have
  a constant mean, variance, and autocovariances – note that when $t_1 = t_2$ we get
  the variance. The autocovariance function measures the degree of comovement
  between observations $t_2 - t_1$ periods apart and depends only upon this time difference when the process is stationary. That is, the covariance between x_t and x_{t-1}
  must be the same as between x_{t-5} and x_{t-6}. The autocorrelation function normal-
  izes the autocovariance by the variance of the process to induce comparability
  across variables:

$$\rho_{t_2 - t_1} = \frac{\gamma_{t_2 - t_1}}{\gamma_0}.$$

  Violations of covariance-stationarity may result from:

- *Nonstationarity in the mean* – the mean of the process is not constant. Many
  macro variables are not mean-stationary, but tend to drift upwards or downwards

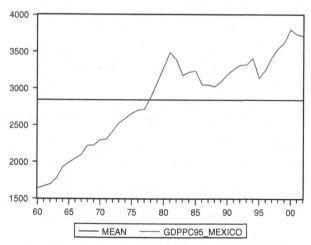

Figure IV-1. Mexico: Real GDP per capita 1960–2002, US$.

over time, often accompanied by some cyclical variation. Consider, for instance, Mexico's real GDP per capita as depicted in Figure IV-1. The series clearly exhibits an upward drift and is therefore not mean-stationary. Calculating the average of the observations would not provide any meaningful information, as the mean would constantly be changing as a result of positive growth. However, the *growth rate* of Mexico's real GDP per capita might well exhibit stationarity. Nonstationarity in the mean could be triggered by:

i. A deterministic time trend – the series increases by a given amount every period.

ii. The presence of a unit root (a stochastic trend) – the variable changes every period by some expected amount, but with random deviations from this average amount (hence the term "*stochastic* trend"). A random walk process, which is often used to describe financial variables such as stock prices and exchange rates, is a special case of a unit root process.

iii. Structural breaks, which are shifts in the level or growth rate of the series.

- *Nonstationarity relative to the variance* refers to time-varying volatility and is often encountered in high-frequency financial data characterized by alternating periods of high volatility and relative stability. An example is provided by the GARCH process described in Part I of this appendix.

2. Common Time-Series Processes

- One of the main building blocks of the time-series processes is *white noise*. Consider a sequence $\{\varepsilon_t\}$ such that

$$E(\varepsilon_t) = 0,$$
$$VAR(\varepsilon_t) = E(\varepsilon_t^2) = \sigma^2, \text{ and}$$
$$E(\varepsilon_t \varepsilon_s) = 0, \text{ where } t \neq s, \text{ implying that } \varepsilon_t's \text{ are uncorrelated over time.}$$

A process satisfying the above conditions is called a white noise process.

- An $AR(p)$ refers to an *autoregressive process* of order p and can be represented as

$$x_t = c + \varphi_1 x_{t-1} + \varphi_2 x_{t-2} + \cdots + \varphi_p x_{t-p} + \varepsilon_t$$
$$= c + \sum_{j=1}^{p} \varphi_j x_{i-j} + \varepsilon_t, \text{ where } \varepsilon_t \sim^{iid} \left(0, \sigma_\varepsilon^2\right)$$

An $AR(p)$ process can be described as a pth order difference equation, in which current value of variable x_t depends on the past realizations of itself and a random component, ε_t.

- An $MA(q)$ stands for a *moving average process* of order q and has the following representation:

$$x_t = \mu + \varepsilon_t + \theta_1 \varepsilon_{t-1} + \theta_2 \varepsilon_{t-2} + \cdots + \theta_q \varepsilon_{t-q}$$
$$= \mu + \sum_{i=1}^{q} \theta_i \varepsilon_{t-i} + \varepsilon_t, \text{ where } \varepsilon_t \sim^{iid} \left(0, \sigma_\varepsilon^2\right).$$

The MA process is thus a linear combination of realizations from a white noise process, ε_t.

- An *ARMA(p,q)* is a combination of *AR(p)* and *MA(q)* processes and has the following form:

$$x_t = c + \varphi_1 x_{t-1} + \varphi_2 x_{t-2} + \cdots + \varphi_p x_{t-p} + \varepsilon_t + \theta_1 \varepsilon_{t-1}$$
$$+ \theta_2 \varepsilon_{t-2} + \cdots + \theta_q \varepsilon_{t-q},$$

where ε_t – white noise: $E(\varepsilon_t) = 0$ $E(\varepsilon_t^2) = \sigma^2$ and $E(\varepsilon_t \varepsilon_s) = 0$, $t \neq s$.
- A *unit root* process is not covariance-stationary. Consider a general AR(1) process:

$$x_t = \varphi x_{t-1} + \varepsilon_t, \tag{IV.1}$$

where ε_t is stationary.

Lag the equation above, $x_{t-1} = \varphi x_{t-2} + \varepsilon_{t-1}$ and substitute it back into (IV.1) to obtain

$$x_t = \varphi^2 x_{t-2} + \varepsilon_t + \varphi \varepsilon_{t-1}.$$

Repeating the lag-substitute exercise T times leads to

$$x_t = \varphi^T x_{t-T} + \varepsilon_t + \varphi \varepsilon_{t-1} + \varphi^2 \varepsilon_{t-2} + \cdots + \varphi^{T-1} \varepsilon_{t-T+1}. \tag{IV.2}$$

Three possible cases can be distinguished:
i. $\varphi < 1 \Rightarrow \varphi^T \to 0$ as $T \to \infty$.
In this case, all shocks to the equation gradually die out and the series is *stationary*. The expression above also suggests that a stationary AR process can be represented as an MA process. We will discuss this later in the context of the Wold decomposition.
ii. $\varphi = 1 \Rightarrow \varphi^T = 1$ $\forall T$.
In such a system, shocks have a permanent effect and never die out; in this case, Equation (IV.1) can be rewritten as

$$x_t = x_{t-1} + \varepsilon_t,$$

and Equation (IV.2) as

$$x_t = x + \sum_{j=0}^{\infty} \varepsilon_{t-j}, \text{ as } T \to \infty,$$

which implies that x_t is an infinite sum of the past shocks to the system with a starting point, x. Such a process is called a "unit root" process.
iii. $\varphi > 1 \Rightarrow \varphi^T \to \infty$ as $T \to \infty$ is an explosive case, as the effects of the shocks increase over time. This case is usually ruled out by assumption in economics and finance in order to obtain convergent equilibria.

If a series contains a unit root, it is said to be *integrated of order one* – *I*(1), meaning that it would need to be differenced once to achieve stationarity. Similarly, an *integrated process of order d* – *I(d)*, must be differenced d times to become stationary. The logarithms of most price-deflated (or real) macroeconomic time-series including GDP, consumption, money, interest rates, etc. are *I*(1), while prices are often found to be *I*(2). The latter would imply that inflation, calculated as a first difference of log prices, $\pi_t = \ln P_t - \ln P_{t-1} \equiv \Delta \ln P_t$ is *I*(1) – contains a unit root and is nonstationary, but the change in the rate of inflation,

$\Delta \pi_t = \Delta \ln P_t - \Delta \ln P_{t-1}$ is stationary. Nominal series often inherit the $I(2)$ character of prices.

More formally, the procedure for obtaining a stationary series is as follows. First, an original series needs to be tested for stationarity in levels using unit root tests (Dickey–Fuller [1979], Phillips–Perron [1988] tests, etc.). If a unit root is present, the series should be first-differenced and a unit root test needs to be applied to the resulting series. If again a unit root cannot be rejected, a second difference transformation is necessary and so on until the unit root test confirms stationarity (rejects the unit root) of the transformed series. The results of such tests, how-ever, need to be taken with caution because of their low power.[1] This particular issue is taken up further in the context of tests for public debt sustainability in Section VII.D.

- *ARIMA* (p,d,q) stands for "*autoregressive integrated moving average.*" For a variable x_t integrated of order one we will construct and *ARIMA* $(p, 1, q)$ model with the following representation:

$$\Delta x_t = c + \phi_1 \Delta x_{t-1} + \phi_2 \Delta x_{t-2} + \cdots \phi_p \Delta x_{t-p} + \varepsilon_t + \theta_1 \varepsilon_{t-1}$$
$$+ \theta_2 \varepsilon_{t-2} + \cdots \theta_q \varepsilon_{t-q},$$

where ε_t is white noise. This *ARIMA* model is equivalent to an *ARIMA* model on first differences of the underlying series. We will use this model below when discussing Beveridge–Nelson trend-cycle decompositions.
- A *random walk* (with no drift) is a special case of a unit root process and can be expressed as

$$x_t = x_{t-1} + \varepsilon_t, \text{ where } \varepsilon_t \text{ is white noise.}$$

Note that a random walk requires an additional restriction on ε_t: it should be serially uncorrelated, that is, white noise, in addition to being stationary. This is a key distinction from unit root processes, which only require that ε_t be stationary. Thus, all random walks are unit root processes, but the reverse is not true. A random walk with drift includes an additional term:

$$x_t = \beta + x_{t-1} + \varepsilon_t, \text{ where } \varepsilon_t \text{ is again white noise, and } \beta \text{ is the drift.}$$

3. Nonstationarity and Univariate Models. Standard regression techniques are valid only when the series and the residuals from the estimated regressions are covariance-stationary. Otherwise, two problems may arise:

i. If the variables used in the analysis are nonstationary, the assumptions necessary for asymptotic theory to hold will be violated and, as a result,
   a. the estimated coefficient may be biased and inconsistent.
   b. the estimated standard errors and tests statistics may be inconsistent.

---

[1] Power of the test is equal to $1 - \beta$, where β is the probability of Type II error – probability of failing to reject a null hypothesis when it is false. Because of low power, stationarity tests are likely to fail to reject the null hypothesis of a unit root, when in fact it is not present in the data.

ii. "Spurious regressions" may result. This refers to obtaining statistically significant coefficients and a high R^2 when, for example, two nonstationary variables are regressed on each other even when they are in fact independent.

As mentioned above, nonstationarity of a time-series could result from the presence of a deterministic time trend and/or a unit root process with or without drift. These alternatives give rise to trend stationary (TS) and difference stationary (DS) models:

i. Deterministic trend or *trend stationary* (TS) model:

The TS model does not assume stationarity of the variable itself, although its fluctuations around the deterministic trend are assumed to be stationary:

$$x_t = \alpha + \beta^* time + \varepsilon_t. \tag{IV.3}$$

ii. Stochastic trend or *difference stationary* (DS) model:

DS model is applicable when the actual series is nonstationary due to the presence of a unit root:

$$x_t = \mu + x_{t-1} + \varepsilon_t.$$

Such a model can be rewritten in terms of first differences:

$$\Delta x_t = \mu + \varepsilon_t, \tag{IV.4}$$

where ε_t is a stationary error process in both cases.

Note that with the TS model, all shocks have a temporary character, while in the DS model, the effects of the shock are permanent. The two models also require different procedures to induce stationarity. Stationarity can be achieved in the TS model by detrending the original series, that is, using the residuals from regression on time as in Equation (IV.3), or in case of DS model – first-differencing the data, as in Equation (IV.4).

Another possible reason behind nonstationarity of the underlying series mentioned above is the presence of *structural breaks*. Those could be modeled separately or incorporated into a TS model using dummy variable analysis. For instance, to model a structural break one would create a dummy variable such as:

$$D_t = \begin{cases} 0, & \text{if } t < \text{break point} \\ 1, & \text{if } t \geq \text{break point.} \end{cases}$$

Such a dummy variable would enable a different intercept and/or coefficient on time before and after the structural break.

How to choose between a deterministic trend and a stochastic trend? A simple way is to conduct unit root tests. The most commonly used tests, available in many econometric software packages, are the Augmented Dickey–Fuller test and the Phillips–Perron test. Others include Kwiatkowski-Phillips-Schmidt-Shin (KPPS 1992) and Ng-Perron (2001). Some of these tests are discussed in Part VII with application to public debt sustainability. Another, less formal, way to differentiate between the two models is to compare the accuracy of out-of-sample forecasts obtained from each of the two models.

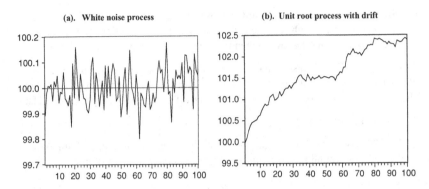

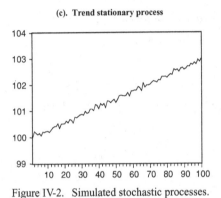

Figure IV-2. Simulated stochastic processes.

For illustration, the graphs in Figure IV-2 depict simulations of white noise, DS, and TS processes.

B. TREND-CYCLE DECOMPOSITIONS, PERMANENT-TRANSITORY DECOMPOSITIONS (WOLD; BEVERIDGE–NELSON)

Wold Representation. After the nonstationary component of a variable has been extracted, what remains is typically a zero-mean covariance-stationary process, x_t. According to the *Wold decomposition* proposition (1938), this portion of the variable denoted x_t can be decomposed into two components represented by the equation

$$x_t = \mu + \sum_{j=0}^{\infty} \psi_j \varepsilon_{t-j}. \tag{IV.5}$$

The first component $\mu = E(x_t/x_{t-1}, x_{t-2}, \ldots, x_{t-p})$ is the optimal linear predictor of x_t based on its past values, and is called the *linearly deterministic component*. The second component $\sum_{j=1}^{\infty} \psi_j \varepsilon_{t-j}$ is an infinite sum of white noise or an $MA(\infty)$ under the assumptions that ε_t is a white noise error made in forecasting x_t as a linear function of its lagged values, $\psi_0 = 1$, and $\sum_{j=1}^{\infty} \psi_j^2 < \infty$. This $MA(\infty)$ component is usually called the *linearly indeterministic component*.

In most practical applications, however, the infinite number of parameters necessary to obtain the right-hand side of Equation (IV.5) cannot be estimated. In this case, a solution would be to find the best fit of the data with a finite number of moving-average terms. This is important for deriving the autocorrelation function for autoregressive processes, one application of which, utilized in Chapter 4, is to assess the speed with which an AR process reverts to some long-run average in response to a shock, that is, the degree of mean-reversion.

Let us introduce a lag operator L such that $Lx_t = x_{t-1}$. Then $L^j x_t = x_{t-j}$. With this notation, a zero-mean $AR(p)$ process

$$x_t = \sum_{j=1}^{p} \varphi_j x_{i-j} + \varepsilon_t$$

can be rewritten as

$$x_t = \sum_{j=1}^{p} \varphi_j L^j x_t + \varepsilon_t,$$

or

$$\varphi(L)x_t = \varepsilon_t, \qquad \qquad \text{(IV.6)}$$

where $\varphi(L) = (1 - \varphi_1 L - \varphi_2 L^2 - \cdots - \varphi_p L^p)$.

Then, the $AR(p)$ process is stationary if it is possible to rewrite Equation (IV.6) above as

$$x_t = \varphi(L)^{-1} \varepsilon_t = \psi(L)\varepsilon_t,$$

with $\varphi(L)^{-1}$ converging to zero. Whether this polynomial converges to zero or not depends on the values of φ_i. More generally, convergence is associated with autocorrelation coefficients, which are functions of $\varphi_i's$ and p, becoming smaller and smaller as the lag length increases, and reaching zero in the limit. Note that $\varphi(L)^{-1}$ will contain an infinite number of terms, which makes $\varphi(L)^{-1}\varepsilon_t$ an infinite MA process, assuming x_t is stationary. In an informal manner, we can measure the speed of mean-reversion by the average lag $\sum_{i=1}^{\infty} i \psi_i$.

Beveridge–Nelson Decomposition. It is frequently of interest to split nonstationary economic time series into trend and cyclical components. A classic example is the estimation of the long-run trend growth rate and cyclical components of GDP (Stock and Watson 1988). While the former is the focus of growth theories trying to explain the forces behind long-run growth dynamics, the latter is studied by business cycle theorists attempting to understand short-run fluctuations and the effects of macroeconomic policies. Other examples include the identification of commodity price booms and busts which feed into commodity export revenues, or cyclical components of government expenditure.

The estimation method of the long-run trend component, and therefore of the cyclical component, which is obtained residually, will depend on the assumptions about the sources of nonstationarity described above (e.g., deterministic trend and TS model, or unit root and DS model, or structural breaks).

- Trend-cycle decomposition in TS model: When the regression model in Equation (IV.3) is estimated on the log of the variable, say real GDP, the coefficient on time yields an estimate of the long-run growth rate for that variable. The cyclical component is obtained as the residual from the estimated regression.

- Trend-cycle decomposition in DS model: The decomposition in this model could be complicated by the serial correlation pattern of the disturbances.
    i. If the errors are white noise, then all innovations have permanent effects on the log level of the variable and there are no cycles around this stochastic trend.
    ii. If, on the other hand, innovations are serially correlated, one can use the decomposition first made by Beveridge and Nelson (1981). Their method implies that any unit root process whose first difference satisfies

$$\Delta x_t = \psi(L)\varepsilon_t = \sum_{j=0}^{\infty} \psi_j \varepsilon_{t-j},$$

where $\varepsilon_t \sim^{iid} (0, \sigma_\varepsilon^2)$ is white noise, can be written as a sum of a random walk process and a stationary process (and some initial conditions):

$$x_t = x_t^p + x_t^s,$$

where x^p is a random walk with or without drift and x^s is a stationary time-series. The superscripts p and s denote permanent (trend) and stationary (transitory) components of x_t, respectively.

To illustrate, consider a unit root process consisting of a driftless random walk with $\varepsilon_t \sim^{iid} (0, \sigma_\varepsilon^2)$ and innovations (or shocks) following a simple first-order moving average process with a constant coefficient $-\theta$. It can be written as follows:

$$x_t = x_{t-1} + \varepsilon_t - \theta \varepsilon_{t-1} \Leftrightarrow \Delta x_t = \varepsilon_t - \theta \varepsilon_{t-1}.$$

Lag and substitute the previous expression to obtain

$$x_t = x_{t-1} + \varepsilon_t - \theta \varepsilon_{t-1}$$
$$= x_{t-2} + (\varepsilon_{t-1} - \theta \varepsilon_{t-2}) + (\varepsilon_t - \theta \varepsilon_{t-1})$$
$$= x_0 + \sum_{i=1}^{t} \varepsilon_i - \theta \sum_{i=0}^{t-1} \varepsilon_i.$$

Let $x_0 = 0$ and $\varepsilon_0 = 0$ to get

$$x_t = (1 - \theta) \sum_{i=1}^{t} \varepsilon_i + \theta \varepsilon_t.$$

Now, the Beveridge–Nelson decomposition is accomplished by letting $x^p = (1 - \theta) \sum_{i=1}^{t} \varepsilon_i$ be the permanent component, and $x^s = \theta \varepsilon_t$ be the stationary component.

With such a specification, each shock to x_t, say of magnitude 1, has a permanent effect to the extent of $1 - \theta$, by which it shifts the stochastic trend. The rest of the shock (amounting to a fraction θ) is temporary and disappears after the first period due to its MA(1) nature. The dynamics are captured in the figure below.

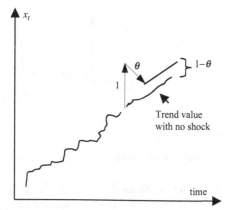

Figure IV-3. Intuitive Illustration of Beveridge–Nelson Decomposition.

Such a representation can be obtained for a more general $ARIMA$ $(p,1,q)$ process.

- For trend-cycle decomposition one can also use filters, such as *Hodrick–Prescott filter, Band-pass filter*, etc. discussed in Module I of this appendix.

V. Hedging and Financial Derivatives[2]

Derivative securities, or derivatives, are financial instruments whose value and pay-off depend upon, or are derived from, the realizations of a more basic underlying variable. This property gives rise to an alternative name – contingent claims. The variables upon which the valuations depend are the prices of underlying securities, goods, or assets.

Futures and options are examples of derivatives and are traded on many exchanges. Forwards, options, and swaps can also be traded in the Over-the-Counter-Market, outside exchanges. *Exchange traded* contracts are standardized, anonymous, and guaranteed by the exchange authorities. *Over-the-counter* (OTC) contracts are private agreements between participating agents. These contracts can be traded among financial institutions, funds, and companies. One of the parties in the contract must take a *long position* and effectively agrees to buy the underlying asset under agreed conditions. The other party takes a *short position* and effectively agrees to sell the corresponding asset under the same conditions.

A. FORWARDS, FUTURES, OPTIONS, AND SWAPS

Forward Contracts. Forward contracts are traded at in the OTC market. *A forward contract* is an agreement to buy or sell a given asset at a future point in time at a predetermined price known as the *delivery price*. Compare such a contract with a *spot contract*, which enables purchase or sale at today's price (the spot price).

---

[2] This section is based on Hull (2000).

Viktoria Hnatkovska

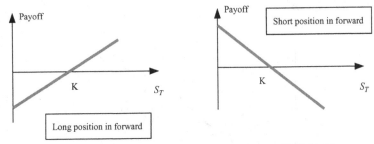

Figure V-1. Payoffs from Forward Contracts. *Source*: Hull (2000).

Another price relevant for the forward contract is *forward price*. The delivery price and forward price will be the same at the moment the contract is signed. Thereafter, the forward price for delivery on the agreed date will vary in line with market trends for the underlying security as the maturity date is approached, even though the delivery price for the contract already signed is fixed. The forward price of the contract thus usually depends on the maturity.

To discuss the payoff from the forward contract, let S_T denote the spot price of the underlying asset at the maturity date of the contract; and K the delivery price set by the contract. Then the payoff from the long position (agreement to buy) is $S_T - K$ implying that since the buyer of the contract is obliged to pay K, she will make $S_T - K$ if the spot price is above the delivery price.

On the other hand, the payoff from the short position will be $K - S_T$ since the seller of the contract, being obliged to sell at K, could have got S_T on the spot market in the absence of the contract. Graphs in Figure V-1 show the payoff schemes from holding forward. Note that they are linear in the price of the underlying asset.

Since the forward contract locks in the agreed delivery price, and is an obligation to transact at this price without any option to back out, it costs nothing to enter and total losses and gains from the contract constitute the overall payoff.

Futures Contracts. *Futures contracts* are similar to forward contracts; the key difference is that unlike forwards, futures are traded at exchanges based on standardized contracts. Yet another difference from the forward contracts is that they do not usually specify the exact delivery date and rather refer to the delivery month.

Options. *Option contracts* differ from the contracts discussed above by providing a right to adhere to the contract rather then imposing an obligation to do so. Therefore, while it is costless to enter into forwards or futures, the holder of an option must incur a cost.

The assets underlying options include stocks, stock indices, commodities, currencies, debt instruments, and futures contracts. In general, two main types of options exist: call options and put options. A *call option* gives the holder the right to buy the asset at a given price, called the strike price, by a certain date, called the *maturity or expiration date*. A *put option* gives the holder the right to sell the underlying asset at a given strike price by a certain maturity date. There are also American and European options, with the former exercisable at any point in time before maturity, and the latter only on the specified expiration date. Options traded on exchanges are mostly American.

As before, a party can take long or short position in call or put options. We consider payoffs from each of these in turn and, for simplicity, focus on European options. As before, S_T denotes the actual price of the underlying asset at maturity date and X, the strike price. Consider a long position in a call option (buying the right to buy the asset at a predetermined price). Such an option will be exercised by the buyer only if the contract provides an opportunity to get it cheaper, that is, only if $X < S_T$, leaving the holder with a payoff equal to

$$\max(S_T - X, 0).$$

The seller of the call option (the party with the short call position) will receive

$$-\max(S_T - X, 0).$$

The payoffs for put options are similarly determined. A long position in a put option (buying the right to sell the asset at the agreed price) would be exercised only if the actual price is below the one preset by the contract, that is, when $X > S_T$. The associated payoff is

$$\max(X - S_T, 0).$$

The payoff to the short position in the put option will pay

$$-\max(X - S_T, 0).$$

Note that the payoff to such instruments is nonlinear in the price of underlying asset, as is evident from the graphs in Figure V-2:

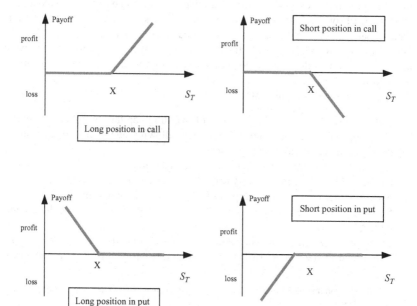

Figure V-2. Payoffs from European Option Contracts. *Source*: Hull (2000).

Table V-1. *Options classification*

	$X < S$	$X = S$	$X > S$
Call option	In-the-money	At-the-money	Out-of-the-money
Put option	Out-of-the-money	At-the-money	In-the-money

Frequently, the terms "in-the-money," "at-the-money," and "out-of-the-money" are used in connection with options. These refer to the relationship between the strike price and the price of the asset, as summarized in Table V-1 with reference to a long position in the particular contract.

Swap Contracts. A swap contract is an agreement between two agents to exchange sets of cash flows in the future with some predetermined periodicity. The amounts of the cash flows usually depend on the future values of some market variable. Most common swaps include interest rate swaps and currency swaps.

The most common swap – "plain vanilla" interest rate swap – specifies the exchange of fixed interest rate payments for a stream of floating interest rate payments. Such swaps are almost always based on a sequence of agreed cash flow exchanges over a given period, that is, every six months for the next five years. The floating rate is usually based on LIBOR[3] as a benchmark, for example, LIBOR + 30 basis points.[4] Gross payments usually do not change hands, rather the difference between the two sets of cash flows is calculated and only these net amounts are exchanged.

The rationale for swap contracts is similar to the comparative advantage argument. Some companies may have a comparative advantage in borrowing in fixed-rate markets, while others, borrowing in a floating rate market. While it is reasonable for the company to go to the market in which it has comparative advantage, this may not always coincide with its needs. It may find it more profitable to borrow at a fixed rate and swap into a floating rate loan rather than borrow directly from the floating rate market.

Other examples of swap contracts include:

- *Currency swaps* originated as a way of avoiding capital controls in different countries and developed into an instrument allowing agents to sell each other desired amounts in different currencies.
- *Commodity swaps* allow the exchange of the cash value of different commodities.
- *Default swaps* are arrangements whereby one party in a swap contract, say A, pays the other party (or counterparty B) but does not receive anything in return from B unless some other party defaults on some other contract, typically a loan, with A.
- *Sovereign debt swaps* – Russian and Argentina attempted sovereign debt swaps in the face of their debt crises to boost liquidity. In case of Russia, the swap

---

[3] LIBOR – London Interbank Offered Rate is the interest rate that banks in the Euromarkets pay each other for deposits.

[4] 100 basis points equal one percentage point, so 30 b.p. is 0.3 percent.

undertaken in July 1998 from short-term ruble treasury bills to long-term dollar Eurobonds was a combination of a maturity and currency swap; in case of Argentina (June 2001), it was just a maturity swap.[5]

- *Total return swaps* involve the exchange of the total return on one asset (equity, fixed income security) for the total return on the other, with maturity of the underlying assets longer than the swap maturity itself.

More complex financial contracts involving swaps include *swaptions*, which are options to enter into swaps at a future date, not swaps of options. In the case of interest rate swaps, for example, the buyer of a "payer swaption" acquires the right, without any obligation, to enter into a swap agreement at some future date with the seller under which the buyer makes payments at a predetermined fixed interest rate while receiving floating interest rate payments from the seller. As with regular options, the buyer pays a seller a premium for such a right. Buying a "receiver swaption" confers the right to enter into an interest rate swap receiving fixed payments from the seller. *Swap futures* are futures on swap contracts.

B. BASIS RISK. To hedge means to reduce the risk associated with the future price movements. Thus, property is a traditional hedge when inflation is high. A commodity producer who agrees to sell her goods at a given price at a specific point in the future and a commodity processor who agrees to purchase these goods enter into a perfect hedge: this completely eliminates the risk of future losses but at the expense of foregoing any possible gains.

This idea extends naturally to the financial markets. The equivalent of a commodity producer is an investor holding a portfolio of stocks and selling futures or option contracts on the stock to protect this portfolio from possible price falls in the future. This is known an a *short hedge*. An equivalent of a commodity processor is an investor who is interested in taking a long position in stocks at some point in the future and wants to insure against possible price increases. This is known as a *long hedge*.

In practice, hedges may not work perfectly for several reasons: the asset whose price is to be hedged may differ from the asset underlying the futures contract; the maturity of the available hedging instrument may exceed that of the time period for which the hedge is needed. All these give rise to *basis risk*.

C. OPTIMAL HEDGE RATIO. The amount of the position in hedging instruments relative to the overall portfolio/ position in the underlying asset being hedged is the *hedge ratio*. It is the number of derivatives that must be held per unit of the underlying asset such that any change in the value of the portfolio triggered by a movement in the price of the underlying asset is exactly offset by a change in the value of the derivatives position in the opposite direction.

The optimal hedge ratio will often be different from one (full hedge) if the objective of the investor is to minimize risk. It will depend on the correlation between the changes in the price of the asset being hedged and the price of the financial

---

[5] See Aizenman, Kletzer, and Pinto (2004) for a discussion of the role played by debt swaps in Russian and Argentinean meltdown.

instrument used for hedging, as well as the volatility of these price changes. If we let:

ΔS – be the change in the spot price of the asset during the life of hedge
ΔF – the change in the price of the instrument used for the hedge during the life of hedge
$\sigma(\Delta S)$ – the standard deviation of ΔS
$\sigma(\Delta F)$ – the standard deviation of ΔF
ρ – correlation coefficient between ΔS and ΔF
h^* – optimal hedge ratio

then the exact formula for the optimal hedge is:[6]

$$h^* = \rho \frac{\sigma(\Delta S)}{\sigma(\Delta F)}. \qquad (V.1)$$

Note how this expression can be rewritten as a slope coefficient in the regression of ΔS on ΔF: $h^* = \frac{Cov(\Delta F, \Delta S)}{Var(\Delta F)}$.

After determining the optimal hedge ratio, the necessary exposure to hedge contracts can be calculated as a product of the position in the asset to be hedged and the hedge ratio. Consider, for instance, a company that needs to buy 1 million barrels of oil in five months. It would obviously lose if the oil price were to rise. However, if it bought call options on oil at a fixed strike price equal to, say, the price it would feel comfortable paying for oil, then rises in the oil price above this level would be offset by the payoff from the call option. The company calculates an optimal hedge ratio from call options to be $h^* = 0.6$. Suppose there are 42,000 barrels per standardized futures contract. Then the company would need to buy $0.6 * \frac{1,000,000}{42,000} = 14.3$ option contracts.

D. CUSTOMIZED INSTRUMENTS. An example of a customized instrument is the *costless collar* discussed in Chapter 5. In general terms, a collar is an options strategy in which an investor hedges his investment in, for example, stocks, by selling an out-of-the-money call option and buying an out-of-the-money put option (recall these terms from Table V-1). The price path obtained resembles a "collar" because it constrains both the potential loss and the potential reward. It is particularly applicable when investor wishes to limit downside risk, but at the same time believes that the value of the investment being hedged will not increase rapidly. The strike prices for the call and put options can be configured in such a way that proceeds from the sale of the call options cover the purchase of the put options, resulting in the costless collar.

---

[6] For a given portfolio $V_P = S^* Q_S + F^* Q_F$, where S and F are prices of share and derivative, the change in value of portfolio is given by $\Delta V_P = \Delta S^* Q_S + \Delta F^* Q_F$. Perfect hedge will eliminate all changes in the portfolio $\Delta V_P = 0$ and would require $\frac{\Delta S}{\Delta F} = -\frac{Q_F}{Q_S}$. To determine the optimal hedge ratio, divide ΔV_P by Q_S to get $\frac{\Delta V_P}{Q_S} = \Delta S + \Delta F^* \frac{Q_F}{Q_S} = \Delta S - \Delta F^* h$, where $h \equiv -\frac{Q_F}{Q_S}$, and minimize $Var(\frac{\Delta V_P}{Q_S})$ with respect to h to obtain the result in Equation (V.1) in the text. See Black and Scholes (1973) for more details.

PART III: MACROECONOMIC AND FISCAL SUSTAINABILITY

This section provides an overview of macroeconomic vulnerability before presenting the fundamentals of public debt sustainability. The focus is on emerging market countries, that is, developing countries with access to the international capital markets. The sequence followed below is dictated by actual events over the past few decades in such countries. The 1980s were dominated by external debt and exchange rate crises, while banking crises and public debt crises were more prominent during the 1990s.[1]

VI. Macroeconomic Vulnerability[2]

A. EARLY WARNING SIGNALS. How to assess the vulnerability to a macroeconomic crisis or debt problem is a perennial topic in country economic analysis. There is a striking pattern in many of the macroeconomic crises (with the exception of East Asia) during the 1990s: a weak fiscal situation combined with current account problems lead to fears of devaluation and default, triggering a speculative attack and bank run which plunges the economy into recession, aggravating the fiscal problem and leading to the possibility of default.[3] Russia's crisis of 1998 and Argentina's crisis of 2001, which are analyzed in Chapters 9 and 10, respectively, conform to this broad pattern. Such crises beg the question of whether an effective early warning system can be designed – economists are often accused of predicting the last crisis instead of the next one!

A sizable literature has emerged in the quest for such a system. It attempts to identify variables that warn of coming macroeconomic problems. These variables are usually classified into the following groups:

Solvency variables – relate to the level of debt and its characteristics. The primary variables of interest in this group include various debt ratios, mainly debt-to-GDP and debt-to-exports. Debt can be calculated at face value or in present discounted value (PDV) terms. Total external debt-to-exports is an especially relevant indicator of debt and repayment capacity since higher external debt implies more strain on the current account and therefore a higher probability of debt problems. External debt-to-GDP is a useful complementary variable as it takes into account the overall resource base.

The measurement of debt can be further refined in several ways: based on currency composition, lenders (public or private), maturity, rates, gross versus net of foreign assets.[4] The share of foreign currency external debt in total external debt

---

[1] This is to a large extent an artificial distinction made for the convenience of presentation. Public debt crises have typically involved both banks and the exchange rate, as in Russia 1998 and Argentina 2001.

[2] This section draws on Sturzenegger (2004) and Sturzenegger and Wolf (2004).

[3] There is an ample literature that relates banking crises with currency crises. See Kaminsky and Reinhart (1996) and Glick and Hutchison (1999). For current account sustainability, see Edwards (2001). For assessing banking soundness, see Caprio, Honohan, and Vittas (2002).

[4] With respect to the latter, Hausmann and Velasco (2002) suggest disregarding foreign assets, as these assets are equally or even less available in times of crises.

provides a rough-and-ready measure of the pressure from exchange rate devaluations on the debt burden.

Private external debt poses a dilemma. Even though it is strictly not a sovereign liability, experience shows that in the wake of macroeconomic crises marked by devaluations and default, governments tend to nationalize or take up part of the external debt burden of the private sector.

The average interest rate on and the average maturity of external debt are useful indicators of the burden of debt as well as the vulnerability to shifting market sentiment. The difference between the interest rate and expected growth rate for the country is an important measure of debt burden.

Liquidity variables are related to the availability of and need for funds in the short-run. The most popular variables in this group include the ratio of short-term external debt to reserves, debt service-to-exports, debt service-to-liquid reserves, and the share of short-term debt in total debt. Global liquidity can be proxied by the GDP-weighted average nominal interest rate in G-7 economies or any international interest rate such as LIBOR. An increase in interest rates in developed economies implies that capital flows may be more likely to remain in or flow back to developed economies, thus increasing the rollover risk in emerging market economies.

Macroeconomic variables characterize the strength of the economy. This group includes indicators of potential current account troubles, such as real exchange rate overvaluation and the level and dynamics of the current account. Political variables, such as future elections or political instability, are relevant as well.

A large empirical literature uses these sets of variables to explain sovereign credit events, such as external debt crises; sovereign noncredit events, such as sudden stops and capital flow reversals as well as currency crises; and public debt crises, also a sovereign credit event which brings in the domestic component of public debt. Each is discussed in turn.

B. EXTERNAL DEBT CRISIS. The external debt crisis has been conventionally associated with a default event. Standard and Poor's defines a sovereign to be in default if the scheduled payment of interest/principal has been missed or delayed and/or a distressed exchange occurs.[5] Manasse, Roubini, and Schimmelpfennig (2003) combine the default classification of Standard and Poor's with the presence of large nonconcessional IMF loans (in excess of 100 percent of quota) to identify debt crises. Pescatori and Sy (2003) define an external debt crisis episode as occurring when a country either defaults or its bond spreads exceed some critical threshold. Detragiache and Spilimbergo (2001), on the other hand, identify a crisis with principal or interest payment arrears on external obligations of more than 5 percent of total commercial obligations and/or rescheduling or restructuring agreement with commercial creditors.

To proxy the probability of the default, empirical studies typically use bond spreads (Edwards 1984) or sovereign ratings (Cantor and Packer 1996).

The following table summarizes empirical results on early warning signals in the context of *external debt crises*. A $+$ ($-$) indicates a significant increase (decrease) in

[5] See Pescatori and Sy (2003) for more details on this and alternative definitions.

Table VI-1. *The literature on early warning signals (external debt crisis)*

	Ades	DS	MRS	PS
Solvency Variables				
GDP growth	−	ns	ns	−
External debt to GDP	+	+	+	+
Budget surplus as % of GDP	−	ns		
Exports to GDP	−			
Overvaluation (RER)	+	+		+
% Multilateral	+			
External debt/reserves			+	
Liquidity variables				
Global Illiquidity	+	ns	ns	
Amortizations/Reserves	+			
Short term debt/Reserves			ns	+
Short term debt		+		
Debt service due		+		
Reserves	−			
Interest on short term debt			+	
Other variables				
Default history	+			
Openness		ns	−	−
Inflation volatility			+	
Dummy for Inflation > 50%			+	
Year with presidential election			+	

Ades: Ades et al. (2000). D-S: Detragiache and Spilimbergo (2001). MRS: Manasse, Roubini, and Schimmelpfennig (2003). PS: Pescatori and Sy (2003).
Source: Sturzenegger F. and H. Wolf (2004).

vulnerability as a result of the factor, while *ns* indicates the variable is not significant, a blank indicates that the variable was not included in the study.

The explanatory power of the early warning signals varies with the definition of crisis used in the study. The two indicators that most consistently appear are external debt-to-GDP and real exchange rate overvaluation. The latter can be estimated as a deviation of the actual real exchange rate from its equilibrium level. The equilibrium real exchange rate is hard to obtain unless a fully specified theoretical model is developed. Another possibility is to use cross-country purchasing power parity comparisons. Many studies simply calculate overvaluation as the deviation of the real exchange rate from its trend.

C. CURRENCY CRISIS. This section discusses statistical criteria for currency crises. As with debt crises, no standardized definition of what constitutes a currency crisis is available. The literature primarily identifies a currency crisis based on one or more indicator variable(s). When these variables exceed a specified threshold over some period of time, a crisis is said to have occurred. The most commonly used variable is the exchange rate. Some studies focus on large and infrequent devaluation episodes; others explore small and frequent devaluations. Other work relies

Table VI-2. *The literature on early warning signals (currency crisis)*

Sector	Variable	Number of studies considered	Statistically significant result
Capital account	international reserves	12	11
Debt profile	short-term debt-to-reserves	3	1
	share of concessional loans	2	2
Current account	real exchange rate	14	12
Financial liberalization	credit growth	7	5
Other financial	m2/international reserves	3	3
Real sector	inflation	6	6
	real GDP growth or level	9	5
Fiscal	fiscal deficit	6	4
	credit to public sector	3	3
Institutional/structural		10	7
Political factors		4	3

Source: Kaminsky, Lizondo, and Reinhart (1998) updated based on findings in Chapter 8 of this book.

on broader measures which include, in additional to devaluations, significant drops in exchange reserves (as in Chapter 8 of this volume[6]), large increases in domestic interest rates, and occurrences of speculative attacks.[7] Crises can also be defined as episodes of exchange rate devaluations accompanied by large falls in output.

There exists a vast empirical literature that tries to identify variables characterizing currency crises and their likelihood. Some indicators that appear to work best are summarised in Table VI-2.[8]

D. PUBLIC DEBT CRISIS. This subsection looks at the usefulness and drawbacks of public debt-related ratios. Ratios like debt-to-GDP or interest-to-GDP must be interpreted with caution. Public debt numbers typically include only "explicit" debt, that is, debt registered in the books of the public sector. However, many governments have hidden fiscal liabilities arising from social security dynamics and pension reform or potential financial sector bailouts, which might come to light only in the wake of a crisis. Most debt analyses omit these items. However, a careful examination should include an assessment of potential fiscal obligations or contingent liabilities of the government. Furthermore, even countries with similar explicit public debt-to-GDP ratios may face very different terms, including interest rates, currency and maturity structure. The interest-to-debt ratio measures the average cost of the debt. This number provides only a first approximation to the yearly cost of the debt. It should be distinguished from the marginal cost of debt, which is the cost of new indebtedness. When a country approaches a debt default situation, the marginal cost of debt typically skyrockets even though average costs might remain relatively stable.

[6] Frankel and Wei use foreign exchange market pressure index, defined as the sum of percentage fall in the value of the currency and percentage fall in reserves to identify crisis episodes.
[7] See Kaminsky et al. (1998) for a comprehensive survey.
[8] See Kaminsky et al. (1998) Table A4 for a more detailed description and additional information.

These considerations are illustratd in Table VI-3 with the experience of selected emerging market economies. These are broken into two groups: the first includes countries that restructured or defaulted on their debt during the 1990s,[9] while the second is a group of countries that did not default.

In the first group, Pakistan had the largest debt burden both in terms of the debt-to-GDP ratio as well as the size of resources absorbed by interest payments in the year preceding the restructuring of its Eurobonds. Ecuador had a slightly smaller debt-to-GDP ratio, but a much lower average interest rate as a result of previous debt restructurings and concessional lending. Yet, as a percentage of tax revenues its interest cost was sizable. Ukraine's interest burden was much lower than Russia's even though its debt-to-GDP ratio was higher. The severity of the debt crisis and the disruption of economic activity have been the greatest in Argentina; while Russia's macroeconomic crisis was severe, it was short-lived. And the debt restructurings in Pakistan and Ukraine were relatively mild, both in terms of the absolute size of the debt restructured and the aftermath.

Interestingly, Columbia's indicators look much worse than those of Argentina. What are not shown are vulnerabilities stemming from a high share of dollar-denominated debt in conjunction with possible real exchange rate overvaluation and contingent liabilities associated with the financial sector. These were key considerations in the Argentine crisis of 2001.

The country examples given above show that debt crises can occur with very different initial conditions. Therefore, one should be careful about relying mechanically on static ratios and rules-of-thumb. In general, recent studies take a conservative view of debt. Reinhart, Rogoff, and Savastano (2003) argue that for emerging market countries with a history of default and high inflation, external debt (public plus private) greatly enhances vulnerability to a crisis once it crosses 15–20 percent of GDP. This finding agrees with that of Pattillo, Poirson, and Ricci (2004), who suggest that external debt ratios in excess of 15 percent of GDP and 65 percent of exports tend to be associated with slower growth. These results have their limitations as they are based on a cross-section of a broad group of heterogeneous countries and do not take into account the output and export growth prospects or the potential for improved fiscal performance. Similarly, IMF (2000) computes the sustainable level of public debt for the median emerging market country based on past fiscal performance to be as low as 25 percent of GDP. While it is helpful to keep such thresholds in mind, the practitioner would also benefit from examining the debt trajectory under a variety of forward-looking alternative scenarios. We describe the rudiments of such approaches next.

VII. Public Debt Sustainability

A good starting point is to distinguish sustainability from solvency. A government's debt position can be regarded as sustainable if the present revenue and expenditure paths can be maintained indefinitely without need for a sudden, drastic increase in the primary fiscal balance (total revenue minus noninterest spending) to either stabilize

---

[9] To make the comparison meaningful for the first group of countries, we include their numbers prior to the debt restructuring or default.

Table VI-3. *Debt burden indicators in selected countries*

| | Restructured/defaulted on debt (year before restructuring/crisis) | | | | | Nondefaulters | | | |
	Argentina (2000)	Ecuador (1998)	Pakistan (1998)	Russia (1997)	Ukraine (1999)	Colombia (2000)	Mexico (2000)	Venezuela (2000)	Poland (2000)
Interest/GDP %	3.4	3.2	7.1	4.8	2.4	5.0	2.6	3.3	2.9
Interest/Taxes %	26.1	44.9	52.2	48.4	7.4	25.3	25.7	18.7	11.0
Interest/Public Debt %	7.5	4.0	7.5	9.0	3.8	9.8	9.4	9.3	7.4
Public Debt/GDP %	44.9	80.0	94.3	52.5	62.8	50.8	27.7	35.3	39.1

Source: Sturzenegger (2004) from IMF, Goldman Sachs estimates.

the debt-to-GDP ratio or reduce it. This means that the current debt trajectory can be maintained without fear of a forced restructuring of debt and/or default. Solvency is a more abstract concept and relates to the question of whether there exists *any feasible* fiscal policy path that allows the government to avoid default given its current debt level.

A. DERIVATION OF THE DIFFERENCE EQUATION FOR PUBLIC DEBT. When governments run fiscal deficits, which means they spend more than the revenues they take in, the deficits have to be financed. The possibilities are to print money – that is, rely on seignorage – borrow, or generate privatization proceeds by selling assets to the private sector. In addition to deficits, governments may incur fiscal costs as a result of contingent liabilities, for example, related to recapitalizing banks or bolstering the financial position of the pension agency or servicing the debt of insolvent public enterprises under guarantees. The focus here is on what happens to public debt and, eventually, the government's ability to service it out of primary fiscal balances, that is, total revenues minus noninterest spending. This relationship is commonly referred to as the government's "intertemporal budget constraint." We present a derivation of the resulting difference equation describing the time path of public debt. For simplicity, we abstract from contingent liabilities. Furthermore, seignorage is typically incorporated into the primary fiscal balance in the form of central bank profits transferred to the government. We shall assume that this is the case here and will not treat seignorage explicitly. A more sophisticated and complete set of derivations can be found in Burnside (2004). We present only the basics here for the practitioner.

The variables are defined as follows (*t* is a time subscript):

GDP_t — Nominal GDP during period t
D_t — Public Debt, end of period t
PD_t — Primary Deficit (noninterest spending minus revenues incl. transferred central bank profits)
$NDFS_t$ — Non-Debt Financing Sources (such as privatization)
g_t — Real GDP Growth Rate
π_t — Domestic Inflation (measured by the GDP deflator)
i_t — Nominal Interest Rate

Debt evolves as shown in (i):

$$D_t = (PD_t - NDFS_t) + D_{t-1}(1 + i_t).$$ (i)

This equation basically says that debt at the end of period t is equal to the primary deficit less nondebt financing plus the starting amount of debt and interest payments on it; note that the fiscal deficit is simply $PD_t + i_t D_{t-1}$.

Divide (i) through by $GDP_t = GDP_{t-1}(1 + g_t)(1 + \pi_t)$ to get:

$$d_t = (pd_t - ndfs_t) + \frac{D_{t-1}(1 + i_t)}{GDP_{t-1}(1 + g_t)(1 + \pi_t)},$$ (ii)

where lower case letters refer to the ratios of the upper case variables to contemporaneous GDP. Subtract d_{t-1} from both sides of Equation (ii) to get:

$$d_t - d_{t-1} = (pd_t - ndfs_t) + d_{t-1}\left[\frac{(1+i_t)}{(1+g_t)(1+\pi_t)} - 1\right]. \tag{iii}$$

Noting that the real interest rate r_t is defined by $(1+r_t) = (1+i_t)/(1+\pi_t)$, (iii) can be simplified to get:

$$d_t - d_{t-1} = (pd_t - ndfs_t) + \frac{(r_t - g_t)}{(1+g_t)}d_{t-1}, \tag{iv}$$

which is Equation (1) in Chapter 9.

Equation (2) in Chapter 9 can be obtained using a shortcut based on continuous time approximations. Let $i_{d,t}$ and $i_{f,t}$ denote the nominal interest rate on the domestic currency portion and foreign currency ("dollar") portion of public debt, respectively. Assume interest payments are made at the end of the year. Let the nominal exchange rate (local currency per dollar) at the end of the year be denoted by x_t and $\hat{x}$ its growth (rate of depreciation) during the year. It follows that

$$r_t = w(i_{d,t} - \pi) + (1-w)(i_{f,t} + \hat{x} - \pi), \tag{v}$$

where w is the share of domestic currency debt in total public debt at the beginning of the period. The last term on the RHS of (v) makes use of (ex post) interest parity and in so doing captures the capital gain or loss on the foreign currency portion of public debt. Defining the bilateral real exchange rate in dollars per local currency, which is the IMF's convention, it follows that real appreciation, ρ, is given by $(\pi - \pi^* - \hat{x})$, where π^* is U.S. inflation measured by its GDP deflator. Adding and subtracting π^* from the last term on the RHS of Equation (v) and using the expression for ρ gives:

$$r_t = wr_{d,t} + (1-w)(r_{f,t} - \rho), \tag{vi}$$

with $r_{d,t} = (i_{d,t} - \pi)$ and $r_{f,t} = (i_{f,t} - \pi^*)$ denoting the real interest rate on domestic currency and foreign currency debt, respectively.

Define $\Delta d_t \equiv d_t - d_{t-1}$ and $\tilde{r}_t = wr_{d,t} + (1-w)r_{f,t}$. For simplicity, set $ndfs_t = 0$. Substituting Equation (vi) into Equation (iv) and rearranging terms gives:

$$\Delta d_t = pd_t + \frac{\tilde{r}_t}{(1+g_t)}d_{t-1} - \frac{(1-w)\rho_t}{(1+g_t)}d_{t-1} - \frac{g_t}{(1+g_t)}d_{t-1}. \tag{vii}$$

Equation (vii) embodies a useful decomposition of the change in the debt-to-GDP ratio into four contributing components: (a) primary fiscal deficits; (b) a real interest rate effect; (c) a real exchange rate effect; and (d) a growth effect. Note that the real interest rate in Equation (vi), which includes the capital gain/loss from real exchange rate movements, has been split into a pure real interest rate effect and a capital gain/loss effect proportional to the share of foreign currency debt in total debt. It is clear from Equation (vii) that a real appreciation ($\rho > 0$) lowers Δd_t and makes public debt dynamics look good; but problems might be building up if the real exchange rate is becoming overvalued. This last point is vividly demonstrated in Chapter 10 on the Argentine crisis; correcting an overvaluation means that ρ

should be negative so that the debt-to-GDP ratio is being "under-reported" relative to the equilibrium real exchange rate. In this case, the debt-to-GDP ratio could jump by a large amount when the correction occurs. For instance, consider again the case of Argentina. In 2001 its debt-to-GDP ratio at the observed exchange rate was 62.2 percent, while the RER was estimated to be overvalued by 45 percent. Correcting for this overvaluation raises Argentina's debt-to-GDP ratio to 90.2 percent, given by 62.2 times 1.45, assuming all public debt is dollar-denominated (see column 5 in Table 10.2, Chapter 10 of this volume).

In terms of practical implementation of the decomposition in Equation (vii), information constraints are likely to be serious. Typically, the analyst is unlikely to have the nominal interest rate separately for domestic and foreign currency debt, just the total amount of interest payments made in local currency. In this case, let $\tilde{i}$ denote the interest rate obtained by dividing total interest payments during period t by the beginning-of-period total debt, D_{t-1}. The shares w and $(1 - w)$ of local and foreign currency debt in D_{t-1} are also likely to be readily available, even though a detailed currency composition may not. Furthermore, if we use the discrete time formula for ρ given implicitly by $(1 + \rho) = (1 + \pi)/[(1 + \pi^*)(1 + \hat{x})$, a more accurate version of the decomposition in Equation (vii) is given by Equation (viii), where the different components explaining the change in the debt-to-GDP ratio correspond to those in Equation (vii). For compactness, the subscript t has been omitted for π, π^*, g, ρ:[10]

$$
\Delta d_t = pd_t + \left[\frac{\tilde{i}}{1 + \pi} - \frac{\pi}{1 + \pi} - \frac{(1 - w)(\pi^* - \pi)}{(1 + \pi)(1 + \pi^*)} \right] \frac{d_{t-1}}{1 + g}
$$
$$
- (1 - w) \frac{\rho}{(1 + \pi^*)(1 + \rho)} \frac{d_{t-1}}{1 + g} - \frac{g}{(1 + g)} d_{t-1}.
$$

(viii)

B. ASSESSING DEBT SUSTAINABILITY. We return to a simplified version of Equation (iv), assuming $ndfs = 0$. In this case:

$$
\Delta d_t = pd_t + \frac{(r_t - g_t)}{(1 + g_t)} d_{t-1}.
$$

(ix)

From Equation (ix) the long run steady-state level of the primary surplus required assuming the debt-to-GDP ratio is constant:

$$
ps \equiv -pd = \frac{(r - g)}{(1 + g)} d.
$$

(x)

Equation (x) is a useful benchmark, but needs to be carefully interpreted. It merely computes the size of the primary surplus needed to stabilize debt. It does not tell us whether this level of primary surplus is achievable or not, or whether the corresponding debt-to-GDP ratio is sustainable. A country may well have to lower its debt-to-GDP ratio.

Equation (x) implicitly assumes that $r > g$, which is almost always the case in practice absent financial repression. We now obtain a simple long-run form of the government's budget constraint, assuming r and g are constant – which simplifies the

---

[10] A detailed derivation is available in Budina and Fiess (2004).

556   *Viktoria Hnatkovska*

algebra without losing any of the essential intuition. Equation (ix) can be rearranged to give a convenient expression for d_{t-1} in terms of d_t which is useful for forward iteration:[11]

$$d_{t-1} = -pd_t + \frac{(1+g)}{(1+r)}d_t. \tag{xi}$$

Define $\delta \equiv (1+g)/(1+r) < 1$ and recall that $ps \equiv -pd$ is the primary fiscal surplus. We now have a standard difference equation that can be solved forward to get an expression for today's debt-to-GDP ratio:

$$d_t = \delta^T d_{t+T} + \sum_{i=1}^{T}\delta^i ps_{t+i} = \sum_{i=1}^{\infty}\delta^i ps_{t+i}. \tag{xii}$$

The final equality in Equation (xii) is obtained taking the limit as $T \to \infty$ of the RHS of Equation (xii) and applying the transversality condition $\lim_{T\to\infty}\delta^T d_{t+T} = 0$. The intuition underlying the transversality condition is that creditors want to be paid, so they will not let future debt grow without bound. This yields the classic solvency condition that initial debt must equal the discounted sum of future primary surpluses so that debt is eventually paid off; the discount rate is none other than the familiar $(r-g)/(1+g)$.[12] An important implication is that a government running primary deficits today must run larger primary fiscal surpluses in the future as future debt financing plays no role. Hence, if debt levels are high and a fiscal adjustment is needed, postponing it will require a much bigger effort in the future. Lastly, if the primary surplus is held constant, solving for this level based on Equation (xii) yields the long-run steady state solution shown earlier in Equation (x).[13]

C. DEBT PROJECTIONS. Some form of the difference equation for debt of the many derived above can be used both to explain how the present debt level was reached and also its future trajectory under various scenarios. See Pinto and Zahir (2004) for an application to India.

D. TESTS OF DEBT SUSTAINABILITY. The sustainability of the path of public debt is of obvious interest to policymakers. How to assess this? We discuss, in turn, simple ways, formal econometric tests, and market signals.

An example of a simple way to test for debt sustainability is to calculate the level of the primary surplus that would stabilize the debt-to-GDP ratio as in Equation (x) above and ask what it would take in terms of spending and tax reform to actually attain that level. Are the needed reforms economically and political feasible? Consider, for instance, a situation where there is a primary deficit, nondebt financing sources are negligible and the real interest rate exceeds the growth rate. Clearly, in the absence of a fiscal correction, the debt-to-GDP ratio will be on an explosive path as can be seen from Equation (iv). Does this mean a crisis is inevitable? Not if the government can easily mobilize additional revenues or cut wasteful spending. Alternatively, growth could speed up through structural reform.

---

[11] Note that this works because $g < r$.
[12] This can be obtained by solving for x from $\delta = 1/(1+x)$.
[13] A more sophisticated analysis may be found in Burnside (2004).

Most of the econometric tests of fiscal sustainability originated from the application for U.S. government debt developed by Hamilton and Flavin (1986). They pointed out that the hypothesis of intertemporal budget balance (Equation xii) is equivalent to the hypothesis that the transversality condition, $\lim_{T\to\infty} \delta^T d_{t+T} = 0$, holds. If this is the case, Equation (xii) becomes $d_t = \sum_{i=1}^{\infty} \delta^i ps_{t+i}$.

The alternative hypothesis would assert that current debt exceeds the discounted sum of future primary surpluses by some positive amount. Hamilton and Flavin implement this idea by assuming that

$$\lim_{T\to\infty} \delta^{t+T} d_{t+T} = a.$$

This implies a particular form of violation of the transversality condition:

$$\lim_{T\to\infty} \delta^T d_{t+T} = a\delta^{-t}.$$

Equation (xii) can now be rewritten as

$$d_t = \delta^T d_{t+T} + \sum_{i=1}^{T} \delta^i ps_{t+i} = a\delta^{-t} + \sum_{i=1}^{\infty} \delta^i ps_{t+i}. \tag{xiii}$$

The Hamilton–Flavin test therefore amounts to testing whether $a = 0$. From an equation analogous to Equation (xiii), they observe that if the discounted path of the future primary surpluses $\{ps_{t+i}\}_{i=1}^{T}$ is stationary,[14] then the process for debt d_t is stationary if and only if $a = 0$. Assuming a constant interest rate, the test reduces to checking for stationarity of the undiscounted primary surpluses and undiscounted debt. Under the assumption of a constant interest rate, stationarity of the undiscounted primary surpluses is sufficient to ensure the stationarity of discounted surpluses. If both series are found to be stationary, a must be equal to zero, and the intertemporal budget constraint holds: fiscal policy is sustainable.

Box TA.1 discusses variations of this test developed by Trehan and Walsh (1991). The interested reader is also referred to Cuddington (1999) for a more detailed discussion, extensions, and a literature overview.

Stationarity tests are now briefly discussed. Stationarity requires that the economic variable of interest does not grow without bound, which can be formally tested by means of *unit root* tests. Several such tests have been developed and became part of standard statistical packages such as Eviews, STATA, RATS, etc. Most common tests include the augmented Dickey–Fuller (1979), Phillips–Perron (1988), and Kwiatkowski–Phillips–Schmidt–Shin (KPSS 1992) unit root tests. We briefly discuss them here. The interested reader may find it useful to first read the time-series section in Part II of this appendix.

E. AUGMENTED DICKEY–FULLER (ADF) TEST. The ADF test, as well as all the other tests mentioned above, posits the presence of a unit root as a null hypothesis. The alternative hypothesis of stationarity is usually chosen. In its original form, Dickey and Fuller suggested running the following regression

$$Y_t = \mu + \beta_0 t + \rho Y_{t-1} + u_t$$

and testing whether $\rho = 1$ to detect the unit root in Y_t.

---

[14] Main time-series concepts are discussed in detail in Part II of this appendix.

Box TA.1. Tests of the Transversality Condition

The following procedure uses the analysis developed in Trehan and Walsh (1991).

1. Constant future interest rate
   - If the path of primary surpluses ps_t is stationary then the present value budget constraint (xii) holds if and only if the process for d_t is also stationary. This implies sustainable fiscal policy. If stationarity of d_t is rejected, then Equation (xiii) is the one that characterizes debt dynamics and the fiscal policy is said to be unsustainable. This procedure is equivalent to the one implemented by Hamilton and Flavin (1986).
   - On the other hand, if the process for primary surpluses ps_t is not stationary, then the process for d_t must be nonstationary as well, and one needs to test for possible cointegration between d_t and ps_t, that is, whether there exists a linear combination of the two processes which is stationary. This can be verified by means of the Johansen cointegration test available in most time-series econometrics software packages. If such a relationship is found, the present value budget constraint Equation (xii) holds and debt dynamics are said to be stationary.

2. Time varying interest rate
   Allowing for time varying interest rate provides a more realistic description of the data generating process but also has important implications for sustainability. In particular, debt sustainability analysis is not based any more solely on testing for stationarity of primary surpluses and debt or the presence of a cointegrating relationship between the two. Rather, it requires stationarity of the inclusive-of-interest (discounted) debt and primary surplus series. This condition ensures the intertemporal budget balance as long as the expected rate of interest is positive.

To implement such a test automatically in most software packages, the regression equation above can be rewritten slightly:

$$Y_t - Y_{t-1} = \mu + \beta_0 t + \rho Y_{t-1} - Y_{t-1} + u_t \quad \Leftrightarrow$$
$$\Delta Y_t = \mu + \beta_0 t + \delta Y_{t-1} + u_t, \tag{xiv}$$

and the unit root test reduces to testing $\delta \equiv (\rho - 1) = 0$.

The augmented Dickey–Fuller (ADF) test expands the regression in (xiv) by including lagged terms of ΔY_t to control for possible higher order serial correlation in series.

$$\Delta Y_t = \mu + \beta_0 t + \delta Y_{t-1} + \beta_1 \Delta Y_{t-1} + \beta_2 \Delta Y_{t-2}$$
$$+ \cdots + \beta_{p-1} \Delta Y_{t-(p-1)} + u_t. \tag{xv}$$

This specification is then used to test the null hypothesis of a unit root in the Y_t series against the alternative of stationarity:

$$H_0 : \delta = 0,$$
$$H_1 : \delta < 0.$$

If δ is significantly different from zero, then the null hypothesis of a unit root, or equivalently, nonstationarity is rejected.

F. THE PHILLIPS–PERRON (PP) TEST. While the above ADF test accounts for the serial correlation in the series by including lagged first difference terms in the variable of interest, the PP test corrects for serial correlation by adjusting the t-statistic on the lagged level coefficient, δ, using nonparametric techniques. As before, finding a statistically significant nonzero coefficient δ permits a rejection of non-stationarity.

Apart from their complexity, econometric tests for unit roots suffer from three drawbacks. First, these tests, which check for explosive trends in the data, have limited power against the alternative hypothesis of a series that is highly persistent, that is, close to being explosive, but which displays mean-reverting tendencies. Returning to the example given above, consider a situation where the primary deficit is positive and the real interest rate exceeds the growth rate so that the debt-to-GDP ratio is on an obviously explosive path. If the government and markets are confident that corrective measures can be taken quickly to dampen the debt trajectory, this may not be a problem, even though unit root tests may detect nonstationarity, that is, an explosive debt path. Bohn (1998) showed that U.S. public debt is sustainable and the debt-to-GDP ratio stationary despite a failure to reject the presence of unit roots based on the standard tests. Second, these tests require long historical series that may often not be available for developing countries. Third, such tests are by nature backward-looking, whereas debt sustainability and solvency are primarily about the future. The utility of these tests therefore derives primarily from their use in conjunction with an assessment of the feasibility of implementing policy corrections to remedy the situation. Two examples of such tests, both applied to India, may be found in Buiter and Patel (1992) and Serven (1996).

Last but not least, for emerging market countries, the market is the final arbiter of whether a given debt trajectory is sustainable or not. Looking at market signals implicit in the pricing of both foreign currency denominated and local currency debt can be insightful about the market's expectations of devaluation and default. Chapter 9 discusses market signals and their interpretation in the context of the Russian crisis of 1998.

VIII. Procyclicality of Fiscal Policy

Often one would like to assess how much deficits vary because of variations in economic activity versus changes in fiscal policy. If government consumption tends to increase in "good times," that is, when economy is booming and output is high relative to trend, while decreasing when output is low relative to trend, then the governments is said to follow a *procyclical* fiscal policy. When government consumption and output move in opposite directions, fiscal policy is said to be *countercyclical*.

A. CORRELATION ANALYSIS. A measure of the degree of the procyclicality of fiscal policy can be obtained from a simple correlation coefficient computed as follows. First, the cyclical component of an indicator of fiscal policy (government purchases, expenditures, primary deficits) must be isolated using any of the trend-cycle decomposition techniques discussed in Part I of this appendix. Then, the cyclical component of a measure of economic activity (GDP, industrial production, etc.) must also be isolated. Once this is done, the comovement between the two can be measured by a correlation coefficient. A positive (negative) correlation indicates procyclical (countercyclical) fiscal policy.

B. REGRESSION-BASED CYCLICALITY INDICATORS. As discussed above fiscal policy cyclicality can be calculated as a correlation coefficient between, for example, Hodrick–Prescott-filtered government spending and output. See Agenor et al. (1999), Stein et al. (1999), Talvi and Vegh (2000), and Chapter 2 of this book for applications. However, Forbes and Rigobon (1998) in their study of stock market comovement and contagion pointed out that such unadjusted correlation coefficients may be inappropriate when crosssectional units under study have different levels of volatility. A robust procedure based on regression analysis should be used instead. The intuition comparing the two approaches is described below:

Consider estimating the degree of fiscal policy procyclicality in two countries, each with a different degree of output volatility, $\sigma_{yy}^h > \sigma_{yy}^l$, where σ_{yy} is used to denote the variance of HP-filtered or first-differenced output and the superscript identifies a country with h (high) or l (low) volatility. Also let g and y denote HP-filtered or first-differenced government expenditure and output respectively. Then if the true data generating process for both countries is given by

$$g_t = \alpha + \beta y_t + \varepsilon_t, \tag{xiv}$$

it follows that $\beta^h = \beta^l$ assuming that the set of classical assumptions for OLS regression is satisfied.[15]

From the equality of βs combined with the standard definition of β, it follows:

$$\beta^h = \frac{\sigma_{g,y}^h}{\sigma_{y,y}^h} = \frac{\sigma_{g,y}^l}{\sigma_{y,y}^l} = \beta^l.$$

The assumption on output volatilities $\sigma_{yy}^h > \sigma_{yy}^l$ implies that the covariance between government spending and output should also be larger in the higher output volatility country.

In turn, the correlation analysis applied to the two countries will yield the following measures of procyclicality:

$$\rho_{g,y}^h = \frac{\sigma_{g,y}^h}{\sqrt{\sigma_{yy}^h \sigma_{gg}^h}} \quad \text{and} \quad \rho_{g,y}^l = \frac{\sigma_{g,y}^l}{\sqrt{\sigma_{yy}^l \sigma_{gg}^l}}.$$

Rewriting these definitions in terms of β's

$$\rho_{g,y}^h = \beta \frac{\sqrt{\sigma_{yy}^h}}{\sqrt{\sigma_{gg}^h}} \quad \text{and} \quad \rho_{g,y}^l = \beta \frac{\sqrt{\sigma_{yy}^l}}{\sqrt{\sigma_{gg}^l}}$$

and combining them with the results above, we get $\rho_{g,y}^h > \rho_{g,y}^l$.

---

[15] Under the set of classical assumptions, OLS estimates of equation (xiv) are unbiased, consistent and efficient in both countries, which implies the equality of β's in the two countries.

It follows that the correlation coefficient will be tend to be higher for countries with higher volatility even when the true correlation between output and government spending is the same. As a result, this correlation coefficient is biased and depends on the variance of y. See Forbes and Rigobon (1998) for a formal derivation of the magnitude of the bias.

On account of these arguments, Lane (2003), Arreaza et al. (1999), and Sorensen et al. (2001) use a regression-based method to measure fiscal procyclicality. In particular, Lane (2003) considers a simple OLS or IV regression of the form

$$\Delta \log(G_{it}) = \beta_0 + \beta_{Gi} \Delta \log(Y_{it}) + u_{it} \quad \forall i,$$

where i (country index) and t (time index). The coefficient $\hat{\beta}_{Gi}$ is an estimator of the elasticity of government expenditure with respect to output growth for country i. A positive value of $\hat{\beta}_{Gi}$ would imply procyclical fiscal policy, and a negative value, countercyclicality. While in his baseline model Lane (2003) uses first differences of the log-transformed output and government spending, he also finds that Hodrick–Prescott-transformed data yield very similar results.

A practitioner may also find it informative to calculate cyclicality indicators for disaggregated components of government finances in order to detect those that are more prone to procyclicality. Such components could include government consumption and its breakdown between wage and nonwage categories, government investment, noninterest government spending, etc. Looking at the aggregate data might be misleading if components tend to move in opposite directions.

C. BLANCHARD'S INDICATOR OF FISCAL IMPULSE. The analysis described above might be sensitive to the choice of the trend-cycle decomposition technique used. In order to check the robustness of the predictions in **A** and **B**, one could use the indicator of fiscal impulse developed by Blanchard (1993).[16] His approach enables the decomposition of the sustainability measure (usually primary balance) into components attributable to changes in macroeconomic conditions, and those due to policy changes. Macroeconomic conditions are captured by the employment level, plus a deterministic trend and a constant. Their impact on the primary fiscal surplus is obtained by using them as regressors in simple empirical models of the primary balance components. Then, the discretionary policy component is given by the difference between the actual primary balance and the primary balance linked to the economy's characteristics.

We next outline the procedure used in the Chapter 10 in this book. Define the variables to be used:

λ ratio of employment to the labor force
T public revenues
G primary expenditure
P GDP deflator
Y real GDP
B primary balance

---

[16] See Alesina and Perotti (1995) and Brunilla et al. (1999) for empirical applications of Blanchard's approach.

To estimate Blanchard's indicator of fiscal impulse, one could use the following steps:

1. Isolate the effect of macroeconomic changes on the expenditure component of primary balance by estimating a time-series regression of real primary expenditures as a share of real GDP on a constant, time trend, and aggregate employment conditions:

$$\left(\left(\frac{G_t}{P_t}\right)\Big/ Y_t\right) = \alpha + \beta \lambda_t + \phi t + u_t.$$

Run an analogous regression for the revenue component of the primary balance:

$$\left(\left(\frac{T_t}{P_t}\right)\Big/ Y_t\right) = \delta + \eta \lambda_t + \varphi t + \varepsilon_t.$$

2. The predicted primary balance is then obtained as a difference between the predicted public revenues and primary expenditures. These two components of the primary balance are calculated as fitted values from the abovementioned regressions by replacing the contemporaneous employment with the previous period's employment.

$$\hat{B}_t = (\hat{\delta} + \hat{\eta}\lambda_{t-1} + \hat{\varphi}t) - (\hat{\alpha} + \hat{\beta}\lambda_{t-1} + \hat{\phi}t).$$

The actual primary balance as a share of real GDP is given by

$$B_t = \left(\frac{T_t}{P_t}\Big/ Y_t\right) - \left(\frac{G_t}{P_t}\Big/ Y_t\right).$$

The component associated with the discretionary policy X_t is then calculated by subtracting the values of the actual primary balance in the previous year from the predicted cyclically adjusted primary balance:

$$X_t = \hat{B}_t - B_{t-1}.$$

In other words, in every period t, X_t as calculated above gives the deviation of the fiscal policy stance from the one that would have prevailed if the macroeconomic environment (as measured by unemployment) had remained the same as in the previous year.

3. Chapter 10 of the book extends the analysis a step further and constructs an indicator of the fiscal impulse as a three-year centered moving average of X_t, in order to smooth out its short-term fluctuations.

$$\Gamma_t = 100 \times \frac{X_{t-1} + X_t + X_{t+1}}{3} = 100 \times \frac{\sum\limits_{i=-1}^{1} X_{t+i}}{3}.$$

The next step is to plot this indicator against time to detect contractionary or expansionary periods of fiscal policy.

REFERENCES

Ades, A., F. Kaune, P. Leme, R. Masih, and D. Tenengauzer. 2000. "A New Framework for Assessing Fair Value in Emerging Markets Hard-Currency Debt." Global Economics, Paper No. 45.

Agenor P., J. McDermott, and E. Prasad. 1999. "Macroeconomic Fluctuations in Developing Countries: Some Stylized Facts." IMF WP/99/35.

Aizenman, Joshua, Kenneth M. Kletzer, and Brian Pinto. 2005. "Sargent-Wallace Meets Krugman-Flood-Garber, Or: Why Sovereign Debt Swaps Do Not Avert Macroeconomic Crisis." *Economic Journal* 115(503):343–67.

Alesina, Alberto, and Roberto Perotti. 1995. "Fiscal Expansions and Fiscal Adjustments in OECD Countries." National Bureau of Economic Research Working Paper No. 5214. Cambridge, MA.

Arreaza A., B. E. Sorensen, and O. Yosha. 1999. "Consumption Smoothing through Fiscal Policy in OECD and EU Countries." In J. M. Poterba and J. von Hagen, eds., *Fiscal Institutions and Fiscal Performance*. Chicago: University of Chicago Press, pp. 59–80.

Auffret, Philippe. 2003. "Catastrophe Insurance Market in the Caribbean Region: Market Failures and Recommendations for Public Sector Interventions." Policy Research Working Paper Series 2963, The World Bank.

Baxter, Marianne, and Robert G. King. 1995. "Measuring Business Cycles: Approximate Band-Pass Filters for Economic Time series." NBER Working Paper No. 5022.

Beveridge, Stephen, and Charles R. Nelson. 1981. "A New Approach to Decomposition of Economic Time Series into Permanent and Transitory Components with Particular Attention to Measurement of the Business Cycle." *Journal of Monetary Economics* 7:157–74.

Black, Fischer, and Myron Scholes. 1973. "The Pricing of Options and Corporate Liabilities." *Journal of Political Economics* 81(3):637–54.

Blanchard, Oliver J. 1993. "Suggestions for a New Set of Fiscal Indicators." In H. A. A. Verbon and F. A. A. M. Van Vinden, eds., *The Political Economy of Government Debt*. Amsterdam: North Holland.

Bohn, Henning. 1998. "The Behavior of U.S. Public Debt and Deficits." *Quarterly Journal of Economics* 13:949–63.

Bollerslev, Tim. 1986. "Generalized Autoregressive Conditional Heterokedasticity." *Journal of Econometrics* 31:307–27.

Brooks, Chris. 2002. *Introductory Econometrics for Finance*. New York: Cambridge University Press.

Brunila, Anne, Juhana Hukkinen, and Mika Tujula. 1999. "Indicators of the Cyclically Adjusted Budget Balance: The Bank of Finland's Experience." Bank of Finland Discussion Papers, 1/99.

Budina, Nina, and Norbert Fiess. 2004. "Public Debt and Its Determinants in Market Access Countries: Results from 15 Country Case Studies." Unpublished paper, World Bank, Washington, DC.

Buiter, Willem H., and Urjit Patel. 1992. "Debt, Deficits and Inflation: An Application to the Public Finances of India." *Journal of Public Economics* 47:171–205; also In Amaresh Bagchi and Nicholas Stern, eds., *Tax Policy and Planning in Developing Countries*. Oxford: Oxford University Press, 1994, pp. 94–131.

Burnside, Craig. 2004. "Fiscal Sustainability in Theory and Practice: Introduction." University of Virginia, manuscript.

Cantor, R., and F. Packer. 1996. "Determinants and Impacts of Sovereign Credit Ratings." *Federal Reserve Bank of New York Economic Policy Review* (October):37–53.

Caprio, G., P. Honohan, and D. Vittas. 2002. *Financial Sector Policy for Developing Countries: A Reader*. Oxford: Oxford University Press, for the World Bank.

564   *Viktoria Hnatkovska*

Cuddington, John. 1999. "Analyzing the Sustainability of Fiscal Deficits in Developing Countries." Economics Department, Georgetown University, Working Paper.

———. 2004. Macroeconometrics Using Eviews Software. Course taught at the World Bank and IMF.

Debt- and Reserve-Related Indicators of External Vulnerability. IMF Paper, March 2000. Available at http://www.imf.org/external/np/pdr/debtres/debtres.pdf.

Deininger, Klaus, and Lyn Squire. 1996. "Measuring Income Inequality: A New Database." *World Bank Economic Review* 10(3):565–91.

Detragiache, Enrica, and Antonio Spilimbergo. 2001. "Crisis and Liquidity: Evidence and Interpretation." IMF "Working Paper" WP 01/2.

Dickey, David A., and Wayne A. Fuller. 1979. "Distribution of the Estimators for Autoregressive Time Series with a Unit Root." *Journal of the American Statistical Association* 74:427–31.

Diebold, Francis X. 2004. *Elements of Forecasting.* Thompson South-Western, Mason, Ohio.

Dollar, David and Aart Kraay. 2002. "Growth Is Good for the Poor." *Journal of Economic Growth*, Springer 7(3):195–225.

Edwards, S. 1984. "LDC Foreign Borrowing and Default Risk: An Empirical Default Risk, 1976–1980." *American Economic Review* 74:726–34.

Edwards, S. 2001. "Does the Current Account Matter?" Prepared for the NBER conference on Crisis Prevention, Florida, January 2001.

Engle, Robert F. 1982. "Autoregressive Conditional Heteroskedasticity with Estimates of the Variance of United Kingdom Inflation." *Econometrica* 50:987–1007.

Forbes, K., and R. Rigobon. 1998. "No Contagion, Only Interdependence: Measuring Stock Market Co-movements." NBER Working Paper 7267.

Ghosh, Atish R., and Holger Wolf. 1998. "Thresholds and Context Dependence in Growth." NBER Working Paper 6480.

Glewwe, Paul, Michele, Gragnolati, and Hassan Zaman. 2002. "Who Gained from Vietnam's boom in the 1990s?" *Economic Development and Cultural Change* 50(4):773–92.

Glick, R., and M. Hutchison. 1999. "Banking and Currency Crises: How Common Are Twins?" Pacific Basin Working Paper Series, Working Paper PB99-07.

Hamilton, James D. 1994. *Time Series Analysis.* Princeton: Princeton University Press.

——— and M. Flavin. 1986. "On the Limitations of Government Borrowing: A Framework for Empirical Testing." *American Economic Review* 76:808–19.

Hausmann, Ricardo, and Andrés Velasco. 2002. "The Argentine Collapse: Hard Money's Soft Underbelly." Mimeo. Kennedy School of Government.

Hodrick, Robert J., and Edward C. Prescott. 1980. "Post-war U.S. Business Cycles: An Empirical Investigation." Discussion Paper 451, Carnegie-Mellon University.

———. 1997. "Postwar U.S. Business Cycles: An Empirical Investigation." *Journal of Money, Credit and Banking* 29(1):1–16.

Hull, John. 2000. *Options, Futures and Other Derivatives.* 4th edition, Englewood Cliffs, NJ: Prentice Hall.

Kaminsky, Graciela, and Carmen M. Reinhart. 1996. "The Twin Crisis: The Causes of Banking and Balance-of-Payments Problems." International Finance Discussion Paper No. 544, Washington, Board of Governors of the Federal Reserve System.

Kaminsky, Graciela, Saul Lizondo, and Carmen M. Reinhart. 1998. "Leading Indicators of Currency Crisis." IMF Staff Papers Vol. 45, No. 1.

Kwiatkowski, Dennis, Peter C. B. Phillips, Peter Schmidt, and Yongcheol Shin 1992. "Testing the Null Hypothesis of Stationarity against the Alternative of a Unit Root: How Sure Are We That Economic Time Series Have a Unit Root?" *Journal of Econometrics* 54: 159–78.

Lane, Phillip. 2003. "The Cyclical Behavior of Fiscal Policy: Evidence from the OECD." *Journal of Public Economics* 87(12):2661–75.

Manasse, Paolo, Nouriel Roubini, and Axel Schimmelpfennig. 2003. "Predicting Sovereign Debt Crises." IMF Working Paper WP/03/221.

Mark, Nelson C. 2001. *International Macroeconomics and Finance. Theory and Econometric Methods.* Malden, MA: Blackwell Publishers.

Ng, Serena, and Pierre Perron. 2001. "Lag Length Selection and the Construction of Unit Root Tests with Good Size and Power." *Econometrica* 69(6):1519–54.

Pattillo, Catherine, Helene Poirson, and Luca Ricci. 2004. "What Are the Channels through Which External Debt Affects Growth?" IMF Working Paper 04/15.

Pescatori, Andrea, and Amadou N. R. Sy. 2003. "Debt Crisis and the Development of International Capital Markets." IMF Working Paper WP/03/xx.

Phillips, Peter C. B., and Pierre Perron. 1988. "Testing for a Unit Root in Time Series Regression." *Biometrica* 75:335–46.

Pinto, Brian, and Farah Zahir. 2004. "India: Why Fiscal Adjustment Now." Policy Research Working Paper WPS 3230, World Bank, Washington DC, March.

Reinhart, Carmen M., Kenneth Rogoff, and Miguel A. Savastano. 2003. "Debt Intolerance." NBER Working Paper 9908.

Serven, Luis. 1996. "Does Public Capital Crowd Out Private Capital? Evidence from India." Policy Research Working Paper Series 1613, World Bank, Washington, DC.

Servén, Luis. 1999. "Macroeconomic Uncertainty and Private Investment in Developing Countries: An Empirical Investigation." Policy Research Working Paper Series 2035, The World Bank.

Sorensen B. E., L. Wu, and O. Yosha. 2001. "Output Fluctuations and Fiscal Policy: U.S. State and Local Governments 1978–1994." *European Economic Review* 45:1271–310.

Stein, E., E. Talvi, and A. Gristani. 1999. "Institutional Arrangements and Fiscal Performance: The Latin American Experience." In J. M. Poterba and J. von Hagen, eds., *Fiscal Institutions and Fiscal Performance.* Chicago: University of Chicago Press, pp. 103–34.

Stock and Watson. 1988. "Variable Trends in Economic Time Series." *Journal of Economic Perspectives* 2(3):147–74.

Sturzenegger, Federico, and Holger Wolf. 2004. "Developing Country Debt. An Overview of Theory, Evidence, Options." Background Paper for the Debt and Volatility Work Program of the Economic Policy Department, Poverty Reduction and Economic Management Network, The World Bank.

Sturzenegger, Federico. 2004. "Tools for the Analysis of Debt Problems." *Journal of Reconstructing Finance* 1(1):1–23.

Talvi, E., and C. Vegh. 2000. "Tax Base Variability and Procyclical Fiscal Policy." NBER Working Paper 7499.

Trehan, B., and C. E. Walsh. 1991. "Testing Intertemporal Budget Constraints: Theory and Applications to U.S. Federal Budget and Current Account Deficits." *Journal of Money, Credit, and Banking* 23(2):206–23.

Wold, Herman. 1938. (2nd edition 1954). *A Study in the Analysis of Stationary Time Series.* Uppsala, Sweden: Almqvist and Wiksell.

Wolf, Holger. 2004. "Accounting for Consumption Volatility Differences." IMF Staff Papers, Vol. 51, Special Issue.

Wooldridge, Jeffrey M. 2002. *Econometric Analysis of Cross Section and Panel Data.* Cambridge, MA: MIT Press.

Index

buffer stocks, 51, 162, 166
Burnside and Dollar growth model, 157
business cycle behavior, 70, 71
buyback/debt exchange programs, 286

CACs. *See* collective action clauses
CAMEL. *See* Capital, Asset, Management,
    Earnings and Liquidity
Cameroon, 18
capital. *See also* human capital
    accounts, 317, 344, 369–374
    investment, 14
    mobility, 56
    physical, 117
    returns on, 2
    shortage of, 225
Capital, Asset, Management, Earnings and
    Liquidity (CAMEL), 259
    -type ratios, 261–262
capital controls, 316, 379, 382
    liberalization of, 364
    reimposing, 372
capital flows, 23, 316. *See also* inflows; outflows
    Argentina's collapse of, 443, 445
    composition of, 326, 347, 365, 374–376
    context of, 252
    controls on, 374
    curbing, 264
    decline of, 443
    effectiveness of, 414
    international, 236
    to Mexico, 343
    non-openness of, 334
    reversal of, 445
    short-term, 375
    sudden stop period of, 315, 364
    unpredictability of, 1
    volatility in, 236
capitalism. *See also* crony capitalism
    American style, 323
    Asian, 323
capital markets
    dominance of, 217
    foreign, 168
    imperfections of, 11
    international, 11
    limited access to, 12
    liquidity of, 169
    open, 30, 347
    Russia's, 427
    sovereign risk and, 8
    symmetries induced by, 8
Caribbean region, 17
cash flow
    expected, 289
    future, 269

promised, 289
relief, 479–480
volatility, 204
causality, influence of, 110
Cavallo, Domingo, 448
CEM. *See* Country Economic Memorandum
Central Europe, 17
CFA franc
    experience, 169
    inflation, 161
    zone, 161, 169
CFC. *See* Common Fund for Commodities
chaebols, 238, 247
    challenges to, 324
    defaults of, 243
channel. *See also* transmission channels
    common lender, 238
    credit, 23
    investment, 10
    monetary policy, 223
    net worth, 222
Chapter 11 bankruptcy, 246
cheaters, taxes and, 409
Chile, 20
    fiscal rules of, 118
Chile Copper Stabilization Fund (CSF), 195,
    200
China, 65
    success of, 324
circuit breakers
    currency market, 264–265
    equity market, 264
Citibank, 489
clause(s). *See* collective action clauses;
    collective representation clauses; cross
    acceleration clauses; majority action
    clauses
climate, political, 1
climatic shocks, 110
CLI. *See* Comprehensive Liquidity Index
cocoa farmers, 163
Cocobod, 165
coefficients
    bivariate correlation, 77
    IV, 88
    OLS, 88
    regression, 78
    slope, 113
    volatility, 78, 82
coffee
    African, 155
    agreements, 165
    bonds, 169
    exporting countries, 153
    exports, 19, 154
    importance of, 153